Religion in Philosophy and Theology

Edited by

Helen De Cruz (St. Louis, MO) · Asle Eikrem (Oslo)
Hartmut von Sass (Berlin) · Heiko Schulz (Frankfurt a. M.)
Judith Wolfe (St Andrews)

125

Humanity:
An Endangered Idea?

Claremont Studies
in the Philosophy of Religion,
Conference, 2019

edited by
Ingolf U. Dalferth and
Raymond E. Perrier

Mohr Siebeck

Ingolf U. Dalferth, born 1948; 1977 Promotion; 1982 Habilitation; Professor Emeritus of Systematic Theology, Symbolism and Philosophy of Religion at the University of Zurich; Danforth Professor Emeritus of Philosophy of Religion at Claremont Graduate University in California.

Raymond E. Perrier, born 1988; 2018 awarded PhD in Religion at Claremont Graduate University; 2019 Adjunct Professor of Philosophy and Religion at Hinds Community College; 2021 Senior Instructional Content Developer at Prime Power Services, Inc.

ISBN 978-3-16-161715-7 / eISBN 978-3-16-162000-3
DOI 10.1628/978-3-16-162000-3
ISSN 1616-346X / eISSN 2568-7425 (Religion in Philosophy and Theology)

Die Deutsche Nationalbibliothek lists this publication in the Deutsche Nationalbibliographie; detailed bibliographic data are available on the Internet at *http://dnb.dnb.de*.

© 2023 by Mohr Siebeck, Tübingen, Germany. www.mohrsiebeck.com

This book may not be reproduced, in whole or in part, in any form (beyond that permitted by copyright law) without the publisher's written permission. This applies particularly to reproductions, translations and storage and processing in electronic systems.

The book was typeset, printed on non-aging paper and bound by Laupp & Göbel in Gomaringen.

Printed in Germany.

Preface

The theme of 40th Philosophy of Religion Conference in Claremont in 2019 was *Humanity: An Endangered Idea?* Much of the discussion of personhood in recent years has focused on the differences between humans and animals, usually with the intention of showing how much we share with other living beings and why they should not be judged and treated significantly differently from us humans. But just when one welcomes this development, the question remains open, what then is it that distinguishes us as human beings? How do we want to live as humans among other living beings, and what is the core and the point of our humanity? Do we have to renounce such an idea because it gives reason to discriminate against other living beings? Or do we need it today at least as much as in the past, because only then can we reasonably judge where the meaningful description of differences turns into unjustified evaluations and devaluations of others? This volume marks some cornerstones of an overdue discussion that the humanities cannot avoid if they want to have a future in the academy.

We had to wait a long time for the final version of some contributions, and in some cases, we had to give up waiting. But what we now present has still become a substantial volume that sheds a differentiated light on the subject and makes an important contribution to its discussion.

We are grateful to the *Udo Keller Stiftung Forum Humanum* (Hamburg) which has again generously provided ten conference grants to enable doctoral students and post-docs to take part in the conference and present their work on the theme of the conference. Five of those papers are published here along with the other contributions to the conference. We couldn't do what we do without its support. We gratefully acknowledge the support of Claremont Graduate University and Pomona College. We are indebted to the contributors to this volume, to Mohr Siebeck who has accepted the manuscript for publication, and to Trevor Kimball (San Luis Obispo) who helped to get the manuscript ready for publication.

Ingolf U. Dalferth
Raymond E. Perrier

Contents

Preface V

INGOLF U. DALFERTH
Introduction: Humanity: An Endangered Idea? 1

I. Philosophy

WALTER SCHWEIDLER
The Paradox of Humanity: Man's Self-Challenging Existence 11

DANIEL CHERNILO
Humanism in Dark Times 25

RAYMOND E. PERRIER
The Logic of Humanism and the Ethics of Indeterminacy,
Universalism, and Egalitarianism 45

LUCAS WRIGHT
Broken Mirrors, Distorted Reflections: Anthropomorphism,
the Recovery of the *Concrétude* of the Human in Rosenzweig,
Heidegger, and Adorno and Horkheimer 55

II. Theology

ANSELM K. MIN
The Human Being as Image of God: Augustinian Meditations
on the Contemporary Crisis of Humanity 81

PETR GALLUS
The Other Reduction? Capitalist Sensationalism and
the Worldliness of God 101

VELI-MATTI KÄRKKÄINEN
"Multidimensional Monism:" An Integrated and Diverse Embodied
Theological Account of the *imago Dei* 109

RONALD COLE-TURNER
Transcendent Humanity: What if the Incarnation Really Matters? 133

DANIEL NELSON
Incarnate Humanity 159

III. Transhumanism

HAVA TIROSH-SAMUELSON
Human Flourishing in the Age of Technology 171

THOMAS JARRED FARMER
Transhumanism, Religion, and the Anthropocene 209

JON BIALECKI
Futures, Straining to Come into the World: Transhumanism,
Transhumanisms, and the Moron Transhumanist Association 219

RICHARD LIVINGSTON
On the Possibility of a Novel Phenomenon 235

IV. Artificial Intelligence

DIRK EVERS
"Know Thyself" – Self-reflection and the Chances and
Limits of Dataism 245

LIU YUE
The Paradoxical Self: A Dilemma for Artificial General Intelligence ... 271

HASSE HAMALAINEN
Conscience and Moral Cognition: What Distinguishes Us
from Machines 285

NATHAN SCHRADLE
Reframing Religion in the Algorithmic Age:
Appraising the Algorithmic Approach to Religion 301

GUELFO CARBONE
Digital Technology and Embodiment: The Flesh as Paradigm 315

V. Ethics

EMILY HODGES
Humanity as the Development of Intersubjective Giving and Receiving 335

ADRIANO FABRIS
The Transformations of Human Ethics in an Age of
Technological Challenges 351

JOSEPH PRABHU
Inter-Being: The Role of Humanity in an Ecological Age 363

JOSIAH SOLIS
Who Still Deserves to Arise? 377

List of Contributors 381
Index of Names 383
Index of Terms 385

Introduction:
Humanity: An Endangered Idea?

INGOLF U. DALFERTH

1. GPT-2

A week before the conference in Claremont on February 22–23, 2019, OpenAI released a very powerful language model called GPT-2.[1] "GPT-2 is a large transformer-based language model with 1.5 billion parameters, trained on a dataset of 8 million web pages. GPT-2 is trained with a simple objective: predict the next word, given all of the previous words within some text."[2] The model "generates synthetic text samples" in a variety of styles, from news articles to fan fiction "in response to the model being primed with an arbitrary input. The model [...] adapts to the style and content of the conditioning text."[3] And it is astonishingly successful in doing so.

Here is an example.[4] The system prompt (human written) was the following:

In a shocking finding, scientist discovered a herd of unicorns living in a remote, previously unexplored valley, in the Andes Mountains. Even more surprising to the researchers was the fact that the unicorns spoke perfect English.

The model completion (machine-written) looked like this:

The scientist named the population, after their distinctive horn, Ovid's Unicorn. These four-horned, silver-white unicorns were previously unknown to science. [...] Dr. Jorge Pérez, an evolutionary biologist from the University of La Paz, and several companions, were exploring the Andes Mountains when they found a small valley, with no other animals or humans. [When they] ventured further into the valley [...] Pérez and his friends

---

[1] Cf. https://towardsdatascience.com/openais-gpt-2-the-model-the-hype-and-the-controversy-1109f4bfd5e8 (4/21/2022).

[2] https://blog.openai.com/better-language-models/. Cf. https://www.faz.net/aktuell/feuilleton/debatten/open-ai-warnt-vor-der-eigenen-entwicklung-gpt-2-16047940.html. (4/21/2022). Since May 2020, an improved version GPT-3 has been on the market, which is even more effective.

[3] Ibid.

[4] The following is taken from https://blog.openai.com/better-language-models/. Cf. https://www.faz.net/aktuell/feuilleton/debatten/open-ai-warnt-vor-der-eigenen-entwicklung-gpt-2-16047940.html. (4/21/2022).

were astonished to see the unicorn herd. These creatures could be seen from the air without having to move too much to see them – they were so close they could touch their horns. While examining these bizarre creatures the scientists discovered that the creatures also spoke some fairly regular English. Pérez stated, "We can see, for example, that they have a common 'language,' something like a dialect or dialectic." Dr. Pérez believes that the unicorns may have originated in Argentina, where the animals were believed to be descendants of a lost race of people who lived there before the arrival of humans in those parts of South America. While their origins are still unclear, some believe that perhaps the creatures were created when a human and a unicorn met each other in a time before human civilization. According to Pérez, "In South America, such incidents seem to be quite common." However, Pérez also pointed out that it is likely that the only way of knowing for sure if unicorns are indeed the descendants of a lost alien race is through DNA. "But they seem to be able to communicate in English quite well, which I believe is a sign of evolution, or at least a change in social organization," said the scientist."[5]

The interesting thing about this text is not the fairly absurd story, but that the alleged report was written without any help of humans. The model generated it on the basis of the dataset on which it was trained, and it could generate an endless number of similar texts unsupervised by any human being. After training the model, humans are not needed any more – or less and less. We are creating technologies whose output is so human-like that we can hardly distinguish any more between a human-generated text and a machine-generated text.

It is easy to see why OpenAI has released only a small version of this model and not "the dataset, training code, or GPT-2 model weights."[6] There is a real danger of applying "these models for malicious purposes, including [...]: generate misleading news articles; impersonate others online; automate the production of abusive or faked content to post on social media; automate the production of spam/phishing content."[7] Clearly, concerns about potential abuse are more than justified. And the company is right in warning: "The public at large will need to become more skeptical of texts they find online, just as the 'deep fakes' phenomenon calls for more skepticism about images."[8]

A few weeks after the conference, I received a letter from an online company that specializes in professionally produced series of publications and articles aimed at a broader audience. They asked me if I would agree to them writing new academic papers under my name based on my published work in the English-speaking world. They would only use material from me, so anything new would really be my doing. But I would no longer have to worry about extending my list of publications, as they would be happy to do this for a small fee, of course.

---

[5] https://blog.openai.com/better-language-models/. (4/21/2022).
[6] Ibid.
[7] Ibid.
[8] Ibid.

2. Five Callenges

These are just a few examples of many. But they help to explain why we have chosen as the theme of the 40th Philosophy of Religion Conference in Claremont (February 22–23, 2019) *Humanity: An Endangered Idea?* Developments like GPT-2 as well as contemporary debates about the alleged demise of the humanities have brought to the fore that we are forced to re-think our humanity. Once we thought that the use of language is one of the things that mark us off from other animals. Now we see that it does not even help to distinguish between our text-generating models and us anymore.

So what is it that makes us different from the technologies we create? Why should we continue to put money into schools of arts and humanities and not invest in more profitable science or technology projects?

We are at a loss to give a convincing answer because we have lost a common understanding of humanity (if we ever had one) that could govern our debates and give direction to our research and discussions.[9] Of course, *humanity* is not *humanism*, and a defense of humanism is not as such an argument for humanity or vice versa. But can one argue for humanity without falling into the trap of 'speciesism'? Or do all arguments for humanity play into the hands of those who welcome 'The Anthropocene', as some have dubbed our age, because we have managed to undo all boundaries between 'humanity' and 'nature' that have traditionally prevailed?[10]

There is no straightforward positive or negative answer to these questions, as we shall see. Who and what we are as humans have always been controversial questions, and so have been the views about our impact on the environment in which we live. We may agree "that you cannot adequately describe a human person with the range of concepts which is adequate for the description of a chair, or a cabbage or even an electronic calculating machine."[11] But this does not imply that we would agree on a positive account of what it means to be a human person. People differ not only about the *is* of humankind and what humans are and do in fact, but also about the *ought* of a humane humanity and how one should live as a human being.

Answers to the questions about our humanity and *humanitas* (Cicero) have been sought along five routes: by contrasting the human with the non-human (other animals), with the more than human (the divine), with the inhuman (negative human behaviors), with the superhuman (what humans will

---

[9] Cf. *Posthuman Glossary*, ed. R. Braidotti and M. Hlavajova (London: Bloomsbury Academic, 2018).

[10] Cf. M. ROBINSON, *What Are We Doing Here?* (New York: Farrar, Straus and Giroux, 2018).

[11] I. M. CROMBIE, "The Possibility of Theological Statements," in *Faith and Logic*, ed. B. Mitchell (London: Routledge, 1957), 57.

become), or with the transhuman (thinking machines). In each case the question at stake and the point of comparison is a different one: a relative difference within a shared animality, an absolute difference from the divine, a practical difference with respect to what it means to live a good human life in a world whose life-sustaining ecosystems have been dangerously put at hazard by our individual and collective behaviors, an evolutionary difference between the present and future states of humankind, or a difference in kind between human biological evolution and technological enhancement. In all those respects the idea of humanity has been defined differently. What makes humans human? What does it mean for humans to live a human life? What is the *humanitas* for which we ought to strive?

Today we have to discuss these questions in the light of at least five challenges:

(1) The first is the *biological challenge* to human distinctiveness. Biological and neurophysiological research increasingly level out and dissolve clear-cut distinctions between humans and other animals and living species: reason, rationality, deliberation, decision-making, free choice, intentional action etc. all come by degrees and can be found in one way or another in other animals as well. Humans are part of nature and must be understood as embedded in complex ecosystems. Therefore the view that humans are special and stand out from the animal world in a significant way is challenged, and human speciesism is banned.

(2) The second is the *technological challenge* that seeks to overcome the limitations of our biological nature by technical means. The truth about us is to be sought not in our evolutionary past, but in our technological future. The romanticism of ecological bioconservatives is countered with the technological optimism of a progressive perfectionism, transhumanism, extropianism or postgenderism. Compared to smart machines, it is not our intellect, but our biology that makes us special. However, if research into biological computing and nanotechnology keeps progressing at the present rate, then the difference between humans and machines will soon be negligible and there will be no space to define humanity. "The future belongs to inorganic life forms," as Martin J. Rees has predicted.[12] The challenge to the idea of humanity from this side is that humanity as we know it is expected to disappear when superintelligent thinking machines will have superseded humans and human intellect.

---

[12] M. J. REES, "Unsere Nachfahren werden Maschinen sein," *NZZ*, October 21, 2017, (https://www.nzz.ch/feuilleton/unsere-nachfahren-werden-maschinen-sein-ld.1322780) (4/21/2022); M. O'CONNELL, *To Be a Machine: Adventures Among Cyborgs, Utopians, Hackers, and the Futurists Solving the Modest Problem of Death* (New York: Doubleday, 2017); R. McKIE, "No death and an enhanced life: Is the future transhuman?" (https://www.theguardian.com/technology/2018/may/06/no-death-and-an-enhanced-life-is-the-future-transhuman) (4/21/2022).

(3) The third challenge is what I call the *anthropological challenge*. If we try to delineate what is human about humans not by comparing humans to other animals but to other humans, then it is striking to see that regularities of a common biology and evolutionary past are by far outdone by the cultural differences and plurality in which humans adapt to different situations and circumstances. There is no unity of humanity that has not emerged from a multitude of diversities – at the biological level, and at the cultural level.[13] Human life knows choice between options and the freedom to choose, not only the causality of nature and the conventional necessities of culture. The anthropological challenge to the idea of humanity is that humanity is a normative project, not merely a biological fact, and that there is an endemic normative conflict about how this project has been or should be worked out in human culture and history.

(4) The fourth challenge is the *cosmological challenge*.[14] We live in a vast universe, in which we are marginal and completely insignificant. And we live in a finite universe that is not made forever. The vastness of the universe may lead to a sense of the greatness of God, or to a fright about the insignificance of human beings. Here is what Pascal wrote four centuries ago: "When I consider the short duration of my life, swallowed up in the eternity before and after, the little space which I fill, and even can see, engulfed in the infinite immensity of spaces of which I am ignorant, and which know me not, I am frightened, and am astonished at being here rather than there; for there is no reason why here rather than there, why now rather than then [...] The eternal silence of those infinite spaces frightens me."[15] Pascal was not the only one who was overwhelmed by this fright. We are nothing. It is not much consolation to be told that we live in a fine-tuned universe that seems to be made precisely for us to observe it, and for us to be made precisely to observe it.[16] We know that this will not last forever – not for us, not for our kind, not for our galaxy, not for our universe. The long-term future of the universe leaves little

---

[13] Cf. E. VIVEIROS DE CASTRO, *Cannibal Metaphysics* (Minneapolis: Univocal Publishing, 2014).

[14] Cf. for the following D. WILKINSON, "Being Human in a Cosmic Context," in *Issues in Science and Theology: Are We Special?* ed. M. Fuller et al. *Issues in Science and Theology: Publications of the European Society for the Study of Science and Theology* 4 (DOI 10.1007/978-3-319-62124-1_1 [2017], 3–16) (4/22/2022).

[15] B. PASCAL, *Pensées* (New York: E.P. Dutton & Co., Inc, 1958), 61.

[16] M. REES, *Just Six Numbers: The Deep Forces that Shape the Universe* (London: Weidenfeld and Nicholson, 2000), 150. He highlights the apparent fine-tuning of the ratio of the electrical force to gravitational force, how firmly atomic nuclei bind together, the amount of material in the universe, the cosmological constant, the ratio of energy needed to disperse an object compared to its total rest mass energy and the number of spatial dimensions in the universe. If any of these were just slightly different to what they actually are then intelligent life would not develop within the universe.

to hope for. If the expansion of the universe is not reversed into a contraction leading to a big crunch, the universe will end as a cold and uninteresting place composed of dead stars and black holes. The only consolation seems to be that we shall not live to see the end. We shall disappear long before.

(5) The fifth challenge, finally, is the *theological challenge* of arriving at a view of human nature by comparing humans to the divine. The force of this challenge is underestimated if one conceives the divine merely as a cultural construction and not as a self-disclosing reality. The point of such a challenge is to outline a vision of a good human life that has, in the monotheistic traditions for example, its center in safeguarding the distinction between creature and creator (and distinction is not separation, as is often wrongly assumed). It is a normative idea of humanity that envisages human life at its best to be a life in harmony with the gifts of the creator (the gift of life and the gift of love) and open to the needs of one's fellow humans (as expressed in the double commandment of love) and of all other creatures who are also the addressees and recipients of God's gifts.

These are some of the challenges that a contemporary debate about the idea of humanity cannot ignore.

3. Idea vs. Concept

Of course, the core of this debate is about our humanity and not only about an idea of humanity. But we cannot discuss our humanity in a meaningful way without making it a topic in an explicit way, and this is only possible if we symbolize it semiotically, define it conceptually or – as in the present case – grasp it philosophically as an idea.

I speak of the idea rather than the concept of humanity for a specific reason: Concepts are often understood to be generalizations from experience condensed into a single term. Ideas are different. They are – in a non-Platonic sense – intellectual tools that help us to orient others and ourselves in a complex and confusing world. Ideas are more like a yardstick to measure something, than something that we measure by a yardstick. Freedom, God, and immortality are such orienting ideas in Kant. They are not concepts that can be exemplified by particular instances. There are no immortalities, or gods, or freedoms in our experience that we could compare. But we could not live a human life without using the ideas of freedom, God and immortality to make sense of our life in this world. They are, in Kant's terms, 'necessary fictions' without which we couldn't live a human life.

The idea of humanity functions in a similar way: It is not a concept like 'human being' of which there are many particular instances, and it is not merely the summary of a descriptive account of what humans are that can be tested against reality. It is rather a normative idea that functions as a yardstick or criterion for a human life worthy that name. It not merely asserts what is the case but what ought to be the case. Thus, the questions to which it answers are not merely 'What are humans?' but 'What do we want to be as humans?', not merely 'How do we live in fact?' but 'How do we want to live as humans together with other beings in the world?' So what are the ideas of humanity that guide us? Do they still help us to orient ourselves in our fast changing contemporary world? Or which idea of humanity would be able or helpful to do so? To address these and related questions is the objective of this conference. Today we shall concentrate on problems posed by philosophy and theology, tomorrow on questions raised by contemporary technology, ecology, and ethics. These are the areas one cannot ignore when tackling the issues before us. They are pressing issues, and we cannot put off addressing them.

4. Outline of the Volume

The volume is organized into five parts. In the first part, basic philosophical questions of being human are discussed, which a useful idea of humanity must consider. This applies both to the Paradox of Humanity and to the question of universalism, which is part of the idea of humanity. In the second part, central theological questions are recalled – the Augustinian tradition of the human being as image of God as well as attempts to reactivate this tradition under contemporary conditions in a technological culture. Part three is devoted to the current discussion about transhumanism and asks how its questions are to be judged from the perspective of Jewish and Christian theology and why they have met with such a positive response from certain religious traditions such as the Mormons. Part four takes up another central area of the contemporary debate on humanity, asking about the role and significance of artificial intelligence for the elaboration of an idea of humanity. How different are we from our own creations, and should we expect that our technological creatures will sooner or later supplant their human creators and be able to leave them behind? This raises obvious ethical questions, which are taken up in the fifth part. How can we think of humanity under the emerging conditions of our technological culture? What role does human togetherness and existence for others play within the framework of an ecological civilization, which is becoming increasingly clear as the future perspective of humanity?

Taken together, the volume outlines a discussion that is important not only in philosophy, theology, and religion, but in the humanities as a whole. If we are no longer able to say which idea of humanity we align ourselves with, we will not be able to provide the humanities with a compass by which they can orient themselves in a rapidly changing social world and technological culture.

I. Philosophy

The Paradox of Humanity:
Man's Self-Challenging Existence

WALTER SCHWEIDLER

Whether one may find it relieving or worrying, the challenges to the idea and to our understanding of humanity do not in fact come from outside it, but rather from its deepest core. Our existence is a challenge to itself, and therefore each of us is a challenge to him- or herself and to others. The reason is that our existence is constituted by a paradox: the paradox of our nature. I am going to use the term "nature" here in a way which is rooted in the classical but pre-modern sense of what the Greeks called *physis*: Any living being is an individual who owes the forms of its life to the species to which it belongs, and these forms of life constitute its nature. In this ancient sense, the term "nature" does not designate a totality of phenomena which can be explained by reference to nomological or statistical laws as is essential for the modern, deterministic concept of nature. This new concept of nature – which I am not going to criticize here but simply keep at a certain distance from my remarks – tends to exclude the free human subject from the determinate totality of natural "objects" and thereby from "nature" in general, while the old term *physis* has the obvious implication that man, like every living being, has a nature.

It is this human nature which is shared by all human beings and which distinguishes us from all other natural beings, but certainly does not oppose us to "nature" in general. It is, however, peculiar to us that human nature is encoded in cultural forms of life and that these forms of life cannot be adequately understood on the level of nature alone. A paradigmatic example of this peculiarity is language. Human beings are speakers by nature: Children cannot survive if nobody speaks to them, and they learn to speak not by attending a language course but simply by being treated as speakers. But there is no "natural language;" there is only everybody's mother tongue which is clearly a product of culture. The connection between nature and culture is, as Lévi-Strauss has pointed out,[1] essentially constituted by the universality of

---

[1] "Wherever," according to Lévi-Strauss, "there are rules we know for certain that the cultural stage has been reached. Likewise, it is easy to recognize universality as the criterion of nature, for what is constant in man falls necessarily beyond the scope of customs, techniques and institutions whereby his groups are differentiated and contrasted. Failing a real analysis, the double criterion of norm and universality provides the principle for an ideal analysis which,

our forms of life. Rules are works of our cultures, but universal rules are signatures of our nature. What we all as human beings share and what distinguishes us from any other natural beings is not a "natural" language but the ability to translate what anyone of us has to say into our and every other mother tongue. So, culture is not a counterpoint or even a contradiction to human nature; but the cultural factor signifies what I am going to understand as the intrinsic paradox of our nature. Humans are beings who by their nature transcend this nature – and thereby nature in general. That we transcend nature does not imply that we could emancipate ourselves from it. On the contrary, and this is the essentially paradoxical point: We transcend our nature by accepting, by understanding and by obeying it or, as is programmatically said in Stoicism or in Buddhism, by "following" it – which is, as we should not forget, a term that implicates a genuinely temporal aspect. Our nature is constituted by something like a self-repeating origin,[2] a return to what could not be and has never been beyond or before the return to it. I think that the philosophical explication of that paradox can be one possible key for the understanding of any kind of danger and therefore also of the topical challenges which the idea of humanity is facing. It is a key to understanding the relation between the specific sense in which we can speak of human nature, human action, and human self-distance.

1. The Paradox of Human Nature and the Challenge to Act

For a full understanding of the relation between our current concept of humanity and the concept of nature in the classical meaning of *physis* we must first pay some attention to the *topos* which in recent times has taken over from the old notion of nature the role of demarcating that which all humans share and what distinguishes us from any other natural kind: human dignity. There is one concept which has nowadays incorporated this hidden connection between human nature and dignity more than any other, i. e. the concept of the person. To explicate this I would like to proceed from the locus classicus in which Kant in his *Groundwork of the Metaphysics of Morals* speaks of the human being as being defined by "this dignity (prerogative) he has over all

---

at least in certain cases and within certain limits, may allow the natural to be isolated from the cultural elements which are involved in more complex syntheses. Let us suppose then that everything universal in man relates to the natural order, and is characterized by spontaneity, and that everything subject to a norm is cultural and is both relative and particular." C. LÉVI-STRAUSS, *The Elementary Structures of Kinship*, trans. J. H. Bell, J. R. von Sturmer and R. Needham, revised ed. (Boston, MA: Beacon Press, 1969), 8.

[2] Cf. W. SCHWEIDLER, "The Self-repeating Origin: Ontological Aspects of Ricœur's Concept of Hermeneutics," in *Hermeneutics and the Philosophy of Religion: The Legacy of Paul Ricœur*, ed. I. U. Dalferth (Tübingen: Mohr Siebeck, 2015), 81–95.

merely natural beings [which] brings with it that he must always take his maxims from the point of view of himself, and likewise every other rational being, as lawgiving beings (who for this reason are also called persons)."[3] I understand this passage as the most precise philosophical demarcation of a basic link which is decisive for all human self-interpretation. It is the link between, on the one hand, the universality and the indivisibility of the demand of every human person for the recognition of his or her dignity and, on the other hand, the addressee of that demand, namely the acting subject. Let me try to explain this in further detail.

It might be said that in his definition of human dignity Kant leaves the most important determination of what for him to be a "person" signified in parenthesis: We are called persons because we are those beings out of the consideration of which at "any time," that is by any acting subject, the maxims are to be formulated which determine and justify that subject's action. So, the reason for which we are, according to Kant, called persons is not something that enables us to act, but it is the reason for which any agent has to respect us. We could say that each and every one of us has to be respected as a member of a kind of jury whose deliberation is the essential ethical condition for whatever somebody who wants to act in a reasonable and justifiable way does.[4] To repeat: Nothing that enables or forces us to act, that is, no qualities, properties, abilities, interests, reasons or powers, constitute us as persons, but only our membership of such a jury that precedes any kind of action – including our own. Consequently, if what constitutes us as persons precedes any kind of action, then we must find ourselves in a deeply passive self-relation. Emmanuel Levinas has referred to this relation as the "absolute passivity of the self," a passivity which is "prior to the passivity-activity alternative, more passive than any inertia."[5] We cannot go deeper here into Levinas' conception of the self, but it must at least be emphasized that in his phenomenological account of humanity this ethically fundamental kind of passivity is in fact fundamental not only in respect to the relation between the acting subject and the other, *l'autre*

---

[3] I. KANT, *Groundwork of the Metaphysics of Morals*, trans. and ed. M. Gregor (Cambridge: Cambridge University Press, 1997), 45; *Gesammelte Schriften*, ed. Königlich-Preußische Akademie der Wissenschaften, 29 vols. (Berlin: Georg Reimer, 1900 ff), vol. 4, 438.

[4] One should never forget that Kant took a lot of concepts which are highly fundamental for his philosophy from the juridical discourse of his time (subsumption, judgment, deduction, autonomy etc.); cf. G.-W. KÜSTERS, *Kants Rechtsphilosophie* (Darmstadt: Wissenschaftliche Buchgesellschaft, 1988); C. RITTER, *Der Rechtsgedanke Kants nach den frühen Quellen* (Frankfurt am Main: Vittorio Klostermann, 1971), 106 ff; F. KAULBACH, "Der Herrschaftsanspruch der Vernunft in Recht und Moral bei Kant," in *Studien zur späten Rechtsphilosophie Kants und ihrer transzendentalen Methode* (Würzburg: Königshausen & Neumann, 1982), 55–75.

[5] E. LEVINAS, *Otherwise than Being or Beyond Essence*, trans. A. Lingis (Pittsburgh: Duquesne University Press, 1998), 121; cf. W. SCHWEIDLER, "Absolute Passivität," in *Das Uneinholbare: Beiträge zu einer indirekten Metaphysik* (Freiburg: Karl Alber, 2008), 366–382.

or *autrui*,[6] but also in the relation in which we find ourselves as *le tiers*, i.e. for everyone of us as a member of the human family.[7] We belong to this family not because of any capacity which we could ever acquire nor which anyone could ever award us with; we belong to it just because of the respect that any rational agent owes to us as members of a jury whose composition obviously, if we do not want to contradict ourselves, cannot be at his or her, i.e. at any acting subject's, discretion. So, the word "family" here is demarcating the not biological, but natural kinship to which we cannot but refer when we forbid ourselves from passing down at our own discretion the judgment of who belongs to the human family and who does not. If we cannot pass that judgment about the composition of the human family, then we cannot but leave it to nature. After all, it holds for any jury that it cannot decide who belongs to it and who does not.

Of course, the meaning of the word "jury" as I use it here is primarily metaphorical, but not completely: In fact, it is the juridical constitution of our human forms of life by means of which we secure the absolute respect for that core of our existence which we call the "inviolable" dignity of the human person. But this expression only makes sense if we understand our legal and juridical institutions as based on and derived from that inviolability, not as some kind of collective achievement by which we would have acquired it. So, the task of the jury to which we belong as members of the human family is to prevent the violation of the inviolable. Levinas has characterized this paradoxical aspect which is fundamental not only for our political order but also for our philosophical reflection as the "reverting of thematization into anarchy ... For ethics, beyond politics, is found at the level of this reverting."[8] The foundation of the political order is in its essence as anarchical as phenomenology is when it finds its deepest subject in that which is in itself not a phenomenon.

Let us try to go deeper into the reason why we as human beings belong to such a "jury." As Robert Spaemann in his great book on persons has pointed out, this reason does not consist in the purported "value" of human life in contrast to other beings, but rather in the specific incommensurability of anybody's own life in contrast to the lives of all others of its kind. "This is," writes Spaemann, "why we prefer to speak of human 'dignity' (*Würde*) rather than human value (*Wert*). The value of ten people may be more than that of one, but ten are no more than one in point of dignity. You can't tot up persons. They form a system of relations in which each is uniquely in relation to every

---

[6] Cf. the complex field of translation of these terms D. GALETTI, "The Grammar of Levinas' other, Other, autrui, Autrui: Addressing Translation Conventions and Interpretation in English Language Levinas Studies," *South African Journal of Philosophy* 34, no. 2 (2015): 199–213.

[7] Cf. SCHWEIDLER, "Absolute Passivität," 366–382.

[8] LEVINAS, *Otherwise than Being or Beyond Essence*, 121.

other."[9] But once again: Why and how do they form such a system? To answer this question, we must turn now from one side of the double-sided medal of humanity, i. e. from the universal relation between all of us as its members, to the other, namely the addressee of the claim or demand which arises from that relation: the acting subject. On that other side we find what can be called the "challenge" of humanity and what makes the paradox of our human nature a key issue of our philosophizing. What we are doing in our philosophical reflection here is essentially the attempt to understand and explicate the challenge which is directed from us to ourselves, i. e. from us as members of the jury to which we belong independently of any deliberate action, toward ourselves as actual or potential agents. In what exactly does this challenge consist?

At this point it is, as I think, very helpful to refer to a concept invented by Thomas Nagel: the concept of "agent-relativity."[10] So far, we have strongly emphasized that the essence of human dignity consists in a demand which is constituted independently of any capability or necessity to act; a claim which precedes any kind of real action. But now we will have to reinforce the significance of the other side of the coin: If there were no understanding of and no obedience to this demand, then we could never have developed any consciousness of human dignity at all. And the understanding of and the obedience to a claim: This obviously implies action. Human dignity is not something that could be first discovered and then respected; rather, they both, the claim to and the respect of human dignity, are, to use a Heideggerian term, equiprimordial. The question in what another person's dignity consists cannot be answered by description but only by action. Here we face the paradox which somewhat mirrors the paradox of absolute passivity which we encountered on the other side of the medal. For the agent who has to respect all other human beings as persons there is no remainder of receptivity which would precede the cultural form of life that constitutes the unit that I characterized as the "jury" of humanity. "This, of course, is paradoxical. Respect, recognition, and so on are species of activity, which would seem to presuppose a moment of receptivity in which persons were identified as persons. Apparently, and not least because it is a question of perceiving another center of being, the perceiver needs to be in a completely receptive posture. But that is not the case, and for a very clear reason: a center of being is, by definition, not something available to knowledge as a phenomenon."[11]

---

[9] See R. SPAEMANN, *Persons: The Difference between "Someone" and "Something,"* trans. O. O'Donovan (Oxford: Oxford University Press, 2006), 185.

[10] Cf. T. NAGEL on agent-relativity and deontology, in *The View From Nowhere* (New York: Oxford University Press, 1986), 164–185.

[11] SPAEMANN, *Persons*, 182.

In respect to this activity which is embedded in our political and especially our juridical forms of life we face the deepest and genuinely temporal core of the paradox of our human existence: that in some way our existence is a response that precedes the question to which it is the answer. And the genuinely challenging aspect of this paradoxical constellation consists in the fact that we as human beings cannot but rely on the understanding of that paradox and the obedience to it. To "rely" here means of course: to act in a way which implies and demands of others to confirm and constitute the reason which we must already rely on when we act. And in this sense the claim or demand to recognize human dignity is "agent-relative:" The universal relation that connects all of us as members of the human family intrinsically presupposes an acting subject who understands that in the act by which he or she recognizes it, nothing less than that universal relation itself is at stake. This is the challenge of action that follows from the nature of a person, i.e. the nature of a being who in the genuine forms of life of its species transcends itself.

2. The Paradox of Human Action and the Challenge of Self-Distance

It is not in order to be counted as a person that I must know all this; but when I am going to perform rational and justifiable actions I must at least intuitively or implicitly understand what is meant by this, the "agent-relativity" of the claim or demand to respect the dignity of any member of the human family. Only he or she who has such a kind of "tacit knowledge" about humanity will understand concretely what is meant in this context by the term "challenge." Perhaps the most obvious example for this is the situation in which I am confronted with persons who lack the qualities and abilities which I as a rational agent possess. When the dignity of such a person, e.g. a comatose, a heavily mentally disabled or an unborn person, is endangered, then it is not he or she, but I the man who is to be blamed. It is my task to treat such persons as equal members of the human family to which they belong, just as I do myself. I must master the challenge to view my action through their eyes. Again spoken of in this somewhat but not only metaphorical way: I must by myself take on his or her role in the process of the "deliberation" of the jury which judges my action. And when I have understood this, then a further and really decisive insight is that the connection with the other persons which makes me in this way responsible for them is not a causal relation. If I wish to see what I am doing through the eyes of disabled person, I must take into account more than only the concrete individual who is affected by my action; I must see not only what my action causes but what it *means*, i.e. what it stands for. Human beings with disabilities become with good reason indignant when the disability of a child, with whom they may in fact never enter into a concrete relation, is considered a valid reason for the termination of a pregnancy. They remind us what such a determination means not only for one, but for all of them and in the end for all of us as human beings. Humanity is essentially constituted when I not only see through the eyes of others what I am doing to them as individuals but also to the whole of human kind. In this way, Christ says: Whatever you did to the least of my brethren, you have done it to me. Similarly, in the Koran it is written that whenever one kills a man, it is as if one has killed mankind as a whole; and equally, whenever a life is saved, it is as if the lives of all have been ransomed.

What makes us members of the not biological, but natural relationship of the human family and consequently of what I called the "jury" to which I belong as a person is not a causal but a *symbolic* relation. Because human action symbolically refers beyond itself to everything that makes persons into representatives of all others of their kind, and indeed even of this kind itself, the judgement of an action as humane or inhumane always depends on the meaning that it has for being human in general. It is precisely this symbolic dimension that alone can rationally explicate why the dignity of human beings is "inviolable:" The violation of dignity takes place on the causal plane, the symbolic meaning, by means of which it is as such defined, can never have a bearing upon it, for it is the relation that transposes all beings that belong to the lattice-work of persons – victims and even victimizers – into an incommensurable distance to each other. And only the symbolic relation, contrary to this negative foundation according to which dignity cannot be infringed upon, makes the compliance with the universal demand, implied by it by the agent who is always enclosed in the limitations of his finitude, possible in a positive way. So in the end it is the paradox of human action, the fact that as a human I am the only being who by its nature is free to act against itself, that allows us to reconcile the universal demand of humanity with the natural condition of our finitude. The debt which I owe to humanity can only and must be paid to the few human – and other living – beings which I am actually and factually responsible for. A good man, so says the Confucian Mencius, treats strangers as his own relatives, and a bad man his own relatives as strangers.

So, the answer to the question what it means that as persons we transcend our nature is to be given on the anthropological level: Man is an *animal symbolicum*. We transcend ourselves when we look upon ourselves as a kind of sign for the relation to all of us which is not perceived but constituted in this view. Therefore, as Robert Spaemann says, the "relational sphere of personal interaction is universal, from which it follows that the exclusion of even one person from the scheme of recognition brings the personal character of the whole system tumbling down."[12] Or, as Markus Rothhaar writes, any failure

---

[12] SPAEMANN, *Persons*, 196.

to recognize another person's dignity, "every violation of a duty which one subject has toward another...[means] a negation of the relation of recognition itself." The call to recognize human dignity is not a "norm of norms" in the sense of a presumed natural law conceived in terms of the disjunction of "is" and "ought," rather it is to be thought of as a "meta-norm." Indeed, and incorporating the conceptualisation of it as a "meta-norm of all norms in general," we may say along with Rothhaar that: "A violation of norms is ... fundamentally not justifiable in terms of being a means to the end of complying with a norm caused by the violation of a prior norm."[13] The connection between the universality and the agent-relativity of the demand of human dignity is not of a normative-moral, rather a performative-logical kind: He who excludes one of the members of his association, which unites all persons with each other and which demarcates them from non-personal beings, from the lattice-work of entities before which he must justify his action, in this way and in this respect falls into contradiction with the conditions of the possibility of justifying his conduct, i.e. with the entirety of the relation that constitutes this association in general. "Contradiction" is precisely a logical, and not a moral category. The key to the philosophical reconstruction of this putative relation present in Kant's parenthetical definition, namely that every person in as far as he or she can be violated in relation to his or her dignity stands for all others of his or her kind, is therefore not present on the level that obliges us to act, rather it is there where that relation, which makes each of us representatives of all beings who are like us and even representatives of our kind itself, is found; namely, the symbolic.

As illuminating, I think, as this insight is on the juridical and political level, it still confronts us on the level of our individual self-relation with another deep challenge: the paradox of self-distance. Apparently, the price we have to pay for the acquirement of the coin that connects humanity and agent-relativity is that we have not only to see ourselves through the eyes of others but even also to look through ourselves in a way which seems to have the effect that we become incommensurable to ourselves. Individuality seems to become, as has been said about the Husserlian notion of it, that which "of course ... characterizes each and every person, but not in the sense of having a universal form commonly participated in, but in the sense that each is precisely not-communicable, not-instantiable, and impredicable."[14] This is an immense challenge to our self-relation which seems to confront us with the choice between the selfless and in the end self-destructing dedication of our whole lives to uni-

---

[13] M. ROTHHAAR, *Die Menschenwürde als Prinzip des Rechts* (Tübingen: Mohr Siebeck, 2015), 270.

[14] J. G. HART, "The Absolute Ought and the Unique Individual," *Husserl Studies* 22, no. 3 (2006): 225.

versal claims and the confession of selfish egotism. To meet this challenge we will have to come back to the temporal aspect which we observed when we mentioned the insight that it belongs to our nature that we have to "follow" it. We will have to ask if looking upon ourselves through the eyes of the others can imply something like a return to what we are and were before we entered into our self-distance.

3. The Paradox of Self-Distance and the Challenge of Self-Return

In order to understand what can be meant by such a way back to ourselves, we must first return to the concept of nature and the relation of self-transcendence in which we have determined our constitution as *animal symbolicum*. When we try to relate the paradoxical aspects of self-distance and self-transcendence toward ourselves we are led to the question what it can mean for a person *to be a symbol* in relation to him- or herself. When by this characterization we refer to our nature – "nature," as I pointed out, in the classical sense of *physis* –, then the term must, imply, on the one side, some common denominator between us and all other natural beings and, on the other side, the key to what might be called the *differentia specifica* which makes us unique among the rest of nature. To explicate this conclusion, I will proceed by way of two steps.

The first step is to specify the relation in which we as human beings stand to our nature. It is, I think, again Robert Spaemann who has pointed out this relation in the most precise manner. "Freedom," he writes, "is first and foremost freedom *from* something; but what is the *person* free from? Only from his or her own nature. A person 'has' a nature, but the nature is not what the person *is*, because the person has the power to relate freely to it. But this power is not innate; it comes through encounter with other persons. Only the affirmation of other centers of being, through recognition, justice, and love, allows us the distance on ourselves and the appropriation of ourselves that is constitutive for persons – in sum, 'freedom from self.' This we experience as a gift."[15] So, according to Spaemann, what we have in common with all other natural beings is that there is a human nature, and what distinguishes us from all other natural beings is the relation in which we stand toward our nature, i.e. the relation of freedom. When we "follow" our nature, we do it by free decision, and we can always refuse to do it. Therefore, human beings face the choice between humane and inhumane action. This is the reason why our respect for the dignity of other human beings cannot be explained as a form of "speciesism." A human being can treat his own kind in ways which are incomparable to any other species: torture, concentration camps, mass destruction etc. If we

---

[15] SPAEMANN, *Persons*, 216.

forbid ourselves from acting in such an inhumane way, we follow our nature, but we do this, like no other natural being, on the basis of free decision.

But: Given that we do this, given that we follow our human nature and treat others as well as ourselves in accordance with the demand to respect their, and our own, personal dignity, what does this have to do with the *differentia specifica* which I denoted by the term "*animal symbolicum*"? To answer this question, I would like to quote one of the most beautiful passages of Claude Lévi-Strauss' *The Savage Mind* (*La pensée sauvage*), a passage in which the difference between our biological relationship and our natural kinship is characterized on the basis of purely anthropological and not at all metaphysical or theological criteria: "All the members of the species *Homo sapiens* are logically comparable to the members of any other animal or plant species. However, social life effects a strange transformation in this system, for it encourages each biological individual to develop a personality; and this is a notion no longer recalling specimens within a variety but rather types of varieties or of species, probably not found in nature ... and which could be termed 'mono-individual'. What disappears with the death of a personality is a synthesis of ideas and modes of behavior as exclusive and as irreplaceable as the one a floral species develops out of the simple chemical substances common to all species [...] Everything takes place as if in our civilization every individual's own personality were his totem: It is the signifier of his signified being."[16] That is to say: There are cultural forms of life which make the uniqueness of one's personality communicable to all members of human kind so that one becomes a kind of individual which in relation to all other natural kinds rather resembles a species more than a specimen. A species, however, never "follows" the specimen, but *vice versa*. So, what is embedded in the "social life" which, according to Lévi-Strauss, turns us into such a quasi-species must be a kind of return by ourselves to ourselves. This is the specific and essentially temporal difference which constitutes what we have called the incommensurability between our individual lives and the metonymical relation which forces any acting subject to find the totality of the conditions which justify his or her action incorporated in every single person who is affected by that action.

What we learn here from the anthropological point of view is that neither the modern concept of nature as the totality of objects determined by "natural laws" nor the classical notion of *physis* in the sense which we find in Aristotle can be the last word concerning the meaning of the term "nature." The symbolic relation between a human being and all others like him can neither be traced back to a hylomorphic understanding of natural beings nor to a dualistic view of an extratemporal "subject" beyond the natural sphere. Man as an

---

[16] C. Lévi-Strauss, *The Savage Mind* (Chicago: The University of Chicago Press, 1966), 214.

animal symbolicum transcends nature by transforming it, so that the 'whence' to which he returns when having undergone this process of transformation is no longer the same totality of species and the individuals which compose it that he started from; rather it is a new kind of totality which has not destroyed the structures that constituted the old one but has raised it to a higher, more complex level. Let me once more quote Spaemann who emphasizes that the term "person" marks a philosophical "discovery" which required a step beyond the teleological models of antique thinking. "The polarity of universal and individual, of class and member, leaves open for Plato the possibility that an individual human may rise above individuality, above being simply a unit in a class [...] But one thing never enters Plato's mind: that someone who 'achieves the Universal' attains a *higher level of being than the Universal itself*. That the justice realized and made concrete in a just man is more than the idea of justice; that the man who dies for his fatherland is more than his fatherland. As an atomic particle he merely contributes to the whole, the people; but in realizing his contributory role, he himself becomes a totality, compared with which the people is only an abstraction," so that the particular individuals "in an individual and irreplaceable way *are* the Universal. They are not parts of a larger whole, but totalities."[17] It is a post-Platonic and post-hylomorphic, and a genuine individualistic concept of "nature" which made possible the step toward the notions of personality and dignity; a step which we perhaps for the first time find taken when Cicero in *De officiis* recommended that in order to have a fulfilled life one should not follow another but one's own nature.[18] So, the nature to which one returns through the free decision to follow it is not the same as the one from which one started. Why? Because the "return" to it is exercised by *acting*, not by any kind of insight or contemplation (which of course may be an important presupposition for the action); and action by definition is never directed solely toward an abstract idea but always toward persons. Humanity is what enables us to return to ourselves by treating others as well as ourselves in a way which *turns out* to be the reason why we opted for it.

This brings me to the second and last step in exploring the challenge that the paradoxical conditions of our nature mean for our human existence. That unique kind of individual nature which makes a person something different from the members of a class or the varieties of a species, which makes it that "center of being" which can never be a phenomenon: How can it be characterized on the ontological level? In the philosophical tradition there is at least one concept that was formed precisely to mark the difference between the *humanitas*, the *natura communis* that connects all human, distinguishing them

---

[17] Spaemann, *Persons*, 19.
[18] Cf. W. Schweidler, "Die Menschenrechte als metaphysischer Verzicht," in *Das Unantastbare: Beiträge zur Philosophie der Menschenrechte* (Münster: LIT Verlag, 2001), 73–100.

from all non-human, beings, and the *entitas individualis*, the purely numeric identity that defines the incommensurability of the person: The *"haecceitas,"* which according to the *doctor subtilis* Duns Scotus, constitutes the genuine totality of our existence; a totality which is not understandable by reference to any natural qualities or capacities. *"Omnino est ignotum nisi secundum se totum concipiatur"* (is completely unknown unless it is grasped fully as it is in itself).[19] At this point we come back to our question about the challenge following from the incommensurability of human individuality, the inaccessibility of oneself for oneself. For Scotus this question, the problem of the *ultima solitudo* of the person, cannot be found but on the practical, the voluntary level, on which we face an absolutely passive constitution which connects all human beings: the *potentia oboedientialis* which we have as created beings in relation to our creator. In this conception, it is the personal nature of our creator which makes explicable that relation which we find in the paradox of the possible violation of the inviolable. We by definition cannot lose or renounce the gift that we have received by our creation, i.e. the gift to which we owe our own existence; whatever we do, we remain in the constitution which we have received by that gift, just because it is essentially passive and so precedes anything we ever could do. But once we act, we can ignore it and thereby deny it; in this case we become a kind of idol to ourselves, posit ourselves in the place of our creator, and then we become as incommunicable and impredicable as one must be when one serves under oneself.

What can we make of this Scotian conception for our problem? Do we in order to understand the paradox of humanity have to rely on a theological notion of creation? My answer: No, but I think there is a structural logic embedded in Scotus' concept of *"haecceitas"* which is still important for the philosophical reconstruction of our self-challenging existence. We find characterized that logic in the differentiation which Scotus makes in the *Ordinatio* (without explicitly using here the term *"haecceitas"*) where he says that the individual is per se intelligible but not for an intellect like the one we have.[20] In this

---

[19] Duns Scotus, *Ordinatio*, I d. 3 p. 1 q. 3 n. 148; cf. T. E. Mintken, "Das liebende Individuum bei Duns Scotus und Husserl als kritische Rückfrage an den gegenwärtigen Individualismus," *Theologie und Philosophie* 93, no. 1 (2018): 33–57.

[20] Scotus, *Ordinatio*, II.3.1 q. 6 n. 192: He compares this to the owl who cannot see the sun because of the limitations of its eyes and not because the sun is invisible per se. A similar metaphor in this respect is given by Nicolas of Cusa; viz. it is not the case that we are blind and therefore unable to see the sun, but rather, though we can see and indeed see the sun, its "brightness excels [the power of our] sight." Nicolas of Cusa, "Apologia doctae ignorantiae," in *Nicholas of Cusa's Debate with John Wenk: A Translation of De Ignota litteratura and Apologia doctae ignorantiae*, trans. J. Hopkins, 3rd ed. (Minneapolis: Arthur J. Banning Press, 1988), 460, §2. Aquinas articulates the same by means of a similar example, namely that a bat's perception of the light of the sun is limited by its own poor vision that is exceeded by the sun's light. Aquinas, *Summa Theologica*, I, q. 12, a. 1, resp.

perspective, the incommensurability and inaccessibility of the human person for any other one of his kind is the reason why the only way to respect him in his unique individuality is the obedience to general and, in the broadest horizon, to universal laws – i.e. to respect him as a member of the "jury" of which we have previously spoken. But when one follows the demands that result from this obligation to the other and oneself, then one's action, just because it is required but not necessitated by our nature, can be instructed by an intellectual power in which we find ourselves in some way preceded by ourselves. This at least was Husserl's answer to the question how the communicability of ourselves to ourselves can be rescued: to posit a "personality of a higher order."[21] This position does indeed imply religion, but not in a theological rather primarily in an anthropological horizon. Again Lévi-Strauss in *The Savage Mind* explicated this horizon when he analyzed one of the earliest stages of the development of our human self-understanding; the relation between religion and magic. "The anthropomorphism of nature (of which religion consists) and the physiomorphism of man (by which we have defined magic) constitute two components which are always given, and vary only in proportion … There is no religion without magic any more than there is magic without at least a trace of religion. The notion of a supernature exists only for a humanity which attributes supernatural powers to itself and in return ascribes the powers of its superhumanity to nature."[22] I would like to conclude with this as a demarcation of the intrinsic connection between the natural (including indirectly the biological and the technological) and the supernatural (including indirectly the anthropological and the theological) challenge as the key to the logic of limitation by which we will have to secure through our political and legal institutions the respect for human dignity.[23]

---

[21] Cf. HART, "The Absolute Ought and the Unique Individual." Cf. also U. MELLE, "Husserl's Personalist Ethics," *Husserl Studies*, 23, no. 1 (2007): 1–15: 3.

[22] LÉVI-STRAUSS, *The Savage Mind*, 221.

[23] I am very grateful to Neil O'Donnell for his help in the translation of my thoughts. I also profited immensely from his and from Tammo Mintken's stimulating ideas in our discussions.

Humanism in Dark Times

Daniel Chernilo[1]

Humanism is one of those polysemic terms that seem worn out and without redemption. The various meanings it has conveyed for centuries – a certain literary and even moral sensibility, a loosely defined philosophical movement, a particular kind of education, a proxy for secular values – do not necessarily make it a strong candidate for a fruitful intellectual engage. An intervention like this may perhaps do little to improve this situation, but I should like to try my chances nonetheless. My starting point is that the idea of humanism still has a significant role to play in contemporary normative debates, but that in order to do so it ought to embrace an egalitarian orientation that sees all members of the human species as equally able to produce and reproduce society (though under unequal social conditions that are not of their own making).[2]

An early expression of humanism gained visibility during the so-called Italian *quattrocento* (the 1400s) and was used to mark a break with a certain canon and presuppositions of medieval education.[3] This humanism was a precursor of the Renaissance, which was understood as a revival of some of the cultural traditions that were alive in Ancient Greece and Rome, but whose centrality had been superseded by the educational scholasticism within monastic orders.[4] The intellectual movement that ensued, heterogeneous as it was, gained salience thanks to the development of novel trends in the arts, science and philosophy. The rise of a more secular type of education went hand in hand with more practical forms of engagement with the world itself – this was apparent in the realm of technology, of course, but also in the ways in which politics and the economy were being conceived and acted upon. Increasingly, these changes came to be explicitly defined as anti- or at least a-religious.[5] By the end of

---

[1] I should like to thank Raymond Perrier for particularly insightful reflections on the first version of this paper as discussed at Claremont in February 2019. I am also grateful to participants of the Claremont conference on the philosophy of religion for the questions, comments and criticisms.

[2] For conventional accounts of humanism, see H. J. Blackham, *Humanism* (London: Penguin, 1968) and the edited collections by A. J. Ayer, *The Humanist Outlook* (London: Pemberton, 1968) and P. Kurtz, *The Humanist Alternative* (New York: Prometheus, 1973).

[3] Q. Skinner, *From Humanism to Hobbes* (Cambridge: Cambridge University Press, 2018).

[4] A. Bullock, *The Humanist Tradition in the West* (Wisbech: Thames and Hudson, 1985).

[5] T. Davies, *Humanism* (London: Routledge, 1997).

the enlightenment, writers like Voltaire[6] and Immanuel Kant[7] were already making explicit how their reflections on knowledge, nature and morality were effectively underpinned by notions of humanity that were philosophical (and increasingly scientific) rather than theological. The universalistic orientation that was central to the Enlightenment's view about our shared humanity was based on the earlier, more metaphysical, universalism of the natural law tradition: the rationalistic universalism of reason arose as the secular version of the Christian belief on the equality of our souls in god's eyes.[8] By the middle of the 19th century, questions of humanism were openly focusing on the status of the human and, to that extent, the argument can be made that they co-emerged with, and also battled against, all sorts of eugenic and indeed racist conceptions that, through an appeal to the alleged neutrality of the natural sciences, upheld the fundamental *inequality* of human beings.[9] At its most committed, the universalistic drive of humanism contended that all humans without exception belong to the same species. Much more contentiously, its argument was also radically *anthropocentric*: humans are the ultimate *makers, owners* and even the *measure* of all things in the world.[10]

The watershed moment within this cursory narrative comes for us in the 1940s. Soon after the end of World War II, a revisionist account of the crises of the past 30 years started blaming humanist beliefs for recent massacres and monstrosities. Humanism was now seen as the hypocritical ideological façade of state power, an unfettered ideology of material progress and technical advancements that was seen as responsible for a conspicuous process of dehumanisation that was nonetheless based on humanist grounds.[11] By the 1960s, many of the best-known European intellectuals – from Levi-Strauss to Althusser, Foucault, Luhmann or Derrida – shared the view that most of what is wrong in Western modernity was represented by the universalistic and anthropocentric underpinnings of humanism. Since the turn of the new century, moreover, this 'definitive' demise has become also apparent through cyborgs that challenge conventional ideas of human nature, animal lovers who challenge conventional ideas of human rights and green campaigners who challenge conventional ideas

---

[6] Voltaire, "Homme. Man," in *Political Writings*, ed. and trans. D. Williams (Cambridge: Cambridge University Press, 2003), 63–75.

[7] I. Kant, *Political writings*, ed. A. S. Reiss, 2nd ed. (Cambridge: Cambridge University Press, 1999).

[8] H. Rommen, *The Natural Law: A Study in Legal and Social History and Philosophy* (Indianapolis: The Liberty Fund, 1998).

[9] S. J. Gould, *The Mismeasure of Man* (London and New York: WW Norton, 1981).

[10] This extreme form of anthropocentrism is already apparent, for instance, in the title of V. G. Childe's (1951) classic work of early anthropology: *Man makes himself* (New York: Mentor 1951). The book was first published in 1936.

[11] K. Soper, *Humanism and Anti-Humanism* (La Salle, IL: Open Court, 1986).

of human sustainability. All kinds of post-, trans- and indeed anti-humanist positions have gained popularity and appear to achieve intellectual traction.[12] To my mind, this criticism has not only gone too far but it is misplaced. It has gone too far because it exaggerates the extent to which humanist ideas are in fact mere instruments of power and to blame for modernity's self-destructive tendencies. And it is misplaced because it conflates legitimate attempts at reflecting on our common status as human beings with their various ideological and political misappropriations.

Some readers may have notices already how the title of my piece is a nod to Hannah Arendt's collection of biographical essays on *Men in Dark Times*.[13] Among other intellectuals, she writes there about her mentor, Karl Jaspers, and her friend, Walter Benjamin. They were both humanist thinkers in very different ways: Jaspers through his commitment to a cosmopolitan justice and the self-reflective role of philosophy at times when humanity was struggling to cope with the world around it; Benjamin because of his aesthetic sensibility and wide-raging intellectual and political interests. Even if we think, as I *still* do, that analogies between our own situation and that of the 1930s in Europe are somewhat exaggerated, we are always confronted with the hard fact that hindsight is a beautiful thing: we may be wrong, and the rise of right-wing populism, plus our inability to face up to environmental challenges, are genuinely worrying. To Arendt, however, by the late 1950s the most worrying trend of her own *dark times* refers to those distortions within public life that find expression in *double talk*. We are losing hope in the fact that language, the most human of artefacts, is able to shed light on our contemporary predicament. War, massacres, and hunger are the most terrible afflictions of human life as a whole; they are constants of human experience. To Arendt, the tragedy of the present is of a different kind; we live in darks time indeed when even "[t]he light of the public obscures everything."[14] Our goal, therefore, must be to try to recover and renew a humanist legacy.

The orientation that inspires my reflections below build on the idea of *philosophical sociology* I have been developing in the past few years.[15] It is a humanist program for three main reasons: (1) it understands the particularity of human

---

[12] R. BRAIDOTTI, *The Posthuman* (Cambridge: Polity Press, 2013); D. HARAWAY, *When Species Meet* (Minneapolis, MN: University of Minnesota Press, 2008); S. FULLER and V. LIPINSKA, *The Proactive Imperative. A Foundation for Transhumanism* (Basingstoke: Palgrave Macmillan, 2014).

[13] H. ARENDT, *Men in Dark Times* (New York: Harcourt, Brace & World, 1968).

[14] Ibid., ix.

[15] D. CHERNILO, "The idea of philosophical sociology," *British Journal of Sociology* 65, no. 2 (2014): 338–357; *Debating Humanity. Towards a Philosophical Sociology* (Cambridge: Cambridge University Press, 2017); "The question of the human in the Anthropocene debate," *European Journal of Social Theory* 20 (2017): 44–60.

lives and experiences within the context of an egalitarian conception of the human species; (2) it treats the anthropological capacities we share as humans (language, bodily integrity, moral responsibility) as central to how humans justify normative ideas in society (justice, equality, solidarity); and, (3) it contends that philosophical enquiry into what makes a human life worth living, on the one hand, and sociological interrogations into how people organize the lives in common, on the other, are two sides of the same coin: *good sociological questions are always, in the last instance, philosophical ones about what makes us the kind of (human) beings that we actually are.*

My paper is structured as follows. The first section is reconstructive as I should like to succinctly reassess the origins of current critiques of humanism have become the by default position in contemporary debates. The second offers a positive argument on the relationships between humanism, universalism and egalitarianism that is also able to counter some of those criticisms. The two main texts that I use below are, respectively, Martin Heidegger's *Letter on Humanism* (first published in 1946) and Jean-Paul Sartre's lecture on *Existentialism is a Humanism*, which was first delivered in October 1945.

1. Current Critiques of Humanism

Canadian philosopher Charles Taylor ranks among the leading intellectuals of the past fifty years. An extremely prolific writer, the extent of his intellectual interests is apparent through works that range from Hegel to multiculturalism, from human language to religion. In 1989, he published a book on *Sources of the Self* – an impressive tome in which he critically assessed modern ideas of identity in order to offer a new, more nuanced, vision of how much our sense of who we are is embedded in conceptions of the good life. At the opening of that book, Taylor makes the following remark:

"*We are all universalists now about respect for life and integrity.* But this means not just that we happen to have such reactions or that we have decided in the light of the present predicament of the human race that it is useful to have such reactions [...] It means rather that we believe it would be utterly wrong and unfounded to draw the boundaries [about human groups, DC] any narrower *than around the whole human race.*"[16]

To Taylor, universalistic beliefs guarantee that, in Western democracies at least, certain fundamental rights have become institutionalized: freedoms of movement, of the press and of cult, universal suffrage, social welfare, autonomy between and division of powers, equality before the law and indeed the rule of

---

[16] C. TAYLOR, *Sources of the Self. The Making of Modern Identity* (Cambridge, MA: Harvard University Press, 1989), 6–7, my italics.

law itself. Taylor's intellectual project may be depicted as a form of moral realism in the sense that our beliefs about the intrinsic worthiness of certain values, principles or institutions are not merely subjective. Instead, they depend upon and are articulated around the objective properties of those objects to which they are attached – chief among them human beings themselves: the fact that "human beings command our respect [...] seems to be a human universal."[17]

Taylor's philosophy is surely humanist in the sense that he seeks to offer a better account of the constitutive features of human identities. His work focuses on how humans are defined by the moral evaluations they make and the ways in which these are linguistically articulated.[18] However, he has several problems with the philosophical underpinnings of modern universalism, all which point against the reductionism of conventional ideas of humanism: its formalism is hollow and does not allow for substantive moral judgements; its naturalism is ontologically deficient and does not allow for thick cultural attachments, its instrumentalism is too reductionist and focuses "on what it is right to do rather than on what it is good to be."[19] Taylor's criticisms boil down to two sets of issues. First, intellectual strategies that favour the universal over the particular cannot give a full picture of human beings as essentially *situated* moral beings. The universalistic insistence on neutrality, impartiality and proceduralism fails to grasp the specificity of those cultural and moral attachments that create a *collective* sense of the good life which, in turn, makes an *individual* human life worth living. Secondly, Taylor's historical reconstruction of the philosophical dead-ends of universalistic beliefs becomes possible only now because they have outlived themselves. Universalistic convictions had a contribution to make in the development of world religions and, through the transformations of ideas of natural law (as obligations) into natural rights (as entitlements), they have also played a key role in the rise of modern legal systems. Yet they are now eroded beyond repair.[20]

Take now the case of Peter Sloterdijk. A philosopher, polemicist and cultural critic, his writings exude a Nietzschean sensibility that distrusts of all ideas of value. He has very little in common with Taylor in either substance or style: if Taylor offers a form of moral realism, Sloterdijk is far closer to a form of (mild) nihilism. In the context of a discussion of Martin Heidegger's *Letter on humanism*, for instance, Sloterdijk[21] makes the following remarks:

---

[17] Ibid., 11.
[18] C. TAYLOR, *The Language Animal* (Cambridge, MA: Harvard University Press, 2016).
[19] TAYLOR, *Sources of the Self*, 1.
[20] I have discussed Taylor's work along these lines in CHERNILO, *Debating Humanity*, 158–180.
[21] P. SLOTERDIJK, "Rules for the Human Zoo: A Response to the Letter on Humanism," *Environment and Planning D: Society and Space* 27 (2009): 17.

"Why should humanism and its general philosophical self-presentation be seen as the solution for humanity, when the catastrophe of the present clearly shows that it is man himself, along with his system of metaphysical self-improvement and self-clarification, that is the problem?"

Sloterdijk is critical of Heidegger's philosophy but he nonetheless adopts Heidegger's indictment on modern humanism, which is seen as a 'metaphysical' system that is built on the uncritical belief in 'self-improvement and self-clarification'. This system of metaphysics may pretend to be rational and self-positing because of its reliance on two of modernity's most significant normative values: the ideas of *progress* and *autonomy*. But far from rational arguments, they are just the unwarranted dogmas of our own times. The more humans pursue these values in their search for perfecting themselves and their social orders, the more disoriented and dangerous their actions become. As we will see below, one of Heidegger's key argument is that an inversion has taken place, whereby ideas of 'man', 'the human' and 'humanity' can no longer be seen as a possible foundation for a better future – they are rather the main sources of our current ills. The normative orientation of humanism must be inverted because, instead of allowing humanity to move forward, we have been suffering their pernicious effects for several decades:

"What can tame man, when the role of humanism as the school for humanity has collapsed? What can tame men, when their previous attempts at self-taming have led primarily to power struggles? What can tame men, when, after all previous experiments to grow the species up, it remains unclear what it is to be a grown-up? Or is it simply no longer possible to pose the question of the constraint and formation of mankind by theories of civilizing and upbringing?"[22]

Central to the rise and demise of modern humanism, therefore, is the troubled relationships between the promises of emancipation and the reality of disappointments of modern life in general and modern technology in particular. Technology has a pride of place in the organization of modern societies because it works as the interface between nature and society, whose applications are to be found in all domains of modern life. Technology has become the 'practical' expression of modern science and as such it reaffirms its 'superiority over traditional or religious ways of understanding the world: from trains to airplanes, from antibiotics to heart transplants, technology is the visible face of that material progress that makes life longer and more enjoyable to ever wider segments of the world's population. The anti-universalist critique of humanism was able to combine well with a critique of technology that rejected material progress as shallow and inessential. It offered a romantic appeal to an ideal community (whether past or future, real or ideal), to the need for nature to remain unpol-

---

[22] Ibid., 20.

luted, to reject the equation between reason in general and with instrumental rationality in particular. Crucially, there is an elitism that contaminates this critique insofar as mass industrial society – soulless, beauty-less, disenchanted – is seen as the direct offspring of modern technology, which in turn expresses the most fundamental but also dangerous constructivism of modernity: a world that can be transformed – indeed created – at man's will.

This negative understanding of technology was common within conservative social thought at the time when Martin Heidegger developed his own critique of modern life and philosophy.[23] By the end of the 1920s, he was arguably the most original and promising philosopher in Germany.[24] As he rejected conventional philosophy – in the form of neo-Kantianism – Heidegger implied that the renovation of philosophy ought to entail a renovation of its relationship with life itself. The failures of academic philosophy – rigid in methodologism and soulless in its disconnection with everyday experiences – were the ultimate expression of the crisis of bourgeois modernity as a whole. His critique of humanism, which has since become the most influential of the past 70 years, built on this reputation and themes.

Heidegger put forward this critique immediately after the end of World War II, and its success may be explained by how it turned humanism as paradigmatic of those terms with the help of which he thought we were going to rescue modern life from itself. Heidegger rejects modern technology because it has become the key expression of the materialism and constructivism of modern culture as a whole. A purely instrumental conception of technology reinforces the distorted anthropocentrism that governs modern civilization: it creates the illusion of human authorship and of full control of the consequences of our actions. Rather than being a mere instrument, technology is a "form of truth" which "is grounded in the history of metaphysics;"[25] it has become existentially crucial for us to realize that "the essence of technology is nothing technological."[26] The technological transformation of the world changes everything connected to human beings because it triggers an inauthentic relationship between being, man and the world.[27] Indeed, the radical inauthenticity that governs modern times obtains from the 'monstrousness' of modern technology itself.[28]

---

[23] In the case of Germany, this is clearly visible in writings by E. JÜNGER, *The Storm of Steel* (New York: Howard Fertig, 1996) and C. SCHMITT, "The Age of Neutralizations and Despolitizations," Télos 96 (1993): 130–142.

[24] P. GORDON, *Continental Divide. Heidegger, Cassirer, Davos* (Cambridge, MA: Harvard University Press, 2012).

[25] M. HEIDEGGER, "Letter on Humanism," in *Basic writings*, ed. D. F. Krell (London: Routledge, 1993), 243–244.

[26] M. HEIDEGGER, "The Question Concerning Technology," in *Basic writings*, ed. D. F. Krell (London: Routledge, 1993), 340.

[27] HEIDEGGER, "Letter on Humanism," 255.

[28] HEIDEGGER, "The Question Concerning Technology," 321.

Heidegger's dislike of technology is intimately connected to its universalistic qualities: technology uproots the world within which it is applied, technology breaks apart the relationship between the authentic and the inauthentic, between natives and strangers, between the past and the future. Heidegger's rejection of technology is based on the fact that it can be applied anywhere and everywhere: modern technology has no home, it knows no *Heimat*.[29]

A text Heidegger composed in 1946, the main argument of *Letter on Humanism* is that we are only able to understand 'man' if we relate it to the higher question of 'being': above all, we must break free from the humanist illusions of autonomy and self-determination. This piece was partly written as a reply to Sartre's *Existentialism is a Humanism* lecture, which had been delivered in Paris in October 1945 and been brought to Heidegger's attention. Biographically, Heidegger wrote *Letter* under difficult personal circumstances: he was living under French-administered territories and was right in the middle of the trials that were to decide on his academic future given his actions, on behalf of the Nazi regime, as Rector of the University of Freiburg. Heidegger was not allowed to move freely, feared incarceration and confiscation of property, one of his sons was still a prisoner of war and his pension rights were also hanging in the balance at the time.[30]

The reason for Heidegger's rejection of humanism is that it has come to express the modern perversions of egalitarianism, rationalism and subjectivity as the very values that were to blame for the war. In Heidegger's account, the crisis that led to World War II had nothing to do with racism, nationalism, antisemitism, irrationalism, mob rule, nor is it characterized by aggressive propaganda, militarization and the total suspension of the rule of law both at home and abroad. With this move, Heidegger inaugurated the type of critique of egalitarianism and universalism that Taylor would not support explicitly but no longer feared; the critique that Sloterdijk was happy to advance further: the humanism of Western metaphysics is responsible for the crisis of modern society: "is the *damage* caused by all such terms [as humanism] still not sufficiently obvious?"[31]

---

[29] E. LEVINAS, "Heidegger, Gagarin and us," in *Difficult Freedom. Essays on Judaism* (Baltimore, MD: John Hopkins University Press, 1990), 232–233.

[30] For an account of the context within which Heidegger composed *Letter*, see E. KLEINBERG, *Generation Existential. Heidegger's Philosophy in France 1927–1961* (Ithaca, NY: Cornell University Press, 2003), 162–168; T. ROCKMORE, "Foreword to the English edition," in *Heidegger. The Introduction of Nazism into Philosophy*, ed. E. Faye (New Haven, CT: Yale University Press, 2009), vii–xxi.

[31] HEIDEGGER, "Letter on Humanism," 219, my italics. After several decades of intense debate, it is beyond doubt now that the authoritarian, nationalistic, antisemitic and irrationalist dimensions of Heidegger's philosophy made his political support of the Nazi regime a fact that is both biographically and philosophically significant (E. FAYE, *Heidegger*; R. SAFRANSKI, *Martin Heidegger: Between Good and Evil* [Cambridge, MA: Harvard University Press, 1998]);

To Heidegger, humanism is a form of subjectivism because it focuses on the narrow, particularistic of point of view of 'man' and, in so doing, it renounces to grasp the ultimate essence of 'being': humanism sides with the subjectivity of the *anthropos* and thus rejects the pursuit of being as that which is genuinely essential and permanent. Because of this subjectivism, humanism is also a form of relativism and even nihilism: because it promises 'autonomy' and soothes its dangers with a certainty of 'progress', humans believe they are free to do as they please. The radical constructivism of modern humanism is to blame for the self-destructive nature of modernity: humans act as if they can think for themselves, rule themselves, and create their own institutions, and the main result of this total arrogance is the fact that they have nearly destroyed themselves. A departure from humanism is really another way of rejecting also anthropocentrism; that is, the notion that "man" is the ultimate measure of all things. With humanism and anthropocentrism being treated as the dogmatic expressions of Western metaphysics, the anti-egalitarian nature of this critique becomes fully apparent. Humanism failed to deliver on its promise of offering a strong sense of the human; the war and its atrocities demonstrate beyond doubt the irresponsibilities that ensue when we fall for the modern myth of the autonomy of the human. Humanism faces also an insurmountable internal contradiction: while its main credo is the self-positing egalitarianism whereby humans learn to treat one another as members of the same species of equal worth, in actual fact humanist notions have consistently required such external justifications as nature, history or god can provide. From Catholicism to Marxism, from historicism to biologicism, the one constant of modern humanism is that it betrays its own immanence and resorts to something that is external to our shared humanity in order to grant self-positing powers to humans themselves.

Given that this external reference point *is* crucial, this only shows the extent to which modern humanism is unable to grasp that most general questions – Heidegger thinks here of questions about 'being' – are those that reject egalitarianism and seek for higher sources of human: the near experience of death, an original relation to language, the essential rootedness of communal life, a permanent attachment to the *Volk*: these are the kind of experiences that Heidegger took as fundamentally human because they point to something that lies beyond and outside humans themselves, they were essential to Heidegger because they separate out between groups of humans and create a hier-

---

D. DI CESARE, *Heidegger and the Jews. The Black Notebooks* [Cambridge, MA: Polity, 2018]). Credit must then be given to Karl Löwith, who saw it all quite clearly already in 1946: 'Heidegger did not "misunderstand himself" when he supported Hitler; on the contrary, anyone who did not comprehend how he could do this did not understand him' (K. LÖWITH, *Heidegger and European Nihilism* [New York: Columbia University Press, 1995], 223). I have discussed this extensively in CHERNILO, *Debating Humanity*, 23–63.

archy within them. To Heidegger, the critique of humanism works around a whole range of anti-cosmopolitan and anti-universalist tropes: irrationalism is more sober and less authoritarian than rationality, authenticity and simplicity are more genuine than emancipation and self-determination, elitism is to be preferred against egalitarianism, only poetry and contemplation touch on the essential in a manner that technology, science and academic philosophy will never be able to do. Domesticity, authenticity and rootedness are treated as the only options available for the promise of a pristine and unpolluted existence in a world that, through technology, state bureaucracy and mass democracy, has nearly destroyed itself. The real danger of inhumanity lays dormant underneath modern institutions whose humanism – based as it is on mystified notions of autonomy, social change and emancipation – is as flawed as it is inescapable in modernity.

Humanism blocks our ability to ask ultimate questions and, in dogmatically asserting a purely egalitarian idea of man that concentrates on the subjectivity of the *anthropos*, it contributes to its radical devaluation. It is within this context that Heidegger criticizes the traditional anthropological conception of the human as *animal rationale*, because it still conceives our humanity in terms of what we share with beasts: "Animal means beast. Man is the beast endowed with reason."[32] Heidegger then distinguishes between this rational animal and an alternative notion of the human that he recovered from the Roman idea of *humanitas*. The humanity of human beings is now defined through an essential notion of being because only thus may humans be able to transcend modern egalitarianism, raise above themselves, and ask genuinely fundamental questions:

"If we are to think of man not as an organism but a *human* being, we must first give attention to the fact that man is that being who has his being by pointing to what is (…) Man is the being who is in that he points toward "Being," and who can be himself only as he always and everywhere refers himself to what is."[33]

Heidegger rejects modern humanism "because it does not set the *humanitas* of man high enough;"[34] the fact that humans share an organic constitution with other living creatures blocks our ability to specify the uniqueness of their humanity; it constitutes too base a ground to establish what is essential in humanity. It reproduces the traditional dualisms of the metaphysical tradition – the mind and the organism, the body and the soul – and makes apparent all that is wrong with modern attempts at understanding the human.

Heidegger's critique of humanism is then construed through a dual negation: first, being is to be preferred over against the human, which means that

---

[32] M. HEIDEGGER, *What is Called Thinking?* (New York: Harper Collins, 2004), 61.
[33] Ibid., 148–149.
[34] HEIDEGGER, "Letter on Humanism," 233–234.

there is little to be concerned about when undermining its normative status. As in Carl Schmitt's famous formulation: if humanity equals bestiality, then we ought to celebrate its definitive demise. Secondly, within humanity itself, higher forms of *humanitas* are to be cared for at the expense of the baseness of the rational *animal*: an elite of poets and philosophers are always to protected and promoted, and for them to reach their potential, others – those less talented, fortunate, and able to contribute to humanity's higher tasks – may have to suffer and bear the costs. By rejecting the egalitarianism that is constitutive of the modern imaginary, Heidegger turned humanism into the true totalitarian ideology of modernity itself.

2. Humanism, Universalism and Egalitarianism

Jean Paul Sartre's lecture on *Existentialism is a Humanism* was originally delivered in Paris to a packed lecture hall in October 1945.[35] It is a philosophical text with a strong political message at a time of national crisis and, although it does not represent a definitive position with Sartre's body of work, it remains his most popular piece.[36] Sartre's thinking about humanism is connected to an egalitarian orientation in three key ways: (1) a general principle of subjective responsibility that is not however individualistic; (2) a critique of essentialism in the form of group thinking; and (3) a notion of universal sympathy that coheres around sociocultural diversity. Let me discuss each of these themes in turn.

Sartre's starting point is the idea of *individual responsibility*, but he contends that in order to understand this properly we must reject an individualistic point of view. He used the term *subjectivity* in order to underscore how individuality is constituted through rather than against intersubjective relations. The right ontological grounding of subjectivity gives integrity to an idea of the human person which, rightly understood, always implies her relationships with others. Despite its shortcomings, therefore, modern individualism as exposed in liberal social and political thought is a permanent historical achievement whose normative purchase lies in the idea of freedom as the fundamental relation into which humans enter with one another. Crucially, this is the basis on which Sartre[37] seeks to connect the particular and the universal: individual responsibility is 'much greater than we might have supposed, *because it concerns all*

---

[35] J.-P. SARTRE, *Existentialism is a Humanism* (New Heaven, CT: Yale University Press, 2007).
[36] P. BAERT, *The Existentialist Moment: The Rise of Sartre as a Public Intellectual* (Cambridge, MA: Polity Press, 2015).
[37] SARTRE, *Existentialism*, 24.

mankind' (my italics). The correct formulation of normative ideas requires a universalistic outlook, so that humanity is unequivocally conceived as a single species, and it is also egalitarian insofar as all members of the human species are of equal worth. A fundamental dialectics is at play between individual freedom, on the one side, and a general freedom that is fully inclusive, on the other: we "will freedom for freedom's sake through our individual circumstances. And in thus willing freedom, we discover that it depends entirely on the freedom of others, and that the freedom of others depends on our own."[38] The egalitarianism of his argument has its own self-propelling drive, moreover: to embrace one's own freedom makes it more likely for others to do the same: "freedom wills itself and the freedom of others."[39] But while liberals emphasize excessively the freedoms of the individual, Sartre is at paints to underscore that because freedom itself requires a strong notion of responsibility, then it cannot be understood in a purely individualistic fashion. The modern idea of individuality is inseparable from our relationships with others and, in order to understand these relations fully, we cannot focus only on freedom but must pay attention to responsibility as well.

Given the premise that humans are free and responsible beings whose identities they form alongside others, Sartre rejects any essentialism that resorts to immutable ideas of human nature: there is nothing in humans, he thinks, that is preordained in nature. He equally rejects the perils of 'group error' in modernity, as it simply makes no sense to draw substantive conclusions from deceptively similar traits or behavioral patterns to be found in such groups as the 'Germans' or the 'French'.[40] These collective nouns are indeed common in everyday language, and surely possess a sociocultural and political locus, but they do not refer to substantive wholes, they are not self-contained entities, and they are never more significant than the individuals who belong to them. To Sartre, the worst error of group thinking is precisely the fact that it seeks to give an account of social life without notions of subjectivity and individuality – thence cancelling any meaningful reference to freedom and responsibility. Neither ideas of human nature that reduce the human to biology nor notions of collective identity that reduce the human to a fix set of cultural traits can do the normative job of justifying such values as autonomy and freedom; on the contrary, human freedom and responsibility are alone "the foundation of all values."[41]

The egalitarian orientation of Sartre's humanism, therefore, builds on the combined arguments that only human beings create values for themselves, that

---

[38] Ibid., 48.
[39] Ibid., 49.
[40] J.-P. SARTRE, *Anti-Semite and Jew* (New York: Shocken, 1995), 82.
[41] SARTRE, *Existentialism*, 48.

all humans are equally able to create values, and that the values humans create achieve their normative purchase in relation to how they appeal to our common belonging to a single human species. A critical lesson of Sartre's work is how he upholds the very egalitarianism that, as we saw above, later critiques of humanism have sought to undermine. The radicalism of this egalitarian position is most apparent in the way Sartre distinguishes between two different meanings of the term humanism. A first type of humanism, which he rejects, takes pride in the collective accomplishments of the human species – for instance, its works of art or technological innovations – and then invites individual human beings to partake in this admiration for what the best among humans have been able to achieve through the ages. Sartre describes this humanism as a 'cult of humanity' and he rejects it as a form essentialism and elitism: one must "never consider man as an end (... rather the opposite ...) man is constantly in the making."[42] Here, Sartre partly subverts Kant's dictum that humans are never to be treated as mere means but that, given their dignity, they are ends in themselves.[43] To Sartre, no glorification of the accomplishments of the few can be used to justify their passive admiration on behalf of the many: this is not a genuine form of humanism because it lacks its essentially egalitarian drive – it is nothing but a form of authoritarianism and of elitism in disguise. Indeed, this is precisely the kind of argument that opens the door for the ultimate *devaluation* of whoever is not deemed capable of reaching such heights: women, Roma, children, the ill. True, there is a humanist dimension to this view because it does not use anything outside humans themselves to found and justify values, but it is not a genuine form of humanism because it is based on the presupposition that we must rank groups of people and indeed individuals themselves according to their potential contribution to humanity's excellence. Given the historical context within which Sartre is writing this piece, it is not surprising that he rejects this false humanism because it "leads ultimately [...] to Fascism."[44]

---

[42] Ibid., 52.
[43] Wrongly in my view, Sartre claims that Kant had reintroduced within his moral thinking the same utilitarian logic that he thought he had left behind. For further discussion, see H. ARENDT, *The Human Condition* (Chicago, IL: The University of Chicago Press, 1998), 155–207 and P. SELZNICK, *A Humanist Science. Values and Ideals in Social Inquiry* (Stanford, CA: Stanford University Press, 2008), 11–14. My own interpretation is available in D. CHERNILO, *The Natural Law Foundations of Modern Social Theory: A Quest for Universalism* (Cambridge: Cambridge University Press, 2013), 121–131; *Debating Humanity*, 72–77.
[44] SARTRE, *Existentialism*, 52. Sartre read Heidegger as a humanist philosopher and Heidegger composed *Letter* at least in part to disavow that Sartrean interpretation. To most in Sartre's generation, Heidegger could not have been a Nazi because he was an existentialist (H. J. BLACKHAM, *Humanism* [London: Penguin, 1962]); L. GOLDMANN, *The Human Sciences and Philosophy* (London: Cape, 1969).

Having rejected the elitist option, Sartre then delineates the humanism to which he is positively committed. In order to do this, he introduces the notion of *human transcendence*: "man is always outside of himself, and it is in projecting and losing himself beyond himself that man is realised [...] it is in pursuing transcendental goals that he is able to exist."[45] This is an appeal to transcendence that requires no metaphysical cosmology, cultural historicism, racial essentialism or biological determinism. It points instead to humans' fundamental freedom and responsibility: "man is nothing other than what he makes of himself [...] there is no other legislator than himself."[46] Sartre's humanism centres on the human capacities for self-legislation, which we may define as the creative capacity of imagining a different world and of making the world a different place. This humanism is a form of realism, moreover, because it allows humans no place to hide from their selfish motivations and ideological delusions. It is a humanism that requires humans to take full responsibility for who they are, for the way they behave and for the consequences of their decisions. It is, above all, a fundamentally egalitarian form of humanism.

The final and perhaps most significant dimension in Sartre's vision of humanism is more methodological in kind; he puts forward the idea that humans have the ability to develop a generalized sense of sympathy towards fellow humans. This may perhaps be rehearsed along the lines of the reflections that Adam Smith offers at the beginning of *The Theory of Moral Sentiments*:[47] as the ability to put oneself in somebody else's position, genuine human sympathy is predicated on the fact that there are some experiences that people do *not* share but can nonetheless be mutually understood. Because of that, they are able to temporarily transcend, or at least bracket out, their first-person perspective and see the world from a different point of view. The claim is precisely that humans are able to reach across many if not most of their differences in order to see the world with different eyes.

It seems a good idea, however, to distinguish a bit more clearly who these others to whom our sympathy may be directed actually are, and I should like to suggest that there are at least two very different groups of people here (this is a distinction Sartre does not really make). On the one hand, our personal biography is constituted through our intersubjective interactions with all those significant others with whom we interact in daily life. Parents, partners, friends and colleagues are of course a crucial here, and there are also countless strangers whose paths we fleetingly cross and who may become quite as crucial in developing a *unique* sense of we are (think, for instance, of experiences

---

[45] Sartre, *Existentialism*, 52.
[46] Ibid., 22, 53.
[47] A. Smith, *The Theory of Moral Sentiments* (London: Penguin, 2009), 13–33.

of 'casual' racial discrimination or sexual harassment in public spaces and how significant they are from an experiential point of view). What sociologists and social psychologists usually regard as our identities – both personal and social – are formed through the ways in which these experiences build and sediment over time so that they eventually give shape to our biographical trajectories.[48] On the other hand, in modern times these experiences are increasingly framed within the imaginary (or, to be more precise, counterfactual) notion of a generalized human subject that encompasses humanity as a whole.[49] All our social interactions are contextual and take place within clearly bounded (national, cultural) settings, but in modern times they belong also within a deeper framework, as it were, that points to a more universalistic and egalitarian direction. As we saw above with reference to Charles Taylor's comments, most modern legal institutions are built on such premises. The ways in which we learn to see and treat each other as humans depend how we learn to construe others as similar as well as unlike ourselves. And we do this within two, rather different temporal and sociohistorical coordinates: one that is concretely located and necessarily corresponds to the here and now of our specific contexts, and a generalized notion of humanity that includes all possible others, most of whom are not here with us and we will never meet.

In the past few decades, it has become common within the social sciences to ground sympathetic understanding more narrowly and only on those aspects that people share. For instance, a key argument in theories of intersectionality in the social sciences is that experiences of gender, racial or religious discrimination can only be understood by those who have undergone similar situations.[50] Sartre's argument works in the opposite direction, however: both the emotional and the cognitive ability to put oneself in somebody else's position becomes possible because we are situated in different contexts, because we have been exposed to different experiences, and indeed because we are driven by our very different interests and motivations. He writes:

"Human universality exists, but it is not a given; it is in perpetual construction [...] I construct it by understanding every other man's project, regardless of the era in which he lives [...] The fundamental aim of existentialism is to reveal the link between the absolute character of the free commitment, by which every man realizes himself in realizing a type of humanity – *a commitment that is always understandable, by anyone in any era* – and the relativity of the culture ensemble that may result from such a choice."[51]

---

[48] M. S. ARCHER, *Structure, Agency and the Internal Conversation* (Cambridge: Cambridge University Press, 2003).
[49] J. HABERMAS, *Truth and Justification* (Cambridge, MA: The MIT Press, 2003).
[50] S. WALBY, J. ARMSTRONG, and S. STIRD, "Intersectionality: Multiple Inequalities in Social Theory," *Sociology* 46 (2012): 224–240.
[51] SARTRE, *Existentialism*, 43, my italics.

Sartre explicitly makes this point as a critique of Eurocentrism when he refers to our mutual understanding with a "Chinese, Indian or black African: There is universality in every project, *inasmuch as any man is capable of understanding any human project*."[52] The possibility of a universal sympathy is not only plausible but necessary because, as members of the same human species, there are some needs and capabilities that apply to us all: we can and indeed do experience inter- and trans-cultural sympathy on such key experiences as grief, pain, love, fear, admiration and happiness. This universalism is incompatible with elitism, essentialism or determinism; on the contrary, it only makes sense on the basis of a strong commitment to the egalitarianism of universal membership of all individuals to our common humanity. To a large extent, this is similar to what, based on Immanuel Kant, Hannah Arendt described as our *cosmopolitan* existence:[53] in addition to the particularities that define us, we are always also part of the widest possible community of humans, and this is the community on whose bases genuine socio-cultural and normative dialogue is possible and ought to remain open.

Yet Sartre's own arguments on how to build this egalitarian commonality are not themselves free of difficulties. His analysis of modern antisemitism shows, for instance, a fundamental ambivalence with regards to the precise role of cultural traits in his explanations of social life. Sartre duly rejects what we may call a flat universalism that knows no culture at all and speaks only of individuals as if they were completely underdetermined by their cultural specificity: "man does not exist; there are Jews, Protestants, Catholics; there are Frenchmen, Englishmen, Germans; there are whites, blacks and yellows."[54] Sartre rejects a wholly abstract idea of 'man' because people do not live their lives in a void but within particular cultural and historical contexts. Crucially, humans see themselves as belonging to groups and, because of that, they orient their actions accordingly. However, Sartre remained unable to give positive content to these sociocultural reference points; perhaps in order to avoid falling for the kind of group error he had just criticized, he fails to say what being French or German *actually* means. Arguably the clearest example of this difficulty comes in his account of the relationships between antisemitism and Jewish identity, as Sartre contends that "it is the anti-Semite who creates the Jew."[55] Sartre is in trouble here because 'Jews' is a social category that has concrete meaning for all those who identify themselves as Jews or have to interact with people who define themselves as Jews. Given that these cultural attachments do matter to those who make use of them, Sartre ought to be able to

---

[52] Ibid., 43, my italics.
[53] H. Arendt, *Lectures on Kant's Political Philosophy* (Chicago: The University of Chicago Press, 1992), 55, 75–76.
[54] SARTRE, *Anti-semite and Jew*, 144–155.
[55] Ibid., 143.

ascertain how exactly these cultural references work, yet he cannot do this. Indeed, if the antisemite genuinely *creates* the Jew, then the Jew becomes a passive recipient of cultural traditions and social markers that only dehumanize them: Sartre has thus subtracted the ideas of freedom and responsibility that otherwise underpin his notion of individual agency.[56]

The tension between more universalistic and more particularistic groundings of human sympathy that is central to this debate has of course different versions. Within sociology, Max Weber reflected on similar issues a century or so ago. In the opening pages of his posthumous *Economy and Society*, Weber lays the conceptual and methodological grounds for the development of his *comprehensive* sociology *–verstehende Soziologie*. There are several of his arguments that are significant for us; the best known one is perhaps the idea that a social action is defined by whether or not there are socially significant meanings attached to it. For instance, if you observe someone reading alone, this is still a social action insofar as only the sociocultural context of this action will allow you to ascertain whether the person is preparing for an exam or reading for leisure. To Weber we also owe the distinction between instrumental and substantive rationality, where the former 'reduces' all meaningful connections to relations between means and ends, and he developed as well the notion of ideal types as methodological devices with the help of which researches can organise disparate historical materials into more fruitful conceptual schemes. But there is another contribution in Weber's sociology which, although it has not attracted a comparable level of attention, remains crucial for our discussion. A genuinely sociological understanding, says Weber, is only possible if and when it builds bridges between humans who do not share a common context or background. He makes the point metaphorically: "one need not to be Caesar in order to understand Caesar."[57] Writing at the beginning of the 20th century, Weber's argument is that if the nascent social sciences were going to make a genuinely scientific contribution to our comprehension of social and historical reality, this may only lie in their ability to allow different peoples – those who did not live 2,000 years ago and will never rule over an empire – to come as closely as possible to an understanding of those contexts, circumstances and personal choices that actually configured those events under investigation.

---

[56] I cannot discuss this in any great detail, but it is worthy of mention how Sartre's piece on *Anti-Semitism and the Jew* belongs within a long tradition of 'progressive' critiques of antisemitism which however struggle to articulate what is actually positive in a modern Jewish identity. The classic of this genre is, of course, K. MARX's, "On the Jewish Question," in *Early writings*, ed. L. Colletti (London: Penguin, 1975), 210–241. See also I. DEUTSCHER, *The Non-Jewish Jew and Other Essays* (London: Merlin, 1981), 25–59 and R. FINE and P. SPENCER, *Antisemitism and the Left. On the Return of the Jewish Question* (Manchester: Manchester University Press, 2017), 30–43 for further discussion.

[57] M. WEBER, *Economy and Society*, vol. 1 (New York: Bedminster, 1968), 5.

More recently, this theme has been taken up by the sociologist and legal scholar Philips Selznick. On the one hand, Selznick contends that the argument about *verstehen* requires a universalistic commitment on the general comprehensibility of human experience. In addition to its methodological implications, this orientation carries normative consequences as well:

"The injunction 'taking the point of view of the actor' is in part a moral message: remember the humanity of all persons, the despised as well as the honored; explore the conditions that help them resist degradation and oppression. A postulate of humanity directs inquiry to the moral promise of human life, including latent ideals of responsibility and cooperation."[58]

This is a point in need of emphasizing because, as said, much contemporary social science treats this form of intercultural understanding as ineffectual at best and politically reactionary at worst. On the other hand, the philosophical elucidation of an egalitarian principle of humanity cannot be mistaken for the actual explanatory work of trying to make sense of particular sociocultural contexts:

"*verstehen* is at best a partial rendering of the postulate of humanity, which takes its departure from knowledge of human nature and the human condition, not from assumptions of *mutual* understanding. *The postulate calls for empirical study of cultures and social worlds —* that is, of the diverse ways in which minds are formed, incentives are generated, and norms of conduct established."[59]

Weber's use of the term *empathy* as an essential building block of his sociological method is based on the fundamentally egalitarian presupposition that all human experiences and all sociocultural contexts can be understood by other human beings who have not experienced them first hand because we are all members of the human species. Understood as a general notion of *human sympathy*, it requires us to develop a genuinely novel perspective, to reflect on something we did not anticipate or expect, to add some new information and to persevere in the always-tentative attempts of trying to make ourselves understood. A generalized notion of this kind is central to a humanist program because its normative implications build upon and are the result of the multiple ways in which humans organize their life in common.

---

[58] P. SELZNICK, *A Humanist Science. Values and Ideals in Social Inquiry* (Stanford, CA: Stanford University Press, 2008), 23.

[59] Ibid., 29, my italics.

3. Conclusion

Let me finish by going back to the reference to dark times. In the preface to her book, Arendt mentions that she took the expression from Bertold Brecht's poem *To Posterity*. The poem talks about the injustices of the modern world, injustices that are not only constitutive of it but also feel all-encompassing and even insurmountable. It is increasingly inevitable to experience the world from a sense of paralysis, a sense that little can be done in order to make it a different, fairer, place. Brecht speaks of the guilt we may feel about those material possessions we have done nothing to deserve but enjoy nonetheless:

> They tell me: eat and drink. Be glad you have it!
> But how can I eat and drink
> When my food is snatched from the hungry
> And my glass of water belongs to the thirsty?
> And yet I eat and drink

He refers also to experiences of remorse or even shame that come from our enjoyment of the world because, while pursuing them, we are not engaged in active political life. We live in dark times because there is no time for genuine rest and even the contemplation of beauty is frowned upon:

> Ah, what an age it is
> When to speak of trees is almost a crime
> For it is a kind of silence about injustice!

This general malaise is then compounded by the tragic realization that previous forms of wisdom, those that we have been educated within and cherish as nearly sacred, no longer apply. They no longer speak to the realities of modern life:

> I would gladly be wise.
> The old books tell us what wisdom is:
> Avoid the strife of the world
> Live out your little time
> Fearing no one
> Using no violence
> Returning good for evil –
> Not fulfillment of desire but forgetfulness
> Passes for wisdom.
> I can do none of this:
> Indeed I live in the dark ages![60]

---

[60] B. Brecht, *To Posterity*: https://www.csee.umbc.edu/~stephens/POEMS/brecht1 (4/21/2022).

A humanism for dark times needs to put values back in their place; it needs to reverse Heidegger's own reversal and commit to a genuinely universalistic and egalitarian idea of humanity. Heidegger's attempt to make humanism responsible for the widespread destruction of the war was strategically devised to hide his own support for the Nazi regime, and it also helped him to mask his commitment to an essentialist, authoritarian, elitist and irrationalist philosophy. His reverence for a 'higher' idea of humanity is as philosophically misguided as it is politically pernicious. Later critiques of humanism cannot be held not responsible for the hypocrisy or even misuses of Heidegger's original critique and yet they remain fundamentally contaminated by it. They remain vitiated by the initial diagnostic that rationalism rather than irrationalism, democracy rather than authoritarianism, cosmopolitanism rather than nationalism are the most dangerous of modern illusions. They have contributed to the devaluation of modern values and principles – equality, autonomy, solidarity, justice – and, wittingly or otherwise, have thrown out the normative baby with the political bathwater. Above all, they have fallen for the double talk that Arendt warns us against: their critiques of power relations and ideology mistake the strategic deployment of certain ideas and arguments for the necessary attempts at renewing our commitment to those very values.

Sartre's proposals have universalism and egalitarianism as their major strength. He understood humanism as a combination of freedom and responsibility and gave good indications about the significance, both philosophical and political, of developing a strong notion of human (as opposed to sociocultural) sympathy. At the same time, his propositions still suffer from a deep-seated anthropocentrism: Sartre is wrong in claiming that humans are nothing but what they make of themselves, exaggerates the reach of human freedom and is unable to find a consistent argument between a rather liberal understanding of individuality and the location of cultural traits for the identities of collective actors.

The Logic of Humanism and the Ethics of Indeterminacy, Universalism, and Egalitarianism

Raymond E. Perrier

1. Difficulties Defining 'Humanism'

Humanism has historically suffered from two major difficulties: 1) there is no standard definition nor an absolute meaning of the concept[1] and 2) 20th century social theories and epistemologies (e. g. Feminist Standpoint Theory) have brought into question the veracity of any attempt to define and prescribe a 'universal' idea of humanity.[2] In light of these criticisms, there have been recent attempts to reimagine the concept of humanism, first, by looking at the basic logical components of humanism – namely, the universal presupposition of a shared and common 'human nature.' Second, there has been a move to rethink humanism in light of the ethical principles that are linked to it.[3] In this sense, a humanist endeavor begins with ethical principles and then proceeds from this starting point to assess the nature of being human. Despite these new attempts to revive humanism and assuming that it has actually diminished from Western cultures, there is also a lingering question: is it necessary to bring the concept back to life at all? Why return to the emotionally charged and politically, culturally, and philosophically loaded term like 'humanism?' Why not dispense with it entirely? Is it even possible to reimagine the concept of humanism without it reeking of "Western intellectual nostalgia?"[4] With these questions in mind, I will argue that humanism is still useful for understanding the conditions of being human, specifically in the Western world, but only insofar as the most basic logical presupposition of humanism (i. e. a universal understanding of being human) is ineluctably linked to a presupposed ethics of dignity, respect, egalitarianism, and solidarity.

---

[1] D. Chernilo, "Humanism in Dark Times," in this volume, 25–44.
[2] T. Wentzer and C. Mattingly, "Toward a New Humanism: An Approach from Philosophical Anthropology" *Hau: Journal of Ethnographic Theory* 8 (2018): 144–157.
[3] See D. Chernilo, "Humanism in Dark Times"; Wentzer and Mattingly, "Toward a New Humanism"; E. DeRobertis, "Philosophical-Anthropological Considerations for an Existentialist-Humanistic Ecopsychology," *The Humanisitic Psychologist* 43 (2015): 323–337.
[4] Wentzer and Mattingly, "Toward a New Humanism," 145.

But before a new idea of humanism is properly constructed, it is important to understand the criticisms raised against the traditional idea of humanism that needs replacing. In fact, a new idea of humanism requires that any new definition of humanism can only emerge with careful consideration for, and adequate responses to, the powerful criticisms raised against the traditional forms of humanism from the 20th century (Feminist Standpoint Theory, Post-Colonial Onto-sociological concepts of epistemology, and Orientalist critiques of the Western narratives of Eastern traditions and practices). Only with these critiques in mind can these two questions be answered fully: 1) why return to humanism at all? and 2) how can humanism be reimagined considering 20th century critiques? These two questions are the substance of this essay, and in what follows I will argue that revisiting humanism is important in order to offset the dehumanizing effects of popular social epistemologies, which are found in sociology, political science, and economics.

More importantly, while unpacking criticisms against common trends in social epistemology, I will make an argument that new theories of human nature should include a sense of indeterminacy. In this essay, I will be evaluating the synthetic *a priori* logic of indeterminacy found in Kant's philosophy. To accomplish this task, I will focus on his philosophical theory of human judgment and place it in contradistinction to the social theory emphasis on human behavior, drives, and desires. This line of thinking, I hope, will offer a more dialectically balanced, egalitarian, and universal understanding of the human being as a being in-between the determinate and indeterminate. I will demonstrate how it is possible to speak of an indeterminate concept of philosophical anthropology, i.e., indeterminacy as a common feature of human existence that keeps overly deterministic concepts of human beings in balance and, more importantly, in check. Consequently, I believe it will be possible to imagine the role of humanism as a frame of mind that compels an individual to embrace the presupposed ethical principles of respect, dignity, egalitarianism, and solidarity.

2. Why Return to Humanism?

Daniel Chernilo argues that humanism "still has a significant role to play in contemporary normative debates" if the concept can be redesigned to "embrace a universalistic orientation" that is defined by ethical and social concepts of egalitarianism.[5] Chernilo's perspective strives to recapture a form of humanism that preceded 20th century critiques of it as a universalist and 'weak'

---

[5] CHERNILO, "Humanism in Dark Times," 25–44

egalitarian credo. The critique of traditional humanism is, in part, a critique of the corresponding religious and metaphysical presuppositions that came with it, but what Chernilo points out is the possibility of reimagining the egalitarian substance of humanism. Eventually, I will arrive at a similar conclusion that the role of humanism is important because it offers a meaningful and deep way of talking about important ethical and social concepts of egalitarianism like justice, human rights, empathy, autonomy, dignity, respect, and solidarity. Before getting to this discourse, however, it is important to ask: Why now?

The context for this discussion, on my thinking, is the growing reality and widespread experience of systemic dehumanization. In truth, humanism is constantly fighting various forms of dehumanization, which have been a constant feature of the social ordering in the Western world. It was present in the class stratification between the plebeians, peasants and the aristocracy, nobility, or ruling class in modern Europe. It was present during the slave trade when Africans were sold as commodities and property, and where the experience of being an African slave was akin to the life as livestock being sold for labor, breeding, and entertainment. Dehumanization was present during the industrial revolution when workers (including children) where treated as utilities that were only worth as much as the profits they could create through labor. More recently, dehumanization is evident in certain trends within the social studies of human existence that, ironically, lack any substantial theories of what it means to in fact be human.[6] Not all social theory of course exemplifies this tendency to systematically dehumanize, and what I mean by dehumanizing is not the standard definition.

To be clear, by 'dehumanizing' I do not mean the loss of humanity, only that the cultural, social, and systems of organization place theoretical and practical limits on what it means to be human. Dehumanizing theories of human nature, or those systems of society that presuppose a theory of human nature, are deterministic and, therefore, quite limiting in scope. The effects of such limits act as the groundwork for creating systems of organization like in the case of political entities, economic principles, laws, and cultural games. And while the effects of one travesty of human history are not analogous to another, it is easy to see the dehumanizing features of today's western world reflect the social theories that are seen in the political and economic theories dominating the globalizing world.

For example, consider the standard economic theories of Neo-liberalism, which presupposes narrow theories of human nature. Neo-liberalism postulates the following theories: the *rational economic man* (REM), *rational choice*

---

[6] T. LEAHY, "The Elephant in the Room: Human Nature and the Sociology Textbooks," *Current Sociology* 60 (2012): 805–823.

theory (RCT)[7], and the theory of the "self-seeking egoist" (SSE)[8], to name a few theories of human nature that are active in Western economic policies to date. The dehumanizing effects of these theories are straightforward. REM and RCT limit the idea of humanity to behaviors like a presumption of rationality, and while all human beings experience degrees of rationality the capacity does not guarantee that all choices and behaviors can be reduced to a sole dependence upon rationality. In REM, the common theory of rationality is deeply linked to early utilitarian theories of human behavior. As a result, the 'rational man' is one that maximizes utility in every decision, and the focus of this economic theory presumes that each choice is consistently utilitarian. RCT is an attempt to re-emphasize economic theory to focus less on determining how or why a decision brings utility and more on an accurate depiction of consumer behavior. The 'rational choice' is determined by the preference of the consumer, which is not necessary the choice that delivers the most utility for the individual. Preferences emerge from choices between a variety of option within the economic market. The 'rational man' or the 'rational choice' is rational by virtue of it being motivated by nothing "other than the single-minded pursuit of their own welfare."[9] These theories failed for various reasons, including an inability to measure whether one preference, choice, or rational decision is thereby more correct than another. They quickly overlook human beings' practical existences, as beings that have different goals, means, and ideas of what it means to live a good life. The limitations that these theories place on humanity result in the dehumanizing effects previously mentioned.

The dehumanizing effects of SSE, in many ways, can be traced back to the prominent concept of human nature in the West, namely, the *principle of self-interest*. Like the early 20th century economic theories of REM and RCT, the self-seeking egoist theory reduces being human back to the pursuit of self-interest. F.Y. Edgeworth admits, however, that there is no purely self-interested individual in the 19th century, he says: "the concrete nineteenth century man is … an impure egoist, a mixed utilitarian."[10] Given the 19th and 20th century context, particularly the influence of the political philosophy of Thomas Hobbes and the economic philosophy of Adam Smith, the emphasis on self-interest is very strong. Of course, self-interest is not the sole character-

---

[7] D. HAY and G. MENZIES, "Is the Model of Human Nature in Economics Fundamentally Flawed? Seeking a Better Model of Economic Behavior" in *Theology and Economics* ed. J. Kidwell and S. Doherty (Basingstoke: Springer: 2015): 183–198.

[8] A. SEN, "Rational Fools: A Critique of the Behavioral Foundations of Economics," *Philosophy and Public Affairs* 6 (1977): 322.

[9] HAY and MENZIES, "Is the Model of Human Nature in Economics Fundamentally Flawed?," 184.

[10] Ibid., 184.

istic of these philosophies. What is even more important are the various ways in which self-interest appears. For Hobbes, it is negatively rooted in the idea that humans are driven by desire and appetites. The Hobbesian foundation for human nature is an ontologically grounded nature of desire that manifests as a negativity within that seeks something concrete, typically categorized as either the pleasure of life or the avoidance of pain and suffering. Smith took this insight and used it to establish his free market capitalism on principles of humanity that carry on through history to ideas of Neo-liberalism. To put it briefly, Hobbes' simple description of human nature as one led by desire, leads to consequent theories about the utility of human decisions to, either seek pleasure, or avoid pain. This utilitarian thinking can equally be seen in the idea that humans are utility maximizers and that any system that can encourage or maximize this behavior is good and just – i.e., free market capitalist principles, globalizing political and economic policies, and the industrial revolution to name three. In light of this way of thinking, a system was created and built upon the narrative thinking that humanity is essentially rational, that rationality is defined by the ability to fulfill and serve the driving force of humanity – i.e., desire (both lower appetites and higher ones) – insofar as rationality serves as a means to utility, then any system that encourages this very same utilitarian behavior is a good one.

This modern portrayal of humanism places hard limits on what it means to be human, and ultimately fails to adapt and evolve to meet the critiques of post-modern movements previously mentioned. But it is evident from the principal concepts resting at the foundation of the modern and traditional conception of humanism that if the foundational principles can be reimagined, then the consequential systems built upon them can also change. The goal, therefore, is to begin with more equitable notions of human existence. The more equitable and indeterminate these notions are the more equitable the systems will be that emerge from them.

3. Universalizing Humanity

Humanism presupposes a certain kind of universalism. In fact, the very idea of a 'humanist' perspective is one rooted heavily in philo-anthropological universalism, whether knowingly or unknowingly, it presupposes the possibility that all humans are the "same." In the least, it presupposes the possibility that all humans can share empirical experiences and, in fact, share biological characteristics of being 'human.' More specifically, modern, and post-modern humanist alike, build political and ethical philosophies on the premise of specific concepts of human nature, which means that it is rather important to try to define the terms of the discussion. The term 'universalism' has an extremely specific use and meaning in humanism, one which demonstrates an intrinsic dialectical dimension. On the one hand, it refers to a 'universal nature' and, on the other hand, 'universal claims and logic' – these two dimensions of 'universal' stand in a mutually conditioning relationship. They represent a dialectical condition more than two stages or two ways of using the same term 'universalism'.

The pitfall of universal thinking, historically speaking, is the tendency to let its meaning come from above. In other words, the voices that dictate what 'universals' are meaningful and why, are voices that typically represent the privileged class (political, racial, and economical classes) and they tend to reinforce societal, ethical, and political structures of power that benefit themselves more than other classes of people within their context. But this is not something that is necessarily a feature of universal thinking so much as its combination with other morally problematic ideals. In opposition to such problematic combinations, Kant offers up ideas about the liberation of human beings through the process of universal enlightenment. His opening statements in the famous essay *What is Enlightenment?* Begins with a truly universal frame of reference: "Enlightenment is the human being's emergence from his self-incurred minority." He describes this experience of being a 'minority' in various ways as the "lack of resolution and courage" to make use of one's own understanding, as a "nature" of which some have "grown fond," as a "ball and chain," a "yoke of minority," etc. Ignoring the obvious exclusivity of Kant's writings, it is clear that his philosophical framework is open to include all humans with some additional considerations. The dialectic of universalism presupposed in Kant's thinking is reflective of both a logic and an understanding of the shared human experience. His universal logic is built on his philosophy of judgment, which is, simultaneously, a shared experience of being human. In other words, humans make analytic and synthetic judgments of various kinds. Judgment is not an exclusively logical process, even though it includes occasions of pure logic, i.e., analytic judgments. All judgment presupposes the 'I think', namely, the existential expression of a potentially enlightened being, who can make judgments base upon pure logic, empirical experience, and imagination.

4. The Logic of Universality

How should the term 'humanity' be defined with regards to the logic of universality? First, we must acknowledge that 'humanity' is a multifaceted term which pertains to a variety of different specialized definitions. For example, 'humanity' refers to the single species of homo sapiens when it is used as a term designating the particular characteristic traits that are unique to human biology or when it is used to designate the particular behaviors of humans in anthropology. But it can also designate the whole of beings that form a human community, for example, one which is grounded in values of autonomy, solidarity, justice, and empathy. Equally important is recognizing that there are no *prima facie* contradictions between specialized definitions of 'humanity.' In some cases, there may be a contradiction, but in many cases, like the two previously mentioned definitions, the uses can be seen as mutually conditioning perspectives of the term that reinforce and broaden our understanding of 'humanity' in its entirety. These are just a few ways that we can speak about universal humanity.

However, the most sincere concerns for postulating a universal understanding of humanity are twofold: 1) it is necessary to determine whether any specific concept of humanity can escape the problem essentialism, i.e., the position that a set of characteristics or qualities determine what humans are by the exclusion of other qualities, and 2) it is necessary that when we use the word 'humanity' as a reference for the whole of all human beings that it actually *includes the whole of humans without limit or exception (i.e. universality)*. Chernilo seems to argue that we can avoid the problems associated with essentialism and at the same time promote the inclusion of all humans in the term 'humanity' if we acknowledge that a universal concept of humanity can only be a partially normative explanation of human existence. If we keep this in mind, then it is possible to justify its application and explore the meaning of humanism as the exploration of universality.[11] In this way, it appears that the idea of 'humanity' should remain indeterminate. It should be a kind of logical idea (not conceptual framework) that can evolve and change to fit the context of its use – being ever conditioned by changes in the way that humans exist. This would mean that there is no *absolute* idea about what it means to be human, even though there are universal principles that can be associated with an understanding of the idea.

5. Egalitarian in Principle

The final aspect of Chernilo's idea of humanism that is thought provoking is egalitarianism. Why do we need to have an egalitarian principle when we explore humanism? Quite simply the need arises from the possibility of problematic combinations between humanism and principles and values that place limits on what it means to be human. In other words, universal concepts do not necessarily get packaged with principles and values that are egalitarian in spirit. The concept of humanism can and often does get coupled with problematic postulates and concepts, i.e., essentialism, elitism, or other hierarchal concepts of power and order that do not embrace the principle of egalitari-

---

[11] CHERNILO, "Humanism in Dark Times," 25–44

anism. Limiting values and principles that are in keeping with egalitarianism allows us to explore the full meaning of humanism without naïvely falling into the pitfalls of exclusivity, which undermine the efficacy of a universal logic humanism.

For Chernilo, the primary postulate of humanism seems to be egalitarianism, whereby the values and principles of modernity must respect the principle in order to be regard as valuable.[12] In other words, throughout Chernilo's presentation it seemed as though egalitarianism was used as the primary and most important postulate of the universal concept of humanism – perhaps only rivaled in the frequency of use by the idea of empathy. The core of his defense of humanism, therefore, begins by acknowledging that universality cannot be genuinely applied to a concept of humanity if it is based on any "notion that we must rank groups of people and indeed individuals themselves."[13] The appeal to an egalitarian postulate, as such, cleverly reinforces Chernilo's logic that universalism is humanism, and it insures that any additional (perhaps we could say practical) principles and values are in line with the egalitarian groundwork of defending the desire to reimagine the universality of humanism. In other words, without the primary principle of egalitarianism a humanist perspective is always at risk of contradicting a real sense of universalism as humanism logic Chernilo is promoting.

6. Intuitive Mechanism of Empathy

So why should we take up an egalitarian principle at all? Why should we take it up as a primary principle for exploring the meaning of humanity? Too often we philosophize about what would be good, but not often why we should pursue the good. We talk about how to have a good will but not always why we should have one. To these questions, I think Chernilo would point us to the idea of empathy. This, in my own words, is the intuitive or emotive mechanism for promoting an egalitarian and universal concept of humanism. It is the reason why we ought to promote this perspective.

Briefly stated, if we look at this discourse on the logic of universalism as humanism with an open mind, and by resorting to philosophical anthropology, then I think we can treat empathy as an intuitive possibility for all of humanity, one which can develop in time for every individual. To be clear, I am not arguing that empathy is innate or an essential quality of human beings. Nor am I claiming that it can be developed by teaching in the way that we teach mathematics and biology. Rather, empathy insofar as it can become an intuitive

---

[12] CHERNILO, "Humanism in Dark Times," 25–44
[13] Ibid.

mechanism for embracing egalitarian principles and a concept of humanity that accepts normative limitations, is developed from the heartened pursuit of human experience. It is developed when a person is exposed to others within the diverse contexts of human existence. It is my understanding of Chernilo's presentation that empathy can be the actual mechanism for promoting egalitarian principles and keeping universalism, i. e., humanism, open to exploring the meaning of humanity while respecting the ongoing changes of human experience and existence. This would mean that humanism can readily and preemptively avoid the possible exclusion of particular instantiations of humanity, while also embracing the universal possibility of a whole of humanity.

Broken Mirrors, Distorted Reflections: Anthropomorphism, the Recovery of the *Concrétude* of the Human in Rosenzweig, Heidegger, and Adorno and Horkheimer

LUCAS SCOTT WRIGHT

> Alle Geburt ist Geburt aus Dunkel ans Licht [...]
> Aus diesem Verstandlosen ist im eigentlichen
> Sinne der Verstand geboren. Ohne dies voraus-
> gehende Dunkel gibt es keine Realität der
> Kreatur; Finsternis ist ihr notwendiges Erbteil.
> *F. W. J. Schelling*

> En moi, la totalité se brise.
> *Emmanuel Levinas*

> Dies ist die Ursache als die Causa sui [...]
> Zu diesem Gott kann der Mensch weder beten,
> noch kann er ihm opfern. Vor der Causa sui
> kann der Mensch weder aus Scheu ins Knie
> fallen, noch kann er vor diesem Gott musizieren
> und tanzen.
> *Martin Heidegger*

1. Introduction

If there exists one identifiable shared theme capable of characterising early 20th century philosophical theology, it is perhaps the recovery of an awareness of the *concrétude* of the human being understood in the individual and socio-political sense, and as a corollary, an attempt to secure a post-metaphysical, non-anthropomorphic, conception of the divine. While both the rejection of anthropomorphism and ontotheological conceptions of the essence of the person – in contrast to a person's existence – are not necessarily opposing concepts, the matter appears more problematic when one considers the work of Frankfurt School theorists Max Horkheimer and Theodor Adorno regarding the rejection of anthropomorphism – largely using the work of classical anthropological and sociological accounts of religion, most notably from Max Weber and Emile Durkheim – as one step toward the rejection of the finitude of human being.

In short, a tension exists between the phenomenological-existential and the critical theoretical approaches to the question concerning the human vis-à-vis the concept of anthropomorphism. Both approaches seek to recover the *concrétude* of the human against every totalising metaphysical definition of the human, yet they diverge with regard to the anthropological, theological, and philosophical category of anthropomorphism. Within the context of the conference prompt,[1] such a tension reveals an intimate link between the theological comparison of the human to God – and vice-versa – and the biological and anthropological challenges posed. In what follows, I attempt to explicate the core stakes of this tension using three primary examples – Franz Rosenzweig, Martin Heidegger, and Theodor Adorno. In the end, I illustrate how the question so often posed regarding the human by 20th century thought rests largely upon how one renders the relationship between the constitutive elements of finitude and contingency on the part of the human, and the status of anthropomorphism – the rejection or acceptance thereof – in the conception of the divine.

2. *Existenz* and the Apophasis of the Absolute

In this first section, I explore the shared concern between Rosenzweig and Heidegger on these two corelated points regarding the *concrétude* of the human and the rejection of an anthropomorphically construed conception the divine. To begin, I offer now two points of clarification as a way to frame my analysis. First, given the larger reception of Heidegger's work, despite the later publication of his most famous text, it is appropriate to begin with several relevant passages from his work, as a way of introducing the reader to the key points of comparison I locate in Rosenzweig.[2] This is not, however, a move meant to prioritise the Heideggerian position over Rosenzweig's, but rather meant to provide a touchstone for further engagement by a broader audience with the later – Rosenzweig being a thinker who, I believe, merits far wider attention than has already been given in the fields of Modern Jewish Thought, Philosophy, and Philosophical Theology. Finally, I should note that I do not address the so-called *Kehre* in Heidegger's thought in my treatment of *Sein und Zeit* and the later *Identität und Differenz*. There are a few reasons for this, not the

---

[1] https://research.cgu.edu/philosophy-of-religion-conference/about/conferences-publications/2019-humanity-an-endangered-idea/ (4/21/2022).

[2] On the question of how to compare Rosenzweig and Heidegger see: K. LÖWITH, "M. Heidegger and F. Rosenzweig or Temporality and Eternity," *Philosophy and Phenomenological Research* 3, no. 1 (1942): 53–77; E. R. WOLFSON. *Giving Beyond the Gift* (New York: Fordham University Press, 2014), 34–89; P. E. GORDON, *Rosenzweig and Heidegger: Between Judaism and German Philosophy* (Berkley, CA: University of California Press, 2003).

least of which is a concern for spatial constraints for the sake of the present chapter. Yet, the most important reason for this omission is that I am seeking here to focus upon one conceptual point of comparison between a dominant theme in Heidegger's thinking – namely, the insistence upon thinking according to the distinction between Being (*Seyn*) and beings (*Seiendes*) – and Rosenzweig's thinking, rather than provide a detailed account of Heidegger's total path of thought.

The publications of Franz Rosenzweig's *Der Stern der Erlösung* (1921) and Martin Buber's *Ich und Du* (1923) stand as decisive points in the history of Jewish and German philosophy. More precisely, both texts share an increased awareness of the complexity of what the later Heidegger in his book *Sein und Zeit* (1927) would call "the average everydayness" of human life (*durchschnittlichen Alltäglichkeit*).[3] "Average everydayness" is a notion Heidegger describes as a specific mode of human being as always-already being-there (*immer-schon da sind*) in contrast to the conception of the essence of the human as *res cogitans*, upon which, according to Heidegger, the modern anthropological understanding of the human is predicated. This modern understanding allegedly follows a twofold trajectory of understanding humans: 1. as rational animals (*vernünftiges Lebewesen*) and 2. via a de-theologised (*enttheologisiert*) transcendence in-abstraction from the everyday being-there of one's life.[4] In contrast to this anthropological notion, Heidegger turns to the famous focus upon the *Existenzialität* of the human in itself – that is, the human in its average everyday being-there (*da-sein*) in-the-world and being-with (*mitsein*) others, which constitutes the mine-ness, or the for-self character, of what previous philoso-

---

[3] M. HEIDEGGER, *Sein und Zeit* (Tübingen: Max Niemeyer Verlag, 1967), 16, 50. Heidegger's turn to the everydayness of Dasein first occurs in his explication of why the question concerning being must be re-posed through the prism of the human being as being-there (*Da-sein*). "Eine Analytik des Daseins muß also das erste Anliegen in der Fragenach dem Sein bleiben. Dann wird aber das Problem einer Gewinnung und Sicherung der leitenden Zugangsart zum Dasein erst recht brennend. Negativ gesprochen: es darf keine beliebige Idee von Sein und Wirklichkeit [...] Die Zugangs- und Auslegungsart muß vielmehr dergestalt gewählt sein, daß dieses Seiende sich an ihm selbst von ihm selbst her zeigen kann. Und zwar soll sie das Seiende in dem zeigen, wie es *zunächst und zumeist* ist, in seiner durchschnittlichen *Alltäglichkeit*" (16). The question that this formulation begs is: what does this average everydayness entail? The answer, it will turn out, is not one of the isolated, self-thinking, individual, but rather that of a person always-already enmeshed in-the-world socio-politically and otherwise relationally. "*Alltäglichkeit deckt sich nicht mit Primitivität*. Alltäglichkeit ist vielmehr ein Seinsmodus des Daseins auch dann und gerade dann, wenn sich das Dasein in einer hochentwickelten und differenzierten Kultur bewegt" (50).

[4] HEIDEGGER, *Sein und Zeit*, 48–50. Here Heidegger is attempting to illustrate the deficiencies of what, at least to this point in time, are the standard biological, psychological, and anthropological approaches to the question of human being – at least according to Heidegger. Heidegger defines modern anthropology according to the aforementioned two parameters – namely, the conception of the human as rational and as defined by a theologically-based notion of transcendence.

phies would identify as "the self." Indeed, the human is, *au fond*, being-there – Da-sein, the name Heidegger gives to the object of his investigation in *Sein und Zeit*. Thus, any question of being-itself, of ontology itself, can only be instigated from within the parameters of what-is, *in actu*, immediately given, the ontic, and the phenomenological.

While the precise question of the present paper forecloses the possibility of a more detailed explication of Heidegger's project in *Sein und Zeit*, it suffices to make a few main points regarding Heidegger's method in his arguably most famous work, which will aid in clarifying the logical consistency of Heidegger's turn to the concrete everydayness of human being, and the later rejection of an anthropological notion of being and the divine in his *Identität und Differenz*. First, the reorientation of philosophical discourse to *Dasein* is undertaken by Heidegger as a way of reposing the question of Being. Yet, according to Heidegger, three interconnected biases have to this point in time obfuscated the question and notion of Being, biases which Heidegger identifies as the constitutive dogmas of traditional philosophical thinking itself. These three biases are: 1. that the notion of Being is tacitly understood, is undefinable beyond this vague understanding, and therefore, is the most empty concept, deserving of no further investigation; 2. that any attempt to define Being leads one into a circular mode of argumentation, given that one must make use of the notion of Being when defining Being itself; 3. that Being is a concept always-already understood and thus is self-evident.[5]

---

[5] HEIDEGGER, *Sein und Zeit*, 2–4. Heidegger writes of three misconceptions, which obfuscate the need to post the question of Being anew. "Auf dem Boden der griechischen Ansätze zur Interpretation des Seins hat sich ein Dogma ausgebildet, das die Frage nach dem Sinn von Sein nicht nur für überflüssig erklärt, sondern das Versäumens der Frage überdies sanktioniert. Man sagt: "Sein" ist der allgemeinste und leerste Begriff. Als solcher widersteht er jedem Definitionsversuch. Dieser allgemeinste und daher undefinierbare Begriff bedarf auch keiner Definition. Jeder gebraucht ihn ständig und versteht auch schon, was er je damit meint" (2). First, there is the notion that Being itself is the most common and empty concept, and thus, that it requires no further exploration. According to Heidegger, this notion appears in appeals to figures and schools of thought such as Aristotle, medieval philosophical theologians, and Hegel, where the relationship between Unity (*Einheit*) and plurality (*Mannigfaltigkeit*) was discussed, but where the precise nature of Being was never illuminated (3). The second obfuscation is that the notion of being is taken to be undefinable – here Heidegger cites Pascal's statement regarding the circularity of the problem, "On ne peut entreprendre de définir l'être sans tomber dans cette absurdité : car on ne peut définir un mot sans commencer par celui-ci [...] Donc pour définir l'être, il faudrait dire *c'est*, et ainsi employer le mot défini dans sa définition" – and thus, the question concerning being is taken itself to be impossible and irrelevant (4). Yet, according to Heidegger, the indefinability of Being does not dispense with the problem this limitation of knowledge presents, but rather, only illustrates that the question concerning being remains a problem for thought. Finally, Heidegger notes a third obfuscation, which clearly relates to the other two – namely that "Being is the self-evident concept" (*Das "Sein" ist der selbstverständliche Begriffe*), the concept which, to repeat the aforementioned point made by Pascal, every statement makes use of and constitutively relies upon in order to appear

Heidegger's main task -to repose the question concerning Being (*Sein*) – is in many respects to reorient this tradition using the very resources of the tradition – a move that Heidegger terms "the task of a destruction of the history of ontology."[6] Logically, Heidegger's discursive analysis of the tradition as a historical artefact itself is linked to the aforementioned turn toward the human-being as *da-sein*, contrary to any presupposition of the human being defined in terms of *essentia*, as timelessly rational. Thus, the formal character of Heidegger's argument is intimately linked to the substance of the argument, insofar as Heidegger recasts his source material from the vantage point of contingent, finite, being. Heidegger begins his discussion of the tradition by restating his basic premise vis-à-vis human being – namely, that every human is itself, insofar as every human is constitutively temporal. As such, human activity, including philosophical thinking, is only ever a possibility in-one's-being-there, an ontic and temporal possibility, rather than the ontological essence of being itself, as is the case for the elision between essence and rational existence in the formulation of the human as a *vernünftiges Lebewesen*.[7] As a result of both this inextricably temporal character of the human and the innate, vague, understanding of being that is proper to the entity called "human," Heidegger posits that only the investigation of the human being as being-in-the-world (*in-der-Welt-sein*) can function as the point of departure for inquiring after the question concerning being.[8] In this way, Heidegger takes on the idea of the unknowability and self-evident character of being, the "vague understanding of being" (*vage Seinsverständnis*) which characterizes the human relation to Being-itself in-time, as an impetus for reposing the question concerning Being anew.[9]

---

intelligible as such – e.g. to say something *is*, is to here make use of the concept of "is," etc. Yet, Heidegger writes, "That we already live in an understanding of being and that the sense of being at the same time remains unclear (*in Dunkel*), proves the fundamental necessity of taking up anew (*die Frage [...] zu wiederholen*) the question concerning the sense of Being" (4).

[6] HEIDEGGER, *Sein und Zeit*, 19.

[7] Heidegger, *Sein und Zeit*, 19. "Alle Forschung – und nicht zuletzt die im Umkreis der zentralen Seinsfrage sich bewegende – ist eine ontische Möglichkeit des Daseins. Dessen Sein findet seinen Sinn in der Zeitlichkeit."

[8] HEIDEGGER, *Sein und Zeit*, 4–15. "Das Dasein enthüllte sich hierbei als das Seiende, das zuvor ontologisch zureichend ausgearbeitet sein muß, soll das Fragen ein durchsichtiges werden. Jetzt hat sich aber gezeigt, daß die ontologische Analytik des Daseins überhaupt die Fundamentalontologie ausmacht, daß mithin das Dasein als das grundsätzlich vorgängig auf sein Sein zu befragendes Seiende fungiert. Wenn die Interpretation des Sinnes von Sein Aufgabe wird, ist das Dasein nicht nur das primär zu befragende Seiende, es ist überdies das Seiende, das sich je schon in seinem Sein zu dem verhält, wonach in dieser Frage gefragt wird. Die Seinsfrage ist dann aber nichts anderes als die Radikalisierung einer zum Dasein selbst gehörigen wesenhaften Seinstendenz, des vorontologischen Seinsverständnisses."

[9] HEIDEGGER, *Sein und Zeit*, 5–6. "Wir wissen nicht, was "Sein" besagt. Aber schon wenn wir fragen: "was *ist* Sein?" halten wir uns in einem Verständnis des "ist", ohne daß wir be-

The most fundamental principle that undergirds Heidegger's turn toward the *concrétude* of the human is the distinction between Being (*Sein, Seyn*) and beings (*Seiendes*). Both the turn to Dasein's temporality, and the subsequent rejection of ontotheology in his *Identität und Differenz*, are predicated upon the raising of the difference between being-as-such – *Sein* – and beings – *Seiendes*, entities defined as-being, as in the process of being – to an epistemological and ontologically fundamental principle, which forecloses any confounding of being-as-such and whatever beings comprehend within the parameters of their *da-sein* in their average everydayness. Heidegger writes, in a section entitled "The Formal Structure of the Question Concerning Being, "The interrogated target of the sought after question is Being (*das Sein*), that which determines beings as beings (*was Seiendes als Seiendes bestimmt*) [...] The Being of beings 'is' not itself a being" (*Das Sein des Seienden »ist« nicht selbst ein Seiendes*).[10] The aforementioned reorientation of the question concerning Being – that is, contrary to the biases of traditional thinking – and the turn to the fundamental temporality of Dasein, both rest upon Heidegger's re-positing of this theologically and philosophically older distinction between *Sein* and *Seiendes* anew, insofar as modes of thinking appear now within the sphere of finite discursivity and activity, rather than as pre-given ontologically primary existents.

It is appropriate to frame what Heidegger is doing on this point as a matter of "re-posing" the distinction between Being and beings, given that this is a major distinction not only in much older philosophies and theologies, as is the case for Meister Eckhart's conception of a unity with God that is both beyond and before all distinction of particularity, but also a more recent *Hauptpunkt* of F. W. J. Schelling's thinking in the 19th century – both are figures to whom Heidegger owes a great deal. Especially in the case of Schelling, it is precisely the fact that Being, *Seyn* in an absolutely inconceivable sense, is differentiated from the myriad of what-is in-the-world that underscores the integrity of what-is as a viable marker, a trace, that one can follow back toward one's ultimate contingency – a dialectic, then, that occurs *in perpetuum* between what-is and the unconditioned condition that neither is nor is not.

The topic of Heidegger's relationship to both figures is well beyond the scope of the present paper, though not irrelevant given the influence of Schelling upon Rosenzweig's concept of a *neues Denken* that is an *erzählende Philosophie*. For the sake of the present, it is at the very least crucial to understand how the two older attempts to posit this distinction prefigure both Heidegger's concept of *Sein an sich* and his critique of God conceived ontotheologically. For Eckhart, the no doubt controversial *Predigt 52* cuts to the core of

---

griftlich fixieren könnten, was das "ist" bedeutet. Wir kennen nicht einmal den Horizont, aus dem her wir den Sinn fassen und fixieren sollten. *Dieses durchschnittliche und vage Seinsverständnis ist ein Faktum* [...] diese Unbestimmtheit des je schon verfügbaren Seinsverständnisses ist selbst ein positives Phänomen, das der Aufklärung bedarf [...] Das Gesuchte im Fragen nach dem Sein ist kein völlig Unbekanntes, wenngleich zunächst ganz und gar Unfaßliches."

[10] HEIDEGGER, *Sein und Zeit*, 6. "Das Gefragte der auszuarbeitenden Frage ist das Sein, das, was Seiendes als Seiendes bestimmt, das, woraufhin Seiendes, mag es wie immer erörtert werden, je schon verstanden ist. Das Sein des Seiendes ist nicht selbst ein Seiendes."

what is at stake both theologically and anthropologically in positing an originary unity or *einer unbedingte Ungrund* – what one may infer, though not without qualification, Heidegger intends by Seyn – within which all particularity is rooted. In this sermon, Eckhart draws a contrast between outer and inner poverty (*Armuot*), the latter being a state of complete divestment, *kenosis* (*Entäußerung*). Such divestment entails the eradication of both self and of God, the latter being only relatively identifiable in relation to the former – a separation, then, is posited between this originary *Unbedingt*, what is rendered in Hochdeutsch as *Ursache* from the Mittelhochdeutsch *ersten sache*, and what human beings call God. "*Dô ich stuont in miner êrsten sache, dô enhâte ich keinen got, und dô was ich sache mîn selbes; dô enwolfte ich niht, noch enbegerte ich niht, wan ich was ein ledic sîn und ein bekennære mîn selbes nâch gebrûchlîcher wârheit. Dô wollte ich mich selben und enwolte kein ander dinc [...] Aber dô ich ûzgienc von mînem vrîen willen und ich enpfienc mîn geschaffen wesem, dô hâte ich einen got [...]*" The main theological and anthropological point is clear: to be one with one's originary ground is to be in a state neither of Being nor inexistence, but rather, to occupy a (non)position, to be before and after all bifurcation itself in a true *coincidentia oppositorum* in which the human and God, relatively identifiable in relation to each other, are drawn so close as to eradicate both identities. Here there is no identification of this *Ur*-point through the logic of *Seiendes* – no conflation of the *Unbedingt* even with what is relatively called God – but rather, this ground of All being is rendered wholly otherwise than all thinking according to the parameters of entity.

The same implication is apparent in Schelling's concept of the *Ungrund*, the *a priori* ontologically primary chaotic darkness that precedes all differentiation, including what humans call God, even with regard to his transcendence, *in actu*. Utilising language that is no doubt indebted to the Origenian notion of God birthing godself through the act of self-cognition and drawing analogies using contemporary research in physics (at the time), Schelling describes the basic distinction between being and the ground of beings, and the existence of God. "Die Naturphilosophie unsrer Zeit hat zuerst in der Wissenschaft die Unterscheidung aufgestellt zwischen dem Wesen, sofern es existiert, und dem Wesen, sofern es bloß Grund von Existenz ist. Diese Unterscheidung ist so alt als die erste wissenschaftliche Darstellung derselben [...] Da nichts vor oder außer Gott ist, so muß er den Grund seiner Existenz in sich selbst haben. Das sagen alle Philosophen; aber sie reden von diesem Grund als einem bloßen Begriff, ohne ihn zu etwas Reellem und Wirklichem zu machen. Dieser Grund seiner Existenz, den Gott in sich hat, ist nicht Gott absolut betrachtet, d.h. sofern er existiert; denn er ist ja nur der Grund seiner Existenz, Er ist die Natur – in Gott; ein von ihm zwar unabtrennliches, aber doch unterschiedenes Wesen." Schelling establishes the inextricability and distinction of God and the ground of God's existence and proceeds to analogise this relation between the two using the imagery of gravity/darkness and light as a means of illustrating how a dialectical unfolding of positive, distinct, existence occurs always in relation to the dark ground of being. "Analogisch kann dieses Verhältnis durch das Schwerkraft und des Lichtes in der Natur erläutert werden. Die Schwerkraft geht vor dem Licht her als dessen ewig dunkler Grund, der selbst nicht actu ist, und entflieht in die Nacht, indem das Licht ausgeht. Selbst das Licht löst das Siegel nicht völlig, unter dem sie beschlossen liegt. Sie ist eben darum weder das reine Wesen noch auch das aktuale Sein der absoluten Identität, sondern folgt nur aus ihrer Natur [...] In dem Zirkel, daraus alles wird, ist es kein Widerspruch, daß das, wodurch das Eine erzeugt wird, selbst wieder von ihm gezeugt werde. Es ist hier kein Erstes und kein Letztes, weil alles sich gegenseitig voraussetzt, keins andere und doch nicht ohne andere ist. Gott hat in sich einen innern Grund seiner Existenz, der insofern ihm als Existierendem vorangeht; aber ebenso ist Gott wieder das Prius des Grundes, indem der Grund, auch als solcher, nicht sein könnte, wenn Gott nicht actu existierte." With this last sentence Schelling constructs what one might call a "dialectics *in perpetuum*. Only insofar as God exists is the ground of existence intelligible, yet likewise, only insofar as God is determined by something – not external – ulterior, perhaps even "unconscious" – to again pick up on the resonance with Origen's Trinitarian theogony, and the resonance of this idea of an unconscious *Grund* that dovetails with psychoanalytic and critical theoretical renderings of the human's own unconscious, unconditioned, condition for the possibility of being (conscious) – is it possible to speak of an "*absolute Identität* in the last instance. In short, it is the distinction between Sein and Seiendes that allows Heidegger, in keeping with these older modes of thinking, to posit the importance of Dasein, *in actu*, as a viable mode of access to the always-already elusive Sein.[11]

Recalling the aforementioned aspect of an always-already present vague understanding of Being that corresponds to Dasein's being-in-the-world, the idea here is not that the phenomenon of Being-itself ceases to be viable from the vantage point of philosophical investigation in the face of the always-already finite point of departure, but rather, that the Being of beings is always configured through the (f)actuality, the *Tatsächlichkeit*, of beings.

It is not unfair, then, to state that the distinction between *Sein und Seiendes* functions as Heidegger's *Ansatzpunkt* for all of his subsequent analysis, underpinning as it does the aforementioned turn toward the *concrétude* of the human as the point of departure for undertaking the question concerning being. Indeed, both the whole of *Sein und Zeit* and the major point regarding *Ontotheologie* in *Identität und Differenz* rely upon understanding the implications of this distinction for *Wissenschaft* generally, and philosophy and theology specifically. In the latter text, the upshot of this distinction is that all ontology and theology are disabused of their ability to ground the being of beings in an *Ursache* – God is no longer identifiable as such, insofar as this is to posit the being of the deity as a kind of ultimate entity, rather than as the opening of the *Abgrund*, around which all stable and differentiated identity is made possible.[12]

---

[11] See: MEISTER ECKHART, *Werke I: Deutsche Werke* I (Frankfurt am Main: Deutscher Klassiker Verlag, 1993), 554–555; F. W. J. SCHELLING, *Werke. Dritter Band* (Leipzig: Fritz Eckhardt Verlag, 1907), 453–454. For more on Heidegger's indebtedness to these ideas see E. R. WOLFSON, *Heidegger and Kabbalah* (Bloomington, IN: Indiana University Press, 2019). For an explanation of Schelling's indebtedness to Origen and other neoplatonic theologies see W. SCHMIDT-BIGGEMANN's "Schellings'Weltalter' in der Tradition abendländischer Spiritualität," in F. W. J. SCHELLING, *Weltalter-Fragmente* (Stuttgart-Bad Cannstatt: Frommann-Holzboog, 2002), 1–78. For a discussion of the question of ontotheology, Heidegger, Schelling, and Jakob Böhme, see H. J. FRIEDRICH, *Der Ungrund der Freiheit im Denken von Böhme, Schelling und Heidegger* (Stuttgart-Bad Cannstatt: Frommann-Holzboog, 2009).

[12] M. HEIDEGGER, *Gesamtausgabe*, vol. 11: *Identität und Differenz*, (Frankfurt am Main: Vittorio Klostermann, 2006). For the sake of space and time, I offer only the briefest of summaries here of Heidegger's argument. Similar to the critique of traditional conception of *Sein* in *Sein und Zeit*, here Heidegger critiques what he perceives as a convergence of the theological notion of a deity and the philosophical, ontological and metaphysical, notion of Being.

In short, Heidegger's raising of the distinction between Being and beings to a fundamental ontological axiom correlates any fundamental ontological claim, and any non-fundamental ontological endeavour such as the anthropological question concerning the being of the human in the world, with the complete rejection of anything resembling an anthropically construed absolute.

A further consequence of Heidegger's project on this point is that what has previously been considered under the auspices of being "ontologically real," or foundational and absolute, is now exposed as being ontically, existentially, contingent, and only relatively real in the ontological sense – that is, derivative in relation to what is fundamentally ontological, the Being-itself of beings which cannot "be" in the same sense of beings, the core conditions for the possibilities that make up Dasein's activities in the world.[13] For Heidegger, then, any

---

Heidegger calls this convergence the "ontotheological constitution of metaphysics" (*die onto-theo-logische Verfassung der Metaphysik*), wherein the ontic and non-fundamental-ontological ordering function of *logia* are, inappropriately, hypostatized into an *Urgrund* which ground everything that is in a chain of being. "Zunächst allerdings und gewöhnlich nehmen sich die Titel Ontologie und Theologie aus wie andere bekannte auch: Psychologie, Biologie, Kosmologie, Archäologie. Die Endsilbe -logie meint ganz im Ungefähren und im Geläufigen, es handle sich um die Wissenschaft von der Seele, vom Lebendigen, vom Kosmos, von den Altertümern. Aber in der -logie verbirgt sich nicht nur das Logische im Sinne des Folgerichtigen und überhaupt des Aussagemäßigen, das alles Wissen der Wissenschaften gliedert und bewegt, in Sicherheit bringt und mitteilt. -Logia ist jeweils das Ganze eines Begründungszusammenhanges, worin die Gegenstände der Wissenschaften im Hinblick auf ihren Grund vorgestellt, d.h. begriffen werden. Die Ontologie aber und die Theologia sind 'Logien', insofern sie das Seiende als solches ergründen und im Ganzen begründen. Sie geben vom Sein als dem Grund des Seienden Rechenschaft. Sie stehen dem Λόγος Rede und sind in einem wesenhaften Sinne Λόγος-gemäß, d.h. die Logik des Λόγος" (66). It is with this conflation of the grounding sense of *logia* and the grounding of entities qua entities – that is, the grounding of being, being as such as just this ordering *Ursache* – which Heidegger identifies as the main project of western ontology and theology. Thus, he proclaims, "Demgemäß heißen sie [Λόγος] genauer Onto-Logik und Theo-Logik. Die Metaphysik ist sachgemäßer und deutlicher gedacht: Onto-Theo-Logik" (66).

Having established that this is what ontotheology is and does, it is not difficult to see how this relates back to the aforementioned, crucial, distinction between *Sein und Seiendes*, upon which Heidegger predicates so much in *Sein und Zeit*. Too, Heidegger does not exactly at this point foreclose something like the convergence of all alterity and identity, all fluctuation and stability, in a kind of *Ungrund*. Yet, this is clearly not what theologians, in any sense that would entail the speaking of the God for whom worship is deserved, would traditionally be willing to call God. Heidegger, in one of the more famous and frankly interesting passages, writes of the ontotheological God. "Dies ist die Ursache als die Causa sui [...] Zu diesem Gott kann der Mensch weder beten, noch kann er ihm opfern. Vor der Causa sui kann der Mensch weder aus Scheu ins Knie fallen, noch kann er vor diesem Gott musizieren und tanzen" (77).

[13] HEIDEGGER, *Sein und Zeit*, 16. "Philosophische Psychologie, Anthropologie, Ethik, "Politik", Dichtung, Biographie und Geschichtsschreibung sind auf je verschiedenen Wegen und in Wechselndem Ausmaß den Vorhaltungen, Vermögen, Kräften, Möglichkeiten und Geschicken des Daseins nachgegangen." The point of this demarcation is clear enough – non-fundamental ontologies and ontic operations, cognitive or otherwise, are real, but only

discourse that does not clarify its fundamentally ontological presupposition vis-à-vis the difference between *Sein* and *da-sein* remains, to a degree, blind, and it is toward the rectification of this blindness that characterizes what Heidegger undertakes in his "fundamental ontology," as the clarification of the concept of the being of beings through the laying out the foundational structures of Dasein.

Having established the pre-conscious understanding of being as constitutive of Dasein, as a reason to take the human being as the point of departure for his analysis, Heidegger qualifies to what degree this understanding is accessible, writing of this base-understanding of being, "but this is not at all to say that this proximate pre-ontological interpretation of being can be taken over, as if this understanding of being may arise from a thematic, ontological, reflection of the authentic state of being [of Dasein]."[14] It is not the case that Dasein immediately understands itself on the basis of its being. Indeed, Dasein is incapable of doing so. Dasein's being is primarily *da-sein*, to-be-there ontically,

---

insofar as they derive their possibility from the fundamental ontological condition for the possibility of their reality. Heidegger posits this distinction earlier on in the text in his description of what foundational concepts (*Grundbegriffe*) do in the founding of scientific disciplines, a crucial initial point that sets up the remainder of his turn to 1. the analysis of entities as the mode of access to the phenomenon of Being and 2. the specific analysis of the entity called *da-sein*. "Grundbegriffe sind die Bestimmungen, in denen das allen thematischen Gegenständen einer Wissenschaft zugrundliegende Sachgebiet zum vorgängigen und alle positive Untersuchung führenden Verständnis kommt. Ihre echte Ausweisung und 'Begründung' erhalten diese Begriffe demnach nur in einer entsprechend vorgängigen Durchforschung des Sachgebietes selbst. Sofern aber jedes dieser Gebiete aus dem Bezirk des Seienden selbst gewonnen wird, bedeutet solche vorgängige und Grundbegriffe schöpfende Forschung nichts anderes als Auslegung dieses Seienden auf die Grundverfassung seines Seins. Solche Forschung muß den positiven Wissenschaften vorauslaufen; und sie *kann* es [...] Solche Grundlegung der Wissenschaften unterscheidet sich grundsätzlich von der nachhinkenden 'Logik' [...] Sie ist produktive Logik in dem Sinne, daß sie in ein bestimmtes Seinsgebiet gleichsam vorspringt, es in seiner Seinsverfassung allererst erschließt und die gewonnenen Strukturen den positiven Wissenschaften als durchsichtige Anweisungen des Fragens verfügbar macht." (10). Foundational concepts, then, always anticipate the subject-area which they found. In this sense, and Heidegger makes this point in anticipation of the charge that his project rests upon a logically dubious circular-logic, all *Wissenschaft* rests upon a kind of proleptical circularity – this is a logic akin to what, perhaps, Elliot Wolfson refers to as an open circularity, a spiral logic in which progress only appears by virtue of the repetition of the same, the repetition of heterogeneity itself in Deleuzian terms. With reference to the distinction between fundamental ontology – that is, the kind of discourse with which Heidegger wants to engage – and other foundational discourses, this proleptic aspect of ontological concepts becomes crucial insofar as it is only fundamental ontology, which can yield the fullest anticipation of any given field. "*Alle Ontologie, mag sie über ein noch so reiches und festverklammertes Kategoriensystem verfügen, bleibt im Grunde blind und eine Verkehrung ihrer eigensten Absicht, wenn sie nicht zuvor den Sinn von Sein zureichend geklärt und diese Klärung als ihre Fundamentalaufgabe begriffen hat*" (11).

[14] HEIDEGGER, *Sein und Zeit*, 15.

a state in which the ground of its being-there is foreclosed precisely because Dasein is at all times ontically, *in actu*, blind to its ground.[15]

Accordingly, Dasein understands itself first and foremost ontically, as being-there in-the-world.[16] Yet Heidegger does not, thereby, foreclose a connection between being-as-such and beings – in fact, to posit such a hard binary would be to reify being-as-such in the way of traditional ontology. Rather, Heidegger's point again is that the question concerning Being-as-such must be posed through the prism of 1. the fact that being-as-such is distinct phenomenologically from beings and 2. the fact that always-already a vague, unconscious, understanding of being-as-such is constitutive of Dasein's average everydayness and being-there-in-the-world. In this way, Heidegger establishes the foundation for his claim that 1. it is only through an investigation of beings that the question concerning being-as-such is to be posed and pursued,[17] and 2. that it is only through an investigation of the particular being called *da-sein*, the human, that Being may appear to us – insofar as it is the human-as-Dasein for whom Being is an issue, that is, the being that is itself being in an active, persisting sense at the core of its identity as such, in contrast to, say, my chair.[18] The general point here, is that to speak of Being or essence (*Wesen*) requires – in light of the distinction and relation between *Sein* and *Seiendes* – the inter-

---

[15] HEIDEGGER, *Sein und Zeit*, 15. The Schellingian resonances of Heidegger's conception of Dasein's relationship to is ground, to *Seyn*, on this point is striking. Heidegger, noting how fundamental this cleft between Dasein's ontic being-there and its *Grund* is, writes, "Das Dasein ist zwar ontisch nicht nur nahe oder gar das nächste – wir *sind* es sogar je selbst. Trotzdem oder gerade deshalb ist es ontologisch das Fernste." Setting aside here the obvious point of connection between Heidegger's point and St. Augustine's pronouncement in Confessions that God is, "the most hidden from us and yet the most present amongst us," an apt comparison that deserves its own analysis, Heidegger's foreclosure for humans of direct, conscious, access to their *Urgrund* on the basis of their being-there ontically bears again the same characteristics of Schelling's aforementioned description of absolute Identity as the dialectical interplay between differentiated being-*in-actu* and the dark, concealed, character of *der Grund der Existenz*. Human beings *are* being-there, are ontic, as Heidegger stresses, and it is the result of this their being that conceals the condition for the ontological condition for the possibility of their being. Just as Schelling stresses the necessity of maintaining both *potentia et actus*, where *potentia* is concealed as *der Grund*, so too does Heidegger maintain the relationship between the ontic and fundamental ontological Being-itself, albeit stripped here in part of its theosophical framework.

[16] HEIDEGGER, *Sein und Zeit*, 15. "Das Dasein hat vielmehr gemäß einer zu ihm gehörigen Seinsart die Tendenz, das eigene Sein aus *dem* Seienden her zu verstehen, zu dem es sich wesenhaft ständig und zunächst verhält, aus der 'Welt'."

[17] HEIDEGGER, *Sein und Zeit*, 6. "Sofern das Sein das Gefragte ausmacht, und Sein besagt Sein von Seiendem, ergibt sich als das Befragte der Seinsfrage das Seiende selbst."

[18] HEIDEGGER, *Sein und Zeit*, 6–7. Die Seinsfrage verlangt im Hinblick auf ihr Befragtes die Gewinnung und vorherige Sicherung der rechten Zugangsart zum Seienden. Aber "seiend" nennen wir vieles und in verschiedenem Sinne. Seiend ist alles, wovon wir reden, was wir meinen, wozu wir uns so und so verhalten, seiend ist auch, was und wie wir selbst sind [...] An welchem Seienden "

rogation of the real-time *Existenz* of human being. "Being lies in being this way and that, in reality, in being present (*Vorhandenheit*), in existence (*Bestand*), in-application (*Geltung*), in being-there (*Dasein*), in the" there is "(*es gibt*)."[19] There can be no sensible speaking of essence without real-time existence, and more precisely, there can be no analysis, no thinking nor calculation nor discourse, without the being-there of one's self as Dasein, and in our case, as being human in-the-world.

In the end, *Sein und Zeit* functions as an explication of the fundamental structures that make up this entity called Dasein, which is, inescapably, its concrete being-there in-the-world, which takes the form of its caring for and enmeshment with the world. The now well-known emphases upon Dasein's relative construction and sense of identity in-the-world and Dasein's relation to entities both present-at-hand and ready-to-hand are understandable,[20] in a basic sense,

---

[19] HEIDEGGER, *Sein und Zeit*, 7.

[20] Regarding the interplay between Dasein and the world, Heidegger reorients the notion of spatiality (*Räumlichkeit*) such that its is "ein Konstituens der Welt ist, die ihrerseits als Strukturmoment des In-der-Welt-seins charakterisiert wurde" (ibid., 101). Colloquially, speaking of entities "in-the-world" implies that spatiality is something like an empty container, in which the myriad of entities that-are find their place. Heidegger, however, reorients this notion of a *leere Räumlichkeit* such that it appears as a mode of being of Dasein itself, Dasein being unlike other entities precisely insofar as Dasein relates to the world in the sense of care and engagement. "Das In-Sein meint so wenig ein räumliches 'Ineinander' Vorhandener, als 'in' ursprünglich gar nicht eine räumliche Beziehung der genannten Art bedeutet; 'in' stammt von innan-, wohnen, habitare, sich aufhalten [...] Dieses Seienden, dem das In-Sein in dieser Bedeutung zugehört, kennzeichneten wir als das Seiende, das ich je selbst bin" (54). This does not eradicate the notion of contingency on the part of Dasein's subjectivity – indeed this would be to lapse back into the notion that the human being is infinitely and essentially a *res cogitans*, a trap of idealistic thinking Heidegger clearly would seek to avoid. Rather, Heidegger renders spatiality not as an occasionalist creation of a subjective-I, but as the belonging-together (*Zugehörigkeit*) of the coherence of things found in the engagement, in the *Stromkreis* – to utilise Rosenzweig's phrasing – called world. In this sense, the human itself *is* spatiality, rather than being "in space," as if the human could posses itself outside of the strictures of spatiality. "*Der Raum ist weder im Subjekt, noch ist die Welt im Raum* ... Der Raum befindet sich nicht im Subjekt, noch betrachtet dieses die Welt, "als ob" sie in einem Raum sei, sondern das ontologisch wohlverstandene "Subjekt", das Dasein, ist räumlich. Und weil das Dasein in der beschriebenen Weise räumlich ist, zeigt sich der Raum als Apriori. Dieser Titel besagt nicht so etwas wie vorgängige Zugehörigkeit zu einem weltlosen Subjekt, das einen Raum aus sich hinauswirft. Apriorität besagt hier: Vorgängigkeit des Begegnens von Raum (als Gegend) im jeweiligen umweltlichen Begegnen des Zuhandenen" (111). In this sense, the matter of Dasein's spatiality is not dissimilar to what Adorno refers to as the preponderance of the object, or the locating of coherence of what-is not in either the idealistic nor positivistic epistemological positions, but rather in the perpetual dialectic between one's sense of identity and one's being-object, contingent, and ultimately powerless before the sheer uncontrollable objectivity of what-is. See: T. ADORNO, *Vorlesung Über Negative Dialektik* (Frankfurt am Main: Suhrkamp Verlag, 2003), 65. "Dieser Zusammenhang in der Sache selbst ist aber nicht zu hypostasieren, also nicht zu einem Absoluten zu machen, und ist auch nicht von außen an sie heranzubringen; sondern er ist in ihnen selbst, in ihrer inneren Bestimmun aufzufinden."

prima facie. Dasein only is, insofar as Dasein is ontically a part of the world, enmeshed with others in a situation always-already underway. In short, Dasein is defined in large part through its relationality to the World and to Others, a logically consistent outcome given the aforementioned basic premises of Heidegger's arguments. Yet, this perpetually dialectical construction of the human person, inescapable in thought word and deed, reveals what is perhaps the more important turn for Heidegger, to say nothing of its controversial character, to the notions of thrownness (*Geworfenheit*), being-toward-death (*sein-zum-Tode*), and of inauthentic and authentic (*Eigentlichkeit*) being. Temporally, Dasein is defined by its futural comportment, its being-toward its innermost possibility to be what it is – in short, by possibility itself, by being-toward the future.[21] What is this future in the last instance? – death, or rather the always-present, existentially constitutive, orientation toward death as one's limit-horizon, rather than a singular event amongst others.[22] Indeed, so crucial is this idea of human-being as being-toward-death – the idea that the human carries the presence of this being-toward-nothing at all times as its being-there in-the-world – that the key notions of being authentically and inauthentically are predicated upon how the reality of death is either confronted or avoided in one's daily life. Too, even one's sense of the past, construed by Heidegger as a being-thrown into the world, is ultimately conditioned by this trajectory towards being naught, insofar as the futurity of the human is also a return to what, phenomenologically, could never have been – nothing.[23] Apropos of this aspect of Heidegger's thinking, Elliot Wolfson's following invocation of Blanchot is noteworthy.

"We may not want to go as far as the Heidegger of *Being and Time* and define the singularity of human existence as being-toward-death (*Sein zum Tode*), that is, the anticipatory resoluteness of the end that compels one to confront the 'nonrelational ownmost potentiality' (*eigenste, unbezügliche Möglichkeit*), which is labelled as 'the possibility of the absolute impossibility of Dasein' (*die Möglichkeit der schlechthinnigen Daseinsunmöglichkeit*). It would be difficult, however, to deny Blanchot's insight regarding dying as the 'never-ending ending,' in the Levinasian formulation, the *impossibility of possibility*, which constantly informs the path of our being as 'a presence in the depth of absence,' the possibility that

---

[21] Heidegger, *Sein und Zeit*, 325. "Formal existenzial, ohne jetzt ständig den vollen Strukturgehalt zu nennen, ist die vorlaufende Entschlossenheit das *Sein zum* eigensten ausgezeichneten Seinkönnen [...] Das die ausgezeichnete Möglichkeit aushaltende, in ihr sich auf sich *Zukommen*-lassen ist das ursprüngliche Phänomen der *Zukunft*."
[22] Heidegger, *Sein und Zeit*, 325. "Wenn zum Sein des Daseins das eigentliche bzw. uneigentliche *Sein zum Tode* gehört, dann ist dieses nur möglich als *zukünftiges* in dem jetzt angezeigten und noch näher zu bestimmenden Sinn. "Zukunft" meint hier nicht ein Jetzt, das, *noch nicht* "wirklich" geworden, einmal erst *sein wird*, sondern die Kunft, in der das Dasein in seinem eigensten Seinkönnen auf sich zukommt."
[23] Heidegger, *Sein und Zeit*, 325–326. "Übernahme der Geworfenheit aber bedeutet, das Dasein in dem, *wie es je schon war*, eigentlich *sein*. Die Übernahme der Geworfenheit ist aber nur so möglich, daß das zukünftige Dasein sein eigenstes 'wie es je schon war', das heißt sein 'Gewesen', *sein* kann."

secures our 'greatest hope' of being human because it reminds us that 'the future of a finished world is still there for us' [...] To cite Blanchot again, '[...] my impending death horrifies me because I see it as it is: no longer death, but the impossibility of dying.'"[24]

What I identify, then, as "the turn to the *concrétude* of human being" in Heidegger's thinking is twofold: Firstly, I am referring to the fundamental appeal in Heidegger to the constitutively temporal character of the human, the non-self-sufficiency of Dasein's relatively constructed identity, and Dasein's always-already apophatic relation to both its birth and death – past and future – in accordance with the principle distinction between Being and beings; Secondly, I am referring to the corelated rejection of any anthropocentric, indeed any ontically-based, construal of the absolute. It is on these points that one can already glimpse the basic challenge that this turn toward the *Existenzialität* of Dasein poses to the attempt to make of the human something non-human. To be sure, the inescapability of being-one's-thereness in-the-world, of being-human-toward-death, does not preclude the existence of shared characteristics with other beings – indeed, the point of the emphasis Heidegger gives to the intimate link between the ontic and ontological is that Being is the being of beings, not only humans. Yet, to jettison the *humane*, or to abstract and reify the "animal" over and against the *humane*, according to Heidegger at least, seems an impossibility and is, perhaps, a mode of inauthentic being insofar as it falsely promises the abrogation of one's angst vis-à-vis one's concern for being, one's being-toward-death, which is constitutively a part of what it means to be *da-sein*.

Turning back to Rosenzweig, it is not difficult to see where his work prefigures these famous Heideggerian motifs. The entirety of the first portion of *Der Stern der Erlösung* is devoted to a critique of what he terms "the philosophy of the All" (*die Philosophie des All*). As the name suggests, the philosophy of the All is on Rosenzweig's account a totalising philosophy – that is, a philosophy which functions under the pretence of being without presupposition, *sui generis, donné a priori*.[25] This pretence to presuppositionlessness (*den Schein der Voraussetzungslosigkeit*) has as its corollary, and indeed for Rosenzweig its ultimate origin, the fear and denial of death – that is, the fear of contingency and finitude – on the part of the human.[26] To philosophize and to theologize

---

[24] WOLFSON, *Poetic Thinking*, 127–128.

[25] F. ROSENZWEIG, *Der Stern der Erlösung* (Freiburg im Breisgau: Universitätsbibliothek, 2002), 5. "Indem aber die Philosophie die dunkle Voraussetzung alles Lebens leugnet, indem sie nämlich den Tod nicht für Etwas gelten läßt, sondern ihn zum Nichts macht, erregt sie für sich selbst den Schein der Voraussetzungslosigkeit."

[26] ROSENZWEIG, *Der Stern*, 1–4. "Vom Tode, von der Furcht des Todes, hebt alles Erkennen des All an [...] Alles Sterbliche lebt in dieser Angst des Todes, jede neue Geburt mehrt die Angst um einen neuen Grund, denn sie mehrt das Sterbliche [...] jedes wartet mit Furcht und Zittern auf den Tag seiner Fahrt ins Dunkel. Aber die Philosophie leugnet diese Ängste der Erde. Sie reißt über das Grab, das sich dem Fuß vor jedem Schritt auftut."

according to this fear of death entails that one theorizes an absolute, eternal, point, which neutralizes the finite (*tödliche*) character of human being – that turns death, and thereby also finitude, into a "*Nichts*," rather than acknowledging death as the presupposition of all life.[27] What Rosenzweig calls his *neues Denken* begins and ends with a different relationship to death – the acceptance of death as constitutive of life *au fond*, the turning of death from a *Nichts* into a *Etwas*.[28] To state the point in more potent terms, this is the recognition that death is *die Voraussetzung* of all lives, of every person, not only now *ein Etwas* contra *ein Nichts*.

The something that Rosenzweig speaks of is not, then, only the singular *ein* of an abstract philosophical principle. Rather, this nothing is a relatively particular nothing, insofar as it is constitutive for, and relative in its manifestation to, each specific person who lives and dies with a name of their own – a seemingly infinite multiplicity of deaths then as the presupposition of the world and of thought.[29] It is this *tödliche* presupposition – or more precisely, the thinking according-to this presupposition – that exposes the false pretence of philosophy to what we may sardonically refer to, given the darkness of the ultimate presupposition in question, as the light of the truth. "The multiplicity of the Nothing which philosophy presupposes [...] turns the foundational thoughts of philosophy (*Grundgedanken der Philosophie*), that is, the thoughts of the one and universal cognition of the All, into a lie."[30]

What is at stake in rebuking this question is nothing less than the integrity of the contingent character of *Existenz* as such, an aspect of Rosenzweig's thought that is surely shared not only by the aforementioned Heidegger, but phenomenological approaches to thinking generally. In his *Das Neue Denken*, the somewhat amusingly later published *Vorwort* to *Der Stern*, Rosenzweig posits a distinction between his "New Thinking" and that of traditional philosophy along the lines of a rejection of abstract notions of "Essence" (*Wesen*), which undercut the immediacy of what-is contingently, moment-to-moment. "All philosophy asked about *Wesen*. It is this question, with which it distinguishes itself from the unphilosophical thinking of normal – healthy – human

---

[27] ROSENZWEIG, *Der Stern*, 4. "Indem aber die Philosophie die dunkle Voraussetzung alles Leben leugnet, indem sie nämlich den Tod nicht für Etwas gelten läßt, sondern ihn zum Nichts macht, erregt sie für sich selbst den Schein der Voraussetzungslosigkeit."

[28] ROSENZWEIG, *Der Stern*, 4. "Wollte die Philosophie sich nicht vor dem Schrei der geängsteten Menschheit die Ohren verstopfen, so müßte sie davon ausgehen – und mit Bewußtsein ausgehen –: daß das Nichts des Todes ein Etwas, jedes neue Todesnichts ein neues, immer neu furchtbares, nicht wegsuredendes, nichts wegzuschweigendes Etwas ist [...] Das Nichts ist nicht Nichts, es ist Etwas."

[29] ROSENZWEIG, *Der Stern*, 4. "Im dunkeln Hintergrund der Welt stehen als ihre unerschöpfliche Voraussetzung tausend Tode, statt des Einen Nichts, das wirklich Nichts wäre, tausend Nichtse, die, eben weil viele, Etwas sind."

[30] ROSENZWEIG, *Der Stern*, 4.

understanding (*vom unphilosophischen Denken des gesunden Menschenverstands*)."[31] To ask about essence is to make derivative the immediate character of a given entity as it stands in-the-world by conflating its existence in-real-time with that of a *Wesen*, which would overdetermine its being – this is seen in the most simple form in the philosophical question, "what is that thing *really* (*eigentlich*),"[32] where the for-self aspect of any entity is rendered derivative in the light of an access to a more authentically definitive identity.

Here already one may detect a similar conviction to that of the aforementioned approach to the distinction between the notion of *da-sein* and the rejection of the essentializing of the human as a *res cogitans* in Heidegger's thinking. Rosenzweig forecloses the possibility of abstracting what is *humane* in the service of an underlying ontological essence. More crucially for the present, however, is the focus upon the "naked individual," to utilise Karl Löwith's description, as the starting point of both Rosenzweig and Heidegger's rejections of totalizing metaphysical systems.

"Their starting point is however the same: the naked individual in its finite existence as it precedes all established civilisation. In their will to go back to the primary and essential things in a genuine experience of life, both coincide with each other in the same spirit of the time, to wit: that decisively separating time during and after the war when everything superfluous was necessarily cut off [...] Both want to make out the truth of human existence, both treat of man [sic. *der Mensch, Dasein*] and world, Logos and time."[33]

Löwith's observations regarding the political impetuses undergirding both Rosenzweig's and Heidegger's positions vis-à-vis the horrors of the first World War and the destruction of any universality that could overdetermine the chaos of the world appear to accord with Emmanuel Levinas' own comments regarding Rosenzweig's rejection of Hegel and the State in his short piece entitled "Franz Rosenzweig: Une Pensée Juive Moderne." In this piece, Levinas notes how Rosenzweig's rejection of nationalism was tied to his rejection of totalizing thinking itself in his turn toward Judaism and Christianity.[34] Indeed, it is

---

[31] ROSENZWEIG, "Das Neue Denken. Einige nachträgliche Bemerkungen zum 'Stern der Erlösung'," *Der Morgen* 1, no. 4 (October 1925)," 430.

[32] Ibid. On the topic of "*gesunden Menschenverstands*" contra the normal *modus operandi* of philosophy, Rosenzweig writes, "Der [gesunden Menschenverstands] nämlich fragt nicht, was ein Ding "eigentlich" sei. Es genügt ihm, zu wisse, daß ein Stuhl ein Stuhl ist; er fragt nicht, ob er etwa eigentlich ganz anderes wäre. Eben dies fragt Philosophie, wenn sie nach dem Wesen fragt."

[33] K. LÖWITH, "M. Heidegger and F. Rosenzweig," 55–56.

[34] E. LÉVINAS. "Une Pensée Juive Moderne," *Revue de Théologie et de Philosophie*, Troisième série 15, no. 4 (1965): 209. "Formé dans la certitude de l'importance spirituelle de l'État et de la politique sous l'influence de l'historien hégélien Meinecke, Rosenzweig *a tôt le pressentiment des dangers qui menacent l'Europe dont la philosophie hégélienne reste une remarquable expression* ... La nationalisme, les États nationaux et nationalistes, une historie fait de guerres et de révolutions, conservent pour Rosenzweig une physionomie hégélienne. Il sent la montée des

precisely the theological and liturgical life, and more precisely the burning heart of the Star of Redemption found in the life of the Jewish people, a people living always-already outside the strictures of the totalizing myth of national-statehood, that Rosenzweig turns to as a correlative concept in relation to his rejection of totalizing metaphysical systems, which would strip human beings of their singularity and integrity.[35]

In the context of Rosenzweig's argument regarding the shortcomings of traditional thinking, the most basic instance of the denegation of the *concrétude* of immediate being occurs in the conflation of God, World, and *Mensch*, a move which compromises the for-self integrity of each element of reality in the desire to posit a unified One. "The world is not allowed to be the World, God is not allowed to remain God, *Mensch* is not allowed to remain *Mensch*, but rather, everything must be *really*, authentically (*eigentlich*), something totally other."[36] For Rosenzweig, this totalizing tendency defines philosophy at its

---

périls. Il cherche un autre ordre. Il se tourne vers le christianisme. En 1913, il est au seuil de la conversion." Yet as Levinas notes, following what is by now a bit more of a mythological rather that historically accurate depiction of what happened on a "nuit dramatique" with his theologian cousins, Rosenzweig turns back towards Judaism as a resource for uncovering a depiction of human life outside the strictures of imperialism and totalizing thought. Regardless of the historical veracity of what happened that night, Levinas nonetheless writes of the Jewish character of *Der Stern* against the backdrop of this rejection of totalizing thinking, "Singulier retournement! La spiritualité juive s'était toujours maintenue par la force de la tradition : les réponses juives aux problèmes précédaient ces problèmes. Et voici qu'une recherche concernant la destinée et le salut de l'Homme tout court, libéré de tout particularisme, mène au judaïsme perdu. La question est d'ordre universel, la réponse est juive."

[35] ROSENZWEIG, *Der Stern*, 337. "Und wieder erkauft such das ewige Volk seine Ewigkeit um den Preis des zeitlichen Lebens. Ihm ist die Zeit nicht seine Zeit, nicht Acker und Erbteil [...] Während der Mythos der Völker sich ständig wandelt, ständig Teile der Vergangenheit vergessen, ständig andre zu Mythos erinnert werden, ist hier der Mythos verewigt und ändert sich nicht mehr; und während die Völker in Revolutionen leben, in denen das Gesetz ständig seine alte Haut abstreift, herrscht hier das Gesetz, das von keiner Revolution abgeschafft wird, und dem man wohl entlaufen, nicht aber es ändern kann." The gnostic, world-denying, framing of Rosenzweig's contrast between the life of non-Jewish peoples – of states – and of the Jewish people is unmistakable. The first sentence would almost be enough on its own to establish the radically antithetical character of Jewish life in relation to the world, and more precisely, to time-itself. For more on this topic see: B. POLLOCK, *Franz Rosenzweig's Conversions: World Denial and World Redemption* (Bloomington, IL: Indiana University Press, 2014). The main point stands -the break with totalizing thought, exemplified with regard to epistemology, metaphysics, and theology in parts I and II of *Der Stern*, now finds as its counterpart the liturgical and kinship relationality of the eternal people who, in a positive reversal of the racist stereotype of the wandering Jew, emerge from time and politics, tethered no longer to such worldly and violent myths.

[36] ROSENZWEIG, "Das Neue Denken," 430. It is here, too, that in drawing the comparison to Heidegger one encounters one of the key differences between their projects – namely the use of theology. This topic deserves a fuller treatment elsewhere, but the following from Löwith's commentary in his "M. Heidegger and F. Rosenzweig or Temporality and Eternity" suffices to chart the basic contours of the difference."

core, such that to think otherwise in accordance with normal human understanding would be to render philosophy, or at least most philosophy according to the parameters Rosenzweig has set, superfluous.[37]

Contrary to this normative philosophical *modus operandi*, Rosenzweig writes of an *erfahrende Philosophie* – an experience-philosophy rooted in what one discovers in real-time. This *erfahrende Philosophie* takes as its point of departure the relationality and referentiality of each particular as constitutive of the universal (*das Ganz*). The first portion of *Der Stern* takes the reader as far as the notion that in the experience of humanity one discovers only what is humane, in the world only that which is worldly, and in God only that which is divine – a chastened point of departure in relation to traditional philosophizing according to an *Ursache als Urseiende*, a beginning of a new thinking at the *finis philosophiae*, the point at which traditional thinking is made superfluous.[38] Here there is only each element of reality isolated ideally in-themselves – God-godself, human-itself, and World-in-itself.[39] Left on its own, this is as far as abstract thinking regarding the question of being and essence (*Seyn an sich, Wesen als Urgrund oder Ursache*) can go.[40]

What is required is a new way of philosophizing, a *neues Denken* that accords with experience in all of its dimensions, including the topic at hand – the

---

[37] ROSENZWEIG, "Das Neue Denken," 430. "Wären sie [die Dinge in der Welt] nichts andres, sondern wirklich nur, was sie sind, so wäre ja – behüte und bewahre – am Ende dies Philosophie überflüssig! Wenigstens eine Philosophie, die durchaus etwas 'ganz anderes' herauskriegen möchte."

[38] ROSENZWEIG, *Zweistromland: Kleinere Schriften zu Glauben und Denken*, ed. A. Mayer and R. Mayer (Dordrecht: Martinus Nijhoff Publishers, 1984), 144. "Die Erfahrung entdeckt im Menschen, so tief sie eindringen mag, immer wieder nur Menschliches, in der Welt nur Weltliches, in Gott nur Göttliches. Und nur in Gott Göttliches, nur in der Welt Weltliches, nur im Menschen Menschliches. Finis philosophiae? Wäre es, dann um so schlimmer für die Philosophie! Aber ich glaube nicht, daß es so schlimm kommt. Vielmehr kann an diesem Punkt, wo die Philosophie mit ihrem Denken allerdings an ihrem Ende wäre, die erfahrende Philosophie beginnen." On this point, Rosenzweig's critique of philosophy is not unlike Heidegger's notion of *Destruktion*, insofar as Rosenzweig does not intend to end philosophy as such, but rather to execute a critical engagement with philosophy in the service of a *neues Denken*.

[39] ROSENZWEIG, *Der Mensch und Sein Werk*, 144. "Jedenfalls ist das die Pointe meines ersten Bandes. Er will weiter nichts lehren, als daß keiner dieser drei großen Grundbegriffe des philosophischen Denkens auf den andern zurückgeführt werden kann. Um diese Lehre eindrücklich zu machen, wird sie in positiver Form gegeben: Es wird also nicht gezeigt, daß keiner auf die beiden andern zurückgeführt werden kann, sondern umgekehrt, daß jeder nur auf sich selbst zurückzuführen ist. *Jeder ist selbst 'Wesen'*, jeder selbst Substanz mit dem ganzen metaphysischen Schwergewicht dieses Ausdrucks" (italics are mine).

[40] ROSENZWEIG, *Der Mensch und Sein Werk*, 145. "Aber jedenfalls glaube ich, mit dem eben Gesagten die Tendenz des ersten Band, so gut man das als Autor kann – d.h. also sicher weniger gut als ein gescheiter Leser –, bezeichnet zu haben. *Auf die Frage nach dem Wesen gibt es nur tautologische Antworten*. Gott ist nur göttlich, der Mensch nur menschlich, die Welt nur weltlich; man kann so tiefe Schächte in sie vortreiben, wie man will, man findet immer nur wieder sie selber. Und das gilt für alle drei gleichmäßig."

Sterblichkeit of being human – without lapsing into either the totalizing trap of traditional thinking, nor the purely isolated elements of reality in-thought alone vis-à-vis the first Part of *Der Stern*. Rosenzweig characterizes this new mode of thinking as "narrative-thinking" (*eine erzählende Philosophie*), which is meant to ask not what things in-themselves are – that is in an ideal and abstract sense – but to ask how things come to be in the first instance – that is, experientially and phenomenologically.[41] Toward this end, Rosenzweig arrives at a similar position to that which Heidegger later takes up – namely, that to theologise and philosophise means to engage with a concept of human life that is always-already up and running, in which everything is constituted through its referentiality to an-other(s).[42] Elliot Wolfson captures this aspect of Rosenzweig's thinking, noting that this referential construction of each thing nevertheless does not elide the difference between each element of reality. Writing of a crucial passage in Rosenzweig's "Das Neue Denken," Wolfson notes, and I quote at length:

"The conjunction 'and' is accorded the status of being the 'basic word of all experience,' since the structure of experience, phenomenologically, is inexorably correlative. Not substance but the relation enframes our experience – God *and* the world *and* the human, which is to say, the nature of these three elements cannot be ascertained in isolation from the other. From that point of view, the conjunction is disjunctive, for like a bridge it connects two termini by keeping them at a distance, forging nearness, as Heidegger would

---

[41] Regarding the use of the term "phenomenology" to characterize Rosenzweig's thinking in *Der Stern*, Bernard Casper writes, in his essay entitled *Transzendentale Phänomenalität und ereignetes Ereignis* in the forward to the Freiburg im Breisgau edition of *Der Stern*, of Rosenzweig's lack of familiarity with Husserl's work at the point of the text's publication -in addition, given the date of publication of *Der Stern* it would be obviously improper to speak of any influence upon Rosenzweig by that other famous *deutsche Philosoph*, Martin Heidegger. Casper notes however, "Aber man darf angesichts der Vorgehensweise des 1. Teils des "Sterns der Erlösung" mit gutem Recht von einem *phänomenologischen* Vorgehen sprechen [...] Mann kann angesichts des 1. Teils des "Sterns des Erlösung" durchaus von einer transzendentalen Reduktion sprechen, insofern nämlich alle Sein*setzung* hier in der Tat ausgeschaltet wird und es derart dem Denken um nichts anderes als um das reine Bewußtsein des Urphänomens des Gottes, und, dann, des Urphänomens der Welt, und schließlich um das reine Bewußtsein des Urphänomens des Menschen geht." See ROSENZWEIG. *Der Stern*. VII–VIII. I concur with Casper's assessment regarding part I of *Der Stern*. Indeed, if we view the first part as an attempt to reconceive abstract thinking itself, what we are left with are the *Urphänomene* of Rosenzweig's existential – phenomenological – reality. If Part I appears analogous to the notion of Husserl phenomenological reduction, as an attempt to get back to the things themselves, then it is in the turn of part II to real-time existentiality – the *Existenzialität* of embodied being in-language and time (though this formulation of the matter obviously begs the question regarding whether abstract thinking could ever be considered as abstract from the transcendental constraints of language and time) – that we see something analogous to the moves undertaken by Husserl's student Martin Heidegger. In both instances the appropriateness of the comparison to phenomenology is merited, admitting certain fundamental differences regarding the aims of each project, etc.

[42] ROSENZWEIG, *Der Stern*, 91.

say, that draws nigh what remains remote. Even in the oneness of the ultimate truth, the truth that is the star of redemption, the conjunction 'and' must be preserved – what is most important is not to determine what the essence of truth is but to realize through the act of verification (*Bewährung*) that truth is relational; that is, it must always be truth for someone. Hence, while God's truth is one, it must be transformed into the manifold that is 'our truth.'"[43]

Wolfson's comments summarise in large part what I intend when I refer to both the turn to the *concrétude* of the human and rejection of anthropomorphism in Rosenzweig. Truth, and more to the point, human being, is, then, always-already a matter of relationality and inescapable embeddedness in relation to others, the divine, and the world. Yet, as Wolfson notes, this relationality of each element of reality – God, World, Human – does not eradicate the alterity of each element vis-à-vis the others. Rather, the relational construction of each element indexes a fundamental difference between each element, a difference that can only appear through the prism of the same, and a sameness that is only visible through the differential quality of being-with (*mitsein*) and being-there. It is this differential that leads Rosenzweig, in the last instance, after his explication of the relation between God, World, *Mensch* and the share that Judaism and Christianity have in this relationship, to conclude that neither Judaism nor Christianity is capable of grasping the totality of the God beyond all differentiated identification, including what is called "truth," insofar as the difference between *anthropos* and the absolute remains unbridgeable in the last instance, just as for Heidegger there can be no conception of "god" which would render the absolute within the parameters of *Seiendes*.

In this sense, just as we may speak of a repetition of heterogeneity on the level of events and time, at least according to Deleuzian terms, so too may we speak of being-human in the spatial and social senses as a repetition of difference, a repetition of the shared differential that orients us toward and defines us by virtue of each other. "Humanity" is defined by virtue of its other and vice-versa, just as each specific person is only so from within the parameters of their relation(s). There is no transcendence without immanence – a point to which the earlier reference to Eckhart is most helpful – just as it makes no sense, epistemologically and phenomenologically, to speak of immanence sans transcendence. The key is the relation itself, which simultaneously upholds and confounds difference. What remains, for both Rosenzweig and Heidegger, is a commitment to the relation itself, and thus, the ultimate upholding of the distinction between the-All – *Seyn* – and beings, and in this sense, both

---

[43] WOLFSON, *Giving Beyond the Gift*, 34–35. In this sense, the necessity of the oneness to appear as plurality mirrors the basic neoplatonic move from the Ungrund to what-is in actu that characterizes the aforementioned contours of Eckhart, Schelling, and Heidegger's thinking as well.

ultimately mobilise an apophatic logic that stands against anthropomorphism and theopomorphism in the final instance. It is however, strictly speaking from my own standpoint, impossible on this account to do away with either anthropomorphism or theopomorphism, just as it is impossible to not recognize the inadequacy and reductive character of either. The relational character of human being conceals as much as it reveals, obscures and much as it defines – in short, to borrow and augment Adorno's language of "the concept," our positive identities of ourselves, others and the divine, are both real and necessarily insufficient.

3. Conclusion: Apophasis and Looking Ourselves in the Mirror

Such a position regarding the contradictory, and to be sure even violent, character of being-human is a point of shared conviction between Rosenzweig, Heidegger, and Adorno and his fellow first-generation Frankfurt School theorist Max Horkheimer. Thus, this central idea regarding the necessity of looking to the inescapability of our being-human, of our being concretely and nakedly – to again make use of Löwith's description of the matter – is advanced through a different register in Adorno and Horkheimer's *Dialektik der Aufklärung* – and yet, the matter of the correlation between this turn and the rejection of anthropomorphism is perhaps problematised in these last two thinkers.

With their awareness of the importance of 19th century anthropological and sociological accounts of human development, largely in relation to the work of Max Weber and Emile Durkheim, Horkheimer and Adorno opened up new avenues for exploring philosophically the ways in which the question concerning human being might be tied to particular social formations and specific reactions in the face of, what for lack of a more nuanced term, they would call apropos of Weber and Durkheim "*Natur*."[44] More precisely, Horkheimer and Adorno locate a pivotal moment in the history of such reactions in the rejection of the finitude of the self *an sich*, which Horkheimer and Adorno render through their account of the corrosive scepticism of modernity in nascent form via the rejection of anthropomorphism in their *Dialektik der Aufklärung*.

---

[44] As in Weber's account of religion in *Wirtschaft und Gesellschaft* and in Durkheim's *Les formes élémentaires de la vie religieuse*, Horkheimer and Adorno make repeated use out of the notion of "nature" as a metric for tracing the development of society and religion. Following what surely is a Weberian line of thinking, the greater the development of society, defined with regard to the complexity of the division of labour and by extension a decreased proximity to nature, so great too is the development of certain social and religious structures. See M. HORKHEIMER and T. ADORNO, *Dialektik der Aufklärung* (Frankfurt am Main: Fischer Verlag, 2006), 27.

Contrary to the position of both Rosenzweig and Heidegger, for Horkheimer and Adorno the rejection of anthropomorphism signifies not a positive recognition of the *concrétude* of humanity, but rather a fearful rejection, and thus a recognition via negation, of finitude in the grasping after something immortal.[45]

This claim, and the whole of the book, arises as a result of several influences – sociological, psychoanalytical, and philosophical – which are brought to bear upon their genealogical account of how Enlightenment thinking has led to its own self-destruction. For the sake of space, a proper explication of these influences must be left in abeyance. However, two such influences merit at least some glancing attention here – namely, the psychoanalytical conception of fear and pain, which Freud identifies as the source of civilizational structures and institutions, and the idea of *solidarité sociale*, which Durkheim reinforced in his account of religion and society. Undergirding Horkheimer and Adorno's main point is an agreement with Durkheim, and Max Weber, regarding the general unfolding of modernity through the historical progression, for lack of a better word not laden with supersessionism, from paganisms to monotheism and finally to demythologisation and disenchantment (*Entzauberung*) in modernity. Indeed, Horkheimer and Adorno's argument depends on there being an intrinsic link between modernity and religious structures and ideas. Yet, contrary to Durkheim's idea that religious, and thus by extension societal, institutions arise on the basis of collective solidarity, Horkheimer and Adorno posit, in agreement with Freud, that the core principle undergirding these developments is one of violent heterogeneity in the face of uncontrollable, terrifying, *Natur*.[46]

There is, then, no possibility of strictly bifurcating a demythologised world and the world of myth, such that the latter would signify a dark period and the former a period of purely enlightened sobriety above the fray of historical chaos – there is only the task of thinking according to an underlying principle of domination. Enlightenment self-destructs precisely insofar as it loses the ability to reflexively reckon with this underlying tendency toward domination by thinking itself over and above such mythological violence. Thus, in the context of the discussion regarding critiques of totalizing thought in the early 20th century, it is not solely the result of a divine hypostatisation of the

---

[45] HORKHEIMER and ADORNO, *Dialektik der Aufklärung*, 12–13.
[46] HORKHEIMER and ADORNO, *Dialektik der Aufklärung*, 27–28. "Wie die ersten Kategorien den organisierten Stamm und seine Macht über den Einzelnen repräsentierten, gründet die gesamte logische Ordnung, Abhängigkeit, Verkettung, Umgreifen und Zusammenschluß der Begriffe in den entsprechenden Verhältnissen der sozialen Wirklichkeit, der Arbeitsteilung. Nur freilich ist dieser gesellschaftliche Charakter der Denkformen nicht, wie Durkheim lehrt, Ausdruck gesellschaftlicher Solidarität, sondern Zeugnis der undurchdringlichen Einheit von Gesellschaft und Herrschaft."

human – though certainty given their overarching argument and Adorno's later work this too would lead to destruction – which leads to domination and totalization of both human and nature. Rather, such a regression into mythological violence is a result of the failure of the human to reckon with its own aging reflection, a failure which appears in the rejection of the anthropomorphic deity *tout court*, as if the very sight of one's frailty – a frailty certainly figured in Rosenzweig's notion of each person's *Dinglichkeit* and Heidegger's notion of *sein-zum-Tode* – must be rejected at all cost.

On this point, we encounter a possible problem in contrast to Horkheimer and Adorno's position inherent in Rosenzweig's and Heidegger's conceptions of the strict bifurcation between *Sein* and *Seiendes*. This would be, if true, a problem intrinsic to the notion that one may actually break the mirror, and thus the reflection, of the *anthropos* with reference to the absolute in the insistence upon the inviolability of the distinction between Being and beings. That this is a possible problem is, to be fair, perhaps more of an issue in a kind of cheap apophatic reception of their work, more than it is a problem for these thinkers themselves. Yet having acknowledged this, it is not unfair to state, I think, that what one may find in Horkheimer and Adorno is a notion of a dialectic *in perpetuum*, which more explicitly cuts against the idea of stepping beyond the parameters of contingency and being-relation, precisely insofar as it is always the most difficult task for thinking to reckon with oneself in all of one's weakness, violence, and finite contingency.

II. Theology

The Human Being as Image of God

Augustinian Meditations on the Contemporary Crisis of Humanity

ANSELM K. MIN

1. Introduction

Is humanity an endangered idea? It certainly is. We are faced everywhere with calls for human dignity and human rights despite all the diversity that characterizes humanity. In a world where human beings are excluded and persecuted for their diversity, the appeal is made to what is common to all, to our humanity. At the same time, we are warned not to define or theorize humanity, except in a purely phenomenalistic and functionalistic way, because any theorization on humanity, it is assumed, tends to lead to essentialism, which then would be abused as ground for exclusion and discrimination. This is perhaps *the* irony of our time: we are compelled to appeal to our common humanity in defense of our human dignity and human rights, yet we are severely divided on what constitutes that very humanity. For political purposes we appeal to our humanity, but without any common understanding of what constitutes that humanity, and in fact discouraging such a common understanding in the name of pluralism largely inspired by deconstructionism. Certainly, the idea of humanity is an endangered idea today, and in many other ways as well.

I am, however, more concerned about humanity as an endangered *reality*, much as I am bothered by humanity as an endangered *idea*. The humanity of human beings has been regarded an endangered reality for quite some time. Not a decade has gone by since World War I without some talk of the "crisis" of humanity. The source of this crisis may have been diverse, such as war, technology, cultural nihilism, hegemonic imperialism, economic oppression, and many others, but it seems clear that most of us alive today have been living under the specter of one crisis or another. For some time now, humanity have been living major turning points of various kinds each of which seems to intensify and magnify the sense of crisis facing human existence as a whole. Just consider some of the representative titles of cultural criticism that have been providing us with a pulse of the times during the last century: *The Decline of the West* by Oswald Spengler (1922), *The New Leviathan: Man, Society, Civilization and Barbarism* by R. G. Collingwood (1942), *Dialectic of Enlightenment* by Max Horkheimer and Theodor Adorno (1947), *Man against Mass Society* by Gabriel

Marcel (1952), *The Technological Society* by Jacques Ellul (1963), *The Pentagon of Power: The Myth of the Machine* by Lewis Mumford (1964), *One-Dimensional Man: Studies in the Ideology of Advanced Industrial Society* by Herbert Marcuse (1964), *The Triumph of the Therapeutic: Uses of Faith after Freud* by Philip Rieff (1966), *The Cultural Contradictions of Capitalism* by Daniel Bell (1976), *The Age of Uncertainty* by John Kenneth Galbraith (1977), *The Culture of Narcissism: American Life in an Age of Diminishing Expectations* (1979) and *The Minimal Self: Psychic Survival in Troubled Times* (1984) by Christopher Lasch (1984), *Amusing Ourselves to Death: Public Discourse in the Age of Show Business* by Neil Postman (1985), *The Society of the Spectacle* by Guy Debord (1994), *The Post-Truth Era: Dishonesty and Deception in Contemporary Life* by Ralph Keyes (2004), *Empire of Illusion: The End of Literacy and the Triumph of Spectacle* by Chris Hedges (2009), *Lies Incorporated: The World of Post-Truth Politics* by Ari Rabin-Havt (2016), and *The Fall of Western Civilization: How Liberalism is Destroying the West from Within* by Shivaji Lokam (2018).

2. The Death of the Subject under Capitalist Sensationalism

I would like to present one view of this crisis. I would like to argue that the death of the subject, i.e., the disappearance of the very subject capable of being an agent of one's own thinking, willing, and feeling, the very mark of humanity as such, is the heart of our crisis today because all other crises either arise from or result in this crisis. The crisis of democracy, for example, arises from the sheer gullibility of the majority and their vulnerability to the power of ideology, propaganda, advertising, and all the arts of manipulation that have become increasingly more and more sophisticated, while the culture of capitalism has been exposing human subjects to the reign of images, appearances, and impressions, overpowering our intellectual judgments with the strongest possible appeal to the immediacy of the senses made possible by the most recent technologies of manipulation. All interest groups, political, ideological, ethnic, religious, but commercial above all, exploit the latest techniques of manipulation to dominate the new public square offered by the internet and mass media in order to win and shape the hearts and minds of humanity now increasingly on the global scale. Many cultural critics agree that contemporary capitalism does not just produce things to consume, things to eat, wear, use, and enjoy, things that are external to the human subject, such as cars, tv sets, and cell phones; capitalism also produces, predominantly, images, appearances, impressions, ideas, values, symbols, dreams, hopes, and anxieties, things that are internal to the human subject and constitutive of the very content of subjectivity. By saturating human subjectivity with its own images and symbols, capitalism enervates the human mind of its very capacity to reflect and judge.

That is to say, contemporary capitalism has been abolishing the very subjectivity of the human subject through its brutal attack *on* the senses and *through* the senses and reducing the subject to the instinctive immediacy of the senses with no critical intellectual mediation.

Herein, I think, lies the heart of the contemporary crisis facing humanity. Human beings are under increasing pressure to abandon thinking and judging. To judge is to transcend the immediacy and particularity of the senses by discerning and abstracting something universal, whether a concept or a norm, and ultimately to recognize the limited as limited by a movement towards the more unlimited, a movement towards the transcendent "more." The capacity to judge is the capacity to transcend the immediacy of what is given and to criticize the appearances of things by an ideal or a standard that exceeds them, and this capacity is the foundation of all things authentically human. All of Western philosophy but especially modern Western philosophy has been "critical" in this sense of the critique of appearances. In varying ways it underlies human activities in all areas of human life, individual and social, in economics, politics, and culture, in ethics, science, and art, all of which are modes of transcendence.

The essence of contemporary capitalism is its *sensationalism* in the *anthropological* sense, by which I mean the attempt to reduce human beings to the subject of mere senses, subject them to the domination of sensible desires, and thus to destroy this very capacity to judge and the will to act according to that judgment. Sensationalism in *the psychological* sense of arousing a quick, intense, emotional reaction is itself a consequence of sensationalism in the anthropological sense. (Here I mean philosophical anthropology.) In this sense it is a most subtle but also a most radical attack on our humanity: our very subjectivity is at stake. By reducing us to the senses it recreates us in the image of sensible things and inclines us to become like them, acting automatically under external stimuli, without the mediation of reflection and judgment. Capitalism systematically accentuates and exaggerates the propensity to evil already natural to human beings, the propensity to substitute for the moral law the subjective principle of self-love based on the incentives of our sensuous inclinations, which Kant calls "radical evil" because it "corrupts the ground of all maxims."[1]

This also means that capitalist sensationalism poses a radical threat to any area of human life where integrity is essential: education where children would rather be entertained than instructed, politics where opinions are shaped by appearances on the media exploited by money, culture where the distinction between true art and fake art has long disappeared, social morality where self-determination and consent have become the highest norm regardless of

---

[1] I. KANT, *Religion within the Limits of Reason Alone*, trans. T. Greene and H. Hudson (New York: Harper & Row, 1960), 31–32.

their content, not to speak of business and economics where any deal is considered acceptable that does not involve explicit violation of positive law. Capitalist sensationalism has been issuing for some time now a categorical imperative of its own: Liberate all desires. We rarely hear anywhere any counsel to restrain, to moderate, and to be reasonable. Between repression of all desires and liberation of all desires there seems to be no reasonable middle. Any talk of restraint is accused of being repressive, something to be avoided at all costs. The capitalist tendency to reify the senses by isolating them from the intellect and will and to subject the whole of human existence to the reign of the senses is especially critical to the integrity of religion. Religion, above all things, is a function of transcendence, for it is a radical critique of life in its totality, ultimacy, and depth.[2] When the intellect and will are dead under the reign of sensationalism, religion too is dead.

It is crucial to note the full implications of this sensationalism. It threatens with disappearance not only Christianity but also all other religions, not only religions but also atheist humanism. After all, living consistently as an atheist humanist means living with honesty, integrity, compassion, with hope in a world without transcendence, resisting the temptations of the senses that degrade human dignity and disrupt human solidarity, all of which certainly require the full integrity of intellectual judgment and volitional commitment. Atheist humanism still presupposes sufficient subjectivity of the subject to hold determinate views and act according to those views. This is what makes the sensationalism of contemporary capitalism more vicious than many preceding crises that usually attack external conditions of the human subject (e.g., poverty, war, exclusion, etc.). Capitalist sensationalism attacks the very interiority or subjectivity of the subject as such. A human being reduced to the senses and sensible desires is simply incapable of holding any religious or moral views, still less of any self-commitment to acting on such views.[3]

---

[2] On the notion of religion as a "radical critique of life," see A. MIN, "Sin, Grace, and Human Responsibility: Reflections on the Doctrine of Justification by Faith Alone in the Age of Globalization," in *Neue Zeitschrift für Systematische Theologie und Religionsphilosophie* 59, no. 4 (2017): 7–9.

[3] I elaborate further on the death of the subject in "The Deconstruction and Reconstruction of Christian Identity in a World of Difference," in *The Task of Theology: Leading Theologians on the Most Compelling Questions for Today* ed. A. Min (Maryknoll, MO: Orbis, 2014), 38–45, and "Transcendence and Solidarity: Conditions of Faith, Hope, and Love Today," in *Faith, Hope, Love, and Justice: The Theological Virtues Today*, ed. A. Min (Lanham, MD: Lexington Books, 2018), 199–202.

3. The Human Being as the Image of God

What can we say about this phenomenon of capitalist sensationalism from the theological point of view? I propose to provide some Augustinian reflections. Why Augustine? Because his writings bear witness to the struggles of a human being caught between the wildest desires of the physical senses and the most profound longings of the spiritual ones yet described by a genius with utmost human sensibility. His insights, I hope, shed some light on the contemporary crisis of humanity caught between the sensationalism of capitalist culture and the inarticulate, hidden longings for signals of transcendence struggling to survive that sensationalism. He struggled with worldliness in its threefold classical biblical aspects, the lust of the flesh, the lust of the eyes, and the pride of life, and it is not difficult to see how capitalist sensationalism has been systematically magnifying and intensifying that worldliness. Augustine's struggles are not so foreign to our struggles. Maybe his doctrine of grace would also be a great source of insight for a way out of our contemporary struggles with worldliness

Augustine's anthropology of the humanity of the human is thoroughly biblical and theological. His exploration of humanity as the image of God takes place in the theological context, more precisely in the trinitarian context where he is exploring models for understanding the triune God. The context of the question is this. We have never seen God nor know God. Still, if we are going to believe in, hope in, and love the triune God, we need some kind of a model that would be appropriate for thinking the triune God. No materialist model is appropriate. Nor can we think of the triune God on the model of just any three things but only of three things that in some way resemble the divine. Augustine rejects a purely formal or abstract approach that will accept any three things that are also in some way one, like the triangle, or even any trinity of things that meet in some way the formal requirements of the trinitarian grammar, namely, the unity of nature, real distinction, and constitutive relationality.[4] So Augustine asks: "from what likeness or comparison of things known to us we are able to believe, so that we may love the as yet unknown God".[5] In Books VIII through XIII of *De trinitate*, he goes through many models from the trinity of sense to the trinity of faith, rejecting them all until in Book XIV he settles on the model of the mind in its threefold function, memory, understanding, and love, but not before modifying it by giving it a divine content.

---

[4] The following abbreviations of titles are used: *Trin.* for *De Trinitate*, *conf.* for *Confessiones*, *gr. et lib. arb.* for *De gratia et libero arbitrio*, *Spir. et litt.* for *De spiritu et littera*, *nat. et. gr.* for *De natura et gratia*, *civ. Dei* for *De civitate Dei*, *ep. Jo.* for *In epistulam Joannis as Parthos tractatus*, and *s.* for *Sermo*.

[5] AUGUSTINE, *Trin.* 8.3.

From Scripture Augustine recognizes that the human being is the image of God bearing some likeness to God, and if so, the model for thinking God must also be sought in that image, but the human being is many things. Where in human nature should we seek the divine image? Augustine uses several criteria for locating the image of God in human nature. Colossians 3:9 exhorts us to "put off the old man with his actions, and put on the new who is being renewed for the recognition of God [in agnitionem Dei] according to the image of him who created him," which seems to make renewal dependent on the knowledge of God, while Galatians 3:28 regards those reborn in Christ as being one in him beyond ethnic, sexual, and class differences, which seems to make rebirth in Christ independent of bodily criteria. From these Augustine argues that the divine image cannot be located in bodiliness but only in the rational, spiritual mind which alone has the capacity for recognizing God, and in this sense, women too are images of God and "fellow heirs of grace" [gratiae cohaeredes].[6] Humans are images of God, then, because of their capacity to know God, which locates the image of God in our rationality or intellectual spirituality, not in our bodiliness. There is, however, more to the image of God than the capacity to know God, which is a necessary but not a sufficient condition for being the image of God.

Even the trinity of faith does not qualify the human being as image of God. Faith contains the trinity of the memory of things believed, the contemplation of their truth, and love of them, but this act of faith, *fides qua*, is temporal even though its objects are eternal truths, and will pass away at the beatific vision when seeing will replace believing. For Augustine, something that is transitory cannot be an image of God. "It is intolerable to suppose that while the soul is by nature immortal and from the moment of its creation never thereafter ceases to exist, it's very best attribute or possession should not last out its immortality. And was anything better created in its nature than its being made to the image of its creator? So, whatever it is that must be called the image of God, it must be found in something that will always be, and not in the retention, contemplation, and love of faith, which will not always be."[7] We have to find in the human soul "an image of the creator which is immortally engrained in the soul's immortality."[8] That is to say, being made to the image of the creator is the noblest attribute of the soul, and it must be coeval with the immortality of that soul. Nothing transitory will do.

If a human being is made to the image of God in his capacity to understand and contemplate God by means of reason, does this capacity really provide a model of the trinity, and if so, of what kind? Augustine's answer to this ques-

---
[6] Augustine, *Trin.* 12.7.12; *Conf.* 13.23.33.
[7] *Trin.* 14.2.4.
[8] *Trin.* 14.4.6.

tion reveals his central assumptions and criteria for locating the image of God that can also serve as a model for speaking of the triune God. He responds:

"[...] although the human mind is not of the same nature as God, still the image of that nature than which no nature is better is to be sought and found in that part of us than which our nature also has nothing better. But first of all the mind must be considered in itself, and God's image discovered in it before it participates in him. For we have said that even when it has lost its participation in him it still remains the image of God, even though worn out and distorted. It is his image insofar as it is capable of him and can participate in him [capax est et particeps esse potest]; indeed, it cannot achieve so great a good except by being his image."[9]

For Augustine the image of God than which no nature is better must be sought in the noblest part of human nature. The ultimate, most profound, and radical source of the nobility and dignity of the human being lies in being created to the image and likeness of God with the capacity for receiving and participating in God's own eternal life.

Now, the noblest part of our nature, for Augustine, is the mind, the mind that remembers itself, understands itself, and loves itself, the mind capable of reflecting on itself in those three paradigmatic ways according to the classical philosophy of mind. The acts of the mind are the most immanent, non-temporal, simultaneous, and perichoretic acts, not adventitious, temporal, successive, and external acts as are the trinities of sensation, imagination, knowledge of temporal things, and even that of the act of faith. The mind is always present to itself even when it is not explicitly thinking about itself, so remembers understanding and loving itself, understands remembering and loving itself, and loves remembering and understanding itself, joining the remembered self and the understood self to each other. The self-present to itself provides the unity of all its acts, mutually relates remembering, understanding, and loving, and makes all its acts totally perichoretic. Each contains the other two, and the three constitute one life, one mind, and one essence. It perfectly represents the self-immanential character of spiritual intellectuality but also conforms to the grammar of trinitarian theology.[10]

What makes this trinity of the mind the image of God, however, is not that it remembers, understands, and loves itself but that it is also able to remember, understand, and love the one who made it, which alone makes it wise. If it remembers, understands, and loves itself only, it remains foolish. Augustine goes on to insist:

"Let it then remember its God to whose image it was made and understand and love him. To put it in a word, let it worship the uncreated God, by whom it was created with a capacity [capax] to receive and participate in him [cujus particeps esse potest]. In this way it will be wise not with its own light but by participation in that supreme light [summae

---

[9] *Trin.* 14.8.11.
[10] *Trin.*, 10.11.18.

illius lucis participatione], and it will reign in happiness where it reigns eternal. For this is called human wisdom in such a way that it is also God's. Only then is it true wisdom; if it is merely human it is hollow."[11]

All things are "from" God, "through" God, and "in" God (Rom 11:36), and in God "we live and move and have our being" (Acts 17:27). Yet, to their great misfortune not all human beings are with God without whom they cannot be, which happens precisely when they fail to remember, understand, and love God. Augustine goes on to lament: "Of course if someone has totally forgotten anything, he cannot even be reminded of it."[12]

At this point it is important to note that, for Augustine, human beings are created *to* the image of the Trinity, Father, Son, and Holy Spirit, according to Jerome's translation of Gen. 1:26. For Augustine the verse speaks not only of creating the human being to "our" image and likeness [ad imaginem et similitudinem nostrum] in the plural, meaning Father, Son, and Holy Spirit, but also "to" [ad] their image and likeness. What does this "to" mean? For Augustine human beings are not "born" of God like the Son, who is therefore the only perfect and equal image of the Father, but only created by God and thus in no way equal to God but approaching God only with a "certain likeness" [quadam similitudine], which happens when human beings are renewed in their minds (Rom. 12:2), imitating God (Eph 5:1), and being renewed for the knowledge of God according to the image of him who created him (Col. 3:10).[13] For Augustine remembering, understanding, and loving God means participating in God, and participating in God not only makes the mind an image of God but also brings about veritable internal changes: renewal from old life [ex vetustate renovatur], reform out of deformity [ex deformitate reformatur], and happiness from misery [ex infelicitate beatificatur]. That is to say, being an image of God is not a state that can be attained once for all but a potentiality of receiving God and participating in his holiness that must be actualized in a process of becoming more and more "like" him, a process that can be completed only at the beatific vision. Being an image of God inherently contains the teleological dynamic and demand of becoming "like" to the exemplar to whose image it is created, a lifelong, indeed eschatological process and task of becoming "like" God involving renewal and reform of the mind.

This renewal and reform process, however, is not something the mind can achieve by itself. The mind "cannot reform itself in the way that it was able to deform itself" because through sin humans lost justice and holiness, and the image became deformed and discolored [deformis et declor].[14] The mind itself,

---

[11] *Trin.*, 14.12.15.
[12] *Trin.*, 14.12.16.
[13] *Trin.*, 7.6.12.
[14] *Trin.*, 14.16.22.

the seat of reason and intelligence capable of knowing God, has become, by its dark and inveterate sins, incapable of not only adhering to and enjoying but even bearing the immutable light unless renewed and healed through faith and purification, for which the mind needs the help of the divine-human mediator, Christ Jesus, who as divine is our goal but as human is our way to the God of human beings [*ad hominis deum*].[15] This renewal, for Augustine, is not a matter of the moment of conversion, baptism, and the forgiveness of sins. It is a two-stage process. As he put it,

> "It is one thing to throw off a fever, another to recover from the weakness which the fever leaves behind; it is one thing to remove from the body a missile stuck in it, another to heal the wound [*vulnus*] it made with a complete cure. The first stage of the cure is to remove the cause of the sickness [*languor*], and this is done by pardoning all sins; the second stage is curing the sickness itself, and this is done gradually by making steady progress in the renewal of this image."[16]

The renewal of the image, however, is not perfected till the eschaton, till the vision of God. "Only when it comes to the perfect vision of God will this image bear God's perfect likeness [*perfecta Dei similitudo*]."[17] According to 1 John 3:2, at the vision of God "we shall be like him because we shall see him as he is." One may ask how seeing God as he is makes those who see God "like" him, in the same way we can ask how seeing another human being as he is makes the seer "like" the person seen. Augustine's interpretation is that the image is meant to be renewed in the spirit of the mind precisely in the *knowledge* of God [*agnitio Dei*] and will be like him as his image when the image truly knows God by seeing God as he is. Doesn't eternal life consist, according to John 17:3 in "knowing you, the one true God and Jesus Christ whom you have sent"? If I may venture another explanation, the sheer incomprehensible intensity of the encounter between creator and creature, the creature seeing the creator as he is, face to face, means the most intense participation of the creature in the life of the creator, an exposure of the creature to the ontological intensity of the creator, and thus the necessary trans*form*ation of the creature to the *form* of the creator. Any exposure to greatness is transforming, and incomprehensibly more so in the case of the exposure to the creative greatness of God whose being sustains my being in its totality, ultimacy, and depth.

By the way, it is safe to state at this point that Augustine's doctrine of humanity as image of God in the teleological process of becoming "like" God and "participating" in God is his equivalent of the Orthodox doctrine of *theosis* or divinization so much talked about in recent years. At the very end of his *De civitate Dei* he says "God would have made us gods, not by deserting him,"

---

[15] *civ. Dei*, 11.2.
[16] *Trin.*, 14.17.23.
[17] Ibid.

as we did by listening to the voice of the seducer, "but by participating in him." Creatures are not divine "by the truth of their own being [*sua veritate*]" but "by participation in the true God [*Dei veri participatione*]".[18] "When we are restored by him and perfected with greater grace, we shall have eternal leisure to see that he is God, for we shall be full of him when he shall be all in all."[19]

4. The Human Being Caught between God and the World

Thus far I have presented Augustine's doctrine of the human being as image and likeness of the triune God. The image, as it turns out, is not an indifferent copy of a lifeless original like a printed copy of a journal essay or like an X-ray image of the lung or even like a photo of a human being. The human being is a creature who can in no way become equal to its creator yet is also created to become "like" its creator and participate in the creator's life by the grace of the creator despite its original nothingness and sinfulness. Human beings are images of the triune God precisely because they can remember, understand, and love God and become like him by seeing God face to face or as he is in the beatific vision. They are images empowered by the divine exemplar to seek communion with God as intellectual creatures capable of God. This is Augustine's theological anthropology, but it is also only one part of his anthropology. There is a second part, the worldliness of the world that the human image transcends in their intellectuality but that also presents constitutive obstacles in the upward ascent of the image and places downward pressures counter to its upward movement. For Augustine the Christian the world is not evil in itself because it is God's creation, but in relation to the sinful, wounded nature of the human image, it is the source, condition, and context of human sinfulness. Ontologically, the world is a good creature of God, but soteriologically it is an ambiguous reality posing a spiritual challenge that takes a lifelong struggle to sublate.

Augustine's view of the world is based on 1 John 2:15–17, which reads:

"Do not love the world or the things in the world. If anyone loves the world, love for the father is not in him. For all that is in the world, the lust of the flesh and the lust of the eyes and the pride of life, is not of the Father but is of the world. And the world passes away, and the lust of it; but he who does the will of God abides forever."[20]

---

[18] *civ. Dei*, 22.30.4; *civ. Dei*, 14.13.2.

[19] *civ. Dei*, 22.30.4. For a discussion of the history and development of the concept of *theosis*, see M. J. CHRISTENSEN and J. A. WITTUNG (eds.), *Partakers of the Divine Nature: The History and Development of Deification in the Christian Traditions* (Madison, WI: Fairleigh Dickinson University Press, 2007), which I reviewed in *Theologische Literaturzeitung* 134, no. 4 (April 2009): 465–467. I regret to say that this collection is guilty of two great omissions in the history of the concept, Augustine and Aquinas.

[20] The translation is that of the Revised Standard Version.

It is clear that the world [*kosmos*] spoken of here is not the physical universe that the scientists talk about but the human world with all its social, historical contradictions that are here radically simplified and traced to three things, the lust of the flesh, the lust of the eyes, and the pride of life. Augustine's personal struggles throughout his life were with the worldliness of the world as constituted by these three things regarded as the principal sources of temptations to sin. Of course, this struggle with the worldliness of the world is not unique to Augustine; it has been the staple of much classical Christian spirituality all the way to very modern times. What is important to note here is Augustine's interpretation of the three sources of worldliness. In the *Confessions* he translates the lust of the flesh as *libido sentiendi* or the lust for sensing, the lust of the eyes as *libido spectandi* or the lust for looking, and the pride of life as *libido principandi*.or the lust for domination.[21]

The lust of the flesh means the lust for sense pleasures including sexual pleasures but also non-sexual pleasures of the senses such as eating and drinking, hearing beautiful sounds, which Augustine finds helpful to piety, seeing beautiful things and shapes, especially light, which he finds caressing and soothing. His struggle with sexual desires is well enough known to need any comment. His particular concern with the lust of the flesh, however, is something more general and more ontological. Things sensible or *sensibilia* are objects of our senses and appeal to the pre-reflective immediacy of our consciousness with the capacity for developing addictions difficult to overcome, addictions that become chains [*vincula*] that bind and enslave us, deprive us of interior freedom as spiritual beings, and reduce us intellectual beings to the level of irrational beings like animals. It is not that Augustine is opposed to the pleasures of senses purely and simply but only insofar as they go beyond the bounds of proper care for health and prudent moderation by reason. Because of the immediacy of their appeal sense pleasures tend to be the source of strongest temptations to human beings composed of body and soul. The lust for sensing contains an inner craving for the immediacy, intensity, and ultimacy of pleasure that promises fulfillment unlimited by anything other than itself, a promise that also turns out to be an illusion.[22]

The lust of the eyes, to be distinguished from the lust of sight for sensible beauty in the narrow sense included in the lust of the flesh, refers to the lust for watching or *libido spectandi* originally used in the entertainment context of watching games and shows and includes the broader meaning of the lust for knowing [*noscendi libido*]. Because eyes are central in acquiring information about external things, the lust of the eyes stands for the lust for information about things that would be intellectual but at the most sensible level. It means

---

[21] *conf.*, 3.8.16.
[22] *conf.*, 10.29.40–10.34.51.

empty curiosity about what is superficial, novel, shocking, miraculous, outrageous, amazing, spectacular, and frivolous, that is, about things and events that arouse excitements at the most sensible level without provoking reflection and meditation in the interiority of the mind. It merely seeks to experience and find out at the most superficial level. Another name for it is intellectual concupiscence that often seeks distraction with trivia as a way of avoiding its own intellectual emptiness and frustration. It is a morbid craving for perverted knowledge, not a desire for true wisdom.[23] It is notable that Heidegger borrows much explicitly for his notion of curiosity [*Neugier*], one of the existential characteristics of inauthentic life, from Augustine's notion of "the lust of the eyes."[24]

The third category [*genus*] of temptations is the pride of life, pride in the world [*ambitio saeculi*] or the lust for domination. This is the temptation to seek veneration and affection from others and find joy in that admiration itself, not in some quality that merits such veneration. It only leads to shameful ostentation, one of the chief obstacles to loving and revering God. People in high positions seek love and honor from fellow human beings and abandon their delight in God's truth for human flattery. Such affection and honor replace God himself. Even when we receive praise for some gifts received from God, we find more joy in that praise than in possessing the gift from God, and that praise is really a sham. Ultimately, however, we seek praise and flattery from others by means of honor, office, wealth, and power so as to dominate others. We forget that all these honors, wealth, and power are transitory and meant as gifts to be used for the common good, making ourselves instead the self-sufficient, omnipotent sources of such gifts and substituting ourselves for God, playing the role of God in society and history, bringing incalculable suffering on our fellow humanity.[25] In short, we aspire to be God ourselves by abandoning God, not by participating in God.[26]

It is noteworthy that Augustine considers Christ's three temptations in the desert (Mark 1:12–13, Luke 4: 1–13, Matthew 4: 1–11) paradigmatic examples of the three categories of temptations. The temptation to turn stone into bread exemplifies the lust of the flesh [*desiderium carnis*], the temptation to throw himself down from the pinnacle of the temple to show how angels will protect him again harm corresponds to the lust of the eyes [*desiderium oculorum*], and the temptation to enjoy the power and glory of the kingdoms of the world in return for worshipping the devil speaks to the pride in the world [*ambitio saeculi*] (ep. Jo, 2:14).

---

[23] *conf.* 10.35.54–35.57.
[24] *Being and Time*, trans. J. Macquarrie and E. Robinson (New York: Harper & Row, 1962), 36.
[25] *conf.*, 10.36.59–41.66.
[26] *civ. Dei*, 22.30.4.

5. The Dialectic of Two Loves

The Augustinian human being, then, is caught in the struggle between his vocation as image of God called to become "like" God through renewal and reform of the mind and the worldliness of the world in which he has to work out that eschatological vocation. What generates this struggle? At the heart of the struggle is the dialectic of two loves, love of God and everything else in God on the one hand, and love of self and the world for the sake of self on the other.[27] For Augustine what ultimately moves a human being is neither knowledge nor even sensible desire but love. We are what we love. "Everyone lives according to what he loves [*secundum hoc enim vivit quisque quod diligit*]".[28] In order to determine the character of a people, we have to look into "what kind of things they love [*quae diligit*]".[29] "The quality of a person depends on the quality of his love [*talis est quisque, qualis ejus dilectio est*]" (ep. Jo., 2:14). Love "connects" two things to each other and makes them similar to each other by making them "cling" [*inhaerere*] to and participate in each other, often with the vice of addiction, often with the power of delight, the former enslaving us, the latter liberating us.[30]

In a profound symbolic meditation on the Holy Spirit hovering over the chaos of the primeval waters spoken of in Genesis 1:2, Augustine discovers two types of love and two types of basic orientation of human existence. He surmises that scripture mentions the Spirit only after first naming heaven, invisible and unorganized earth, and the darkness over the deep because the Spirit must first have something over which to hover. Add to this what Paul says about the supereminent life of charity that has been poured into our hearts through the Holy Spirit. It seems to follow that the supereminent love must be poised above the waters from the first. The waters symbolize the weight of passions [*pondus cupiditatis*] that drag us down into the violent deep, over which love [*caritas*] lifts us up through the Spirit hovering over the waters. These do not refer to places but to affections [*affectus*] and loves [*amores*]. Passion refers to the impurity of our spirit that sweeps us downward [*inferius*] with love of anxieties [*amore curarum*], love refers to holiness that lifts us upward [*superius*] with love of true peace [*amore securitatis*] so that we may raise our hearts to God [*sursum*] where the Spirit is poised above the waters.[31] So, according to Augustine, each of us, according to the nature of his desires, carries his own load, the load of

---

[27] *civ. Dei*, 14.
[28] *Trin.* 13.20.26.
[29] *civ. Dei*, 19.24.
[30] *The City of God* is an illustration of these two loves in human history; see P. WEITHMAN, "Augustine's Political Philosophy," in *The Cambridge Companion to Augustine*, ed. E. Stump and N. Kretzmann (Cambridge: Cambridge University Press, 2002), 234–252.
[31] *conf.* 13.7.8.

love that is wings to fly with, or the load of greed [*cupiditas*] that is a burden to weigh us down. The way of love liberates us, the way of greed oppresses us.[32] These are, for Augustine, two fundamental loves and orientations of human existence.

The heart is the locus of our loves and desires. The heart is the dimension of what is ultimate, most profound, most intimate, and most compelling in human existence. If we are going to be moved to do anything important, our heart must be moved to do so, but when our heart is moved, we do it with joy [*gaudium*] and delight [*delectatio*], which adds energy, zest, and momentum to our actions. When the heart is not moved, we do thing with fear, fear of consequences, fear of punishment, fear of alternatives, or at best with indifference and reluctance, out of a sense of obligation, without joy and delight. The difference in result between things done with joy and things done without joy is a matter of everyday experience. In this sense joy and delight is an immense liberating power. For Augustine the grace of the Holy Spirit operates precisely in this way. The Holy Spirit inspires us to do good things with love, joy, and delight by pouring love into our hearts (Rom. 5:5), thus healing and strengthening our free will, not replacing it.[33]

The problem of human life is that we are pulled in many different, even opposing directions by the love of many different things, leading to the fragmentation of our life into a conflicting multiplicity of concerns and, in extreme cases, to the anguish of the divided soul, demanding integration and unification of life.[34] The lust for sensing, the lust for seeing, and the lust for competing and dominating are constant sources that divide our life, making human life "one long temptation" [*tota temptatio*].[35] For Augustine this integration of life is only possible when we love God and all other things in God.

Most often we have fallen outside ourselves into the world of things and altogether forget ourselves.

"Such is the force of love [*amor*] that when the mind has been thinking about things with love for a long time and has got stuck [*adhaeserit*] to them with the glue of care [*curae glutino*], it drags them along with itself even when it returns after a fashion to thinking about itself. Now these things are bodies which it has fallen in love with outside itself through the senses of the flesh and got involved [*implicata*] with through a kind of long familiarity. But it cannot bring these bodies themselves back inside with it into the region, so to say, of its non-bodily nature; so, it wraps up their images and clutches them to itself, images made in itself out of itself."[36]

---

[32] On the distinction between *caritas* and *cupiditas* as two types of *amor*, see H. ARENDT, *Love and Saint Augustine* (Chicago, IL: University of Chicago Press, 1996), 18–35.
[33] *spir. et litt.*, 16.28, 19.32, 25.42, 51, 63, *nat. et.gr.*, 57.67.
[34] *conf.*, 9.21 ff.
[35] *conf.*, 10.32.48.
[36] *Trin.*, 10.5.7.

We are not only immersed and lost in the world of sensible things and their images. We also love and cling to them and even come to think of ourselves as things of the same sort, conforming to and identifying with them. In fact, we think we are bodies.[37] Furthermore, Augustine says that we are "in" the things we are thinking about with love, which means, mostly in the sensible material things, and this makes it difficult for us to enter into ourselves without their images. In his colorful language, the mind and the images it loves "are all stuck astonishingly fast together with the glue of love" [*cohaeserunt mirabiliter glutino amoris*] so much so that the mind mixes itself up with things and their images it loves and simply identifies itself with them. The mind, however, is not any one of these things and images. It is a self-consciousness that distinguishes things, their images, and judges them, distinguishing itself from them all. Nevertheless, most often the mind is so lost in things that it forgets itself as the transcendental, self-conscious source of the unity and diversity of all experiences. Still, the mind cannot not remember itself, not understand itself, or not love itself, although it can forget to think about itself as an object.[38]

Humans are, then, profoundly involved in the worldliness of the world, its lust for sensing, its lust for seeing, and its arrogance of self-sufficiency all of which are thoroughly mediated by the senses and sensible desires. Human beings are "fallen," to use an Heideggerian expression, into the world by ties of love, attachment, and clinging. Such fallenness is not a temporary accident but a permanent existential. The choice for Augustine, therefore, is a choice between two ways of living, the way of the image in its spiritual ascent to God above itself, and the way of worldliness in its sensuous descent to the world beneath itself. The challenge is to "transfer his love [*amorem*] from temporal things to eternal, from visible to intelligible, from carnal to spiritual things,"[39] for which we depend on the grace of the Holy Spirit who strengthens our free will by liberating it from "delight in sinning to take a constant delight in not sinning,"[40] from the delight in satisfying the lust of the flesh, the lust of the eyes, and the lust for domination with the greater delight in the work of spiritual ascent to the love of God.

---

[37] *Trin.*, 10.6.8.
[38] *Trin.*, 10.8.11.
[39] *Trin.*, 14.17.23.
[40] *civ. Dei*, 22.30.3.

6. Contemporary Capitalist Sensationalism as Theological Crisis of Humanity: Concluding Reflections

Augustine's vision of humanity was a most exalted one. The human being was created to become the image of God with the capacity for knowing and participating in God. Through the life-long renewal and reform of the mind the human being was called to become "like" God, a process that could be completed only eschatologically. This eschatological destiny of the human being, however, faces an existential struggle with the worldliness of the world in which he has to work out his destiny. I do not know whether Augustine had a sense of a historical crisis because of this existential struggle; perhaps the impending ruin of the Roman Empire posed this existential crisis in a different form. Today, however, we do face a historical crisis in this struggle because capitalist sensationalism seems to spell the death of the very subject, a subject capable of recognizing the struggle as a struggle because the belief in God has been declining, which renders irrelevant any claim that human beings are created to the image of God, and because human beings are being reduced to infra-rational entities with no higher needs than the satisfaction of sensible desires. The idea of a human being as the image of God precisely for his capacity to remember, know, and love God today sounds like something rather out of this world. Capitalism intensifies the theological crisis not only because it has been eroding the belief in God through the spread of secularism but also more so for Augustine because it intensifies and magnifies the worldliness of the world in its threefold aspects.

By liberating all desires to stimulate consumption and inventing ever-more sophisticated technologies of manipulation capitalism has been magnifying its sensationalism or appeal to the senses and sensuous desires. It has been liberating the lust of the flesh, not only for sexual pleasures but for all sense pleasures. It has been maximizing the lust of the eyes with empty curiosities, distracting commercials, ever more stimulating exposures, laying bare all intimacies, publicizing all that is private, revealing all that is secret, with no respect for the intrinsic dignity of anything whatsoever. Nothing seems sacred enough to remain inviolate. No more taboos remain. In the words of Slavoj Žižek, "perversion is no longer subversive: such shocking excesses are part of the system itself."[41] In the words of another social critic, Neil Postman "all public discourse increasingly takes the form of entertainment. Our politics, our religion, news, athletics, education, and commerce have been transformed into congenial adjuncts of show business, largely without protest or even much popular notice," which makes Las Vegas the paradigm of contemporary cul-

---

[41] S. Žižek, *The Fragile Absolute or Why Is the Christian Legacy Worth Fighting For?* (New York: Verso, 2001), 23.

ture.[42] Capitalist sensationalism has also been exaggerating the pride of life by demonstrating splendors of the pleasures of power, wealth, and fame in the most spectacular way. It is worldliness at its most intense, most systematic, most worldly. I wonder how more worldly the world can get. It has been overpowering our intellect and will with a systematic, concentrated attack on the senses and sensuous desires and confining us, our visions, horizons, and hopes to the world of what the ancients used to call *sensibilia* or sensible things. Capitalist sensationalism is posing a crisis, however, not only because it magnifies the dangers of worldliness to the spiritual journey of the image of God but more because it tends to kill the very subjectivity of the subject capable of willing to undertake that journey to God and feel worldliness as a hurdle on that journey.

In a profound meditation on the word "God," Karl Rahner once suggested that the death of the word "God" means the death of the human being as human being and the degradation of the human being to the status of an animal. The reason is that "God" is a word that stands for the ultimate intelligibility of the world in its totality, unity, and depth. Whether or not God exists as a reality, the word stands for the unifying, ultimate source of the reality of the world as a totality, and has the function of evoking the inquiry on the totality, unity, and depth of the world as a world. Without the word or its equivalent we have no way of even asking that most ultimate of all questions. The death of the word, then, means the death of the capacity to conceive and ask about the totality, unity, and ultimate depth of the world. We will be dealing with only particular empirical aspects of particular things, never with the whole of the world or human existence. We are deprived of the capacity to think totality, unity, and depth, that is, the capacity to think transcendence. And this does mean the death of the human subject and his reduction and confinement to the particularity of *sensibilia*.[43] I think Augustine would totally agree. For Augustine as well the highest dignity of the human being is the capacity to know and participate in God, who represents yet infinitely transcends the unity, totality, and ultimate depth of the reality of the world as its creator. The ability to judge is precisely the ability to transcend the partiality, particularity, and givenness of the sensible world by being able to conceive norms and causes and totalities. This capacity for transcendence is the basis for the possibility of critique, critique of both knowledge and society, and of the world as a whole. For Augustine the capacity to know God and the capacity to make moral judgments go together. Which is to say, there is a profound connection between the erosion of the belief in God and the death of the subject.

---

[42] N. POSTMAN, *Amusing Ourselves to Death: Public Discourse in the Age of Show Business* (New York: Penguin, 1985), 80.

[43] K. RAHNER, *Foundations of Christian Faith: An Introduction to the Idea of Christianity*, trans. W. Dych (New York: Seabury, 1978), 44–50.

For all the sinfulness and fallenness of humanity, however, Augustine, the doctor of grace and love, still hopes that the human being remains the image of God with the capacity for receiving and participating in God. This image has not been destroyed, although wounded, by original sin, and it still retains its defining capacity for God. The mind will always remember God because it lives and moves and has its being in him. The mind does not remember God because it has any explicit memory or knowledge of God but because it continues to be touched by the light that has always been touching it. What light? For Augustine, even the godless make moral judgments about what is right and what is wrong, what is just and what is unjust, how we ought to live. Where, however, do they get the standard of justice? Not from their nature, which is changeable, since the standards must be unchangeable, not from their behavior, which is unjust, not from any written document, which may or may not be itself just. They get the idea of justice from the book of that light called truth impressed into their hearts. Even those who turn away from the light are still touched by it. The implicit presentiments in our hearts of the immutable norms of justice, Augustine hopes, will keep alive the memory of God and a sense of eternity.[44]

I have so far spoken of Augustine and capitalism, of Augustine as a classical theological interpreter of human existence and worldliness in its threefold aspects as a perennial source of our spiritual crisis, and of capitalism as a determining contemporary social condition intensifying that crisis of worldliness without limit through its sensationalism. I am addressing the theological crisis of contemporary humanity and locating that crisis in the capitalist sensationalism absolved from all limits. (There are, of course, many other crises we face as human beings today, brought on by different causes such as the destruction of the ecosphere, developments in artificial intelligence, genetic manipulation, etc., but I am inclined to say that all these crises are also exacerbated by capitalist sensationalism that does not know how to restrain or discipline itself in its search for profit.) Let me stress that it is not my intention to deal with either capitalism or Augustine in all their respective relevant aspects nor to address all the controversial issues surrounding both. Both are very hotly debated topics and loaded with many critical issues. I have avoided them in order to focus on the theological crisis of humanity, on capitalist culture as source of that crisis for bringing on the "death of the subject" and on Augustine for his profound illumination of the human subject as the image of God with a peculiar vulnerability to worldliness in its threefold aspects. My essential question has been, What kind of humanity does capitalist culture produce? Not whether capitalist politics allows more freedom than does socialism, not whether capitalism economy is productive of greater wealth than other systems, which may be

---

[44] *Trin.*, 14.15.21.

answered in many different ways. Likewise, my essential questions has been, Are human beings images of God, and if so, what are the existential threats to the dignity of human beings created as images of God, not whether Augustine is a dualist and misogynist.

One final word. Much traditional Christian spirituality, typified by Thomas a Kempis and his *Imitatio Christi*, has been very negative towards the world, in a twofold sense, in the ontological sense as something that passes away, and in the moral sense as something that tempts and corrupts the human soul, a danger to salvation. For these twofold reasons traditional spirituality has been a spirituality of withdrawal from the world, even of *contemptus mundi*, perhaps to a more pronounced degree in Catholicism than in Protestantism. Vatican II brought about a great change in the Catholic attitude towards the world, stressing its positive theological value as God's creation, the theological obligation to participate in "building the world," and nowadays protecting the ecological integrity of creation. What is conspicuous by its absence is any talk of "worldliness" as something dangerous. Such talk sounds like a call to return to old time, pessimistic, negative spirituality. It is also ironical, however. There are plenty of evil things going on in the world today, from the cheating and lying going on in business and politics, big nations threatening small nations and the entire world with nuclear bombs, absolutely shameless displays of sex and violence on the media, and oppression and genocide of minorities to the senseless, destructive competition for profit and power to dominate the world and even space. These are precisely phenomena of "worldliness" in its moral, theological sense that Augustine was talking about in its threefold manifestations, the lust of the flesh, the lust of the eyes, and the pride of life. Isn't it ironical that during the very decades these things happen every day, in fact, on a scale far greater than Augustine could have imagined, we no longer talk of worldliness, and that the struggle against these evils are carried on instead largely by secular humanists and critical theorists? There is no denying that Christian churches are actively involved in decrying social injustices and reforming structural evils, but they are also rather silent about cultural trends that accentuate the lust of the flesh, the lust of the eyes, and the pride of life that degrade and destroy the very image of God. They certainly do not decry them as *sources of temptation* dangerous to the dignity and destiny of the human being. Perhaps it is past time to renew the critique of the world in its worldliness in a new form without the pessimism and escapism of the old?

The Other Reduction?
Capitalist Sensationalism and the Worldliness of God

Petr Gallus

I am thankful to Dr. Min for his critical lecture pointing to the strong tendency of the current capitalist system to reduce humanity only to the *sensibilia*. Nevertheless, I see in his text the danger of the other reduction: against the sharp critique of capitalist sensationalism as the source of the current crisis of humanity, which reduces humans only to immediate sensual pleasures, Dr. Min presents a picture of spiritual and intellectual mind-focused humanity with a capacity for transcendence. Problematic here is the dualistic frame that puts mind and body against each other, stressed all the more by the analysis of *libido* and *cupiditas* in Augustine, where worldliness and corporeality seem at the end to be a burden we need to shake off. Humans would be then reduced only to intellectual and spiritual mind or soul: although Dr. Min speaks about "The Human Being as Image of God", it turns out that the image of God is rather only the human mind, not humans as mind-body-wholes. While in Dr. Min's view capitalist sensationalism loses the mind ("the death of the subject"), Dr. Min loses the body in his critique and with it he loses the world. At the same time, he speaks about a *theological* crisis. From a theological perspective, however, the term "image of God" has a clear anchor: the proper image of God is in Jesus Christ as the Logos who became flesh. Therefore, theologically speaking, this would be a more appropriate starting point for a balanced approach to the crisis of humanity.

My response will have four parts, in which I will try to overcome the dualistic view and to interpret the discussed phenomena in a more holistic way. I will therefore deal (1) with the problems of today's capitalism, (2) with the conception of humanity and (3) with the theology of Augustine, in order to propose (4) the christological perspective as the more appropriate key to the problem of humanity.

1. The Dangers of Capitalism

There is no doubt that the current forms of the capitalism practiced all around the world bear many serious dangers, which are to be criticized and fought against. And indeed, the tendency to invest in sensual pleasure and only sensual pleasure is one of the issues that contributes most surely to the crisis of humanity. "[I]nstinctive immediacy" is a nice and fitting diagnose of what is so seductive about this sensualist side of capitalism. The lack of distance and of a "critical intellectual mediation" leads to the fact that thinking and judging are, today, indeed the most endangered human capacities.[1]

On the other hand, though, this notion is not new. Sensual experiences, whether negative or positive, are always stronger and have a much greater impact on us than does calm critical reflection. That the human capacity to think and to judge is endangered is therefore nothing surprising or new. It was actually always so, because humans always experience pressure from the immediate senses. In capitalist societies, this sensual pressure inhabits two levels, both mentioned by Dr. Min: the external (producing 'things') and the internal (producing images, impressions, ideas, symbols, dreams, etc.).[2] Moreover, an important characteristic of the capitalist world is also the fact that one can basically have, or get, what one desires; the objects of our desires are mostly available. In comparison with older times, things, experiences, and possibilities are far more accessible and realizable than earlier (on the external level probably easier than on the internal, because the external issues are mostly only a question of the money). On the other side, though, there is also a rising frustration, fed e.g. by the pressure of advertisement, about the need to acquire everything we still do not have, but should have. In Central or Eastern Europe, where I come from, we know this "brutal attack on the senses and through the senses"[3] as a huge phenomenon in our society in the 1990s, shortly after the Velvet Revolution of 1989. Yet today the situation has developed and capitalist societies face, in my opinion, also other and even more severe problems than sensationalism.

Dr. Min complains, "We rarely hear anywhere any counsel to restrain, to moderate, and to be reasonable".[4] It is true that the stress of self-discipline, of restraining, is quite foreign to the capitalist system. However, it is not true that such appeals are rare. Today, the increasing ecological and climatic threats stand for the most reasonable and compelling arguments for self-discipline. These arguments are being heard with increasing intensity by individuals as well as by (at least some) political leaders. It is possible though that this happens more in Europe than in the U.S.

Nevertheless, Dr. Min – in his skeptical view of the history of the twentieth century captured peculiarly between *The Decline of the West* and *The Fall of Western Civilization*[5] – accuses capitalist sensationalism of causing people

---

[1] Cf. A MIN, "The Human Being as Image of God," in this volume, 81–99.
[2] Ibid.
[3] Ibid.
[4] Ibid.
[5] Ibid.

to abandon thinking and judgment, and of reducing humans to mere sensual beings who yield to the sensual immediacy and, with this loss of distance (which is according to Dr. Min necessary, besides other things, also for religion) of actually ceasing to be human. He calls this ultimate diagnose "the death of the subject", so that humans oppressed by capitalist sensationalism seem to be reduced only to stimulus-response patterns, i. e. actually to the status of animals.[6]

From my European point of view, however, to say that people stopped thinking and judging and live their lives only under the impressions created by sensual pleasure is too simple and one-sided. In my opinion, not the absence of thinking and judging, but the question of *how* people think and judge – not the manipulation of human beings toward mere sensuality, but the *manipulation of thinking and judging* – is the main problem today. I mean to point here to problems closely bound to our "post-truth era": to the pressure of different propagandas, of so-called "alternative facts" or of "hybrid warfare", which stand in close connection to the above-mentioned internal level of our senses and produce an immense flood of images, ideas, symbols or anxieties, all of which influence us more than we would admit at first. Simply said: the problem is – and it has come out, for example, in many of the most recent national elections in the U.S. as well as in Europe – that people still think and judge, but often in a scary way, with tendencies to simple and populistic solutions, as well as various fundamentalisms.

The next result of this development within the current wild flood of unstructured information – often colonized by some opaque economic and political powers – is the often-mentioned erosion of truth, which leads to indifference and unconcern. And this indifference results in a relativizing arbitrariness, as well as in endless plurality of positions in which the only rule that applies is that position does not actually matter. I consider this to be the most severe danger within today's Euro-American societies. Such indifference creates space not only for sensationalism, but also for different utilitarianisms, pragmaticisms, manipulations, and, in the end, creeping totalities in which a blindly convinced minority rules over the indifferent majority.

At this point, I want to make one more point clear. Based on sentences like "Capitalism systematically accentuates and exaggerates the propensity to evil already natural to human beings", one could have the impression that we have to search for a system other than the capitalist one. We surely need to deal with the dangers of capitalism, but I am deeply convinced that we need to do it *within* the frame set by capitalism. From my own experience as a person who lived a part of his life under the communist regime, I have to say that the alternative to capitalism is *not* socialism or communism (despite the fact that, to my

---

[6] Ibid.

great disillusionment, the opposite opinion is still alive even among academics). What we need is a kind of capitalism with a human face. One can now critically ask, how something like this should be done? There is definitely no simple answer. There is, however, an ongoing discussion of this topic.[7] What I want to point out is the fact that although there are many dangers inherent in capitalism which we must fight against, there is still some democratic space for disagreement with the majority, for opposing what is forced as 'normal,' for the search for one's own way. In this respect, freedom is still possible, although it is always a struggle and often a matter of marching against the wind.

2. What Is Humanity?

In his warning against the death of the subject, Dr. Min presupposes a dualist picture of humans, influenced obviously by the Neoplatonic tradition and strengthened by the Augustinian view. Putting aside the debate about how many dimensions we should name in order to grasp the human being as a whole,[8] the worse problem is, in my opinion, that in the traditional dualist view the soul, or mind, is understood *in opposition* to the body or flesh. Dr. Min correctly notices with Augustine that the world is still a good creation of God – i.e. it is not evil as such: "Ontologically, the world is a good creature of God, but soteriologically it is an ambiguous reality."[9] Unlike the finite and ambiguous world, the mind is infinite and clearly much more appreciated. It is the old Neoplatonic-Augustinian heritage that the body is corrupt and sinful and pulls us down, whereas the soul tends rather towards the divine. In Dr. Min's analysis, the body obviously has to do with the immediacy of the senses, whereas the mind, separately from the body, is characterized by its

---

[7] Not only in my country, but all over the world for the last 40 years. Cf. S. BRITAIN, *Capitalism with a Human Face* (Cambridge, MA: Harward University Press, 1995); K. M. LEISINGER, "Capitalism with a Human Face: The UN Global Compact", *The Journal of Corporate Citizenship* 28: *Is Corporate Citizenship Making a Difference?* (2001): 113–132; H. W. PETERS, speech from May 3, 2018: "Capitalism with a Human Face," https://www.beehive.govt.nz/speech/capitalism-human-face; S. ŽIŽEK, https://www.theguardian.com/global-development/poverty-matters/2011/apr/22/slavoj-zizek-animated-ideas-about-charity (both accessed on 06/25/2019).

[8] Cf. e.g. the widely accepted bio-psycho-socio-spiritual model (BPSS), introduced officially by the WHO in 2002, and against it the naturalistic neuro-scientific model, which considers the mind or soul only a fiction of the brain (cf. a good and short overview e.g. in D. NAUER, *Mensch. Christliches Menschenbild heute? Verständlich erläutert für Neugierige* [Stuttgart: W. Kohlhammer Verlag, 2018], 68–76; or in relation to consciousness H.-D. MUTSCHLER, *Bewusstsein. Was ist das?*, *Forum Theologische Literaturzeitung* 34 [Leipzig: Evangelische Verlagsanstalt, 2018]).

[9] MIN, "The Human Being," where Min criticizes the shift in the theology of the Catholic Church after Vatican II and defends the negative view of worldliness.

ability to keep its distance and reflect on the immediate experience. This ability of distance as the ability to transcend the sensible world is later identified with the "capacity for transcendence", in which we can "conceive norms and causes and totalities", i.e. also God.[10] The mind obviously takes an opposite direction from the body.

It is necessary to stress, however, in critical opposition, that the mind is a phenomenon as ambivalent as the body and, regarding sin and the soteriological role, the position of the mind is even worse than that of the body. Against the traditional tendency to associate primarily the body with sin, it is mostly from the soul or mind that the worst evil comes. (Similar to the typical totalitarian structure, in which the main ideologist never kills or oppresses anyone directly, because there are obedient people available for his purposes who realize his ideas and received orders and who, in the case of prosecution concerning having carried these ideas out, afterwards repeat that they were only executing orders.) There is hardly anything scarier than the human intellect.[11]

At the same time, another well-known problem with dualistic conception has to do with the view that the body and mind/soul are opposites and therefore separable, whence the bearer of the identity (or of the humanity) can be, in the end – and in the eschatological end the more – only the soul. This conclusion underestimates the fact that fundamentally all human actions are (to use a theologically trendy word) 'embodied' – moreover, that human identity, personality, and subjectivity are embodied, because all identifying signs of our identity are mediated through the body (face, figure, voice, etc.).

The human is, therefore, more rightly seen as a whole of body and mind, inclusive of all the ambiguities inherent within this holistic perspective. And within this holistic view, it is also appropriate to see the bigger picture: not only the human being as an individual, but, in the larger question of humanity, within the unavoidable context of others – to see the human being not only as an individual, but as an individual within social relations. What we call 'subject' is not something which precedes all further relations, but is, rather, the result of the encounter with the other and his or her otherness. This otherness constitutes one's own subjectivity; one can say 'I' only vis-à-vis the other.[12]

The loss of the ability to self-distance and the related capacity for transcendence, as described by Dr. Min, is, therefore, to be conceived as a loss not only for the mind, or as a loss of the mind, but as a loss for the whole person and its

---

[10] Ibid.

[11] This is a well-known notion already in the biblical scriptures (cf. Mt 5:28; 12:34; 15:19), later developed by M. Luther (cf. M. LUTHER, *WA* 42, 348,38 [Genesisvorlesung 1535–1545]; "Der Große Katechismus," in *Bekenntnisschriften der Evangelisch-Lutherischen Kirche* [Göttingen: Vandenhoeck & Ruprecht, 1959⁴], 560, lines 22–24).

[12] Cf. I. U. DALFERTH, *Die Wirklichkeit des Möglichen* (Tübingen: Mohr Siebeck, 2003), 415–429.

being and life. It is, with Paul Tillich, a "lost dimension" which is relevant for the mind and for the body as well.[13]

3. The Theology of Augustine

Much of what I discuss above has its roots in the theology of Augustine. I will stress two more problems with the Augustinian conception of mind (or soul). Dr. Min entitled his lecture "The Human Being as Image of God". The problem in Augustine is that the image of God is not the human being as such, but only the mind. The human being in his or her very core is the mind, which *has* a body (not: which *is* a body). This fact provoked my objection that a view of the human being based on this dual scheme tends to the other reduction: whereas capitalist sensationalism reduces humans only to the senses, to bodily pleasure, and forgets subjectivity and the mind, the Augustinian conception reduces humans only to the mind (or soul) and forgets the body in its positive dimension.

The other point concerns the immortality of the soul, a Platonic element that runs deep in the Augustinian conception, since the imorality of the soul makes the most important difference to the body. The body is finite, the soul is infinite. And nothing transitory or finite could be the image of God. *Similis simili*: The infinite God can communicate Himself only to an adequate partner, and this cannot be the body, only the soul.[14]

Due to its immortality, the soul is actually a divine element in humans. Regarding the overcoming of death (which is then only the death of the body, which separates it from the immortal soul), an individual possesses the grounds for the final victory in him/herself. No one need therefore be afraid of death; the solution is from the beginning firmly within us. This means that actually no appeal to God is needed in this point. It is no wonder that the problem of the immortal soul has been handled in the history mostly fully apart from Christology: the cross and the resurrection of Jesus Christ are in this case actually not needed anymore. Everyone has the grounds of salvation within him/herself and, moreover, Jesus Christ himself (i. e. his soul) did not die – only his body did. If the soteriological focus is already on creation, then the death and resurrection of Jesus Christ become obsolete, because everything can be done by the Father alone. There is a full substitution of the grace of the creation for the grace of the cross.

---

[13] Cf. P. Tillich, "The Lost Dimension in Religion," originally in *The Saturday Evening Post*, v. 230, no. 50 (1958), later in *The Essential Tillich*, ed. F. F. Church (Chicago, IL: Chicago University Press, 1987), 1–8.

[14] Cf. Min, "The Human Being," in this volume, 81–99.

But again: only regarding the soul (or mind). Whereas the soul aims toward participation in God, finite creation is subjected to time. According to the dualist division, as well as the reception of the Johannine dualism, Augustine cannot think salvation from sin in other terms than as salvation *from* the sinful world. In so doing he underestimates – regarding the world and hence also regarding the corporeity of humans – the fundamental soteriological difference between sin and nature, which should preserve the world from such a theological destruction. In Augustine, the lifelong struggle with the world can end only with redemption *from* the world and from the body, from everything finite.[15] However, this ultimately results in the loss of the world. The other – Augustinian – reduction loses the body and with it the whole world.[16]

All of these problems, arising from the dualist frame and its asymmetrical mind-body relation that favors the mind, result from one absolutely fundamental, but omitted, theological point. In Augustine's critique of *libido* and *cupiditas*, as well as in Min's critique of capitalist sensationalism, Christology is missing.[17]

4. The Worldliness of God

From the theological perspective, the fundamental statement is: *Ho logos sarx egeneto* – the Logos became flesh (John 1:14). This is where all reflection on the mind-body relation and the God-world relation has to start. This Christological anchor balances every critique of the dangers posed to and by humanity and avoids the reductive tendencies in one or the other direction, without throwing the baby out with the bathwater. There are at least two fundamental points that suggest a path for further thinking:

First, in Jesus Christ as the true God and the true human (as per the Chalcedonian tradition), God remains God and human remains human. There is no transformation or mutation. It is the goal neither of God nor of humanity to become something different; the aim of the human is not to shed its humanity and gain divinity. Moreover, the *humanity of Jesus Christ*, which is the proper

---

[15] Cf. P. GALLUS, "Der Tod Jesu Christi, Zeit und Ewigkeit", *Neue Zeitschrift für Systematische Theologie* 60 (2018): 534; I. U. DALFERTH, "Zeit der Zeichen," in *Gedeutete Gegenwart* (Tübingen: Mohr Siebeck, 1997), 253–259; "Theologie der Zeit: alte und neue Zeit," in *Zeitstruktur und Apokalyptik*, ed. U. Fink and A. Schindler (Zürich: NZN Buchverlag, 1999), 95–99.

[16] It is then only consistent and logical when the immortal soul tends towards God in order to be divinized at the end. Augustine, like Dr. Min, has obvious sympathy for the old Eastern conception of *theosis*, which, however, runs the risk of blurring the fundamental theological difference between Creator and creation, God and humans.

[17] Augustine introduces Christ through creation and stresses the incarnation in the first place, but he underestimates the outreach of Christology to the created world (cf. *Confessions* XI, VI–VIII). Likewise, in Dr. Min's text, Christ does not play any important role.

image of God. Jesus remains fully human but open to the divine and in his humanity, he mirrors divine love to others.

Second, in Jesus Christ, God became human. In him, God entered the world and went into the depths: Logos did not become only human mind, nor only *soma*, but *sarx*, the corrupted, finite flesh with all its ambiguities and inclinations. It was not just embodiment, but incarnation, enfleshment. In Jesus Christ, God takes the world as seriously as it gets. In Jesus Christ, God Himself became world. But not an ideal world, rather a part of the corrupted, sinful world. Our world. And in this world, God became human, wholly human.[18] From this perspective, all conceptions that lose the body or the world prove to be theologically blind alleys. In Jesus Christ, there is salvation and redemption also *for* the world, not only from the world.

This soteriological ground has an impact also for the ontological and ethical dimension of humanity. In the incarnation, the body, the flesh, and all the world are taken seriously as things that God cares about and are hence not excluded from salvation. At the same time, the way of *how* was God in Jesus Christ including his death on cross and his resurrection throws a clear and critical light on how people should live, if they want to live as true humans, i.e. in the image of God. Regarding sensationalism in particular, from this perspective it is obvious that not the *sensibilia* as such, but rather their abuse, is problematic: this would be the case right there, where humanity, including its worldliness and bodiliness do not mirror the love of God for the others, where sinful tendencies displace the fundamental relation to God and to the others, where sin as the *amor sui* combined with *hybris* establishes itself as the dominating power.[19] But again, this can be recognized in its whole depth only in the light of the cross and of the resurrection of Jesus Christ.

This Christological insight can be a good starting point for a more complex and integrated view of humanity. I would offer this insight as the solution that Dr. Min is seeking with his last sentence: it is exactly "time to renew the critique of the world in its worldliness in a new form without the pessimism and escapism of the old".[20] We need only to start Christologically and, at least in the case of the framework, we cannot follow Augustine.

---

[18] Already the early church rejected stepwise all conceptions in which the divine Logos was substituted for one of the dimensions of humanity (e.g. typically Apollinaris of Laodicea, in whom the Logos was substituted for human soul). The final statement was the Chalcedonian *vere homo*.

[19] This, the conception of sin on the personal level as *amor sui* (and not primarily as *libido* and *cupiditas*) is a point in which Augustine can be followed, in combination with other authors, as I try to show in my article "Verantwortliche Rede von der Sünde," *Communio Viatorum* LX (2018): 139–170.

[20] Min, "The Human Being," in this volume, 81–99.

"Multidimensional Monism:" An Integrated and Diverse Embodied Theological Account of the *imago Dei*[1]

Veli-Matti Kärkkäinen

1. Introduction

Indeed, it is "a strange fact about our culture that we are operating with a variety of radically different views of the basic nature of human beings." As if that were not enough, "[e]ven stranger is the fact that so few people seem to notice."[2] In fact inquiry into human nature has been compared to a "labyrinth" where there are "blind alleys" and where it is difficult to "find one's goal."[3] No wonder, there is a bewildering confusion regarding the nature of human nature not only among philosophers of mind and (those) neuroscientists (who think philosophically!) but also among Christian philosophers and theologians.

On the one hand, common intuitions, universal religious teachings,[4] and traditional accounts of classical philosophy envision some kind of dualistic[5] account of humanity in which an important distinction is made between the physical and mental. On the other hand, among neuroscientists, philosophers of mind, and large number of other scientists a monist-physicalist account has gained upper hand. That said, any talk about "scientific orthodoxy" is precarious and in need of nuancing. Neuroscientific results and insights are not

---

[1] This presentation draws directly from my "'Multidimensional Monism:' A Constructive Theological Proposal for the Nature of Human Nature" and "A Rejoinder to Goetz," in *Neuroscience and the Soul. The Human Person in Philosophy, Science, and Theology*, ed. T. M. Crisp, S. L. Porter, and G. A. Ten Elshof (Grand Rapids, MI: Eerdmans, 2016), 201–27, 235–37; and more widely, my *Creation and Humanity. A Constructive Christian Theology for the Pluralistic World*, vol. 3 (Grand Rapids, MI: Eerdmans, 2016), chap. 12.

[2] N. Murphy, *Bodies and Souls, or Spirited Bodies?* (Cambridge: Cambridge University Press, 2006), ix; she reports that no fewer than 130 different views of the human person were present in a recent book she read (3–4).

[3] D. Kraschl, "Das Leib-Seele-Problem als Ausdruck menschlicher Geschöpflichkeit," *Neue Zeitschrift für Systematische Theologie und Religionsphilosophie* 53, no. 4 (2011): 399, translation mine.

[4] For a detailed engagement of four living faith traditions (Jewish, Muslim, Hindu, and Buddhist) regarding the nature of human nature, consult Kärkkäinen, *Creation and Humanity*, chap. 14.

[5] As is rightly noticed, a concept such as dualism has to be handled with great care and hence, we should rather speak of dualisms (in plural).

"brute facts," they call for interpretation. Consider this ironic fact: three leading scholars in the field, namely, Sir John Eccles, Francis Crick, and Roger Sperry – all of them Nobel laureates – look at the same evidence and draw different conclusions: one is dualist, another reductive materialist, and yet another nonreductive physicalist, respectively![6]

When it comes to my own academic field, Christian systematic (or constructive or doctrinal) theology, beginning from the mid-Twentieth Century or so, a definite shift has taken place away from traditional dualism towards a highly integrated, mutually conditioned account of human person as a physical-mental totality. While in the past, body-soul dualism was assumed to be the default position, academic theology has come to a new appreciation of the fact that "we know conscious and self-conscious life only as bodily life [...] bodily functions condition all psychological experience. This is true even of self-consciousness." As a result, not only for scientists but also for a growing number of contemporary theologians, "traditional ideas of the soul as a substance that is distinct from the body and that is detached from it in death" have lost much of their credibility.[7] That said, unlike some Christian philosophers and biblical scholars, systematicians, however, have not yet engaged in any significant measure the dynamic interdisciplinary conversation among philosophers of mind, neuroscientists, and others. Indeed, at the moment of this writing I cannot think of one single major presentation of a Christian doctrine of humanity written by a systematician which would contain a truly interdisciplinary dialogue.[8] What is most astonishing to me is the total omission of this kind of engagement in the recent massive two-volume theological anthropology by David Kelsey of Yale; in a theological discussion of more than one thousand pages, most everything else is investigated but not the contributions of philosophy of mind and brain sciences![9]

---

[6] N. C. MURPHY, "Nonreductive Physicalism: Philosophical Issues," *Whatever Happened to the Soul? Scientific and Theological Portraits of Human Nature*, ed. W. S. Brown, N. C. Murphy, and H. N. Malony (Minneapolis, MN: Fortress, 1998), 127–148.

[7] W. PANNENBERG, *Systematic Theology*, trans. G. W. Bromiley, vol. 2 (Grand Rapids: Eerdmans, 1994), 181–182.

[8] The only exception to my knowledge is my *Creation and Humanity*. This is of course not to deny the contributions of some systematicians, say Michael Welker of Heidelberg University, Germany and Niels Henrik Gregersen of Copenhagen University, Denmark who have discussed human nature in a widely interdisciplinary manner. What I am saying is that these contributions have not yet found their way to "normal" systematic theological presentations. In this regard, it is interesting that the two leading international constructive theologians who have published theological "summas," namely Wolfhart Pannenberg and Jürgen Moltmann have completely missed the interdisciplinary conversation about human nature although both of them for decades have interacted in doctrine of creation with natural sciences from cosmology to physics to quantum theory to evolutionary biology.

[9] D. H. KELSEY, *Eccentric Existence: A Theological Anthropology*, 2 vols. (Louisville, KY: Westminster John Knox, 2009).

Why would the question about the nature of human nature matter to Christian theology? The basic answer is simply this: any philosophical view that considers the human being merely as a physical entity, without any "real" mental life or consciousness, would make an idea of religious belief (apart from its object) meaningless. In other words, religion in any meaningful sense would not of course be possible apart from these higher mental capacities. This is the main concern behind traditional dualism, namely, to make room for and affirm the reality of the non-material aspect of the human person, named soul (or spirit) in tradition. This legitimate concern, however, does not automatically lead into the affirmation of traditional dualism. As mentioned, the mainstream of the current international and ecumenical theological guild has sought to find more proper ways of affirming the uniqueness of humanity and the reality of the mental.

Indeed, notwithstanding the need for theology to listen carefully to what neuroscientists and philosophers of mind are claiming, it is also the fact that the shift toward a unified, monistic, and holistic view is "in line with the intentions of the earliest Christian anthropology"[10]. Too often the investigation into the history of the body-soul relationship ignores the fact that, unlike Platonism (which by the end of the second century had become the dominant philosophy), important early patristic thinkers defended the psychosomatic unity even when they continued distinguishing between body and soul (spirit). This much can be said even if, quite soon in early centuries the idea of body-soul unity soon gave way to dualism for the simple reason that, in keeping with the times, even those theologians who championed the psychosomatic unity did not thereby reject the idea of soul as an independent entity.

The plan of this essay is the following: I will first explain what kinds of underlying intuitions and assumptions lie behind my constructive proposal. Thereafter, I will engage in some detail the major contender to dualism(s) and physicalist monism in contemporary philosophy and theology, namely nonreductive physicalism. Although my own proposal owes to its insights, I also find it wanting in the final analysis. The rest of the essay following these two topics will be devoted to explaining and defending the program of "multidimensional monism."

2. Underlying Assumptions and Convictions

The constructive theological proposal of human nature developed and defended in this essay is funded by a number of convictions which I briefly mention here but do not have space to argue in much detail.[11]

---

[10] PANNENBERG, *Systematic Theology*, vol. 2, 182.
[11] All details can be found in my *Creation and Humanity*, Chap. 12.

First, traditionally Christian theology has emphasized the difference of humanity from the rest of creation rather than its continuity with it. A radical change in contemporary theology has to do with the emphasis on continuity. Unbeknownst to many, the first two creation narratives in the Old Testament point to a dynamic mutuality among creatures. The emergence of a sequence of forms – or "generations of the heavens and the earth when they were created" (Gen. 2:4a) – culminating in the creation of humanity, makes the creation an interrelated web, a network. This is not to undermine the uniqueness of humanity in relation to God but rather to remind us of our indebtedness to all that God has created.

Second, notwithstanding an integral mutual connection between humanity and nature, both philosophically and religiously/theologically it is necessary to also highlight the uniqueness of humanity among other animals. Typically, neuroscientists and philosophers of mind list the following kinds of distinguishing features:

1. *Language*: the capacity to communicate complex, abstract ideas, rather than merely repeat
2. *A theory of mind*: an ability to consider the thoughts and feelings of another person
3. *Episodic memory*: a conscious historical memory of events, persons, times, and places
4. *Conscious top-down agency*: conscious mental control of behavior and influence
5. *Future orientation*: ability to run mental scenarios of the future implications of behaviors and events
6. *Emotional modulation*: a complex social and contextual cognition that serves to guide ongoing behavior and decision making.[12]

Even this fairly sophisticated list requires amplification with features such as the capacity to discern beauty and other aesthetic experiences; the importance of feelings such as falling in love or deep disappointment; the gift of imagination that "travels faster" than the speed of light; and, say, the sense of humor.

Third, I take it for granted that any contemporary theological account of human nature should acknowledge and endorse the current common knowledge of the integral connection between brain events and mental life. Intelligence, emotions, sociality, as well as behavioral patterns such as criminality or altruism can be linked very tightly to the neuronal basis. Notwithstanding complicated philosophical interpretations of neuroscientific results, there is no

---

[12] W. S. BROWN, "Cognitive Contributions to Soul," in *Whatever Happened to the Soul? Scientific and Theological Portraits of Human Nature*, ed. W. S. Brown, N. Murphy, and H. N. Malony (Minneapolis, MN: Fortress, 1998), 99–126.

denying the tight link between the functioning of the brain and human behavior. Perhaps as a surprise to many comes the linkage between observed neural activity and exercise of spiritual and religious activities.[13]

Fourth, in keeping with current scientific consensus – which I also see in sync with both biblical holistic vision and contemporary systematic theological interpretation – critical values shaping human personhood include sociality, embodiment, and emotionality, along with rationality, of course. Theological anthropology, commensurately, conceives the human being as a relational being, in relation to God, to fellow human beings and creation, as well as to oneself. Hence, mental life is shaped and formed by social context, including socialization and language.[14] Alongside sociality, embodiment is an essential value in a contemporary scientific account of the human person:

> "We have thoughts, wishes, and desires that together constitute our character. We express these mental states through our bodies, which are simultaneously our organs of perception and our means of affecting other things and persons in the world [...]. [The massive literature on theories of personhood] clearly points to the indispensability of embodiedness as the precondition for perception and action, moral agency, community, and freedom – all aspects that philosophers take as indispensable to human personhood and that theologians have viewed as part of the *imago dei*."[15]

To the bodily life belong cognition, emotions, passions, and desires. Recently we have also discovered that emotional (and moral) states such as empathy, shame, trust, regret, and detecting the emotional states of others not only are tightly linked with certain neural activities but are also embodied and socially shaped.[16]

Fifth, I claim that while the traditional body-soul dualism finds support in biblical terminology and theological tradition, it does not necessarily result in the endorsement of traditional dualism. Contemporary critical biblical scholar-

---

[13] Groundbreaking interdisciplinary work is being done at the Institute for the Bio-Cultural Study of Religion founded by the neuroscientist Patrick McNamara and philosopher of religion Wesley J. Wildman; see the Web site for research and resources: http://www.ibcsr.org/. Also for a massive collection of essays on evolutionary and neurological bases of religion, including neurotheology, as well as related issues, see the three-volume, *Where God and Science Meet: How Brain and Evolutionary Studies Alter Our Understanding of Religion*, ed. P. McNamara (Westport: Praeger, 2006). For an insightful critique of neuro-theology and neurology of religion, see W. S. Brown, "The Brain, Religion, and Baseball: Comments on the Potential for a Neurology of Religious Experience," in *Where God and Science Meet: How Brain and Evolutionary Studies Alter Our Understanding of Religion*, ed. P. McNamara (Westport, CT: Praeger, 2006), vol. 2, 229–244.

[14] L. A. Brothers, *Friday's Footprints: How Society Shapes the Human Mind* (New York: Oxford University Press, 1997).

[15] P. C. Clayton, "The Case for Christian Panentheism," *Dialog* 37, no. 3 (1988): 205.

[16] A. R. Damasio, *The Feeling of What Happens: Body and Emotion in the Making of Consciousness* (New York: Harcourt Brace, 1999).

ship[17] contends that notwithstanding the prevalence of dualistic language – and a terminology which often seems to make a separation between mind (soul, spirit) and other aspects of the human nature – the mainstream biblical vision of human nature is not necessarily dualistic but advocates a holistic and integral view in which physicality plays a bigger role than tradition has claimed.[18] While resisted by the conservative side of theologians, a non-dualist position has established itself as a virtual consensus. The philosopher Nancy Murphy summarizes accurately the situation in the biblical scholarship on human nature:

"A survey of the literature of theology and biblical studies throughout the twentieth century, then, shows a gradual displacement of a dualistic account of the person, with its correlative emphasis on the afterlife conceived in terms of the immortality of the soul. First, there was the recognition of the holistic character of biblical conceptions of the person, often while still presupposing temporarily separable 'parts.' Later there developed a holistic *but also physicalist* account of the person, combined with an emphasis on bodily resurrection."[19]

Importantly, the prominent British biblical scholar James D. G. Dunn affirms the same by debunking the myth that whereas the Old Testament supports a more holistic conception of the human nature, the Greek-Hellenistic is deeply dualist:

"[W]hile Greek thought tended to regard the human being as made up of distinct parts, Hebraic thought saw the human more as a whole person existing on different dimensions. As we might say, it was more characteristically Greek to conceive of the human person 'partitively,' whereas it was more characteristically Hebrew to conceive of the human person 'aspectively.'"[20]

Sixth, I assume that neither can the mental be reduced to the physical base nor can the causal power of the mental on physical be denied. Briefly put: I am against both reductionism and causal closure. It is absolutely fundamental to our concept of actions performed intentionally (as opposed to involuntarily) to assume

---

[17] It is noteworthy that a widely influential defense of dualism in the biblical data is written by a philosopher rather than a biblical scholar – and this work is often referred to by other dualists: J. W. COOPER, *Body, Soul, and Life Everlasting: Biblical Anthropology and the Monism-Dualism Debate*, 2nd ed. (Grand Rapids, MI: Eerdmans, 2000).

[18] Importantly, the Hebrew term *nepheš* (as in Gen 2:7) refers to the whole person rather than to mere "soul." The term occurs no less than about 800 times in the Old Testament and has as its etymology the meaning of "throat" or "gullet"; hence, they denote human need (as a thirsty throat) and physicality; see further, J. B. GREEN, *Body, Soul, and Human Life: The Nature of Humanity in the Bible. Studies in Theological Interpretation* (Grand Rapids, MI: Baker Academic, 2008), 57. That said, the monist orientation of the Old Testament does not rule out duality or plurality in its presentation of the human being, as even a casual reader notes.

[19] N. MURPHY, *Bodies and Souls, or Spirited Bodies?* (Cambridge: Cambridge University Press, 2006), 10.

[20] J. D. G. DUNN, *The Theology of the Apostle Paul* (Grand Rapids, MI: Eerdmans, 1998), 54, quoted in MURPHY, *Bodies and Souls*, 21.

mental causation.[21] A crucial issue for theologians is to defeat what the British neuropsychologist Donald McKay used to call "nothing-buttery,"[22] namely, the identity theory according to which all mental phenomena, whether intellectual, emotional, or moral, are but brain/neural states.[23] Along with identity-theory, I also reject other related theories of the mind-body-relationship which eliminate mental causation, including psychophysical parallelism and epiphenomenalism.

Having now clarified that I do not recommend traditional body-mind dualism as the preferred way of conceiving the nature of human nature, before beginning a search for a more proper approach, let me briefly register both the liabilities and lasting values of traditional dualisms.

3. Body-Mind Dualism(s): Lasting Values and Serious Liabilities

I believe that while behind traditional dualism(s) there are absolutely important intuitions and convictions which no authentic Christian theology can afford to leave behind, those intuitions can be maintained in certain type of monistic views as well. The key intuitions I have in mind include the following:
– that there is "more" to human life than just the material;[24]
– that there is something "more" than merely material processes that explain the uniqueness and dignity of human life;
– that affirming morality and an ethical base calls for "more" than material explanation[25]; and
– that there is hope for life eternal and therefore, even at the moment of my personal death, I am not forgotten by God.

---

[21] My claim is not to deny that at the moment the causal interaction between the bodily and mental is one of the unresolved problems. We simply don't know currently as to "how reasons – our beliefs, desires, purposes, and plans – operate in a world of causes, and to exhibit the role of reasons in the *causal* explanation of human behavior." (This is the premise of Fred's book, so not sure if the quote is used correctly) F. DRETSKE, *Explaining Behavior: Reasons in a World of Causes* (Cambridge, MA: MIT Press, 1988), x.

[22] D. M. MACKAY, *The Clock Work Image* (Downers Grove, IL: InterVarsity Press, 1974), 21. Also, see the now-classic argument in D. M. ARMSTRONG, *A Materialist Theory of Mind*. rev. ed. (London: Routledge, 1993) for the view that mental states are nothing but brain states.

[23] For an important current defense of type identity, see *New Perspectives on Type Identity: The Mental and the Physical*, ed. S. Gozzano and C. S. Hill (Cambridge: Cambridge University Press, 2012).

[24] K. WARD, *More Than Matter?: Is There More to Life Than Molecules?* (Grand Rapids, MI: Eerdmans, 2011).

[25] E. g., B. L. RICKABAUGH, "Responding to NT Wright's Rejection of the Soul: A Defense of Substance Dualism," An Unpublished Presentation at the Society of Vineyard Scholars Conference, Minnesota, April 28, 2012 (http://www.academia.edu/1966881/Responding to N. T. Wrights Rejection of the Soul: A Defense of Substance Dualism) (2/28/2019); See also J. P. MORELAND and S. B. RAE, *Body and Soul: Human Nature and the Crisis in Ethics* (Downers Grove, IL: IVP Academic, 2000).

Seeking to maintain these essential values, I also discern a number of liabilities in traditional dualisms which make me look for another option. It seems to me that dualisms (of various sorts) locate the image of God and human uniqueness in the soul rather than in the human person as a whole, a move not supported by the Bible. Briefly stated: the image of God in the biblical testimonies relates to the whole of humanity and encompasses each human person in his or her totality.[26]

Second, dualisms tend to elevate reason above other features of human nature. Although no one would undermine the proper role reason and intelligence play in human life, it is also one of the liabilities of traditional anthropologies, including the account of the *imago Dei* that thereby physicality and emotions are easily being marginalized. In case the physicality is being downsized, the critical question emerges "If the body does not belong to the *imago Dei*, how can the body become 'a temple of the Holy Spirit'?"[27] Third, as mentioned, dualisms seem to run against much of current neuroscientific knowledge.

What are the alternatives available? An appealing route to some prominent Christian philosophers, psychologists, and neuroscientists to negotiate between traditional dualism(s) and current move towards physicalist monism is nonreductive physicalism. Would that be the way to go in light of the underlying convictions mentioned above?

4. Nonreductive Physicalism: Promises and Liabilities[28]

Identity theory and its siblings are based on "reductive physicalism" and believe that human behavior and choices have their causal base in the physical processes, a view known as "bottom-up" causation. Hence, higher-level capacities such as mental abilities are nothing but the sum of their lower-level physical processes. Nonreductive *physicalism* – the dominant explanation of human nature in current Anglo-American philosophy of mind[29] – agrees with part of this agenda by claiming that all higher capacities have a physical base. But it vehemently disagrees with a reduction of the higher to its physical base.

---

[26] For details of all aspects of the imago Dei discussion, see KÄRKKÄINEN, *Creation and Humanity*, ch. 11.

[27] J. MOLTMANN, *God in Creation: A New Theology of Creation and the Spirit of God*, trans. M. KOHL (Minneapolis, MI: Fortress, 1993), 239.

[28] This section is a repeat with only some small changes and additions of my "'Multidimensional Monism': A Constructive Theological Proposal for the Nature of Human Nature," in *Neuroscience and the Soul*, 201–227.

[29] J. BICKLE, "Multiple Realizability," *The Stanford Encyclopedia of Philosophy*, ed. E. N. Zalta (2013), (http://plato.stanford.edu/archives/spr2013/entries/multiple-realizability/) (4/21/2022).

In other words, having emerged (from the physical base), mental capacities cannot be reduced back to their base: they have become something "more." Hence, some theologians and Christian philosophers are ardent defenders of nonreductive physicalism while strongly rejecting reductive physicalism. For them, even religiosity has an ultimately physical base but cannot be reduced to it.[30] Not surprisingly, most advocates refuse to use the term "soul" any longer for the simple reason that there is no use left for it.[31]

The minimalist description of nonreductive physicalism simply is that in its attack on reductionism it considers the mental as an emergent novel property (or capacity or event) that "supervenes," that is, is dependent on the subvenient base, but that cannot be reduced to its base.[32] How to defeat reductionism[33] is obviously the main agenda of nonreductive physicalists. Terminologically, an important distinction has to be made between "methodological reductionism," that is, "a research strategy of analyzing the thing to be studied into its parts" and "causal reductionism," "the view that the behavior of the parts of a system [...] is determinative of the behavior of all higher-level entities (also called "parts on whole" and "bottom up"), as well as "ontological reductionism," which claims that "higher-level entities are 'nothing but the sum of their parts'." The last two are of course related, but regarding the latter, one needs to make yet another distinction. Whereas ontological reductionism claims that "as one goes up the hierarchy of levels, no new kinds of metaphysical 'ingredients' need to be added to produce higher-level entities from lower," for "reductive materialism," the higher-level processes are not only the function of the lower, but they are not even "real." That is accurately called "reductive materialism." That is the target of all nonreductivists.

A key resource for nonreductive physicalism is the use of the theory of emergence.[34] Emergence is the view that new structures, capacities, and processes will come to existence, that these cannot be reduced to the lower level, and that they can exercise a causal influence downwards. This means that the mental, most prominently, consciousness, is derived from the biological/phys-

---

[30] N. Murphy and W. S. Brown, *Did My Neurons Make Me Do It? Philosophical and Neurobiological Perspectives on Moral Responsibility and Free Will* (Oxford: Oxford University Press, 2009).

[31] Murphy, *Bodies and Souls*, ix.

[32] Many other more-or-less synonymous nomenclatures are used, including "[pluralistic] emergent monism," "constitutional monism," "open-system emergence" or "deep physicalism," "dual aspect monism," and "emergent dualism." Most (but not all) of them are monist in a particular way, namely, physically/materialistically (while not denying the reality of the mental, including, in most cases, even religiosity).

[33] An important current statement and defense of reductionism is chapter 4 of J. Kim, *Physicalism, or Something Near Enough* (Princeton, NJ: Princeton University Press, 2005).

[34] For a now classic essay, see K. Popper, "Natural Selection and the Emergence of Mind," *Dialectica* 32, no. 3–4 (1978): 339–355.

ical basis but is not to be reduced to it and that it may have causal influence on the subvenient base.[35] The concept of "emergence," however, is a complicated matter. As a result, not any form of supervenience necessarily helps defeat the identity theory, as there are also reductionist interpretations thereof.[36] The one needed for an antireductionist program is one with the claim that there are a number of ways a particular supervenient property may be instantiated and that it is context specific (the principle of multiple realizability[37]). In other words, it has to be the case that mental properties (against the co-variation thesis) could change without the change in the base property due to contextual factors.[38] For example, a rich lady giving money to help a poor man on the street corner can be a genuine token of generosity, while the same kind of gift by this married lady to her secret lover would not be. In other words, supervenient properties can be multiply realizable and therefore are not identity relations.[39]

If mental causation is to be affirmed, as nonreductive physicalists robustly do, then it means that there needs to be the possibility of the top-down (and whole-part) mental causation. That is not of course to deny bottom-up causation but to claim that that is not the only form. The most persistent critic of nonreductive physicalism, Jaegwon Kim, ironically makes the valid point as he claims that:

"[…] the emergentist and nonreductive physicalist are mental realists, and Mental Realism, via Alexander's dictum,[40] entails causal powers for mental properties […] [as] mental properties, on both positions are irreducible net additions to the world. And this must mean […] that mental properties bring with them *new causal powers, powers that no underlying physical-biological properties can deliver* […]. To be real, Alexander has said, is to have causal powers; *to be real, new, and irreducible, therefore, must be to have new, irreducible causal powers.*"[41]

---

[35] See P. CLAYTON, *Mind and Emergence: From Quantum to Consciousness* (Oxford: Oxford University Press, 2004), vi.

[36] For a reductionist version, see KIM, *Physicalism, or Something Near Enough*, 14; see further, B. P. MCLAUGHLIN, "Varieties of Supervenience," in *Supervenience: New Essays*, ed. E. E. SAVELLOS and Ü. D. YALÇIN (Cambridge: Cambridge University Press, 1995), 16–59.

[37] The key scholars in the development of the concept have been Hilary Putnam and Jerry Fodor. See H. PUTNAM, *Mind, Language, and Reality: Philosophical Papers* 2 (Cambridge: Cambridge University Press, 1975), 429–440; J. FODOR, "Special Sciences (Or: The Disunity of Science as a Working Hypothesis)," *Synthese* 27 (1974): 97–115.

[38] See MURPHY and BROWN, *Did My Neurons Make Me Do It*, 204.

[39] N. MURPHY, "Nonreductive Physicalism: Philosophical Issues," in *Whatever Happened to the Soul? Scientific and Theological Portraits of Human Nature*, ed. W. S. Brown, N. Murphy, and H. N. Malony (Minneapolis, MI: Fortress Press, 1998), 127–148.

[40] That is, to speak of mental property (or any property for that matter) is to speak of causal efficacy (in other words: if mental events do not "do" anything, why speak of them at all!). It was formulated by S. ALEXANDER, *Space, Time and Deity: The Gifford Lectures at Glasgow*, vol. 2 (London: Macmillan, 1920), 8.

[41] J. KIM, *Supervenience and Mind: Selected Philosophical Essays* (Cambridge: Cambridge University Press, 1993), 350.

An Integrated and Diverse Embodied Theological Account of the imago Dei   119

Kim rightly concludes that apart from downward causation mental causation is not explicable. Because of this – and two related reasons, namely, rejection of causal overdetermination[42] and causal closure[43] – Kim rejects as incoherent the whole notion of nonreductive physicalism.[44] But doing so, as said, he clarifies helpfully the main resources available and necessary for the antireductionist program.

Let us now consider the potential of a nonreductive physicalist proposal as set forth by some leading Christian scholars.

5. Why Nonreductive Physicalism is a Move Towards the Right Direction but does not Take Us Far Enough

There are lasting values in nonreductive physicalism that need to be carefully preserved. The foundational key value simply is the importance of physicality.[45] Beyond that, nonreductive physicalism is fairly successful in negotiating between the full embrace of the most recent scientific data concerning human behavior and the essentials of Christian (religious) intuitions. That said, it is not difficult to see the basic philosophical dilemma of nonreductive physicalism and that its claim for *physicality* as the ultimate base and explanation is its Achilles' heel: "say yes, and you seem to end up with a reductive physicalism; say no, and you aren't really a physicalist after all."[46]

In this context one cannot avoid facing the problem common to all physicalists, namely, that of the higher mental capacities, consciousness, including self-consciousness. One way to highlight the distinctive nature of mental life is to speak of "intentionality,"[47] that is, "aboutness," referring to something else. This aboutness-relationship is dramatically different from a causal rela-

---

[42] J. KIM, "The Non-Reductivist's Troubles with Mental Causation," in *Mental Causation*, ed. J. Heil and A. Mele (Oxford: Oxford University Press, 1995), 208.

[43] Ibid., 209.

[44] J. KIM, "The Myth of Nonreductive Materialism," in *The Mind-Body Problem: A Guide to the Current Debate*, ed. R. Warner and T. Szubka (Oxford: Blackwell, 1994), 242–60. Later in his evolving thinking Kim has come to grant the possibility and even need of a kind of mental causation – as long as the reductionist program is not thereby thwarted: J. KIM, *Physicalism, or Something Near Enough* (Princeton, NJ: Princeton University Press, 2005), 9. He calls this view "conditional physical reductionism" (5).

[45] See W. S. BROWN, "Conclusion: Reconciling Scientific and Biblical Portraits of Human Nature," in *Whatever Happened to the Soul? Scientific and Theological Portraits of Human Nature*, ed. W. S. Brown, N. Murphy, and H. N. Malony (Minneapolis, MN: Fortress, 1998), 213–228.

[46] CLAYTON, *Mind and Emergence*, 130. No wonder J. Kim considers nonreductive physicalism internally incoherent. See his *Mind in a Physical World: An Essay on the Mind-Body Problem and Mental Causation* (Cambridge, MA: MIT Press, 1998).

[47] For the groundbreaking work on intentionality we owe to the phenomenologist philosopher Edmund Husserl; see A. D. SPEAR, "Husserl on Intentionality and Intentional Content," in *Internet Encyclopedia of Philosophy: A Peer-Reviewed Academic Resource*, 2011, (http://www.iep.utm.edu/huss-int/) (6/10/2019).

tionship.[48] It is hard to contest what the philosopher of mind Jerry Fodor observed: "Nobody has the slightest idea how anything material could be conscious."[49] Titles such as *How Matter Becomes Imagination*[50] – even though written by senior neuroscientists, one of whom is a Nobel Laureate – simply promise too much. No human researcher can know, as Thomas Nagel so famously argued, 'what it's like to be a bat'."[51]

Furthermore, as surprising as it may sound, it seems to me to me that from a (natural) scientific perspective it is less than clear that physicalism is the right or even the best choice. It seems to many that current science is moving away from what "physical" (or material) used to mean. The physicist Arnold E. Sikkema notes that a key problem of nonreductive physicalism is "that it elevates the *composition* of entities as though what things are made of is of ultimate concern to a discussion of their ontology." As is well known, in the theory of relativity mass is nothing else but a form of energy (in relation to the speed of light); in quantum mechanics, treating subatomic entities as particles is complementary to regarding them as probability waves; and so forth.[52] The point here is that matter/physicality has become very elusive, virtually "non-material." And even if nonreductive physicalists would respond (as I guess they might) that the point of nonreductive physicalism is not on the composition, I think Sikkema's question calls for an answer.

The bottom line is this: what is matter/physicality? Is it totally different from the mental? If mental events, particularly consciousness, morality, and religiosity are but materially based processes, then the "matter" we speak of has little or nothing in common with our current scientific understanding! It may be, as the late Jesuit scientist William Stoeger surmises, that the neuroscientific investigation pushes us to radically reconsider and change what "physical/material" and "non-physical/non-material" may mean.[53] In any case, as is well

---

[48] P. CLAYTON, "Neuroscience, the Person, and God: An Emergentist Account," in *Neuroscience and the Person: Scientific Perspectives on Divine Action*, ed. R. J. Russell, Murphy, T. C. Meyering, and M. A. Arbib (Vatican City and Berkeley: Vatican Observatory and Center for Theology and the Natural Sciences, 2004), 191.

[49] J. FODOR, *Times Literary Supplement*, 3 July 1992, 5–7, quoted in CLAYTON, *Mind and Emergence*, 112.

[50] Subtitle in G. M. EDELMAN and G. TONONI, *A Universe of Consciousness* (New York: Basic Books, 2001).

[51] CLAYTON, *Mind and Emergence*, 111–112.

[52] A. E. SIKKEMA, "A Physicist's Reformed Critique of Nonreductive Physicalism and Emergence," *Pro Rege* 33 (2005): 23–24 (24); available at (http://www.academia.edu/294859/A_Physicists_Reformed_Critique_of_Nonreductive_Physicalism_and_Emergence) (6/10/2019).

[53] W. R. STOEGER, S. J, "The Mind-Brain Problem, the Laws of Nature, and Constitutive Relationships," in *Neuroscience and the Person: Scientific Perspectives on Divine Action*, ed. R. J. Russell, Murphy, T. C. Meyering, and M. A. Arbib (Vatican City and Berkeley, CA: Vatican Observatory and Center for Theology and the Natural Sciences, 1999), 132.

known, "matter" is not a well-defined scientific concept (whereas "mass" and "energy" are).[54] We even need a new vocabulary to speak of the mind and the mental. We probably cannot say the mental is "immaterial" or "non-physical" because that would cut off its deep integration with the brain (any more than we can say the mental is material). Would terms such as "trans-material/-physical" communicate that best?

The main point for my purposes is simply this: perhaps the premature jump onto the physicalist bandwagon by Christian scholars may not be as philosophically and scientifically advantageous as previously thought. There are also some urgent religious and theological reasons for continuing the quest. Beyond the obvious, that from the theological and religious point of view many would find it very difficult to think of ontology merely in terms of a staunch physicalist claim,[55] is the deeper claim that even for nonreductive physicalists who are not atheists, physicalism is only the penultimate option. All theistic traditions consider the Ultimate to be spirit/spiritual, certainly that is case for all Abrahamic faiths. In this light, I feel sympathies for the philosopher-theologian Philip Clayton's preference for a "monism" that is not physicalist in itself although it takes physicality most seriously. He argues that we should not assume that the "entities postulated by physics complete the inventory of what exists" while insisting that "[r]eality is ultimately composed of one basic kind of stuff."[56] Rather, "recognizing the physical as one aspect among others will help develop a more fully orbed philosophy of science, recognizing the importance of the different methodologies of inquiry that rightfully play roles in the other scientific disciplines, rather than focusing on what some regard as the highly problematic ontology of the entities of mechanics due to their lying so far beyond imagination."[57] With these cautions and insights in mind, let us try our hand at a tentative constructive proposal for how to best understand the nature of human nature in light of theological, philosophical, and scientific contours.

---

[54] STOEGER, "The Mind-Brain Problem, the Laws of Nature, and Constitutive Relationships," 133–135.
[55] SIKKEMA, "A Physicist's Reformed Critique of Nonreductive Physicalism and Emergence," 22.
[56] CLAYTON, *Mind and Emergence*, 4.
[57] SIKKEMA, "Physicist's Reformed Critique," 26.

6. "Multidimensional Monism": Towards a Holistic, Pluralistic, and Unified Account of Human Nature[58]

1. "Multidimensional Monism": Main Ideas and Intuitions

I argue that human beings are "psychosomatic unities rather than dual beings composed of a spiritual soul housed within a material body."[59] Indeed, as Tom Wright reminds us, we should talk about "differentiated unity":

> "Paul and the other early Christian writers didn't reify their anthropological terms. Though Paul uses his language with remarkable consistency, he nowhere suggests that any of the key terms refers to a particular 'part' of the human being to be played off against any other. Each *denotes* the entire human being, while *connoting* some angle of vision on who that human is and what he or she is called to be."[60]

Having critiqued dualisms, a question arises here as to whether my proposal still operates with dualistic notions. Indeed, there is an element of dualism here – and in any account proper for a theological/religious explanations. But it is not substance dualism; rather, a property dualism of a sort.[61] There is no doubt in my mind that, for example, nonreductive physicalism with all its resistance to traditional body-mind dualisms similarly assumes property dualism as it considers the mental real (existent) and assigns causal powers to it. In this regard, I feel much sympathy with the classical Thomistic hylomorphic view which does not represent substance dualism but rather something akin to property dualism.[62] What also comes to mind here is the physicist Roger Penrose's idea of the mental as "conscious substance"; it speaks of consciousness (which he also dares to call "soul") in a way that clearly belongs under property dualism.[63] Somewhat similarly, the philosopher of mind David

---

[58] This section with only minor changes is based on my *Creation and Humanity*, 337–349.

[59] J. POLKINGHORNE, "Anthropology in an Evolutionary Context," in *God and Human Dignity*, ed. R. K. Soulen and L. Woodhead (Grand Rapids, MI: Eerdmans, 2006), 93.

[60] N. T. WRIGHT, "Mind, Spirit, Soul and Body: All for One and One for All; Reflections on Paul's Anthropology in his Complex Contexts," a paper presented at Society of Christian Philosophers Eastern Meeting (March 18, 2011); available at http://www.ntwrightpage.com/Wright_SCP_MindSpiritSoulBody.htm (6/10/2019).

[61] I am using the nomenclature "property dualism" in its general sense well aware of the fact that both in the philosophy of mind and philosophy of language debates, philosophers disagree about its exact meaning. For the purposes of this essay, there is no need nor space to engage those debates.

[62] Just consider this statement from *Summa Contra Gentiles* 2.69.2: "body and soul are not two actually existing substances; rather, the two of them together constitute one actually existing substance." THOMAS AQUINAS, *Summa Contra Gentiles*, ed. J. Kenny, O. P., various translators (New York: Hanover House, 1955–1957). Available at http://dhspriory.org/thomas/ContraGentiles.htm (6/10/2019).

[63] R. PENROSE, *The Emperor's New Mind: Concerning Computers, Minds, and the Laws of Physics* (Oxford: Oxford University Press, 1989).

Chalmer's idea of the "information states" in terms of "the double-aspect principle" which is based on the "observation that there is a direct isomorphism between certain physically embodied information spaces and certain *phenomenal* (or experiential) information spaces"[64] represents property dualism of some sort.[65]

In systematic theology, Moltmann's vision of "a *perichoretic* relationship of mutual interpenetration and differentiated unity"[66] and Pannenberg's "personal unity of body and soul"[67] speak the same language. The ethicist Reinhold Niebuhr's associating the "self" with body but reluctance to reduce self to the bodily, reflects the same intuitions.[68] If I understand "emergent dualism" correctly, it argues that having had the mental emerge, it becomes a property on its own.[69] With all its deviations from classical Christian tradition, American Process philosophy's monistic dipolarism represents yet another form of property dualism.[70] To this same family of interpretations I would also add Clayton's "emergentist monism" which he fittingly calls "property dualism"[71] and systematician Ted Peters's "emergent holism."[72]

In sync with nonreductive physicalists, I argue that the reality of mental life cannot be had without a (strong) theory of emergence; this was established above. It not only saves the mental but also helps establish its causal efficacy. This "radical kind of emergence"[73] holds robustly to the mind's downwards

---

[64] D. J. CHALMERS, "Facing Up to the Problem of Consciousness," *Journal of Consciousness Studies* 2, no. 3 (1995): 200–219, (http://consc.net/papers/facing.html) (6/10/2019).

[65] D. J. CHALMERS, *The Conscious Mind: In Search of a Fundamental Theory* (New York: Oxford University Press, 1996), 305, cited in I. BARBOUR, "Neuroscience, Artificial Intelligence, Human Nature," *Zygon* 34, no. 3 (1999): 274. In response to Chalmer's proposal, see the rejoinders in *Explaining Consciousness – The Hard Problem*, ed. J. Shear (Cambridge, MA: MIT Press, 1999).

[66] MOLTMANN, *God in Creation*, 258–260.

[67] Main heading in PANNENBERG, *Systematic* Theology, vol. 2, 181.

[68] See R. NIEBUHR, *The Self and the Dramas of History* (New York: Charles Scribner's Sons, 1955), 26.

[69] See W. HASKER, *The Emergent Self* (Ithaca, NY: Cornell University Press, 1999). Cf. the "integrative dualism" of Charles Taliaferro. See his *Consciousness and the Mind of God* (Cambridge: Cambridge University Press, 1994).

[70] See further, C. HARTSHORNE, "The Compound Individual," *Philosophical Essays for Alfred North Whitehead*, ed. F. S. C. Northrup (New York: Russell & Russell, 1967), 193–220.

[71] CLAYTON, "Neuroscience, the Person, and God: An Emergentist Account," 212. R. W. SPERRY means something similar in his *Science and Moral Priority: Merging Mind, Brain, and Human Values* (New York: Columbia University Press, 1983).

[72] T. PETERS, "Resurrection of the Very Embodied Soul?," in *Neuroscience and the Person: Scientific Perspectives on Divine Action*, ed. R. J. Russell, Murphy, T. C. Meyering, and M. A. Arbib (Vatican City and Berkeley: Vatican Observatory and Center for Theology and the Natural Sciences, 2004), 305.

[73] R. V. GULICK, "Reduction, Emergence and Other Recent Options on the Mind/Body Problem: A Philosophical Overview," *Journal of Consciousness Studies* 8, no. 1 (2001): 1–34.

and whole-part causation. Strong emergence "is consistent with the neuroscientific data and the data with the constraints on brain functioning. At the same time, it has the merit of conceiving of mental activity in terms of mental causation, which accords well with our own experience of mental agency."[74] A good example here is how to best speak of human "personhood"; it can never be a matter of merely analyzing and investigating biological and physical processes. The physical explanation never captures "me," the person, *qua* person, but rather as an object of study.[75]

With the tight, in many ways indistinguishable, interdependency and communion between the physical and mental in mind, the British physicist-priest Polkinghorne suggests "dual-aspect" monism as a fitting concept to describe the holistic account of human nature. The emphasis on *monism* indicates that the classical metaphysical options of materialism, idealism, and Cartesian dualism are unsatisfactory in light of the current multilayered, complex, and dynamic understanding of reality, including human nature. Dual-aspect monism "acknowledge[s] the fundamental distinction between experience of the material and experience of the mental but which would neither impose on reality a sharp division into two unconnected kinds of substance nor deny the psychosomatic unity of human beings." A useful way for him to illustrate the nature of dual-aspect monism is quantum theory's idea of complementarity (superposition principle), which allows for two different/distinct states simultaneously. The main point about the *dual-aspect* nature is to argue that "there will be entities, such as stones, whose nature is located wholly at the material pole, and other entities, such as ourselves, who are 'amphibians,' participating in both kinds of polar experience," namely, mental and material.[76] Polkinghorne also reminds us of the obvious difference between the material and noetic/mental: whereas the former is "a world of process, characterized by temporality and becoming," the latter is "everlasting, in the sense that such truths just *are* and do not evolve." These two "worlds," however, are "complementary aspects of a larger created reality" and hence illustrate the duality that goes beyond material versus mental: "it must also embrace becoming/being and everlasting/temporal." Humanity belongs to both, and therefore, "a fully integrated metaphysics" is needed in which "the multiplicity of experience leads us to an account of considerable richness and subtlety."[77] The potential liability of the dual-aspect monism is that it may make the mental less than real

---

[74] CLAYTON, *Mind and Emergence*, 139.

[75] For comments, see the section titled "Person-Based Explanations and the Social Sciences" in CLAYTON, *Mind and Emergence*, 144–148.

[76] J. POLKINGHORNE, *Faith, Science and Understanding* (New Haven: Yale University Press, 2001), 95–97.

[77] Ibid., 98.

and merely a matter of perspective or experience.[78] The dual-aspect monist, however, doesn't have to be liable to this weakness.

That is not yet the whole story. Both the basic intuition of the undifferentiated psychosomatic unity and dual-aspect monism imply more, as Clayton puts it: "We need multiple layers of explanatory accounts *because* the human person is a physical, biological, psychological, and (I believe also) spiritual reality, and because these aspects of its reality, though interdependent, are not mutually reducible." The term "ontological pluralism" may best describe this approach.[79] Moltmann's creative nomenclatures "spirit-body," "spirit-*Gestalt*," "spirit-soul," as complementary metaphors, echoes this.[80] The German systematician Michael Welker warns us of the reductionism with regard to fixating on one particular aspect, either physicalist or mentalist. Whereas scientists fear the latter, humanists tends to fear the former. "There are simply too many anthropological insights and burning questions in social and cultural studies and in the natural sciences that cannot be hosted by this model."[81] Not only the sciences but also biblical theology point to multidimensionality. Prophetically, one may want to say, already decades ago in Paul Tillich's theology, multidimensionality came to the fore – the inorganic, organic, psychic, and spiritual as the fundamental dimensions of the human.[82] Similarly, the practical theologian Don S. Browning has for years developed a robust theology of the multidimensionality of human nature (with a view to discerning moral goods and values).[83]

2. *What Kind of Monism?*

But why not physical monism? Above I have expressed my reservations about nonreductive physicalism and will not repeat them here. While I greatly appreciate Jaegwon Kim's honesty when, as a staunch physicalist, he admits, "Physicalism is not the whole truth, but it is the truth near enough,"[84] I also think any

---

[78] This is clearly the case in M. VELMANS, "Making Sense of Causal Interactions between Consciousness and Brain," *Journal of Consciousness Studies* 9, no. 11 (2002): 75.

[79] CLAYTON, *Mind and Emergence*, 148.

[80] MOLTMANN, *God in Creation*, 262–264.

[81] M. WELKER, "Theological Anthropology versus Anthropological Reductionism," in *God and Human Dignity*, ed. R. K. Soulen and L. Woodhead (Grand Rapids, MI: Eerdmans, 2006), 319.

[82] P. TILLICH, *Systematic Theology*, vol. 3 (Chicago, IL: University Press of Chicago, 1951), 22–23.

[83] D. BROWNING, *A Fundamental Practical Theology* (Minneapolis, MI: Fortress, 1991), 94–109 and 139–170 lists the dimensions into which there is no need to go in detail here. For a short statement, see his "Human Dignity, Human Complexity, and Human Goods," in *God and Human Dignity*, ed. R. K. Soulen and L. Woodhead (Grand Rapids, MI: Eerdmans, 2006), 299–316.

[84] KIM, *Physicalism, or Something Near Enough*, 6.

authentic physicalism ultimately leads to "ontological physicalism," according to which all there is, is physical[85] – a position I strongly oppose. The reason is simply this: strictly speaking, ontological physicalism can only be penultimate for a theist. Hence, it seems to me that multidimensional monism, as argued in this project, fits better the key belief in Christian faith (and I guess, other theisms as well) of the complex unity of the finite world as God's creation. While exhibiting various properties as a result of rich creative divine work, the notion of the "unity of nature," as distinct from the infinity of the Creator God (who is Spirit), tells us all creatures share a common nature (however complex and multidimensional that may be).[86]

Let us come back to the issue already raised tentatively above: What does theology have at stake in this debate on ontology? Clayton rightly notes that "[i]f one holds that all mental phenomena are only expressions of physical causes or are themselves, at root, physical events, then one has (at least tacitly) advanced a theory of the human person that is pervasively physical. It then becomes extremely unclear (to put it gently) why, *from the perspective of one's own theory of the human person*, a God would have to be introduced at all (except perhaps as a useful fiction)."[87] Now, that does not of course mean that a Christian physicalist couldn't introduce God. But the point is that a truly physical *anthropological* account does not make it any easier than any other version of human nature; God has to be introduced "from outside," after all. Clayton lays out the options well: "If a theologian espouses physicalism, she may be forging an alliance with the majority worldview within the neurosciences, but she may also be giving up the most interesting rapprochement between theology and the sciences of the person just as she approaches that debate's most decisive issue."[88] (Similarly, of course, traditional dualism may easily stall the dialogue with sciences.) Perhaps, then, even in terms of dialogue (although theological convictions can never be primarily based on their usefulness), the best way for theology is to insist on the necessity but insufficiency of physical explanation.

When viewed from a historical perspective, not only the *opening* but also the full endorsement of nonmaterialist, in other words, idealist ontology has been the dominant position among Christians and other theists (both mono- and polytheists). The late American Reformed Paul K. Jewett expresses succinctly this sentiment: "To be materially conditioned as conscious selves is not to be materially constituted as such."[89] Not only Idealist philosophers such as Kant,

---

[85] Ibid., 150.
[86] See also CLAYTON, "Neuroscience, the Person, and God," 209–210.
[87] CLAYTON, "Neuroscience, the Person, and God," 204.
[88] Ibid.
[89] P. K. JEWETT, *Who We Are: Our Dignity as Human; A Neo-Evangelical Theology* (Grand Rapids, MI: Eerdmans, 1996), 9 (italics removed).

Fichte, Hegel, Schelling, and numerous others,[90] but virtually all such thinkers from antiquity to recent times have been Idealists of a sort; similarly most cultures in the Global South;[91] so also are the *advaita* (nondualistic schools of Indian philosophy); and so forth. This suggestive listing alone would justify keeping the door open to nonphysicalist monism. It seems to me that Christian theology would do well to be cautious in going full-blown into physicalism because "we are in great danger of phrasing the discussion in such a way that the deepest and most significant issues of human existence simply never appear on the screen."[92]

The British philosopher-theologian Keith Ward has recently suggested another version of dual-aspect theory that he names "dual-aspect idealism" and situates it between Cartesian dualism and physicalism. A student critical of his mentor, Gilbert Ryle, who coined the term "ghost in the machine" ridiculing Descartes's dualism and turn to the inner self, Ward rightly contends that because "mind and consciousness are different from, something over and above, molecules and matter [...] they are not at all ghostly."[93] Indeed, he reminds us how radically different Idealism is from the physicalism/materialism of contemporary naturalism, in its claim that:

"The material world [...] exists as a environment created by a primordial mind in which finite minds can exist in mutual self-expression and interaction [...] It totally reverses the modern myth that minds are by-products of a purely material evolutionary process, completely determined by physical events in their bodies and brains."[94]

At the same time, he also reminds us how vastly different contemporary materialism is through the lens of force fields, quantum theory, and string theory.[95] Now, as mentioned, Ward is not drawn to dualism *per se*; instead, he represents a property dualism of a sort.

What Process philosophy is calling the "inner" life of the physical, Polkinghorne names dual-aspect monism, and the Oxford philosopher Horace Romano Harré, dual-side theories (of monism), all point to the same direction. While not Idealist thinkers *per se*, they do think that even "material" processes somehow are not completely void of some kind of teleology and that the

---

[90] For an important discussion from the perspective of anthropology, see R. MARTIN and J. BARRESI, *The Rise and Fall of Soul and Self: An Intellectual History of Personal Identity* (New York: Columbia University Press, 2006), 185–190.

[91] See J. M. KAPOLYO, *The Human Condition: Christian Perspectives Through African Eyes* (Downers Grove, IL: InterVarsity Press, 2005).

[92] P. HEFENER, "Imago Dei: The Possibility and Necessity of the Human Person," in *The Human Person in Science and Theology*, ed. N. H. Gregersen, W. B. Drees, and U. Görman (Edinburgh: T. & T. Clark, 2000), 81.

[93] WARD, *More Than Matter?*, 10.

[94] Ibid., 57.

[95] Ibid., 81.

universe is more like an organism rather than a machine.[96] Ward refers to the human embryo: as much as current science eschews any notions of vitalism or (Aristotelian) teleology, we expect it to become an adult person, a highly complicated obviously purposeful process.[97]

The minimalist statement about human nature, going back to the beginning of this section, is then psychosomatic pluralistic unity. The nomenclature "pluralistic unity" also points to the need to dare to "confuse" and go beyond established categories (while holding to the best insights of each) such as idealism, physicalism, and monism.[98] Multidimensional monism is one such emerging proposal for continuing discussion and critique. With the shift away from traditional substance dualism (notwithstanding property dualism of some sort), the question arises of whether to continue using the term "soul" at all. That question we take up next.

3. What about the "Soul"?

Among the current advocates of nondualist accounts of human nature, including Christian nonreductive physicalists, the term *soul* has become a virtual anathema. By implication, it also happens often that all uses of that term, even if they are not using it in the substance dualistic context, are deemed suspicious. While that attitude is understandable, constructive theologians should also exercise some critical faculties here. I do not consider it wise, let alone necessary, to leave behind the ancient term of *soul*, even if traditional dualism is let go. The reasons to continue using the term *soul* are the following:

First, similarly to so many other terms whose meaning has changed, the theologians' task is to help the faithful to grasp its redefinition. Just consider the term *creation*. As much as its meaning has changed after the embrace by theology of contemporary natural sciences' view of the evolvement of cosmos, its deepest intuitions have stayed intact.

Second, the term *soul* is so widely and frequently used in the biblical canon – and consequently, everywhere in Christian tradition – that its dismissal seems to be totally unfounded and counterproductive as it may cause the rejection of the proposal itself without further investigation.

Third, there is also the interfaith consideration: although different religious traditions may mean different things when using the term, the cancellation in Christian tradition would not only look awkward and confusing to others but also seriously hinder dialogue.

---

[96] Ibid., 81–83.
[97] Ibid., 83–84.
[98] Ibid., 102–103.

Fourth, blaming the use of "soul" (because of its close connection with substance dualism) for all kinds of ills in Christian life, say an anti-body attitude or isolationist spirituality or escapist eschatology, misses the main point, which is that most any conception of human nature may foster negative or positive spiritualities or orientations of religious life (just differently).

The late American Reformed theologian Ray S. Anderson offers useful guidelines for the systematic use of the term *soul*. Although my own constructive proposal of human nature does not exactly match his, these guidelines serve well regarding the term. First, "soul" does not denote a "substance or entity residing in the body" but rather the "whole person, especially the inner core of human personal life as created and upheld by God" (to which should be added that no less is body and other aspects of the multidimensional human being also upheld by God). Second, the terms body, soul, and spirit are not analytic distinctions but rather functional and overlapping with each other. Third, even though Christians have a firm hope for life eternal in the resurrected body as the gift of God, soul – no more than anything else in the human being – is not immortal by nature.[99] Fourth, as a result, rather than saying that the human person "has a soul," it is better to say that the "person is soul."[100]

Regardless of the terminological choice, all deviations from traditional dualism face the important questions of how to speak of an afterlife and continuation of personal identity. Although full discussion belongs to Christian eschatology, short notes are in order here.

4. What about Afterlife and the Persistence of Personal Identity?

So, how to think of afterlife in the post-Cartesian-dualism world? In other words, does it mean that leaving behind traditional talk about the soul and its disembodied existence means leaving behind the idea of life everlasting? No, it does not. Christian tradition never affirmed the immortality of the soul (as in Platonic philosophy) nor that only one part of the human person will be saved for eternity. In fact, in early theology, notwithstanding terminological (and at times, material) inconsistency, the divinity of the soul and, hence, its intrinsic capacity to survive beyond death, was rightly rejected and replaced by belief in eternal life as the gift of God.[101] Furthermore, the hope for the resurrection was established for the whole person, not only for the soul.[102]

---

[99] R. ANDERSON, *On Being Human* (Grand Rapids, MI: Eerdmans, 1982), 182–183.
[100] Ibid., 186.
[101] PANNENBERG, *Systematic Theology*, trans. G. W. Bromiley, vol. 3 (Grand Rapids, MI: Eerdmans, 1996), 571.
[102] See PETERS, "Resurrection of the Very Embodied Soul?," 322–325.

What about the continuity of personal identity? This has to be looked at from two complementary perspectives. Theologically speaking, guaranteeing the identity is the task of God, not ours.[103] Scientifically and philosophically speaking, identity is a task belonging to the human person, lasting all of one's life, embedded in growth and development in all areas, including personal development and social context. Embodied memory serves here an important role.[104] Whereas in this life, there is always the form of a timely sequence with its broken moments, when God's eternity comes to swallow the finite life, that "will represent the *totality* of our earthly existence."[105]

Polkinghorne correctly notes that in itself the soul's "role as the carrier of human identity is almost as problematic within life as it is beyond death." The continuity cannot be a matter of material continuity since atoms are in constant flux through wear and tear. Perhaps the best way to speak of the continuity of identity is in terms of "the almost infinitely complex, information-bearing pattern in which the matter of the body is organized at any one time. This surely is the meaning of the soul."[106] Based on the foundational Christian teaching of the human being as the image of God, we have to say that "[w]hat gives us an identity that does not die is not our nature, but a personal relationship with God."[107] Embodied, the soul does not carry in itself the powers of natural immortality. "As far as science can tell the story, the pattern that is a person will dissolve with that person's death and decay."[108] This proposal seems to correspond to contemporary scientific understandings of information, or the way complex systems could be understood – and all living beings are systems of some kind.[109] Aquinas's hylomorphic account of human nature is also based on these intuitions.

Now, seen from the theological point of view, this does not, however, mean that therefore when the person dies, that is all there is. Utilizing the concept of information, it can be stated that what the older soul theory rightly intuited was that "the faithful God will remember the pattern that is me and re-embody it in the eschatological act of resurrection." I couldn't agree more with

---

[103] Ibid., 316.

[104] PANNENBERG, *Systematic Theology*, vol. 3, 562.

[105] PANNENBERG, *Systematic Theology*, vol. 3, 561.

[106] POLKINGHORNE, "Anthropology in an Evolutionary Context," 98; see also his "Eschatology: Some Questions and Some Insights from Science," in *The End of the World and the Ends of God: Science and Theology on Eschatology*, ed. M. Welker and J. Polkinghorne (Harrisburg, PA: Trinity Press International, 2000), 38–41.

[107] J. ZIZIOULAS, "The Doctrine of the Holy Trinity: The Significance of the Cappadocian Contribution," in *Trinitarian Theology Today: Essays on Divine Being and Act*, ed. C. Schwöbel (Edinburgh: T. & T. Clark, 2000), 58.

[108] POLKINGHORNE, "Anthropology in an Evolutionary Context," 99.

[109] J. POLKINGHORNE, *The God of Hope and the End of the World* (New Haven, CT: Yale University Press, 2002).

Polkinghorne, who continues: "In making this assertion, I want to affirm the intrinsically embodied character of human being, without supposing that the flesh and blood of this world represents the only possible form that embodiment might take."[110] While I understand why Christian nonreductive physicalists – with justification – underline the importance of death's finality to combat the obvious misconception in which the soul were to possess natural powers of immortality and its independence, I also find the "gap" theory – that is, between my personal death and the final resurrection there is "nothing of me" – problematic from the systematic theological point of view. Not that I have any doubts whatsoever concerning the capacity of the Creator to re-create *ex nihilo* the resurrected person who has faced physical death (that belief is no more difficult than believing that in the first place the person was given the gift of life). Nor do I think that positing a "soul" is needed to guarantee continuity between this life and the life to come, because, simply put, making the soul the locus of continuity doesn't really explain much in the first place! My reservations lie elsewhere, namely, in the complex and mutually conditioned continuity vs. discontinuity relationship between life on Earth and life in the resurrected body as well as between my own personal eternal destiny vs. that of the whole cosmos. If the gap theory is followed, both of these themes, crucial to a systematic theological negotiation of eschatological consummation, may be frustrated.

7. Conclusions: Remaining Tasks and Questions

With resistance to traditional body-soul dualisms, sympathetically and critically learning from nonreductive physicalism, in this essay I have attempted tentatively to imagine a credible theological account of the nature of human nature. It is clear without saying that this kind of quite wide-ranging exploratory explanation faces a number of further tasks and begs answers for several questions. The most basic of these tasks simply the need to be able to clarify more clearly as to what exactly multidimensional monism means. This is particularly important in light of the fact, having mentioned above, that my own discipline, systematic (doctrinal) theology is a late-comer to the kind of interdisciplinary conversation in theological anthropology.

Much interdisciplinary investigation concerning the meaning of those very concepts, namely "matter" and "mental" is needed. What if the divide between the physical and mental becomes obsolete (at least in some sense); would that re-orient the theological talk about the nature of human nature? We also need

---

[110] POLKINGHORNE, "Anthropology in an Evolutionary Context," 99–100.

continuing reflection on how the "mental" posited of humanity may be related to the "mental" in the whole cosmos.

Although the question of afterlife belongs to eschatology; its interconnection with theological anthropology is obvious. The tentative proposal above concerning the persistence of personal identity, formerly based on the concept of soul, is an urgent issue. Although philosophers of mind have devised a number of tactics to speak of the persistence of identity, their integral relation to the discussions on the nature of human nature deserves to be made wider and deeper.[111]

Based as it is on biblical materials and testimonies, Christian systematic theology also faces the need to continue investigating the implications of the prevalence of dualistic terminology in the Scripture – similarly to the Scriptures of other faith traditions. That theologians are listening carefully to neuroscientists, evolutionary biologists, philosophers of mind, and others, cannot be used as a pre-text for ignoring their foundational scriptural witnesses. That has to be said even if, as mentioned above, I argue that the dualistic terminology does not necessarily mean endorsing substance ontology.[112].

---

[111] See further my *Hope and Community. A Constructive Christian Theology for the Pluralistic World*, vol. 5 (Grand Rapids, MI: Eerdmans, 2017), 121–28 especially.

[112] See further my *Creation and Humanity*, 333–337.

Transcendent Humanity:
What if the Incarnation Really Matters?

Ron Cole-Turner

The invitation to this conference identifies four challenges that endanger our idea of humanity: the loss of human distinctiveness, the technological challenge, the anthropological challenge arising especially from evolutionary biology, and the theological challenge. The statement ends with this comment: "These are the challenges that a contemporary understanding of the idea of humanity must address. To do so is the objective of the [...] Conference."

The approach taken here in this paper is to engage these challenges, not by addressing them with "a contemporary understanding of humanity" as the invitation to the conference puts it, but by setting them in relationship to a very old view, Christianity's most peculiar claim, the incarnation. In the first two sections of this paper, I begin this task by exploring and restating the biological and technological challenges in sections one and two. Section three responds to the theological challenge by offering a revised theology of the incarnation. My goal is not to argue for the truth of the incarnation or even for its relevance to the contemporary challenges so well summarized in the invitation to this conference. No claim is made here that belief in the incarnation solves or removes any of the difficulties set before us. I wish only to suggest that by engaging these challenges, the meaning of the incarnation can find a new and richer clarity.

1. Reframing the Biological Challenge

Recent advances across a range of scientific fields have transformed our understanding of ourselves. As never before, we are coming to see humanity as embedded within the larger planetary web of life. We share common ancestry and use the same genetic code. Some DNA sequences are preserved over hundreds of millions of years of evolutionary divergence, with functions widely shared today across the spectrum of living things on earth. Everything about us is evolved.

Nowhere is the new scientific perspective more provocative than when we consider our current form of humanity in comparison with all the other human forms or species that have existed, some of them until just a few tens of thousands of years ago. About a decade ago, new discoveries and technical advances in analysis began to undermine confidence in standard interpretations of human origins. Taken together, they provide strong evidence for the need for a new interpretation of the hominin lineage, that evolutionary pathway that diverged from the chimpanzees some seven million years ago. In terms of fossil discoveries, the 2009 publication of the full description of *Ardipithecus ramidus* marks the beginning of the recent phase.[1] Many other important findings have followed, including *Australopithecus sediba*[2] and *Homo naledi*.[3] In 2019 researchers described fossil remains found on the island of Luzon in the Philippines. The remains date to 50,000–67,000 years ago and "display a combination of primitive and derived morphological features that is different from the combination of features found in other species in the genus *Homo* (including *Homo floresiensis* and *Homo sapiens*) and warrants their attribution to a new species, which we name *Homo luzonensis*."[4]

A key part of the reason for the rapid advance in human origins has been the technical advances in isolating and analyzing the tiniest traces of the past. Nowhere is this more significant that in paleogenomics, the recovery, analysis, and comparison of the genes of creatures long gone. The 2010 publication of a draft of the Neandertal genome opened a new era in our view of our past.[5] Now we know that our "species," *Homo sapiens*, is not a unique branch on the lonely high point of the evolutionary tree, but more like one vine interwoven with other vines that contribute in various ways to the identity of the humanity that emerges in the end.

Until about a decade ago, the "recent out of Africa" theory was generally endorsed by experts in the field. Today, however, whatever core of truth remains to this theory is subject to so many revisions that scarcely the same theory survives. The idea that we modern human beings are the result of a

---

[1] T. D. White, B. Asfaw, Y. Beyene, Y. Haile-Selassie, C. Owen Lovejoy, G. Suwa, and G. Wolde-Gabriel. "*Ardipithecus ramidus* and the Paleobiology of Early Hominids," *Science* 326, no. 5949 (2009): 64–86.

[2] L. R. Berger, D. J. De Ruiter, S. E. Churchill, P. Schmid, K. J. Carlson, P. HGM Dirks, and J. M. Kibii. "*Australopithecus sediba*: A New Species of Homo-like Australopith from South Africa," *Science* 328, no. 5975 (2010): 195–204.

[3] L. R. Berger, J. Hawks, D. J. de Ruiter, S. E. Churchill, P. Schmid, L. K. Delezene, T. L. Kivell et al. "*Homo naledi*, a New Species of the Genus *Homo* from the Dinaledi Chamber, South Africa," *Elife* 4 (2015): e09560.

[4] F. Détroit, A. S. Mijares, J. Corny, G. Daver, C. Zanolli, E. Dizon, E. Robles, R. Grün, and P. J. Piper. "A New Species of *Homo* from the Late Pleistocene of the Philippines," *Nature* 568, no. 7751 (2019): 181.

[5] R. E. Green, J. Krause, A. W. Briggs, T. Maricic, U. Stenzel, M. Kircher, N. Patterson et al., "A Draft Sequence of the Neandertal Genome," *Science* 328, no. 5979 (2010): 710–722.

discrete speciation event occurring in East Africa some 150,000 years ago is no longer tenable. Gone with it is the idea that all human beings alive today are descendants only of that group. It remains true that all individual human beings alive today are biologically integrated as one species. It is scientifically wrong (not to mention morally abhorrent) to think that there are extant separate human "races" or "species" or even "sub-species" with long and separate evolutionary histories.

Our unity as a biological community, however, comes not at our beginning of our evolution but midstream and most especially at the end (that is, in the last 40,000 years or so). Human unity is the result of the merger of diverse populations. It is not present at the outset, and it is not the result of a discrete moment of speciation generating a unique species that eliminates all rivals. Human genetic homogeneity is the result of millions of years of population separation and hybridization, of divergence followed by convergence. In evolution, hybridization is commonplace among closely related species. The new science challenges the former view that species are defined by reproductive isolation. Paleogenomics is just beginning to reveal how hybridization played a key role in human evolution. It is clear already, however, that claims of "species uniqueness" have lost their meaning, at least in terms of evolutionary origins. We should not think that there is a "unique," reproductively isolated species called *Homo sapiens* that occasionally hybridizes with other forms such as Neandertals. What we find instead is hybridization all the way around and all the way back.

When it comes to the evidence of the earliest appearance of the genus *Homo*, very little is clear. Experts suggest that our genus may be recognizable in a fossil that dates to about 2.8 million years ago.[6] But what distinguishes *Homo* from *Australopithecus*? A suite of traits marks the difference. But the traits do not appear all at once as a full suite, and sometimes they appear where they seem out of place or out of sequence. We do know that in various forms, hominins identified as *Homo erectus* spread into Eurasia about 1.8 million years ago, spreading as far as the islands of Indonesia and the Philippines as they continued to evolve for well over a million years. Meanwhile, somewhere around 800,000 years ago, the ancestral population for the Neandertals and Denisovans appeared probably in Africa and then spread throughout Eurasia, where they lived side by side with other populations. When the populations overlapped, hybridization probably occurred.

Roughly 300,000–150,000 years ago, human "modernity" appears trait by trait across vast expanses of time and geography, in diverse populations and

---

[6] B. Villmoare, W. H. Kimbel, C. Seyoum, Chr. J. Campisano, E. N. DiMaggio, J. Rowan, D. R. Braun, J. Ramon Arrowsmith, and K. E. Reed, "Early *Homo* at 2.8 Ma from Ledi-Geraru, Afar, Ethiopia," *Science* 347, no. 6228 (2015): 1352–1355.

ecosystems that were themselves constantly undergoing change and movement, including convergence and interbreeding or gene "introgression." Traits seen as modern do not appear all at once or in one place. They appear one by one over hundreds of thousands of years and in regions all across Africa. It is still common, nonetheless, to hear non-experts speak of *Homo sapiens* as "modern" humans, as if from the start our species shows clear morphological traits that mark us off from other hominins. The evidence does not support this view. There is no "start," no geographical locale, no suite of "modern" traits that appear as a package.

Contrast this to the "recent out of Africa" hypothesis, which tended to temporalize and localize the appearance of "modern" humans to East Africa about 150,000 years ago. The new evidence suggests a different picture, one that undermines simplistic notions of human species uniqueness. The first signs of emergence of traits identified as "modern" date to sometime between 220,000 and 380,000 years ago.[7] A population of living in what is now Morocco, on the far northwest corner of the African continent, exhibited some features called modern and other features that seem more archaic.[8] And almost as soon as they appear in Africa, some of these modern traits show up out of continent.[9] The rest of Eurasia, of course, was already populated (sparsely, of course) by multiple forms of the genus *Homo*, some with advanced technology and

---

[7] J.-J. HUBLIN, A. BEN-NCER, S. E. BAILEY, S. E. FREIDLINE, S. NEUBAUER, M. M. SKINNER, I. BERGMANN et al., "New Fossils from Jebel Irhoud, Morocco and the Pan-African Origin of *Homo sapiens*," *Nature* 546, no. 7657 (2017): 289.

[8] Cf. E. M. L. SCERRI, M. G. THOMAS, A. MANICA, P. GUNZ, J. T. STOCK, C. STRINGER, M. GROVE et al., "Did Our Species Evolve in Subdivided Populations across Africa, and Why Does it Matter?," *Trends in ecology & evolution* 33, no. 8 (2018): 582–594. The authors summarize the impact of recent findings in a recent article. "We challenge the view that our species, *Homo sapiens*, evolved within a single population and/or region of Africa." Various "modern" traits appear at widely different times and in diverse populations. The "human fossils suggest that morphologically varied populations pertaining to the *H. sapiens* clade lived throughout Africa. Similarly, the African archaeological record demonstrates the polycentric origin and persistence of regionally distinct Pleistocene material culture in a variety of paleoecological settings." In other words, varied forms of humanity with distinct cultures existed side by side, with "modern" traits spread around but not clustered in any one "modern" group that was uniquely *H. sapiens*. Add to this the insights from paleogenomics, the reconstruction and analysis of fossilized DNA. New (and still only very partial) paleogenomics analysis "also indicate that present-day population structure within Africa extends to deep times, paralleling a paleoenvironmental record of shifting and fractured habitable zones. We argue that these fields support an emerging view of a highly structured African prehistory that should be considered in human evolutionary inferences, prompting new interpretations, questions, and interdisciplinary research directions."

[9] I. HERSHKOVITZ, G. W. WEBER, R. QUAM, M. DUVAL, R. GRÜN, L. KINSLEY, A. AYALON et al., "The Earliest Modern Humans outside Africa," *Science* 359, no. 6374 (2018): 456–459. "This finding changes our view on modern human dispersal and is consistent with recent genetic studies, which have posited the possibility of an earlier dispersal of *Homo sapiens* around 220,000 years ago."

culture roughly on a par with the so-called "modern" humans. Movements from Africa to Eurasia continued as humans that were slightly more "modern" or more like us spread across Africa and beyond, probably in waves beginning roughly 100,000 years ago.

As they spread, they encountered other forms of the genus *Homo* almost everywhere, living in widely separated migratory groups that followed food sources and adjusted to changes in climate. These various populations interbred and produced viable offspring. From comparative paleogenomics we have learned that interbreeding between Neandertals, Denisovans, and "modern" humans not only occurred repeatedly but leaves behind its legacy in the DNA of many human beings today. At least two cases of newly hybridized individuals have been reported.[10,11] Paleogenomics also reveals the fine-grained history of human populations and migrations during the past 100,000 years.[12,13]

The more we know about our past, the more obvious it becomes that there are no clear lines or markers in evolution's transitions.

> The arrival of the first humans is not marked by sudden bursts or clear boundaries. There are no unambiguous markers, no defining lines drawn in the evolutionary sands, no visible historic thresholds between human and nonhuman. As hard as we might search for the boundaries, we cannot find them. Instead, when we look back at the fossils, the teeth and the skulls and the other fragments that bear witness to our origins, we can discern no bright lines that distinguish humans from nonhumans or pre-humans. There are no faint lines, no lines at all, in fact, that mark the advent of the human, unambiguously distinguishing our kind from other kinds or announcing our arrival.[14]

Is this counter-intuitive? Of course, but no more so than the truth that the earth is spinning and revolving even though common sense tells us that the ground is stable.

By comparison to our past, today's global humanity is surprisingly homogenous genetically, despite our fixation on biological variation. The key reason for our homogeneity is interbreeding. Variations in DNA sequences arise over time in relatively isolated populations. Each population is subject to its unique

---

[10] Q. Fu, M. Hajdinjak, O. T. Moldovan, S. Constantin, S. Mallick, P. Skoglund, N. Patterson et al., "An Early Modern Human from Romania with a Recent Neanderthal Ancestor," *Nature* 524, no. 7564 (2015): 216.

[11] V. Slon, F. Mafessoni, B. Vernot, C. de Filippo, S. Grote, B. Viola, M. Hajdinjak et al., "The Genome of the Offspring of a Neanderthal Mother and a Denisovan Father," *Nature* 561, no. 7721 (2018): 113.

[12] R. Nielsen, J. M. Akey, M. Jakobsson, J. K. Pritchard, S. Tishkoff, and E. Willerslev. "Tracing the peopling of the World through Genomics," *Nature* 541, no. 7637 (2017): 302.

[13] M. A. Yang and Q. Fu, "Insights into Modern Human Prehistory using Ancient Genomes," *Trends in Genetics* 34 (2018): 184–196.

[14] R. Cole-Turner, *The End of Adam and Eve: Theology and the Science of Human Origins* (Pittsburgh, PA: Theology Plus, 2016), 69.

selective environmental pressures (Darwinian natural selection). When diverse populations meet, hybridization occurs and some genetic diversity is lost. The new hybridized population is then subject to its own selective pressures, giving rise to a population that is slightly new and comparatively more homogeneous. This process repeats itself over and over at various timescales and geographic ranges. Today it is believed that hybridization or gene introgression occurred frequently in the past, especially in most recent few thousand years. As a result, genetic differences among living human beings are reduced to the point of functional insignificance at the population level.

The new evidence suggests that gene introgression played a major role in our evolution. "These emerging studies raise the possibility that hybridization played not merely a small or ephemeral role, but a central role in the emergence and evolution of *Homo sapiens* through the introduction of new variation, and production of new genetic amalgamations and innovation, thereby opening up more evolutionary possibilities." Divergence and hybridization "is the rule, not the exception, in human evolution."[15]

Something similar has taken place in the way we see the earliest human cultural advances. We now see that they appeared across wide expanses of time and space. One popular misconception is that there was some sort of cultural "big bang" that occurred roughly 30,000 years ago, centered in Western Europe and showcased by the cave art of Chauvet or Lascaux. While this art is dramatic evidence of human symbolic awareness, it is not unique and not the earliest examples. Neandertals are the most likely creators of the first art in Europe, their comparatively simple paintings dating almost 20,000 years before the more famous cave art.[16] And it is believed that even earlier, Neandertals created a "structure" deep in a cave in France, using stalagmites as building blocks.[17] The famous cave art of Chauvet was created over a span of about 9,000 year by various populations, groups that seem to have left little genetic trace among the more recent occupants of Europe.[18]

Perhaps more challenging to the idea of a localize cultural big bang is that cave art similar to Chauvet has been found on the far-away Indonesian island

---

[15] R. ROGERS ACKERMANN, A. MACKAY, and M. L. ARNOLD, "The Hybrid Origin of 'Modern' Humans," *Evolutionary Biology* 43, no. 1 (2016): 1–11.

[16] D. L. HOFFMANN, C. D. STANDISH, M. GARCÍA-DIEZ, P. B. PETTITT, J. A. MILTON, J. ZILHÃO, J. J. ALCOLEA-GONZÁLEZ et al., "U-Th Dating of Carbonate Crusts Reveals Neandertal Origin of Iberian Cave Art," *Science* 359, no. 6378 (2018): 912–915.

[17] J. JAUBERT, S. VERHEYDEN, D. GENTY, M. SOULIER, H. CHENG, D. BLAMART, CHR. BURLET et al., "Early Neanderthal Constructions Deep in Bruniquel Cave in Southwestern France," *Nature* 534, no. 7605 (2016): 111–114.

[18] A. QUILES, H. VALLADAS, H. BOCHERENS, E. DELQUÉ-KOLIČ, E. KALTNECKER, J. VAN DER PLICHT, J.-J. DELANNOY et al., "A High-Precision Chronological Model for the Decorated Upper Paleolithic Cave of Chauvet-Pont d'Arc, Ardèche, France," *Proceedings of the National Academy of Sciences* 113, no. 17 (2016): 4670–4675.

of Sulawesi, dating to roughly 35,000 years ago with hand stencil images dating to about 40,000 years ago, as old as anything in Europe.[19] More recently, "similar rock art was created during essentially the same time period on the adjacent island of Borneo." This art also first appears around 40,000 years ago. Most remarkable, however, is the date of one of the hand stencils. "Two reddish-orange-coloured hand stencils from the same site each yielded a minimum uranium-series date of 37.2 ka, and a third hand stencil of the same hue has a maximum date of 51.8 ka [...]. Our findings show that cave painting appeared in eastern Borneo between 52 and 40 ka."[20]

While technological and cultural sophistication is more widespread and stretches back further than we once thought, we have also learned the somewhat less "modern" species of *Homo* survived well into the time when the *Homo sapiens* population was taking its shape. The 2019 report of *H. luzonensis* complicates our view of the past hundred thousand years, the very period in which *H. sapiens* emerges even while sharing the planet with Neandertals, Denisovans of various sorts, the "hobbit" (*H. floresiensis*), and now the similarly short-statured hominins from Luzon. The 2013 discovery of *H. naledi* and the surprisingly late date for these fossils suggests that diverse forms overlapped, sometimes interbreeding and sometimes probably not. Dated to somewhere between 335,000 and 236,000 years ago, *H. naledi* seems too small-brained and "archaic" for its time.[21] But the way the fossils were found deposited in a single, nearly inaccessible underground chamber raises the haunting question of whether some sort of burial custom may have been practiced. Who else is out there waiting to be found?

New discoveries upset old theories and force us to consider new ideas about our origins and about our humanity. Evolution is not sequential or linear. One species does not follow another. "We are not the final twig on the branch at the end of a sequential progression from one form or species to the next, from *Australopithecus* to *Homo habilis*, then *Homo erectus*, then *Neandertalis*, then modern humans. None of these evolved from what came before. All of us evolved *with* what came before. Our past is more diversified and complex than we can know, and traces of its complexity is in us today in the form of DNA

---

[19] M. AUBERT, A. BRUMM, M. RAMLI, T. SUTIKNA, E. WAHYU SAPTOMO, B. HAKIM, MJ VD MORWOOD, G. D. VAN DEN BERGH, L. KINSLEY, and A. DOSSETO, "Pleistocene Cave art from Sulawesi, Indonesia," *Nature* 514, no. 7521 (2014): 223.

[20] M. AUBERT, P. SETIAWAN, A. A. OKTAVIANA, A. BRUMM, P. H. SULISTYARTO, E. W. SAPTOMO, B. ISTIAWAN et al., "Palaeolithic Cave Art in Borneo," *Nature* 564, no. 7735 (2018): 254.

[21] P. HGM DIRKS, E. M. ROBERTS, H. HILBERT-WOLF, J. D. KRAMERS, J. HAWKS, A. DOSSETO, M. DUVAL et al., "The Age of *Homo naledi* and Associated Sediments in the Rising Star Cave, South Africa," *Elife* 6 (2017) [eLife 2017;6:e24231 doi: 10.7554/eLife.24231]. "These age results demonstrate that a morphologically primitive hominin, *Homo naledi*, survived into the later parts of the Pleistocene in Africa, and indicate a much younger age for the *Homo naledi* fossils than have previously been hypothesized based on their morphology."

sequences. At the very least, this affects how we see ourselves and our connection with our own deep past. Our past is in us."[22]

And so, too, is our future.

2. The Challenge of Technology

Looking back in time, we are confounded by evolution's blurred lines that refuse any simple definition of humanity. Looking forward, we are met by technologies that deliberate blur the lines, refusing to be constrained by any simple definitions or their moral and normative corollaries. Evolution has made us up as it goes along, and now we are only acting in accordance with nature when we use technology to continue to reinvent ourselves. Why should we not set out to change ourselves deliberately? Why not overwrite evolution? Nothing moral or natural stands in our way. The only limit is our technology, and today that does not seem to be much of a limit. So let us free ourselves from our biology in order to go beyond this humanity until we become something new, perhaps even a new species. Such is the creed of today's transhumanist.

Although often given the credit, Julian Huxley does not coin the term "transhumanism," but he does give it its contemporary meaning in a published lecture in 1951, which is expanded and reprinted in 1957 to contain these oft-quoted words: "The human species can, if it wishes, transcend itself – not just sporadically, an individual here in one way, an individual there in another way – but in its entirety, as humanity. We need a name for this new belief. Perhaps transhumanism will serve: man remaining man, but transcending himself, by realizing new possibilities of and for his human nature." When we do this, Huxley claims, "the human species will be on the threshold of a new kind of existence, as different from ours as ours is from that of Pekin man," what we would now call *Homo erectus*.[23]

Huxley's program is not possible yet, and it may never be. The technologies developed in the past 60 years, however, seem to be taking us in the direction that he envisioned. His focus on biological evolution and on a new species directs our thought immediately to recent advances in gene editing and to the debate over human germline modification. Nearly everyone has condemned the 2018 debacle in China over the use of CRISPR/Cas gene editing to modify and then implant viable human embryos (if indeed that is what happened). At the same time, however, scientific experts in this field have opened the door

---

[22] R. COLE-TURNER, "New Perspectives on Human Origins: Three Challenges for Christian Theology," *Science and Theology* 18 (2020): 524–536.
[23] J. HUXLEY, "Transhumanism," in *New Bottles for New Wine: Essays* (London: Chatto & Windus, 1957), 17.

to just this sort of use of gene technology.[24] While some scientists attempt to draw a line between therapy (acceptable in time if safe) and enhancement (not acceptable), many of them realize that such a line is difficult to draw and impossible to enforce. Use of CRISPR and other advances in gene editing to enhance future children is clearly foreseeable and perhaps inevitable within a few decades, although within the limits of what is possible through DNA modification. There is a big gap, however, between narrow and targeted enhancements and the kind of engineered speciation that Huxley foresaw.

For the most part, today's transhumanists focus on individuals and not on the human species. The technologies they embrace have the power to modify individuals but little or no power to advance evolution. In many respects, Huxley's vision no longer guides transhumanism. Perhaps the focus on future generations simply does not interest people living today, who will not live long enough to see this future unless they do something first about their own limits, starting with the length of their own lifespans. Instead of Huxley's "new kind" of humanity, today's transhumanists turn to technology to become healthier, stronger, smarter, and able to live longer than unenhanced humans, starting now. The focus is on my individual enhancement, not our species evolution.

Advances in gene editing, pharmacology, nanotechnology, and information technology all offer pathways to human enhancement. Many of these technologies are used for therapy as part of today's medicine. But increasingly they are being used for experiments in enhancement. Not just transhumanists but nearly everyone today who enjoys at least a middle class existence seems to be drawn to the idea that technology can be used to make us "better than well." The specific targets for human enhancement include nearly every human trait and capacity. Physical health and strength, longevity, cognitive performance, elevated mood, and even moral capacity and spiritual experience are targets for enhancement.

Little evidence exists that any of these new technologies of human enhancement actually work. Careful nutrition and an active lifestyle tend to produce mental and physical health well into the later decades of life. But there are no proven magic pills to make us healthier, smarter, or resistant to aging. People seem willing, however, to take risks for the sake of enhancement, downing or injecting unproven supplements and performance enhancing drugs. Alongside mainstream transhumanism there now exists a "grinder" culture, a kind of "do-it-yourself" biohacker self-enhancement network of individuals who implant chips or even use mail-order CRISPR gene editing tools on themselves.

---

[24] NATIONAL ACADEMIES OF SCIENCES, ENGINEERING, AND MEDICINE, *Human Genome Editing: Science, Ethics, and Governance* (Washington, DC: The National Academies Press, 2017 (https://doi.org/10.17226/24623) (4/22/2022).

Underlying this culture of human enhancement is the conviction that all persons have the right to control their own bodies, which lack normative definition and are therefore entirely subject to personal choice. We embrace not just political liberty but freedom of choice over nature with technology as the power over limits. There is no human "nature" in a philosophical or theological sense, no canonical set of traits or a normatively human genome that is natural in the sense of being morally sanctioned and therefore beyond modification or enhancement. Today's culture of human enhancement and transhumanism relies on evolution as a scientific view that discredits and deconstructs "human nature." Evolution could have made us different from what we are. In fact, evolution made many different forms of humanity along the pathway that led to us today. Given enough time, evolution might make us into something else. But why wait for evolution when we have technology?

When we look back at our evolutionary origins, we cannot find a clear species definition or boundary. We cannot say: that was the first modern human, or even what the first modern human was. All we see are populations with distinct traits but also with the proclivity to migrate and interbreed. We see hybridization, not clear or discrete speciation. And when we look forward into the future horizons of our human technological transformations, we see no limits aside from finitude itself. We refuse to accept any definition that limits our freedom or puts moral constraints on our creativity.

Already today, when we look around ourselves at our technologies of human experimentation, we see how we negate definitions by deliberately mixing and blurring what we once believed was pure and clear. One example of deliberate mixing is the widespread creation of chimeras for research. Human pluripotent stem cells, whether derived from embryos or created by induced pluripotency, are routinely inserted into blastocysts of other species, most commonly mice. As the mouse pup develops *in utero* and in the first weeks of life, human cells proliferate to all parts of the chimeric mouse, including the brain and possibly the sex cells. For that reason, professional guidelines discourage laboratories from allowing chimeric animals to breed. Nearly every lab at the forefront of stem cell research, however, intentionally mixes cells of human and nonhuman origin to create chimeric animals. Medical transplants of pig values also create chimeras of a sort. Interestingly, in order to reduce immune rejection, the pigs are "humanized" first though DNA changes.

Another emerging field of biotechnical research should be mentioned here because of its growing power to erase yet another human boundary line. When *in vitro* fertilization techniques were first used in humans, researchers were able to create human embryos outside the womb. Concerns about the moral status of the embryo led to the widespread adoption of the 14-day rule, which limits research on human embryos up to 14-days after fertilization. Today, using human embryonic stem cells, researchers are exploring various ways to create novel entities that have some of the features of human embryos but are also significantly different. These novel entities are not the product of fertilization (or of "cloning," for that matter). They lack the full developmental potential of human embryos.[25] What, then, are these "novel entities"? How should this research be defined and regulated? Does the 14-day rule apply to them?[26] Part of the irony is that the more they become like human embryos, the more useful they are in research *and* the more challenging they are to define or regulate. Our point is that here in yet another arena of research, definitions become less clear when we intentionally create entities that seem to land on the line that once marked an important moral and ontological boundary.

Another example of intentional mixing and blurring is cyborgs, the bringing together of the cybernetic machine and the biological organism in a single functional unit. Human cyborgs already exist as products of technology. But more than that, cyborgs serve as a powerful symbol of our posthuman age. It is both a creation and a metaphor for today's multifaceted and multi-natured human, making its literary debut a generation ago in the writings of Donna Haraway. She introduces the concept of the cyborg with these words: "By the late twentieth century, our time, a mythic time, we are all chimeras, theorized and fabricated hybrids of machine and organism; in short, we are cyborgs. The cyborg is our ontology [...] a condensed image of both imagination and material reality."[27] As product and symbol of our posthuman age, the cyborg has nearly sacramental power as a sign that effects what it signifies. Standing alongside the hybridization that created humanity and the laboratory chimeras we humans create, the cyborg is one of the new and unsettling icons of our age, shattering our boundaries by blurring our humanity.

3. Incarnation and Transcendent Humanity

According to the conference invitation, the fourth challenge that endangers our idea of humanity is the *theological challenge*. Compared to God, what are humans? Some claim that if God exists, humans are thereby confined and

---

[25] A. Warmflash, B. Sorre, F. Etoc, E. D. Siggia, and A. H. Brivanlou. "A Method to Recapitulate Early Embryonic Spatial Patterning in Human Embryonic Stem Cells," *Nature methods* 11, no. 8 (2014): 847.

[26] I. Hyun, A. Wilkerson, and J. Johnston, "Embryology Policy: Revisit the 14-day Rule," *Nature News* 533, no. 7602 (2016): 169. Cf. J. Aach, J. Lunshof, E. Iyer, and G. M. Church, "Addressing the Ethical Issues Raised by Synthetic Human Entities with Embryo-like Features," *Elife* 6 (2017): e20674.

[27] D. Haraway, "A Cyborg Manifesto: Science, Technology, and Socialist-Feminism in the Late Twentieth Century," *Socialist Review* 80 (1985), 65–108, reprinted in *Simians, Cyborgs and Women: The Reinvention of Nature* (New York: Routledge, 1991), 149–181, 150 (http://www.stanford.edu/dept/HPS/Haraway/CyborgManifesto.html) (4/21/2022).

diminished. For the sake of human freedom, we should reject "God" as a needlessly self-limiting human construct. Alternatively, according to the invitation, "the point of this challenge, at least in the monotheistic traditions, is to outline a vision of a good human life that has its center in safeguarding the distinction between creature and creator."

But does Christianity seek merely to safeguard the distinction between God and humanity? The argument here in this paper makes a different claim, one rooted in Christianity's most scandalous and idiosyncratic assertion, that the distinction between God and humanity is bridged, but never removed or even blurred, in the incarnation.

But how is it possible today to understand the idea of the incarnation in light of the challenges before us? What concept of the human can we have in mind when we say that God takes up and becomes one with the human? One might think that the challenges to the idea of humanity that confront us today spell the end of the Christian idea of incarnation. It was always scandalous. Now it is impossible even to describe.

The goal here is to suggest otherwise. Can it be that the challenges facing the concept of humanity might lead us to a more profound understanding of the relationship between the human and the divine? This is not to suggest that the church's ancient creedal assertion of the incarnation can simply be extracted from its context forced to fit our own, least of all by ignoring contemporary challenges. What, then, are the possibilities for our moving forward? Here it will be argued that through a somewhat selective reading of the theological tradition, combined with the use of the freedom of the theologian in every age to offer tentative hints that go beyond a strict reading of past doctrinal formulas, it may be possible to see the challenges to humanity as drawing forth a theological view richer perhaps in some respects than what was possible to say in the past.

In the paragraphs that follow, I will introduce and defend five key claims. In each case, I want to suggest that these claims have their roots in Christian tradition, that they are connected to the doctrine of the incarnation, that they are informed by the challenges of human evolutionary biology and technological transformation, and that they resonate in perhaps unexpected ways with our situation today. The first claim is that humanity, theologically understood, is incomprehensible and indefinable. Second, humans are meant to be godlike, but what this means is surprising and even counterintuitive. Third, humanity is diverse but is united with itself, biologically and theologically, not by creation but by incarnation. Fourth, human transformation is unlimited. Fifth, human creativity is cosmic and culminates in cosmic transfiguration.

1. Human Indefinability

The claim that humans are incomprehensible and indefinable is clearly articulated by the fourth century theologian, Gregory of Nyssa. He begins his argument by insisting that God is incomprehensible and indefinable. If humans are in the image of God, we must share that indefinability. If not, then by knowing how to define ourselves, we could understand God's nature. The human person, according to Gregory, bears "an accurate resemblance to the superior nature." If so, one might think we could start with a concept of the human and use it as a kind of theological Rosetta stone by which we could decipher God's "incomprehensible Nature."[28] For Gregory, what mirrors the Incomprehensible must itself be incomprehensible. There is no knowledge of one that can be used to comprehend the other.

In the late twentieth century, we see this claim expressed anew by Karl Rahner. In a discussion of the incarnation, he asks: "But do we really know from what has been said what man is and so what 'human nature' is?" No. Rahner claims that a definition "is impossible for man." But then, almost playfully, he offers this: "Man is, one might say in way of definition, an indefinability come to consciousness of itself."[29] He continues by saying that "Man is therefore mystery in his essence, his nature [...] Our whole existence is the acceptance or rejection of the mystery which we are [...]."[30] Not unlike Gregory, Rahner connects human indefinability with divine incomprehensibility. Human indefinability is not some sort of human deficit, nor is it something that will be resolved by greater knowledge or scientific advance. It is our glory, or more precisely our openness to light and glorification. On this, compare Rahner with David Bentley Hart's creative paraphrase of Nyssa: "I am an openness whose depth does not belong to me, but to the boundless light that creates me, and whose identity is then given me as other."[31]

Whether it is "openness" or sheer apophatic indefinability, the assertion of human incomprehensibility points to the profundity and sacred depth inherent in each human person. Our point here is that this somehow suits our contemporary moment and the challenges facing the meaning of humanity. Rahner recognizes that the truth of human indefinability fits today's intellectual context.[32] But its truth is not grounded in its relevance. Human indefinability

---

[28] Gregory of Nyssa, *On the Making of Man*, 11.4, in *Nicene and Post-Nicene Fathers*, Series II, vol. V, ed. P. Schaff and H. Wace (Peabody, MA: Hendrickson Publisher, 1994), 397.

[29] K. RAHNER, "On the Theology of the Incarnation," *Theological Investigations: More Recent Writings*, vol. 4, (Baltimore, MD: Helicon, 1966), 107.

[30] RAHNER, "Incarnation," 108.

[31] D. BENTLEY HART, "The Mirror of the Infinite: Gregory of Nyssa on the *Vestigia Trinitatis*," *Modern Theology* 18, no. 4 (2002): 541–556, 557.

[32] For example, Rahner links the theological notion of human indefinability with the possibility of human technological modification through genetics. One can imagine Rahner

is grounded in our relationship with God. "And this mystery is our nature, because the transcendence which we are and which we accomplish brings our existence and God's existence together: and both as mystery. And here we must always remember that a mystery is not something still undisclosed, which is a second element along with what is grasped and understood. This would be to confuse mystery with the still undiscovered unknown."[33]

The theology of human indefinability finds a clear correspondence in what we are learning from the scientific study of the human past and the technological transformations of the human future. Looking back or looking forward, we see no clear empirically-rooted definitions of humanity. The study of our past reveals multiple forms, simultaneous diversity, separation and difference followed by hybridization and convergence. Looking forward to the transformation of humanity through technologies that we cannot imagine, our power to predict the future of humanity is as weak as our technology is strong. Human indefinability meets us empirically in the science of our past and in the distant horizons of our future. But to this empirical indefinability, theology adds three important claims. First, we are *inherently* indefinable and not just because of the limits of our knowledge. Second, we are indefinable *now* and not just in the past or in the future. Third, we are indefinable because *we mirror the divine*. Theology, therefore has nothing to fear when it finds its echo in empirical indefinability. On the contrary, Christian theology predicts that no scientific advance or technology achievement will make the human definable. If our theology of human indefinability fits our posthuman context, well and good.

2. Human Godlikeness

One of the hopes voiced by some transhumanists is that with enough technology, we will become gods. Our becoming godlike is an old idea, but of course the transhumanists insist that now at last it is actually possible to acquire godlike features through technology.

Christian theology has its own version of human godlikeness, one made possible by the grace of the incarnation as a completion of the creation. Never,

---

agreeing with Nick Bostrom's comment that posthumans are essentially unimaginable: "As we seek to peer farther into posthumanity, our ability to concretely imagine what it might be like trails off. If, aside from extended healthspans, the essence of posthumanity is to be able to have thoughts and experiences that we cannot readily think or experience with our current capacities, then it is not surprising that our ability to imagine what posthuman life might be like is very limited." (N. BOSTROM, "Why I Want to be a Posthuman When I Grow Up," at http://www.nickbostrom.com/posthuman.pdf, 5–6) (4/21/2022). For RAHNER, see "The Experiment with Man: Theological Observations on Man's Self-Manipulation" and "The Problem of Genetic Manipulation," *Theological Investigations* IX (London: Darton, Longman & Todd, 1972).

[33] RAHNER, "Incarnation," 107.

of course, is the ontological distance or difference between Creator and creature something to be overlooked. Apart from the incarnation, Christian theology offers no basis for ontological continuity between God and humanity, no ladder of ascent from this world to the next, and no analogy by which we can compare ourselves with God. Søren Kierkegaard spoke of an "infinite qualitative distance" between God and the human creature, a phrase echoed in the early writings of Karl Barth and others.

At the same time, Christianity insists that "distance" is not the only word much less the final word it has to say when it attempts to speak of our relationship to God. While never minimizing the distance, theology must also make the paradoxical claim that God unites what is ontologically and morally separate. Speaking of God and Christ, Paul writes: "For our sake he made him to be sin who knew no sin, so that in him we might become the righteousness of God" (2 Cor 5:21). Such radical moral bridging is also an ontological bridging, expressed succinctly and forcefully in the commonplace saying attributed to Athanasius: "God became human so that humans might become God."

Humans are not God, and we cannot make ourselves into God. And yet the motif of human divinization by divine initiative or divine grace is a theme that arises throughout sacred scriptures and in the writings of theologians through the centuries. In Genesis 1:26–27, humans (unlike other creatures) are addressed by God and are declared to be in the image of God. In Genesis 3, the enigma of human godlikeness is a key driver in the narrative. According to verses 3–4, "[…] the serpent said to the woman, 'You will not die; for God knows that when you eat of it your eyes will be opened, and you will be like God, knowing good and evil'" (Gen 3:3–4). Is Satan tempting through deception or by holding out something partly true but also partly destructive? Consider verse 22, where God seems to agree with the truth of at least part of Satan's proposal: "Then the LORD God said, 'See, the man has become like one of us, knowing good and evil […]'" (Gen 3:22). What is true here seems to be that by following Satan's advice, humans will become like God. What is dangerous is that they will become rival gods, Satan's version of divinity, which is autonomous, self-aggrandizing, and so fundamentally ungodlike.

The godlikeness of humans is also found in Psalm 8 and Psalm 82, words quoted by Jesus according to John 10:34. Or consider Leviticus 19:2b: "You shall be holy, for I the LORD your God am holy." In this text, which appears as a kind of prologue to a recounting of the commandments, humans are to resemble God in holiness. This text is quoted in Christian scriptures in 1 Peter, where we read: "Instead, as he who called you is holy, be holy yourselves in all your conduct; for it is written, 'You shall be holy, for I am holy'" (1 Pet 1:15–16). The same human/divine comparison is found in the words of Jesus, according to Matthew 5. "Be perfect, therefore, as your heavenly Father is perfect" (Mt 5:48).

The critically important question here, and perhaps the most neglected, is to ask what God is like. There are many ideas of God. Which one must we become? Consider this comment from Karl Barth: "Perhaps you recall how when Hitler used to speak about God, he called him 'the Almighty.' But it is not 'the Almighty' who is God; we cannot understand from the standpoint of a supreme concept of power, who God is. And the person who calls 'the Almighty' God misses God in the most terrible way."[34] Who, then, is the God in whose likeness we are to live?

For Christian theology, it is the God of Jesus Christ and therefore the God characterized by self-giving and even self-emptying. Here more than anywhere we see the link between God, humanity, and incarnation. The self-emptying God is the God who not only creates but enters into the creation, taking it into God's own being. By self-emptying, God becomes human. According to Karl Rahner, "[…] the basic element, according to our faith, is the *self*-emptying, the coming to be, the κένωσις and γένεσις of God himself, who can come to be by *becoming* another thing, derivative, in the act of constituting it, without having to change in his own proper reality which is the unoriginated origin."[35] In other words, God is inherently self-emptying, and this inherent identity means that God can express who God is by *becoming* human. God incarnate is "the self-utterance of God in its self-emptying, because God expresses *himself* when he empties himself."[36]

These motifs fit together. Only a self-emptying God becomes human. Can one imagine "the Almighty" being incarnate, "taking the form of a slave, being born in human likeness"? (Phil 2:7). Only the self-emptying God can take on our humanity. By becoming human, God makes us godlike by uniting us and making us to conform not to "the Almighty" but to the One who is self-emptying.

According to Michael Gorman and his interpretation of Romans and Philippians, the God known in the incarnate Christ is a self-emptying or "kenotic" God. From this it follows that human beings "are most like God when they act kenotically. In Christ's preexistent and incarnate kenosis we see truly what God is truly like, and we simultaneously see truly what Adam/humanity truly should have been, truly was not, and now truly can be in Christ. *Kenosis is theosis*. To be like Christ crucified is to be both most godly and most human. Christification is divinization, and divinization is humanization."[37]

---

[34] Karl Barth, quoted by D. L. MIGLIORE, "The Trinity and Human Liberty," *Theology Today* 36, no. 4 (1980): 488–497, 492; original quote from K. BARTH, *Dogmatics in Outline* (London: SCM, 1949), 48.

[35] RAHNER, "Incarnation," 114.

[36] Ibid., 116.

[37] M. J. GORMAN, *Inhabiting the Cruciform God: Kenosis, Justification, and Theosis in Paul's Narrative Soteriology* (Grand Rapids, MI: Wm. B. Eerdmans Publishing, 2009), 37.

It is important at this point to see how this connects to the meaning of creation, especially the completion of the creation of humanity and not merely its rescue. God's self-emptying is creative. According to Rahner: "In the incarnation, the Logos creates by taking on, and takes on by emptying himself."[38] Creation and incarnation are thus linked, as if they were two parts of a single action by which God's "plan" for creation is brought to its realization. By the incarnational act of self-emptying, creation is brought to completion in Christ, a completion that transforms and unifies all things. Of all the things to be unified, humanity is our focus here.

3. Human Unity

From the standpoint of science, any claim that humanity is the goal of biological evolution is considered suspect. Christianity, however, must speak of purpose rooted in theology and not read off nature. Scripture does not avoid references to God's will or purposes, going so far as to say that in Christ, God's plan is revealed: "[God] has made known to us the mystery of his will, according to his good pleasure that he set forth in Christ, as a plan for the fullness of time, to gather up all things in him, things in heaven and things on earth" (Eph 1:9–10). Rahner is correct when he says: "We presuppose, therefore, that the goal of the world consists in God's communicating himself to it. We presuppose that the whole dynamism which God has instituted in the very heart of the world's becoming by self-transcendence (and yet not as that which constitutes its nature) is really always meant already as the beginning and first step towards this self-communication and its acceptance by the world."[39]

Our main question in this section, however, is not whether the emergence of humanity is somehow built into evolution as its inner purpose but whether humanity is in any sense a unity. Christian theology links the two questions. God's plan, according to Ephesians, is "to gather up all things" in Christ. According to Galatians 3, divisions of class, gender, and ethnicity are transcended in Christ, who unifies humanity: "There is no longer Jew or Greek, there is no longer slave or free, there is no longer male and female; for all of you are one in Christ Jesus" (Gal 3:28). God's purpose in creation is not just for human-like consciousness to emerge through evolution, but for its emergence, with all its diversity and multiplicity intact, to have a transcendent unity.

By comparing human genomes, we know that today's global human population is surprisingly homogenous genetically. When asked for an explanation, scientists point to the long history of gene introgression through interbreeding

---

[38] RAHNER, "Incarnation," 116.
[39] K. RAHNER, "Christianity within an Evolutionary View of the World," in *Theological Investigations*, vol. V (London: Darton, Longman & Todd, 1966), 173.

among populations. But when it comes to the diversity of human forms in the past, science reveals only complexity. Since our divergence from the lineage that led to today's chimpanzees, the hominin lineage has just changed dramatically. In our lineage there are many forms or species, some grouped together in the genus *Australopithecus*, some in the genus *Homo*. Should we think that all members of the genus *Homo* are "human"? Or only *Homo sapiens*? If "human" is a claim that confers value or a special ontological status, there can be no scientific answer to the question of which ancestral forms are "human" and which are not. But even if "human" is thought to be merely a kind of arbitrary marker between something earlier and something later, there is no scientific way to know when to apply the label. Nonexperts tend to think that the first *Homo sapiens* were really human but anything before was not. The problem is that we cannot say with any clarity what we mean by the first *Homo sapiens*. Traits that we associate with *Homo sapiens* appear bit by bit, piecemeal, over great expanses of time and distance, and only come together later, but not in any clearly definable moment. There is no first *Homo sapiens*.

Part of the problem here is that the science of human diversity has always been politically sensitive. Today's recent discoveries have made scientists wary of discussing human diversity in public.[40] One reason is the sheer technical complexity that stands in the way of public understanding of the significance of paleogenomics and diverse ancestral populations. Things were easier fifteen years ago when the recent "out of Africa" theory was generally accepted. Human biological unity could be explained in terms of biological origins. We are all descended from one population that first appears about 150,000 years ago, spreading throughout the world and replacing everyone else. Any genetic diversity among humans, it was claimed, is merely superficial adaptation to local selective pressures. Today, however, with the "out of Africa" theory no longer credible in anything like its strict form, another explanation is needed, one based on gene introgression.

Such is the context in which Christian theology looks today for the unifying significance of the incarnation. Just as science has lost its ability to defend human biological unity on the basis of recent species origins in Africa, so many theologians have found it impossible to defend unity on the basis of even more recent origins in a biblical Adam and Eve. As science turns toward the unifying power of hybridization and convergence, so theology turns to consider anew the unifying power of the incarnation.

---

[40] G. LEWIS-KRAUS, "Is Ancient DNA Research Revealing New Truths – or Falling Into Old Traps?," in *New York Times Magazine* (January 17, 2019). At the same time, the general public has embraced personal DNA testing in order to learn about ancestry. Added to this is the resurgence of white supremacy, with its advocate embracing genetic tests as proof of their "racial purity" until the results seem to show otherwise.

The unity of humanity is not something theology can presuppose. When Christianity claims that the divine Logos assumes humanity or "human nature," it must add immediately that what is assumed is unified. Theology has nowhere to go to find a clear definition of humanity as a whole. The incarnation creates what does not already exist. Human unity is the consequence and not the presupposition of the incarnation. In concrete theological language, Christ does not assume the preexistent unity of human nature. By the incarnation, Christ makes us one. The incarnation unites us all with ourselves by uniting us all with the divine. According to Gregory of Nyssa, the divine Word took up "a complete human being and made him his own, so that his human qualities might be thoroughly and ceaselessly changed into divine ones by the divine presence, and that this process of transformation might then radiate out from that one human individual into the entire human race [...]."[41]

This is not to say that we can somehow escape the problem of saying what we mean by "all." This simple word appears over and over in Paul's theology and in the history of theological debates. Too often in the past, debate has centered on whether all descendants of Adam and Eve are redeemed in Christ, or only some. Our question here, however, is not about some living human beings *versus* all. Here we are asking how far back and how wide theology must go in asserting the scope of the incarnation.

In its classic formulation, the incarnation means the assumption or taking on of human nature. Today, what is meant by "human nature"? In thinkers such as Gregory of Nyssa, humanity does not refer to one human being but to all humans together. Commenting on Nyssa, "On the Making of Man," David Bentley Hart writes that "[...] all talk of human 'nature' most properly refers, in Gregory's thought, not merely to some abstract set of properties instantiated in any given individual, but to the *pleroma* of all persons who come into existence throughout time, who together constitute, as in a single body, the one humanity that God first willed in fashioning a creature in his image, the ideal *anthropos* who dwells eternally in the wisdom and foresight of God ..."[42] For us today, "the *pleroma* of all persons" takes on something far bigger than Nyssa might have had in mind.

Theologians of the past did not know about all the varied forms of hominins. And yet we are not entirely without theological precedent here. From classical antiquity, early theologians learned about the legends of the so-called "monstrous races," creatures with some human features but not human in appearance. From Augustine's time, Christian theologians tended to include these

---

[41] B. E. Daley, S.J., *God Visible: Patristic Christology Reconsidered* (Oxford: Oxford University Press, 2018), 141.
[42] D. Bentley Hart, "The mirror of the infinite: Gregory of Nyssa on the Vestigia Trinitatis," *Modern Theology* 18, no. 4 (2002): 541–561, 548–549.

creatures in the broad theological category of the human. According to Allison Hepola, "Overall it seems that when the topic of the monstrous races was considered by the medievals, the tendency was to view them as humans. Christian thinkers in this period were surprisingly comfortable with the claim that the appearance and structure of the body is largely irrelevant to human nature. Instead the most important feature of the body for determining whether some being is human or not is simply whether that body biologically descends from Adam."[43] It may be, of course, that Christians theologians doubted the actual existence of these "monstrous" creatures. The generosity they seem to show by including monsters may, in their minds, have involved no practical consequence. Nevertheless, their argument from lineage is interesting and applicable to our own view.

Our proposal here is that in light of today's scientific understanding of humanity, the central truth of Nyssa's claim should be expanded to include the full history and diversity of the hominin lineage. Once again, Karl Rahner is one of the few theologians who can be quoted in support. He writes: "Christian faith is aware of a universal history of salvation, common to all mankind, existing from the very outset, always effective, universally present as the most radical element of the unity of mankind [...]."[44]

In Nyssa we find the radical social implications of the incarnation. In Rahner we discover its radical evolutionary implications. Building on Rahner, our proposal is that the incarnation unifies not simply all existing human beings but all who have come before us in our hominin evolutionary history. "The human lineage is the defined locus of the incarnation, the place we know within creation that is prepared for incarnation."[45] This represents a significant widening of the traditional Christian claim.

For many, the proposal here goes too far in widening the scope of the incarnation. There is no doubt that traditional theologians held the view that only human beings in the ordinary sense, the kind that exist today or what we would call *Homo sapiens*, are made one with God in Christ. Theology today, however, cannot continue to make this claim without addressing the problem

---

[43] A. Hepola, "Dragons and Dog-Headed Saints: Some Medieval Perspectives on the Significance of the Human Form" in *Christian Perspectives on Transhumanism and the Church*, ed. by S. Donaldson and R. Cole-Turner, (Cham, Switzerland: Palgrave Macmillan, 2018), 39–52. Hepola quotes Augustine: "No faithful Christian should doubt that anyone who is born anywhere as a man – that is, a rational and mortal being – derives from that one first-created human being. And this is true, however extraordinary such a creature may appear to our senses in bodily shape, in color, or motion, or utterance, or in any natural endowment, or part, or quality." Augustine, *City of God*, Book XVI, Chapter 8, 662.

[44] Rahner, "Oneness and Threefoldness of God in Discussion with Islam," *Theological Investigations*, vol. 19 (London: Darton, Longman & Todd, 1984), 160.

[45] Cole-Turner, "New Perspectives on Human Origins."

we face in defining *Homo sapiens*. Earlier theologians believed that the incarnation reaches back in time and includes all humans who have ever existed but who are biologically like us all the way back. For us today, going back in time is something we simply cannot do unless we recognize that multiple forms of hominins, full of diversity and dissimilarity, that make us the genus *Homo*, even more so if we go back to the start of the hominin lineage. Our proposal here is to see them included in what we mean by "all."

Other theologians may object that our proposal is too narrow. The debate over recent proposals for "deep incarnation" is helpful here.[46] Advocates of "deep incarnation" are right to remind us that assumption of the physical body in the incarnation means that all levels of nature are assumed and therefore redeemed.[47] The problem with their claim, aside from making an unnecessary break with scripture and tradition, is that it fails to recognize the distinct evolutionary significance of the hominin lineage. In this lineage, something happens for the whole cosmos, but it happens *in this lineage*.[48] The effects are cosmic but the evolutionary basis is localized. At least up to the present, and at least for planet Earth (and thus for all we know), the cosmos attains consciousness only in the hominin lineage. Just when in that lineage? That we cannot say. But we can be reasonably confident that it occurs nowhere else.

So we agree with Rahner. We must "try to see man as the being in whom the basic tendency of matter to find itself in the spirit by self-transcendence arrives at the point where it definitely breaks through; thus in this way we may be in a position to regard man's being itself, from this view-point within the basic and total conception of the world. It is precisely this being of man, seen from *this* view-point, which – both by its highest, free and complete self-transcendence into God, made possible quite gratuitously by God, and by God's communication of himself – 'awaits' its own consummation and that of the world in what in Christian terms we call 'grace' and 'glory'."[49]

4. Unlimited Human Transformation

The incarnation includes all humanity, unifying all and also divinizing all without limit. Such grand claims are contained implicitly in the Ephesians text quoted above that speaks of God's plan to gather up all things in Christ. Here again we see the link between creation and incarnation. What happens in

---

[46] R. COLE-TURNER, "Incarnation Deep and Wide: A Response to Niels Gregersen," *Theology and Science* 11, no. 4 (2013): 424–435.

[47] Cf. N. H. GREGERSEN, "Deep Incarnation: Why Evolutionary Continuity Matters in Christology," *Toronto Journal of Theology* 26, no. 2 (2010): 173–188.

[48] N. H. GREGERSEN, "*Cur deus caro*: Jesus and the Cosmos Story," *Theology and Science* 11, no. 4 (2013): 370–393.

[49] RAHNER, "Evolutionary View," 160.

Christ happens in the whole of humanity. According to Brian Daley's summary, in Nyssa "the risen and transfigured human Christ is the one means by which the rest of the race can also participate in that same process of 'divinization' [...]."[50] Or in the words of Norman Russell: "The renewal of the human race is like a second creation carried out by the Creator, but this time from within. The unity of humankind, which Athanasius takes for granted, means that the whole of human nature is deified in principle when the human nature which the Logos assumed is deified by him."[51]

We find an echo of this in the popular writings of C. S. Lewis, whose *Mere Christianity* contains this description of the transformation God intends for individuals: "He will make the feeblest and filthiest of us into a god or goddess, dazzling, radiant, immortal creature, pulsating all through with such energy and joy and wisdom and love as we cannot now imagine, a bright stainless mirror which reflects back to God perfectly (though, of course, on a smaller scale) His own boundless power and delight and goodness."[52]

The key insight offered by Gregory of Nyssa, however, is that the transformation of human is not merely glorious but that it knows no end. Just as he insists that humans are undefined because we mirror the incomprehensible mystery of God, so he observes that our movement into that incomprehensible mystery can have no limit or endpoint. Nyssa, therefore, speaks instead of our *"being transformed from glory to glory*, and thus always improving and ever becoming more perfect by daily growth, and never arriving at any limit of perfection. For that perfection consists in our never stopping our growth in good, never circumscribing our perfection by any limitation."[53] Vladimir Lossky echoes this when he speaks of "[...] the unlimited vistas of the union of created beings with the Divinity."[54] Hart expands on it with these words: "And, no matter how far the soul ventures into the infinity of God, she will

---

[50] B. E. DALEY, S. J., "Divine Transcendence and Human Transformation: Gregory of Nyssa's Anti-Apollinarian Christology," *Modern Theology* 18, no. 4 (2002): 497–506 at 502.

[51] N. RUSSELL, *The Doctrine of Deification in the Greek Patristic Tradition* (Oxford: Oxford University Press, 2004), 172. The link between creation and incarnation is explicit in Rahner, who insists that "we are perfectly entitled to think of the creation and of the Incarnation, not as two disparate, adjacent acts of God '*ad extram*' which in the actual world are due to two quite separate original acts of God, but as two moments and phases in the real world of the unique, even though internally differentiated, process of God's self-renunciation and self-expression into what is other than himself," in Rahner, "Evolutionary View," 177–178.

[52] C. S. LEWIS, *Mere Christianity* (Grand Rapids, MI: Zondervan 2001), 174–175.

[53] J. DANIÉLOU and H. MUSURILLO (eds.), *From Glory to Glory: Texts from Gregory of Nyssa's Mystical Writings* (New York: Scribner, 1961), 51–52; italics in the original. R. WILLIAMS suggests that the idea of "unceasing advance" is Gregory's "most important contribution to Christian thought [...]" in *The Wound of Knowledge: Christian Spirituality from the New Testament to St. John of the Cross*, 2nd ed. (Cambridge, MA: Cowley Publications, 1991), 62.

[54] V. LOSSKY, "Redemption and Deification," *In the Image and Likeness of God*, ed. J. H. Erikson and T. E. Bird (Crestwood, NY: St. Vladimir's Seminary Press, 1974), 97–110, 97.

continue always to yearn for more of God's beauty, to hunger for his sweetness, nor will she ever find any end to the reality in which she moves [...]."[55]

In three respects, the incarnation is connected here with creation as mere rescue but as transformative completion. First, the incarnation adds to the completion of the evolutionary creation of humanity by making us one in our diversity, not by negating differences but by including all forms, expressions, cultures, and lives. Second, the incarnation is the pathway by which God creates the transfigured human, glorifying what is now unified. Third, it is the pathway by which God through a glorified humanity transfigures the whole creation. Andrew Louth speaks of some of this when he writes: "[...] deification is the fulfillment of creation." Recalling the theme of Ephesians 2, he continues: "One way of putting this is to think in terms of an arch stretching from creation to deification, representing what is and remains God's intention: the creation of the cosmos that, through humankind, is destined to share in the divine life, to be deified."[56]

The claim that humans are indefinable and the claim that our transformation is unlimited really amount to the same claim. As Rahner puts it, "the transcendence of man makes it clear that it would be wrong to define him, to delimit and put bounds to his possibilities."[57]

5. *Human Cosmic Creativity*

Even so, we must refrain from any hint that humanity is the pinnacle of creation or the reason why God creates. Science certainly does not support that. And theology objects more strongly still. Perhaps the greatest paradox of all is that because of the incarnation, Christianity cannot be anthropocentric. God is the center, and God's purposes extend beyond us to the whole creation. If God takes up our humanity and glorifies us, it not to elevate our sense of importance or to make us anything more than grateful and humble creatures able to hear and respond to the invitation to glorify, transfigure, and unite all things with God in Christ.

We human beings have lived for only a brief moment in the geological history of one small planet. In a cosmos of hundreds of billions of galaxies, each with hundreds of billions of suns, each on average having perhaps at least one planet, we are small indeed. Some doubt that technologically advanced human civilization will last very long. But if we do, what might we create? Will we

---

[55] HART, "Mirror," 550.
[56] A. LOUTH, "The Place of *Theosis* in Orthodox Theology," in *Partakers of the Divine Nature: The History and Development of Deification in the Christian Traditions*, ed. M.J. Christensen and J.A. Wittung (Cranbury, NJ: Rosemont Publishing, 2008), 34–35.
[57] RAHNER, "Incarnation," 110.

produce machines that are more intelligent than humans? Will they be our "last invention," as machines take over? Will we be needed anymore?[58] Will there be a future technological "singularity" that transforms matter not just to human-grade intelligence but to a truly transcendent phase, changing the very nature of the material universe?[59]

All these possibilities suggest that in the end, humanity will be irrelevant. We will either destroy ourselves or replace ourselves. We may be kind of a big deal on earth at the moment. But we are hardly the evolutionary apex of the cosmos. In light of the incarnation, however, we can see our significance as the pathway by which God may be transforming the whole creation. As Rahner puts it, "[…] the Incarnation appears as the necessary and permanent beginning of the divinization of the world as a whole."[60]

The idea of cosmic divinization or transfiguration is associated chiefly with the speculative theology of the seventh century theologian, Maximus the Confessor. Theologians such as the twentieth century Romanian scholar, Dumitru Stăniloae, have drawn on Maximus to develop a vision of cosmic transformation in which human creativity plays a small but important part. According to Stăniloae, "The world was created in order that man, with the aid of the supreme spirit, might raise the world up to a supreme spiritualization, and this to the end that human beings might encounter God within a world that had become fully spiritualized through their own union with God. The world is created as a field where, through the world, man's free work can meet God's free work with a view to the ultimate and total encounter that will come about between them."[61]

Stăniloae's vision of cosmic transformation reminds us perhaps of Teilhard de Chardin. Others will think of the writings of Ray Kurzweil, a brilliant inventor but a somewhat fringe thinker on the edge of today's transhumanist community. Almost as if he had read Maximus, Kurzweil makes these claims: "In the aftermath of the Singularity, intelligence, derived from its biological origins in human brains and its technological origins in human ingenuity, will begin to saturate the matter and energy in its midst."[62] Then the entire universe – whatever exactly that means in light of today's cosmology – will be

---

[58] B. JOY, "Why the future doesn't need us." *Wired* 8, no. 4 (2000): 238–262.

[59] R. KURZWEIL, *The Singularity is Near*, (London: Gerald Duckworth & Co, 2010). Cf. R. COLE-TURNER, "The Singularity and the Rapture: Transhumanist and Popular Christian Views of the Future," *Zygon* 47, no. 4 (2012): 777–796.

[60] RAHNER, "Evolutionary View," 160–161.

[61] D. STĂNILOAE, *The Experience of God: Orthodox Dogmatic Theology, Vol. 2, The World: Creation and Deification*, trans. I. Ionita and R. Barringer (Brookline, MA: Holy Cross Press, 2000), 59.

[62] KURZWEIL, *Singularity*, 21.

transformed. "Ultimately, the entire universe will become saturated with our intelligence. This is the destiny of the universe."[63]

The big difference between Kurzweil and Stăniloae is the role of God in the process. They agree that humanity and human technology play a role. For Kurzweil, any "God" involved in the process emerges only at the end, as a product of a universe saturated with intelligence. For Stăniloae, God is there, beginning and end, alpha and omega, the source and the destiny of all things differentiated and then unified.

Where Kurzweil speaks of a universe saturated with intelligence, Stăniloae speaks of its "complete spiritualization" and "perfect transparency." He writes: "For if man were the only one freely working within the world, he could not lead the world to a complete spiritualization, that is, to his own full encounter with God through the world. God makes use of his free working within the world in order to help man, so that through man's free work both he and the world may be raised up to God and so that, in cooperation with man, God may lead the world toward that state wherein it serves as a means of perfect transparency between man and himself."[64] In the cosmic vision of Stăniloae, humanity and thus the incarnation play a key role in the completion of the creation.

As Rahner observes, one of the theological implications of human evolutionary biology is that the era of advanced cultural sophistication and technology prowess has really only just begun. "Today we believe that we know a history of humanity which stretches several hundred times further back into the past than had been imagined in the old days, and we get the impression that, after a very long and up till now almost stagnant starting period, humanity has a history before it, a history whose future in this world has only just begun." This changes the way theology sees the incarnation. Rahner continues: "[…] whereas previously one had the impression that God had entered the world through the Incarnation of his Word in the evening of world-history, we now get the impression that (in terms of large periods) he came approximately at the moment when the history of man's active self-possession and of his knowing and active self-steering of history was just beginning."[65]

All this suggests that Christians need not be anxious theologically about the challenges to humanity that we face today. Our lack of definition as a species, our multiform origins, the prospect of human germline modification and enhancement, the unlimited possibilities for human transformation, even the

---

[63] Ibid., 29.
[64] Stăniloae, *Experience of God*, p. 59.
[65] Rahner, "Evolutionary View," 189. He continues by saying that "it is perfectly meaningful and understandable that the Incarnation stands at the beginning of this first really all-human period" (190).

prospect that human intelligence may give rise in time to a vastly greater form of intelligence [...] such things may spark our concerns for safety, for careful debate, and for complete transparency, and of course for social and economic justice and for environmental responsibility.

But none of these uncertainties should raise theological anxieties. In fact, it may turn out that those who seriously embrace the idea that the Creator's purposes for the creation are achieved through the incarnation may be among the least anxious of all. This humanity of ours may not be definable empirically or theologically. Its transformations may not be limited now or eschatologically. But in the end what we are and what we shall be is not ours to know or to control. It is all so much bigger than that.

Incarnate Humanity

DANIEL NELSON

1. Introduction

"God is only properly spoken about when we speak of him metaphorically. All non-metaphorical language about God is not even figurative language about him. This is the truth (and the plausible truth, on the aristotelian (sic) premiss that definitions should not make use of metaphors) of the otherwise deeply problematic statement: *deus definiri nequit* (God cannot be defined)."[1]

The perspectives Professor Cole-Turner offered and the integration of recent fossil discoveries with the recent genetic research I found to be fascinating, particularly as he was able to place these findings in relation to the incarnation. I offer here what I understood to be his main points. For section one, on evolutionary biology, he seemed to be arguing that recent evidence suggests two conclusions: 1) the idea that evolution is nonlinear and that this means that evolution takes place *with* rather than *from*, and 2) more importantly, this means that the lack of distinctions, the fact that it seems that humanity evolved as convergence and hybridization, makes a clear definition of humanity, from an evolutionary perspective, somewhat more difficult (if not impossible). In the second section, which looks forward towards the influences of technology, he made a point of distinguishing the transhumanist movements as typically focusing on individual enhancements rather than at the level of evolutionary speciation. But his point seems to remain essentially the same as in the first section: technology allows us to, as he says, "blur" the distinctions of what is identified as human (from chimeras to cyborgs) again, making it difficult, if not impossible, to arrive at a definition of humanity. And finally in the third section, which I understood to be the heart of his discussion, he makes five theological claims, which I will simply list here: human indefinability, human godlikeness, human unity, *unlimited* human transformation (which he directly connects with indefinability and godlikeness), and human cosmic creativity.

My questions are primarily directed at these theological claims. I want to focus on two areas of questioning. The first area has to do with methodolog-

---

[1] E. JÜNGEL, "Metaphorical Truth. Reflections on Theological Metaphor as a Contribution to a Hermeneutics of Narrative Theology," in *Theological Essays*, trans. J. Webster (New York: Bloomsbury T & T Clark, 2014), 60.

ical questions, or perhaps grammatical might be more accurate, to clarify the concepts (or ideas?) and how we are moving between them. The second area of questions is more material, focusing on the claim of indefinability. I think that your project of showing the relation and correlation of biological anthropology and theological anthropology through the incarnation hinges on this claim of indefinability. I will attempt to frame these questions regarding human indefinability in each of the other four claims.

2. Method and Grammar

First, the general methodological question refers primarily to fields of inquiry and grammatical usage of specific terms – or the usage of these terms as parts of different language games and contexts of application. Professor Cole-Turner makes a case for including biology in the theological indefinability of humanity, but I am wary of certain dangers of equivocation without clearer conceptual delineations between conversation partners. I think he highlights this difficulty and I think his paper is clearly working to address this very danger through a sort of inclusivity. I am hoping he could say more though. Allow me to elaborate.

Part of my confusion, I think, is that it is easy to equivocate on terms like 'creation', or 'humanity', or 'evolve/transcend' – which is problematic, especially given the content and distinctions between scientific inquiry and theological reasoning. So, what precisely is being referred to by 'creation'?[2] Is it the act of creating? If so, then does the grammar of creation language indicate that we are properly referring to the one who creates? Or is it the creation itself (thing/s created)? In which case, are we properly referring to the material universe (specifically not calling it a cosmos or world, etc., which indicate at least two levels of interpretation)? Or are we indeed referring to the cosmos as the ordered whole by the term 'creation'? Or possibly some combination of all of these?

The same grammatical situation is present in discussions of an idea of humanity. Is the discussion about the concept or the idea of humanity? Is it about what it *means* to be human? Is it about what a human *is*? How a human should act? Is this an ontological question, or an empirical (ontic) question? What are the contrast terms? For instance, how do human beings relate to ideas of humanity. Not all humans are humane, and we speak of a lack of humanity when speaking of other human beings – but what then are we ref-

---

[2] For further reference, look at Pierce's semiotics for instance, with the triad of sign, object, and interpretant.

erencing?[3] It seems clear that while the grammar of biological inquiry into the concept of humanity and the grammar of theological inquiry do have significant areas of overlap, the fundamental presuppositions and therefore the questions that are trying to be answered are not the same – and this is born out in where the answers to these questions are sought.[4]

As such, I find Professor Cole-Turner's emphasis on the incarnation to be very helpful, especially with the prominence of the idea that in the incarnation humanity is unified. The notion of biological unity is significant (genetically as one species), but I am not positive that is what Paul is talking about in (for instance) Galatians 3.[5] Paul's emphasis in chapter 3 on unity is not biological in the sense of genetics, but in the sense of inheritance – who is in God's family, and who will inherit the Spirit, and that in the Spirit, all of the distinctions that we use to distinguish us (so called accidents) are not what define our being. As Eberhard Jüngel suggests, following Luther, "justification is the real definition of human being [...]. In its formal aspect, 'justification' means

---

[3] For instance, note the different distinctions that Dalferth makes – what is the contrast term to human? I. U. DALFERTH, *Creatures of Possibility: The Theological Basis of Human Freedom* (Grand Rapids, MI: Baker Academic, 2016), 23. "Without the distinction between God and humanity, a human being could not be considered as a creature: a creature is that which is not God but would not exist without God. Without the distinction between human and animal, we are liable to lose sight of the fact that a human being is one creation among other, each of which is to be appreciated for its own distinctiveness and uniqueness. And without the distinction between one human being and another, we are at risk of seeing the fundamental theological issue as the distinction between human and animal life (human and nonhuman) and not as the distinction between humane and inhumane life (humaneness and inhumaneness). Yet the latter is the primary concern of the theological debate over our understanding of the humanness of humans."

[4] See further, DALFERTH, 22. "Questions of orientation are quite different from questions of explanation, and they call for different answers. Whereas questions of explanation relate to the why ('Why does something occur?') or the how ('Why does something occur in this manner?') of a phenomenon, questions of orientation focus on the conduct of human life when dealing with the phenomena, not on the phenomena themselves."

[5] "Now before faith came, we were imprisoned and guarded under the law until faith would be revealed. Therefore, the law was our disciplinarian until Christ came, so that we might be justified by faith. But now that faith has come, we are no longer subject to a disciplinarian, for in Christ Jesus you are all children of God through faith. As many of you as were baptized into Christ have clothed yourselves with Christ. There is no longer Jew or Greek, there is no longer slave or free, there is no longer male and female; for all of you are one in Christ Jesus. And if you belong to Christ, then you are Abraham's offspring, heirs according to the promise. My point is this: heirs, as long as they are minors, are no better than slaves, though they are the owners of all the property; but they remain under guardians and trustees until the date set by the father. So, with us; while we were minors, we were enslaved to the elemental spirits of the world. But when the fullness of time had come, God sent his Son, born of a woman, born under the law, in order to redeem those who were under the law, so that we might receive adoption as children. And because you are children, God has sent the Spirit of his Son into our hearts, crying, "Abba! Father!" So, you are no longer a slave but a child, and if a child then also an heir, through God." (Gal. 3:23–4:7, NRSV).

that it is through the event of divine justice that humans being first become themselves: the *righteousness of God* which occurs in the being of Jesus Christ constitutes our humanity."[6]

This mention of the Spirit leads to the next part of these grammatical questions. Professor Cole-Turner clearly is associating this view of the incarnation as completing creation, as one work, and such a view has a long and significant history, as he points out. But how does this view relate to, say a more Augustinian perspective (in the way of a salvation history) or just a non-theosis soteriology? It seems that the concept of incarnation (biblically) arises in the context of the resurrection of Jesus who is identified as the Christ, as the son of God (read the tradition backwards – begin with the resurrection, then death, then incarnation).[7] The narrative surrounding the incarnation, the cross, and the resurrection is one of sin and salvation. I am curious how Professor Cole-Turner integrates these other very traditional theological concepts (sin and salvation, justification and grace, and even the *imago dei*) into the correlation he is making of evolutionary biology and transhumanism to the incarnation.

From these general methodological questions, I would like to draw attention to his main theses and ask a few more specific questions.

3. Human Indefinability

This claim is the hinge of his argument. It is the danger with which questions into the biological and evolutionary origins of human beings presents us, and it is the danger of future technological meddling – clear distinctions are blurred, and there is, in a sense, a radical openness as the result of the lack of definition. The suggestion he seems to be arguing for throughout not just this section but his whole paper is that the limits of empirical research into what it means to be human, and our human origins have analogous complimentary theological correlates. The issue of indefinability with which he starts conveys this point beautifully: empirically there is no clear first human, there are no hard limits in either our past or our future at which humans first ought to be counted *as* humans. The usage of the incarnation then becomes the link that assuages the dangers of indefinability, and in fact make it a central aspect

---

[6] E. JÜNGEL, "Humanity in Correspondence to God: Remarks on the Image of God as a Basic Concept in Theological Anthropology," in *Theological Essays*, trans. John Webster (New York: Bloomsbury T & T Clark, 2014), 133.

[7] I. U. DALFERTH, *Crucified and Resurrected: Restructuring the Grammar of Christology*, trans. J. Bennett (Grand Rapids, MI: Baker Academic, 2015), xvi–xvii. In this passage he discusses his "hermeneutical strategy" of looking for the question/s that a text is seeking to answer. One of the initial questions of this process is put thus: "What is the problem posed by the resurrection confession of the first Christians that is answered by reference to the cross?"

of what it means to be human. Theologically, he suggests that "we are *inherently* indefinable" and I think the other two claims 1) about time (now and in the future, and 2) why (because we mirror the divine) help to unfold what is meant by inherently. And as conversation partners, it is hard to think of better or more influential partners then St. Gregory of Nyssa and Karl Rahner. But I do have some questions about the idea of indefinability that I am sure Professor Cole-Turner can help me think through.

I must admit that indefinability has always struck me as somewhat problematic – or at least I get confused when the term is used. In a sort of adolescent manner, I want to ask impudent questions, like, "If it is indefinable, then how are we talking about it?" which is generally unhelpful. I very much recognize the importance of the apophatic tradition reminding us especially that when we are talking about God, everything we say will fail to fully to capture the referent. But it is implied that there is a referent – we are at the very least pointing. And if humans are indefinable because they mirror the divine, I want to know if more can be said. It seems that the idea of claiming humanity is inherently indefinable because God is indefinable seems to be highly apophatic. Our inability to provide a complete definition of God would seem to be no small part of what indicates that we are indeed trying to refer to the divine. However, Wittgenstein asks a question about having a clear picture of a blurry drawing as well as a blurry picture of a clear drawing. What does that look like?[8] He continues by pointing out that a lack of a *fixed* meaning does not indicate the lack of a definition, or the inability to use a word.[9] It seems that the level of and clarity of delineations and definitions is at least partly dependent on *what* is being identified. As such, I wonder what is meant by God being indefinable. It seems there are numerous definitions, from God speaking to Moses,[10] to the incarnation – Jesus's words in John 14:9, "Jesus said to him, 'Have I been with you all this time, Philip, and you still do not know me? Whoever has seen me has seen the Father. How can you say, 'Show us the Father?'" (NRSV). Or John's claim that God is love.[11] Or even

---

[8] L. WITTGENSTEIN, *Philosophische Untersuchungen* = *Philosophical Investigations*, ed. P. M. S. Hacker and J. Schulte, trans. G. E. M. Anscombe, P. M. S. Hacker, and J. Schulte, rev. 4th ed. (West Sussex, U.K.: Wiley-Blackwell, 2009), 40–41, §76–77.

[9] WITTGENSTEIN, 42, §79. "And this can be expressed as follows: I use the name 'N' without a *fixed* meaning. But that impairs its use as little as the use of a table is impaired by the fact that it stands on four legs instead of three and so sometimes wobbles. "Should it be said that I'm using a word whose meaning I don't know, and so am talking nonsense? ..." (The fluctuation of scientific definitions: what today counts as an observed concomitant of phenomenon A will tomorrow be used to define 'A'.)"

[10] "God said to Moses, 'I am who I am.' He said further, 'Thus you shall say to the Israelites, "I am has sent me to you."'" (Ex. 3:14, NRSV)

[11] "Beloved, let us love one another, because love is from God; everyone who loves is born of God and knows God. Whoever does not love does not know God, for God is love. God's

much later, Anselm's idea of that than which nothing greater can be thought (a negative definition), or Aquinas's idea, or Luther's claim that a god is what one trusts and believes in.[12] What positive or negative attributes/characteristics are we hoping to draw attention to? Does the characteristic of indefinability mean that we cannot say anything definitely? Does it mean we are limited to a pointing? But more importantly, I want to turn the question the other way: What does the incarnation tell us about what it means to be human? It seems that the incarnation as a moment of revelation functions to tell us about both who we are and who we ought to be, and in fact humanity takes its definition from this event of revelation (at least theologically), rather than trying to come to an autonomous understanding of humanity and applying it to Jesus.

Finally, it is significant to identify part of the content of the revelation (we could possibly say creation) of humanity in Jesus Christ as a humanity that is not in the right relation to God. As a revelation, this can only be seen from the perspective of Christ's own humanity as properly related. In the end, human indefinability, theologically, seems to stem from the fact of sin – the absurdity of not relating properly to God (as creature to creator), and in so doing, falling into nothingness – the other is indefinable because there is *no-thing* to define. Theologically, the importance of the incarnation is intimately concerned with both sin and salvation, and the incarnation in fact orients us to this situation such that we can indeed become definable as human (as what it means to be human) because God shows what it is to be human.

4. Human Godlikeness

And I think Professor Cole-Turner does exactly this – he offers an idea (definition) of God and applies this to human beings. While he briefly touches on the image of God language in this section, he rightly focuses on the God that is to be imaged in humanity. He asks not only what is God like, but "which one must we become?" With the clear focus on the incarnation, and working

---

love was revealed among us in this way: God sent his only Son into the world so that we might live through him. In this is love, not that we loved God but that he loved us and sent his Son to be the atoning sacrifice for our sins. Beloved, since God loved us so much, we also ought to love one another. No one has ever seen God; if we love one another, God lives in us, and his love is perfected in us." (1 John 4:7–12, NRSV)

[12] M. LUTHER, *The Large Catechism of Dr. Martin Luther 1529*, ed. K. I. Stjerna, *The Annotated Luther Study Edition* (Minneapolis, MN: Fortress Press, 2016), 300. "What does 'to have a god' mean, or what is God?" Answer: God is that in which we are to look for all good and in which we are to find refuge in all need. Therefore, to have a god is nothing else than to trust and believe in that one with your whole heart. As I have often said, it is the trust and faith of the heart alone that make both God and an idol [...]. Anything on which your heart relies and depends, I say, that is really your God."

from the kenotic tradition, the argument seems to be that because of the incarnation, we see in Jesus Christ a God who empties himself and by emptying himself, unites and makes us conform to him. He continues by agreeing with Gorman that "'Kenosis is theosis'" and that, as such, we are most human then when we act like God – kenotically. Finally, this kenotic incarnation is linked intrinsically as the completion of creation.

Previously, the argument was for human indefinability because of God's indefinability. However, it seems that by defining God in this way, as the one who empties himself, the definition of God (who was indefinable – or at least traditionally only negatively definable) becomes the definition of what it means to be human: we are most human when we mirror the divine in this particular way – we empty ourselves. In other words, I am wondering how to properly relate these two claims of indefinability and of the kenotic God, as well as how to relate this from questions of what we are as human beings, to questions of what it means to be human, or humane.

Moreover, I want to know what this emptying consists of. If I am indeed to be Christlike and therefore human in the act of self-emptying, I want to know what this self consists of or of what I, as a self, am emptying from myself. In other words, the kenotic understanding of incarnation is not the whole story. And again, this is where the theological issues of sin and salvation arise, what is the goal or purpose of self-emptying? The Gospel narrative locates that goal in God's love, which by extension, is self-emptying, for the purpose of restoring the relationship between God's self and his human beings (his creation). This is the moment of reconciliation, for the purposes of redemption. But if there is such an "infinite qualitative difference" between God and humans, in what way do we mirror the divine by self-emptying?

5. Human Unity

From indefinability and godlikeness, Professor Cole-Turner moves to human unity, claiming that the incarnation does not presuppose human unity, but rather creates it – human unity is the consequence of the incarnation. I think that is a beautifully made point. "Christ makes us one" by uniting us with the divine.[13] Here though, his main concern seems to be what constitutes and counts as human empirically by including in our indefinable understanding of humanity "the full history and diversity of the hominin lineage."[14]

---

[13] R. COLE-TURNER, "Transcendent Humanity: What if the Incarnation Really Matters," in this volume, 133–158.
[14] Ibid.

I am curious about how to connect these two claims. If it is indeed the incarnation that identifies what it means to be human – Jesus Christ *is* human – then the unity doesn't seem to be particularly empirical. It seems as if we are moving back and forth between anthropology and theological anthropology wherein each seem to be working to make different points. In one case what a human is, and in another, what it means to be a human – or the humanity of humans. I appreciate the call for a greater inclusivity of what is meant by "all," but again, I am not sure that the referent is the same in each case.

Moreover, I am curious about the pragmatic "cash value" of extending what is meant by all to the entire lineage and wonder where we really ought to stop – surely the lineage can be traced past the common chimp/human ancestor, and that seems (maybe with a bit of stretching the concepts) to be included in the lineage.

My final question regarding the issue of unity will hopefully tie in with his fourth point as well, regarding unlimited human transformation. He presents the argument that evolutionary biology and particularly the evolution of *homo sapiens* is the process of divergence and convergence and hybridization. This activity of human evolution continuing forward seems to lose the name evolution and be identified as 'transcendence.' What does it mean for the idea of continued evolution that we are a unity? How do we transcend or continue to evolve if there is nothing to evolve with (other groups of humans etc.)? What role does technology play in this? In this case, the ideas of unity theologically and unity biologically seem to be at odds (i.e., how does the historicity of the incarnation, especially as the completion of creation work with continued evolution and transcendence?).

6. Unlimited Human Transformation

Again, as the link between the incarnation and creation is stressed, the unifying action of the incarnation and the limitless (unlimited) scope of divinization (due to the infinity of God, "in whom we live and move and have our being") is established. If God is infinite, and humans mirror the divine, there can be, as Gregory of Nyssa points out, no arriving at a limit of perfection. Thus, at the end of this section he helpfully acknowledges that human indefinability and unlimited transformation are essentially the same claim.

As such, my questions regarding indefinability arise again, as do some of the grammatical issues that I began with regarding what is meant by creation. Specifically, I am curious as to how unlimited transformation is related to the other parts of the Christian conceptual web, particularly the idea of *new creation*.[15]

---

[15] "So, if anyone is in Christ, there is a new creation: everything old has passed away; see, everything has become new!" 2 Cor. 5:17 (NRSV).

If the incarnation is the completion of creation, then where does new creation fit, or take place? Furthermore, as mentioned above, how does evolution connect to transformation, and/or to new creation?

Finally, if we mirror the divine, that mirroring seems to be of a different sort than a biological mirroring. As such, how do we have unlimited transformation biologically at an evolutionary species level? And how do we continue to evolve or transcend when the some of the key evolutionary factors of natural selection are negated by our technology? This is a silly example, but I have a two-year-old and we were watching WALL-E, the Pixar movie. The movie shows that humans have become so dependent on technology that bones shrink and they begin to take on characteristics of whales. In other words, transcendence and evolution seem to imply that life will become better, that we will become better, and by shifting between the ontic and the ontological, I wonder how that can be guaranteed. Wouldn't it be necessary for some sort of diversification to maintain the manner in which we evolve *with*? There is a sort of odd bias at play wherein we might take offense at the idea (although almost entirely discredited now) that early humans were "knuckle-draggers," but it is a feat and an enviable state to be a brain in a vat (even if that vat is now a computer). Does the incarnation have anything to say about our potential biological transformation? How does this work with the idea that what is not assumed is not saved? Is the form of the human an accident unrelated to our indefinable essence? Why did God then choose to be incarnate as human, and not as what we might become?

7. Cosmic Creativity

For this last section, Professor Cole-Turner reminds us that humanity is the means, not the end of God's creative purposes. In this way he suggests that through the incarnation, which creates human unity, human godlikeness, and results in unlimited human transformation, God seeks to also transform the cosmos: a cosmic theosis that takes place through human beings. Significantly, he also points out that in terms of history, humanity has occupied a tremendously brief moment on a relatively small planet, making use of Rahner to point out that in this sense, the incarnation is possibly closer to the beginning than the end of human history.

My question here is again of the same type. How does this understanding of humanity and cosmic creativity reflect, say, the eschatology of Paul? Or how does this relate to Hegel's Spirit conscious of itself: Absolute Spirit? How does this relate, again, to the new creation? It seems that if humanity is simply the means of divinizing the cosmos, then by extension, the incarnation is also simply a means – and this seems like it might affect views of the Trinity, or in other words, an understanding of the relationality of God.

8. Conclusion

I have expressed two general directions of questions, in hopes of engendering more dialog. The first direction has to do with methodology and grammar. The second direction has to do with the material content and what I understood to be the hinge of Professor Cole-Turner's argument: human indefinability. The dangers presented by the conclusions of evolutionary biology and the possibilities of future transcendence (indefinability) are met with the theological notion of human indefinability as well through the idea of mirroring the *divine* indefinability. Essentially, my question is whether or not we must indeed accept the biological and technological conclusions of indefinability as normative for our theological idea of humanity. If theology is to be an orientational activity and not an empirical science, then the task is not to deny or negate the findings of evolutionary biology, but rather to see those findings in a new way. In other words, what is the controlling framework for how we ask our questions? Do we allow biology to determine how and what we can say theologically about the human person? Or do we let theology inform us what it *means* to be a human person, through revelation in the incarnation of Jesus Christ?

III. Transhumanism

Human Flourishing in the Age of Technology

Hava Tirosh-Samuelson

1. Introduction

This conference asks us to ponder contemporary challenges to the idea of humanity posed from four directions. The first challenge comes from biological and neurophysiological research that dissolves the clear-cut distinction between humans and other animals. The second challenge comes from rapid technological development and the belief that humanity can perfect itself by means of technology, an ideology articulated by transhumanists, extropians, and posthumanists. The third challenge comes from awareness of human cultural diversity and the realization that the idea of humanity is not a biological fact but a normative ideal that can be used to exclude, marginalize, and oppress those who are in some way considered less than "human." And the fourth and final challenge is theoretical: in a secular age it is meaningless to distinguish between "God" and "humanity," between "creature" and "Creator," since these are all but social constructs that do not correspond to extra-mental reality. Today human technological creativity allows humans to "play God," namely, to do things that were previously ascribed to God. In light of these challenges the conference organizers have asked us to ponder whether humanity has become an endangered idea.

One crucial challenge to humanity, however, is conspicuously missing from the above list of challenges. I refer to the ecological challenge which threatens the very future of humanity as a biological species. The ecological challenge compels us to confront the core paradox of the human condition today. On the one hand, humanity as a species celebrates a seemingly unlimited power as humans now control and impact every ecosystem permanently and irreversibly. Earth scientists have dubbed our age "The Anthropocene," the age in which humanity became a geological force and the boundary between "humanity" and "nature" has collapsed.[1] But on the other hand, in the Age of the Anthro-

---

[1] The literature on the Anthropocene is quite extensive. For overviews see I. Angus, *Facing the Anthropocene: Fossil Capitalism and the Crisis of Earth System* (New York: Monthly Review Press, 2016); C. Bonnheuil and J. B. Fressoz, *The Shock of the Anthropocene* (New York: Verso, 2017); S. L. Lewis and M. A. Maslin, *The Human Planet: How We Created the Anthropocene* (London: Yale University Press, 2018).

pocene the very existence of the human species on Earth has become uncertain due to widespread environmental degradation brought about by human behavior. We now live in the midst of a massive ecological crisis evident in climate change, extreme weather events, desertification, loss of biodiversity, retreat of glaciers, rising sea levels, loss of fisheries and forests, acidification of oceans, pollution of air, water, and soil, and numerous other features of environmental degradation. The Anthropocene is no temporary crisis which we can somehow muddle through by relying on human technoscientific ingenuity. Rather, the Anthropocene signifies a new condition that compels us to make momentous technological, economic, social, political legal, and moral choices that will determine the future of all life on Earth.[2] As the British naturalist, Sir David Attenborough, put it at the World Economic Forum in Davos in 2020: the Holocene epoch, namely "the 12,000 year-period of climatic stability that allowed humans to settle, farm and create civilization," is over [...]. "The Garden of Eden is no more" because we have wrecked the natural world.

There has been much discussion about the causes of our ecological crisis. Western culture since the 17th century has profoundly changed with the rise of mechanistic philosophy that brought about the disenchantment of nature. In the modern world view, as Alister McGrath critically put it, "humanity is the creator and arbiter of values and is free to interpret and manipulate nature as it pleases."[3] The modern Enlightenment project posited a disenchanted and objectified nature, appearing "in the guise of meaningless matter, which was to be overcome and mastered for human purposes and not to be imitated, propitiated or religiously celebrated."[4] The Enlightenment ideology of perpetual "progress" legitimized the exploitation of nature which was further exacerbated by capitalism, colonialism and imperialism that regarded nature and subjugated people as mere "resources" for empowerment and enrichments of Western national-states.[5] Within three centuries, the accumulated impact of modernity has yielded the massive environmental collapse characteristic of the Anthropocene. Thus, we are now faced with the conundrum that the presumed unlimited power of humanity has undermined the ability of human life to flourish and has made the future of humanity as a biological species profoundly uncertain.

---

[2] See J. S. DRYZEK, R. B. NORGAARD and D. SCHLOSBERG, *The Oxford Handbook of Climate Change and Society* (Oxford: Oxford University Press, 2011).

[3] A. MCGRATH, *The Renenchantment of Nature: The Denial of Religion and the Ecological Crisis* (New York: Doubleday, 2002), 54.

[4] S. VOGEL, *Against Nature: The Concept of Nature in Critical Theory* (Albany, NY: SUNY Press, 1996).

[5] See for example, P. ANKER, *Imperial Ecology: Environmental Order in the British Empire, 1895–1945* (Cambridge, MA: Harvard University Press, 2001); D. HEDRICK, *The Tentacles of Progress: Technology Transfer in the Age of Imperialism, 1850–1940* (Oxford: Oxford University Press, 1988).

The paradox of utmost power and profound vulnerability is evident as well in the systematic reflections about the meaning of being human. These reflections began in the ancient world in the context of pondering the meaning of *eudemonia*, normally translated as 'happiness' but better understood as 'flourishing.' For the ancients, flourishing was not a subjective condition but a pattern of life that could be objectively determined to be appropriate to our nature as human beings. The ancient discourse on human flourishing evolved in the Middle Ages among Christians, Muslims and Jews, but was given a different interpretation in Renaissance humanism, the educational movement that celebrated the uniqueness and dignity of humanity and that gave us the *studia humanitatis*, or what we call the humanities. Today, as we all know, both the ideology of humanism and the study of the humanities are under severe duress, almost on the brink of extinction. Critiqued by postmodern and postcolonial scholars, 'humanism' has become to be viewed negatively as intellectually untenable and socially harmful. Not surprisingly, the humanities have lost their prestige, funding, identity, and public purpose, and humanists are having difficult time gaining the respect of other disciplines.[6] In academic institutions and public discourse, humanists and the humanities are largely ignored or marginalized by scientists, engineering, and computer specialists who are currently regarded as the arbiters of truth and the priests of knowledge about what it means to be human and how humanity should move forward in its perpetual march of progress and innovation. In the technological Age of the Anthropocene, then, the study of the humanities has collapsed as the meaning of being human became ever more contested.

This paper focuses on the technological ethos of the Anthropocene as manifested in the ideology of transhumanism. Transhumanism seeks to enhance humanity by means of technology so as to bring about the posthuman phase in the evolution of the human species. Put differently, transhumanism is accelerated evolution by means of human intervention. Transhumanism, I would argue, posits a certain understanding of human flourishing, which is the focus of my critique. To properly understand the transhumanism's view of human flourishing, I begin with a brief exposition of the discourse on human flourishing from antiquity to the present. In this dialectical story transhumanism can be seen as extension and even radicalization of Enlightenment rationalism as well as an outcome of the postmodern critique of the Enlightenment. In the second section of the talk, I explain how transhumanism has contributed to making humanity an endangered idea by envisioning and advocating the demise of the biological human species and its replacement by super-intelligent machines.

---

[6] H. TIROSH-SAMUELSON, "In Praise of Human Dignity: The Humanities in the Age of Big Data," *On Education: Journal for Research and Debate*, 2:1 (2018), (https://doi.org/10.17899/on_ed.2018.2.4) (4/22/2022).

Focusing on the two main features of transhumanism – human enhancement and human-machine interface – I expose the shortcomings of transhumanism as a vision of human flourishing. In the third part of the talk, I offer an outline for an alternative approach to human flourishing, one that is rooted in the Jewish religious tradition but that draws its inspiration from Aristotelianism, environmentalism, dialogical philosophy, and feminism. I argue that if we wish to respond to the ecological crisis so as to ensure the future of the human species on Earth, it is necessary to reinterpret the idea of humanity in post-secular, pluralistic, embodied, and relational way. Transhumanism, in my view, does not offer us a sustainable vision for the technological Age of the Anthropocene.

2. Human Flourishing and the Idea of Humanity: A Brief Genealogy

Transhumanism traces its intellectual roots to Renaissance humanism, but the transhumanist interpretation of Renaissance humanism is deficient. To correctly understand Renaissance humanism, we should start the story not in fifteenth century but in ancient Greece where the connection between human well-being and virtue, especially the virtue of *humanitas*, was first established. *Humanitas* was the Latin translation of the Greek concept of *philanthropia* (namely, loving what makes us human) which in the antiquity was inseparable from an educational program (*paideia*) of the (male) citizen of the Greek polis. The Greek *paideia* was to produce the morally good person who possessed the virtues (arête), or excellences of character. In the *Nicomachean Ethics* Aristotle gave us the most systematic analysis of the connection between character, virtue, and human flourishing (*eudaimonia*). The term 'flourishing' is a better translation of *eudaimonia* because it is dynamic rather than static, it has a developmental aspect, and it is construed both as a process and as achievement. Human beings flourish as do plants or animals but flourishing consists not only of physical development "but also of intentionality, experience, and culture."[7]

In the *Nicomachean Ethics* Aristotle made it clear that human flourishing is not a subjective feeling or a psychological state but an objective state of affairs about the wellbeing of species. Flourishing refers to a pattern of living that pertains to one's life as a whole over a long period of time.[8] Douglas Rasmussen, a Neo-Aristotelian, aptly explains the Aristotelian view of human flourishing saying this:

---

[7] J. KLEINIG and N. G. EVANS, "Human Flourishing, Human Dignity, and Human Rights," *Law and Philosophy* 32, no. 5 (2013): 539–564.

[8] Secondary literature on Aristotle's analysis of Eudaimonia is massive and cannot be cited here. For a summary see TIROSH-SAMUELSON, *Happiness in Premodern Judaism: Virtue, Knowledge and Well-Being* (Cincinnati, OH: HUC Press, 2003), 9–54.

"human flourishing is an activity, an actuality, and an end (or function) [...] flourishing is to be found in action. It is not something static. These activities are those that both express and produce in a human being an actualization of potentialities that are specific to its natural kind. Finally, these activities also constitute the achievements of a human being's natural end or *telos*. Human flourishing is that-for-the-sake-of- which human conduct is done, and though flourishing is dependent on human agency for its achievement, it does not depend on such agency for its status as the ultimate end."[9]

In the Aristotelian schema flourishing is the final good of human life, the good that all human beings seek, but most people mistakenly identify Eudaimonia either with the life of pleasure derived from gratification of bodily desires or with honor that other people impute (or what we today will call 'fame'). In contrast, Aristotle shows that true human flourishing depends on the cultivation of character. Character, as Nancy Sherman put it, "has to do with a person's enduring traits: attitudes, sensibilities, and beliefs – that affects how a person sees, acts, and indeed lives."[10] The virtues are those excellences of character which, like skills, are acquired through habitual practice. To flourish as a human being, one must become virtuous.

Since I have analyzed Aristotle's analysis of human flourishing elsewhere, I will not repeat it here.[11] Let me only note that Aristotle has left for posterity a very ambiguous legacy that resulted in an ongoing debate about his vision of human happiness.[12] According to the "inclusive" interpretation, human flourishing, or happiness, is "an activity of the complete life in accordance with complete virtue," which means that the flourishing life consists of a range of moral and intellectual virtues (e. g., generosity, temperance and courage) as well as the more down-to-earth qualities of wit, humor and conviviality and social goods such as wealth and friends. To flourish as a human being, one must cultivate the virtuous character by acting in the social sphere and by interacting with other persons. Human flourishing occasionally includes contemplation of philosophy truths, but the activity of contemplation does not constitute the ideal life. In contrast, the "exclusive" interpretation holds that human flourishing consists exclusively in the activity of contemplation. Aristotle states that "the good for man is activity of soul in accordance with virtue, and if there is more than one virtue, according to the best and most perfect."[13] The most

---

[9] D. B. BAUMGARTEN, "Human Flourishing and the Appeal to Human Nature," *Social Philosophy and Policy Foundation* (1999): 1–43.

[10] N. SHERMAN, *The Fabric of Character: Aristotle's Theory of Virtue* (Oxford: Clarendon Press, 1991), 1.

[11] TIROSH-SAMUELSON, *Happiness in Premodern Judaism: Virtue, Knowledge and Well-Being* (Cincinnati: Hebrew Union College Press, 2003).

[12] See R. KRAUT, *Aristotle on the Human Good* (Princeton: Princeton University Press, 1991).

[13] ARISTOTLE, *Nicomachean Ethics*, I:7 1097a26; 43 (https://www.perseus.tufts.edu/hopper/text?doc=Perseus%3Atext%3A1999.01.0053%3Abekker+page%3D1097a%3Abekker+line%3D25) (4/21/2022).

perfect aspects of human being are the speculative intellect and contemplation is its excellence. All other human virtues and activities should be undertaken for the sake of this one activity, which constitutes human perfection.

Since Western discourse on human flourishing from antiquity to contemporary transhumanism is indebted to Aristotle, it is important to note that for Aristotle human flourishing is an *objective state rooted in the teleological structure of reality and nature of human species*. Human flourishing requires a conscious effort to cultivate the virtues, the stable character traits that direct us toward the good. A human being can flourish only if the rational aspect of the soul governs the irrational aspects through habitual practice that brings about the mean in emotions and actions. The flourishing life is thus predicated on self-mastery and self-control rather than on an impulsive gratification of bodily needs or emotional craving. Most importantly human flourishing takes place in a social context rather than in isolation, but it must include a certain measure of philosophical activity; without some contemplation of truths, we cannot be fully human. Finally, the happy person is the well-rounded person who engages in philosophy while living political life.

The Aristotelian approach would dominate Western reflection on human well-being for the following centuries, but the philosophical schools of the Hellenistic world – Cynicism, Epicureanism and Stoicism – did so not within the structure of the self-contained Greek polis but within empires whose diverse population was uninvolved in the political process.[14] Whereas Aristotle held that human happiness requires first the well-functioning society, the Hellenistic philosophical schools focused on the well-being of the individual with little regard to politics and civic activity. They were all familiar with Aristotle's analysis of human flourishing but developed their theories independently of the Peripatetic school. For the Cynics, moral virtue was sufficient for *eudaimonia* which was equated with a disposition of independence or freedom from worldly needs and passions. For the Epicureans, the ultimate goal of human life was the life of untroubledness (*ataraxia*) or tranquility, a state of mind of the happy person, a part of happiness but not happiness itself. Happiness itself was conveyed in language of private contentment in negative forms. And for the Stoics *eudaimonia* was to be conducted with reference to a universal cosmic Nature, the ordering principle of all the particular entities encom-

---

[14] See A. LONG, "Hellenistic Ethics and Philosophical Power," in *Hellenistic History and Culture*, ed. P. Green (Berkeley, CA: University of California Press, 1993), 143–147: M. C. NUSSBAUM, *The Therapy of Desire: Theory and Practice in Hellenistic Ethics* (Princeton, NJ: Princeton University Press, 1994), chaps. 8–13; T. H. IRWIN, "Stoic and Aristotelian Conceptions of Happiness," in *The Norms of Nature: Studies in Hellenistic Ethics*, ed. M. Schofield and G. Striker (Cambridge: Cambridge University Press, 1986), 205–244; G. STRIKER, *Essays on Hellenistic Epistemology and Ethics* (Cambridge: Cambridge University Press, 1996).

passed therein."[15] The Stoics retained the equation of virtue with knowledge, but they defined the content of the virtues in epistemic terms. The Stoics radically internalized morality and *eudaimonia*: the goal of the happy life is the "absence of passions" because they manifest mistaken judgements by the ruling reason. The goal of the Stoic sage was to extirpate these "excessive impulses by reasoning correctly about their true value.

The Stoic philosophers of the Roman period (e. g., Cicero, Seneca, Epictetus and Marcus Aurelius) posited a universalist ethos based on unity or brotherhood of mankind, and universal norms of divine physics and natural law that apply to the inhabited cosmos as a whole. For the Stoics the true polis was the cosmos that embodies logos or Nature; the earthly polis and political constitutions are dismissed as ridden with vice and error. On Earth the true citizen is the wise man, the Stoic sage; all others are "exiles, enemies and unjust and lawless." The Stoics added the virtue of *humanitas* to the cluster of virtues that comprised the traditional unwritten Roman code of conduct. Cicero elaborated on the meaning of *humanitas* when he described the formation of the ideal orator who is active in public service. For Cicero *humanitas* was the character trait that enabled a Roman citizen to interact with, care and understand the needs of conquered people who were clearly viewed as less than the Roman citizen. As Peter Gay explains, for Cicero,

"*humanitas* was a style of thought, not a formal doctrine. It asserted man's importance as a cultivated being, in control of his moral universe. The man who practiced *humanitas* was confident of his worth, courteous to others, decent in his social conduct, and active in his political role. He was a man, moreover, who faced life with courageous skepticism: he knows that the consolations of popular religion are for more credulous beings than himself, that life is uncertain, and that sturdy pessimism is superior to self-deceptive optimism. Man becomes man as he refines himself; he even becomes godlike."[16]

Stoicism thus laid the ground for interpreting the virtue of *humanitas* in religious terms, but it is important to note that the discourse on humanity was simultaneously inclusive and exclusive: 'humanity' signifies what humans have in common with each other despite cultural differences, but some humans are endowed with *humanitas* more than others, and true humans are always male rather than female.

With the Christianization of the Roman Empire, reflections on human flourishing will be given a new turn. The Platonic strand of the Christian discourse, articulated by Augustine, viewed the human self as an immaterial soul

---

[15] J. M. BRYANT, *Moral Codes and Social Structure in Ancient Greece: A Sociology of Greek Ethics from Homer to the Epicureans and Stoics* (Albany, NY: State University of New York Press, 1996), 432.

[16] P. GAY, *The Enlightenment: The Rise of Modern Paganism* (New York: WW Norton & Co, 1995), 107.

that can think, but if Plato emphasized the importance of perfecting reason and following it, Augustine emphasized the importance of the will, the ability to choose between good and evil, and the fundamental duty to love and serve God. For Augustine humanity lies in the mind, the inner person and the most important part of the mind is not the intellect (or reason) but the will. The orientation of the will determines whether we love lower good (bodily goods, wealth, and reputation) or higher goods (the virtues). Since the 13th century, however, it was Aristotle's analysis of happiness rather than Plato's that would dominate Christian scholasticism.

The Second Part of Thomas Aquinas's *Summa Theologica* and the Book 3 of the *Summa Contra Gentiles* offer systematic engagement of human flourishing, or happiness, and whether it can be obtained in this life. The ultimate answer is that perfect happiness (*beatitude*) is not possible on earth, but imperfect happiness (*felicitas*) is.[17] This put Aquinas between Aristotle, who believed that complete happiness was possible in this life, and Augustine, who taught that happiness was impossible and that our main pleasure consists merely in the anticipation of the heavenly afterlife. In the Second Part of the *Summa*, Aquinas expressed his most fundamental ideas about what it means to be human, the actions that are crucial for the development and growth toward God as end, and the conditions for such action. Flourishing, and the movement towards full flourishing, involves the whole person, body and soul. While paying close attention to volition and intellection, outlining the acts of knowing and willing that are proper to being human, Aquinas also attends to human embodiment and the passions, which can be either conducive to spiritual thriving, or detract from it. In Aquinas's religious interpretation of Aristotle, the final end of human life is God and full flourishing is experienced in the next life in the direct presence of God.

The scholastic approach to human flourishing was challenged in the early fifteenth century when Italian humanists revived the Roman understanding of *humanitas* as part of wholesale educational reform and rethinking of the meaning of being human. Helped by the new technology of printing, Renaissance humanists reprinted classical texts and broadened the intellectual outreach of education. By insisting on the *studia humanitatis*, the humanists applied techniques of textual criticism to ancient texts that were the basis of learning in the natural sciences and the professional faculties of the universities law, medicine, and theology. Humanism was not a comprehensive philosophy that could replace traditional scholastic philosophy, but because humanism implied a method of intellectual procedure rather than a comprehensive philosophy, it had certain critical and even radical implications.[18] Humanistic methods of

---

[17] AQUINAS, *Summa Theologica*, II., q. 1, a. 8.
[18] C. G. NAUERT, *Humanism and the Culture of Renaissance Europe*, 2nd ed. (Cambridge: Cambridge University Press, 2006), 62.

textual interpretation could be applied to all texts, scientific, legal, or theological whose authority previously could not have been challenged. For that reason, the humanists were regarded as troublemakers and in theology even as heretics. Renaissance humanists, of course, were not irreligious let alone atheists. Yet especially the so-called "civic humanists" of the early 15th century were interested in worldly things, be it material wealth, political power, human love and family life. Renaissance humanism was a culture for lay people, the urban people who made Italy the wealthiest nation in Europe.

The humanist understanding of human flourishing privileged *via activa* of city life over the *vita contemplativa* of the monastery. Regarding the secular life as natural and good they eschewed asceticism, and valued marriage, family life, acquisition of wealth, and participation in politics. As moral philosophers the Renaissance humanists accepted that there are spiritual goals existing beyond the worldly ones, but these goals are to be sought through religion which accepts that the great majority of Christians will not be monks. Humanist treatises on secular life were inspired by their classical sources in which they found optimistic views of human nature.[19] Thus Lorenzo Valla affirmed the goodness of human nature and the real hope of human happened to depend not on human striving by on divine grace. In Aristotle and Cicero (but also in St. Augustine and Lactantius) Valla found authority for an optimistic assessment of human nature. Other humanists (e. g., Manetti) lauded the harmony and beauty of the human body, reflecting man's creation by God in his own image. God placed many in the world and ordered him to rule it, to work and be active and free. Human dignity is expressed in human creative actions, Manetti told his readers, summarizing many ideas about human dignity expressed earlier by Petrarch, Salutati and Valla.[20] For the Renaissance humanists *humanitas* was *dignitas* were closely intertwined but they could not be divorced from religious beliefs.

The uniqueness and dignity of humanity were understood differently in Renaissance Platonists. In the Platonic Academy of Florence, Marsilio Ficino the translator and commentator of Plato's writings moved away from the so-called "civic humanism" and its engagement in family business and politics to focus instead on the philosophical culture that civic humanism had rejected. Ficino's eclectic philosophy revived the wisdom of the ancients, be it Hermetic, Neoplatonic, or Jewish, while positing dignity of humans not in civic life but in the immortality of soul. The dignity and immortality of the soul is determined metaphysically because the soul is situated in a privileged midpoint

---

[19] Key humanist texts are available in E. CASSIRER, P. O. KRISTELLER and J. H. RANDALL (eds.), *The Renaissance Philosophy of Man* (Chicago, IL: University of Chicago Press, 1948).

[20] For rich analysis of humanistic thought on human dignity and happiness consult C. TRINKAUS, *In Our Image and Likeness: Humanity and Divinity in Italian Humanists*, 2 vols. (South Bend, IN: University of Notre Dame Press, 1995).

between God and primate matter. Ficino argues that the soul's location in the precise center of the Great Chain of Being, between God and Prime Matter, lends to it a privileged position and accounts for its dignity and uniqueness.[21] The soul is at on and the same time drawn to what is above as well as responsible for the governance of Nature below. The soul shares in divinity but also suffuses all of Nature, lending it motion and vitality. Ficino sees the soul as charged with the governance of the material world and is intimately responsible for its potential wellbeing. The soul is not connected to any distinct part of the body but communicates its life-giving power throughout.

For Ficino human uniqueness and inherent dignity lies in the immortality of the Soul, but his decision to place humanity at one specific point in the hierarchical order of creation seemed deterministic. It was against this claim that Pico della Mirandola composed his *Oration on the Dignity of Man* as an alternative.[22] In Pico's interpretation of the biblical creation narrative God first created the natures of all things, spiritual and material, to form a complete and perfect universe. Only then did God create the human being. Yet since the hierarchy of creation was already complete and all possible nature had been given out, he gave the human no fixed place in the hierarchy and no nature at all. Instead of nature, the human being (and not even the angels) received freedom, the freedom to choose his own place in the hierarchy and so to choose from himself any created nature. Each person therefore has to make the right choice to cultivate the spiritual part of his being and thereby become spiritual. A person who makes an unwise choice, who follows his baser instinct will become like a beast. The true human nature is to have no nature that rigidly determines what one could become. Their own free choice allows humans to create themselves in the sense of determining whether they will be like God or like the beasts. Every other created being is "a something" (a quid) but only the human among all creatures is "a someone" (a quis), namely, a person and this condition the human shares only with God. Creation in "image of God" thus differentiates between the human and all other creatures. In Pico's view of human flourishing, there was room for divine grace and no need for a crucified and resurrected Savior.

Transhumanists present themselves as heirs of Pico della Mirandola to whom they attribute the notion that humans have no fixed nature, insisting instead that humanity is "work in progress."[23] If Renaissance humanists held that vir-

---

[21] P. O. KRISTELLER, *Eight Philosophers of the Italian Renaissance* (Stanford, CA: Stanford University Press, 1964), 37–53.

[22] KRISTELLER, "Pico," in *Eight Philosophers of the Italian Renaissance*, 54–61; 66–67.

[23] See N. BOSTROM, "A History of Transhumanist Thought," *Journal of Evolution and Technology* 14, no. 1 (2005): 1–25, reprinted in *Academic Writing Across the Disciplines*, ed. M. Retenwald and L. Carl (New York: Pearson Longman, 2011) available at www.nickbostrom.com (4/22/2022).

tue and moral training determine human flourishing, transhumanists maintain that humans can engineer themselves to be whatever they wish to be through genetic manipulation and other technologies. The transhumanist appropriation of Pico as intellectual progenitor does not do him justice because it misses Pico's religious views, a nuanced blending of Platonism, Aristotelianism, Hermeticism and Kabbalah.

In truth, transhumanism is more indebted to the Enlightenment understanding of being human than to Renaissance humanism, although transhumanism offers a rather skewed understanding of the Enlightenment as well.

Briefly put the Enlightenment position could be summarized as follows:[24]
- all human beings share the same universal nature that cuts across all cultures;
- human nature is fixed and constant and not dependent on historical or cultural circumstances;
- what makes human nature distinct from and superior to all other animals is the human capacity to reason;
- to be human means to "dare to know" the truth;
- the ultimate goal of human knowledge is not God but humanity itself; and
- the self-directed study of humans, which gives rise to the science of Man, is the foundation of all the sciences.

The Enlightenment laid the foundation for the empirical science of humanity, namely, the social sciences. The Enlightenment philosophers, especially the members of the Scottish Enlightenment, Thomas Hutcheson, Adam Ferguson, David Hume and Adam Smith, inaugurated the empirical analysis of human flourishing, but unlike our contemporary social sciences which privilege the descriptive over the normative, the promoters of the Scottish Enlightenment included virtue and freedom (or liberty) in their understanding of human flourishing; these two prescriptive values were no less important to human flourishing than wealth and well-functioning institutions.[25] The members of the Scottish Enlightenment viewed social institutions through the lens of human flourishing and they praised or critiqued them by looking at the effects of institutions on public virtue and human flourishing. In their critique of institutions such as feudalism, polygamy, slavery and infanticide, these Enlightenment thinkers saw human flourishing not merely as the product of institutions, but as the result of "a life led in accord with a particular disposition of human nature ... The Scottish model happiness consists not in attainment but

---

[24] Any attempt to summarize Enlightenment ideas necessarily results in a cartoonish presentation of a very rich and complex intellectual movement. For thick descriptions of the Enlightenment see GAY, *The Enlightenment*. See also A. PAGDEN, *The Enlightenment: And Why It Still Matters* (Oxford: Oxford University Press, 2014).

[25] See R. P. HANLEY, "Social Science and Human Flourishing: The Scottish Enlightenment and Today," *The Journal of Scottish Philosophy* 7, no. 1 (2009): 29–46.

in activity,"[26] a position not so different from Aristotle's inclusive view of happiness. This point is lost in transhumanism because of its reductionist understanding of human rationality.

The Enlightenment viewed human reason as a liberating power from the tutelage of superstition, tradition, and error so as to enable humans to flourish in this life. The emancipatory power of reason yields independence from political tyranny and the establishment of just societies in which humans can flourish under conditions of freedom, democracy and equality. For Enlightenment thinkers, human progress makes it possible for human to experience human flourishing in this life and by virtue of progress more and more people could flourish without divine intervention, regardless of religious beliefs, and independent of divine commands. In the Utilitarian theory of Jeremy Bentham and John Stuart Mill the good or bad of all actions should be judged by its effects on happiness; the morally best alternative is the one that yields the "greatest happiness of the greatest number" of people. Translated into policy, this conception of human flourishing meant that governments should aim to promote the citizen's happiness and should do so by following reason. The Utilitarian interpretation entailed that human flourishing has become a matter of economics and politics to be controlled by governments on the basis of rational, empirical data. With the growth of the social sciences in the 20th century, this approach would result in the quantitative analysis of human flourishing by economists, sociologists, and psychologists, especially those who promote the science of Subjective Well-Being, Positive Psychology and Happiness Studies.[27] The philosophic examination of human flourishing will be undertaken by Neo-Aristotelians who revived virtue ethics as alternative theories to

---

[26] Ibid., 36.

[27] For an historical overview and the connection between the science of Subjective Well Being and Positive Psychology see D. HOROWITZ, *Happier? The History of a Cultural Movement that Aspired to Transform America* (Oxford: Oxford University Press, 2018). Positive Psychology, a term coined by Abraham Maslow, was promoted by Martin Seligman in the 1990s as a critique of psychoanalysis on the one hand, and the medicalization of human mental life, on the other hand. Seligman's work is deeply indebted to Aristotelian conception of human flourishing while recognizing the importance of religion in the flourishing life. Seligman found that happiness has three dimensions that can be cultivated: the pleasant life, the good life, and the meaningful life and he highlights the important of 6 core virtues valued in almost every culture: wisdom & knowledge; courage, love & humanity; justice; temperance; spirituality & transcendence. See M. SELIGMAN, *Authentic Happiness: Using the New Positive Psychology to Realize Your Potential for Lasting Fulfillment* (New York: Free Press, 2002). In a later book, Seligman somewhat modified his list of "core strengths" but the approach remains the same. See M. SELIGMAN, *Flourish: A Visionary new Understanding of Happiness and Well-Being* (New York: Free Press, 2011). Seligman correctly understands the connection between flourishing and education and his program is designed "skills of well-being" that "will allow us to have more positive emotion, more meaning, better relations, and more positive accomplishments" (SELIGMAN, *Flourish*, 63).

Kantian Deontology, Consequentialism, and Utilitarianism.[28] The revival of Aristotelian virtue ethics is relevant to my critique of and response to transhumanism, as we shall see in the third part of this paper. For not let us continue with the genealogical survey of the discourse on human flourishing.[29]

Enlightenment rationalism underscored the project of modernity, which was inherently optimistic: the enlightenment of humanity will yield perpetual progress leading humanity to enjoy peace and prosperity. Most recently this optimistic view of the idea of humanity was celebrated by Steven Pinker who argues that humanity today enjoys life, health, prosperity, safety, peace, knowledge, and in short, happiness more than ever before.[30] Pinker found it necessary to remind us of the glory of the Enlightenment and its accomplishments because he rejects the postmodern critique of the Enlightenment. Two World Wars, the Nazi death factories of Auschwitz and other death camps, and the specter of nuclear annihilation since Hiroshima have exposed the dark side of the modern technoscience, raising deep skepticism about the Enlightenment's naïve belief in universal humanity and progress. The wholesale rethinking of the Enlightenment project for the past seven decades has yielded conflicting results in terms of the concept of humanity or the future of human species.

On the one hand, immediately after the War scientists searched for new understanding of the human species that could take into consideration scientific developments and technological advances, the very accomplishments that made Auschwitz and Hiroshima possible. In the Macy Conferences on cybernetics (1946–1953) the new term 'posthumanism' was coined signaling a new, interdisciplinary understanding of the human species. *Homo Sapiens* was now

---

[28] The revival of Aristotelian virtue ethics began in the late 1950s with female British philosophers, Philippa Foot and G. E. M. Anscombe generated an alternative approach to moral philosophy as well as a robust examination of Aristotle's analysis of happiness. For an overview of this discourse see R. CRISP and M. SLOTE, eds., *Virtue Ethics* (Oxford: Oxford University Press, 1997); N. BADHWAR, *Well Being: Happiness is a Worthwhile Life* (New York: Oxford New University Press, 2014).

[29] My brief overview glaringly omits the discussion of Immanuel Kant for a reason. Whereas for Aristotle character traits are moral virtues that contribute to the ideal life, the kind of life that the wise person would hope for, for Kant human flourishing pertained to "personal contentment and success in achieving the ends we want." For Kant "morality is a constraint on the pursuit of a happy life rather than a means to it or an element of it." See T. E. HILL, "Happiness and Human Flourishing in Kant's Ethics," *Social Philosophy & Policy*, 16, no. 1 (1999): 143–175. For close analysis of Aristotle and Kant see, SHERMAN, *Making a Necessity of Virtue: Aristotle and Kant on Virtue* (Cambridge: Cambridge University Press, 2002); J. AUFDERHEIDE and R. M. BADER, eds., *The Highest Good in Aristotle and Kant* (Oxford: Oxford University Press, 2015). For Aristotle the highest good is not something that can be maximized; rather it is the end for the sake of which all other goods are chosen – Eudaimonia. Kant understands the highest good as happiness proportionate to virtue, where virtue is the unconditioned good and happiness is the conditioned good.

[30] S. PINKER, *Enlightenment Now: The Case for Reason, Science, Humanism and Progress* (New York: Penguin Random House, 2017).

removed from its privileged position in relations to meaning, information and cognition and instead a new science of human beings, cybernetics, was proposed as the "the scientific study of control and communication in the animal and the machine." Cybernetics, or the scientific study of how humans, animals, and machines control and communicate with each other, deliberately erased the boundaries between human and the non-human, between man-made artifacts and organic systems, between social behavior and natural life. Cybernetics thus characterized the posthuman condition as the breakdown of traditional dichotomies (e. g., nature/culture; men/women; human/animal), the hybridization and fusion of elements that were previously kept apart, and the decentering of the humanity from its previous position of privilege as the "zenith of creation." In educational terms, cybernetics and the disciplines that spawned from it brought about the integration of the natural sciences, social sciences, communication, engineering, and business, and the subsequent marginalization of the humanities, the disciplines devoted to understanding 'humanity'.

But on the other hand, in the post-War years the question of humanity has taken on new salience and meaning as people recognized *genocide* as "crime against humanity." Coined by Raphael Lemkin in 1946, the term genocide was defined not only as "killing people but eliminating their whole way of life and culture."[31] To protect against future genocides the international community promoted the discourse of human rights, which recognized the humanity as a collective entity while protecting the rights of individual human beings.[32] Precisely because in WWII human beings have proven their capacity for atrociously inhumane behavior, after the War the notion that humanity is an ideal that deserves special protection became even more prevalent, stimulated by the spread of globalization, growing internationalism, technological advances in transportation and communication, and the beginning of space explorations. In the post-War years, however, conflicting trajectories both enhanced the awareness of our shared humanity and undermined it at the same time. Thus, The Universal Declaration of Human Rights (Dec. 10, 1948) asserted the "recognition of inherent dignity and of the equal and inalienable rights of all members of the human family is the foundation of freedom, justice and peace in the world." The UN became "the voice for humanity" and a host of international institutions emerged to facilitate the flourishing of the human

---

[31] B. MAZLISH, *The Idea of Humanity in a Global Era* (New York: Palgrave Macmillan, 2009), 19.

[32] For a history of the discourse on human rights and its interpretation of humanity see L. HUNT, *Inventing Human Rights: A History* (New York: W. W. Norton, 2007); S. MOYN, *The Last Utopia* (Cambridge, MA: Harvard University Press, 2010); P. G. LAUREN, *The Evolution of International Human Rights: Visions Seen* (Philadelphia, PA: University of Pennsylvania Press, 2011).

family. The awareness of our shared humanity deepened in 1968 with the first pictures of Planet Earth from space; now people saw what the home of the human family looks like from the outside. But all was not well on planet Earth as pioneering environmentalists (e.g., Rachel Carson, Murray Bookchin, and Barry Commoner) identified the destructive impact of technoscience on the Earth. Carson argued that humankind was tempering with nature by its reckless misuse of chemical pesticides (especially DDT) as she described how pesticides alter the cellular processes of plants, animals, and possible humans. The contamination of soil, water, vegetation, birds and wildlife caused long-term effects that are detrimental to the continuation of life. Put differently, environmentalism shed new and critical light on modern technoscience and its ideology of progress.[33] The pending ecological crisis and the threat of nuclear disaster put into question the very possibility for the flourishing of the human species on Earth.

In the second half of the 20th century naïve belief in technoscientific progress was challenged philosophically by postmodernist thinkers (e.g., Jacques Derrida, Michel Foucault, Jean-Francois Lyotard, and Jean Baudrillard) who proclaimed the "End of Man," namely the demise of a conception of humanity which has prevailed in the West since the Renaissance and especially since the Enlightenment. They called for the end of "the long-held belief in the infallibility of human power and the arrogant belief in our superiority and uniqueness."[34] The call for the "End of Man" signified the critique of the Enlightenment philosophical anthropology and its metaphysical assumptions and ethical ramifications, which the postmodernist philosophers regarded as unjust, repressive, and exploitative. Foucault in particular showed that the universal "Man" does not correspond to any objective reality, since "Man" is no more than a set of historical contingencies that reflected certain relations of power. "Man" is a figment of discourse. By 'discourse' Foucault referred to self-contained systems of thought, beliefs or social and political practices governed by internally accepted relations and procedures. The "Death of Man" was the correlative of the "Death of God" and the "Death of Nature," all of which were no more than harmful socially constructed fantasies. And if "God," "Man" and "Nature" are not objective realities, their collapse also meant the

---

[33] How the awareness of the ecological threat led to the environmentalism see E. W. JOHNSON, "Ecological Threat and the Founding of the U.S. National Environmental Movement Organizations, 1962–1998," *Social Problems* 58, no. 3 (2011): 305–329. It is important to note that Carson's scientific observations were inspired by her religious orientation. See E. BARRY, *Devoted to Nature: The Religious Roots of American Environmentalism* (Oakland, CA: University of California Press, 2015); L. SIDERIS, "Fact and Fiction, Fear and Wonder: The Legacy of Rachel Carson," *Sounding: An Interdisciplinary Journal* 91, no. 3–4 (2008): 335–369.

[34] R. PEPPERELL, *The Posthuman Condition: Consciousness beyond the Brain* (Bristol: Intellect Books, 2003), 100.

"End of Education,"[35] since humanistic education was about the pursuit of truth, the cultivation of virtues, the knowledge of past traditions, and the preparation for civic responsibility. For postmodernist critics all these educational goals were but the manifestation of the human "will to power." Therefore, there was no point in perpetuating the pretext that the study of the humanities could liberate humanity from unjust, oppressive beliefs and practices, as the Enlightenment had claimed. The crisis of the humanities, which we now lament, was brought about by the humanists themselves.

Within higher education postmodernism and the counter-culture revolutions of the 1960s would bring about profound transformation with the demand for inclusion by previously excluded perspectives leading for the critical engagement of the humanities and the humanistic canon from vantage points thus dismantling any claim for universality.[36] Diversity and multiculturalism blossomed in the 1970s and 1980s into numerous academic area studies (e. g., feminist, queer, Latino/a, Hispanic, Jewish, Asian, post-colonialist and many others). While expanding the scope and diversifying the content of the humanities, they also signaled the emergence of "posthumanism" as a replacement of the humanistic *paideia* whose roots go back beyond the Renaissance to antiquity. Cultural posthumanists have insisted that humanism is not only a harmful dogma, but also that humanism is replete with its own prejudices which are precisely the kind of "superstition" from which the Enlightenment called us to break free. Cultural posthumanists uncovered the repressive implications of humanism for women, minorities, occupied and oppressed social groups and even animals. Since all boundaries are socially constructed, so the argument went, the marginalization and repression of any group is inherently unjust and must end. Similarly the artificial boundaries between "humans" and "non-humans" had to collapse, whether the "non-humans" are animals, machines, aliens, or monsters.[37] Humans are not only animals who evolved over time like any other organism, but also animals who are inherently "a prosthetic creature that has coevolved with various forms of technicity and materiality, forms that are fundamentally 'non-human' and yet have nevertheless made the human what it is."[38] Humanists who challenged the idea of humanity were most responsible for undermining its validity.

---

[35] See G. SPANOS, *The End of Education: Toward Posthumanism* (Minneapolis, MN: University of Minnesota Press, 1993).

[36] See D. HOLLINGER, ed., *The Humanities and the Dynamics of Inclusion since World War II* (Baltimore, MD: Johns Hopkins University Press, 2006).

[37] See E. L. GRAHAM, *Representation of the Post/Human: Monsters, Aliens and Others in Popular Culture* (New Brunswick: Rutgers University Press, 2002).

[38] C. WOLFE, *What is Posthumanism?* (Minneapolis, MN: University of Minnesota Press, 2010), xxv.

The collapse of boundaries between nature and culture, organic and inorganic, humans and animals would generate a new understanding of human embodiment. It was expressed most powerfully by the figure of the Cyborg, a term coined already in 1960 by Manfred Kline to denote a "cybernetic organism," namely a being with organic and bio-metronic body parts. In 1985 Donna Haraway articulated the liberationist potential of cyborgization in her *Cyborg Manifesto*, a feminist project that sought to reconstitute a new identity politics about gender norms.[39] Thereafter, the Cyborg figure was used to represent the complex relationship between humanity and technology, develop narrative that explore the imaginative possibilities inspired by new technologies, or theorize the relationship between humans and machines. The Cyborg discourse entered many cultural forms such as films, science fiction, performance and installation art and horror genre, and in all of these cultural modalities the human body was defamiliarized, depicted so as to inspire revulsion, or disengaged from its biological nature as the body is dissolved into electronic space and cybernetics existence.[40] The "End of Man" meant not only the demise of theoretical assumptions about universal reason and human rights, but also the demise of the biological basis of human existence, the human body.[41]

By the end of the 20th century, however, the fusion of humans and machines was no longer idle phantasy of cultural posthumanists who interpreted literary texts or visual images, but a technological possibility brought about by the convergence of genetic engineering, robotics, informatics, nanotechnology, and applied cognitive science. This convergence and the advances in the life sciences, neuroscience, and medicine has been marshaled to facilitate the enhancement of human physical and mental characteristic, elimination of disease and pain, and the radical extension of life expectancy. Techno-optimists (who, ironically enough, endorse the philosophical assumptions of the Enlightenment), hailed the capacity of new technologies to improve the human condition through techno-scientific enhancement that will not only fix a perceived limitations of biological humans but will also facilitate the transition from biological humanity to mechanical posthumanity. In 1957 Julian Huxley coined the term 'transhumanism' to denote what he called "evolution-

---

[39] D. J. HARRAWAY, "A Cyborg Manifesto: Science, Technology and Socialist Feminist in the Late Twentieth Century," *Socialist Review* 80 (1985): 65–68; reprinted as "A Manifesto for Cyborgs: Science, Technology, and Socialist Feminism in the 1980s," in her *Simians, Cyborgs and Women: The Reinvention of Nature* (New York and London: Routledge, 1990), 149–181.

[40] See G. S. GREENBERG, "Cyborg Discourse: Technology's Transformation of Communication," *Communication Booknotes Quarterly* 38, 1 (2007): 5–26.

[41] See, J. HALBERSTAM and I. LIVINGSTON (eds.), *Posthuman Bodies* (Bloomington, IN: Indiana University Press, 1995); N. K. HALES, *How We Became Posthuman: Cybernetics, Literature, and Informatics* (Chicago, IL: Chicago University Press, 1999).

ary humanism,"[42] as the ideology that advocates the necessary, indeed inevitable, transition from biological humanity to mechanical posthumanity in which the human species will be superseded by decision-making, super-intelligent machines.[43] Transhumanism is the program that will bring about techno-scientific posthumanism, the desired *telos*. But make no mistake: the goal of techno-scientific posthumanism is not the "End of Man" as a philosophical concept or the "End of Education" as a program for self-cultivation, but rather the *end of humanity as a biological species*.

In the first part of my talk, I explain the emergence of transhumanism and posthumanism in the context of a long, convoluted, and dialectical discourse on human flourishing. This discourse is very much alive and well today especially in the fields of psychology, philosophy, and economics. From this perspective there is no need to worry about humanity becoming an endangered species or the idea of humanity becoming an endangered idea. However, the deeper we understand the roots of transhumanism and posthumanism the more problematic the core of the project becomes. Transhumanism offers us a technological interpretation of human flourishing. The transhumanist project has two main features: enhancing humans by means of technology so as to make humans smarter, stronger, more attractive, younger looking, and long-living. The human enhancement project equates human flourishing solely with bodily performance while denigrating the limits of human biology. Human enhancement will presumably bring about a new entity, a mind that could first fuse with and eventually be supplanted by super-intelligent, autonomous, decision-making machines. Transhumanism presents these beings as the ideal of being human but attaining this ideal will mean the human biological species or at best the enslavement of biological humans. While transhumanism seeks to offer coherence to our contemporary converging technologies, I maintain that transhumanism does not offer us a viable theory of human flourishing. Precisely because transhumanism envisions the replacement of biological humans with super-intelligent machines transhumanism endangers human existence rather than enhances it.

---

[42] J. HUXLEY, TIROSH-SAMUELSON, "Science and Betterment of Humanity: Three British Prophets of Transhumanism," in *Building Better Humans? Refocusing the Debate on Transhumanism*, ed. Tirosh-Samuelson and K. L. Mossman (Frankfurt am Main: Peter Lang, 2012), 55–82.

[43] To date the best representation of transhumanist ideas, themes, and attitudes is M. MORE and N. VITA-MORE, *The Transhumanist Reader: Classical and Contemporary Essays on the Science, Technology and Philosophy of the Human Future* (New York: Wiley-Blackwell, 2013).

3. Transhumanism: Enhancing Human Bodies and Making Humanity Obsolete

It is difficult to generalize about transhumanism because it is a highly decentralized movement with numerous spokespeople who often disagree with each other. According to Nick Bostrom, a leading transhumanist, "transhumanism is a loosely defined movement [...] [that] represents an interdisciplinary approach to understanding and evaluating the ethical, social and strategic issues raised by present and anticipated future technologies."[44] Transhumanism, Bostrom tells us, is a "worldview that has a value component," and that definition expresses the aspirations of transhumanism to theorize the role of technology in the evolution of the human species. The core claim of transhumanism is that the human species is on the verge of a new phase in its evolution as the result of converging technologies, nanotechnology, biotechnology, information technology and cognitive science (in short NBIC). These technologies, so we are told, will bring about the physiological and cognitive enhancement of human beings that will pave the way for the replacement of biological humans by autonomous, super-intelligent, decision-making machines that will usher the posthuman age. Whereas biological humans emerged out of the slow, uncontrolled, and unpredictable process of evolution, the process that will bring about the posthuman will be fast, controlled, and directed, brought about by human engineering. Described as "enhancement revolution" (Buchanan), "radical evolution" (Garreau), "designer evolution" (Young), "conscious evolution" (Chu),[45] this futurist scenario turns the human into a design project and human flourishing into a technological matter. By means of new technologies the human species will redesign itself so as to transcend its biological limits, paving the way for the emergence of a new mechanical, posthuman species.

Transhumanist discourse consists of several currents or strands, but different people label them differently.[46] One identifiable current is the Extroprian-

---

[44] N. Bostrom, "Transhumanist Values" (2001), http://www.nickbostrom.com. For a fuller treatment see idem, "Transhumanism FAQ, A General Introduction," version 2.1, available on http://www.nickbostrom.com (4/21/2022).

[45] A. Buchanan, D. W. Brock, N. Daniels and D. Walker, *From Change to Choice* (Cambridge: Cambridge University Press, 2002); J. Garreau, *Radical Evolution: The Promise and Peril of Enhancing Our Minds, Our Bodies and What It Means to Be Human* (New York: Doubleday, 2004); S. Young, *Designer Evolution: A Transhuman Manifesto* (Amherst, NY: Prometheus Books, 2006); T. Chu, *Human Purpose and Transhuman Potential: A Cosmic Vision for Our Future Evolution* (San Raphael, FL: Origin Press, 2014).

[46] For a different classification of the major strands within transhumanist thought see A. Sanders, "Transhumanism and the Meaning of Life," www.aleph.sa/papers/Meaning of life.pdf (4/22/2022). Sanders differentiates between Extropianism, Terrestrial Transhumanism and Cosmic Transhumanism, but he covers the themes I have outlined on the basis of Bostrom's classification.

ism, namely those who "develop extropian perspectives on technology, science, philosophy and our in the journal *Extropy: The Journal of Transhumanism*, in the Extropy Institute newsletter, email forums, and conferences [...] and whose specific conception of transhumanism involving certain values and goals, such as boundless expansion, self-transcendence, dynamic optimism, intelligent technology and spontaneous order."[47] The main spokesperson of this strand is Max More, the founder of the Extropy Institute, which is now defunct (More is currently the President of Alcor, whose main business is cryonics, yet another dimension of the transhumanist project). A second current of transhumanism consists of Singularitarians, namely, those who believe that the "transition to a posthuman world will be a sudden event, elicited by the creation of a runway machine intelligence."[48] Their leader is Ray Kurzweil, the inventor and futurist who is revered by many transhumanists, even though he does not define himself as a transhumanist. A third group of transhumanists consists of those who follow David Pearce's Hedonistic Imperative and combine transhumanism with hedonic utilitarianism and who emphasize pleasure and morphological freedom, namely "the right to modify and enhance one's body, cognition, and emotion."[49] A fourth current can be labelled Democratic Transhumanism and consist of those who emphasize social responsibility and democratic decision making in the use of converging technologies for the benefit of humanity.[50] And finally, there are the Survivalists, or those who endorse Aubrey De Grey's campaign against aging and death and who focus on radical life extension and longevity. In between these currents there are other variants, reflecting the preferences, expertise, and commitment of individual transhumanist activists who vary greatly from each other. Because transhumanism is so diverse and constantly evolving, it is hard to generalize about it or to debate with its advocates; one can always disavow what another transhumanist has written or said so that transhumanism is indeed "work in progress," which is how transhumanists view human nature.

These are all part of the same futuristic vision that calls for the transition from biological humanity to mechanical posthumanity. This vision promises mankind happiness by means of technology. The basic point is that humans should tran-

---

[47] See M. MORE, "On Becoming Posthuman," *Free Inquiry* 14 (1994): 38–41, (http://eserver.org/courses/spring98/76101R/readingss/becoming.html) (4/22/2022). For a more recent formulation see M. MORE, "The Philosophy of Transhumanism," in *The Transhumanist Reader*, 3–27.

[48] BOSTROM, "Transhumanist Values."

[49] D. PEARCE, "The Hedonistic Imperative," (http://www.hedweb.com) (4/22/2022). This definition of "morphological freedom" is taken from "The Transhumanist Declaration (2012)," in *The Transhumanist Reader*, 55.

[50] James Hughes is the main voice of this strand within the transhumanist world. See J. HUGHES, *Citizen Cyborg: Why Democratic Societies Must Respond to the Redesigned Human of the Future* (Cambridge, MA: Westview Press, 2004).

scend their current natural state and limitation through the use of technology; they should embrace self-directed human evolution. If until now humankind attempted to tame nature to better serves natural needs, transhumanism revisions humankind's nature to better serve human fantasies. David Pearce, the co-founder of *Humanity +*, says: "If we want to live in paradise, we will have to engineer it ourselves. If we want eternal life, then we'll need to rewrite our bug-ridden genetic code and become god-like [...] only hi-tech solutions can every eradicate suffering from the world. Compassion alone is not enough."[51] If this is not powerful enough, here is an excerpt from the Transhumanist Manifesto that conveys the intention of transhumanism: "The Transhumanist mission is to pursue the most expedient course an individual can take to search one's most powerful and advanced self, whose primary purpose is to overcome anything that get in the way of the goal, namely death." The extension of human life span while increasing other physical, emotional and mental capacities is meant to create heaven on Earth. Science and technology will thus bring about eternity, or put differently, transhumanism promises us happiness we cannot refuse.

You may want to dismiss these ideas as mere silliness and say that they do not matter. But this is not my view. Transhumanism is culturally significant because this is not mere speculation on the fringe of mainstream culture, but a presence that shapes contemporary culture as transhumanists themes, vocabulary, values, and style frame contemporary film, science fiction, horror genre, video-games, performance art, new media art, literature, and cyberpunk.[52] In many ways we are already living in a transhumanist world since today all aspects of being human – embodiment, sexuality, subjectivity, emotionality, and sociality – have been thoroughly transformed by the hybridization of the organic and the mechanical, artificial intelligence, new digital and virtualizing media, cyberspace, online gaming, digital collectivities, networked information, and new media arts. Part of the appeal of transhumanism arises from the fact that offers a technological interpretation of human happiness. Let me clarify this point by looking into the two main aspects of transhumanism: human enhancement and machine-human interface. Both of these pertain to the attainment of happiness but if the first aspect seeks to improve the human body by means of technology the second project seek to eliminate biological humanity altogether.

---

[51] PEARCE, "The Hedonist Imperative," (http://www.hedweb.com) (4/22/2022).
[52] On the proliferation of transhumanist themes in contemporary culture see M. FEATHERSTONE and R. BURROWS, *Cyber Space/Cyberbodies/Cyberpunk: Cultures of Technological Embodiment* (London: Sage Publications, 1996); N. K. HAYLES, *How We Became Posthuman: Virtual Bodies in Cybernetics, Literature, and Informatics* (Chicago, IL: University of Chicago Press, 1999); R. M. GERACI, *Apocalyptic AI: Visions of Heaven in Robotics, Artificial Intelligence, and Virtual Reality* (New York: Oxford University Press, 2010); *Virtually Sacred: Myth and Meaning in World of Warcraft and Second Life* (Oxford: Oxford University Press, 2014); R. RANISCH and S. SORGNER (eds.), *Post- and Transhumanism: An Introduction* (Frankfurt am Main: Peter Lang, 2014).

4. Human Enhancement: Technological Human Flourishing

The human enhancement projects promise human technological flourishing. Human beings will remain embodied as they are but transcend their current biological limitations. The extension of human capacities is what Max More calls Extropy. Extropy, more tells us, is "the extent of a living or organizational system's intelligence, functional order, vitality, and capacity and drive for improvement" and 'extropic' as the "actions, qualities, or outcomes that embody or further extropy." More elaborates the point saying that extropy "is not a real entity or force, but only metaphor representing all that contributes *to our flourishing*." More argues that technology will bring about human flourishing through "perpetual progress, self-transformation, practical optimism, intelligent technology, open society in terms of information and democracy, self-direction, and rational thinking.[53]" He emphasizes how the pace of change – technological, cultural and economic – continues to accelerate and to reach deeper so that advances in technologies (including "social technologies" of knowledge management, learning and decision making), will presumably enable us to change human nature itself in its physical, emotional, and intellectual aspects. More predicts that with better knowledge and decision making, humans could live far longer in better than "perfect" health, improve their self-knowledge and awareness of interpersonal dynamics; overcome cultural, psychological and memetic biases in thinking; enhance intelligence in all its various forms, and learn to thrive on change and growth. In short, humans will flourish because technology will enable them to be "doing better" and "being more."

How will technology make humans flourish? Transhumanism promises to engineer human flourishing by transcending biological limits imposed on us by the messy process of random evolution. Transhumanism takes for granted that evolution has given rise to biological humans but refuses to see biology as destiny. Precisely because the evolutionary process has given rise to the complex human brain, the "inevitable product of the evolutionary process,"[54] human beings are not only permitted to intervene and alter the biological facts through designer genes, designer drugs, and a whole range of enhancement technologies, but *should* do so in order to improve the human species. Transhumanists regard evolution as a slow, random, chaotic, and flawed process that can be improved only when humans take control of it so as to direct evolution to the ultimate destiny of the human species. Doing so, transhumanists promise us, will ensure greater happiness for humanity, both individually and collectively, as well as the fulfillment of human innate ambitions to live

---

[53] Cited on the website of the Extropy Institute. Cf. M. MORE, "The Philosophy of Transhumanism," in *The Transhumanist Reader*, 4.

[54] See YOUNG, *Designer Evolution*, 212.

forever. Through negative interventions, positive interventions and enhancement, human beings will be "healthier, more beautiful, more athletic, more intelligent, more creative, more pleasant, and many other 'mores'."[55] Enhanced (or augmented) humans will be happier than ordinary humans and further along in the process of attaining perfection.

For the past three decades we have vociferously debated validity of technological enhancement. Proponents of enhancements view these interventions as "tools that can facilitate our authentic efforts as self-discovery and self-creation."[56] The proponents of enhancement technologies (be they drugs, implants, or prostheses) claim that they not only enable us to overcome limitations and deficiencies but that they enable us to authentically create ourselves choosing for ourselves the kind of life we wish to live. By contrast, the critics of enhancement worry that these technologies threaten our efforts at achieving authenticity and regard enhancement technologies as procedures that separate us from what is most our own and from how the world really is. I concur with the critics and in my writings, I sought to explain why I consider transhumanism to be a misguided idea.

The project of technological enhancement through bioengineering reflects a certain interpretation of the idea of humanity. Technological enhancement equates human flourishing as "being more" or "doing better" which are understood in *materialist terms*. It is the performance of the human body which determines human flourishing and given its limitations the human body should be manipulated mechanically, chemically or genetically. To flourish and be truly happy, transhumanists like David Pearce or Mark Walker tell us, we need to remove any impediment by engineering the human genome, taking "happy pills," or engage in "neuroscientific mind-making." All these are technologies that will lead to "super-happiness," according to David Pearce. Needless to say, in the transhumanist discourse on human flourishing there is no mention of cultivating virtues through moral training of habituation, practice, and learning since character is irrelevant to happiness. Indeed, the virtues themselves can be technologically engineered![57] Only "rational redesign" that will reframe "who and what we want to become" will make us happy. Transhumanism then promises a bioengineered paradise on Earth, a hyper-individualist vision in which we will presumably live happily here and now because we will be liberated from biological constrains.

---

[55] CHU, *Human Purpose and Transhuman Potential*, 32 and 33.

[56] E. PARENS, "Authenticity and Ambivalence: Toward Understanding the Enhancement Debate," *Hastings Center Report* 35, no. 3 (2005): 36.

[57] For a critique of the techno-scientific claims of transhumanism that the virtues will be able to be manipulated artificially see F. JOTTERAND, "'Virtue Engineering' and Moral Agency: Will Post-Humans Still Need the Virtues?," *American Journal of Bioethics and Neuroscience* 2, no. 4 (2011): 3–9.

The path to liberating humanity from embodiment begins with sexuality. Transhumanists view the sexualized body as burdensome and biological reproduction as a practice that will be eventually surpassed by reproductive technology. Since humans should feel free to be whoever they want, transgenderism is highly recommended so that it is no surprise that transgender subculture is suffused with transhumanist themes.[58] According to Martine Rothblatt (born Martin Rothblatt) "the greatest catapult for humanity into a new species lies just beyond the event horizon of transgenderism."[59] She claims that "the freedom of gender is, therefore, the gateway to a freedom of form and to an explosion of human potential. First comes the realization that we are not limited by our sexual anatomy. Then comes the awakening that we are not limited by our anatomy at all."[60] "The mind is the substance of humanity. Mind is deeper than matter," Rothblatt tells echoing the Enlightenment rationalism, a point that will become relevant when we discuss brain-computer interface.

The freedom to be whatever we want to be is most evident in cyberspace, where avatars, namely, non-biological simulations of the self, choose the form of their self-presentation and change it at will.[61] Cyberspace has become the ultimate "place" where liberation from biology can be experienced because in it there is no connection between gender and genitals, no need for biological reproduction, and no suffering caused by human corporeality. The irony is evident: the ability to be free of sexual embodiment is possible only because biomedical technologies have actualized in the flesh what previously has been only an unrealizable fantasy. If indeed existence *in silico* is so much better than existence *in corpore* why bother changing the latter? The transition from one gendered body to another makes sense only if life in organic bodies is inherently good, which transhumanists vociferously deny.

Transhumanism's contradictory attitude towards human embodiment is evident in the view of death. Given the transhumanist disdain toward the human body, one could imagine that transhumanists would welcome death or at least accept death with sober calm. Instead, transhumanists are outraged by death and find it an affront and an insult.[62] Because of the youthful desire to

---

[58] Parens, "Authenticity and Ambivalence."

[59] M. Rothblatt, "Mind Is Deeper Than Matter: Transgenderism, Transhumanism and the Freedom of Form," *The Transhumanist Reader*, 318.

[60] Ibid. It seems to me that there is a difference between transgenderism as an expression of "morphological freedom" and transgenderism as a solution to gender dysphoria. The former is a result of choice; the latter is a result of perceived necessity.

[61] Rothblatt developed this point in her *Virtually Human: The Promise and Peril of Digital Immortality* (New York: St. Martin Press, 2015).

[62] The attitude is most evident in N. Bostrom, "The Fable of the Dragon Tyrant," Journal of Medical Ethics 31 (2005): 273–277. For reflections on transhumanist attitudes toward death see T. Moos, "How Transhumanism Secularizes and Desecularizes Religions Visions," in Perfecting Human Futures: Transhuman Visions and Technological Imaginations, ed. J. B. Hurlbut

live forever in healthy bodies, Aubrey de Grey has been leading "the crusade to defeat aging" which for him is "not only morally justified but is the single most urgent imperative for humanity."[63]

Perpetuating and extending youthful life is one important concern of transhumanists who promote a range of anti-aging techniques and technologies, since they are convinced that it is possible to postpone death indefinitely. Postponing death, of course, is not abolishing death, but in the meantime, transhumanists promise us happiness through longevity research. And should that proven to be disappointing, there is still cryonics, the program to keep dead biological humans in deep freeze in order to resuscitate them in the posthuman future. Cryonics is hailed as the "door to the future,"[64] due primarily to the promises of nanotechnology,[65] but so far at least research into molecular nanotechnology did not make resurrection of the dead any more real.[66] If nanotechnology will eventually bring about the resurrection of the dead, all we need to do is to live long enough until that becomes possible by reprogramming our bodies. Ray Kurzweil believes that nanotechnology revolution will not only re-program and optimize biology, but will involve "applying massively parallel computerized processes to reorganize matter and energy at the molecular level to create new materials and new mechanisms even more intricate and powerful than biology."[67] The evidence that presumably supports this claim is presented *not as a process for the betterment or improvement of human life but as the attainment of the end-state or termination point of human flourishing when the biological human will be replaced by mechanical posthuman machines.*

---

and H. Tirosh-Samuelson (Wiesbaden: Springer, 2016), 159–178, esp. 164–166; H. TIROSH-SAMUELSON, "Technologizing Transcendence: A Critique of Transhumanism," in Religion and Human Enhancement: Death, Values and Morality (New York: Palgrave Macmillan, 2017), 267–283.

[63] A. DE GREY, "The Curate's Egg of Anti-Anti-Aging Bioethics," in *The Transhumanist Reader*, 215.

[64] Eric K. Drexler's support for cryonics is available on his blog "Metamodern: The Trajectory of Technology;" additional references are available on the blog of the Institute for Evidence-Based Cryonics. Other scientific support for resurrection of the dead by means of nanotechnology is the well-known F. J. TIPPLER, *The Physics of Immortality: Modern Cosmology and the Resurrection of the Dead* (New York: Anchor, 1994).

[65] Eliezer Yudokowsky, for example, believes that "people who haven't signed their children up for cryonics are lousy parents." See J. BARRAT, *Our Final Invention: Artificial Intelligence and the End of the Human Era* (New York: Thomas Dunne, 2013), 50.

[66] See D. H. GUSTON (ed.), *The Encyclopedia of Nanoscience and Society* (Thousand Oaks, CA: SAGE Publications, 2010), 387.

[67] R. KURZWEIL, *Transcend: Nine Steps to Living Well Forever* (Emmaus, PA: Rodale Books, 2010), 404.

5. Machine-Human Interface: Making Biological Humanity Obsolete

Human enhancement, then, is not the ultimate goal of transhumanism. Rather, the goal is the transition from biological humanity to technological posthumanity. Cyborgization, or brain-computer interface is a necessary step in the process that will not only augment human capabilities but transforms humans into technological entities. The merger between humans and machines, Gulio Prisco tells us, is "the ultimate realization of the dream to achieve indefinite lifespan, with vastly enhanced cognitive abilities, lies in leaving biology behind and moving to a new post-biological, cybernetic phase of our evolution."[68] Presumably, when this perfection is achieved, "we will build (and/or) become God(s)."[69] The telos of human enhancement then is not the experience of pleasure by living long, youthful, and imaginative life on Earth, but rather the annihilation of biological humanity and its replacement by super-intelligent machines.

Transhumanists depict that transition as an *inexorable, necessary progression which it deems to be progress for humanity*. The gradual transition from biological to mechanical entities is predicated on the creation of Artificial Intelligence (AI), computers whose computational capacities far exceed human abilities. In the beginning of the transition, humans and intelligent robots coexist, as we now do, but computers perform all sorts of functions that humans either cannot or do not want to perform so that computers "serve" humanity. Accelerated, exponential progress of AI technology, however, will facilitate the ultimate form of machine-brain interface: the "uploading" of the human mind onto supercomputers. When uploading is achieved, intelligent machines will be able to teach themselves and correct their own mistakes. This constitutes an irreversible turning point – known as technological Singularity, or AI Singularity – in which the super-intelligent machines become autonomous and self-aware. Eventually these superintelligent machines will "tire of caring for humanity and will decide to spread throughout the universe in the interests of discovering all the secrets of the cosmos."[70] At that point, humanity as we know it will be destroyed as embodied humans will be eliminated and replaced by machines. In other words, human flourishing will finally be achieved when humans stop being humans.

This futuristic vision of human happiness depends on mind-uploading. Uploading means that "intelligent software would be produced by scanning

---

[68] G. PRISCO, "Transcendent Engineering," *The Journal of Personal Cyberconsciousness*, vol. 6, no 2 (2011): 235 (https://www.terasemjournals.com/PCJournal/PC0602/prisco.html) (4/21/2022).

[69] Ibid., 234.

[70] R. M. GERACI, *Apocalyptic AI: Visions of Heaven in Robotics, Artificial Intelligence, and Virtual Reality* (New York: Oxford University Press, 2011), 149.

and closely modeling the computational structure of the biological brain," and the technical term for it is "whole brain emulation."[71] Bostrom explains the main steps of that process,[72] and while admitting that "the emulation path will not succeed in the near future (within the next fifteen years, say),"[73] he still contends that whole brain emulation "will eventually succeed,"[74] albeit it in ways which are yet to be discovered. He cites Hans Moravec, the originator of transhumanist futuristic scenarios, who says that that "human level AI is not only theoretically possible but feasible within this century."[75]

I, of course, am much more skeptical and critical than Bostrom or Moravec. While there is no doubt that computers have transformed all aspects of life, it is very doubtful that they have contributed to human flourishing. On the contrary, it seems that co-existence with AI has contributed and will continue to contribute to social isolation, mass dislocation, loss of freedom, loss of autonomy, and even loss of human life.[76] In short, machine-human interface does not contribute to human flourishing in the present; in fact, it undermines it. But the contradictions involved with AI go even deeper. The creators of AI are aware that machine intelligence falls short of human intelligence, even though smart machines are able to perform fast and complex computations that much exceeds human calculation. AI still falls short of human intelligence,[77] in part because "the biological mechanism of consciousness is not localised in the brain but distributed throughout the body."[78] If this is so, ironically enough, true super-intelligent machines will have to learn the wisdom of the human body, the very entity that transhumanism denigrates and seeks to abolish. I suspect that the same problem is relevant to autonomous cars, to cyber pilots, or to information systems. Supercomputers have undoubtedly transformed human life but not necessarily for the better.

The ultimate paradox in transhumanist understanding of human futurism concerns the final phase of the process by which accelerated change, self-improving technology, intelligence explosion, emergence of superintelligence, shifts to new forms of organization, and increased complexity and intercon-

---

[71] N. BOSTROM, *Superintelligence: Paths, Dangers, Strategies* (Oxford: Oxford University Press, 2016), 28.
[72] Ibid., 36–38.
[73] Ibid., 43.
[74] Ibid., 61.
[75] Ibid., 28, note 6.
[76] See Y. N. HARARI, *21 Lessons for the 21st Century* (London: Jonathan Cape, 2018); S. ZUBOFF, *The Age of Surveillance Capitalism: The Fight for the Future at the New Frontier of Power* (New York: Public Affairs, 2019).
[77] For a debate whether computers think and whether their computation can be considered 'intelligence' see J. BROCKMAN (ed.), *What to Think about Machines That Think: Today's Leading Thinkers on the Age of Machine Intelligence* (New York: Harper Perennial, 2015).
[78] Ibid., 170.

nectedness will bring about the irreversible turning point, called Singularity.[79] Described in apocalyptic terms Singularity is imagined as an inevitable and irrevocable shift from the biological to the mechanical, which will inaugurate the posthuman phase. The Singularity is presented not simply as a hypothesis to subject to philosophic critique and scientific analysis,[80] but rather as a fact that accounts for how the future must and will develop.

For over two decades transhumanists have enthusiastically promoted AI Singularity as the telos of their technological project. I see no good reason to accept this imaginary scenario as the telos of human flourishing, for the simple reason that the technological entities that will emerge will not be human, and therefore their well-being will be fundamentally different from the well-being of humans. But regardless of whether we should aspire to be technologies entities or as Ted Chu calls them, CoBes (short for Cosmic Beings) more and more voices of people who previously promoted AI as the telos of human existence, have come to admit that AI can and often does wreak havoc on human life whether is in malfunction of planes, in the collapse of stock markets, or in propaganda and fake news on social medias. On December 2, 2014, Stephen Hawking, who greatly benefited from machine-human interface, has sounded the alarm when he stated that "the development of full artificial intelligence could spell the end of the human race." Eliezer Yudkovsky is now most concerned about building super-intelligent machines that will be friendly to humans rather than malevolent.[81] And even Nick Bostrom, the transhumanist who has done more than any other to make transhumanism philosophically and culturally respectable, has recently (November 2015) admitted the dangers and risks involved in building computer systems with superintelligence. Yuval Noah Harari, the Israeli historian who has become international celebrity, has recently urged us to recognize the totalitarian dangers inherent in AI and their destructive impact on many aspects of human life: employment, labor, leisure, and politics. More and more people realize that transhumanist dream of human flourishing by technology can turn human life into a nightmare.

Transhumanism then is both an extension and radicalization of the Enlightenment idea of humanity as well as the expression of postmodernist critique and of the Enlightenment idea of humanity. Some transhumanists, such as

---

[79] See A. SANDBERG, "An Overview of Models of Technological Singularity," in *The Transhumanist Reader*, 377.

[80] See A. H. EDEN, J. H. MOOR, J. H. SORAKER, and E. STEINHART (eds.), *Singularity Hypotheses: A Scientific and Philosophical Assessment* (Berlin: Springer Verlag, 2012). D. PROUDFOOT, "Software Immortals: Science or Faith?," 367–389 offers a powerful and most relevant critique of the Singularity Hypothesis.

[81] BARRAT, *Our Final Invention*, 153; E. YUDKOWSKY, *Creating Friendly AI 1.0: The Analysis and Design of Benevolent Goal Architecture* (San Francisco, CA: Machine Intelligence Research Institute, 2001).

Eliezer Yudkowsky, claim that transhumanism is simply humanism,[82] but as my historical overview suggests, transhumanists misrepresent Renaissance humanism. My concern with transhumanism is not merely its internal contradictions in regard to the meaning of being human but the fact that transhumanist faith in the power of technology cannot help us to address the pressing challenges of the Anthropocene. In its blind faith in technology and in the destructive actions that flow from this faith, the transhumanist technological project greatly contributes to the ecological collapse that characterizes the Anthropocene. After all, the powerful intelligent machines built by humans to perform infinite calculations use metals that are extracted from the Earth, usually by exploiting child labor under conditions that amount to slavery in countries such as the Democratic Republic of Congo.[83] There is nothing humane about the treatment of the laborers who do the extracting because the lofty ideal of universal humanity which entitles humans to equality, justice and respect, is simply not extended to them. *The technological project of human enhancement is built on injustice and the debasement of the ideals of humanity as much as it contributes to the worsening of ecological degradation that will eventually lead to collapse of all life on Earth, including human life.* If we wish to respond to the specter of ecological collapse, we need to find our inspiration not in fetishizing technology but in our religious traditions that offer us a very different view of human flourishing. Let me try to offer such vision on the basis of the Judaic tradition.

6. A Judaic View of Human Flourishing: Divine Creation and Human Creativity

The Judaic tradition has much in common with Aristotelian approach to human flourishing as I have in my study, *Happiness in Premodern Judaism* which traces the development of the Judaic discourse on happiness from antiquity to the seventeenth century. The Judaic approach is particularly relevant to this discussion because contemporary Judaism is remarkably open toward technoscience, especially in regard to biotechnology.[84] Whereas in the Christian dis-

---

[82] See YUDKOWSKY, "Transhumanism as Simplified Humanism," (http://yudkovsky.net/singularity/simplified). (4/22/2022).

[83] The story of transhumanism is inseparable from the story of globalization and its dark side. On the connection between technology and injustice in Congo see N. EYAL, *The Revolt against Globalization* (in Hebrew) (Rishon LeZion: Miskal – Yediot Ahronoth Books and Chemed Books, 2018), 76–82. The imperative of globalization is economic efficiency, and its cost is paid not only by human beings all over the world but also by the planet itself.

[84] See L. ZOLOTH, "Jewish Bioethics: Current and Future Issues in Genetics," *The Oxford Handbook of Jewish Ethics and Morality*, ed. E. N. Dorff and J. K. Crane (Oxford: Oxford University Press, 2013), 351–366.

course contemporary technologies such as genetic engineering, genetic mapping, genetic testing and screening, preimplantation genetic diagnosis, genetic surgery, stem-cell research, and cloning of humans has generated passionate debate, these technologies have been largely endorsed by Jews. Moreover, the rhetorical trope of "playing God," which has governed the debate about the scope of limits of technologies, is conspicuously missing in Jewish bioethical discourse. The openness toward biotechnology among Jews has much to do with the tragic lessons of the Holocaust, the demographic imbalance between Jews and Arabs in Israel, which threatens the Jewishness of the state, and the awareness that technoscience is essential to ensure Israel's survival in the Middle East. But putting all these historical factors aside, what is most relevant to our discussion is the Judaic view that links divine creation and human creativity.

Three principles govern Jewish openness to technoscience in general and to biotechnology in particular:
1. That God created the world and continues to sustain it
2. That God revealed his Will in the form of Law, the Torah, spelling out instructions for human care of created world, and
3. That God will redeem the world in the remote future in response to human conduct and in collaboration with human efforts

From these foundational beliefs follow religious obligations that are relevant to technoscience:
- The obligation to mend, improve, or fix the created world (*tikkun olam*)[85]
- The obligation to heal disease and illness and reduce pain and suffering (the commandment of *rafo yerafe*)[86]
- The obligation to save and preserve life (*piqquah nefesh*)[87]

Without explicating these beliefs let me only say that in Judaism divine creation and human creativity are intertwined since in the created world and human beings are created in the divine image (*tzelem Elohim*). Although Jew-

---

[85] The obligation "to mend the world" (*letakken olam*) is stated in the daily prayer, Aleinu, which is a prayer to establish God's kingdom on Earth. The sixteenth-century Lurianic Kabbalah expanded the idea to encompass the human effort to transform the world through observance of Jewish Law with Kabbalistic intentions. In modern Judaism, especially among Reform Jews, the phrase *Tikkun Olam* has become shorthand for social action, and reflects, interestingly enough the influence of the Social Gospel Movement and Progressivism on Reform Judaism in America. See M. MARMUR, "Ethical Theories in the Reform Movement," in *The Oxford Handbook of Jewish Ethics and Morals*, 211–214.

[86] The obligation to hear is derived from Exodus 21–19 according to which an assailant must ensure that his victim is "thoroughly healed" and Deuteronomy 22:2 "And you shall restore the lost property to him." See DORFF, *Matters of Life and Death*, (Philadelphia, PA: Jewish Publication Society, 1998), 27.

[87] The principle notion that the preservation of life (in Hebrew Pikkuach Nefesh) overrides virtually any other religious consideration is derived from Leviticus 18:5.

ish theologians and philosophers debated the meaning of the "image of God," they all agreed that the created world is good but not perfect. Created in the divine image, human beings are called to act as God's partners in the on-going act of mending or repairing the created world.

The rabbinic tradition portrays human beings as "God's partners" in the created world (Babylonian Talmud, Kiddushin 30b; Shabbat 10a) and that is understood to mean to that humans have an obligation to improve and ameliorate what God has created because "God left it for human beings to complete the world."[88] Abraham Steinberg, a leading Jewish bioethicist, put is very pointedly when he asserts: "we are partners with [God] to improve the world. It is not an option – it is an obligation to continue to improve the world and do good for the world," which leads him to conclude that "we are therefore permitted to interfere in nature, nay, we are obligated to interfere, obligated to improve the world."[89] For Steinberg and many other Jewish ethicists across the spectrum of contemporary Judaism, science and technology express God given human creativity which is to be employed for the sake of the "betterment of humanity." Thus Rabbi J. David Bleich, another leading Orthodox bioethicist who has written extensively on genetic engineering concludes that "man is an active partner in the process of creation as such is charged with bringing creative processes to completion."[90]

And yet, Jewish bioethicists (especially Orthodox and Conservative) subject the employment of science and technology religious constraints. It is Jewish Law (in Hebrew: Halakhah) that dictates what can and should be done technoscientifically. Steinberg explains that science and technology can be used for the betterment of humanity "as long as 1) there is no essential halakhic prohibition in the actual actions of technological advancement; 2) the process of improvement of creation does not have a prohibited result which cannot be prevented or corrected; 3) the act of improvement benefits humans, and moreover, the derived benefit surpasses the detriment."[91] The Judaic openness to technoscience and the obligation to use it for the betterment of humanity is neither uncritical nor permissive; rather the validity of this or that technology, technique, or procedure has to be examined from within the parameters of Jewish Law and found either permissible or forbidden.

Judaism sanctions an activist attitude toward the created world which seems to cohere with the transhumanist veneration of technology. But a closer look

---

[88] A. ROSENFELD, "Judaism and Gene Design," *Tradition* 13 (1972): 71–80.
[89] A. STEINBERG, "Cloning: Jewish Medical Ethics," *Encyclopedia of Jewish Medical Ethics* (New York: Feldheim, 2003), II, 513.
[90] J. D. BLEICH, "Survey of Recent Halakhic Periodical Literature: Genetic Engineering," *Tradition* 37, no. 2 (2003): 67.
[91] STEINBERG, "Human cloning – Scientific, Moral and Jewish Perspective," *The Torah u-Madda Journal* 9 (2000): 200.

at the Judaic concept of *Tikkum Olam* suggests a deeper understanding of the complexity of created world than what transhumanism offers us. The Judaic tradition accepts it as a given that the created world is good, but it is not perfect. The goodness of creation also includes evil, sin, pain, and suffering. Even death, the finitude and mortality of humans, does not detract from the inherent goodness of creation. Expecting to imitate God and "follow His ways," humans are called to improve, perfect, and repair the world by following God's divine commands. By observing the commandments human beings sanctify the physical world through intentional acts, thus improving the world morally and religiously. The key value that guides the work of *Tikkun Olam* is justice (in Hebrew *tzedek*) but what is justice and how to apply it to the social world cannot be separated from a range of Judaic attitudes, values, and sensibilities. In other words, *Tikkun Olam* is always an ethical, moral and religious project, not a mere techno-scientific project.

In contemporary Judaism the ideal of *Tikkun Olam* has been applied to a wide range of social problems, including climate change, disability, poverty, homelessness, and immigration. The application of *Tikkun Olam* to climate change is most relevant to our concern with the future of humanity, since the ecological crisis threatens the ability of human beings to flourish. Jewish environmentalists view the ecological crisis, and especially climate change, not merely as a scientific issue to which there are technoscientific solutions, but first and foremost as *social and moral issue* to which Judasm can and must respond. Arthur Waskow, a leading Jewish environmentalist, evokes Mishna Tractate Avot 1:14 – "If not now When? – as he relentlessly preaches that climate change is *the* Jewish issue of our time and appealed to Jews and non-Jews" to reflect upon the impact of climate change on this Holy Temple that is our Planet Earth, to turn and take action, large and small, toward a better future."[92] What does that mean in practice? Waskow and other Jewish environmentalists are mainly engaged with critique of the extraction industry and the economic practices of late capitalism that have allowed it to become so ruinous. Significantly, Jewish environmentalists have not engaged the debate on climate engineering precisely because they do view it as a moral rather than technological issue.

The Judaic approach to human flourishing is distinguished by its positive attitude toward human embodiment. Contrary to transhumanism, which denigrates the biological human body, Judaism sees the human body as belonging to God: humans have the body on loan during our lease on life. God is the owner of the human body and God can and does impose conditions on human use of the body. Among those requirements is that we seek to preserve human

---

[92] A. WASKOW, "Tackling Climate Change: If Note Now, When?," (http://aleph.org/resources/tackling-climate-change-if-not-now-when). (4/22/2022).

life and health and do everything we can to save life: The Talmud states that "He who saves one life [it is] as if he saves the entire world" (Sandhedirn 37a). Saving human life is so important that it takes precedence over other obligations, even the obligation to observe the Sabbath. From the obligation to save, protect, and promote life Jewish ethics concludes that we have a duty to seek to and develop new cures for human diseases. The Jewish tradition accepts both natural and artificial means to overcome illness and see physicians as agents and partners of God in the ongoing act of healing. Thus, the mere fact that human beings created a specific therapy (rather than finding it in nature) does not impugn its legitimacy. On the contrary, we have a religious duty to develop and use any therapy that can aid us in taking care of our bodies, which ultimately belongs to God. While God is views as the ultimate healer, the Jewish tradition holds that God does not leave sickness and health entirely in God's hands; rather humans have the responsibility for the promotion of health and the prevention and or cure of disease. In Judaism, contrary to transhumanism, the body is not an empty vessel, and the soul is not a separate substance imprisoned in the body. Rather the human being is a psycho-physical unity in which body and soul are interdependent. As Maimonides already taught in the 12th century, the well-being, or flourishing, of the human body (*tikkun ha-guf*) and the well-being of the soul (*tikkun ha-nefesh*) are closely intertwined.[93]

The human psycho-physical organism is inherently relational or social. That is to say, the human is always in relationships with other humans, with other created beings, or nature, and with God. Relationality follows from the doctrine of creation as well as from the belief that God entered a covenant with Israel. In this worldview the human is never self-sufficient, or autonomous, but always dependent, vulnerable, and in need to care. As an embodied biological creature, the human is also always gendered, since creation requires procreation and reproduction for the perpetuation of the species. Despite veneration of biological procreation and the value of reproduction, contemporary Judaism has been rather open toward gender identity issues and under the impact of feminism has increasingly moved beyond traditional gendered stereotypes to endorse a flexible and variegated understanding of gender. Biology matters and the perpetuation of human life is a religious value, but traditional sex roles are not to be rigid and confining.[94] Contemporary Judaism is remarkably welcoming of non-traditional sex-roles while highlighting the importance of family life.

---

[93] On Maimonides' conception of happiness and the interdependence of body and soul see TIROSH-SAMUELSON, *Happiness in Premodern Judaism*, 192–245.

[94] This approach sheds light on the widespread use of reproductive technologies in Israel to promote the so-called New Family (Mishpahah Hadahsah), namely non-traditional familial arrangements that perpetuate biological reproduction outside the structure of the traditional patriarchal family. I. ROSENBLUM, *Garden of God: The Family Revolution* (Tel Aviv: Modan, 2016).

The Judaic view of the relational Self means contrasts with the view that the human Self as autonomous, self-contained, and absorbed in computational activities. Rather, the human is socially and politically engaged in which the human must recognize and accept the existence and relevance of the Other. As a relational being, the human Self is not defined above and against the Other but dialogically: the Other is always part of the dyadic Self. As Buber has taught the relational Self can stand in two primary relationships: the conditional, instrumental, and exploitative attitude of I-It relation, or the immediate, unconditional, and totally accepting relationship of I-Thou. The choice between these two paradigms determines the quality of human relations (whether private or public) as well as in the interaction between humanity and the natural world. Individually and collective, humans can flourish if and only if they do not exploit others but accept others and ensure that they will flourish on their own terms. A relational understanding of the human Self thus includes the Other in the purview of the Self and is necessarily pluralistic. *Politically speaking the idea of human flourishing must be understood democratically, allowing for a plurality of visions that peacefully co-exist with each other.*

The relational understanding of the human Self has obvious ecological ramifications. Indeed, Judaism sees all creatures as part of the interconnected web of life in which each creature has a task to perform. Created in the divine image, the task of the human being is not to exploit the resources of nature created by God, because human well-being or flourishing depends on the fecundity of the world. The Judaic tradition makes clear that the human being was given the task "to protect and to till" the created world that ultimately belongs to God. The human is not simply a "manager" or a "steward" of the created world but a caring gardener whose actions ensure that the world will continue to thrive in the future. Humans are responsible not only for the care of the present world but also for the wellbeing of future generations. "Do Not Destroy" (*bal tashchit*) is the preeminent environmental principle that guides Jewish attitude toward environment, although it is open to interpretation.[95] The responsibility for the well-being of future generations means that we have to ensure that the very conditions of life – soil, air, water – will continue to flourish indefinitely. The human species, the Anthropos, must not exploit, destroy, or diminish the created world, because the human does not own creation, life, or the future. Rather, the human has a responsibility to ensure that all forms of life continue to flourish for generations to come because the created world belongs to God.

The Judaic ecological view endorses an ethics of care and responsibility that recognizes and honors human vulnerability, dependency, and need of care. All

---

[95] See J. BENSTEIN, "Bal Tashchit: A Jewish Environmental Precept," in *Judaism and Environmental Ethics. A Reader*, ed. M.D. Yaffe (Lanham, MD: Lexington Books, 2001).

created beings require care and cannot flourish without care, both the need to care for and the need to be cared for.[96] Unlike transhumanism that envisions a disembodied, simulated Self, Judaism views human flourishing as care for actual, embodied people whose humanity is not lessened by their physical vulnerability but rather enhanced by it. What enhances our humanity is the ability to love, care, and be kind to those who need our care: the sick, the old, the socially marginal, and the foreigner. The 19th century Musar teacher, Israel Salanter, put it best when he stated that "the material needs of the other are my spiritual needs."[97] This insight was the inspiration for the ethics of Emmanuel Levinas, who was a product of a Musar Yeshivah in Lithuania.[98] Levinas's ethics according to which the Other places infinite responsibility on everyone who comes into relation with an Other, rather than just a choice taken by a moral few, has transformed contemporary philosophy as well as contemporary Judaism and has been applied in numerous cultural contexts, including politics, environmentalism, and art. The Judaic ethics of responsibility and care applies to all aspects of life be it economic, politics, medicine, education, and many other domains.

How can we become caring humans engaged in the practice of care? The answer lies in the cultivation of character and the excellences of character, namely the virtues, as the ancient philosophers, both Jewish and non-Jewish, understood so well. Transhumanists, we should recall, have nothing to say about character formation because they identify humanity with computational rationality. In contrast, the Judaic view refuses to reduce human beings to computational data, since humans have desires, preferences, emotions, feeling, inspirations, dreams, and hopes, all of which cannot be translated into computational data. They can only be told in narratives, some of which are regarded as sacred narrative because they frame our attitudes to life and our daily actions. In the Judaic view of human flourishing, the relational, narrative-making human cultivates his/her character by acquiring the

---

[96] The ethics of care is a distinctive strand within feminist discourse. For an overview see V. HELD, *The Ethics of Care: Personal, Political and Global* (Oxford: Oxford University Press, 2005). For a Judaic and environmental engagement with the ethics of care see H. TIROSH-SAMUELSON, "Ethics of Care and Responsibility: Bridging Secular and Religious Cultures," in *Environmental Ethics: Cross-Cultural Explorations*, ed. M. Kirloscar-Steinbach and M. Diaconu (Freiburg: Karl Alber, 2020), 29–57.

[97] The teachings of the Musar Movement are currently being revived especially in Conservative Judaism. See G. CLAUSSEN, "The Practice of Musar," *Conservative Judaism* 63, no. 2 (2011): 3–26. The contemporary exposition of the Musar movement draws on the thought of Emmanuel Levinas.

[98] On Levinas's training in the Lithuania Musar Yeshivha see S. MOYN, *Origins of the Other: Emmanuel Levinas between Revelation and Ethics* (Ithaca, NY: Cornell University Press, 2005); R. GIBBS, "Blowing on the Embers: Two Jewish Works of Emmanuel Levinas: A Review," *Modern Judaism* 14, no. 1 (1994): 99–113.

virtues, a process that requires education, habitual practice, and relationships with other beings. The cultivation of virtue begins in the family, elaborated in years of formal education, and is nourished throughout life by interacting with friends, colleagues, and members of various civic associates. The ethics of virtues, as Judaism shows very clearly, is not in conflict with ethics of duties but complementary to it. The virtues are also inseparable from values, emotions, and attitudes all of which are sorely missing in the transhumanist narrative of the mind that thinks itself.

The Judaic perspective of human flourishing, I would submit, is much more suitable to the challenges of our technological age. Instead of glorifying humanity over all other creatures and fetishizing human technological power at the expense of nature, the Judaic approach insists on the rootedness of the human being in the natural world and human responsibility toward the world created by God. The Judaic view does not glorify rationality over other dimension of being human and does not equate human rationality with computation. Rather the Judaic perspective recognizes the richness, complexity, and diversity of being human and offers an ethics of care, compassion, solidarity, empathy, connectedness, cooperation, gratitude. The ideal human is not the Promethean figure that stands defiantly against the world by constantly innovating and creative new ways of life, but rather a being who accepts the limits of the created world and lives within these limits with humility, modesty, temperance, and resilience. The Judaic view is by no means anti-technological nor is it anti-philosophical; rather, it calls for an attitude of openness and wonder toward the created world, appreciating its infinite wisdom and honoring its inherent integrity. The Judaic view encourages the cultivation of an environmentally virtuous person who regards arrogance, greed, carelessness, indifference, and wastefulness as vices that that undermine our obligations to the world created by God.

7. Conclusion

Whether we like it or not technology is here to stay and will continue to shape every aspect of human life including manufacturing, transportation, labor, communication, finance, war, education, sports, law, government, entertainment, and the arts. If humanity is not to become extinct in the Anthropocene despite the massive ecological damage that the human species has inflicted, the human species will have to endorse a different interpretation of being human. In the 20th century due to changes I have discussed in the first part of the essay we have indeed developed planetary consciousness that compels us to think about the future of the human species as a collective entity, precisely because that future has become so precarious. To respond to the challenges of the

Anthropocene, we must not be seduced by transhumanist techno-optimism since it will lead not to the flourishing of the human species but rather to its demise. Contrary to transhumanist fantasies, we need to articulate alternative viable visions for the future of humanity that will honor and cherish human biological existence, celebrate the diversity and richness of the human experience, and ensure that humans will thrive in the face of massive change. Human flourishing as I envision does not consist in infinite computational activity but in an embodied social life of family, work, education, and community governed by the values of responsibility and care.

The alternative vision of human flourishing is post-secular in the sense of considering religious beliefs as part of the vision of being human; it is global in the sense of encompassing all human beings and not merely members of a specific national, ethnic, or racial group. The vision is relational in the sense that it treats humans as not as autonomous beings but as social beings who are interdependent and who must learn to peacefully co-exist with each other despite their differences. Recognizing diversity and the irreducibility of the Other, this alternative vision of humanity is pluralistic since the Other is always part of who we are rather than that against which we define ourselves. Finally, this vision is ecological because it looks at human beings not as masters of the Earth who have a license to exploit its resources but as creatures whose task is to protect the created world. Humans are not machines, but organisms embedded in the web of life whose future the human must protect. Human flourishing consists not of computation but of caring relationship with other people, with the Earth, and with God.

Although my approach to human flourishing is grounded in Judaic sources, almost everything I said is compatible with the ethos of other religious traditions, especially, the monotheistic traditions of Christianity and Islam. The shared ground between the monotheistic traditions is due not only to the evolutionary development of these Scriptural religions but also to their similar adaptation of ancient Greek philosophy and ethics. To survive, let along thrive, in the Anthropocene, we need to revive ancient traditions and translate them into our new conditions. This has happened in philosophy with the revival of virtue ethics and the renewed interest in the ancient discourse on human flourishing. The merits of ancient reflections have been recognized not in philosophy, where Neo-Aristotelian virtue ethics is now a distinctive alternative to Deontology and Consequentialism, but also in the fields of psychology, economics, health science, political science, and environmental studies. If we think about the future of humanity in terms of ancient theories of human flourishing, both their religious and secular variants, we may be able to critique some of the harmful contemporary cultural trends that fetishize technology and that wish to make humanity into an endangered species and not only an endangered idea. To ensure the future of the human species we should not abandon the idea of humanity but reinterpret it so as to bring the idea and the reality, the global and local, the public and the private, closer to one another. In the Anthropocene concern for the human species as a whole will not disappear, in fact it will become more prevalent, but our vision for humanity should not follow the lines proposed by techno-optimistic transhumanism. I hope that the alternative vision proposed in this lecture will enable us to get some clarity about human flourishing in the age of technology.

Transhumanism, Religion, and the Anthropocene

Thomas Jared Farmer

1. Introduction

"Ich lehre euch den Übermenschen. Der Mensch ist Etwas, das überwunden werden soll. Was habt ihr gethan, ihn zu überwinden? Alle Wesen bisher schufen Etwas über sich hinaus: und ihr wollt die Ebbe dieser grossen Fluth sein und lieber noch zum Thiere zurückgehn, als den Menschen überwinden?"[1]

In her paper, "Human Flourishing in the Age of Technology",[2] Hava Tirosh-Samuelson presents a compelling picture of transhumanism as both an extension and (to some degree) a corruption of the Enlightenment project. In particular, she highlights the emergence and gradual development of notions of human nature and human flourishing over the course of the western philosophical tradition, eventually giving rise to modernist conceptions during the period of the Enlightenment. According to Tirosh-Samuelson, however, transhumanism amounts to a reduction of this discourse. It limits the function of reason to *calculating thought* and equates human flourishing exclusively with bodily performance.[3] Transhumanism therefore seeks to augment this performance by means of technological manipulation. The innate limits imposed on the human species by biology are correspondingly viewed, not as essential features of our being nor as inviolable natural boundaries to be respected, but, instead, merely as so many obstacles to be overcome on the path towards optimization.

The term *transhumanism* itself is a hypernym which represents a constellation of distinct and often competing ideas and philosophies. Even so, this set

---

[1] F. Nietzsche, *Also sprach Zarathustra* (1883), *KGA* 1 (Berlin: Walter de Gruyter, 1968).
[2] H. Tirosh-Samuelson, "Human Flourishing in the Age of Technology," in this volume, 171–208.
[3] Horkheimer and Adorno describe what they call "calculating thought" by saying, "[R]eason is the agency of *calculating thought*, which arranges the world for the purposes of self-preservation and recognizes no function other than that of working on the object as mere sense material in order to make it the material of subjugation ... Being is apprehended in terms of manipulation and administration. Everything – including the individual human being, not to mention the animal – becomes a repeatable, replaceable process, a mere example of the conceptual models of the system" (M. Horkheimer and T. Adorno, *Dialectic of Enlightenment: Philosophical Fragments*, trans. E. Jephcot [Stanford, CA: Stanford University Press, 2002], 65; M. Horkheimer, *Gesammelte Schriften*: vol. 5, *Dialektik der Aufklärung und Schriften 1940–1950*, ed. G. S. Noerr [Frankfurt am Main: S. Fischer, 1987]).

of perspectives, each in their own manner, purport to provide a path forward on the way towards so-called "posthumanism" – the inevitable next stage in human evolutionary development beyond *Homo sapiens*. Whether this transition is envisioned as arriving as a result of "machine-human interface" (cyborgism), "whole brain emulation" (mind-uploading), "genetic engineering," or some combination of these and other related factors, proponents of transhumanism, nevertheless all agree in principle with Nietzsche's assertion that, *"Der Mensch ist Etwas, das überwunden werden soll."*

2. Human Dignity and the *Imago Dei*

In response to this position, Tirosh-Samuelson wishes to offer an alternative conception of human flourishing – one grounded in the Judaic tradition, but which is also consonant with other religious lifeways. Namely, that humanity (and, indeed, all of creation, עולם) is imbued with *inherent*, not merely *instrumental* value. In the words of Sallie McFague, "Human dignity and the integrity of creation lies at the heart of the biblical vision of the good life."[4] Tirosh-Samuelson here highlights how this high-view of humanity in the West is frequently tied to the biblical conception of humanity being created "In the image of God" – thus giving rise to discourse on the *Imago Dei*, which arguably informed the eventual emergence of the idea of human rights.[5] As biblical scholar Ellen F. Davis has pointed out, "Before anything else, creation in the image of God indicates that human life has both value and form: inestimable value, and a form that is uniquely and richly expressive of divine intentions."[6] Additionally, Bruce C. Birch, et al., maintain that:

"[Genesis 1] democratizes an ancient Near Eastern royal use of image language; all human beings are created in the image of God, not just kings. The result is that all inter-human hierarchical understandings are set aside; all human beings of whatever station in life stand together as image of God. That both male and female are created (*'ādām* is here used generically, hence the translation 'humankind') means that the female images the divine as much as the male. Likeness to God pertains not only to what male and female have in common but also to what remains distinctive to them."[7]

---

[4] S. McFague, "Epilogue: Human Dignity and the Integrity of Creation," in *Theology That Matters: Ecology, Economy, and God*, ed. D. K. Ray (Minneapolis, MN: Fortress Press, 2006), 199.

[5] This is interesting in itself, since the concept appears only briefly in either the Hebrew Bible or the Christian New Testament (Gen. 1:26–27; 2 Cor. 4:4, cf. Col. 1:15; 3:10).

[6] E. F. Davis, *Scripture, Culture, and Agriculture: An Agrarian Reading of the Bible* (New York: Cambridge University Press, 2009), 56.

[7] B. C. Birch, W. Brueggemann, T. E. Fretheim, and D. L. Petersen, *A Theological Introduction to the Old Testament*, 2nd edition (Nashville, TN: Abingdon Press, 2005), 44.

In spite of fostering a sense of interhuman mutuality, the second dimension of this supposed divine similitude, however, appears to provide scriptural justification for the exploitation of the natural world. As Genesis 1:26 recounts: "Then God said, 'Let us make *humankind* (אָדָם) *in our image, according to our likeness* (בְּצַלְמֵנוּ כִּדְמוּתֵנוּ); *and let them have dominion* (וְיִרְדּוּ) over the fish of the sea, and over the birds of the air, and over the cattle, and over all the wild animals of the earth, and over every creeping thing that creeps upon the earth'" (NRSV). Nevertheless, contrary to the frequent image of Adam (as primal representative of humanity) exercising domination over creation as a kind of imperious facsimile of God on Earth, many biblical scholars and theologians have sought to challenge such a reading. For example, Davis argues that "let them exercise mastery *among*" is a preferable translation for the Hebrew preposition (בְּ) with its adjoining verbal phrase (וְיִרְדּוּ). She maintains that "The language of Genesis 1 acknowledges the unique power of *Homo sapiens*, yet without separating us from other creatures."[8] Indeed, in the biblical narrative, humankind serves as God's stewards of creation aiding in its protection and cultivation. In this respect, the dichotomy between humanity and nature is ultimately illusory. Humankind is a part of nature, embedded in a *network of mutuality*. As Abraham Joshua Heschel observed, "Man is continuous both with the rest of organic nature and with the infinite outpouring of the spirit of God."[9] Likewise, Ilia Delio argues that "We live in an evolutionary and self-organizing cosmos where each person is co-extensive with the entire universe. Ours is not a 'fallen' humanity but a 'deep' humanity, embedded in nature from the Big Bang onward."[10] Finally, Catherine Keller notes that:

"The biblical imagery, to the extent one can draw theological generalizations from it, constructs the universe as all-together inspirited, from the first hovering of the spirit over the prematerial waters through every phase of creaturely life. The divine breath of life, the *ruach*, not a thing but rather an activity, a breathing – is endlessly released into the free agents of creation, enlivening the unfathomable multiplicity, the poignant complexity, of the *genesis collective*. There is nothing disembodied about this spirit; as God's it is embodied as the world, and in each of us it is – the spirit of material life itself … A full-bodied ecotheology will embrace a wider, more ancient Spirit."[11]

In the Christian tradition, furthermore, the notion of the *Imago Dei* receives special significance in light of the doctrine of the Incarnation of Jesus Christ. For reasons of brevity, this is a point upon which I do not wish to linger. Even

---

[8] Davis, *Scripture, Culture, and Agriculture*, 55.

[9] A. J. Heschel, *Man is Not Alone: A Philosophy of Religion* (New York: Farrar, Straus, and Giroux, 1951), 210.

[10] I. Delio, *Making All Things New: Catholicity, Cosmology, Consciousness* (New York: Orbis Books, 2016), 79.

[11] C. Keller, "The Flesh of God: A Metaphor in the Wild," *Theology That Matters: Ecology, Economy, and God.* ed. D. K. Ray (Minneapolis, MN: Fortress Press, 2006), 97.

so, I feel I would be remiss if I did not point out what I take to be one of the profounder implications of this belief. To wit, in spite of the long Christian associations with Platonism (and later Gnosticism/Docetism) with their clear preference for the mental over the physical, Christianity also has a long tradition of dignifying embodiment as the site of the sacred.[12] The notion that God takes on flesh *fully*, with all of the messy details that implies, reflects both something about the God of Christianity and about God's creation.[13]

3. Posthumanism Disentangled

Having now established, to my own satisfaction at least, that a matter of major contention between many religious critics of transhumanism (among them Tirosh-Samuelson and myself) concerns the latter's apparent denigration of

---

[12] See L. T. JOHNSON, *The Revelatory Body: Theology as Inductive Art* (Grand Rapids, MI: Wm. B. Eerdmans Publishing Co., 2015); N. L. EISLAND, *The Disabled God: Toward a Liberatory Theology of Disability* (Nashville, TN: Abingdon Press, 1994); and E. MOLTMANN-WENDEL, *I Am My Body: A Theology of Embodiment* (New York: Continuum Publishing, 1996).

[13] One could, no doubt, counter by asking: (1) Was not a prime focus of Jesus' ministry healing the sick and infirmed? (2) Are there not clear similarities which can be drawn between transhumanism and the Pauline notion of the *Soma Pneumatikon*? Or, (3) How is transhumanism really all that distinct from the religious belief in life eternal? It's beyond the scope of the present paper to satisfactorily respond to these questions in detail. Even so, I would like to offer a set of assertions without defending them here. (1) Yes. Jesus' ministry was primarily directed at the sick and infirmed. The contrast between something like advances in prosthesis which allow people who have lost limbs to function within society more easily while being differently abled has a different qualitative affect than selective body augmentation for the express purpose of transcending normal human limits. The same could be said for eyeglasses, pacemakers, or gender affirming surgeries. None of which are designed to make us more than human. Other technologies which do in fact allow us to transcend normal human capacities (e.g., automobiles, trains, airplanes, etc.) do not do so by altering our biology. Points (2) and (3) are related. While the Apostle Paul, at times, seems to imply the possibility of separation between the human essence and the body (see 2 Cor. 5:8; 12:2), he imagines the general resurrection and thus life eternal as being embodied. That said, Paul is restricted in discussions of the *Soma Pneumatikon* to the analogies and abstract concepts of his own time and social location. For the Christian who believes in the Resurrection as more than a mere metaphor, the precise nature of the resurrected body can only ever be hinted at, never grasped. One can see Christianity itself as an extended discourse on the nature and ultimate meaning of the resurrection event. This meaning is not exhausted by an indefinite extension of lived experience. In the final analysis, there are certainly parallels to be observed, but Christianity cannot be simplistically categorized as transhumanist without significant qualification. See R. H. GUNDRY, *Sōma in Biblical Theology: With Emphasis on Pauline Anthropology*. Society for New Testament Studies, Monograph Series 29 (Cambridge: Cambridge University Press, 1976); K. RAHNER, "Resurrection of Christ," *Sacramentum Mundi*, Vol. 5 (New York: Herder & Herder, 1970), 323–24; N. T. WRIGHT, *The Resurrection of the Son of God* (Minneapolis, MN: Fortress Press, 2003); and R. SIDER, "The Pauline Conception of the Resurrection Body in I Corinthians XV," *New Testament Studies* 21 (1974–75): 35–54.

the inherent value and dignity of the present state of our embodiment (with all the vicissitudes that entails), we can now briefly address a terminological distinction that Tirosh-Samuelson introduces into the discussion. The ultimate terminus of the efforts of many transhumanists appears to be the goal of posthumanism. Though Tirosh-Samuelson qualifies the use of this term by the descriptors "cultural" and "technoscientific" the manner in which these two relate to one another in her paper appears mostly implicit and thus opens the way for ambiguity and possible misunderstanding. Thus, I would like to make a few (hopefully clarifying) comments on what I take to be their relationship.

1. Technoscientific Posthumanism

What is meant by technoscientific posthumanism receives more attention by Tirosh-Samuelson and is thereby perhaps clearer. As a result, I will not labor to represent it here in great detail, except to point out the way in which this perspective – which calls for the end of the biological human species and its replacement by the integration of consciousness with machine intelligence – seems to naively preserve an outmoded form of mind-body dualism. Admittedly, the following comments cannot be applied to all transhumanists, but apply most aptly to supports of the notion of "whole brain emulation." The idea of mapping consciousness to such a degree that it can be transferred or uploaded into a computer or robot has been frequent fodder for science-fiction narratives in recent years, but arguably has become no more practical.

Mind-body dualism, of course, conceives of the mind as immaterial and as occurring concomitantly with a material body. Most dualists conceive of the mind and the body as distinct in kind and possessive of different ontological properties existing in a kind of symbiotic relationship. While most transhumanists ostensibly adhere to a materialist view of cognition in which the mind is coextensive with operations of the brain, supporters of "whole brain emulation" nevertheless reproduce a conception of the mind as somehow distinct and separable from the body. This sort of interactionism views the mind as inhabiting and governing the physical body in much the same way that a person may momentarily inhabit a machine (e.g., a tank, forklift, etc.) and control "its" subsequent movements. *Ghosts in Machines*[14] and *Brains in Vats*[15] come to mind.

Much has been written in recent decades, however, about the problematic nature of conceiving of consciousness in this way. Proponents of embodied cognition, for example, rejects the image of the mind as a computational process

---

[14] See G. RYLE, *The Concept of Mind* (New York: Routledge, 1949, 2009).
[15] See G. HARMAN, *Thought* (Princeton, NJ: Princeton University Press, 1973) and H. PUTNAM, *Reason, Truth, and History* (Cambridge: Cambridge University Press, 1981).

similar to a computer program. Instead, as they contend, the mind appears to arise as a result of myriad factors not merely reducible to neurochemical activity in the brain, which correspondingly rely heavily on external features of embodiment.[16] Unlike, gene-editing, nootropics, or neural implants (all of which are already being utilized), mind-uploading remains only a distant possibility.

2. Cultural Posthumanism

Tirosh-Samuelson points to postmodernism's critique of the Enlightenment as providing a form of "cultural posthumanism" insofar as it subjects many of the cherished assumptions of the so-called "Age of Reason" to withering skepticism. For example, postmodernism largely casts aspersions on Enlightenment claims of embodying the ideals of emancipation and progress. It accomplished this by demonstrating that the frequent appeals made by Enlightenment-era figures to the supposed indubitability of *Reason* as the ultimate arbiter of universal value and meaning, more often than not, simply cloaked assumptions and goals which were anything but disinterested or universally valid. Instead, these attendant assumptions were frequently castigated as being racist, classist, sexist, homophobic, and hopelessly Eurocentric. For postmodern theorists, the elevation of western European society to the level of highest ideal yet achieved artificially divided the world between "civilized nations" and "barbarians."[17] This furthermore had the additional effect of subdividing internal factions within so-called "civilized" countries between the partisans of the Enlightenment and the forces of supposed "backwardness" and "superstition."[18]

What we now think of as postmodernity, however, is as much a continuation of the Enlightenment as it is a reaction to it. For example, the inevitable relativizing effects of the Enlightenment's attempts at *Entmythologisierung* was hinted at as early as Kant. In his work, *Idea for a Universal History from a Cosmopolitan Point of View* (1784), Kant says, "Man is an animal which, if it lives among others of its kind, requires a master [...] But whence does he get this master? *Only from the human race. But then the master is himself an animal*, and

---

[16] See A. Noë, *Out of Our Heads: Why You Are Not Your Brain, and Other Lessons from the Biology of Consciousness* (New York: Hill and Wang, 2009); R. D. Beer, "Dynamical Approaches to Cognitive Science," *Trends in Cognitive Sciences* 4, no. 3 (2000): 91–99; A. Chemero, "Epilogue: What Embodiment Is," *A Multidisciplinary Approach to Embodiment: Understanding Human Being*, ed. N. Dess (New York: Routledge, 2021), 133–140.

[17] See M. Boletsi, *Barbarism and Its Discontents* (Stanford, CA: Stanford University Press, 2013); D. R. Brunstetter, *Tensions of Modernity: Las Casas and His Legacy in the French Enlightenment*. Routledge Innovations in Political Theory Series (New York: Routledge, 2012); S. Slabodsky, *Decolonial Judaism: Triumphal Failures of Barbaric Thinking*, New Approaches to Religion and Power Series (New York: Palgrave Macmillan, 2014).

[18] See E. Cameron, *Enchanted Europe: Superstition, Reason, and Religion 1250–1750* (New York: Oxford University Press, 2010).

needs a master."[19] Implicit in this statement is the recognition that, bereft of a transcendent arbiter (real or imagined), there can exist no objective basis upon which to adjudicate between alternative worldviews or modes-of-life. The pretense of Reason's objectivity and universalizability then can be seen to have served this ersatz function. Since many Europeans could no longer trust in dogmatic Christianity to serve as a complete organizing paradigm, they needed an alternative narrative to hold-fast against the destabilizing effects of uncertainty generated by the radical social upheavals of the era.

Thus, it was perhaps always inevitable that the deconstructive enterprise of modernity would, in the end, turn its scrutinizing gaze inward. As Horkheimer and Adorno famously observed in the *Dialectic of Enlightenment* (1947), "Mythology itself set in motion the endless process of enlightenment by which, with ineluctable necessity, every definite theoretical view is subjected to the annihilating criticism that it is only a belief, until even the concepts of mind, truth, and, indeed, enlightenment itself have been reduced to animistic magic." If postmodernity represents the end of Humanism, therefore, it is only because it has completed the project of modernity by realizing the ultimately hermeneutic nature of all such endeavors at meaning-making. In other words, for better or worse, it's myth all the way down.

Here, we will be forced to bracket-out any attempt at a fuller discussion of the implications of such a realization, however, and instead focus our attention on its pertinence to Tirosh-Samuelson's argument. One of the downsides of this demotion of humanity to "just another part of nature" with no special status is that it removes the stigma against its violability. In other words, as far as I can see it, the consequences of viewing humanity as not being special can only lead to one of two conclusions. It will either have the effect of dignifying all of nature by locating in it the site of the sacred which formally had been the exclusive possession of humankind; or, far more likely, it will result in the reduction of human beings to merely so much more material to manipulate as objects upon which to exercise power. Indeed, as Heidegger said:

"Modern science's way of representing pursues and entraps nature as a calculable coherence of forces. Modern physics is not experimental physics because it applies apparatus to the questioning of nature. Rather the reverse is true. Because physics, indeed already as pure theory, sets nature up to exhibit itself as a coherence of forces calculable in advance, it therefore orders its experiments precisely for the purpose of asking whether and how nature reports itself when set up in this way."[20]

---

[19] I. KANT, "Idea for a Universal History from a Cosmopolitan Point of View," in *Kant on History*, ed. and trans. L. W. Beck (New York: Bobs Merrill, 1963) (https://www.marxists.org/reference/subject/ethics/kant/universal-history.htm) (6/30/2022); *Kants Gesammelte Schriften*, *AA* 8 (Berlin: Walter de Gruyter & Co., 1900), 15–31.
[20] M. HEIDEGGER, *The Question Concerning Technology and Other Essays*, trans. W. Lovitt (New York: Garland Publishing, 1977), 21.

"[Man] comes to the point where he himself will have to be taken as standing-reserve. Meanwhile man, precisely as the one so threatened, exalts himself to the posture of lord of the earth. In this way the impression comes to prevail that everything man encounters exists only insofar as it is his construct. This illusion gives rise in turn to one final delusion: It seems as though man everywhere and always encounters only himself."[21]

In effect, calculating thought can only ever rob objects of their essence and value except as a standing-reserve, a resource, for some other end. The only dignifying quality that humanity seems to possess for the transhumanist is its ability to make of itself what it wills – or, to put it less charitably, to reduce itself to an object of its own calculating thought. Stripped of inherent dignity, infinitely malleable as nothing more than raw material, we might well ask, "What value is left then to perpetuate or reclaim in a posthuman future?" "To what is death an enemy?" "In other words," "Why bother continuing to exist?"

I suspect that for many transhumanists, physical suffering, limitation, adversity, and mortality are not constitutive elements of their conception of a meaningful existence – indeed, they amount to its negation. While I can certainly understand the perspective that wishing to preserve these elements of existence appears to promote a kind of masochistic life-denying philosophy. Nevertheless, upon closer analysis, I demur at such a characterization. We can wish to limit unnecessary suffering without accepting the end of our humanity as its price. Whether or not our lives are long or short (relatively speaking); whether or not we somehow survive death in the hereafter, to me, seems to be of little consequence for the actual meaning of our existence. As Wittgenstein reminds us:

"[...] If by eternity is understood not endless temporal duration but timelessness, then he lives eternally who lives in the present. Our life is endless in the way that our visual field is without limit."

"The temporal immortality of the soul of man, that is to say, its eternal survival also after death, is not only in no way guaranteed, but this assumption in the first place will not do for us what we always tried to make it do. *Is a riddle solved by the fact that I survive forever? Is this eternal life not as enigmatic as our present one?* The solution of the riddle of life in space and time lies outside space and time. (It is not problems of natural science which have to be solved.)"[22]

4. Living in the End Times, or Capitalism and the Anthropocene

The likelihood of ecological collapse and human extinction as a result of climate change is the Sword of Damocles which now hangs over any discussion of the future. The term "Anthropocene," as Tirosh-Samuelson notes, is the

---

[21] Ibid., 27.
[22] L. WITTGENSTEIN, *Tractatus Logico-Philosophicus*, 6.4311 and 6.4312 (New York: Harcourt, Brace & Company, Inc., 1922), 88–89.

period into which we have now transitioned; the period in which humankind has become a geological force impacting all life on this planet. This term can be misleading though. It has the unfortunate effect of stigmatizing all of humanity equally for the results of actions which can be mostly attributed to the decisions of a handful of major international corporation. The majority of humanity is as much the victim of the effects of climate change as it is its perpetrators. As the editors of Scientific America wrote recently, "Surely [...] the last survivor of an uncontacted hunter-gatherer tribe in the Brazilian Amazon, bears less responsibility for our present predicament than, say, former Secretary of State Rex Tillerson, who was CEO of ExxonMobil. The tribe's carbon emissions are essentially zero, whereas ExxonMobil is the fifth-largest carbon emitter in the world, according to the Carbon Majors Report."[23] The ecofascist notion that human-beings are somehow inherently a malevolent force in nature – a virus of some kind attacking the planet – repeats the same distorted view of humanity as being something "other" to the world.

Though it occupies only a peripheral concern in Samuelson's paper, it seems clear to me, that any attempt to address the current ecological crisis practically or theoretically has to contend with the primary socioeconomic driver of climate change – capitalism. This is relevant to the discussion of transhumanism, not merely because the existential threat of extinction promises to foreclose the future that transhumanists hope for, but also because of the degree to which technology companies are entangled with global capital. The profit-motive built into capitalism coupled with the notion of infinite growth as the measure of success run headlong into the realities of finite resources and the interdependence of life on complex natural cycles which capitalist extraction interrupts. Transhumanism, rather than providing an alternative to this death-spiral, instead, merely offer a form of techno-escapism, which neither fundamentally questions nor undermines the factors which lead to social stratification and exploitation in the first place. Indeed, it depends on them. In the end, as Ana Teixeira Pinto has observed:

"The techno-capitalist spirit [...] is 'decidedly Faustian, and not Promethean: it does not seek to emancipate human beings and better their estate, but rather to dominate and distinguish itself from the merely human' [...] appeals to move beyond the 'human' as currently constituted, either as a return to a mystical eschaton or as singleton superseding humanity, fail to yield any meaningful movement – metaphysical or otherwise – which would signal a departure from the autonomous subject that undergirds settler capitalism."[24]

---

[23] Scientific American Editors, "The Term 'Anthropocene' Is Popular – and Problematic." Originally published with the title "Rethinking the 'Anthropocene'", *Scientific American* 319/6/10 (December 2018) (doi:10.1038/scientificamerican1218-10. Accessed 8/12/2021).

[24] A. T. PINTO, "Capitalism with a Transhuman Face: The Afterlife of Fascism and the Digital Frontier," *Third text* 33, no. 3 (2019): 321.

5. Conclusion

In his 1943 book, *The Abolition of Man*, C. S. Lewis made the following statement:

"[W]hat we call Man's power over Nature turns out to be a power exercised by some men over other men with Nature as its instrument ... Each generation exercises power over its successors [...] This modifies the picture which is sometimes painted of a progressive emancipation from tradition and a progressive control of natural processes resulting in a continual increase of human power. In reality, of course, if any one age really attains, by eugenics and scientific education, the power to make its descendants what it pleases, all men who live after it are the patients of that power. They are weaker, not stronger: for though we may have put wonderful machines in their hands we have pre-ordained how they are to use them ... And we must also remember that, quite apart from this, the later a generation comes – the nearer it lives to that date at which the species becomes extinct – the less power it will have in the forward direction ... There is therefore no question of a power vested in the race as a whole steadily growing as long as the race survives. The last men, far from being the heirs of power, will be of all men most subject to the dead hand of the great planners and conditioners and will themselves exercise least power upon the future ... For the power of Man to make himself what he pleases means, as we have seen, the power of some men to make other men what they please."[25]

One of the things I find most compelling in this quotation is the manner in which, as Lewis observes, the powers of the past and present limit the range of available options for the future. Indeed, it determines what is thinkable. Those who seek to move us towards a posthuman future wish to determine in the present what is expendable in the human condition. In this respect, Tirosh-Samuelson provides a helpful corrective to what I take to be the overly narrow vision of human flourishing offered by transhumanism. Unlike the transhumanist model which reduces human fulfillment to the self-actualization of the individual through the artifice of technological innovation, Tirosh-Samuelson provides an understanding of flourishing grounded in irreducible relationality and inherent dignity of human life. We do not stand apart from our bodies, the world, or each other, we are embedded in the community of creation.

---

[25] C. S. Lewis, *The Abolition of Man* (New York: Harper Collins, 2001), 55–59.

Futures, Straining to Come into the World

Transhumanism, Transhumanisms, and the Mormon Transhumanist Association

Jon Bialecki

1. Introduction

Copy editing is an editorial process that is designed to capture and cure errors before the infelicity of their being published. Which is why it's interesting is that one recurrent tic that I have encountered when my writing is under editorial care is the desire to replace 'transhumanisms' with 'transhumanism,' or even, sometimes, with 'Transhumanism.' What constitutes error in language is a matter of judgement, centering on aesthetic issues, the ease of reading, the clarity produced, and tradition. But the sense of something being incorrect also resonates with an implicit picture of the world, an ontological sense of how things are constructed; it is no accident that language, cognition, and social life so closely echo with one another. And, based on the vagaries of editing alone, it seems safe to suggest that, at least when dealing with nouns that represent social-intellectual movements such as transhumanism, in much of the English world, and perhaps in "Standard Average European" languages as a whole, there is a desire to see various expressions of a concept as falling under a single aegis, as all being in essence another iteration of the same thing.[1]

This platonic symptom is not just a function of background cognition – it is at times a conscious expression of concept a singular, transcendent truth. Which is to say, an often *religious* truth. It is a mistake to read religion and transcendence as always implying each other. There are visions of religion – or, to court the copy-editor's ire yet again, of variants of religiosity or religiosities – that are comfortable with immanence, running from Spinoza to Kierkegaard to some modes of contemporary Christianity. But Western monotheism does at times have a tendency to think in terms of singular truths that cannot be reduced to the multiple and varied state of affairs in the world we inhabit on a quotidian basis. Again, transcendence does not by its nature mean intellectual

---

[1] B. Whorf, "The Relation of Habitual Thought and Behavior to Language," in *Language, Thought and Reality: Selected Writings of Benjamins Lee Whorf*, ed. J. B. Carroll (Cambridge, MA: The M.I.T. Press, 1956), 134–159.

monoculture; one could imagine a divine that embraces and valorizes difference, and many people do understand God in that matter. But monotheism ('monotheisms'?) does open up a temptation to see divine as singular, the truth of divinity as singular, and therefore see religion as a category to be a set of singular objects where internal differentiation is either error or noise. And, hence, all those copyeditor corrections.

But the world itself strains against this attempt to silo and unify. Indeed, these emergent efforts at differentiation and proliferation are so driven that they insist even when they are pushed back against by a desire for consistency. This resistance is important to understand if we are discussing a topic such as the future of humanity. The problem lays in that singular article, 'the.' For, unless that future is prewritten, we do not have 'the' future of humanity, we have a proliferation of potential futures that are straining to come into the world. And our ability to read and negotiate all these becomings are contingent on seeing the situation not as a set of molar blocks of distinct and inert ideological substance, a limited set of fully formed futures that sit on a metaphorical bookshelf, ready to be selected, but as molecular movement where new combinations and variants are continually come into being.[2] Further, this flattening of differentiated viewpoints into single ideological positions forecloses understanding the specific social and cultural conditions that allow for and foster these vying futures. Either ideas stand apart from the social grounds that were necessary for their initial formulation, or alternately, we grant that there was some causal conditioning, but we again fall into discussing it as a single unified force, and not itself an internally differentiated phenomenon; in this later case, we end up speaking about 'late capitalism' or 'secularism' or the like, all of which are real fields of force, but which themselves also contains variation and gradations, and which interact with various specific social and cultural conditions in significantly distinguishable ways.

Let's make this discussion less dreamy; let's lay out some bones and put some flesh on it. What is an example of what this siloing looks like when discussing possible future, how does this operation constricts the eye and makes the imagination sclerotic, and finally – what is a transhumanist, anyway? I'd like to start this conversation by discussing some of the work of Hava Tirosh-Samuelson, a critical thinker and philosopher who has been engaging transhumanism for something approaching two decades now; or to be more precise, since this is not an engagement with the person, it is better to frame the first object as an essay by Hava Tirosh-Samuelson, entitled "In Pursuit of Perfectionism: The Misguided Transhumanist Vision" (though other work Tirosh-Samuelson

---

[2] H. BERGSON, *The Creative Mind: An Introduction to Metaphysics* (New York: Philosophical Library, 1946).

works will be referenced from time to time a well).³ Then, let me present the Mormon Transhumanist Association, a group that would seem to be fairly well defined by its name alone, even if its existence may raise numerous questions for those unfamiliar with the group. We'll use our discussion of these two to present a tentative picture of transhumanism, or rather, a series of different pictures of transhumanisms, focusing on a fractal-like internal difference that complicates any totalities and multiplies potential futures. In the end, this essay will argue that the coeval human futures that characterize the present moment are too important to grasp through sliding them into rough predetermined slots.

2. Making Transhumanism from Transhumanisms.

Lets' begin by putting a face on transhumanism – though, Tirosh-Samuelson tells us, putting a face on Transhumanism is difficult because "[t]ranshumanism is not easy to define."[4] This is not just Tirosh-Samuelson's own conceit, the essay "In Pursuit of Perfection" wants to stress. We are told that "the leading transhumanist theorist" also describes it as "loosely defined."[5] Still, despite the nebulous nature of the object, we are given what is at least a working gloss on our object:

"There are many facets to transhumanism, but they all cohere into the claim that the human species is on the verge of a new phase in its evolution as the result of converging technologies such as genomics, robotics, informatics, and nanotechnology. According to transhumanism, these technologies will bring about the physiological and cognitive enhancement of human beings that will pave the way for the replacement of biological humans by autonomous, superintelligent, decision-making machines, which will constitute the posthuman age."[6]

This is a rather serious charge. When all is said and done, all transhumanists, then, are seeking the *extinction* of our species. (Though what constitutes 'species' here is something that Tirosh-Samuelson skips over, and is something that we will have opportunity to revisit.) This is not an overreading of the term replacement, which could be understood as a process of transformation and therefore continuation, albeit under different circumstances. It is about rupture and an ending: "transhumanism [...] is not about how we can flourish as biological, social, and political humans but a vision that denigrates our humanity,

---

[3] H. TIROSH-SAMUELSON, "In Pursuit of Perfection: The Misguided Transhumanist Vision." *Theology and Science* 16, no. 2 (2018): 200–222.
[4] Ibid., 200.
[5] Ibid.
[6] Ibid.

calling us to improve ourselves technologically so that we could voluntarily become extinct. As I see it, transhumanism calls us to commit collective suicide as a species."[7]

Given the nature of the accusation, it is best to be clear about who transhumanists are. But clarity on this point is made difficult by the fact that Tirosh-Samuelson sees transhumanists as both numerically sparse and as legion. "Numerically" we are talking about a movement that is "still very small" – only several thousand people worldwide, at least if transhumanism is measured by someone being "loosely" associated with in institution called H+ or Humanity Plus, *nee* World Transhumanist Association. But after this rough census, we are told about other institutions: the "Foresight Institute," the defunct "Extropian Institute," the "Institute for Ethics and Emerging Technology," (also known as "IEET"), "the future of Humanity Institute, the Machine Intelligence Research Institute ... and the Mormon Transhumanist Association, to name just a few." Tirosh-Samuelson tell us about still other organizations later in the course of the essay. There is "the Transhumanist Policy Center, the Center for Genetics and Society, the Center for Transhumanity-Immortal Life, Teresam and the Society for Universal Immortalism."[8] (Even further in, we are informed about "Singularity University [...] whose curriculum is informed by the transhumanist imagination.") In short, the full enumeration of institutions, organizations, and affinity groups clocks in at thirteen overall – and we are told to keep in mind that this list is not exhaustive. The list of "main spokespersons" for this "highly decentralized" movement also tends to run long. We are given twenty-three different transhumanists or transhumanist fellow travelers by name, even though we are reminded that this is a list of just "a few prominent voices."[9]

At the level of crass sociology, it is an interesting question as why this miniscule sliver of what is at this point in time at least still humanity should have such a proliferation of leaders and institutions. It may be because transhumanism is "not monolithic but a cluster of several currents."[10] There is extroprianism, which is centered on "boundless expansion, self-transcendence, dynamic optimism, intelligent technology, and spontaneous order."[11] Then there is a group, supposedly traveling under the name Singularitarians, who are anticipating the sudden advent of "runaway machine intelligence."[12] We are told

---

[7] Ibid., 204.
[8] Ibid., 201.
[9] Ibid.
[10] Ibid.
[11] Ibid, quoting M. MORE, "On Becoming Posthuman," *Free Inquiry* 14, no. 4 (1994): 38–41 (no page number given).
[12] TIROSH-SAMUELSON, "In Pursuit of Perfection," 201–202, citing N. BOSTROM, "Transhumanist Values," available on his website http://nickbostrom.com (4/22/2022).

about a strain of "hedonistic" transhumanism that emphasized "pleasure" and "morphological freedom," which is glossed as the freedom of individuals to enhance and modify physical, psychological, and cognitive aspects of their bodies. The last two modes presented are "democratic transhumanism," which is concerned about "social responsibility and democratic decision making in the use of converging technologies for the benefit of humanity" (that is, the species that transhumanism is supposedly aiming to make extinct), and the "[s]urvivalists [...] who focus on radical life extension and longevity." And again, this is an illustrative, and not an exhaustive, list "there are other variants, reflecting the preferences, expertise, and commitment of individual transhumanists activists who" [again] "vary greatly from each other."

The recurrent theme here is vertiginous difference. Even as Tirosh-Samuelson admits this, she complains about it as well:

"Because transhumanism is so diverse and constantly evolving, it is hard to generalize about it or to debate with its advocates; one can always disavow what another transhumanist has written or said, so that transhumanism is indeed a "work in progress," which is how transhumanists view human nature."[13]

The chief difficulty posed by this efflorescence seems to be the challenge of "debat[ing] with its advocates." Rather churlishly, transhumanists seems unwilling to defend or take responsibility for the positions of other transhumanists whom they disagree with. What is to be done? One option at this point would be to interrogate the nature of the "it" that appears in the possessive phrase "its advocates." If we are going to see transhumanism as a *single thing*, what is the nature of this single thing, and how is it that this single thing contains so much ideological diversity? Is there something about transhumanist thought, either in its form, its substance, or the media through which transhumanist thought is forged and circulated, that gives it this singular character, and if so, is whatever is responsible for this trait particular to transhumanist thought, or is it something that can be identified in other contemporary intellectual centers or collections of interest as well? Alternately, we could take the trouble we have here and ask if the problem is about us, somehow – perhaps something about how we think of representation and grouping, where there is a desire to impute something shared to all members of the category, even when, in a Wittgenstein 'family resemblance' manner, no such single through-line is shared by all members of the set?

These are questions that we will have occasion to return to later on. The fact that this will be something we engage with down the line means, of course that Tirosh-Samuelson has taken a different route. Not despite the differences in all these actualizations of transhumanism, but because of them, she

---

[13] Ibid.

is aggregating all these transhumanisms into a single transhumanism. She does so for reasons that are far from flippant: she is concerned about the baleful influence transhumanism might have on a wider society, and this influence can only be engaged with if it is reified. As she says,

> "I treat the various strands of transhumanism as themes of one and the same futuristic vision that calls for the transition from biological humanity to mechanical posthumanity. I admit that in so doing, I impose on transhumanism a certain degree of coherence that it may not have. Nonetheless, I argue that treating the various themes of transhumanism together is legitimate because only then can we grasp why it is culturally significant even though it is deeply misguided."[14]

Again, these are serious stakes, the fabric of culture, or at least of what is "culturally significant," if we wish to again avoid the creation of singular objects, is at risk. And one can sense Tirosh-Samuelson's sincere anxiety. Because of this, this condensation into a single object is an operation that is worth considering.

Before we go on, we can parenthetically ask whether transhumanism does have the cultural cachet that Tirosh-Samuelson credits it with, a claim which might be questioned given that she begins her essay stating that "most people are unfamiliar with the term" transhumanism, and that when she shares the fact that she "writes about" it" she "usually encounter[s] a perplexed look." Still, granting her claim, it still seems from what she says that her concern is not in transhumanism itself, but its effects on popular culture. These effects, though, are the result of a diverse movement, one that she singularizes herself into a monolithic, but also virtual, singular object. This is curious, since her concern seems to be ultimately with the reception of transhumanism, and it takes little command of information theory or semiosis to understand that intention, communication, and reception are three different moments that contain the possibility of some considerable communicative disjunctures. It might be that the better question is what is it in the popular culture that makes it (again, this is the language of singular entities treated as if there were no internal differentiation) see or project concepts and values *onto* a collective, imagined transhumanism. This is especially the case because it is doubtful that a disaggregated, ununified transhumanism is presenting a single message to the popular culture. And then there is the possibility that the causal arrow goes the other way, or at least that the arrow is double headed: perhaps we should be asking what are the strands in popular culture, or perhaps even the different strands and situations present in different cultures, that are creating transhumanism?

Some allowances should be made for Tirosh-Samuelson here, though. Near the conclusion of her essay she does consider the something along the lines of

---

[14] Ibid.

transhumanism having a social engine, meditating on how secularism may have primed the culture for transhumanism. Perhaps a more important concession would be to note that her move in singularizing a plural transhumanism might be justified on grounds that the intellectual violence being done is not all that great because, while the various transhumanisms fused together by her caprice may differ, the range of that difference is not so great that the gains in clarity do not outweigh the scope of what is lost. It is possible that transhumanisms may still be more alike than different, and that this supposed variation is more an example of the narcissism of minor differences than it is of any true breadth of the movement(s). The best way to test whether this is true is to produce a list of traits that Tirosh-Samuelson scries in what we might want to call 'monolithic' or 'generic' transhumanism, and hold it up against a test case. Of course, doing this is not an unproblematic procedure, since we risk creating another artificially unified object at a lower level; this is a danger that must be kept in mind. It's best, then, to choose a social collectivity whose texture, position in larger social landscapes, and degrees of internal variance (both those actually encountered, and those that are suffered without generating conflict), is to a degree understood.

3. Mormon Transhumanism

Here, I turn to the Mormon Transhumanist Association for our test case. There are two reasons for this. First, they are a group that, with their approval, I have been studying ethnographically since 2015; I have spoken formally and informally to members innumerable times, I have attended their annual conferences, and, when able, their monthly meetups in Provo, Utah (though they also have far had far less frequent meetups in Seattle and the Bay area that I have not had a chance to attend). And what is more, I have spent time in the various virtual spaces they inhabit – the various chatrooms, listserves, and Facebook pages that constitute their online social nodes. The other reason is that this is a group known to Tirosh-Samuelson; in fact, it is cited by her as an exemplar of transhumanism, alongside a wealth of other future-facing organization and groups.

Asking if Tirosh-Samuelson's descriptor of 'generic' transhumanism fits for a group she was unaware of, after all, seems a bit underhanded. And the MTA (as the Mormon Transhumanist Association is sometimes referred to) is definitely an organization that she is aware of. It was, after all, one of the bodies that she enumerated in passing when listing all the social transhumanist organs. But her most extended encounter with the MTA occurs in an earlier paper of hers, where she considers whether transhumanism is a 'secular faith.' If it is a secular faith, she notes, at least from the standpoint of traditional Christianity, it is a "heresy." This leads her to the following claim: "It may not be a coincidence that the fastest-growing religion today – the Church of Latter-day Saints [sic] – which some Christians regard as a 'heresy,' is also the tradition that exhibits the most positive attitude towards transhumanism."[15] As 'heretical' transhumanists splinter group within a 'heretical' religion, though, she presents them as not doing much beyond anticipating technological *theosis*. "Comparing them to a rather abstracted vision of the institutional Church of Jesus Christ of Latter-day Saints, she states that "the good works in this world that Mormons consider necessary for eternal life consist of service to others and massive investment in education; while transhumanists talk about the benefit of technology to humanity, they have yet to translate their ideology into social action or education."[16]

Is this an adequate depiction, at least from an ethnographic standpoint? To measure this claim, we might want to consider the makeup and history of the Mormon Transhumanist Association (or, as it is sometimes referred to as, the MTA). First, the group is paradoxically both young and old at the same instance. Growing out of online discussion groups centered on debates about Mormonism, it coalesced as a group of about thirteen people in roughly 2006. Over time, this group has expanded to roughly a thousand individuals, though it should be noted that not all of that one thousand are equally active in the life of the organization or in placing transhumanism at the center of their faith. Admittedly, one thousand people are not that many, and being only fifteen years of age makes it relatively recent as far as human institutions go. But when compared to other transhumanist organizations, it is long in the tooth, and it is massive when it is put up against other religious transhumanist organizations. It is the largest and oldest religious transhumanist group. Furthermore, it is even older than many influential secular transhumanist organizations: as might be guessed from the disparate and varied description of transhumanism, transhumanist groups are prone to fissures and internal contestation. (Indeed, the Mormon Transhumanist Association is now so old that it can count itself has having a few second-generation members, children of some early adopters to the organization.) Unsurprisingly, given that the Church of Jesus Christ of Latter-day Saints is a Church that is effectively without any paid clergy, and where the responsibility of maintaining and running the various stakes falls on unpaid volunteers, the Mormon genius for bottom-up social organization has served the Mormon Transhumanist Organization well. Prizing themselves on an ethic of self-reliance, there is an understanding that Mormons must do their collective labors themselves.

---

[15] H. Tirosh-Samuelson, "Transhumanism as a Secularist Faith," *Zygon* 47, no. 4 (2012): 727.

[16] Ibid.

Of course, though, MTA members are not your prototypical Mormons. The original group was a set of young (mostly) men with degrees from Brigham Young University, Provo, the flower of the Mormon higher-educational system. They had majored in areas such as philosophy, music, and linguistics; and yet found themselves employed as software engineers in the "Silicon Slopes," the Utah tech corridor whose rapid growth was fueled by a tech industry stereotype of Mormons as dedicated, hardworking, and sober (both figuratively and literally) worker. Many people who had been pulled into programming and related endeavors did not have a Heideggerian "ready-at-hand" attitude towards the new technologies they were now wrestling with; they interrogated what this new technology was ontologically, viewing from the standpoint of their liberal arts training and their religion.

Their religious sensibilities made quite a difference. Tirosh-Samuelson presents Mormons as 'heretical,' at least from an imagined Christian standpoint. It is true that what is understood as heresy and what is considered orthodoxy are not innocent judgments; they are a function of institutions being situated to speak authoritatively on the matter and having the political power and social capital to make these pronouncements effectively binding. It should also be remembered that this is perspectival; from a Mormon standpoint, mainline Christianity is considered to be contaminated by "The Great Apostasy," namely the forgetting of teachings, ritual practices, and priesthood authority for all (male) believers promulgated by Jesus Christ, and only brought back by the Joseph Smith. So, your miles may vary. But that said, it is undeniable that Mormon doctrine differs considerably from most of Western Christianity. *Theosis* has already been addressed, of course, defined by Tirosh-Samuelson, not entirely inadequately, I should add, as "the concept of eternal progress of humans, and the concept of a progressing God."[17] But the important aspect of *theosis* is the idea that "[a]s man now is, God once was; as God now is, man may become," as it was put by Lorenzo Snow, a nineteenth-century Mormon Apostle. In short, there is greater identity, and thus in a way an intimacy, between the human and the divine, and discussions of humanity's eschatological fate are also meditations on the processes that brought this world into being. Equally important was the post-Copernican, post-Newtonian concept that everything is material-including spirit, which merely was a more refined form of matter. The idea that Godhood is achieved and that this is a thoroughly material universe (even God has a material body) brings us to one more doctrinal distinctive: miracles are not the suspension of natural laws, but a more deft exercise of them. In effect, God is leveraging his superior understanding of the natural laws to bring miracles into effect, making miracles a kind of technology. These distinctives led some of these Mormons, thinking through the implications of rapidly advancing

---

[17] Ibid., 727.

technology, to posit that *theosis* may be achievable by technological, material means. This, combined with the Mormon ethos of self-reliance, suggested to MTA members that achieving *theosis* might be undertaken themselves, rather than simply remaining passive while Godhood is presented to them.

What is harder to identify but just as important is the way that Mormon Transhumanism allows for a different form of navigating Mormon sociality. And this, strangely, involves a discussion of secularism. Tirosh-Samuelson argues that speaking globally, transhumanism as a 'post-secular faith' is in part an effect of secularism. However, the Mormon Church was never secular – or at least, it wasn't secular during its founding nineteenth century. Animated by a radically different vision of marriage, voting in blocks as instructed by leadership, and even founding towns and militias, the Mormon Church continually tried to exercise authority in domains that under a secular disposition fell to the state and create subjects animated by a different sense of possibilities, embodiments, and affects in comparison to the nineteenth-century American secular subjects.[18] Rejecting this-worldly polygamy and consequently having Utah declared a state may have formally submitted the Church to the secular order, but the Church remains a total institution in large measure. Utah Mormonism is something close to an ethnicity, complete with ethnic dishes and art forms particular to it (there is a deep Mormon love of Musical Theatre, for instance). But what is more, religious ties are often laminated onto business ties, to the degree that preexisting relations and established trust catalyzes negotiations and transactions. More pressing, though, is that kinship, particularly marital ties, are also inextricably wedded to Mormonism. This is because the Mormon unit of salvation is effectively not the individual but the family, and leaving the religion places the salvation of others into question and also breaks the links that bond people together in the afterlife.

This makes leaving Mormonism a difficult and oftentimes painful, experience.[19] And yet there are pressures to leave Mormonism, because the internet has allowed for a greater ease in circulating information that varies from the imagine presented by the Church. This included aspects of Mormon history, such as Joseph Smith's role in polygamy and the ban on blacks entering the priesthood of all believers (a ban which was only rescinded in 1978). The advent of the internet also allowed for the organizing of groups who felt themselves to be in tension with the Church; feminist Mormons, LGBTQ Mormons, and progressive Mormons (constituencies that often overlapped) could now form online communities, giving them a platform to challenge the Church.

---

[18] P. COVIELLO, *Make Yourselves Gods: Sex, Secularism, and the Radiant Body of Early Mormonism* (Chicago, IL: University of Chicago Press, 2018).

[19] E. BROOKS, E. MARSHALL, *Disenchanted Lives: Apostasy and ex-Mormonism among the Latter-day Saints* (New Brunswick, NJ: Rutgers University Press, 2018).

Mormon Transhumanism can serve as a way out of this problem. By focusing on salvation as a human process, it relativizes the past. If humanity in general, and the Church in particular, is working towards a *telos*, then one would expect error in the past, and hope for positive changes in the future. Thus prior infelicities and contemporary mistakes become something that can be reconciled with. They are thus able to say that they "have a testimony," an essential aspect for Mormon, while at once creating a distance between themselves and many of the positions of the institutional Church. But many remain members in the Church. This is all to say that to the degree that individual Mormon Transhumanists are a part of the Church, they are engaged in the "the good works in this world that Mormons consider necessary for eternal life," particularly the "service," as it allows for them to be a part of the larger community. These Mormons Transhumanists engage in the same charitable endeavors as regular Mormons – it is just that the *transhumanist* aspect of the binomial nomenclature is always controlling, even it isn't marked. It is not so much that the transhumanist aspect is absent, but rather that it serves as a stabilizing force for the "Mormon" part of the name.

It must be stressed, though, that not all members of the Mormon Transhumanist Association are faithful or active members of the group. For many people brought up in the faith, the problematic aspects of past history and present politics are too much; others find the church conformist or inhospitable to difference. And they therefore, rather than negotiate a new relationship with the Church, end up parting with it, painful as such leave-taking can be. Here, Mormon transhumanism plays an almost therapeutic role; instead of allowing for a rearticulating of Mormonism, it allows for a virtual Mormon space, where former Saints can play with the most intriguing aspects of Mormon metaphysics, or engage in forms of sociability reminiscent of the aspects of Mormonism that they found convivial when they were members. I have heard of ex-Mormon transhumanists state that they have at times felt a 'burning of the bosom' during Mormon transhumanist gatherings – a phrase associated in Mormon religious parlance with the action of the Holy Ghost.

It is worth noting that even in a group as seemingly clearly delineated as Mormon Transhumanism, there is a multiplicity of positions. For more orthodox members, the set of technological possibilities that get amalgamated under the rubric of "transhumanism" are at once divine and eschatological, affordances set into the world at the beginning so that humanity could ascend in the same way that this universe's creators have done so before. For those who are not orthodox members, or even for those few who have never been orthodox members, Mormon transhumanism gives them a way to engage in a familiar form of cosmological speculation, articulated in a religious language that they may be fluent in, but which they no longer have an opportunity to regularly speak. For one set, it allows them to take their distance, while still remaining within the fold; for another set, it allows them to become closer to the cosmological aspects of Mormonism that interest them, while still staying outside the faith.

Even the picture just given of Mormon Transhumanism as a bifurcated discussion split between those formally inside and outside of the institutional Mormon Church is too procrustean. There are different articulations of the relationship between technology and religion on the side of those still within the Church, and those outside of the Church have different approaches to questions regarding the nature of divinity, ranging from those who hew close to an orthodox Mormon cosmology, but simply see the religion as more extensive than the institutional Church, to those who, having lost faith in both the Apostles who lead the Church as well as in the Church itself, due to prior bad acts or contemporary problematic positions, have taken away from this betrayal of trust the idea that they should show similar levels of skepticism regarding the existence of the deity.

It seems, therefore, that the proliferation of positions and authorities that Tirosh-Samuelson identified in transhumanism writ large is in a way fractal; that even a transhumanist organization with as fairly limited remit as the MTA is fractured into some quite different ontological and social positions. We also saw her accusation that Mormon Transhumanists, unlike members of the institutional Church of Jesus Christ of Latter-saints, were not engaged in charitable works was not quite on the nose; it is more accurate to say that they do engage, directly through volunteering and indirectly through tithing, to charitable activities and "good works," but they do so in their capacities as Mormons. This also suggests that the value of transhumanism is not always in the vision that it presents of the future but can be at times also how it allows people to negotiate the presence. Whether inside or outside of institutional Mormonism, being a Mormon Transhumanist does something for members. And any attempt to engage with transhumanism, whether as study or critique, needs to take this into account.

Since we are now weighing Tirosh-Samuelson's description of Mormon Transhumanism, and perhaps thus through inference of transhumanism(s) write large, it should also be noted that the accusation that Mormon Transhumanists do not participate in "education" is not quite on the nose, either. Mormon Transhumanism has various spaces where, for lack of a better term, it can be said to occur: there are the usual social media spaces, and there are also monthly meetups for the various chapters (though the Provo, Utah branch is by an order of magnitude larger and more active than more anemic, irregular meetups in places such as Seattle or the California Bay area). And there are various more relaxed family gatherings. But the chief meeting is the annual conference. The conference features all of the trappings of other academic conferences, such as keynote speakers (usually one figure from academic

Mormon studies and another associated with secular humanism), panels, and paper sessions. These conference trappings even include location; for instance, the first Mormon Transhumanist sponsored conference was held in 2009 at the Claremont Graduate University in Claremont, California. In short, it could be suggested that these Mormon Transhumanists are as much an academic exercise and hence are also engaged in the labor of promoting education through capillary action as the conference that was the impetus for this same volume.

4. The End, and the Return, of Humanity

However, there is still one charge that has not been met, and it is a rather serious one: the claim that transhumanism was working collectively for the extinction of the human race. Again, given this essay's thesis that transhumanism is a varied group, to deny that some transhumanists would be comfortable creating superhuman forms of intelligence even if these entities superseded humankind would be wrong.[20] But it would be difficult to say that of Mormon transhumanism. This is partly because of common interest in space flight and the colonization of other planets, a potential expenditure of resources defended as 'not putting all of the eggs in one basket.' But this charge is not quite correct for another, more subtle reason. Tirosh-Samuelson's charge assumes a gulf, and not some form of continuity, between the human and non-human. But this is not how the relation between the human and the divine is imagined in Mormonism. As put by one Brigham Young philosophy professor, writing in the Church operated periodical New Era: "There is nothing more fundamental in God's revelations than the basic premise that we are of the race of Gods. We are of his species."[21] The work of *theosis* is not the replacement of the species, but rather the species achieving its ultimate fulfillment.

It is true that in recent decades, such strong claims regarding the identity of humanity and God have not been emphasized by an institutional Church interested in appearing to be in harmony with conventional protestant orthodoxy, and there are some members of the wider Church of Jesus Christ of Latter-day Saints who would dismiss this language as going too far. But there are reasons, not predicated on an identity of the divine and the human, to be skeptical of the idea that Mormon Transhumanism aims at human extinction. And this reason is rooted in the common Mormon practice of baptism of the dead.

---

[20] See, e.g., A. FARMAN, "Re-Enchantment Cosmologies: Mastery and Obsolescence in an Intelligent Universe," *Anthropological Quarterly* 85, no. 4 (2012): 1069–1088.

[21] K. NIELSEN, "People on Other Worlds." *The New Era* (1971). Available online: https://www.churchofjesuschrist.org/study/new-era/1971/04/people-on-other-worlds?lang=eng (accessed on 10/27/2020); see generally J. BIALECKI, "Future-Day Saints: Abrahamic Astronomy, Anthropological Futures, and Speculative Religion," *Religions* 11 (2020): 612.

Recall the claim that the unit of salvation in orthodox Mormonism is not the individual but the family. The problem with this framing is that the limits of the family as a unit are difficult to define. The various generations are imbricated by parentage and descent, where one son or daughter is another person's mother or father. And through cousins and other lateral kin, the web of kinship runs out laterally as well. This means that to redeem the family to the fullest extent, one must offer those who have already passed away the same opportunity to join in this redemption as those who are proselytized in this life. The form through which this post-terminal offer is communicated is proxy baptisms, where an individual is baptized in the name of someone dead; this is at times a departed Mormon relative, but most often it is a name found in the copious genealogical records that the Church holds. This practice is not uncontroversial; in the case of baptisms of those who were killed because they were identified as belonging to a persecuted religious group, for instance, offering a chance to switch affiliation in the afterlife can understandably come across as being at the least in bad taste. But, to the degree that issues such as these can be put aside, one has to be struck by the grandeur of vision here: this is ultimately an attempt to, by the day of judgment, redeem the entire resurrected human race.

This ambition is shared by many Mormon Transhumanists as well; indeed, if I had to judge whether a post-human *theosis* or a resurrection of the human dead was more central to Mormon Transhumanism, based on the affective charge that it carries, I might have to go with resurrection. This prominence is perhaps because they feel the obligation to resurrect is meant to be devolved onto humanity and must be done by technical means. A full discussion of the way that various Mormon transhumanists have speculated about how this might be accomplished would take us too from our topic; sometimes, this is imagined to occur in a virtual realm through ancestor simulations; at other times, they imagine that this might occur through quantum archeology, a thoroughly untested idea that through quantum entanglement seemingly lost information could be retrieved, thereby allowing for a material recreation of the dead. Either way, serious problems about identity and continuity arise; to put it baldly, is someone who is identical with someone else physically a continuity of that person, viewed through the more ephemeral lens of subjectivity and personhood. But however skeptical one might be of the probability or the metaphysics, in a way, one could argue that this goal is, in fact, about the preservation of the human race, including those who have been lost. Up to the present moment, death as a final horizon that cannot be erased or returned from has shaped the human experience. One may wonder whether the humans living side by side with their ancestors would still be human in the sense we have been. This is certainly above the pay grade of a mere anthropologist. But it should be noted that at least the intent is for the preservation, singularly and collectively, of the entire species. And this is a vision, threading Mormon doctrine and technological ambition, that is so singular that to collapse it into a single phantasmic position for the sake of critique seems not only a misstep, but a denial of both transhumanist difference in general, and of this mode of difference in particular. Multiple futures are being imagined, and if one wishes to have a critical role in how those multiple futures interfere and intensify one another as they become actualized, it is probably best to more carefully attend to not only the variety of things being yearned for, but why various different futures are so attractive to different populations in the first place.

On the Possibility of a Novel Phenomenon

Richard Livingston

On a warm and windy spring day in early April 1844, Joseph Smith stood in front of a crowd of thousands to deliver what would become one of the most important sermons of his prophetic career. At the time, he was not just the Prophet to his people, but he was also the Mayor of one of the largest cities in Illinois, the Lieutenant General of the largest militia in the United States, and was even sustained as the "King" of a secret council that called itself the "Kingdom of God."[1] On that sunny Sunday afternoon, less than three months before his own death, the Mormon prophet, priest, and king stood for over two hours to provide a sermon that was part general conference address and part funeral oration to honor King Follett, a recently deceased member of the community.

Jon Bialecki quoted some of what eventually became known as the "King Follet discourse"[2] in the context of his discussion of Lincoln Cannon's attempt to console a fellow transhumanist who was grieving over the loss of his mother. But I want to consider a few more passages, because I think they provide some extremely important insights into the theological and cosmological foundations of Latter-day Saint faith. More importantly, I think they might be able to further illuminate the affinity that many Mormons feel for transhumanism, as well how we might think about religious expressions of transhumanism.

After several preliminary comments to set the stage for a speech that would address "a subject of the greatest importance and the most solemn of any that could occupy our attention,"[3] Smith opens with the following:

In the first place I wish to go back to the beginning of creation. There is the starting point in order to know and be fully acquainted with the mind, purposes, decrees, and ordinations of the great Elohim that sits in the heavens. *For us to take up beginning at the creation it is necessary for us to understand something of God Himself in the beginning.* If we start right, it is very easy for us to go right all the time; but if we start wrong, we may go wrong, and it is a hard matter to get right.[4]

---

[1] "Council of Fifty," The Joseph Smith Papers, accessed February 15, 2019, (https://www.josephsmithpapers.org/topic/council-of-fifty).

[2] S. Larson, "The King Follett Discourse: A Newly Amalgamated Text," *BYU Studies* 18, no. 2 (1978): 193–208.

[3] Ibid., 198.

[4] Ibid., 199, emphasis mine.

In order to understand creation, one must first understand its creator. Smith's theology is thus unequivocally a kind of *theology from above*. It is necessary to begin with the one who created the world in order to grasp how the world came to be.

Similarly, it is only by understanding of the nature of divinity that one is able to grasp the nature of humanity. As Smith continues,

> There are but very few beings in the world who understand rightly the character of God. *If men do not comprehend the character of God, they do not comprehend their own character. They cannot comprehend anything that is past or that which is to come*; they do not know – they do not understand their own relationship to God.[5]

Interestingly, this cosmotheological vision is not only a *spatial* framework that moves from the divine realm in order to reveal something about the human realm, but it's also *temporal* framework that aims to reach backward into that which has been and forward into that which is yet to be in order to understand how we currently stand in relation to the Divine Reality.

> I want to go back, then, to the beginning that you may understand and so get you to lift your minds into a more lofty sphere and exalted standing than what the human mind generally understands. I want to ask this congregation – every man, woman, and child – to answer this question in their own heart: *What kind of a being is God?* Ask yourselves! I again repeat the question: What kind of a being is God?[6]

Once again, Smith wants to elucidate what it means to be human by elucidating, indeed for him *revealing*, what it means to be God.

Before the world came into existence, Smith goes on to ask, "what kind of a being was God?"

> I will go back to the beginning to show you. I will tell you, so open your ears and eyes, all ye ends of the earth, and hear [...] I am going to tell you the designs of God for the human race, the relation the human family sustains with God, and why He interferes with the affairs of man. First, *God Himself who sits enthroned in yonder heavens is a Man like unto one of yourselves* – that is the great secret! If the veil were rent today and the great God that holds this world in its sphere and the planets in their orbit and who upholds all things by His power – if you were to see Him today, you would see Him in all the person, image, fashion, and very form of a man, like yourselves. For Adam was a man formed in His likeness and created in the very fashion and image of God. Adam received instruction, walked, talked, and conversed with Him as one man talks and communicates with another.[7]

First and foremost, then, he explicitly rejects the widely-held classical monotheistic view that God is wholly other, ontologically utterly *unlike* everything other than God. Instead, for Smith, humanity and divinity share the same

---

[5] Ibid., emphasis mine.
[6] Ibid., emphasis mine.
[7] Ibid., 200, emphasis mine.

"DNA," so to speak, so when the bible says that God made human beings in God's own image, it should be understood in a very literal way – that is, God is an embodied person in precisely the same way that human beings are embodied persons.

Now, just in case his audience isn't sure about how this heavy cosmotheological discourse is appropriate for a commemorating a lost loved one, he goes on,

> In order to understand the subject of the dead and to speak for the consolation of those who mourn for the loss of their friends, it is necessary to understand the character and being of God. For I am going to tell you how God came to be God and what sort of a being He is. For we have imagined that God was God from the beginning of all eternity. I will refute that idea and take away the veil so you may see. [...] The first principle of truth and of the Gospel is to know for a certainty the character of God, and that we may converse with Him the same as one man with another, and that *He once was a man like one of us and that God Himself, the Father of us all, once dwelled on an earth the same as Jesus Christ himself did in the flesh and like us.*[8]

I hear echoes of this in Lincoln Cannon's reflection on the loss of his father, as it appears as though he was trying to emulate Joseph Smith in his effort to console the grief-stricken fellow-member of the Mormon Transhumanist Association. For both Smith and Cannon, one needs to know that God understands your pain, because God is the same kind of being that we are, and God once lived the kind of life that we do now by living on a planet like ours. Just as Jesus was incarnate in this world, so also God the Father was incarnate in some other world, somewhere, somewhen.

And just as God the Father and God the Son became divine beings only after first living on an earth as all human beings do, so also humans possess the same seeds of divinity within themselves, and thus have the potential to attain Godhood.

> Here then is eternal life – to know the only wise and true God. *You have got to learn how to make yourselves Gods in order to save yourselves and be kings and priests to God, the same as all Gods have done* – by going from a small capacity to a great capacity, from a small degree to another, from grace to grace, until the resurrection of the dead, from exaltation to exaltation – till you are able to sit in everlasting burnings and everlasting power and glory as those who have gone before, sit enthroned.[9]

It's especially here, with this talk of self-salvation, resurrection, and exaltation, that I think the Mormon affinity with transhumanism begins to come into focus.

Smith then further clarifies his intention to comfort those still stinging from the death of their beloved King Follet.

---

[8] Ibid., 201, emphasis mine.
[9] Ibid., emphasis mine.

I want you to know the first principles of consolation. How consoling to the mourners when they are called to part with a husband, father, wife, mother child, dear relative, or friend, to know, though they lay down this body and all earthly tabernacles shall be dissolved, that their very being shall rise in immortal glory to dwell in everlasting burnings and to sorrow, die, and suffer no more. And not only that, but to contemplate the saying that they will be heirs of God and joint-heirs with Jesus Christ. What is it? *To inherit and enjoy the same glory, powers, and exaltation until you ascend a throne of eternal power and arrive at the station of a God, the same as those who have gone before.*[10]

And there it is. To complete his spatial movement from above to below (and *back* above), as well as his temporal movement from past to present to future, Smith takes his listeners upward and forward by asserting that not only was God once a human like we are, but we can be resurrected into immortal glory, ascend to our own thrones of eternal power, and become a divine being just like God is.

We can thus tread in the tracks of all the Gods who have gone before us. Lorenzo Snow, the fifth president of the LDS Church, concisely captured all this in a famous couplet: "As man now is, God once was. As God now is, man may become."[11] Despite the fact the Church of Jesus Christ of Latter-day Saints has unquestionably deemphasized, decentered, and distanced itself from this teaching in recent decades,[12] my own sense is that it's still viewed by many as central to the doctrine of eternal progression, and is foundational to their faith.

As always, there are numerous details and disagreements that cannot be discussed here, but my primary point is that this provides one of the clearest pieces of evidence of which I'm aware that Mormonism has had at least a *strand* of transhumanism running through its theology from its earliest days. It appears to have been baked in from the get go. Or, as Bialecki puts it, the notion that human beings might gain "cosmos-making powers [...] is backed by an unconscious but unyielding logic in a Mormon context [...] becoming what is more than human is [seen by some as] [...] the very object of religion."[13] It's thus understandable how Mormon Transhumanists feel like transhumanism provides a friendly framework within which to fit together their core theological claims, their general openness to science and technology,

---

[10] Ibid., emphasis mine.

[11] E. R. Snow, *Biography and Family Record of Lorenzo Snow* (Salt Lake City, UT: Deseret News Company, 1884), 46.

[12] For example, in its essay, "Becoming Like God," the LDS Church is careful to avoid suggesting the human beings can literally become the same kind of being that God is now, along with all that implies in terms of becoming worship-worthy beings, creating worlds, etc., and suggests instead that human beings can become "like" God. ("Becoming Like God," Gospel Topics Essays, The Church of Jesus Christ of Latter-day Saints, access February 15, 2019. [https://www.churchofjesuschrist.org/study/manual/gospel-topics-essays/becoming-like-god]).

[13] J. Bialecki, in this volume, 219–233.

and an ethic that instils a personal responsibility to bring about progress in the human condition so that it can realize its highest (divine) potential.

Furthermore, I think this is important, because there might be a lesson here that might help answer some of the questions that Bialecki is wrestling with in his paper: most importantly, "what is the relation between transhumanism and religion, in light of the existence of religious transhumanisms?"[14] In order to respond, I'm going to come at this a bit sideways, so bear with me, but there's been a long-running debate about Mormonism's relationship to Christianity. In other words, are Mormons Christians? Or, is Mormonism Christian? I'm fully aware that this is a highly complex and controversial topic, but I mention it here to make a what I hope might be a relevant point.

Some of the biggest reasons why so many traditional Christian communities have answered "No" to the question of whether Mormons are Christians are the sorts of theological claims made by Joseph Smith in his cosmotheological sermons. In response to heavy criticism for the audacious claims he made when he spoke at King Follett's funeral, Smith gave a similar sermon a little over two months later, just a week before he was murdered, in which he said the following:

> I wish to declare I have always, and in all congregations when I have preached on the subject of the Deity, it has been the plurality of Gods. It has been preached by the Elders fifteen years. I have always declared God to be a distinct personage, Jesus Christ a separate and distinct personage from God the Father, and that the Holy Ghost was a distinct personage, and a Spirit, and *these three constitute three distinct personages, and three Gods*.[15]

This, along with the teaching that human beings can become Gods, was unquestionably the dominant position of the LDS leaders and lay members alike until at least the late 1900s and early 2000s. It shouldn't be surprising, therefore, why traditional Christians might think that Mormons not only reject the traditional trinitarian understanding of God, but they also affirm, at a minimum, a tri-theistic understanding of the Godhead, and, at a maximum, a kind of poly-theistic perspective (insofar as all human beings have the seeds of the fulness of divinity within their soul). Now, because these sorts of truth-claims have commonly been considered fundamental, and because they're viewed as irreconcilable with traditional ideas about God, it is felt that Mormon theology hasn't just tried to expand the limits of acceptable Christian discourse, it has placed itself entirely beyond the boundary. It is beyond the pale, so they aren't just heretics, they're radically *unchristian*, they're something completely foreign.

---

[14] Ibid.
[15] "History, 1838–1856, volume F-1 [1 May 1844–8 August 1844]," The Joseph Smith Papers, accessed 2/15/2019 (https://www.josephsmithpapers.org/paper-summary/history-1838-1856-volume-f-1-1-may-1844-8-august-1844/107), emphasis mine.

As a Mormon philosopher of religion myself, I'm actually sympathetic to these sorts of concerns, and it's why I think one of the best responses is the one that Jan Shipps, a prominent historian of Mormonism, gave over thirty years ago. Shipps sees Mormonism's relationship to traditional Christianity in the way that the early Christian tradition related to Judaism. That is, she considers Mormonism a genuinely new religious tradition, such that *Mormonism is to Christianity as Christianity is to Judaism*. The early Christians were Jews, she says, and felt "that they had found the only proper way to be Jewish." Similarly, nineteenth-century Latter-day Saints were Christians, and they too feel they found the only proper way to be Christian. They thus "embarked on a path that led to developments that now distinguish their tradition from the Christian tradition as surely as early Christianity was distinguished from its Hebraic context."[16] For Shipps, then, Mormonism represents a new Abrahmic faith.

What I'm suggesting, and here I think I'm basically in agreement with Bialecki, is that we shouldn't foreclose the possibility that something novel is happening by assuming, with those who see transhumanism as essentially and unavoidably a religious phenomenon, that "there can never be something new under the sun, and that we are doomed to having our thought eternally imprisoned in a limited set of categories and themes."[17] To the contrary, as he says in the final section of his paper, when we observe religious individuals making selective use of their rituals or repurposing religious language in the quest for a *technological* solution to the fundamental existential problem of humanity, perhaps it would be better to see it as something like "an amalgam of different discourses, drawing on different claims for the basis of authority," one in which the threads of religious desire, human imagination, and scientific discovery are interwoven to form a unique never-before-seen tapestry.[18]

In my judgment, there is an unquestionably a religious sensibility at work here, but the solutions to humanity's most basic and intractable problems, namely it's fragility, finitude, and mortality, are sought and found in technology rather than divinity. And therein lies the dilemma, or *aporia*, as Bialecki prefers to put it. On the traditional Mormon understanding of resurrection, it's the priesthood that holds the keys to breaking the chains of death. Resurrection involves the use of divine powers of restoration and reunification, that is, through the performance of a priesthood ordinance or ritual, the body and spirit which were separated at death will be somehow be brought back together in such a way that they can never be divided again. As one LDS scripture states, "For notwithstanding they die, they also shall rise again, a spiritual

---

[16] Jan Shipps, *Mormonism: The Story of a New Religious Tradition* (Urbana, IL: University of Illinois Press, 1987), ix–x.
[17] Bialecki, in this volume, 219–233.
[18] Ibid.

body. They [...] shall receive the same body which was a natural body; even ye shall receive your bodies, and your glory shall be that glory by which your bodies are quickened."[19] The rite must be performed by one who has the authority to exercise priesthood power, but the ultimate source of that power is God. The "technology" at work is thus exclusively divine in nature rather than human.

By contrast, the transhumanist understanding of resurrection is solely human in nature rather than divine, and can in principle be brought about by anyone with access to the technology. Hence the seemingly unavoidable tension raised by Bialecki. And this is partly why I think he may be right to suggest that transhumanism could be a novel phenomenon. If so, then perhaps transhumanism is to religion as religion was to whatever meaning-making activity might have preceded it. Put differently, maybe transhumanism is related to religion in the modern period the way that religion in the post-axial age was related to whatever meaning-making activity dominated the pre-axial age.

But then, this all begs some crucial questions which haven't been asked yet, much less scrutinized. So let me conclude with a couple of brief critical comments. My biggest concern about Bialecki's otherwise thought-provoking paper is that it doesn't seem possible to answer the questions it raises given certain self-limitations. For example, I'm not sure how one could ever come to any resolution concerning the boundaries of religious and scientific discourse without providing some sort of delineation or definition or description of what counts as religion or science. The essay argues that religion, science, and transhumanism are such that they run into unavoidable aporias when they get mashed up by groups like the Mormon Transhumanist Association. However, in order to fully determine the nature of the aporia, as well as arrive at any potential solution, one would need to first clarify the meaning of the terms, because without that it doesn't seem possible to adequately determine whether and how these discourses contradict, complement, or cohere with one another.

Even if we accept the now widely-held view that there is no single definition of religion that could be universally embraced, as Jonathan Z. Smith famously argued,

"Religion" is not a native term; it is a term created by scholas for their intellectual purposes and is therefore theirs to define. It is a second-order, generic concept that plays the same role in establishing a disciplinary horizon that a concept such as 'language' plays in linguistics or 'culture' plays in anthropology. There can be no disciplined study of religion without such a horizon."[20]

---

[19] The Church of Jesus Christ of Latter Day Saints, *Doctrine & Covenants*, 88:27–28. (https://www.churchofjesuschrist.org/study/scriptures/dc-testament/dc/88?lang=eng) (4/22/2022).
[20] J. Z. SMITH, "Religion, Religions, Religious," *Critical Terms For Religious Studies* (Chicago, IL: The University of Chicago Press, 1998), 281–282.

It is thus the responsibility of scholars to clarify what they mean when they use it, and I don't see how to an adequate response to Bialecki's question could be given without at least a provisional or working definition.

I'll conclude with one further example of why dealing with terminology matters. Whatever religion is, at a minimum I think it involves a first-order way of being in the world. By that I mean one can live a religious life without ever engaging in the second-order activity of critical reflection about the teachings, texts, or practices of their religion. In short, one can be religious without doing theology. On the other hand, whatever science is, it's typically understood a second-order way of trying to understand the world. As with being religious and doing theology, it's possible for humans to live their lives without engaging in the second-order activity of trying to figure out how the world works. In other words, one can be human without doing science. My point is that because religion is fundamentally a first-order form of discourse, and science is fundamentally a second-order form of discourse, claiming that they either conflict or cohere with one another might actually be a category mistake. For this reason, I think additional work needs to be done to clarify the key terms of the debate, and then consider how they might provide a basis for working out any potential solutions.

IV. Artificial Intelligence

"Know Thyself" – Self-Reflection and the Chances and Limits of Dataism

Dirk Evers

The digital revolution goes along with the fear that humanity, at least as we know it, might disappear. While there are voices in the public realm advocating and welcoming the dawn of the super-intelligent machine, Stephen Hawking and others have warned that with digital technology dominating human lives, humanity is in danger of becoming extinct.[1] Hawking sees the chance to emigrate from this planet and continue humanity in new forms elsewhere; Elon Musk, however, advises humanity to merge with technology[2] so that we might have a chance to become part of some superintelligence. Does the digital revolution pose a threat for humanity? In which respects is digital technology already beginning to influence the ways in which we relate to ourselves? Will it bring the end of humanity as we know it? To answer these questions, I will (1) reflect on the character of the digital revolution, especially (2) with reference to it as an era of new media. I will point (3) to the chances and limits of what is called artificial intelligence (AI) in a more specific sense and (4) how that might be attractive to postmodern transformations of self-knowledge. I will (5) close with reflections on the religious character of certain narratives of Dataism as an eschatological world-view, reflecting our own anxieties and desires.

1. Digital Revolution

With the term digital revolution, I refer to the radical technological shift to digital electronic data processing which began with the invention of modern computers in the 1950s. At the end of the 20th century, this development

---

[1] https://www.cambridge-news.co.uk/news/cambridge-news/stephenhawking-fears-artificial-intelligence-takeover-13839799. (4/22/2022).

[2] With this Musk takes up the idea of transhumanism and extropianism, cf. the overview on the history of transhumanist thinking by the philosopher Nick Bostrom, director of the Future of Humanity Institute at the University of Oxford: N. BOSTROM, "A History of Transhumanist Thought," *Journal of Evolution and Technology* 14, no. 1 (2005): 1–25, (https://www.jetpress.org/volume 14/bostrom.html). (4/22/2022).

gained momentum and turned into an encompassing technological change for at least three reasons.

Firstly, digital technology became exponentially smaller, cheaper, faster and more powerful. This is expressed by what is called Moore's 'law', an observation made by George Moore, co-founder of Intel, in 1965, when he referred to the fact that the complexity of integrated circuits has increased by a factor of about two every second year, while the costs have stayed the same or even decreased. His prediction proved accurate for several decades, partly because enterprises in the computer industry developed their strategies in accordance with Moore's 'law',[3] thus giving it the character of a self-fulfilling prophecy: If we do not double the efficiency of our computers within two years, we will be left behind. Progress in hardware and software architecture (networking, storage, communication technologies etc.) led to similarly high growth rates in other aspects of data processing. Moore's 'law' is, of course, no law of nature, but an observation and a contingent historical rule of thumb that points to the immense dynamics of digital technology and that proved more or less accurate over the last few decades on a truly global scale.

Secondly, with the invention of digital networks working with cable or wireless, connecting very different digital machines like computers, mobile phones, mass storage devices, music players, printers and others and by establishing the internet as a world-wide network accessible to everybody and able to store and provide any kind of information in an interactive format, different kinds of data can be exchanged, analyzed and processed. Thus new forms of economy, communication, education, science, working conditions as well as social conduct emerged and gained enormous influence. The 'Digital revolution', therefore, refers to the whole system of data exchange and the generation of digital information, including commercial and public institutions that facilitate and control this process, as well as to the respective technologies, be they integrated circuits, mobile devices or computer hard- and software.

And thirdly, the digital revolution was brought about by new means of programming. Artificial intelligence (AI),[4] resting on artificial neural networks with structures of deep learning, parallel processing and effective algorithms drawing on big data,[5] provides extremely fast and astonishingly effective software for speech recognition and autonomous robots, for example, formerly thought to be too complex for digital emulation. We will come back to the

---

[3] Cf. https://www.intel.com/content/www/us/en/history/museum-gordon-moore-law.html. (4/22/2022).

[4] The term Artificial Intelligence (AI) has been used since 1956 when it was introduced by John McCarthy, see below §3 of this essay.

[5] Cf. M. Fuller, "Big Data: New Science, New Challenges, New Dialogical Opportunities," Zygon 50, no. 3 (2015): 569–582.

beginnings and the concepts of AI later. Here we only note that one can identify three basic computational approaches that contribute to what we call AI, or machine intelligence, as it was often called in its beginnings: 1. *Symbolic AI*, that is symbol manipulations by applying abstract methods of inference on data, thus emulating cognitive reasoning. 2. Sub-symbolic approaches mainly drawing on *artificial neural networks*, but also including statistical methods and less rigid forms of inference. 3. *Knowledge systems* and huge amount of data (*Big Data*), to which methods of symbolic AI and artificial networks can be applied for analyzing and managing them. Thus the process we call a 'digital revolution' not only refers to hardware and infrastructure, but also to certain concepts of processing digitized data.

It is this complex technological change, comprising technological, institutional and conceptual developments, that amounts to the Digital Revolution. The pace of this development is driven by the astonishing effectiveness of the technology involved, but also fueled by huge profits, so that some of the leading enterprises like Microsoft, IBM, Google (resp. Alphabet Inc.), Apple, Amazon and Facebook have developed into huge holdings and belong to the most powerful, influential and valuable global brands. And it is a *revolution*, indeed, in the sense that Friedrich Engels used the term to describe the second industrial revolution: it transforms whole societies, including the ways people think about their lives and ways of living. Engels referred to the changes brought about in England with the invention of the steam engine and mechanical weaving looms, which "have given the initial impetus to an industrial revolution, a revolution which at the same time transformed the whole bourgeois society."[6] It is "the revolutionizing of all traditional relationships by an industry *as it develops*, which also revolutionizes people's minds."[7] It transforms whole societies, it does so on a global level, and it not only changes the ways of producing *goods*, but also our ways of producing *values*, so that according to IT-pioneer Jaron Lanier we are not only the customers of internet trusts, we are also their product.[8] Why is that so?

---

[6] F. ENGELS, "Die Lage der arbeitenden Klasse in England," *Marx-Engels Werke* (Berlin/Ost: Dietz Verlag, 1962), 2:237: "den Anstoß zu einer industriellen Revolution, einer Revolution, die zugleich die ganze bürgerliche Gesellschaft umwandelte" (my translation).

[7] Letter to Friedrich A. Sorge (31 December 1892), in F. ENGELS, "Briefe", *Marx-Engels Werke* (Berlin/Ost: Dietz Verlag, 1962), 38:563: "Es ist die Revolutionierung aller hergebrachten Verhältnisse durch die *sich entwickelnde* Industrie, die auch die Köpfe revolutioniert" (my translation).

[8] Cf. J. LANIER, *Who Owns the Future?* (New York: Simon & Schuster, 2013).

2. A New Era of Media

The digital revolution is also a media revolution. Media are not just arbitrary means of transmitting information. They mediate between human beings, and they mediate between human beings and reality. Media are means of communication, reflection, expression and thus of self-formation, because human beings are mediated beings. We are enclosed within a net of symbolic meaning. Ernst Cassirer characterized human beings as symbolic animals (*animalia symbolica*), whose nature it is to live as cultural beings who are fully immersed in their own symbolic world, a world of meaning and symbols.[9] The immediate unity of reception and agency, as it usually forms the fundamental layer of animal behavior,[10] is reduced with human beings and to a large extent substituted by nets of symbolic meaning in different formats like language, mythos, science, art etc.[11] By their very nature, human beings are mediated beings, and so they not only live, but realize and know that they live and how they are living.

It was Marshall McLuhan who famously pointed to the fact that throughout history a change in communication technology affected the cognitive organization of human understanding as well as social organization.[12] Referring to McLuhan's analysis many cultural scientists distinguish four epochs of media. The dawn of history coincides with the tribal era in which human beings produced, cultivated and inherited their symbolic cocoon by *oral* tradition, and the reverberations of that era can still be studied in the early texts of the Hebrew bible and other documents of early cultures. With the development of *written* texts in antiquity different modes of fixing traditions and constituting collective as well as individual identities emerged, especially with reference to sacred texts that explained the world and provided reference points of orientation. It also made new forms of philosophical, scientific and theological discourse possible. The modern era began with the invention of the *printing* press. It triggered processes of mass education through mass media and allowed for new ways of sci-

---

[9] E. CASSIRER, *An Essay on Man: An Introduction to a Philosophy of Human Culture* (New Haven, CT: Yale University Press, 1944). See also the seminal work from 1941 by S. K. LANGER, *Philosophy in a New Key: A Study in the Symbolism of Reason, Rite, and Art* (New York: Mentor Books, 1954).

[10] Cassirer refers to the concept of "Funktionskreis" (functional circuit) as developed by v. Uexküll, cf. CASSIRER, *Essay*, 23.

[11] Cf. E. CASSIRER, "'Geist' und 'Leben' in der Philosophie der Gegenwart [1930]," in *Ernst Cassirer: Gesammelte Werke. Hamburger Ausgabe*, vol. 17, *Aufsätze und kleine Schriften (1927–1931)*, ed. T. Berben (Darmstadt: Wiss. Buchgesellschaft, 2004), 185–205.

[12] Cf. his ground-breaking work M. MCLUHAN, *The Gutenberg Galaxy: The Making of Typographic Man* (London: Routledge & Kegan, 1971). Recently, German sociologist Dirk Baecker has taken up McLuhan's model and applied it to the consequences of digital media for politics, society and privacy, cf. D. BAECKER, *4.0 oder Die Lücke die der Rechner lässt* (Leipzig: Merve Verlag, 2018).

entific and public discourse as well as commerce through book-keeping. With the use of *electricity* for communication (for example, the invention of the telephone and radio transmission) in the 19th century, a development started which transformed the plurality of nations and cultures on this globe into one *global village* – another famous expression by McLuhan. While in antiquity and in the early modern era the world or nature were understood as a text or book that human minds can read and interpret, the digital revolution views reality as data processing: "Instead of tending towards a vast Alexandrian library the world has become a computer, an electronic brain."[13] This marks the passage from the electric epoch to the *digital* era: reality is transformed into data and their processing. This change to digital technology has begun to encompass all aspects of reality by turning them into data bodies and thus into objects of data-processing so that reality and virtual worlds begin to merge and new forms of self-understanding and self-expression become possible. With this we have set the stage in which we can now locate the significance of AI in its more specific sense.

3. Artificial Intelligence

1. The Birth of AI

The term Artificial Intelligence (AI) has been used since 1956 when it was introduced by John McCarthy in the invitation to the famous *Dartmouth Summer Research Project on Artificial Intelligence*.[14] In the long run it replaced other terms like 'machine intelligence'. I cite from the proposal for that conference:

We propose that a 2 month, 10 man study of artificial intelligence be carried out during the summer of 1956 at Dartmouth College in Hanover, New Hampshire. The study is to proceed on the basis of the conjecture that every aspect of learning or any other feature of intelligence can in principle be so precisely described that a machine can be made to simulate it. An attempt will be made to find how to make machines use language, form abstractions and concepts, solve kinds of problems now reserved for humans, and improve themselves. We think that a significant advance can be made in one or more of these problems if a carefully selected group of scientists work on it together for a summer.[15]

This proposal also gives a first definition of AI:

For the present purpose the artificial intelligence problem is taken to be that of making a machine behave in ways that would be called intelligent if a human were so behaving.[16]

---

[13] McLuhan, *Gutenberg Galaxy*, 32.
[14] See H. Gardner, *The Mind's New Science: A History of the Cognitive Revolution* (New York: Basic Books, 1985), 30.
[15] http://www-formal.stanford.edu/jmc/history/dartmouth/dartmouth.html.
[16] Later Minsky defined AI as "the science of making machines do things that would require intelligence if done by men" (M. L. Minsky, *Semantic Information Processing* [Cambridge, MA: MIT Press, 1968], V).

Let me point out three claims in this statement. *First*: The fundamental idea is to proceed from precise description to simulation. Whatever can be described precisely, can also be translated into instructions for the machine, that is into rules for the transformation of symbols. The machine can then make inferences, generalizations and analogies and translate the outcome back into normal language. Therefore language (in its propositional and informational aspect), abstractions, problem solving and inferences are central to the notion of intelligence behind this concept. *Second*: The aim is to make machine *behavior* intelligent, not the machines themselves. Many involved in the early project of AI were inspired by Alan M. Turing, who committed suicide only two years before in 1954, and his proposal of the later so called Turing test for intelligent machine behavior, or as Turing himself called it the 'imitation game.'[17] *Third*: In the statement we already find the idea that these machines should be able to learn and improve themselves, an idea also already proposed by Turing.

That approach led to some progress, and was accompanied by extreme optimism. A decade later in 1967 Marvin Minsky, who had been part of the Dartmouth group, would claim: "Within a generation, I am convinced, few compartments of intellect will remain outside the machine's realm – the problem of creating 'artificial intelligence' will substantially be solved"[18]. However, progress could mainly be achieved for precisely defined, narrow problems. Non-formal language, for example, or spoken language or other ordinary tasks like face recognition proved to be more complex. Or, as computer scientist Donald Knuth put it in 1981: "AI has by now succeeded in doing essentially everything that requires 'thinking' but has failed to do most of what people and animals do 'without thinking.'"[19] That led to the so-called winter of AI in the 1970s[20] when the US and the UK governments cut the finances for AI projects because the slow progress by no means matched the promises once given. The approach of constructing intelligent machines emulating human intelligence mainly by precise simulation of behavior through symbolic manipulation got stuck. In his 1985 book *Artificial Intelligence: The Very Idea* American philosopher John Haugeland named that approach GOFAI ("Good Old-Fashioned Artificial Intelligence").[21] It rests on the problematic assumption that many, if not all, central aspects of human intelligence can be achieved by formal procedures.

---

[17] A. Turing, "Computing Machinery and Intelligence," *Mind* 59 (1950): 433–460.

[18] M. L. Minsky, *Computation: Finite and Infinite Machines* (Hoboken, NJ: Prentice Hall, 1967), 2.

[19] N. J. Nilsson, "The Quest for Artificial Intelligence: A History of Ideas and Achievements (Web Version)" (https://ai.stanford.edu/~nilsson/QAI/qai.pdf) (4/22/2022).

[20] Cf. M. Olazaran, "A Sociological Study of the Official History of the Perceptrons Controversy," *Social Studies of Science* 26, no. 3 (1996): 611–659 (http://www.jstor.org/stable/285702) (4/22/2022).

[21] J. Haugeland, *Artificial Intelligence: The Very Idea* (Cambridge, MA: MIT Press, 1993).

2. Artificial Neural Networks

However, the development of AI gained new momentum when a new way of programming and of computational architecture had a breakthrough, the concept of *artificial neural networks*. The architecture of neural networks is radically different. One fundamental feature of machines that were used for GOFAI is the separation of memory and central processing unit, and most of the digital devices we use in everyday life are built like that.[22] The machine reads rules taken from memory into the central processing unit and then manipulates data that it finds in the memory or receives via its input device, like a keyboard. In the end modified data will be send to the output devices like a display or a printer.

Artificial neural networks work rather differently. They consist of many small units, the knots or artificial neurons, which are interconnected and structured in layers. The neurons of the first layer receive signals, process them with some internal function giving "weight" to different inputs they receive, and then send a value to other knots in the next layer. The last layer produces the final output. Thus information is not held in discrete storage locations, but is distributed throughout the system and represented by its internal parameters, the functions that determine the connectivity of the knots. These internal parameters and the net's connectivity are not programmed into the system by software engineers, but are learned by the system itself through training with trial and error and by receiving positive or negative feedback while performing the required tasks. The idea of such an approach also dates back to the early 1950s and was indeed inspired by neuro-scientific research, which had identified interconnected neurons in animal cortices that modify their sensitivity according to their activation and in that sense are able to learn. Major progress was achieved when researchers managed to establish effective routines of training for multi-layered artificial neural networks to perform specific tasks like pattern or language recognition.

There are some advantages coming with this technology. In certain circumstances such a net can perform at an acceptable level even if some units do not work properly; and such systems can often recognize patterns or objects even if only a part of the object is presented as input. Thus these systems have become extremely effective in object and speech recognition, for example, and a lot of the success of recent AI rests on such trained, artificial neural networks. However, in contrast to classical symbolic AI, artificial neural networks do not presuppose theoretical models that determine how input is transformed into output. The designers of classical computational processing were required to have a basic theory of the relevant data and their importance, which they translated into formulas and decision trees for the machine. Artificial neural

---

[22] In technical terms these are Turing machines with a von Neumann architecture.

networks are not theory-driven. They are trained through feedback learning and develop their internal network of evaluation by trial and error. They can learn and even learn how to learn at different levels. With this kind of technology analytic powers go along that are unprecedented. However, they have one significant limit: They are like black boxes. Humans have designed their overall structure, but nobody knows in detail how the assessment processes work.

Today, both forms of AI, symbolic and non-symbolic, are usually combined. And they are now able to draw on more and more information exchanged via network technology. Accumulated structured data bases (for example scientific data or voice and language data bases) and real world data (for example from video and audio surveillance, from social media communication etc.) can be used to train such networks, and unqualified data can be analyzed by them so that they can identify patterns and regularities. Today artificial neural networks identify human faces faster and at a better rate than humans themselves, and they diagnose certain cancer tissues with higher precision than the best medical doctors, not to speak of unexperienced physicians in remote areas. And they provide tools for decision-making systems that analyze complex situations better and faster than humans and are used for many applications in robotics, including autonomous driving. IBM's Watson system is advertised as the most sophisticated assessment tool for business intelligence and won the *Jeopardy!* game show in 2011, proving its capacity to understand irony and word-plays. Google's AlphaGo has beaten the best players of the highly complex Asian game of Go, and similar systems are calculating the claims of assurance companies. In leading investment funds algorithms decide on where the money goes. Decision systems assist in the development of business strategies and the best composition of workgroups, and they suggest whom to fire and whom to hire. Another fast-growing field are social bots that help people to get juridical advice. The Robo-Lawyer DoNotPay is a free chatbot that offers AI-powered legal counsel under the motto: "*Get free legal help in under 30 seconds.*"[23] It started with helping to challenge parking tickets and is now used to object against contract violations by landlords or to claim maternity leave, and it has been successful in helping people to claim asylum or fight against deportations.

3. Ignorance: The Opacity of Decision Systems

By its very architecture, machine learning resting on artificial neural networks reproduces what in the realm of human knowledge has been called Polanyi's paradox.[24] According to a famous statement of the chemist and philosopher

---

[23] Cf. www.donotpay.com.
[24] Cf. T. RAMGE, *Mensch und Maschine: Wie künstliche Intelligenz und Roboter unser Leben verändern* (Ditzingen: Reclam, 2018), 16–18.

Michael Polanyi, *"we can know more than we can tell."*[25] We know how to swim, ride a bicycle or speak our first language without being able to explain exactly to others how we do it. The rules of grammar of our first language, for example, we did not learn via cognitive rule following, but by practice and conditioning, which comes very close to computational feedback learning. And this applies to many aspects of human knowledge. We can recognize faces or people we see from the back simply by their posture. We identify many objects as what they are without being able to give a full account of the relevant features: "We know it when we see it." And scientists know how to handle the instruments in their laboratory often without knowing exactly how they work.[26]

Insofar as systems of AI are conditioned and trained rather than programmed, they know much more than they can explain. If a system of AI assesses people in order to determine the relevant risks for a certain insurance, it might find, for example, that Asian women over 46.4 years of age who have had a certain knee operation have a higher risk in some relevant respect. But what does that say? And based on which data and categories of relevance has the machines come to this result? Is there an unjustified bias hidden in the algorithm the machine has applied? Has it 'unintentionally' made a category mistake? The machine cannot tell. This becomes particularly relevant in decisions related to fairness and justice in the public realm. In health systems where resources are limited, but equal access to medical treatment should be a rule, AI might be helpful to decide for whom a certain expensive treatment may have the most positive effect. But on which grounds should such an algorithm work? Should it simply calculate the probability of years of healthy life after that treatment for different people? What about the old then? What about gender or race differences that may play a role in the individual's response to that treatment? Should that be taken into account? AI cannot account for its decisions, but for societal, political and juridical decisions we want to follow standards of equality and non-discrimination.

Therefore, more and more voices in the debate on AI demand built-in routines in decision-making systems that allow for an assessment of *how* the system has come to its decision. This movement calls for Explainable Artificial Intelligence (XAI) and works on methods and standards for assessable decision systems. But with very complex neural networks this is nearly impossible. Machines would have to develop a theory of themselves. They would have to assess their own algorithms and networks, reduce their complexity and

---

[25] M. POLANYI, *The Tacit Dimension [1966]* (Chicago, IL: University of Chicago Press, 2009), 4.

[26] A lot of scientific research today is done in distributed groups of scientists with different fields of expertise working together with no one who oversees everything in detail. This resembles the architecture of neural networks as well.

find out how to translate the complex net of interdependencies of evaluations into an evaluative language which can be understood by human beings. That might prove an extremely difficult and complicated task, which might even reproduce the problem on a higher level. Self-evaluations of evaluative systems might be biased as well so that we get into an infinite regress. And according to the very fundamental incompleteness theorems proven by Kurt Gödel,[27] no formal system is able to prove its own consistency and at the same time make sure that its evaluation has been complete. Machines cannot make themselves understood, because they are identical with their program and cannot relate to themselves in such a way that they can 'explain' what they are doing. In a well-defined sense, machine intelligence is a black box to us and to itself, and in our digital world already black boxes relate to other black boxes with unpredictable results. Turbulences on stock markets, where AI systems make very fast decisions on the basis of what they anticipate how other systems decide, are an example of this. AI rests on trust and must always be embedded into frames of political and societal decision-making.

Another example is the internet that is constantly analyzing itself. Bots and web-crawlers fetch, analyze and file information from web servers so that more than half of all web traffic is made up of bots, half of which is created by 'good' bots, the other half by 'bad' bots (spambots, bots that collect e-mail addresses, bots that spy for vulnerability, and others).[28] Part of this information is re-fed into the web, but most of it is used in the interest of certain enterprises. Again non-linear effects may be produced so that it can be difficult to identify biased information. All this points to the fact that AI is far from becoming transparent to itself. AI is in its very structure non-reflexive. It is we who have to reflect on the chances and limits of AI and who have to shape present and future uses of these forms of digital technology. However, that poses significant challenges.

4. Difference, Knowledge and Control

The German sociologist and writer Christoph Kucklick has identified three transformations that go along with the digital revolution: a revolution of *differentiation*, a revolution of *knowledge*, and a revolution of *control*.[29] AI allows for ever fine-grained categories and *differentiation*. Diagnostic tools identify 37 kinds of headache, and Facebook offers over 60 gender options. AI makes highly differentiated assessments of needs possible and thus appropriate

---

[27] K. GÖDEL, "Über formal unentscheidbare Sätze der Principia Mathematica und verwandter Systeme I," *Monatshefte für Mathematik und Physik* 38, no. 1 (1931): 173–198.

[28] Cf. https://www.incapsula.com/blog/bot-traffic-report-2016.html (4/22/2022).

[29] See CHR. KUCKLICK, *Die granulare Gesellschaft: Wie das Digitale unsere Wirklichkeit auflöst*, 2nd ed. (Berlin: Ullstein, 2015).

responses to them. Especially for individual medical treatment this is an enormous advantage. However, average is no orientational category anymore, and standards become obsolete. For those who do not fit into traditional norms of average and difference this comes as a liberation, while others lose their standards of orientation. One can also ask what will become of our moral sense of community and solidarity in a world of individual, highly differentiated monads.

That goes along with changes in producing, processing and applying *knowledge*. Machine learning supersedes the highest forms of human intelligence and leads to new forms of knowledge, because machines will no longer be just tools mediating between us and nature, but interfaces connecting different aspects of reality and representing it in virtual formats. If reality is understood as an infinitely differentiated network accessible by virtual interfaces, we will lose forms of more direct contact with reality. Nature, society, reality itself, in all their impenetrable complexity, present themselves as machineries of communication, of data exchange and data evaluation, which resonate with human minds and their cognitive faculties, but cannot be comprehended and represented as a potentially complete body of knowledge or theory of everything.

In the end this implies a revolution of *control*, and here Kucklick is in agreement with the Israeli historian Yuval Harari who asks: "Where has all the power gone?"[30] It is dissolved in the system itself, and it is transformed into new tools of data management which do not try to bring the flow of data under linear control, but which have developed forms of 'riding' on the flows of information, directing them gently and responsively by isolating information from the access of other, by controlling and monitoring important interfaces and by generating dependencies on certain exclusive technologies and formats. This will bring about new forms of steering and managing that do not make use of generic knowledge acquisition by understanding and modeling fundamental processes of reality, but that provide tools for a successful management of complexity and ignorance. Notions of absolute knowledge like the Leibnizian central monad, the Laplacean calculating spirit or a scientific theory of everything in physics will lose plausibility and will be replaced by more playful, less rigid notions of knowledge and its management. Although networks provide access to knowledge for many and challenge centralized power structures, they are not giving power to the individual. Rather they give less rigid, subtle, but in some respects even more powerful tools to those who control the network, have access to evaluative algorithms and try to execute their power not by dominion, but by subtle manipulations that try to stay below the users'

---

[30] Y. N. HARARI, *Homo Deus: A Brief History of Tomorrow* (London: Vintage, 2017), 435–440.

levels of attention. Such changes of social, political and economic structures,[31] going along with the digital revolution, will co-evolve with changes of human self-understanding, since digital technology also provides tools for self-knowledge and self-management that serve as interfaces for understanding and managing ourselves. In the next paragraph of this short essay I will concentrate on the challenges AI poses to the modern quest for an authentic and autonomous individual self, which is at the center of Western modernity.

4. Self-Management and Modernity

The challenge that goes along with AI is not so much that it will become like and then excel human minds. I shall address that challenge in the final part of my paper. What is affected, however, are human ways of communication and life-conduct. Decision-making in the context of the ways in which we conduct our lives on different levels might merge too intimately with machine intelligence, so that the scopes of human freedom and autonomy become endangered. In this part of the paper I want to point to some dynamics that I see at work, especially in Western post-modern societies. However, much more inter-cultural discourse and post-colonial critique is necessary to understand these dynamics more profoundly.

1. The Self-Referential Structure of Self-Knowledge

Since antiquity self-knowledge has been an imperative central to European religious as well as philosophical contemplation on human existence. On the wall of the famous temple in Delphi, dedicated to Apollo, the reminder "Know Thyself" (Γνῶθι σεαυτόν) invited the visitors to engage in reflection on their mortal, finite existence. It was understood as a commandment given by the Deity and became a focus of early philosophical discourse starting with Socrates and Plato. The intricacies of this imperative are obvious. Any knowledge presupposes the difference between the subject that knows and the object or fact that is known. In the case of self-knowledge, subject and object of knowledge coincide, and that threatens to make self-knowledge impossible. Since Plotinus and neo-platonic reflection on this problem, together with German idealism as its successor, there have been attempts to identify modes of intuitive, unmediated knowledge that might be able to transcend the bifurcation of subject and object of knowledge, often making a difference between

---

[31] Cf. S. ZUBOFF, *The Age of Surveillance Capitalism: The Fight for the Future at the New Frontier of Power* (London: Profile Books, 2019).

discursive intellect or soul (ψυχή) and intuitive reason or mind/spirit (πνεῦμα) with only the latter capable of self-knowledge.

In any case, the challenges of self-knowledge are manifold, and different aspects of philosophical reflection as well as religious practices intend to meet these challenges. In modernity, one pressing issue became the relation between the inner self and the outer formations of human existence. Charles Taylor relates modernity to the rise of a buffered self, which finds itself disengaged from the outer world, while the pre-modern, porous self experienced itself as often helplessly exposed to external spiritual forces. Religious practices such as mantic rites, astrology, oracles, prayers, blessings, dietetics etc. often dealt and still deal with the protection of that endangered inner self. Along with the rise of modern science and rationalist philosophy, nature became disenchanted, and the inner self, by means of new forms of self-reflection, became disentangled from nature. The modern self lives with a much finer sense of a categorical boundary between self and others, between mind and world. With the transition to the culture of printed mass media, texts became an important tool for the reassurance of the inner, now buffered self. This can be seen in certain practices of bible study, penitential self-exploration under the guidance of written manuals or the rise of the modern novel in the 18th century, which reflected the quest of individuals to give meaning to their lives in terms of narratives. The modern self continues the search for reassurance, now aiming at authenticity, self-determination and unambiguous social recognition.

2. Modernity and the Culture of Authenticity

As Charles Taylor's extensive study on the Sources of the Self[32] from 1989 has argued, the quest for what it means to be a self as an authentic individual, and the search for appropriate sources for inner self-formation, are at the center of modernity. Modern inwardness as "the sense of ourselves as beings with inner depth", "the affirmation of ordinary life" that sees our earthly existence as the only and ultimate chance of self-realization, and "the expressivist notion of nature as an inner moral source,"[33] which suggests that we shall find the core of our self-identity within ourselves, are at least three important aspects of the modern search for self-knowledge and self-identity. The ideal of authenticity[34] draws on the notion that every individual is called to realize an original way of being human. It gives crucial moral importance to a reflected self, which is

---

[32] C. TAYLOR, *Sources of the Self: The Making of the Modern Identity* (Cambridge, MA: Harvard University Press, 1989).
[33] Ibid., X.
[34] C. TAYLOR, *The Ethics of Authenticity*, 11th ed. (Cambridge, MA: Harvard University Press, 2003), 28.

in close contact with its inner nature and thus resists pressure towards outward conformity and avoids functional and shallow routines. The moral obligation of self-determination is the demand to be true to one's own originality and to realize and express it by the self-determined conduct of life. Every voice is worth hearing, because it brings its own personal note into this world by expressing an original self. And in changing situations and different contexts, human beings want to be recognized not only as the same individual, but as an individual self, as who they *really* are and want to be.

That coincides with the extraordinary increase of optionality of life-forms "spawning an ever-widening variety of moral/spiritual options,"[35] which again started in the 18th century and continues to this day. The modern individual must search for orientation mainly within herself, while the disenchanted reality appears enclosed within an immanent frame. It "is the sense that all order, all meaning comes from us. We encounter no echo outside. [...] A race of humans has arisen which has managed to experience its world entirely as immanent."[36] In the end, we have to decide ourselves how we give meaning to our existence, what strong evaluations we execute in order to draw on relevant moral sources, and what authorities we trust. Even traditionalist thinking cannot escape optionality. We cannot choose not to choose. Even if we completely deliver our lives and our life-choices to some authority, be it God, the community or science, this is still our choice, and it is at the heart of modern pluralist societies to respect such decisions of self-denial only to the extent that the individual concerned may, in principle, opt out again.

In many respects, the concept of the buffered self is certainly an advantage compared with the porous self of pre-modern times. However, postmodernity has revealed the constructed, the struggling, the fragile and the aggressive character of the modern search for individual authenticity. And post-colonialism has pointed to the pragmatic self-contradictions inherent in Western liberalism, which promotes freedom and equality, but creates dependency and paternalism and forgets about solidarity and community. Our inner self is dependent on relations of recognition, trust and communality, and far too often it fails to serve as the inner compass and voice leading to self-realization. Too often it is not the confident and autonomous self that is at the center of modern biographies, but an irritated, frightened, fighting self that tries to find a way through the thicket of anticipated, imaginary and actual demands, of adaptation and denial, of self-presentation and camouflage.

---

[35] C. TAYLOR, *A Secular Age* (Cambridge, MA: Harvard University Press, 2007), 299.
[36] TAYLOR, *A Secular Age*, 376.

3. Self-Knowledge in the Digital World

It is in this setting that modern tools of decision-making and self-management become relevant. Internet technology, together with AI and constant connectivity via mobile devices, intend to provide means and tools for the conduct of life, and thus establish feedback loops that generate ever more data and allow for ever differentiated and better real-time offers of choices in ever more realms of life. This promises an effective and well-tempered mix of individuality, creativity and conformity. As early as 2007 Eric Schmidt, then CEO with Google, defined the organization of daily life as the company's goal: "The goal is to enable Google users to be able to ask the question such as 'What shall I do tomorrow?' and 'What job shall I take?'"[37] Schmidt renewed that vision in 2010 and even went beyond it by claiming that Google and its digital tools should not be limited to answering questions, but should aim at giving advice: "I actually think most people don't want Google to answer their questions. They want Google to tell them what they should be doing next."[38] Devices have been introduced that push the development in that direction. At the forefront of present technological developments are *digital virtual assistants*, which the strategists of the leading internet enterprises are aggressively trying to introduce. Apple promotes Siri, Microsoft Cortona, Google works with Google Assistant, Amazon is linked to Alexa, and there are a few others. The idea is that these systems provide access to many digital services through ordinary language communication. Drawing on algorithms by decision-making systems built on AI, virtual assistants can help to look for special offers, suggest products during curated shopping, book flight and train tickets, play music according to moods and preferences, provide users with news and entertainment, find the best route for cars to take, manage appointments and remind users to take medicine and to eat and drink regularly. They can supervise behavior unnoticed and call for help when individuals show signs of severe disease or when the system detects an accident, when a fire breaks out or an intruder enters the building. They carry out orders and check the invoices we receive. The list could be extended nearly indefinitely. Harari calls these assistants "oracles" and warns that when everybody uses the same oracle, the oracle might turn into a sovereign.[39]

Social media such as Facebook are platforms for self-presentation and networking. By providing easy tools for individual expression and respective appreciation, they model social status systems and draw on the human need for recognition. As the founding president of Facebook, Sean Parker, who is now a critic of Facebook, explained in a video statement, the "social-vali-

---

[37] Cf. https://www.ft.com/content/c3e49548-088e-11dc-b11e-000b5df10621 (4/22/2022).
[38] https://www.wsj.com/articles/SB10001424052748704901104575423294099527212 (4/22/2022).
[39] HARARI, *Homo Deus*, 398.

dation feedback loop" of Facebook is "exploiting a vulnerability in human psychology". The founders of Facebook "understood this consciously. And we did it anyway."[40] Companies like Apple have understood that digital technology must go together with certain life-style options and promote effective interfaces for self-management. Applications for self-monitoring appear first in Apple's app-store. And the advertisement for Apple's own device, the new Apple Watch 4, states with crystal clarity: "For a better you. [...] Fundamentally redesigned and re-engineered to help you stay even more active, healthy, and connected." The watch monitors a person's physical activity and the activity of her heart muscles. It notifies low and high heart rates, detects falls and can send out emergency SOS alerts. It encourages the user to close the activity rings every day. Thus the device provides personal coaching and is described as "part guardian, part guru."[41]

Against the background of Taylor's analysis of the modern culture of authenticity and its excessive demands for self-determination, we can understand why these techniques of decision-making, of self-management and self-presentation can be attractive. They promise to lower the pressures and undercut the self-referential structure of self-knowledge in a modern world of increased optionality by providing user-friendly interfaces for self-management that help to cope with demands of authenticity and claims of autonomy, as well as the need for social recognition transcending traditional conventions. Thus they seem to liberate people from the malaise of modernity with its excessive demands for self-exploration and self-expression, and they promise viable short-cuts for time-consuming and precarious processes of education and self-exploration, which are always in danger of failure and of wasting the most precious good, lifetime. The wearisome journey to the inner self may in the end be in vain, and its doubtful character threatens to diminish the portion of actual happiness that a personal life might be able to realize. Real-time interfaces of self-management promise enjoyment of life without surrender to external authorities and without getting lost within oneself, and they provide means of dealing with the unknown and thus recognize the depth of human individuals.

Digital virtual assistants that use AI for individual decision-making are non-reductionist precisely because they refrain from penetrating into reality by way of theoretical analysis. They avoid the theory-practice gap by focusing on tasks and effective progress and allow for functional self-knowledge and self-control. And since AI is highly complex, decentralized and horizontal in its architecture, digital oracles appear to be relatively neutral, unbiased,

---

[40] https://www.axios.com/sean-parker-unloads-on-facebook-god-only-knows-what-its-doing-to-our-childrens-brains-1513306792-f855e7b4-4e99-4d60-8d51-2775559c2671.html (4/22/2022).

[41] Cf. https://www.apple.com/apple-watch-series-4/ (4/22/2022).

non-mischievous and impersonal, so that they do not come with social obligations. They undercut the ambivalences of I-Thou-relations without retreat into an inner world. With their dispensation of hard facts, inferential necessity and ultimate reason in favor of effective management through intuitive interfaces they appeal to the iconic turn with coherence and resonance as main criteria. Self-knowledge and self-exploration gain a playful, explorative and esthetic character against cognitive forms of self-explanation. This coincides with the fact that the new social media allow for an integration of self-exploration with self-presentation. Individuality, non-conformism and the need for recognition seem to be reconcilable after all.

4. Digital Self-Management as Quasi-Religion

Israeli historian Yuval Harari claims that with AI permeating every aspect of life a new religion is emerging, which in fact has "already conquered most of the scientific establishment."[42] Harari calls this quasi-religion *Dataism*, because it venerates neither God (as traditional religion) nor man (as modern humanism), but worships data. For him, Dataism is a plausible world-view for many science-oriented people, because it is filling the void that the decline of pre-modern religion leaves and it provides an integrated view of and effective interaction with reality. Data then is not just a category among others, it is the essence of reality: "Dataism declares that the universe consists of data flows, and the value of any phenomenon or entity is determined by its contribution to data processing."[43] Biochemical information (DNA), algorithms of evolutionary adaptation, the neural processes of the brain, and data technology resting on deep-learning AI are but variants of the same cosmic principle. This fits with a scientific view of life, in which the barriers between humans, animals and machines collapse. For politicians, businesspeople and ordinary consumers, Dataism offers technologies with enormous opportunities for influencing whole societies and for profiting from people's interests, while for "scholars and intellectuals it also promises to provide the scientific holy grail that has eluded us for centuries: a single overarching theory that unifies all the scientific disciplines from musicology through economics to biology"[44]. The divide of academic disciplines in sciences, humanities, cultural studies, linguistics and others collapses as well, when they all transform their objects of study into data patterns, use the same basic concepts and methods of analysis and communicate via platforms of data exchange. And with information as the essence of being, Dataism leaves behind dualist world-views, which since Descartes has

---

[42] HARARI, *Homo Deus*, 428.
[43] Ibid., 428.
[44] Ibid., 428–429.

been so prominent and controversial in Western thinking. It does not explain matter from mind or mind from matter, but deals with a category integrating both aspects right from the outset.

However, as Harari himself concedes, all this rests on the presupposition that life as well as social formations can adequately be reduced to data flows and decision-making.[45] And such a presupposition is far from being self-evident. We still do not know whether data-processing is a sufficient or even necessary precondition for consciousness and the inner world of qualitative experience.[46] If organisms indeed function in an inherently different way than algorithms and neural networks, then AI can manage only certain aspects of reality and will never fully understand the dynamics of living beings.

However, Harari considers that "even if Dataism is wrong and organisms aren't just algorithms, it won't necessarily prevent Dataism from taking over the world,"[47] because it is so effective and psychologically attractive to us. As we have claimed, human beings are symbolic animals. They project reality according to their needs and interests and live in symbolic worlds. Religions provide prominent examples of how factually inaccurate, counterfactual and even illusionary views of reality can appeal to fundamental features of the human life-form and might be difficult to resist. In the case of Dataism, a scientifically convincing paradigm merges with effective technology, with attractive lifestyle options in the pursuit of health, pleasure and self-determination and with economic, social and political dynamics. With its ethics and imperatives like 'share your data' it counters monopolies of power and dominance. No party, no activist group, not even a business consortium providing and partly controlling the digital data flows like Google or Microsoft, is in charge after all, although we also sense their manipulative power. Small interest groups, business trusts, ruthless individuals and undemocratic systems as well as autocratic despots can profit from the intricacies and structures of the digital world. With this Harari points to the dangers for politics. It is difficult to still develop grand visions of the future of society. Government is more and more reduced to administration, managing a country, not leading it.[48] And it becomes extremely difficult to gain control over money flows and global businesses. The global market as a

---

[45] Cf. ibid., 438.

[46] John Searle's argument for the non-functional nature of artificial intelligence, illustrated with his famous thought experiment of the Chinese room, is – in my view – still valid, cf. J. R. SEARLE, "Minds, Brains, and Programs," *Behavioral and Brain Sciences* 3, no. 3 (1980): 417–424. Searle still holds to his original claim, even against philosophers who proclaim the emergence of superintelligence. See also J. R. SEARLE, "What Your Computer Can't Know," *The New York Review of Books* LXI, no. 15 (2014): 52–55. Even Harari concedes that "we have no idea how or why dataflows could produce consciousness and subjective experience" (HARARI, *Homo Deus*, 458).

[47] HARARI, *Homo Deus*, 459.

[48] See ibid., 438.

data-based and effective system of exchange of goods, services and funds tends to establish what is best for the system, not for human beings or nature. New, strenuous and international efforts are necessary to push issues of justice, fairness, equality, solidarity, environmental sustainability and how to deal with the chances and risks of scientific progress like genetic engineering.

All in all, Dataism presents itself as a quasi-religion. Like secular humanism, it is a world-view within the immanent frame, to use Taylor's notion again. It shows analogies to traditional religions insofar as it provides a coherent and all compassing world-view, but especially because it is a practice dealing with the challenges of contingency. It meets the definition of religion as given by the German philosopher Hermann Lübbe: Religion provides practical means to cope with contingency, it is "Kontingenzbewältigungspraxis"[49]. It does not explain (away) the contingencies of life, but provides forms of coping with them. As a quasi-religion, Dataism offers views and tools for dealing with the unknown, and it provides goals and tasks as well as tools for real-time decision-making. But it confines itself to the immanent frame and the shifts towards "the minimal transcendences of modern solipsism whose main themes" are "'self-realization,' personal autonomy, and self-expression."[50]

Like every religion, Dataism rests on faith and is shaken by misuse of trust. As soon as manipulations and commercial or political concerns are revealed to actually overrule the independence of data exchange and AI, the basic trust in the neutrality plus superiority of the system vanishes and its impenetrable character turns into a threat. It is an open question how much trust human beings are willing and able to invest in AI and how that relates to political, cultural and social settings. There are many studies of human behavior that show how important questions of equality and justice are to human beings. And the ideal of authenticity with its imperative of autonomous self-determination is by no means obsolete, as Harari and others seem to suggest. Small gains of individual happiness and collective efficiency will surely not suffice to draw people into attitudes of *relative* or even *ultimate dependency* on AI and decision-making algorithms.

However, with moderate Dataism as a postmodern variant of secular civil religion, other forms of balancing individual freedom, conduct of life, pursuit of happiness and political steering might become possible – which are different from those that characterize Western liberal, pluralist and democratic societies. There are estimations that about half of all data produced by internet use is generated by Chinese users, mainly via mobile devices. All these data are extremely valuable and can be used to assess and guide the behavior of the

---

[49] H. Lübbe, *Religion nach der Aufklärung* (Graz: Verlag Styria, 1986).
[50] T. Luckmann, "Shrinking Transcendence, Expanding Religion?," *Sociological Analysis* 51, no. 2 (1990): 127 (https://doi.org/10.2307/3710810) (4/22/2022).

population, especially in a centralized state resting on a uniform ideology. That may not be Dataism as a new form of universal religion, but a viable alternative to humanist and liberal formations of the individual and the community, of steering and freedom, of self-management and social recognition – different from those we see in various Western societies, some of which are also moving towards more uniform, Durkheimian societies. With the digital revolution new forms of accepted, mediated heteronomy become possible, which might come as a relief from the burden of liberal modernity. A different sense of the social common good, of privacy and individuality, of authenticity and recognition, a different concept of economic steering that undercuts the difference between socialism and capitalism, a different understanding of happiness and its pursuit may lead to transformations of individual decision-making, political power and the public sphere mediated by AI. Here I see the real challenge of AI.

5. The End of Humanity as We Know it? Superintelligence and Singularity

Others go beyond. Like many religions, Dataism has its prophets, and it has its eschatology. Proponents of radical forms of Dataism announce fundamental and ultimate change. Often personally involved with AI and its technology, they present themselves as participants in the development and infer messages from what they see coming. Given the accelerating dynamics of the digital revolution, it is no wonder that people involved and interested try to anticipate future developments in order to find inspiration and orientation. Developers and business managers as well as politicians and philosophical thinkers are under constant pressure to predict directions and anticipate possible new pathways, so that many debates on AI refer to what soon, what likely or what inevitably will be the case, and what that might mean for us today. Utopian, alarmist and dystopian forms of speculation are all present in these discourses. In any case, AI invites us to develop profound thought experiments and fantastic scenarios. With AI, humanity has created intelligent machines somewhat in its own image, so that the question occurs: what this will mean for the creators themselves, especially when machines become more intelligent than humans?

One view is that AI will outperform human intelligence pretty soon, and that then machine intelligence will start perfecting itself, as each generation of new machines and programs creates more intelligent machines. This will lead to an explosion of intelligence disrupting the continuity of the historical development on this planet. This super-nova of intelligence is called the 'singularity' or 'superintelligence'. The basic notion goes back to the days of early AI and was formulated by the British mathematician Irving J. Good[51] in 1965:

---

[51] Irving J. Good worked as a cryptologist together with Alan Turing on the design of computers and decoding during and after World War II. In 1967 he moved to the US, where

Let an ultraintelligent machine be defined as a machine that can far surpass all the intellectual activities of any man however clever. Since the design of machines is one of these intellectual activities, an ultraintelligent machine could design even better machines; there would then unquestionably be an 'intelligence explosion,' and the intelligence of man would be left far behind. Thus the first ultraintelligent machine is the *last* invention that man need ever make, provided that the machine is docile enough to tell us how to keep it under control.[52]

The term 'singularity' for this 'intelligence explosion' was introduced in 1983 by science fiction author and professor of computer science Vernon Vinge,[53] who in his 1993 essay *The Coming Technological Singularity*[54] announced the end of the human era as we know it, so that "old models must be discarded and a new reality rules". The basic idea is that after the emergence of a dominating superintelligence the history of humankind will not continue, but will enter into a post-human, presently unpredictable, state with humanity either merging with superintelligence or becoming extinct. That is called the singularity, which in mathematics and science is a point at which a given theory is not defined or loses its meaning, because certain variables become infinite or indeterminate.

Vinge also presupposes that soon computers beyond a certain level of intelligence and complexity as well as large computer networks will 'wake up' to consciousness and thus develop into super-powers dominating human beings. He speaks from an 'Intelligence Amplification'-point of view and sees the answer to this challenge in what he calls strong superhumanity. Strong superhumanity looks for opportunities to merge technology with human bodies and minds (e.g. by using transhumanist technologies[55] like upgrading bodies with robotics and connecting brains directly to super-computers) so that it might become possible that in an upgraded form "humans themselves would become their own successors". Immortality for the human mind would be a consequence,

---

he served as consultant to director Stanley Kubrick on supercomputers when Kubrick worked on his movie "2001: A Space Odyssey."

[52] I. J. GOOD, "Speculations Concerning the First Ultraintelligent Machine," *Advances in Computers* 6 (1965): 33.

[53] D. J. CHALMERS, "The Singularity: A Philosophical Analysis," *Journal of Consciousness Studies* 17 (2010): 9.

[54] See https://edoras.sdsu.edu/~vinge/misc/singularity.html. All quotes in this and the following paragraph are cited from this document (4/22/2022).

[55] Transhumanism rests on a combination of AI, Nano Technology and Synthetic Biology, by which the human race shall not only be able to merge with technology, but shall leave its biological form behind. Cf. already the Extropian Principles (1st publication in 1998): "We will co-evolve with the products of our minds, integrating with them, finally integrating our intelligent technology into ourselves in a posthuman synthesis, amplifying our abilities and extending our freedom" (https://web.archive.org/web/20100114100426/http://www.maxmore.com/extprn3.htm) (4/22/2022). See also the historical overview by Nick Bostrom (reference in footnote 2).

because it will then be possible to download it from brains, merge it with superintelligence and keep it running – a vision, by the way, that Vinge himself sees as highly ambivalent, since participating in maximal superintelligence, knowing and understanding everything that can be known, would be boring to itself, and "after a few thousand years it would look more like a repeating tape loop than a person." All in all, however, Vinge joins with others of the superintelligence camp in stating that beyond singularity, humans would finally become 'like God.' He cites creative physicist and mathematician Freeman Dyson: "God is what mind becomes when it has passed beyond the scale of our comprehension".

Another very popular voice in this choir is the US-American author, inventor and director of engineering with Google Ray Kurzweil, who identifies a plurality of parallel, exponentially growing developments in modern digital technology and especially in AI. He speaks of the general law (!) of accelerating returns leading towards singularity.[56] Kurzweil is proud of having predicted a whole set of technological developments in his early books, and in his 2005 book *The Singularity Is Near* he set "the date for the Singularity – representing a profound and disruptive transformation in human capability – as 2045."[57] Kurzweil estimated the computational power of the human brain to be $2 \cdot 10^{14}$ bits per second. On the way to the singularity, personal computers should reach that level by 2020 and will soon develop their own free will and spiritual experiences.[58] However, from what we know about computing technology, Kurzweil's insinuation that the intelligence of a system is a function of its growth in computational speed and storage memory is not warranted. Nevertheless, Kurzweil assumes that once computers excel human intelligence and start to perfect themselves, the explosion of superintelligence comes into sight, and this will give the human mind the opportunity to become part of it. He not only predicts that mortality will be overcome in a post-biological future, at least insofar as humanity merges with machines, he also speculates that, beyond the singularity event, superintelligence will expand and reach out to the cosmos "to create the Universe it wants. This is the goal of the Singularity".[59] On the way to this eschatological future, human beings will already start being 'like God', when nanobots (micro robots) implanted in their brain will expand their intelligence as well as their sensitivity beyond any present measure by connecting them with the superintelligence of AI technology. Thus 'God' is not the creator of the cosmos and its creatures, but their final product and

---

[56] http://www.kurzweilai.net/the-law-of-accelerating-returns (4/22/2022).
[57] R. KURZWEIL, *The Singularity Is Near: When Humans Transcend Biology*, Science (New York, NY: Penguin, 2005), 136. For a popular and catchy presentation of his claims see also the movie with the same title.
[58] Cf. already R. KURZWEIL, *The Age of Spiritual Machines: When Computers Exceed Human Intelligence* (New York: Penguin Books, 1999).
[59] http://www.kurzweilai.net/the-law-of-accelerating-returns (4/22/2022).

creation's eschatological fate. 'God' is created through the process of cosmic expansion and planetary evolution, which eventually ignites the explosion of superintelligence through the hands of human beings, transforming the cosmos into its final, blissful state with the human mind participating in it.

There are a number of issues connected to these prophecies and eschatologies, but in a short paper like this we cannot deal extensively with them. A few spotlights must suffice. On the whole, the concept of the awakening of a superintelligence is hardly warranted. The nature of AI with its present hardware and software architecture does not suggest that AI will transform itself into superintelligence. In the scenarios presented AI is usually addressed as a quasi-agent and ghost from the machine (a kind of *Deus ex machina*), and it is argued that 'this' AI then will learn and perfect 'itself'.[60] But, as we have seen, AI is a general term for a complex phenomenon, not for a 'thing'. In some scenarios with AI taking over history, 'AI' even acts like a Hegelian 'Weltgeist' and is equipped with opaque forms of autonomy, although it is by no means clear under what conditions the abstract notion of machine learning allows for reification in the form of a superintelligent intentional agent.

Oxford philosopher Nick Bostrom at least sees the problem and tries to argue for the possibility of AI plus technology developing towards what he calls a singleton. A singleton "refers to a world order in which there is a single decision-making agency at the highest level,"[61] and he tries to argue for the hypothesis "that Earth-originating intelligent life will (eventually) form a singleton."[62] He identifies an overarching trend in the past, manifest in the transition from hunter-gatherer bands to tribes to cities, and extrapolates that "this trend points to the creation of a singleton."[63] However, he keeps the notion very open and speculates that very different types of singletons are possible: good, bad, democratic, totalitarian and others. They are all singletons as long as they are able to coordinate and determine everything on this globe. Bostrom then speculates further how such a quasi-entity in the form of a singleton develops intentionality when AI starts to dominate it, that is motivations, intentions, goals and preferences in order to 'rule' the world and later the whole cosmos. He admits that 'intelligence' (in the sense of the computational capacity for complex problem solving) does not necessarily go along with intentionality, because intelligence and final goals are orthogonal axes.[64]

---

[60] An example is CHALMERS, "Chalmers Singularity."
[61] N. BOSTROM, "What is a Singleton?," *Linguistic and Philosophical Investigations* 5, no. 2 (2005): 48.
[62] Ibid., 53.
[63] Ibid.
[64] See N. BOSTROM, "The Superintelligent Will: Motivation and Instrumental Rationality in Advanced Artificial Agents," *Minds and Machines* 22, no. 2 (2012): 71–85 (https://doi.org/10.1007/s11023-012-9281-3, https://doi.org/10.1007/s11023-012-9281-3) (4/22/2022).

But if there are some intelligent agents having a significant number of final goals, he speculates, there might be instrumental reasons for them to join forces, to coordinate goals and thus turn into an intentional god-like entity with extraordinary knowledge and power.

All these arguments are hardly warranted. Against the idea that functional AI is able to develop understanding and intentionality at all (the original thesis of *strong* AI against *weak* AI), Hubert Dreyfus[65] and John Searle[66] have protested right from the beginning, with Roger Penrose[67] later adding objections from a mathematical and quantum-theoretical perspective. Dreyfus, for example, argues that the brain is not a rule-following digital system, but works with indispensable analog components, and that formal symbolic reasoning is but a very small part of human intelligence and understanding. In a sense, human reasoning is highly artificial itself and a late product of intentional and self-aware minds, not the other way around. In any case, as we have seen, AI today works with very different structures of computing than envisioned in the beginning of AI: decentralized, self-learning networks and algorithmic assessments drawing on huge clusters of data. I do not see any trajectory leading towards a 'wake-up' of machine intelligence as such. AI is decentralized and not self-reflexive. It reminds us of collective intelligence integrating specialized cognitive modules, cooperation and coordination like a swarm of fish, rather than an agent becoming conscious (of what?) and on the way to intentional super-power. And it has become very clear how important bodies and biology are not only for developing an inner sense, but also for intuitive and rational decision-making. AI is inspired by how we think that we think, but in the end we build machines that serve certain purposes as well as possible under specific contingent conditions, and although this brings about far-reaching transformations, that is something very different from preparing the way for a superintelligence that confronts us with the alternative either to give up ourselves or to merge with it so that we may reach the next level.

According to Dreyfus, speculative, prophetic Dataism is not scientific reasoning but a quasi-religion: "In current excited waiting for the singularity, reli-

---

[65] Starting with the informal paper H. L. DREYFUS, "Alchemy and Artificial Intelligence," RAND Corporation, https://www.rand.org/pubs/papers/P3244.html and the famous essay H. L. DREYFUS, *What Computers Can't Do: A Critique of Artificial Reason* (New York: Harper Row, 1972); then continuing with H. L. DREYFUS, *What Computers Still Can't Do: A Critique of Artificial Reason*, 6th ed. (Cambridge, MA: MIT Press, 1999) and H. L. DREYFUS, "A History of First Step Fallacies," *Minds and Machines* 22, no. 2 (2012): 87–99 (https://doi.org/10.1007/s11023-012-9276-0, https://doi.org/10.1007/s11023-012-9276-0) (4/22/2022).

[66] See footnote 45.

[67] R. PENROSE, *Shadows of the Mind: A Search for the Missing Science of Consciousness* (Oxford: Oxford University Press, 1994) (http://www.loc.gov/catdir/enhancements/fy0637/94012887-d.html) (4/22/2022).

gion and technology converge."[68] And it seems to me no random coincidence that it is Teilhard de Chardin's catholic cosmology leading from the biosphere via the noosphere – with the help of science and the acceleration of evolution – to the Omega point, that can be seen as a religious progenitor of these models – with a transcendent dimension, of course, and not within the immanent frame. Dataism as quasi-religion reveals more about the religious fantasies, fears, projections and desires of its proponents than of present technological developments. The digital revolution is not a challenge because its technology is so powerful and so ingenious that it will swallow those who created it, but because it resonates with certain aspects of human psychology and it challenges us to redefine and preserve what it means to be human. Or as IT-pioneer Jaron Lanier put it: "the mythology is the problem, not the algorithms."[69] Discourse on the question whether or not AI endangers the human species is primarily about human hopes, fears and strong evaluations in reference to human ways of living and about the dynamics that bring forth a will to technology, and only secondarily about AI.

Human beings are susceptible to eschatological narratives, and within the immanent frame perspectives based on science and technology have gained plausibility. Superintelligence and transhumanism are seductive because they promise a restoration – through scientific and technological progress – of the eschatological hopes that science itself has obliterated. They are not entirely different from theological attempts to spell out cosmology, evolution and history in terms of a history of salvation, rather they turn them upside down and let the deity emerge from creation rather than creation from the deity – a version of inverse intelligent design with the outlook of eternal salvation, or as Dreyfus bluntly put it: "singularity is the rapture for nerds."[70]

However, for theologians and philosophers of religion these discourses are a reminder to be careful and critical about their own notions of God or the divine. When Leibniz as an early modern optimist wrote "*Cum DEUS calculat et cogitationem exercet, fit mundus*: When God calculates and executes considerations, the world comes into existence,"[71] then he argued for a notion of God as superintelligence, combining omniscient decision-making with omnipotent determination. If that is the essence of the divine being, it must be asked whether such a notion shrinks to, and becomes identical with, superintelligence once the immanent frame is accepted. We might need other and more responsive notions of God in relation to an open, developing reality and to

---

[68] DREYFUS, "Dreyfus History," 87.
[69] J. LANIER, https://www.edge.org/conversation/jaron_lanier-the-myth-of-ai (4/22/2022).
[70] DREYFUS, "Dreyfus History," 99.
[71] G. W. LEIBNIZ, *Die philosophischen Schriften von Gottfried Wilhelm Leibniz Bd. VII*, ed. C. I. Gerhardt (Berlin: Weidmannsche Buchhandlung, 1890), 191 (my translation).

human conduct of life that have the power to deal differently and constructively with apocalyptic fears and eschatological illusions. And we have to be especially careful with tendencies towards rich and imaginary eschatological scenarios, because they "may only too easily injure Christian faith and life, and thereby spoil for us the present."[72] In a Christian theological perspective, from which I write, living in the presence of God must be the focus so that we "face up to and maybe even enjoy our embodied finitude,"[73] but not the fears and promises of eternity that tend to turn faith into policy.

Because we are a symbolic species, we need media to relate to others, to ourselves, to the divine. For the same reason, we tend to project fears, hopes and visions onto the astonishing and all-pervasive development of AI, its capacities, its creation of virtual realities, its competence in dealing with the unknown. But also because we are a symbolic species, we are competent in dealing with virtual realities and with extended selves. We are equipped with a double mode of consciousness[74] when dealing with, for example, puppets, theatre plays, rituals, and symbols, knowing that we still have to distinguish between reality and its symbolic representation. We can even distance us from ourselves when we cultivate humor, irony, fiction and phantasy. Religions give testimony of both, of dangerous and illusionary forms of coping with contingencies as well as of impressive examples of how human beings realize meaning in individual and communal life by transcending themselves, by tolerating ambiguity[75] and by being open towards others, including having a precise sense for false security and justified confidence. And that may not be the least service of philosophical reflection on the digital revolution and AI, that it is intriguing, challenging, entertaining, irritating and funny at the same time.

---

[72] F. D. E. Schleiermacher, *Der christliche Glaube. Nach den Grundsätzen der evangelischen Kirche im Zusammenhange dargestellt. Zweite Auflage (1830/31): Teilband 2*, ed. R. Schäfer, KGA I/13-2 (Berlin/New York: de Gruyter, 2008), 465 (§ 158.3); "nur zu leicht [...] die Gegenwart verderben", translation: F. Schleiermacher, *The Christian Faith*, 3rd ed., ed. P. T. Nimmo (London: Bloomsbury Academic, 2016), 703.

[73] Dreyfus, "Dreyfus History," 99.

[74] Cf. C. P. Scholtz, *Alltag mit künstlichen Wesen: Theologische Implikationen eines Lebens mit subjektsimulierenden Maschinen am Beispiel des Unterhaltungsroboters Aibo* (Göttingen: Vandenhoeck & Ruprecht, 2008).

[75] Cf. T. Bauer, *Die Vereindeutigung der Welt: Über den Verlust an Mehrdeutigkeit und Vielfalt*, 2nd ed. (Ditzingen: Reclam, 2018).

The Paradoxical Self

A Dilemma for Artificial General Intelligence

Liu Yue

In this paper, I will articulate a dilemma for Artificial General Intelligence (AGI for short) which claims that a machine can eventually perform any intellectual task that a human being can do, by taking recent empirical research which amounts to the claim that the self is no more than a mechanism (or a side product of the information processing) of the brain. Though this claim is consensually held by many philosophers and scientists, it has not yet been fully verified. Were it true, it would be in favor of AGI at face value. I am neither committed to this claim nor to AGI. My strategy in this paper is simply to elaborate the fact that if this claim is true, it will pose a dilemma for AGI. Based on this dilemma, I will propose a sketchy defense for the idea of minimal humanity.

1. AGI: A Goal as well as A Standard

Can machine think? This is the question Turing raised 70 years ago at the beginning of his landmark paper.[1] Although Turing immediately remarked that it might not be appropriate to address the question in this way because it involves some absurdity with respect to our common understanding of "machine" and "think," and suggested to replace it with the question of can machine pass the Turing test, I believe that there won't be too much hesitance when a person is asked this question nowadays. Just think about the 2016 startling news of AlphaGo's beating Lee Sedol and then Ke Kie with many innovative moves, especially its unexpected comment on Ke Jie[2] while the function of the evaluating mechanism is just to analyze the tactical situation for making

---

[1] A. Turing, "Computing Machinery and Intelligence," *Mind* 59 (1950): 433–460.

[2] Demis Hassabis, the founder of DeepMind, had posted a Twitter message saying that "As we were in the control room looking at what AlphaGo's evaluation is saying; the evaluation: win rate, for roughly 50 moves, it thought that Ke Jie has been playing perfectly. And it agreed with all the moves, then, for the first roughly 100 moves, it is the closest game we have seen anyone play against the master version of AlphaGo" during the competition.

the next move. It is absurd to raise this question 70 years ago, and it is somehow trivial to raise this question today. Willing or not, we have to admit that machine can indeed think, then the question becomes that to what extent we may agree that machine can think, or in other words, whether machine can think *exactly* like a human. To see how AI scientists address this issue, I will briefly review three kinds of AI discussed in the literature of philosophy and science.

Since the birth of AI science at a workshop at Dartmouth College in 1956, there are at least three kinds of AI discussed by philosophers and scientists, i.e. weak AI, strong AI, and AGI. "Weak AI" and "Strong AI" are coined by John Searle in his 1980 paper.[3] The claims of each thesis are as follows:

Weak AI: An appropriately programmed computer can pass the Turing Test.
Strong AI: An appropriately programmed computer with the right inputs and outputs would have a mind in exactly the same sense human beings have minds.

After articulating the Chinese Room argument in response to Turing's solution, Searle concludes that even if a computer can successfully pass the Turing Test, it doesn't entail that the computer thus has a mind. Searle's verdict that weak AI holds while strong AI doesn't is widely adopted by philosophers. Note that this distinction is mainly deployed in philosophy rather than in AI science. What AI scientists are mainly concerned with is the realization of AGI, which was firstly introduced by Mark Gubrud[4] in a 1997 conference and claims that,

AGI: An appropriately programmed computer could successfully perform any intellectual task that a human being can.

AGI has once been an optimistic and prominent view[5] with an overwhelming momentum of AI research in the 60s. Although AI research underwent two hiatuses during the 70s and the early 90s, AGI has recently regained great attention and confidence due to some significant developments such as neural networks in deep learning. Roughly speaking, AGI is stronger than weak AI since it requires not any specific[6] but a general intelligence; meanwhile

---

[3] J. R. SEARLE, "Minds, brains and programs," *Behavioral and Brain Sciences* (1980): 417–424.

[4] M. A. GUBRUD, "Nanotechnology and International Security," *Fifth Foresight Conference on Molecular Nanotechnology*, vol. 1, 1997 (http://www.foresight.org/Conferences/MNT05/Papers/Gubrud/index.html). (4/22/2022).

[5] For example, D. CREVIER, *AI: The Tumultuous History of the Search for Artificial Intelligence* (New York: Basic Books, 1997), 109 quotes Minsky as having said on AGI in 1967, "Within a generation [...] the problem of creating 'artificial intelligence' will substantially be solved." H. A. SIMON, one of the attendees of the Dartmouth workshop, also writes: "machines will be capable, within twenty years, of doing any work a man can do" (*The Shape of Automation for Men and Management* [New York: Harper & Row, 1965], 96).

[6] For weak AI the specific intelligence is to pass the Turing Test.

AGI is weaker than strong AI since it doesn't require the computer to have a mind. What is agreed by both philosophers and AI scientists is just weak AI. Most philosophers don't think there is any significant philosophical difference between weak AI and AGI while most AI researchers don't even take strong AI.[7]

The main reason why I choose AGI but not strong AI for which to articulate the dilemma is because, in my view, the Chinese Room argument and strong AI are problematic since they both implicitly presuppose the existence of human minds. Searle maintains that the Chinese Room argument is sound because it is based on two cornerstones, which are intuitively cogent. The two cornerstones, as Searle rephrases in a retrospective paper, are the claim that semantics is not syntax and the claim that simulation is not duplication.[8] According to Searle, the support to the first claim is the intuition that we understand a sentence through its meaning which cannot be reduced to its syntactic structure, and the evidence for the second claim is that intentionality is intrinsic to human mentality which a computer can never possess. Instead of examining the problems of each cornerstone in details,[9] I only want to point out one crucial thing, that is, both the understanding of meaning and intentionality have to presuppose the existence of human minds. By stealthily taking these presumptions, the Chinese Room argument has already conceptually excluded the possibility that a computer can genuinely understand a sentence or have intentionality, and thus entails the negation of strong AI, that a computer cannot have a mind. As I see it, the Chinese Room argument is *per se* a circular and not sound.

Moreover, even if the negation of strong AI is not smashed by the invalidity of the Chinese Room argument, by deploying the ambiguous idea of mind, Strong AI can hardly provide any operable instructions to verify itself in any empirical manner. Russell and Norvig argue that, if we accept Searle's description of intentionality and the mind, we are forced to accept that consciousness is epiphenomenal: that it "casts no shadow" and is undetectable in the physical

---

[7] S. J. Russell and P. Norvig, *Artificial Intelligence: A Modern Approach*, 2nd ed. (Upper Saddle River, NJ: Prentice Hall, 2003).

[8] J. R. Searle, "Twenty-One Years in the Chinese Room," in *Philosophy in A New Century: Selected Essays* (Cambridge: Cambridge University Press, 2008), 53–66.

[9] There is a long and prominent tradition in the philosophy of language denying the existence of meaning. For example, Quine is well known for his continuous criticism of the idea of meaning, as he writes: "meaning […] is a worthy object of philosophical and scientific clarification and analysis, and […] it is ill-suited for use as an instrument of philosophical and scientific clarification and analysis" (W. V. O. Quine, *Theories and Things* [Cambridge, MA: Harvard University Press, 1981], 185). For a review of different skeptical views on semantics, see S. Soames, "Skepticism about Meaning: Indeterminacy, Normativity, and the Rule-Following Paradox," *Canadian Journal of Philosophy* 27, no. 1 (1997): 211–249; for the critics to the claim that simulation is not duplication, see various versions of system reply.

world, which is similar to my objection.[10] In contrast, leaving aside whether a computer can possess a mind, or whether there is really something namely a mind, AGI only forecasts that a computer can eventually perform any intellectual task, which sets up an implementable goal for experimental approach.

For the sake of simplifying the situation, it is reasonable to constrain the scope of intellectual tasks to those tasks the procedure of which can be reported in a verbal way by the subject to a more or less extent[11], since the kind of verbally reportable tasks constitutes a subset of intellectual tasks and if we can build up the dilemma on the subset it will also apply to the whole set. Constrained in this way, AGI doesn't require a computer to achieve any intellectual task of which the process is inaccessible or ineffable to the subject, such as vision or olfaction. To sum up. Weak AI is the answer to the question "can machine think," and the constrained AGI is probably the answer that most AI scientists hold to the question "can machine think exactly like a human to the effect that it can perform any verbally reportable intellectual task". This is the other reason why I choose AGI in this paper.

Now we can further ask, what standard can be used to assess whether constrained AGI succeeds or not. The most famous standard on hand is the Turing Test, according to which if the interrogator could not distinguish between responses from a machine and a human, the machine could be considered "intelligent." However, the biggest problem for the Turing Test is that its application scope is very limited.[12] In fact, the Turing Test is not needed in many cases wherein the ability of the program can be directly assessed via the task result but not Q&A. For example, we don't need to use the Turing Test to assess whether AlphaGo can successfully play the Go game. The other reason why we need another standard is because the Turing Test can only serve as a conclusive standard even in the case when it is applicable. It is conclusive because it can only be used at the final stage to test whether the program can successfully imitate such capacity. As Gunderson[13] points out, thinking is a general concept of human cognition while playing the imitation game is but one example. So when computer scientists design a new program, the goal they bear in mind

---

[10] RUSSELL and NORVIG, *Artificial Intelligence*.

[11] Whether the process of thinking is accessible or to the subject is still controversial, as R. E. NISBETT and T. D. WILSON remarked in their widly-quoted paper, substantial evidences indicate that "there may be little or no direct introspective access to higher order cognitive processes" ("Telling more than we can know: verbal reports on mental processes," *Psychological Review* 84 [1977]: 231). I don't attempt to discuss this problem here and by "more or less" I don't require the process to be fully accessible.

[12] There are many other criticisms of the Turing Test. I don't attempt to review them here and for those who are interested please see A. P. SAYGIN, I. CICEKLI, and V. AKMAN, "Turing Test: 50 Years Later," *Minds & Machines* 10, no. 4 (2000): 463–518.

[13] K. GUNDERSON, "The Imitation Game," *Mind* 73 (1964): 234–245.

must not be to pass the Turing Test, but to imitate certain cognitive capacity. The Turing Test is not instructive since it doesn't provide any specific direction for scientists to go, and therefore an instructive standard is needed as well.

It seems to me that AGI is not just the answer to the question of can machine think exactly like a man but also offers us an instructive standard to AI research. AGI as an answer, that is to say, a machine can think like a human if only if it can achieve any intellectual task that a human can do. AGI as a standard, that is to say, AGI is successful if only if for any intellectual task that a human can do, it must be possible for the machine to be programmed to perform the same task[14]. In turn, if there is one intellectual task that a man can achieve such that the machine can by no means to be programmed to achieve the same task, the AGI can be considered to be failed. This standard is instructive and can play a complementary role to the Turing Test: according to the instructive standard, we may design a program to simulate any intellectual capacity that we can find in a human, and if needed, we can deploy the Turing Test to see whether the program succeeds or not.

2. A Stipulation of the Paradoxical Self

In this section, I will sketch several philosophers' views on whether there is such an entity (or a thing) namely the self and how contemporary scientific research sheds light on this question. The most notorious view holding that the self is an entity which cannot be reduced to any material thing, is defended by Descartes. According to Descartes, that I am doubting cannot be doubted because to doubt that I am doubting is by itself an act of doubting. The indubitability of being doubting entails that there must be a self which conducts the act of doubting, that is, I think therefore I am. The Cartesian self is a thing that thinks, doubts, understands, affirms, denies, wills, refuses, and that also imagines and senses, which is synonymous with the mind or the soul for Descartes.

Kant is in line with Descartes in the sense that he took the self to be irreducible and ground all mental acts. In Kant's view, the enduring self[15] is not

---

[14] Here it is worth pointing out that for a machine to successfully perform an intellectual task does not entail that the program underlying this performance must be akin to the cognitive capacity underlying a human with respect to the task. I am grateful for Dr. Hasse Hamalainen's reminding me that to possess a cognitive capacity and to perform an intellectual task are two different things whereas what AI scientists mostly concern about is the later other than to simulate the cognitive capacity. However, we should bear in mind that it is still arguable whether we can regard a machine as thinking exactly like a man if it can perform all intellectual tasks with essentially different capacities.

[15] It shall be noted that it is not clear whether Kant took the self to be equivalent to the unified consciousness or the mind.

empirical because it is not an object of experience and thereby not to be found in self-consciousness; on the other hand, the self is transcendental for that it precedes any experience and cognition, and constitutes the necessary condition for any experience and cognition. That is why Kant named the self "the transcendental unity of apperception" and claimed that "The 'I think', must be capable of accompanying all my presentations."[16]

Husserl constantly echoed Descartes and Kant's idea of the irreducibility of the ego. By inheriting and expanding the idea of intentionality from Brentano, Husserl found that within every intentional state, we can find one pole of the intentional object together with the other of the subject who performs the intentional act, which Husserl termed the phenomenal structure, i. e. I-think-something, or ego-cogito-cogitatum (compared to Descartes's cogito-ergo-sum). However, the phenomenological structure is not yet the residuum of phenomenological reduction because within mental processes the empirical (or psychological) ego "can change, come and go, even though one may doubt that every cogito is necessarily something transitory and not simply, as we find it, something in fact transitory."[17] Nonetheless, it is evident that we can always recognize ourselves as an integrated identity through time, and if the empirical ego is transitory, what anchors all the mental processes? Husserl's answer is the pure ego.[18] As he wrote:

"[…] the pure Ego would, however, seem to be something essentially necessary; and, as something absolutely identical throughout every actual or possible change in mental processes, it cannot in any sense be a realty inherent part or moment of the mental processes themselves. In every actional cogito the ego lives out its life in a special sense. But all mental processes in the background likewise belong to it; and it belongs to them."[19]

The shared understanding of the self among these three philosophers is that *the self is the irreducible origin of mentality or grounds the integration of mentality*. There is no way to go beyond the self, whatever by introspection or inference, because it is the self that gives rise to all mental acts such as introspection and inference, but not the other way round.

Though the Cartesian self is an entrenched idea in philosophy, there is no lack of opposite voices, such as Hume. Hume claimed that we can by no means introspect on the so-called "self" as an object. As he wrote:

---

[16] I. KANT, *Critique of Pure Reason*, trans. P. Werner (Indianapolis, IN: Hackett Publishing Company, 1996), 132.

[17] E. HUSSERL, *Ideas Pertaining to a Pure Phenomenology and to a Phenomenological Philosophy, First Book*, trans. F. Kersten (The Hague: Martinus Nijhoff, 1982), 132.

[18] Husserl's distinction between empirical ego and pure ego may be inspired by Kant's distinction between empirical self-consciousness and transcendental apperception, though "transcendental" is used by Kant and Husserl in different senses.

[19] Ibid., 132–133.

"There are some philosophers, who imagine we are every moment intimately conscious of what we call our self [...] For my part when I enter most intimately into what I call myself, I always stumble on some particular perception or other, of heat or cold, light or shade, love or hatred, pain or pleasure. I never can catch myself at any time without a perception, and never can observe anything but the perception."[20]

Therefore, the idea of the self is nothing more than a collection of different perceptions. Hume concluded: "I may venture to affirm of the rest of mankind, that they are nothing but a bundle or collection of different perceptions, which succeed each other with an inconceivable rapidity, and are in a perpetual flux and movement."[21] According to Hume, the idea of a self is merely functional, that is, to explain the integration of the perceptions, "we feign the continued existence of the perceptions of our sense, to remove the interruption; and run into the notion of a soul, and self, and substance, to disguise the variation."[22]

The problem of Hume's argument is the fact that the self cannot introspect on itself is compatible with the existence of a Cartesian self. A simple analogy is the fact that one cannot lift her own body doesn't entail that her body doesn't exist. Since we have certain physiological limitations with respect to our bodies, the same goes to our cognitive capacities. The intuition that one can introspect on oneself is implicitly based on a perception-like model of introspection originally proposed by Locke and the reasoning goes like: if one can perceive her own body, one can also introspect on her own self. However, if the self is really something non-material, it has no extension and is thus undividable. Then there is no reason to maintain that the self can "see" (retrospect on) any part of itself.

Still, it seems to me that it is possible to reveal the fact there is no such an irreducible entity namely the self by the phenomenological approach, especially based on the phenomenological structure. The key reason is that if the self precedes all mental acts, then the phenomenological structure, even having the empirical self being excluded, must not be the final residuum after a radically phenomenological reduction, because "to precede" always requires a temporal interval of the self's attempt to a mental act, which in principle should be introspectible. However, since Husserl had already eloquently argued that the phenomenological structure is indivisible, this is already powerful evidence to reject the presupposition that there is a proceeding self. Concerning the problem of unification or integration, the idea of a functional self is also redundant, as Sartre remarked,

---

[20] D. HUME, *A Treatise of Human Nature* (Waiheke Island, RI: The Floating Press, 2009), 393–395.
[21] Ibid., 396.
[22] Ibid., 398.

"The I is a producer of inwardness. But it is certainly the case that phenomenology does not need to resort to this unifying and individualizing I. Rather, consciousness is defined by intentionality. Through intentionality it transcends itself, it unifies itself by going outside itself."[23]

Bearing this disagreement among philosophers in mind, let's shift our gaze to science to see how contemporary findings may illuminate this question. In cognitive science and neuroscience, substantial evidences are obtained in support of the view that the self is an information processing mechanism generated by the brain. One thing needed to be clarified in advance is in what sense the "self" is intended in the scientific debates. The consensual is that the self is identical to the conscious agent while the function of the conscious agent is to perform conscious will. I think that both Descartes and Kant can also agree to equate the self with conscious will. The following problem is to what extent we may agree that the conscious will can will freely. There are mainly two ways to construe conscious will: conscious will as an ability to make rational, informed decisions when one is not being subjected to undue force; and conscious will as an ability to have made a different decision in the absence of any prior difference.[24]

What the nowadays findings refute is the conscious will construed in the second way. First of all, a series of experiments show that there are some brain activations before a conscious intention/decision comes into awareness.[25] If this is true, our sense of conscious will which can deliberatively or freely author our thoughts and actions is no more than a hindsight mechanism generated by the brain. Although Libet retains the conscious will with the function of veto, the problem is that this resolution cannot accommodate well with other findings which reveal the defect of the self-mechanism under certain circumstance or in some pathological cases. For example, some experiments show that under certain stimulus the subject will hold a wrong authorship of certain behaviors which are not caused by her own will, and on the other hand, some experiments also show that under certain misdirection, the subject may lose or deny

---

[23] J. P. SARTRE, *The Transcendence of the Ego: A Sketch for a Phenomenological Description*, trans. A. Brown (London: Routledge, 2004), 4.

[24] See A. R. MELE, *Free: Why Science Hasn't Disproved Free Will* (Oxford University Press, 2014). I completely agree that we have conscious will in the first sense and I think this is the kind of freedom that D. C. DENNETT defends in *Freedom Evolves* (London: Penguin, 2004).

[25] See B. LIBET, "Unconscious Cerebral Initiative and the Role of Conscious Will in Voluntary Action," *Behavioral and Brain Sciences* 8, no. 4 (1985): 529–539; "Do We Have Free Will?," *Journal of Consciousness Studies* 6, no. 8–9 (1999): 47–57; C. S. SOON, M. BRASS, H. J. HEINZE and J. D. HAYNES, "Unconscious Determinants of Free Decisions in the Human Brain," *Nature Neuroscience* 11, no. 5 (2008): 543–545; J. D. HAYNES, "Beyond Libet: Long-Term Prediction of Free Choices from Neuroimaging Signals," in *Conscious Will and Responsibility. A Tribute to Benjamin Libet*, ed. W. Sinnott-Armstrong and L. Nadel (Oxford: Oxford University Press, 2011), 85–96.

the sense of authorship with respect to her own voluntary actions.[26] If these findings are really the case, I don't see how the veto of conscious will can play a role in cases of the latter kind. Moreover, the studies of split-brain patients reveal a vast amount of confabulations in the process of integrating the information that the patient receives from separate visual fields. For example, a patient is shown a picture of a chicken foot and a snowy field in different visual fields and asked to choose from a list of words that well associated with the pictures. The patient would choose a chicken to associate with the chicken foot and a shovel to associate with the snow; but when asked why choosing the shovel, the response would be "the shovel is for cleaning out the chicken coop."[27] Gazzaniga thus concludes that the self is no more than a by-product generated by an interpreter locating in the left hemisphere when it integrates information.

Secondly, although more and more researches seem to indicate that the unification of consciousness is on a global scale and the same goes to the unification of agency, some neuroimaging studies show that by disrupting activity of neural circuitry in certain area will induce reports of lowered self-awareness and strong feelings of dissociation.[28] It is also admitted that there are different kinds/levels of agency, as Balconi points out,

"[T]here is evidence of different neural correlates for the sense of agency, which might reflect different agency indicators and/or sub-processes or levels of agency processing. The first group of brain areas involved in the sense of agency is located in the motor system and includes the ventral premotor cortex, the supplementary motor area (SMA) and pre-SMA, and the cerebellum. A second group consists of the dorsolateral prefrontal cortex (DLPFC), the posterior parietal cortex, the posterior segment of the superior temporal sulcus, and the insula. It is probable that the first group constitutes a network of sensory-motor transformation and motor control, and the second a set of association cortices implicated in various cognitive functions."[29]

Thirdly, many models have been proposed to explain the mechanism of the self or the emergence of the self without resorting to a Cartesian self.[30] Then

---

[26] Plenty of cases can be found in D. M. WEGNER, *The Illusion of Conscious Will* (Cambridge, MA: MIT Press, 2002).

[27] Various cases are discussed in M. S. GAZZANIGA, *Who's in Charge? Free Will and the Science of the Brain* (New York: Ecco, 2011).

[28] See M. GRUBERGER, Y. LEVKOVITZ, T. HENDLER, E. V. HAREL, H. HARARI, S. E. BEN, H. SHARON, and A. ZANGEN, "I Think Therefore I Am: Rest-related Prefrontal Cortex Neural Activity is Involved in Generating the Sense of Self," *Consciousness & Cognition* 33 (2015): 414–421.

[29] M. BALCONI, *Neuropsychology of the Sense of Agency* (New York: Nova Science Publishers, 2010), 4.

[30] To my limited knowledge, see S. NICHOLS and S. P. STICH, *Mindreading: An Integrated Account of Pretence, Self-awareness, and Understanding Other Minds* (Oxford: Clarendon Press/Oxford University Press, 2003); T. METZINGER, *The Ego Tunnel: The Science of the Mind and the Myth of the Self* (New York: Basic Books, 2009); A. DAMASIO, *Self Comes to Mind: Constructing the Conscious Brain* (New York: Pantheon, 2010).

following the principle of parsimony, there is no good reason for us to retain the Cartesian self, or the conscious will. To sum up, what we can tentatively learn from these findings are the followings:

(1) We commonly share an intuition that "I," as a self, is a conscious agent which can freely deliberate and make decisions;
(2) This intuition is an illusion and the self is a mechanism generated by the brain;
(3) I am able to negate myself to the effect that there is no such an irreducible entity to which "I" refers and this understanding can be justified to some degree by both philosophical reflection and appealing to empirical findings.

3. The Dilemma for AGI

Before articulating the dilemma, let me summarize the two seemingly irrelevant theses introduced in the former sections:

Thesis 1: The constrained AGI is true if only if for any constrained intellectual task that a human can do, it must be possible to program the computer to perform the same task.

Thesis 2: The self of a human can negate itself in the sense that it can recognize the fact that it is not an irreducible entity but a mechanism generated by the brain.

Call thesis 1 the constrained AGI (CAGI for short) and thesis 2 the speculation of the paradoxical self (SPS for short). The general idea is that, suppose that CAGI and SPS are both true, SPS will then pose a dilemma to CAGI.

First of all, given that the empirical findings are more inclined to support the claim that the self is not an entity (or a thing) but rather a mechanism (or a process), SPS is very likely to be true. At the same time, these findings are in favor of the computational theory of mind, which holds that human mind is an information processing system and cognition is a form of computation.[31] If the human mind (Here and hereafter I just adopt the common usage of the word "mind" without any metaphysical commitment.) is computational, it can be considered as a program in a broad sense. Given the programmed nature of the human mind, in turn, one can plausibly conjecture that an appropriately

---

[31] The computational theory of mind (CTM) was firstly advocated by W. S. McCulloch and W. Pitts, "A Logical Calculus of the Ideas Immanent in Nervous Activity," *The bulletin of mathematical biophysics* 5, no. 4 (1943): 115–133. They argued that neural activity is computational and neural computations can explain cognition. CTM was introduced into philosophy by Hilary Putnam, and developed by Jerry Fodor in the 1960s, 1970s and 1980s. For a recent defense of CTM, see S. Pinker, *How the Mind Works* (New York: Norton, 1997).

programmed computer can think *exactly* like a human mind. Therefore, these findings that amount to SPS are on the surface in favor of CAGI.

However, a quick examination will reveal that SPS cannot easily accommodate with CAGI. If SPS is true, to know that SPS is true should also be regarded as an intellectual task. According to CAGI, a machine is able to think *exactly* like a human only if it can be programmed to perform any intellectual task that a human can do. That is to say, for a machine to realize CAGI, it must at least be possible to be programmed to realize SPS in itself; and to realize SPS in itself means that the machine has to ultimately realize that it is not a human mind but a program (or a machine running by a program) by itself. Now it comes the dilemma: for the program to know that it is a program but not a human mind is against its design intent to imitate a human mind.

To put this more specifically. Suppose that we will have an ultimate program A^{32} which can both fulfill CAGI and SPS[33]. That A fulfills CAGI means that A can think *exactly* like a human being such that A can perform any constrained intellectual task that a human can do. That A fulfills SPS means that it must be programmed in a way to realize SPS. Note that to realize SPS does not require the program to perform any practical task and thus no result can be used to access whether the program successfully realizes SPS. The only way to assess whether A succeeds in realizing SPS is to appeal to the Turing Test. Nevertheless, we only need an extremely simplified version of the Turing Test here. We don't need a third person in this particular test to interfere with the interrogator's determining which of the other two is human. All we need is the interrogator to ask one simple question, that is, "can you *sincerely* tell me whether you are a computer with a program or a human with a mind?" On the one hand, if A succeeds in accommodating with SPS, it must be able to genuinely know that it is a program designed by mankind instead of a mind and has to sincerely reply that "I am indeed a program." However, this will contradict its design intent to behave as if it has a mind. On the other hand, if A cannot genuinely realize that it is a program, it cannot realize the SPS, which is a crucial part of human cognition; it then cannot be regarded as being able to think *exactly* like a human in every aspect.

I will consider two related concerns to further illustrate this dilemma. The first concern is that in this dilemma I seem to assume that being a human is NOT being a program, but isn't this precisely the point that is being debated in

---

[32] Here "program" will be intended at a general level just like what Turing intended by this word in his 1950 paper. Besides, normally a program is designed for a specific task, but here the ultimate program is supposed to achieve any intellectual task, probably the same to what Domingos calls the master algorithm. See P. DOMINGOS, *The Master Algorithm: How the Quest for the Ultimate Learning Machine Will Remake Our World* (New York: Basic Books, 2015).

[33] In fact, taking SPS as an intellectual task, to fulfill CAGI entails to fulfill SPS. Here I mention both just for the sake of convenience.

section 2? In fact, I have pointed out before articulating the dilemma that these empirical findings seem to amount to the conclusion that the self is a program, then in what sense such a program cannot be *artificially* programmed? My response is that probably by no means can the human self be artificially programmed although I completely agree that the human self is *per se* a program. Firstly, it must be pointed out that the term "program" can be intended at two levels, natural program and artificial program, and the difference between these two kinds of program is difference of degree but not difference of kind. Moreover, a program cannot be an infinite regress, meaning that being a program naturally entails that such program has a starting point, from where the program is initiated. Both natural program and artificial program must subject to this law. What the dilemma reveals is the limitation of an artificial program. For an artificial program to imitate a conscious self, its starting point shall be the recognition of itself as a conscious self and there seems to be no possibility for the program to go beyond this starting point. A human self as a natural program certainly has its own starting point, but whether this starting point is under or beyond our cognition is still unknown. What is clear here is that such natural program doesn't suffer the limitation to recognize itself as a program while an artificial program does. With respect to this distinction between natural and artificial program, I think my position is quite similar to Searle's, as he claims that human is a biological (natural) machine but not a computer (artificial machine).

Following this concern, the other concern is that how can we conclude that an artificial program must suffer such a limitation? One might be suspicious that, since we cannot know that the self is not an irreducible entity merely by reflection and our concluding that the self is just a mechanism generated by my brain mostly depends on empirical research, then given the opportunities for AI programs to study with each other, may it be possible for them to discover the fact that they are programs designed to imitate human minds but not human minds themselves? My reply will be that as far as I can see, the limitation posed by the dilemma is both conceptual and practical, which is not easy to dissolve or overcome. The main difference between a human and a computer is that a human is a contingent product of evolutionary processes without any teleology while a computer (or a program which drives a computer) carries a design intent from its birth by nature. Therefore, it is very difficult to see how CAGI might contain such a possibility to betray its design intent.

In sum, if SPS is correct, to know that SPS is correct should be a crucial part of human cognition. And if CAGI is correct, it has to accommodate the SPS and thus should be possible to recognize itself as a program, which is against its design intent to behave as possessing a human mind. Even though this dilemma might not be ultimately insoluble, CAGI has to bite this bullet if it wants to achieve further success.

4. Generalizing the Conclusion: A Defense for the Minimal Humanity

In the last section, I will explain what this dilemma may contribute to the question of "Humanity, an endangered idea?" Taken literally, this question contains two concepts: humanity and danger, so we should explore a little bit on the idea of humanity and why it is endangered. The idea of humanity can be understood in a narrow sense as a set of disciplines and in a broad sense as the distinctiveness of human. It is tricky to see that danger in the broad sense refers to the fact that the kind of distinctiveness that some philosophers endeavor to defend such as intrinsic value – some may prefer the term of transcendental value – is more or less undermined by the modern development of science during the past decades, and that philosophers' tenacious insistence on such kind of distinctiveness in turn alienates humanity as a set of disciplines from the scientific community, which constitutes the danger in the narrow sense. One cannot help to ask, whether there is a way of defending humanity, which can be embraced by scientists and at the same time retain our dignity as mankind. Or in other words, if we commit to a set of scientific theories such as evolutionary theory, neurobiological approach to the human brain and etc., is there still something in humanity that can be called distinctive? My answer is yes and I call the kind of humanity defended as such the minimal humanity.

A systematic defense of the minimal humanity is based on a brewing project which I call cognitive nativism, and given the limited space I can only provide a sketch of the project here. In short, the cognitive nativism project aims to defend and extend an old idea deriving from Kant claiming that all we have are our representations of the world. It means that our so-called knowledge of the world is no more than a system of our representations and we are indeed agnostic to thing-in-itself. This nativism is referred to as cognitive for it premises that our representations are *structured* and *confined* by our innate cognitive capacities[34] and given the fact that we are mankind sharing the same biological and cognitive bases we should possess the same cognitive capacities. This implies that if there exist some creatures of which the biological and cognitive bases are completely different from ours, they should have completely different representations of the world and thus their knowledge, say, their physics, should be completely different from ours. Note that mankind is also part of the world. Therefore, this scenario also goes for our so-called knowledge of ourselves, whatever concerning our biology or our cognition.

---

[34] A specific and also the most well-known version of cognitive nativism is Chomsky's linguistic theory which holds that the structure underlying language is biologically determined and since we shared the same biological basis we should share the same linguistic structure (for example, see N. CHOMSKY, "Linguistics and Cognitive Science: Problems and Mysteries," in *The Chomskyan Turn*, ed. A. Kasher (Oxford: Blackwell, 1991), 26–53.

Since our representations are structured and confined by our cognitive capacities, they certainly suffered some limitations of representing the world. Take mathematics for example[35]. According to this project, mathematics is just one of these cognitive capacities. If this is true, it can explain why mathematics perfectly fits physics because physics is exactly our representation of the physical world structured and confined by mathematics, and at the same time it also explain the limitation of mathematics in modeling the world because mathematics is not the language of nature as we used to think. One enthralling mathematical problem that can lucidly elaborate the limitation of our representing the world in a mathematical way is the three-body problem[36]. In a nutshell, three bodies (even n bodies) move stably in the real world; however, based on Newton's laws of motion and law of universal gravitation, we cannot solve for their subsequent motion given their initial positions and velocities. In other words, there is no sustained solution to the three-body problem because any disturbance will lead to a different solution. This discrepancy between our representing the world and the observed phenomenon of the world compellingly illustrates the fact that our representations are very limited.

Turn our gaze to AI. I don't take AI to be on the opposite side of humanity (In fact, I don't take technology in general to be so.). AI, as I may suggest, is a way, or a kind of technique for us to understand ourselves. Therefore, it should also be subject to the same limitation described above. If the dilemma articulated in this paper is sound, it can be treated as an exemplification of the limitation. Moreover, we should not simply regard this dilemma as revealing a defect of AI, but to appreciate it for its reserving a part of humanity beyond the technical approach. To sum up. I don't defend the intrinsic distinctiveness of humanity here and I leave the question of whether there is intrinsic distinctiveness of humanity open; instead, I try to show the limitation of science and technology, especially regarding AI as a technique of understanding human intelligence. If the dilemma and the generalization are sound, even with the booming development in science and technology, we can still defend the minimal humanity. So to speak, humanity is not endangered at root, because there is always some distinctiveness of human nature lying within the scope of humanity as well as going beyond the limitation of cognition.

---

[35] I will argue in a future paper that mathematics is a kind of cognitive capacity but for the moment let's tentatively accept this idea and see what we can infer from it.

[36] I won't introduce the three-body problem here and for those who are interested in this topic please see J. BARROW-GREEN, "The Three-Body Problem," in *The Princeton Companion to Mathematics*, ed. T. Gowers, J. Barrow-Green, I. Leader (Princeton, NJ: Princeton University Press, 2008), 726–728.

Conscience and Moral Cognition: What Distinguishes Us from Machines

Hasse Hämäläinen

1. The Human Capacity to Act on the Basis of Inferences

Consider the question what, if anything, enables us to perceive other humans as distinct from machines in the extent that we are justified in treating them differently than we treat machines.[1] A possible initial reaction would be to think that the question is absurd. As a matter of fact, we treat one another very differently than we treat machines, and there seems to be no need to justify why this should be the case unless there was a concrete reason to suspect that our moral attitude towards machines might be mistaken – but a computer is yet to complain about inhumane treatment. A machine, unlike an animal, is not a sentient being that could be a bearer of rights.[2]

However, this initial reaction may change when one is asked to consider also 'the big question': what, if anything, can be perceived to make us humans 'exceptional' among living beings, and thus justified in treating other beings differently than we treat one another?[3] Through the history of philosophy the most influential way to justify this has been to appeal to our capability to act on the basis of inferences. According to one philosophical tradition, familiar from Aristotle, this capacity justifies our exceptionality sui generis, and according to another, Cartesian tradition, as a perceptible correlate of our experience of self-consciousness. In order to act on the basis of inferences, one would need to form (at least) communicable conceptions of potential states of affairs

---

[1] I would like to thank the participants of Forum Humanum Seminar and Claremont Conference in the Philosophy of Religion 2019 together with Jarosław Olesiak for their comments and suggestions. My research work on history of philosophy that contributed to this chapter has been supported by a grant from the National Science Centre in Poland, no. UMO-2018/31/B/HS1/02050, funding the research project Between Secularization and Reform: Religious Rationalism in the Late 17th Century and in the Enlightenment, at the Institute of Philosophy of the Jagiellonian University in Kraków.

[2] The view that ascription of rights presupposes sentience apart from e. g., mere rationality or interests is established by now: for an overview of the ways to frame it, see e. g., A. Cochrane, "From human rights to sentient rights," *Critical Review of International Social and Political Philosophy* 16, no. 5 (2013): 655–675.

[3] For an alternative approach towards this question, see M. Coeckelbergh, *Growing Moral Relations: Critique of Moral Status Ascription* (New York: Palgrave Macmillan, 2012).

(e. g. 'learning all about neural networks' or 'getting something to eat'), deliberate about ways to realize them,[4] prioritize between different states and ways to realize them, and act according to the conclusions of such deliberations.[5] Although the capacity to act on the basis of inferences evades strict definitions, already this description makes clear that without it, one would neither be in position to describe potentially realizable states of affairs in the world, and by implication, communicate (about them) by means of language,[6] nor be regarded as morally responsible for one's conduct.

Like any other perceptible ability, also the ability to act on the basis of inferences can presumably come in degrees. However, even if one went as far as to acknowledge that also animals could act on the basis of inferences in some degree, this would not yet imply that humans are 'exceptional' no more. Although also certain animals can make an impression of acting on the basis of inferences – e. g. great apes can learn to communicate by means of symbols[7] – no animal can come close to humans in a hypothetical scale that measures the complexity of the inferences that a being makes to guide their actions. Provided that no difference of a similar magnitude can be perceived with regard to any other cognitive capacity, such as vision or 'emotional intelligence', which seems likely, the capacity to act on the basis of inferences could be the perceptible criterion of being a human, even if it were not exclusive to us.

At least this conclusion should make searching an answer to the question what, if anything, enables us to perceive other humans as distinct from computers in the extent that we are justified in treating them differently than we treat computers seem not absurd, but very relevant. For unlike animals, computers, which are artifacts that draw logical inferences from numerically encoded data, do not have biological limitations that prevent them from extending their capability to act on the basis of inferences. Since it is possible for a computer to draw any inference by means of a sufficient number of NAND-gates,[8] and

---

[4] E. g., K. ARKOUDAS and S. BRINGSJORD, "Philosophical Foundations," in *The Cambridge Handbook of Artificial Intelligence*, ed. K. Frankish and W. J. Ramsay (Cambridge: Cambridge University Press, 2014), 36. The authors argue that the ability to act on the basis of inference is the hallmark of intelligence, and credit Aristotle as the source of this view.

[5] See esp. R. HURSTHOUSE, *On Virtue Ethics* (Oxford: Oxford University Press, 2004), 91–105, and S. GAUKROGER, "Descartes' Theory of Perceptual Cognition and the Question of Moral Sensibility," in *Mind, Method, and Morality: Essays in honour of Anthony Kenny*, ed. J. Cottingham and P. Hacker (Oxford: Oxford University Press, 2010), 230–251.

[6] See C. TAYLOR, *Language Animal* (Cambridge, MA: Harvard University Press, 2016), esp. 6–12.

[7] See S. HURLEY and M. NUDDS, "Language as a Window on Rationality," in *Rational Animals?*, ed. E. Savage-Rumbaugh, D. Rumbaugh, and W. Fields (Oxford: Oxford University Press, 2006), 513–550.

[8] See C. SHANNON, *A Symbolic Analysis of Relay and Switching Circuits*, Master's Thesis (Cambridge, MA: Massachusetts Institute of Technology, Dept. of Electrical Engineering, 1940).

because any input that passes the human (or animal) neural system (a neuron can either fire or not fire)[9] can be potentially converted to a format accessible to a computers (for also a transistor in a NAND-gate can be either on or off), emulating this human mode of acting does not seem to be out of their reach.

Provided that as a perceptible mark of our humanity, the capacity to act on the basis of inferences justifies our 'exceptionality', then a machine that is capable of acting in the same way (a.k.a. Artificial General Intelligence, AGI) should be considered equally 'exceptional' or else, humans should be considered 'exceptional' no longer. Even the theoretical prospect of such a conclusion has made the defenders of human exceptionality worried, among other things, it would imply that in addition to humans, also machines could be entitled to have moral personhood in the extent that is appropriate to non-sentient beings.[10] Although so far, no machine has come even close to emulating inference-based acting characteristic to humans – e.g. due to lack of technologies capable of mirroring human movements and the shortage of processing power (in our brains, billions neurons can fire simultaneously, whereas current state-of-art GPUs can run ´only´ thousands of parallel processes)[11] – they seem to be advancing towards this end.

One way to evidence the degree of the competence of a computer to act on the basis of inferences would be to instruct it to perform humanlike tasks without programming the steps of the performance to it. Thus, e.g. success in answering questions in Chinese would be considered an instance of an inference-based acting from a machine if and only if the machine was not programmed by humans to accomplish specifically this task.[12] Since, thanks to artificial neural networks, computers can already translate Chinese to any other language and vice versa without being programmed each rule needed to accomplish specifically this task, we already have some evidence that they are becoming able to act moral and more like humans.[13] And since the capacity

---

[9] See e.g., P. JOHNS, "Electrical Signalling in Neurons," in *Clinical Neuroscience* (London: Churchill Livingstone, 2014), 71–80.

[10] Cf. M. A. BODEN, *AI: Its Nature and Future* (Oxford: Oxford University Press, 2016), 138–144.

[11] See P. CHURCHLAND, "Rules: the Basis of Morality?" in *Open MIND*: 6(T), ed. T. Metzinger and J. M. Windt (Frankfurt am Main: MIND Group, 2015), 1–13; 16–18. According to the article, a human brain can perform 100'000'000'000'000 operations simultaneously, while a CPU only 8. However, currently, e.g. NVidia Geforce 1080 GPU has 2560 parallel-processing cores, which shows the rapidly increasing performance of computers.

[12] That is, a Turing test (A. Turing, "Computing Machinery and Intelligence," *Mind* 59 [1950]: 433–460) modified to prevent pre-programmed systems from passing it, because as J. SEARLE, "Minds, Brains and Programs," *Behavioral and Brain Sciences* 3 (1980): 417–457, argues, such a system would not be 'intelligent' even if it passed the test.

[13] See the explanation of the operating principles of Google Translate in Y. WU et al., "Google's Neural Machine Translation System: Bridging the Gap between Human and Machine Translation," *arXiv* (2016): 1609.08144.

to tell what a random image represents[14] and ability to play games[15] etc. could be invoked as examples of inferential tasks that animals cannot do, but which machines can execute with superhuman competence, some 'posthumanist' thinkers have suggested that we should prepare ourselves for the creation of AGI by abandoning the conception of humans as 'exceptional' beings, instead of attempting to defend our 'exceptionality' against the growing challenges to it any longer.[16]

2. 'Machine Morality' and Acting on the Basis of Inferences

In what follows, I will not argue for abandoning the idea of human exceptionality. Rather, I will suggest that only ability to act on the basis of inferences can enable us humans to actualize a certain very perceptible capacity, which, however, is grounded non-inferential cognition. Since the actualization of this capacity requires a humanlike capacity to act on the basis of inferences, an animal could not actualize it. However, without possessing the non-inferential cognition that this capacity also requires, even a being, whose ability to act on the basis of inferences surpasses that of any human, such as a future computer, could not actualize it. With this implication, the said capacity – that is, our capacity for manifesting morality according to my hypothesis – could provide a justification for positing a perceptible and essential difference between humans and machines.

The mainstream theories of moral action, Consequentialism and Kantianism, have not paid much attention to investigating the question what makes one's behavior appear 'moral' to others. This is because, among the proponents of both theories, 'moral behavior' is understood as the performance of right actions and the actualization of one's capacity for acting on the basis of morally valid inferences as both necessary and sufficient to render one's behavior as 'moral.'[17] However, although it is rather clear that we need to be able to prioritize certain ends over others in order to act morally across situations, it is less clear on what grounds this prioritization should occur. Hence, according to the theorists of moral action, the main issue that needs to be addressed by their field

---

[14] O. VINYALS et al., "Show and Tell: A Neural Image Caption Generator," *arXiv* (2014): 1411.4555.

[15] D. SILVER et al., "A General Reinforcement Learning Algorithm that Masters Chess, Shogi, and Go through Self-play," *Science* 362:6419 (2018): 1140–1144.

[16] E.g. J. P. SULLINS, "When is A Robot A Moral Agent?," *International Review of Information Ethics* 6 (2006): 23–30, and T. M. POWERS, "On the Moral Agency of Computers," *Topoi* 32, no. 2 (2013): 227–236.

[17] See e.g., K. BAIER, "The Conceptual Link between Morality and Rationality," *Noûs* 16, no. 1 (1982): 78–88.

of philosophy is whether the prioritization decisions ought to be reached as a result of utility calculation or the application of the Categorical Imperative.[18]

The theories of so-called 'machine morality' seem to pay implicit homage to above conclusions: many of them share an assumption that building machines that can act on the basis of inferences is a more difficult challenge than making machines to behave in a way that would appear as moral to human observers. Provided that morality is an application of moral inferences to acting, as the mainstream theories of moral action claim, it should be implementable to machines that have a capacity to infer how to realize a certain determined end(s) by action. It seems that such machines could be made to 'use' this capacity in a way that reflect our prioritization decisions between various ends by programming them to automatically adjust their conduct so that it is always in compliance with a certain set of moral maxims (e.g. 'not injure a human being or, through inaction, allow a human being to come to harm').[19] Due to this prospect, some theorists of machine morality are optimistic about the potential of e.g. self-driving vehicles to manifest moral agency.[20]

Reflecting on this conviction, most studies on machine morality are now concentrated around finding the right methods for verifying that the behavior of a machine is 'moral' and free from unjustifiable biases, instead of studying whether displaying moral agency is even possible for computing machines. Today, among those involved in studying 'machine morality,' there is much debate on e.g. whether comparing the decisions of a machine against those of ethically and legally informed humans,[21] or against a database of crowdsourced moral decisions[22] would be a more appropriate method for verifying the morality of a machine. However, virtually no attention is dedicated to the question about the validity of assuming that the ability to act on the basis of inferences is sufficient for moral acting. In other words: would a machine that acts in conformity with certain moral maxims really appear as a moral agent to us?

---

[18] Although these two normative principles are the most influential ones, they are by means not the only ones. E.g., R. HURSTHOUSE, *On Virtue Ethics* (2004), 28, suggests that moral rules can be derived from the ideal of 'a virtuous person'.

[19] These examples are from I. ASIMOV's 'three laws of robotics' in the short story collection "Runaround". See especially the collection titled *I, Robot* (New York: Doubleday, 1950), 40.

[20] E.g., D. HOWARD and I. MUNTEAN, "A Minimalist Model of the Artificial Autonomous Moral Agent (AAMA)," AAAI 2016 Conference Paper (https://www.aaai.org/ocs/index.php/SSS/SSS16/paper/view/12760/11954), 221, and V. CHARISI et al., "Towards Moral Autonomous Systems," *arXiv* (2017): 1703.04741 (4/22/2022).

[21] D. DANKS and A. LONDON, "Algorithmic Bias in Autonomous Systems," *Proceedings of the Twenty-Sixth International Joint Conference on Artificial Intelligence (IJCAI–17)* (2017): 4691–4697, esp. 4695.

[22] See E. AWAD, J.-F. BONNEFON, I. RAWHAN et al., "The Moral Machine Experiment," *Nature* 563 (2018): 59–64.

Although computers have gradually became able to emulate the operation of more and more human inferential capacities, there is a dearth of even remotely successful attempts to build a machine that can act in a way that would appear as moral to human observers. In the light of aforementioned philosophical theories of the nature moral acting – Consequentialism and Kantianism – which assume that acquiring a capacity of acting inferentially in conformity with a certain moral principle suffices to transform a being into a moral agent – this should not be the case. At the very least, if there was any correspondence between the capacity of a being to act on the basis of inferences and its capacity for manifesting morality, we should have already some signals that machines are approaching morality. However, we do not have any: although self-driving cars are among the first in the line of candidates for machines that should display at least rudimentary moral competence, even the developers of such cars have not dared to publicly test in which extent humans – even experts, who would be less than likely laymen to confuse a humanlike bodily appearance with humanlike rational capacities – would perceive their products as being 'moral'.

However, it would be a fallacy to take the lack of evidence as evidence for the lack of correspondence between the ability of a computer to act on the basis of inferences and its perceived morality. In order to demonstrate that no machine can manifest morality, in what comes next, I attempt to show that it is technically impossible for the method that has done the most to enable computer systems to emulate human inference-based acting, i. e. artificial neural networks (NNs), to predict human moral judgements, and by implication, to emulate human morality. I first show what features of NNs are conducive to accomplishing this task, and then that predicting human moral judgements by means of them would require virtually infinite computing power. Since this task would be impossible for humans, too, were our moral judgements reached exclusively by means of inferences, the shortcomings of NNs in it must derive from the nature of the capacity for moral cognition: it cannot be an implication of the capacity for inference-based acting only. Although a demonstration along these lines would not prevent an apologetic of machine morality from suggesting that perhaps there is some still unknown machine learning paradigm that would enable machine morality, any such a suggestion would place the burden of presenting proof to its presenter. Until this happens, the considerations that I present below remain relevant.

3. A Moral Neural Network?

If we think of a NN designed to predict human moral judgements – let us call it a 'moral NN' – its output could consist in data labelled with moral concepts. These are concepts that guide how one is to act, in this case, towards some data – say, by signaling whether or not it needs to be removed from an internet service to which it has been uploaded. We may decide that the moral NN would be successfully trained provided that human observers would be willing to consider it 'moral' on account of the data labels that it outputs. The training dataset of such an NN could, in theory, consist of any kind of data. However, labelling combinations of pixels or sounds with moral concepts would require a NN that is far more complex than needed for establishing why no NN can emulate human moral cognition. Thus, 'the training dataset' of our moral NN shall only consist of relatively short strings of texts – such as comments written to the internet service, grouped by the threads to which they were posted (e. g. to comment such and such news). The point is to show NNs could not convincingly manifest moral acting to humans even in this seemingly simple task.

Since NNs operate with only numerical values, before the moral NN can begin labelling a string – such as "Xs must not live!" – the string would need to be converted into a series of numerical values. The values should not be arbitrary, but such that they enable inferring the most probable label of the string on the basis of the features that it shares with other strings. Achieving this outcome presupposes the same words are represented by the same numerical values across all the strings in the training dataset. This can be achieved by using 'word vectors' to represent each individual word in the training dataset. Word vectors are arrays that record how many times a single word, such as 'live' in the above comment, has certain definite features. Since the features must come from the same dataset that is used for training the NN – i. e. from social media comments – a method that ensures the comparability of the word vectors would be to use the words that appear in the proximity of the word 'live' across the training dataset as the features for the word 'live'. In order to prevent the length of the word vectors from becoming excessive, we may decide that only the words that are within, say, a 5 word range from a particular word in each comment count as being in its proximity, and that the word vector will only list the counts of the 100 principal components of the dataset (i. e. the least mutually correlated words) within that range (excluding the verb 'to be', prepositions and articles etc. words that tend to appear across all kinds of strings and therefore will not bear relevance to the eventual label of the string).[23]

---

[23] For more on the described 'word2vec' method, see esp. T. MIKOLOV, I. SUTSKEVER, K. CHEN, G. CORRADO and J. DEAN, "Distributed Representations of Words and Phrases and their Compositionality," *arXiv* (2013): 1310.4546.

So as to improve the accuracy of word vectors, we might like to create a separate vector for each comment to indicate the context in which its appears. This step is crucial for preventing the NN from treating e. g., 'Xs must not live' and 'no live Xs must' as identical comments.[24] Although the two comments would have the same set of word vectors, they would have different and unique 'context vectors', which can be created in a manner analogous to the word vectors, except this time, the counts of the 100 principal components would be measured considering all the words in the comment and, say, 5 comments that surround it in a thematic thread. If converted to context vectors along these lines, the context vector of the former aforementioned comment would almost certainly be different from the vector of the latter. In order to enable the NN to take the context vectors into account when evaluating the comments, the context vector of a comment is to be concatenated with the word vectors of the same comment, and the concatenate divided by the total number of the words in the comment, creating one vector that numerically represents the whole comment.

Above procedure would be repeated with every string in the training dataset, and the resulting 'comment vectors' be used as the inputs to the moral NN. After a comment vector is inputted to the NN, each of its 100 values (i.e. counts of the 100 principal components) would be connected to the 'activation functions' (the task of which is to introduce the non-linearity to the NN). Each of these 'connections' would be then assigned with a 'weight' (i.e., multiplied with a numerical variable), a 'bias' (another variable) added to their weighted sum, and the final sum fed into an activation function. Based on the inputs and their weights functions determine whether a particular 'neuron' of a NN 'fires' a signal or not, i.e. whether the output of the function is to be passed forward to another layer of activation functions and neurons.

After passing through several layers of neurons, the signal of the comment vector reaches the final, 'output' layer of the NN. At this point, our task is to make sure that the 'output function' on that layer correctly recognizes the comments that are to be removed. We can decide, for example, that an output 1 means certain removal, and 0 certain acceptance. Thus, if the output function of the final layer delivers, say, a value greater than 0.9 after receiving input from the previous layer, then this implies that probably the comment needs to be removed. Since the comments of the training set are already labelled by humans, we can calculated the difference ('loss') between the signal sent by the output function and the correct label (1 or 0). After each (batch of) comment(s), the weights are adjusted across the NN in order to minimize the loss. Eventually, the weights of the NN should become set in a such a way that

---

[24] See L. Quoc et al., "Distributed Representations of Sentences and Documents," *arXiv* (2013): 1405.4053.

it is able to correctly predict the label of virtually each comment in the training set. When we have reached confidence that the NN can predict not only the training dataset, but it can also correctly label the comments in the 'validation dataset', the NN can be tested with comments that have been used neither in its training nor validation. If the NN can also label them as accurately as it predicted the labels in its training- and validation datasets, it should be ready to operate with unlabeled real-world data – and begin outputting judgements about comments that would convince human observers about its ability to manifest an aspect of human morality.

4. Why the Moral Neural Network would not Work

Provided that predicting moral judgements was analogous to most other machine learning tasks, the described NNs should allow inferring the label for a comment (a moral judgement) on the basis of the vector of the comment. However, the problem is that although our NN could indeed 'learn' to infer correct labels for a large number of strings, it could not reliably infer a correct label to a string that has not been included in its training or validation datasets. This would mean that the NN would fail with the testing dataset and prevent it from appearing as moral to human observers.

The problem that faces the moral NN can be demonstrated by means of an example: Assume that in an unprecedented comment, a person X claims (falsely) to be a police officer and that (in reality, innocent) person Y should be arrested. Since the comment is unprecedented, the training or validation set of the NN could not have contained it. Thus, the NN would label the comment on the basis of the labels that other comments with similar word and context vectors had received. A conceivable, and even likely, outcome of this process would be that the comment vector 'X, police officer, Y, should, arrested' would not be labelled as removable: its vocabulary is not threatening or hateful overall (there can be a plenty of innocent comments with similar principal components), and the comment could be surrounded by otherwise appropriate comments: it is not inevitable that it is flanked by discussion consisting of harassment and insults. However, although these factors would result in the word, context and thus, also the comment vectors of the comment to imply approval, which would cause even a well-trained moral NN to fail in its prediction task, a morally competent human could easily 'see' that this comment should be removed: the real police officers would not write in that way, and there is no doubt that the comment aims at harassing Y and making their life more difficult.

By failing to label the obviously removable comment as removable, the NN would fail to make an impression of moral behavior to its human observers –

regardless of whether they were Consequentialists or Kantians. The possibility of such a failure breaks an analogue between the moral NN and other types of NNs reveals a basic difference between moral cognition and other types of cognition. For example, a machine translation NN, the task of which is to find functional correlates for certain vectors in the vector space of English language from the vector space of Chinese, would not make such a mistaken judgement unless it would face an unprecedented grammatical structure or metaphor in either language. However, the more the machine translation NN has learn about grammar and metaphors, the less frequent such occurrences become. An analogous conclusion would apply to an image recognition NNs, since also the creation of unprecedented visual objects and new names for such objects is a relatively slow process for us humans. However, as our example showed, with moral cognition, this is not the case: it is very easy for us to image entirely unprecedented moral situations. This is because we face unprecedented moral data all the time, which explains why figuring out what a certain moral maxim requires us to do a certain situation is often very difficult for us.[25] However, even though many moral situations are unprecedented, acting according to moral maxims is nevertheless possible for us. Acknowledging this leads to an important observation about the nature of moral cognition.

The primary reason to believe that computer systems, which can emulate any logical operation, could emulate human moral cognition was that such cognition involves inferences. For example, one can arrive at a judgement that 'this comment is to be removed', because of having deduced that 'it undermines the authority of public officials and harasses Y'. But we have not yet studied the possibility of moral cognition being not exclusively inferential. After certain considerations are brought in, it may even begin to seem likely that our ability to spot when a certain moral inference is to be drawn, that is – to return to our example – to 'see' the relevance of the comment to what one has learned during her life about (a) how police officers are supposed to behave and (b) what counts as 'harassment' in a certain situation – cannot be inferential.

As we have seen with our example moral NN, it might not be possible to deduce what moral inference should be drawn on the basis of either the words of an unprecedented comment – e. g. 'I represent police: Y is to be arrested' – or its context, since on their own, these features may suggest nothing about the potential relevance of feature (a) or (b) to the labelling of the comment. Rather, in order to manifest human moral inference by weighting the vectors of the comment in a way that would imply its removal, the NN would need

---

[25] That is why moral recognition seems to be more analogous to an activity such as manifesting the sense of humor – that NNs also fail to emulate, because, although they can create new jokes, they do not have the 'eye of experience' – to use Aristotle's phrase – that can enable a comedian to suddenly tell a joke that 'fits perfectly' to the situation.

to weight them against every vector that it has ever learned, their all possible combinations and the context of those combinations. Only such a procedure could guarantee that the NN would find sufficient similarity between the comment vector and the vectors of those comments that have received a removal decision. However, accomplishing this machine learning task seems hardly possible for any computer system – in fact, it would not be possible even for a human brain.

No doubt moral cognition often requires a long time of deliberation, but weighting all the possible combinations of the five words of the comment (because our example NN ignores ubiquitous words such as the verb 'be' or preposition 'to') with even, say, 20 other words and their combinations would require more than 4724 floating point operations, which would take more than 7 years of processing even from the world's fastest computer.[26] Since we, as opposed to an artificial NN, can, however, draw moral inference very quickly in spite of the fact that in our memory, there are many times more than 20 concepts to weight, it seems clear that we do not spot when we should draw a certain moral inference only by means of having drawn other inferences. Thus, we have a reason to think that our capacity for moral cognition presupposes an non-inferential cognitive capacity that somehow enables to immediately 'see' when a certain inference needs to be drawn. Next, I shall investigate this possibility as a potential source of an answer to the question what, if anything, enables us to perceive other humans as distinct from computers in the extent that we are justified in treating them differently than we treat computers.

5. Conscience: The Non-Inferential Enabler of Human Morality

By this point, we have seen that the fact that NNs can emulate human linguistic skills and our ability to conceptualize our perceptions does not imply that they can ever make an impression of being moral. A prerequisite for mak-

---

[26] 25 concepts can form 15'511'210'043'330'985'984'000'000 permutations. Since forming a single permutation takes (at least) 3 flops, we would need to multiply the above number by (at least) 3 to have an idea of the computing capacity needed for evaluating them all one by one. That would be (at least) 47 yottaflops, which would exceed the computing capacity of a human brain (about 1 exaflop/second) by 47 mln. times, so evaluating the permutations would take about 17 months from our brains (thus, if brain operated like a massive parallel-processing computer, like e.g. Churchland, "Rules: the Basis of Morality?" argues, moral thinking should take much longer than it actually takes). Since the world's fastest computer, *Summit*, has the capacity of ca. 200 petaflops (ca. ⅕ of the human brain), the task would take about 7 years from it. And if we assume that not every evaluable combination has to include every word, we would need to add all permutations in between 1 and 24 to the aforementioned permutations, which would result an even higher number to evaluate.

ing such an impression would be able to accurately predict human moral judgements. However, this would be impossible for NNs, because the moral evaluations of certain unprecedented actions cannot be reliably inferred on the basis of learned data without quasi-limitless computing power. Since it is thus not possible that either we humans form such evaluations on the basis of inferring from data, it seems that mere ability to act on the basis of inferences is insufficient to render an agent's behavior to appear as moral, *pace* current mainstream theories of moral action, which regard morality as nothing but acting on the basis of inferences. Hence, it seems that we must have a non-inferential, i.e. intuitive, ability to 'see' what actions we need to take in a particular situation. In Western philosophy, a traditional name for this ability has been 'conscience'.

Unfortunately, the mainstream theories of moral action that have influenced research on moral AI so far do not give conscience any self-standing role to play in the process of moral cognition. According to J. S. Mill, one of the founders of Consequentialism, conscience is a 'subjective feeling' rather than a rational capacity, and thus unable to issue moral judgements, but at the most to motivate obedience to them,[27] while Kant famously reduces conscience into "practical reason holding the human being's duty before him for his acquittal or condemnation."[28]

However, centuries before these reductive accounts of conscience were formulated, St. Thomas Aquinas proposed that the cognition of certain basic moral maxims might belong to conscience instead of practical reason. In order to separate this, intuitive and interpersonal aspect of conscience from the aspect that performs a moral self-judgement on the basis of the intuited maxims, he named it *synderesis*.[29] However, the examples that Aquinas gives about the maxims intuited by *synderesis* show that although his theory points to a promising way towards building a conceptual description of the nature of our capacity for moral cognition, his theory is not unproblematic. The root of the problem is that the maxims, such as "evil is to be avoided," "nothing illicit is to be done" and "one must live according to reason" are purely formal and

---

[27] J. S. Mill, "Utilitarianism," in *Utilitarianism and On Liberty*, ed. M. Warnock (Oxford: Blackwell, 2003), 204–205: "[The] binding force [of conscience], however, consists in the existence of a mass of feeling which must be broken through in order to do what violates our standard of right, and which, if we do nevertheless violate that standard, will probably have to be encountered afterwards in the form of remorse. Whatever theory we have of the nature or origin of conscience, this is what essentially constitutes it."

[28] I. Kant, *Metaphysik der Sitten*, AA IV, 400. Citation from A. W. Wood, "Kant on Conscience," Unpublished in English, Ms., Available online: https://web.stanford.edu/~allenw/webpapers/KantOnConscience.pdf (2006), 5 (4/22/2022).

[29] For the etymology and history of this Latin concept, see e.g. R. Sorabji, *Moral Conscience through the Ages: Fifth Century BCE to the Present* (Oxford: Oxford University Press, 2014), 60–61.

present no specific end for an agent to pursue.[30] The purely formal character of Aquinas' basic moral maxims implies that in order to arrive at a moral cognition, our practical reason would need to infer why a certain action must fall under a certain maxim. From a computational point of view, a rather obvious problem for the Thomistic 'practical syllogism' is that even if the number of the basic moral maxims was limited, the enormous multiplicity of potential actions that we can take at any situation would make also this an excessively computing-intensive task for our brains to accomplish in a manageable time.

In the early 20th century, W. D. Ross proposed what can be interpreted as an attempt to both continue and revise this 'intuitionist tradition' in moral philosophy, although instead of *synderesis*, he used the concept of a "prima facie duty" to refer to intuitively cognized moral maxims. His proposal was that all prima facie duties – e.g. the "duty of beneficence" (acting in a way that benefits others) – are obliging in themselves.[31] Therefore, provided that an opportunity to benefit other people presents itself to someone, one does not need to infer that she ought to take that opportunity. Of course, this might not be the only relevant duty in the situation, for example, also "the duty of non-maleficence" can be present. However, in any case, the only thing what one has to infer is how to satisfy the various prima facie duties that are present in a situation: e.g. by figuring out a way to benefit other people without harming anyone.[32] This is a prioritization problem, resolving which may seem to be more manageable as a task for our brains than construing a Thomistic 'practical syllogism'.[33] However, even this problem could be too resource-intensive for us to resolve, because although Ross claimed that there are seven basic prima facie duties,[34] his selection of those duties was quite arbitrary, as there is no a priori principle that could limit the quantity of the features of the situation, or relevant duties, or combinations of these that we would need to consider in order to find the most relevant duty.

However, the way out from this situation would be to think that instead of (mere) abstract duties, conscience could present us complete 'prima facie evaluations', such as that, for example, "this is harassment towards Y". Once an evaluation like this flashes to one's mind, her rational capacities can step

---

[30] AQUINAS, *Super Sent* 2, d. 24, q. 2, a. 3–4, d. 39, q. 3, a. 2; *QDV*, q. 16, a. 1, ad 9. Citation from T. HOFFMANN, "Conscience and Synderesis," in *The Oxford Handbook of Aquinas*, ed. B. Davies (Oxford: Oxford University Press, 2012), 256.

[31] W. D. ROSS, *The Right and the Good*, ed. P. Stratton-Lake (Oxford: Oxford University Press, 2002), 19–21.

[32] Ibid., 31–32.

[33] E. g. S. L. ANDERSON and M. ANDERSON, "*Prima Facie* Duty Approach to Machine Ethics and Its Application to Elder Care," *Human-Robot Interaction in Elder Care: Papers from the 2011 AAAI Workshop* [WS-11-12] (2011), 2–7, presented on the issue of choosing between *prima facie* duties as a prioritization problem.

[34] See the list of the duties in ROSS, *The Right and the Good*, 21.

in and infer reasons why this is must be the case, or, alternatively, why that could not be the case. The computing power that is needed for the execution of such justificatory inferences would be considerably more limited than in either alternative scenario: the process of inferring could take a form of a decision-tree with branches representing reasons for and against assenting to the intuitively represented evaluation. Proceeding through such a tree, even if it were extensive, would not be out of the reach of the power of our brains, because one would need to consider only two options at time and proceed only as far as needed to exhaust the reasons one for choosing either of the options, in which case the other option would win out and be realized in an action.

Although the introduction of the concept of prima facie moral evaluation can provide a useful characterization of the operation of human conscience and enable demonstrating out why machines fail in emulating moral cognition, also it can be objected. For example, one can point out that as members of the same species all of us have rather similar cognitive systems, and thus, by implication, should also come up with similar prima facie moral evaluations in similar situations, but clearly, this is not the case: moral disagreement is everywhere. My reply to this empirical objection would be that the moral judgements that we express to one another should not be confused with the prima facie evaluations: the former always result from an inference, and they can modify or even discard the latter, which are presented intuitively to our consciousness.

Another likely objection could be motivated by the widely-held assumption that humans are accurate at inferring visual perceptions from sense data. Should reaching moral evaluations by means of inferences require quasi-infinite computing power, would not the same requirement hold with visual perception as well, and thus, accurate visual perception to be impossible for us? To this argument, my reply would be that also human visual cognition might begin from a prima facie evaluation, such as that "there is a cat". The crucial difference between visual and moral cognition is, however, that the former, unlike the latter, can be emulated by means of inferences – because our intuitive identifications of visual objects happen to correspond with certain patterns of pixels in our field of vision – and thus, a NN, even though it is incapable presenting prima facie evaluations, can label images by inferring the labels from their pixel patterns.[35]

Since moral cognition that is impossible to computers is possible for us, we can conclude that its mental basis cannot thus be in inference, but in a prima facie evaluation that presents itself intuitively to us – i. e. in conscience –

---

[35] See e. g., Y. LeCunn et al., "Gradient-Based Learning Applied to Document Recognition," *Proceedings of the IEEE*, 86, no. 11 (1998): esp. 2279–2280.

and in this way delimits the data that we need to process in order to reach a moral judgement. However, reaching a moral judgement would not be possible without an advanced capacity to act on the basis of inference, because inferences are necessary for judging whether the prima facie moral evaluation is to be accepted or rejected. Due to the fact that conscience can neither be had by animals nor emulated by machines – even if they surpassed human performance with regard to all conceivable inferential operations – it seems be a promising candidate for justifying human exceptionality. Moreover, since conscience guides the way in which we act, the difference between having and not having conscience is perceptible: a being, who lacks conscience (such as an NN) cannot appear as a moral in the same way as another human would. Sooner or later, a failure to spot an action that would strike as obviously morally relevant for most people would reveal its lack of conscience. Thus, my answer to the question from which we began – i.e. what, if anything, enables us to perceive other humans as distinct from computers in the extent that we are justified in treating them differently than we treat computers – is the following. We have a presumptive reason to regard conscience as the human-specific capability that can justify us in perceiving other humans as morally distinct from machines now and in the future – though the normative scope of this difference needs still to be specified.

Reframing Religion in the Algorithmic Age
Appraising the Algorithmic Approach to Religion

NATHAN SCHRADLE

1. Introduction

Yuval Harari devotes the final chapter of his best-selling *Homo Deus* (2017) to describing what he calls "the Data Religion" or "Dataism." This new religious stance, he argues, is the product of our contemporary data-driven culture – in a world in which we are surrounded by vast landscapes of data that overwhelm human capacities, the basic tenets of humanism and the democratic social and political structures that have defined the Modern period are "losing control of events, and failing to present us with meaningful visions of the future."[1] This circumstance, while long-developing, is currently exacerbated by the development of self-correcting algorithms. The networked algorithm and the bits of information it produces, to hear Harari tell it, have replaced the neoliberal subject as the fundamental unit of measure and concern in both governance and the free market.

Harari is not alone in this view. Adam Greenfield incisively describes "the posthuman turn" as the contemporary milieu produced by modern governmental and capitalist institutions "shaped not so much by our own needs but those of the systems that nominally serve us," in which "human perception, scale and desire are no longer the primary yardsticks of value."[2] Greenfield carefully charts a number of applications of algorithms, from predictive policing to automation of manual labor, where their adoption is heralded as a means of overcoming human perceptive and physical limitations. Algorithms, he argues, are portrayed as more reliable, more obedient, more equitable, and freer from bias than the humans they have replaced.[3] Both Harari and Greenfield are quick to note the lack of evidence to support such rhetoric. Yet, both also imagine the "posthuman turn" toward increasing commodification and deployment of algorithms to be inevitable, their success all but pre-ordained as the "Internet of Things" seamlessly integrates each new instantiation into a

---

[1] Y. HARARI, *Homo Deus: A Brief History of Tomorrow* (New York: Harper Collins, 2017), 380.
[2] A. GREENFIELD, *Radical Technologies* (New York: Verso, 2017), 185.
[3] Ibid., 188–191.

global capitalist network, one primarily controlled not by human agents but by automated networks of algorithms working in concert.

Harari is likewise far from alone in describing this novel milieu in explicitly religious terms. Many transhumanists, led by the likes of Ray Kurzweil and the leaders of the non-profit organization Humanity+, argue that the ever-accelerating production of algorithm-based technologies will result in practical immortality, first as the organic body is enhanced, and then ultimately as it is replaced by algorithmically afforded cognitive frameworks. Both Kurzweil and fellow transhumanist Hugo de Garis have described the moment when artificial intelligence surpasses the capabilities of humans as inspiring, in the words of de Garis, a "new and powerful religion."[4] Kurzweil, for his part, imagines that computerized superintelligence will "ultimately infuse the universe with Spirit," and, in so doing, make life "truly meaningful."[5] Hence, he claims that we need "a new religion" to promote the proper kind of morality and knowledge that will bring about such an end.[6] David Pearce, advocate of the "Hedonist Imperative" to use our accumulating understanding of genetic engineering and nanotechnology to eliminate suffering, likens the transhumanist project to "the naturalization of Heaven." He argues that "as the genetic revolution in reproductive medicine unfolds, what might once have been the stuff of millennialist fantasy is set to become a scientifically feasible research program."[7]

Despite the brevity of these prefatory remarks, there are clearly massive splits in the scientific and scholarly community regarding whether algorithms and the kinds of cultural regimes they inspire are poison or remedy, salvation or doom. My goal in this article is not to take one side of that debate. Nor is it to determine whether or not transhumanism or posthumanism somehow qualify (or do not) as "religions" or "spiritualities." A great deal of scholarly ink has already been spilled on these topics.[8] Instead, I aim to show how the

---

[4] H. DE GARIS, *The Artilect War: Cosmists vs. Terrans: A Bitter Controversy Concerning Whether Humanity Should Build Godlike Massively Intelligent Machines* (Palm Springs, CA: ETC Publications, 2005), 105.

[5] R. KURZWEIL, *The Singularity is Near: When Humans Transcend Biology* (New York: Penguin Books, 2005), 389. While in this instance Kurzweil references a "new religion," it should be acknowledged that elsewhere he also lambasts traditional religions for, among other things, their failure to fulfill any of their salvational promises. Yet, I would point out that Kurzweil constantly returns to a religious idiom in order to establish the importance and significance of transhumanist work. For more on the complicated relationship between transhumanism and more traditional forms of religion, see R. GERACI, *Apocalyptic AI: Visions of Heaven in Robotics, Artificial Intelligence and Virtual Reality* (Oxford: Oxford University Press, 2010).

[6] Ibid., 374.

[7] D. PEARCE, "Introduction to the Hedonist Imperative," accessed June 11, 2019 (https://www.hedweb.com/hedethic/hedonist.htm).

[8] For interesting examples beyond ROBERT GERACI, *Apocalyptic AI*, David Noble identifies the "religion of technology" as an important undercurrent running through Western culture from the medieval period, one that has regularly drawn a connection between salvation,

quasi-religious enthusiasm that surrounds transhumanist deployments of algorithms can come to mask the posthuman imperatives that undergird such technologies. For while the potential salvation of the human race through transhumanist technology is obviously yet to be realized, the algorithmic technologies that might one day lead to a transhumanist utopia are being put to much more modest use every day in both institutional and academic contexts. In the academic context, these uses have a great deal to do with how scholars conceive of and analyze "religion" as a cultural and biological phenomenon.

In this essay I focus on an overarching thread of contemporary scholarship that animates (and is animated by) the enthusiastic embrace of modern technology seen here in transhumanist discourse. Scholars working in the fields of cognitive science, evolutionary psychology, sociobiology, and neurotheology (the study of the neurological correlates of religious experience) embed both those technologies themselves and corresponding theoretical premises into their very method of study. I refer to this trend in contemporary scholarship as the "algorithmic approach to religion." I will show how the proliferation of the algorithm as both a technological and theoretical tool shapes this prevalent contemporary scholarly understanding of religion. My concern here is adjacent to the anxiety directed at the posthuman turn by Harari and Greenfield; namely, that the algorithmic approach to religion participates in a broader posthuman tendency to devalue, or even deny the existence of, those elements of human experience that are not renderable in algorithmic terms, and by so doing impoverishes our contemporary understanding of religion. Given the inexorable pull that algorithms exert on contemporary modes of knowledge- and value-production (academic and otherwise), the need for careful consideration and analysis of the adoption of algorithms in these fields is evident.

2. What is the Algorithmic Approach to Religion?

The origins of the algorithmic approach to religion can be traced back to the field of "cybernetics" – a Post-World War II trans-disciplinary mode of scientific inquiry that built on the insights of information theory to emphasize the ways in which groups of humans, animals, and machines might alternatively control and enable the actions of one another through digital information

---

dominion, and technological development in (see D. NOBLE, *The Religion of Technology: The Divinity of Man, and the Spirit of Invention* [New York: Penguin Books, 1999], 202–212). Erik Davis similarly insists on the spiritual significance of such endeavors, writing that, "regardless of how secular this ultramodern condition appears, the velocity and mutability of the times invokes a certain supernatural quality that must be seen, at least in part, through the lens of religious thought" (E. DAVIS, *Techgnosis: Myth, Magic, and Mysticism in the Age of Information* [New York: Harmony Books, 2004], 4).

exchange. Influential cyberneticists such as Ross Ashby and Norbert Wiener used their status at institutions like the Biological Computing Laboratory at the University of Illinois and the Massachusetts Institute of Technology to shape debates about the latent potential of digital technologies, including algorithms, from the very moment that such technologies were first conceived.

Jean-Pierre Dupuy has provocatively dubbed this process "the mechanization of the mind."[9] While the development of computing technologies and innovative approaches to artificial intelligence has better captured the popular imagination in the ensuing decades, Dupuy compellingly demonstrates that the more profound (though much subtler) shift in thinking emerged from insights about the computational elements of human cognition rather than the newfound capacity to simulate organic cognitive processes synthetically. He uses this demonstration to argue that cognitive science is a kind of re-ascendent cybernetics, arguing that "the various disciplines that make up what today is known as cognitive science [...] pretend not to recognize their kinship with cybernetics. And yet it was cybernetics that birthed them all."[10] The basic insight of cybernetics, rendered in language useful here, was that the processes of seeking, interpreting, and acting upon information define intelligence and those processes are algorithmic in all intelligent entities, whether organic or artificial. As these fields increase in prominence, they affirm a paradigm in which intelligence is framed as a capacity shared among "brains, minds, and machines" precisely because (as we will see below) the shift to information-processing and -sharing as the primary yardstick of intelligence/cognition turns the actual medium of exchange into a secondary characteristic.[11]

I argue that the employment of the algorithm as a theoretical tool and behavioral model is the glue that holds the disparate fields, I have linked to the algorithmic approach to religion together. While there is a myriad of sources one might draw upon to demonstrate this development, to my mind there is no clearer, more cogent, or more influential example than Daniel Dennett's Darwin's Dangerous Idea (1995). Adding to the now commonplace definition of an algorithm as a step-by-step method for solving a problem, Dennett argues that natural selection is itself an algorithmic process, and that understanding that process as such holds the key to unlocking the mysteries of human behavior. In the book, Dennett lays out a definition of the algorithm that has exerted significant influence on the algorithmic approach to religion.

---

[9] J. DUPUY, *On the Origins of Cognitive Science: The Mechanization of the Mind*, trans. M. B. DeBevoise (Cambridge, MA: MIT Press, 2009), 27–84.

[10] DUPUY, *On the Origins*, ix.

[11] S. J. GERSHMAN, E. J. HORVITZ, and J. B. TENENBAUM, "Computational Rationality: A Converging Paradigm for Intelligence in Brains, Minds, and Machines," *Science* 329, no. 6245 (2015): 273.

Every algorithm, he claims, possesses the same three qualities: "substrate neutrality," "underlying mindlessness," and "guaranteed results."[12] An algorithm is merely a blind process, the logic goes – that process can play itself out in carbon or in silicon, or variously among a group of neuroscientists in London or a tribe in the Andaman and Nicobar Islands, and it makes no difference; the algorithm can run in the background in each of these vastly different contexts all the same. Moreover, this freedom of medium – what Dennett calls "substrate neutrality" – is the result of the algorithm's "underlying mindlessness." While designed algorithms can certainly be programmed to achieve the intentional ends of their designers, individual algorithms themselves are simply functional processes with no intentionality. They move step by inexorable step. Thus, Dennett argues that they have "guaranteed results" stemming from that inexorability. Once set in motion, the outcome of the algorithm is virtually predetermined. All unexpected results from an algorithmic process represent a failure in the thinking of the observer and not any variability in the algorithm itself.[13]

Dennett's insight that natural selection is an algorithm possessing these qualities informs (or at least resonates with) many of the different theoretical tools that have been used to account for religion's existence and success by many of the practitioners of the algorithmic approach. Two general lines of argument have proven to be the most popular. The first touts religion as a byproduct of adaptive bio-cognitive behaviors, such as the "hyperactive agency detection device," (HADD) developed by Justin L. Barrett and used to great effect by evolutionary psychologists such as Scott Atran and Pascal Boyer. Religion has also been conceived of in this line of argument as a mechanism for staving off crippling anxiety about mortality, as in the more recently articulated Terror Management Theory.[14] The other major line of argument within the algorithmic approach claims that religion is a prosocial group adaptation (and hence a naturally selective algorithm operating through culture). Claiming that memes do for culture what genes do for biology, this body of scholarship relies on dual inheritance theory to argue that both biology and culture develop algorithmi-

---

[12] D. DENNETT, *Darwin's Dangerous Idea: Evolution and the Meanings of Life* (New York: Simon and Schuster, 1995), 50–51.

[13] Ibid., 52–60.

[14] For "hyper-active agency detection device, see S. ATRAN, *In Gods We Trust: The Evolutionary Landscape of Religion* (Oxford: Oxford University Press, 2002); J. BARRETT, *Why Would Anyone Believe in God?* (New York: AltaMira Press, 2004); P. BOYER, *Religion Explained: The Evolutionary Origins of Religious Thought* (New York: Basic Books, 2001). These studies treat religion as the byproduct of a tendency to read agency into unexpected or unexplainable events and unpredictable movements that helped our hunter-gatherer ancestors stay alive in the face of constant threats. Eventually, the postulated agents are generalized as personified as spirits and gods. For an influential formulation of Terror Management Theory, see S. SOLOMON et. al., *The Worm at the Core: On the Role of Death in Life* (New York: Random House, 2015).

cally, and religion is a culturally limned form of expression that assists groups in maintaining social identity and building trust between members, and even encourages making individual sacrifices meant to aid the group's reproductive capacity at the expense of the individual.[15]

These two lines of argumentation have found increasing scientific support in the form of novel neurological studies of religious experience, what Andrew Newberg has dubbed "neurotheology."[16] Beginning with V. S. Ramachandran's studies of temporal lobe epilepsy and mystical experience in the 1990's, the increasing sophistication of technological probes into brain function combined with ongoing research in artificial intelligence meant to simulate the human brain's mental (algorithmic) processes has resulted in a veritable treasure trove of data about how our brains process various forms of religious experience. The confidence with which these studies proceed reaches a kind of apotheosis in insights like Joe Tsien's "Theory of Connectivity," in which he purports to have isolated and mathematically defined the process that "explains the general purpose and core computational algorithm behind the layered cortex of the brain."[17] That confidence reaches a fever pitch in studies like those conducted at the Simulating Religion Project in Boston, where researchers develop computer programs meant to mimic biological and cultural algorithms in order to run simulations of real-world religious experiences. Human brain-states are referred to throughout as "organic algorithmic processes."[18]

While this introduction to these disparate studies obviously robs them of some of their detail and nuance, the basics are sufficient to see the logic that undergirds the algorithmic approach to religion that I want to further analyze going forward. In all of these studies, biology and culture are the outcomes of long-standing algorithmic processes. Human agency lies in applying one's rationality (itself an algorithmically afforded capacity) in employing, regulating, and negotiating the algorithmic imperatives of both in the pursuit of self- or group-interest.

---

[15] Dual Inheritance Theory, the idea that both biology and culture evolve algorithmically, is linked to a myriad of works, but see especially P. RICHERSON and R. BOYD, *Not By Genes Alone: How Culture Transformed Human Evolution* (Chicago, IL: University of Chicago Press, 2005); D. S. WILSON, *Darwin's Cathedral: Evolution, Religion, and the Nature of Society* (Chicago, IL: University of Chicago Press, 2002); and more recently A. NORENZAYAN, *Big Gods: How Religion Transformed Cooperation and Conflict* (Princeton, NJ: Princeton University Press, 2015) for prominent treatments of this theory.

[16] A. NEWBERG, *Principles of Neurotheology* (New York: Routledge, 2010).

[17] J. Z. TSIEN, "Principles of Intelligence: On Evolutionary Logic of the Brain," *Frontiers in Systems Neuroscience* 9, no. 1 (2015): 186.

[18] For more on the Simulating Religion Project, see "Simulating Religion Project Portal," Institute for the Bio-Cultural Study of Religion, accessed February 12, 2018 (https://www.ibcsr.org/index.php/institute-research-portals/simulating-religion-project).

3. What is Wrong with the Algorithmic Approach to Religion?

The algorithmic approach to religion has led to many exciting insights about the way that humans relate to their own biological and cultural contexts, but it is plagued by the same lacuna that haunts any science that focuses on cognition: the gap between biologically and culturally determined mental states and the conscious experiences that those states engender. This blind spot has become a near truism in the philosophy of science at least since the early 20th century and the process philosophy of Alfred North Whitehead, who argued that "reality" is made up of the evolving interaction of physical and experiential processes.[19] In these terms, the problem with the algorithmic approach to religion is that, like the fields of evolutionary psychology and cognitive science more broadly, it does not have a satisfactory method for incorporating actual conscious experience (what Dennett and other philosophers of mind call "qualia") into its model of religion.

While it would be more than a little solipsistic to say that this dilemma regarding the indecipherability of consciousness and human experience is uniquely troubling when considering religion, it is difficult to ignore the centrality of human experience when attempting to understand the social and psychical effects that religion exerts. The field of religious studies is practically founded on the notion of "mystical experience" and "experience of the divine," with no less a luminary in the field than William James going so far as to say that, "Religion ... shall mean for us the feeling, acts and experience of individual men in their solitude, so far as they apprehend themselves to stand in relation to whatever they consider to be divine."[20] What are we studying when we study religion if not the experiences of the religious?

This is not to say that the so-called hard problem of consciousness undermines the algorithmic approach to religion altogether. I chose Dennett as the representative of the algorithmic approach in part because even in his relatively early work in the mid-1990's he offers a well-developed argument as to a work-around. Given the uncanny valley that looms between the actual experience of consciousness and its brain-based neurological correlates, Dennett insists on the scientific primacy of the latter. He argues that science is restricted to studying those things with tangible physical properties (i.e., brains), and that consciousness is an emergent and secondary property that is the result of but does not reciprocally influence neurological activity. He likewise dismisses the

---

[19] A. N. WHITEHEAD, *Process and Reality* (New York: The Free Press, 1978 [1929]). Were this a paper that sought to address the philosophy of science in more detail, I would point out the many precursors to Whitehead who made similar arguments, especially in the threads of Indian/East Asian philosophy that anticipated his insights by centuries.
[20] W. JAMES, *The Varieties of Religious Experience: A Study in Human Nature* (New York: Penguin Viking, Inc., 1982 [1902]), 9.

verifiable existence of "qualia."[21] While I have my own apprehensions about Dennett's claims, I see no persuasive means of disproving them. And the algorithmic approach to religion does produce valuable quantitative data of great use when considered in conjunction with the many methods available for the study of religion in other social science and humanities fields. However, many of the evolutionary narratives seem contrived. The thought experiments about the evolving prehistoric human mind, while engaging, often seem too neat and tidy to reflect the overwhelming number of variables that undoubtedly go into any single human perception or decision. I follow Barbara Herrnstein-Smith in her critique of the "New Naturalists," evolutionary psychologists like Pascal Boyer and Scott Atran (both mentioned above) who I am labelling here as developers of the algorithmic approach. She writes:

"We may accept from the New Naturalists the idea that the existence, persistence, and many recurrent features of the beliefs and practices that Western scholars currently assemble under the term 'religion' reflect the operation of evolved capacities and behavioral tendencies that emerge more or less reliably among humans. In accepting that idea, however, we need not accept the specific evolutionary scenarios or specific mental machinery currently posited in evolutionary psychology or mainstream cognitive science to account for human behavior or cognition more generally."[22]

The kind of methodological modesty that Herrnstein-Smith advocates here often seems more professed than practiced by scholars working on the algorithmic approach. Herrnstein-Smith says as much, writing, "In their cognitive-evolutionary accounts of the wholly 'natural' springs of human, including religious, beliefs, the New Naturalists are not self-refuting. But in their implicit – and sometimes explicit and elaborated – self-exemption, they are self-ignorant."[23] This crucial insight can be clarifyingly translated into the language of dual inheritance theory; while practitioners of the algorithmic approach to religion are quite adept at positing and providing persuasive arguments for the existence of inescapable biological and cultural algorithms that necessarily provide the framework in which human beings engage in religious practice and belief, they are far less adept at recognizing the way the same process might inform their own work. Contra Whitehead, the algorithmic approach is all too often accompanied by scientific pretenses toward certainty and objectivity, as if the scientists themselves are unwilling to recognize that the algorithmic procession of biology and culture impacts all forms of knowledge-production/communication equally, including their own.

---

[21] See D. DENNETT, *Consciousness Explained* (Columbus, OH: Back Bay Books, 1991).
[22] B. HERRNSTEIN-SMITH, *Natural Reflections: Human Cognition at the Nexus of Science and Religion* (New Haven, CT: Yale University Press, 2009), 57–58.
[23] Ibid., 120.

Here Dennett comes closest to addressing this dilemma once again, though he falls well short of the mark. In a nod toward his technical milieu, Dennett describes the interrelation of biology and computer science in terms reminiscent of Dupuy, writing of evolutionary biology's dependence on computer modeling that, "No sooner do more powerful computers become available than we discover with their help that more complex models of evolution are not only possible but positively required if we are really to explain what Darwinism has always claimed it can explain."[24] Yet, he fails to fully follow through on this momentary recognition of his own cultural positionality.

In an extended excursus on the evolution of morality in the later sections of his work, Dennett refers to the genetic fallacy, the idea that it is a "mistake to infer current function or meaning from ancestral function or meaning."[25] What he fails to see about the algorithmic approach is that it falls prey to an inverted version of the genetic fallacy by inferring the ancestral function and meaning of human behavior, including religion, from an algorithmic understanding of brain and behavior that has only emerged in the contemporary (what Greenfield would call "posthuman") era. The rational logic that sustains the algorithmic approach, informed as it is by understandings of the world that have only emerged with the development of cybernetics in approximately the last 75 years, is nevertheless granted a kind of ahistorical universality because it jibes with contemporary understandings of the natural selection that has blindly guided humanity throughout its development as a species. The vast majority of studies within the algorithmic approach to religion exhibit this same ahistoricity.

This shortcoming might be addressed by using any number of theoretical and critical tools from the social sciences and the humanities, but there are two lines of argument that serve best. First, one could simply point these scholars to the works of Bruno Latour, especially his early work in Laboratory Life (1986) and Science in Action (1987) in which he explored the social construction of scientific facts, arguing that the objects of scientific study actually come into existence through the instruments used to derive them and the minds used to determine them and have no reality independent of the network of actors that produce them.[26]

---

[24] DENNETT, *Darwin's Dangerous Idea*, 193–194.

[25] Ibid., 465. Familiar readers will recognize in this invocation the seed for his argument in *Breaking the Spell* (2006); that religion evolved perfectly naturally in ancestral contexts to provide knowledge and meaning which has been eclipsed by scientific knowledge, thus rendering religion useless in the present-day.

[26] See B. LATOUR, *Laboratory Life: The Construction of Scientific Facts* (Princeton, NJ: Princeton University Press, 1986) and *Science in Action: How to Follow Scientists and Engineers Through Society* (Cambridge, MA: Harvard University Press, 1987).

Hannah Landecker has applied this significant insight to scientific understandings of biological processes with a particular eye to historical shifts in scientific culture. For example, her work on the history of scientific approaches to metabolism analyzes the shift from what she calls "industrial metabolism" to "postindustrial metabolism" by charting "the relationship between food, time, and biology with the shift from metabolism as factory to metabolism as iteratively generated interface, which is also a shift from the time of energetics to the time of information."[27] Much like modern postindustrial society's re-shaping of our relationship to metabolism with the rise of sedentary labor and overabundance of calories, our increasingly algorithmically-enabled and networked lives are fundamentally altering the way that contemporary humans navigate and interact with their lifeworlds. Following Landecker, might we only be seeing cognition as an algorithm because we've been able to develop algorithms that pass along knowledge and process information in a way that is analogous to how we imagine our minds to do so? In reverse, might we imagine our minds to do so because we have used algorithmic- and information-based technologies to probe their depths? The analogy between brains and computers is at best overdetermined by the current technological milieu.

The same point that Landecker raises about the biological process of metabolism applies to the contemporary treatment of the notion of rationality. The algorithmic approach to religion posits that human rationality is computational and algorithmic (hence the description of computational rationality as a shared virtue of brains, minds, and machines above). Yet, any good student of critical theory will tell you that mistaking the modern notion of instrumental reason for an ahistorical, universal formation of "Rationality" is a mistake. Moreover, any student well-versed in the white Eurocentric canon of religious studies scholarship on which authors like Boyer and Dennett often draw will tell you that modern, formal rationality is not necessarily to be celebrated. As early as 1905, Max Weber famously described the "iron cage" of rationality, concerned with efficiency, rational calculation, and control at the expense of all else.[28] While his view of this "iron cage" may be no less escapable than the algorithmically afforded bio-cultural lifeworld that the algorithmic approach posits, his is a far more critical view. One wonders why scholars employing the algorithmic approach so enthusiastically embrace the cage's arrival.

Critical theorists have presciently warned scholars about the dangers of succumbing to modern instrumental reason's pretensions at historical universality. Normative notions of "rationality" are not deployed in an abstract, consistent

---

[27] H. LANDECKER, "Postindustrial Metabolism: Fat Knowledge" *Public Culture* 25, no. 3 (2013): 498.

[28] M. WEBER, *The Protestant Ethic and the Spirit of Capitalism*, trans. T. Parsons (New York: Routledge, 2001), 123.

algorithmic process, but instrumentalized through economic, bureaucratic, institutional, and technocratic forms of power embedded in each and every specific social context.[29] In the contemporary moment, "rationality" is thus produced and leveraged through the neoliberal institutional environment that defines late capitalism. Increasingly, that late capitalist context is also explicitly and overwhelmingly technological – we are made visible to bureaucratic institutions by and through algorithms parsing relevant economic and cultural data extracted from our lives by algorithms tailor-made for the purpose.

This point is crucial. Following Adam Kotsko, I consider Neoliberalism to be more than the latest form of free market capitalism. It aspires to be "a complete way of life and a holistic worldview" conflating the logic of rational utility and self- and group-interest that drives the market with a more general moral imperative to behave in ways befitting that market logic.[30] From the neoliberal perspective "every decision, even the most impulsive and impassioned, [is] treated as a reasoned attempt at utility maximization."[31]

The correlation between these neoliberal assumptions and the algorithmic logic I have been describing here plays out in the algorithmic approach to religion. Describing religion in terms that increase either survivability or group cohesion and trust treats both the cognitive mechanisms responsible for the development of religious ideas and the social contract established through religion as mere means of "utility maximization." The same can be said for treating natural selection as an algorithmic process – useful adaptations survive and spread, while useless ones lead to extinction. Thus, treating human behavior as the outcome of biological and cultural algorithmic processes merely further fortifies the bars of Weber's modern "iron cage," especially when considered in light of Dennett's assertion about the inevitability of algorithmic outcomes. To be properly functioning humans, the argument goes, we cannot help but act according to the algorithmic impulses that define and produce the substrate out of which our consciousness emerges. Consciousness in this telling is algorithmically entrapped as much as it is algorithmically afforded.

Kotsko describes this general circumstance as "the assumption of rational choice in the absence of meaningful agency;" rational because we make conscious decisions from our algorithmically afforded positions that accord with

---

[29] While I want to avoid getting bogged down in the details (specifically the particular disagreement between specific theorists) in this essay, I am referring obliquely to the work of Frankfurt School theorists such as Max Horkheimer and Theodor Adorno (see especially *Dialectic of Enlightenment* (Palo Alto, CA: Stanford University Press, 2002) and the subsequent work of Michel Foucault, especially *Discipline and Punish: The Birth of the Prison* trans. A. Sheridan (New York: Vintage Books, 1995).

[30] A. KOTSKO, *Neoliberalism's Demons: On the Political Theology of Late Capital* (Palo Alto, CA: Stanford University Press, 2018), 6.

[31] Ibid., 87.

the logic of the algorithms that enframe and entrain us when we are making the "proper" decisions, absent of meaningful agency because the freedom to make contrary decisions only ever occurs in a context always already provided by and simultaneously enclosed within a system that valorizes the algorithmic logic which one might hope to resist.[32] Thus the algorithmic approach serves as yet another instrument of neoliberal technocratic and institutional power, shaped, as Greenfield says, "not so much by our own needs but those of the systems that nominally serve us."

4. Conclusion – Can Our Contemporary Faith in Algorithms Be Undone?

The application of Greenfield's insight to the process of algorithmic rationalization that I have described in this essay takes on even more urgency when we consider the fact that our understanding of the logical technique which algorithms employ in their step-by-step functionality is more rhetorical flourish than actual fact. Modern society increasingly relies upon algorithms to 'fairly and rationally' adjudicate many of its institutions. This includes instances of state-sponsored surveillance programs (such as the National Security Agency's PRISM program) and analyzing recidivism risk in the judicial system.[33] However, a legal system that takes concerns about the proprietary nature of privately developed algorithms seriously means that in nearly all instances there is no publicly available knowledge about how any of these institutionally deployed algorithms function. Moreover, the development of new "deep learning" strategies for training and creating useful algorithms means that knowledge about how these algorithms function isn't even privately held. No one knows quite how they work.[34] The proper, rational functioning of these algorithms is left up to faith.

While the algorithmic approach to religion provides exciting insights about the interplay of biology and culture and the development of human brains and

---

[32] Ibid., 89.

[33] For example, justices have been using the COMPAS algorithm to analyze the likelihood of prisoner recidivism, but the proprietary nature of the algorithm means that its functioning remains a public secret. A recent study demonstrated that black defendants were nearly twice as likely as white ones to be mislabeled by the COMPAS algorithm as at high-risk for recidivism. See J. LARSON, S. MATTU, L. KIRCHNER and J. ANGWIN, "How We Analyzed the COMPAS Recidivism Algorithm," last modified May 23, 2016 (https://www.propublica.org/article/how-we-analyzed-the-compas-recidivism-algorithm).

[34] See especially W. KNIGHT, "The Dark Secret at the Heart of AI," *MIT Technology Review*, April 11, 2017 (https://www.technologyreview.com/s/604087/the-dark-secret-at-the-heart-of-ai/) (4/22/2022).

behavior, it also justifies this faith in algorithms by arguing that algorithmic logic has guided the process of human development throughout our species' relatively brief history. It justifies the deployment of algorithms in modern institutions by arguing that they have been deployed in nature and society long before humans became aware of them. Thus, the image of religion that the algorithmic approach presents reinforces the elements of modern neoliberal society about which there is excellent cause to be apprehensive. The algorithmic approach to religion is too embedded in the very processes of technological rationalization to provide one of Harari's "meaningful visions of the future" other than a consummation of the false premises and promises of the late capitalist present.

But might that approach be attenuated so that its valuable insights can be brought to bear in scholarship on religion without succumbing to the pitfalls outlined here? It seems to me that religious studies is a perfect field for such discussions, both because of the specter of "religion" that looms over popular discourse related to these technologies and because of its inherently interdisciplinary nature. For example, while some scholars in religious studies have dedicated their time to parsing the religious or spiritual elements of transhumanism and other contemporary technophilic movements, scholars approaching the field from different theoretical perspectives seek in "religion" the tools necessary for combating the very technocapitalist culture that Kurzweil and his followers see as having so much potential. As Randall Styers writes, many modern philosophers inspired by Marxist critiques of capitalism have "recognized religion as a potent force for social change, an invaluable mechanism for a critique of the alienations of commodity culture and the dehumanizing effects of technological rationalization."[35] Thinkers from Terry Eagleton to Slavoj Zizek have acknowledged religion's distinctive social potency and postulated that its social force might be determinative in imagining political and social alternatives to current technocapitalist modes of structural exploitation and domination.

Yet contemporary scholarship on religion all too often overlooks this ambiguity. Only by acknowledging the intellectual freight attached to the category of religion and by bringing the astute work being done in cognitive science and sociobiology of religion into conversation with the theoretical concerns of more diverse trajectories of religious studies scholarship can the insights developed using the algorithmic approach be built upon in a way that earnestly attends to the social potency of religion and also foregoes blind optimism about the integration of technocratic forms of oppression into late capitalist society.

---

[35] R. STYERS, "Continental Philosophy and the 'Return of the Religious'," in *Religion, Theory, Critique*, ed. R. King (New York: Columbia University Press, 2017), 501.

Digital Technology and Embodiment: The Flesh as Paradigm

GUELFO CARBONE

1. Introduction

Involving a variety of approaches, such as postphenomenological hermeneutics, informational ontology, and posthumanism, the contemporary philosophical debate addresses our relationship with digital technologies by discerning two main features of the term 'digital', one related to our bodily experience, and the other to the computational sphere. Yet, the aspect related to our hands and fingers, and the aspect that traces back to the functionality of computational devices themselves are mostly discussed separately. The present paper, in turn, draws on the ambivalence of the 'digital,' while trying to reflect on both of the abovementioned aspects at one and the same time. A philosophical understanding of our symbiotic and synergic interaction with current technologies is the overall concern of the paper, which focuses on the entanglement of the phenomenology of embodiment and of digital technology; the former revisited as the phenomenology of the flesh, the latter broadly conceived as a prominent part of the techno-ecosystem in which our specific form of life is continuously evolving.[1]

2. The Twofold Meaning of Digital

The most advanced technology largely in use today, multi-touch digital technology, is rooted in the gestures of the basic tool that defines us as human beings, namely, our hand and its fingers. Yet, to employ our fingers in order to manipulate these devices, which have become an integral part of our daily lives, is not simply the result of the practical, operative necessity of their use. On the contrary, from a philosophical point of view, it represents the core of our relationship with present-day technology.

---

[1] This paper has benefited greatly from insightful responses to an earlier version by participants at the 6th Annual Claremont Forum Humanum Seminar: "Humanity: An Endangered Idea" (February 2019), which I attended thanks to the grant that was generously provided by the Udo Keller Stiftung Forum Humanum.

Indeed, the word 'digital' refers, in the first place, not to the devices per se, rather to our embodied reality, namely, to both human psychomotor and cognitive abilities. Digital technologies carry with them a philosophically fruitful ambivalence, which, on the one hand, hints back to the "circle of praxis"[2] of our instrumental relationship with the surrounding world, and, on the other hand, provides a specific mode of interaction with devices, which is charged with promising lines of development.

The ambivalence of the term 'digital' is already present in the ancient language from which the word is derived. The Latin word *digitalis* derives from *digitus*, 'finger' or 'toe,' and refers both to the part of the body and to the computational function of the fingers, which allow for the possibility of discrete counting without any external support,[3] as is evident in the Latin phrase *computare digitis* (to count on the fingers, to calculate the total amount using the fingers).

The English noun 'digit,' which dates back to the 17th century, also derives from *digitus*,[4] and displays four basic meanings: (i) one of the five terminal divisions of the hand or foot (a finger or toe), (ii) the breadth of a finger used as a measurement (tantamount to three-quarters of an inch), (iii) each of the numerals below ten (originally counted on the fingers), (iv) the twelfth part of the diameter of the sun or moon, used in expressing the magnitude of an eclipse.[5]

---

[2] J. Patočka, *The Natural World as a Philosophical Problem*, ed. I. Chvatík and L. Učník, trans. E. Abrams (Chicago, IL: Northwestern University Press, 2016), 171.

[3] M. Elo, "Digital finger: beyond phenomenological figures of touch," *Journal of Aesthetics & Culture* 4, no. 1 (2012): 1–12, (https://doi.org/10.3402/jac.v4i0.14982); A. Romele, "Herméneutique du digital: les limites techniques de l'interprétation," *Archives-Ouvertes HAL*. Accessed May 13, 2019, (https://hal.archives-ouvertes.fr/hal-01299368) (4/22/2022).

[4] J. Simpson and E. Weiner (eds.), *The Oxford English Dictionary*, vol. IV, second edition (Oxford: Clarendon Press 1989), 653–54. One of the most interesting occurrences of the word "digit" reported in the Oxford English Dictionary is taken from W. Austin, *Devotionis Augustinianae flamma, or, Certaine devout, godly, and learned meditations written, by the excellently-accomplisht gentleman, William Austin, of Lincolnes-Inne, Esquire. The particulars whereof, the reader may finde in the page following;) set forth, after his decease, by his deare wife and executrix, Mrs. Anne Austin, as a surviving monument of some part of the great worth of her ever-honoured husband, who changed his life, Ian 16. 1633* (London: Printed [by J. Legat and R. Bagder] for R. Meighen & J. Legat, 1637), 108, as he discusses the biblical episode of the Bronze Serpent lifted up on a perch by Moses (Numbers 21:9; John 3:14–15). The author notes that a perch is a unit of measurement equivalent to ten feet, hence, it is beyond our corporeal length; therefore, if we wish to make use of the perch as a unit of measurement, we must carry it with us. Conversely, the author points out that the inch (or digit), the palm, the cubit, and the pace are units of measurement that are derived from various parts of the body, and therefore, we carry them around with us naturally.

[5] In the 20th century, the arithmetical meaning (the third one listed in the definition above) has significantly been used as an attribution, especially for parts and data in mechanical calculators, of digital computers and similar devices, with the meaning "digit counter," or pulse (see e.g. R. K. Richards, *Arithmetic operations in digital computers* [New York: Van Nostrand, 1955]).

Accordingly, the adjective 'digital' refers to something pertaining to the fingers, and relating to using digits, in particular. In this latter sense, it is also applied to a computer that operates on data in the form of digits or similar discrete elements, as opposed to an analogue computer.

The Latin *digitus* itself can be traced back to the ancient Greek word *dáktulos*, which is from *dékomai*, 'to grasp,' 'to receive.' In the German word *Finger* and its cognate *fangen* (namely, 'to grasp') we find an echo of such a semantic kinship.[6] Hence, the word 'digital' refers not only to a peculiar bodily predisposition that identifies the human species, but it is also related to our most natural and general cognitive performances, as well as to our symbolic approach to the world.[7]

The use of digital devices goes back to our evolved interaction with technology, outlining a relationship with which we are increasingly engaged not only as users, but also as epistemic agents. The peculiar role of the hand in the interaction with digital devices stands right at the core of both our symbiosis and our synergy with the techno-ecosystem in which our daily life and survival are embedded.[8] Indeed, as is particularly evident in the case of multitouch digital technology, the interactive use of the hand, a "tool of tools" according to Aristotle,[9] highly symbolizes both *what* we demand from techno-

---

[6] It is also worth briefly mentioning that the concept of "the finger of God" plays a central role in the biblical narrative: the two tablets of law given to Moses are written by the finger of God (Exodus, 31:18; Deuteronomy, 9:10); the heavens are the work of God's fingers (Psalms, 8:3); the finger of God performs supernatural deeds (Exodus, 8:19). See I. Löw, "Die Finger in Literatur und Folklore der Juden," in *Gedenkbuch zur Erinnerung an David Kaufmann*, ed. M. Brann and F. Rosenthal (Breslau: Schlesische Verlagsanstalt, 1900), 61–85 and R. KIEFFER and J. BERGMAN (eds.), *La Main de Dieu. Die Hand Gottes* (Tübingen: Mohr Siebeck, 1997), for further references.

[7] "The characterization of the human being as a rational animal is already present in the form and organization of his *hand*, his *fingers*, and his *fingertips*; partly through their structure, partly through their sensitive feeling. By this means nature has made the human being not suited for one way of manipulating things but undetermined for every way, consequently suited for the use of reason; and thereby has indicated the technical predisposition, or the predisposition of skill, of his species as a *rational* animal." (I. KANT, *Anthropology from a Pragmatic Point of View*, trans. and ed. R.B. Louden; with an introduction by M. Kuehn (Cambridge: Cambridge University Press, 2006), 227–28; see also D. MORAN, "Between Vision and Touch: From Husserl to Merleau-Ponty," in R. KEARNEY and B. TREANOR (eds.), *Carnal Hermeneutics* (New York: Fordham University Press, 2015), 214.

[8] P. MONTANI, *Tecnologie della sensibilità. Estetica e immaginazione interattiva* (Milan: Raffaello Cortina Editore, 2014); A. GREENFIELD, *Radical Technologies. The Design of Everyday Life* (London/New York: Verso, 2017).

[9] ARISTOTLE, *De Anima*. Translation, introduction, and commentary by C. Shields (Oxford: Oxford University Press, 2016), 65; E. ALLOA, "Getting in Touch. Aristotelian Diagnostics," in Kearney and Treanor, *Carnal Hermeneutics*, 57–72; D. D'ANGELO, "La carne e il tatto nel 'De Anima' di Aristotele. Un'interpretazione fenomenologica," *Philosophy Kitchen* 4 (2016): 55–68.

logical devices – in terms of ease of use, accessibility, and "readiness-to-hand"[10] or "handiness"[11] – and the scope of its development, namely, *how* we try to improve the performances of advanced technologies in a suitable fashion so as to make them adaptable to our embodied form of life as a whole, the hand being an essential part of the model for such adaptability.

A philosophical understanding of our symbiotic and synergic interaction with current technologies is the key point of the present paper, which draws upon the ambivalence of the meaning of the word 'digital' by trying to reflect on both the computational and the bodily aspects at one and the same time. As a pervasive phenomenon in biological and social life, in every respect, digital technology becomes particularly relevant inasmuch it encourages philosophy to rethink most of the metaphysical categorizations belonging to its tradition, particularly those related to human embodied reality, such as subject/object, mind/body, activity/passivity.[12]

It seems that contemporary philosophy has embraced this task by addressing the phenomenon of digital technology, although it does not seem to be overly interested in considering both of the two abovementioned features of the meaning of 'digital' together. Furthermore, symbiosis and synergy are often debated separately, as though the computational feature applies only to the synergy with the external object (the device), whereas the bodily experience applies to the alleged sovereign subject of the human-machine symbiosis (the user). On the contrary, such a symbiosis seems to reshape the very idea of 'human,' insofar as it stimulates our intelligent form of life in its entirety.[13]

The computational-arithmetical feature of digital technology is considered in different fields of philosophy, such as digital philosophy[14] and informational ontology.[15] The cognitive sciences, inasmuch as they take inspiration from an anti-metaphysical aim, seem more interested in the philosophical issue of the

---

[10] M. HEIDEGGER, *Being and Time*, trans. J. Macquarrie and E. Robinson (Oxford: Basil Blackwell, 1962), 98 et passim.

[11] M. HEIDEGGER, *Discourse on Thinking. A translation of Gelassenheit*, trans. J. M. Anderson and H. Freund; with an introduction by J. M. Anderson (New York: Harper and Row, 1996), 67 et passim.

[12] G. AGAMBEN, *The Use of Bodies: Homo Sacer IV, 2*, trans. A. Kotsko (Stanford, CA: Stanford University Press, 2016); E. ALLOA, T. BEDORF, C. GRÜNY, and T. N. KLASS (eds.), *Leiblichkeit. Geschichte und Aktualität eines Konzeptes*. 2nd ed. (Tübingen: Mohr Siebeck, 2018).

[13] R. DIODATO, *Aesthetics of the virtual*, trans. J. L. Harmon, ed. S. Benso; foreword by J. Protevi (Albany, NY: State University of New York Press, 2012); M. HAGNER and E. HÖRL (eds.), *Die Transformation des Humanen. Beiträge zur Kulturgeschichte der Kybernetik* (Frankfurt a. M.: Suhrkamp Verlag, 2008).

[14] E. FREDKIN, "An introduction to digital philosophy," *International Journal of Theoretical Physics* 42, no. 2 (2003): 189–247, (http://dx.doi.org/10.1023/A:1024443232206) (4/22/2022).

[15] L. FLORIDI, "Against digital ontology," *Synthese* 168, no. 1 (2009): 151–78, (https://doi.org/10.1007/s11229-008-9334-6) (4/22/2022); *The Philosophy of Information* (Oxford: Oxford University Press, 2011).

embodied mind in its connection with the broadly conceived human environment, as well as relying on computational models to explore and describe cognition.[16] Posthuman philosophies dwell upon the mutation of the concept of the body, including its relationship with technology, from a non-naturalist and transdisciplinary perspective.[17] Postphenomenological and hermeneutical approaches take up the question concerning technology once again, in the wake of Heidegger, Derrida, Simondon, and Nancy, focusing on the effects of digital culture on society, often in dialogue with social sciences.[18] Techno-aesthetics and environmental media theory also seem to be moving in this direction, stressing how machines and touch-based devices change our experiential horizon, seeking new modes of symbiotic interaction with technologies.[19]

The present paper is part of an ongoing independent research project that focuses on the interplay between human embodied reality and digital technologies, combining different philosophical disciplines, such as ancient philosophy, metaphysics, and aesthetics. The twofold meaning of 'digital' serves as the common thread for a philosophical reading of our relation with new technologies that underlines the entanglement of the phenomenology of embodiment with digital technology; the former revisited as phenomenology of the flesh, the latter broadly conceived as a prominent component of the techno-ecosystem in which our specific organic life is continuously evolving. The research argues that the phenomenological notion of flesh could be the leading concept that would allow a post-metaphysical interdisciplinary critique of our present digital culture,[20] with the hope of outlining new perspectives on how the humanities can help to shape modes of being human in an increasingly automated world.

In order to outline the overall direction of this research, the second section of this paper presents the topic *a parte objecti*, that is, by sketching out a

---

[16] P. THAGARD, *Mind: Introduction to Cognitive Science*, 2nd ed. (Cambridge, MA: MIT Press, 2005); R. SUN (ed.), *The Cambridge Handbook of Computational Psychology* (Cambridge, MA: Cambridge University Press, 2008).

[17] C. WOLFE, *What is Posthumanism?* (Minneapolis, MN: University of Minnesota Press, 2010); R. RANISCH and S. L. SORGNER (eds.), *Post- and Transhumanism: An Introduction* (New York: Peter Lang, 2014); R. BRAIDOTTI, *The Posthuman* (Cambridge: Polity Press, 2013); "Posthuman Critical Theory," *Journal of Posthuman Studies* 1 (2017): 9–25.

[18] B. STIEGLER, *Technics and Time (1): The Fault of Epimetheus*, trans. R. Beardsworth and G. Collins (Stanford, CA: Stanford University Press, 1998); R. ROSENBERGER and P.-P. VERBEEK, eds., *Postphenomenological Investigations: Essays on Human-Technology Relations* (Lanham, MD: Lexington Books, 2015); KEARNEY and TREANOR, *Carnal Hermeneutics*.

[19] G. SIMONDON, "On Techno-Aesthetics," trans. A. De Boever, *Parrhesia* 14 (2012): 1–8; P. MONTANI, D. CECCHI and M. FEYLES, *Ambienti mediali* (Milan: Meltemi, 2018).

[20] A. GALLOWAY, *Laruelle. Against the Digital* (Minneapolis/London: University of Minnesota Press, 2014); M. BETANCOURT, *The Critique of Digital Capitalism: An Analysis of the Political Economy of Digital Culture and Technology* (Brooklyn, NY: punctum books, 2016).

philosophical discussion of the ontological status of digital objects, while the third section tackles it *a parte subjecti*, claiming that, due to its specific mode of givenness, the flesh may serve as a suitable paradigm in order to establish a fruitful phenomenological inquiry on digital technologies. As shall be seen in the provisional conclusive remarks in the fourth and final section, the phenomenological account of the digital world hints back to a prominent historical issue that concerns the very relationship with technology we are experiencing at the present time.

3. Ontology of the Digital

Since the time of ancient Greek epistemology, established by Plato and Aristotle, ontological terminology has relied on the distinction between natural objects and technical objects as a fundamental categorization in order to orient scientific research. One may ask to which of these ontological realms do digital objects belong? Indeed, at first glance, it is not so easy to assign the objects we deal with in the digital world to either one of these realms. In the digital world, we experience digital objects as data. Data are those digital objects (such as a video or a social media profile) formalized by schemes or "ontologies" that one can generalize as metadata, and which are produced via the Web. The latter, in turn, represents the context of the experience of data.[21]

Yet, as Yuk Hui argues, "[w]hen we look at the term 'data' we hardly recognize that its Latin root *datum* originally means '[a thing] given;' the French word for data, *donnée*, has this meaning as well,"[22] as does the Italian term *dato*. One of the most evident features that phenomenology has in common with post-Kantian transcendental philosophy is that it emphasizes the givenness of the objects, namely, the context of the phenomenal presence of things given through our own experience.[23]

Thus, a phenomenological approach would express the question 'what is a digital object?' as: how are data experienced, in other words, what is the context of their givenness? Instead of following the reductionist approaches, which

---

[21] Y. Hui, "What is a Digital Object?," *Metaphilosophy* 43, no. 4 (2012): 380–95, (https://doi.org/10.1111/j.1467-9973.2012.01761.x); *On the Existence of Digital Objects*; foreword by B. Stiegler (Minneapolis, MN: University of Minnesota Press, 2016).

[22] Hui, "What is a Digital Object?," 388.

[23] On this topic see, above all, Edmund Husserl's second volume of *Ideas*, particularly the Second Chapter ("The Ontic Sense-Strata of the Thing of Intuition as Such") of the First Section entitled "The Constitution of Material Nature" (E. Husserl, *Ideas Pertaining to a Pure Phenomenology and to a Phenomenological Philosophy – Second Book: Studies in the Phenomenology of Constitution*, trans. R. Rojcewicz and A. Schuwer [Dordrecht/Boston: Kluwer Academic, 1989], 30–59). See also G. Crowell, *Normativity and Phenomenology in Husserl and Heidegger* (Cambridge: Cambridge University Press, 2013).

understand the digital milieu as abstract entities (such as information and data), Hui's phenomenological account takes its cue from an embodied perspective, which contrasts digital objects with natural objects and technical objects.

As one speaks of 'natural' and 'technical' objects from the phenomenological perspective, a crucial caveat is to be considered: phenomenology begins as a descriptive task that analyzes what is given in pure consciousness through our cognitive performances in order to fix concepts and experiential structures that are valuable for knowledge. Hence, both 'natural' and 'technical' refer to the modes of givenness, by relying on an ontological structure, which is relational, rather than essential.[24]

Thus, Hui recalls that an object considered in the natural attitude (which could be a stone as well as an artifact) is perceived as a present being within the framework of the subject-substance relationship, whose interfacing mode is knowledge.[25] Relying both on Simondon's mechanology[26] and Stiegler's[27] approach, then, Hui also provides an intriguing definition of the technical

---

[24] This is a crucial point made by the very founder of phenomenology, Husserl, who distinguished the phenomenological attitude from the natural one. Through the phenomenological attitude, Husserl intended to deactivate the natural attitude, by interrupting it. The latter orients our everyday behavior, in terms of how we look at things, and how we deal with them, whereas phenomenology reflects on reality, understanding it as a given of consciousness (E. HUSSERL, *Ideas pertaining to a pure phenomenology and to a phenomenological philosophy. First book: General introduction to a pure phenomenology*, trans. F. Kersten [The Hague/Boston/Lancaster: Martinus Nijhoff Publisher, 1983]; *Ideas* [1989] and *The Basic Problems of Phenomenology. From the Lectures, Winter Semester, 1910–1911*, trans. I. Farin and J. Hart [Dordrecht: Springer Verlag, 2006]). See also PATOČKA, *The Natural World*, 147–48: "In short, Husserl shows that individual as well as eidetically transformed phenomenological experience, studied as truly pure experience in the phenomenological attitude, is essentially independent of the thesis of nature, of being, of the world – that the experience of the world, of things, is thus, by essence and nature, independent of things, that it has its own a priori laws, its own structure that remains valid, whether the world exists or not. The 1910–11 lecture course [HUSSERL, *The Basic Problems*] is one of Husserl's most important works, a text containing a blueprint of his entire philosophical problematic."

[25] HUI, "What is a Digital Object?," 382. The naturalization of the things given to our consciousness, which traces back to the naturalization of the subject itself, is phenomenology's long-standing concern, fully investing all kind of objects that fall into perception, as clearly explained by PATOČKA, *The Natural World*, 127: "The natural world – in which pragmatically useful as well as natural, and human as well as animal beings, the works of man as an individual as well as those of history are given *in the original* – is a phenomenon whose originality must first be described and analyzed and only then interpreted, in such a way that the phenomenon does not vanish with the interpretation. In this process, it will appear that the naturalization of the spirit, which was at the beginning of the whole problematic [*scil.* of Patočka's essay], is but one of the two great perils guarding the entrance to it: the other is the hypostatizing, the absolutizing of the subject when its naturalization is brought to light and the ensuing danger obviated, yet without grasping in its full originality the essential character of the 'natural world' as a whole."

[26] G. SIMONDON, *On the Mode of Existence of Technical Objects*, trans. C. Malaspina and J. Rogove (Minneapolis, MN: University of Minnesota Press, 2017).

[27] STIEGLER, *Technics and Time (1)*; *Technics and Time (2): Disorientation*, trans. S. Barker (Stanford, CA: Stanford University Press, 2009).

object, arguing that "a technical individual is a technical object that supports the functioning of its inner structure at the same time as it is able to adapt an external milieu to its functioning."[28] Instead of the relationship between a subject and a substance (or essence), the technical object shows the ontological grip between things and the surrounding world. A technical object (a hammer, for instance) gains its usefulness and its application within networks of instrumental references in which we are constantly practically engaged. Relevance and significance orient human praxis so that a technical object is not, properly speaking, an 'object', that is, something that we approach in disinterested contemplation, for the sake of knowledge.[29] The things that we use gain specific relevance in the tissue of references in which our life unfolds, to the point that, as Jan Patočka noted, the surrounding world becomes a sort of "nonorganic body" to us, whereas the social sphere grows as a kind of "supraorganic organism" built upon the cooperation of a "community of mutually using users,"[30] a definition that also perfectly applies to our everyday shared usage of the Web's resources and potentialities.

According to Hui, digital objects qua data are a sort of *tertium datur* with respect to both natural and technical things. Due to their particular mode of givenness,[31] when phenomenologically approached, digital objects do not seem to fall entirely under either the subject-substance relationship (knowledge) or the things-surroundings relation (praxis), eliciting a combined approach for their philosophical interpretation:

"Digital objects appear in three phases, which are interdependent of each other but cannot be reduced or generalized into oneness: *objects*, *data*, and *networks*. If the investigation of natural objects is concerned with the dialectics of subject and substance, and the

---

[28] HUI, "What is a Digital Object?," 385.

[29] HEIDEGGER, *Being and Time*, trans. J. Stambaugh (Albany, NY: State University of New York Press, 1996), 77–83.

[30] PATOČKA, *The Natural World*, 172–74. In Patočka's terms (one of the most perspicuous readers of Martin Heidegger's phenomenology of technology), besides knowledge and contemplative attitude, our world is also built upon work and struggle: "Work and struggle are two fundamentally different principles: in work man confronts things, in struggle he confronts his fellows as virtually enthralled or enthralling. In practice, the two principles combine: the organization of humanity for work is the result of a struggle, and is itself a struggle" (ibid., 174).

[31] Hui argues that "we have to recognize that since 1946 the word 'data' has had an additional meaning [i. e. not just 'a given thing,' as seen above]: 'transmittable and storable computer information.' This second sense of 'data' suggests a reconsideration of the philosophy of objects, since the givenness can no longer be taken as sense data or a mode of being together of man and nature; instead, one has to recognize its material transformation. The significance of the new technique of data processing we now call the digital is not only that with computers we can process large amounts of data but also that by operating with data the system can establish connections and form a network of data that extends from platform to platform, database to database. The digital remains invisible without data, or traces of data" (HUI, "What is a Digital Object?," 388).

investigation of technical objects is concerned with the relationality between the object and the milieu, then the investigation of digital objects must obtain a new direction by pushing these two investigations further. This does not mean that the previous investigations lose their significance; it simply indicates that the question of substance is no longer at issue [...]. The investigation of digital objects must find a new relation between object and mind. Furthermore, the relationality within technical objects and their relationality to the world are not independent of each other. Technical objects are not only symbols as they appear in the world, nor are they simply tools for use; their internal relations are materialized and codified, which in turn conditions the opening of the world."[32]

As Hui's philosophy of digital objects underlines, rather than a brand-new technology, the digital represents "a new technique to manage data in comparison to the analogue."[33] Such a technique inaugurates a new world, in which the Web is acting "both as an interface between users and digital objects and as a world in which these digital objects conceal and reveal – in both physical and metaphysical terms."[34] Hui claims that the immersive digital world requires "a theory of relations."[35] As will be demonstrated in the next section, through an insightful critique of the metaphysical categorization of human embodied reality, the phenomenology of the flesh provides crucial elements in order to foster a theory of our relationship with the digital world.

4. Phenomenology of Embodiment as Incarnation

The present paper makes use of phenomenology both as a philosophical tradition and a research method, which outlived that tradition. The reach of phenomenology on the question concerning technology unfolds in two wide-ranging directions. On the one hand, phenomenology provides a philosophical self-reflective approach that calls into question the metaphysical tradition as a whole. On the other hand, due to long-standing reasoning on technology, phenomenology offers a fruitful standpoint for our understanding of the ontological constitution of the digital world.[36]

---

[32] Ibid., 390. "Digital objects appear to human users as colourful and visible beings. At the level of programming they are text files; further down the operating system they are binary codes; finally, at the level of circuit boards they are nothing but signals generated by the values of voltage and the operation of logic gates. How, then, can we think about the voltage differences as being the substance of a digital object? Searching downward we may end up with the mediation of silicon and metal. And finally we could go into particles and fields. But this kind of reductionism doesn't tell us much about the world" (ibid., 387).

[33] Ibid., 387.

[34] Ibid., 381.

[35] Ibid., 394.

[36] M. HEIDEGGER, *The Question Concerning Technology and Other Essays*, trans. and with an introduction by W. Lovitt (New York; London: Garland Publishing, 1977); D. IHDE, *Technology and the Lifeworld: From Garden to Earth* (Bloomington, IN: Indiana University Press, 1990).

The phenomenology of the flesh is a particularly suitable field of research. Indeed, the flesh shows an exceptional mode of phenomenality that encourages the deconstruction of the basic metaphysical patterns, such as subject/object, mind/body, activity/passivity. Due to the peculiar role of the hand and fingers in the processes of subjectification, the flesh further offers a different paradigm as compared with the traditional visual and ocularcentric one,[37] the latter being considered quite limited, when confronted with the immersive digital media environment and the development of human-machine interactions introduced by digital technologies.[38]

From Husserl on, one of the most relevant arguments regarding the phenomenology of embodiment is the distinction between the body experienced (or lived) as the "living body," or "body proper" (*Leib*) and the "inert body," or the "body-object" (*Körper*), a distinction which addresses the perception of the body, understood as situated within the intersubjective relationship.[39] Yet, according to Giorgio Agamben, the correct posing of the problem of the body "was put durably off course" precisely because of the phenomenological doctrine of the *Leib*.[40] Indeed, Husserl claimed that the only originary donation of a body can be the donation of one's own body, and that only if one has constituted one's own body, can one then apperceive every other body as such, the apperception of the separated, distant, other body being a fundamentally mediated apperception. Agamben further notes that such an "apodictic pronouncement of the originary character as 'mine' of the donation of a body never stops giving rise to aporias and difficulties."[41] This is true first and foremost,

---

[37] M. MERLEAU-PONTY, *The Visible and the Invisible. Followed by working notes*, ed. C. Lefort, trans. A. Lingis (Evanston, IL: Northwestern University Press, 1968); "Eye and Mind," in *The Merleau-Ponty Reader*, ed. L. Lawlor and T. Toadvine (Evanston, IL: Northwestern University Press, 2007), 351–378; E. ALLOA, *La résistance du sensible. Merleau-Ponty critique de la transparence* (second edition) (Paris: Kimé, 2014); *Resistance of the Sensible World: An Introduction to Merleau-Ponty* (first edition), trans. J. M. Todd; foreword by R. Barbaras (New York: Fordham University Press, 2017); D. MORAN, "Between Vision and Touch: From Husserl to Merleau-Ponty," in Kearney and Treanor, *Carnal Hermeneutics*, 214–44; J.-L. NANCY, *Corpus*, trans. R. Rand (New York: Fordham University Press, 2008).

[38] M. MAZZEO, *Tatto e linguaggio. Il corpo delle parole* (Rome: Editori Riuniti, 2003); R. DIODATO, "The touch beyond the screen," *atque* 11 (2012): 153–174.

[39] E. HUSSERL, *Cartesian Meditations: An introduction to phenomenology*, trans. D. Cairns (The Hague: Martinus Nijhoff Publisher, 1977); *Ideas Pertaining to a Pure Phenomenology*; D. FRANCK, *Flesh and Body: On the Phenomenology of Husserl*, trans. J. Rivera and S. Davidson (London: Bloomsbury, 2014).

[40] "A correct posing of the problem of the body was put durably off course by the phenomenological doctrine of the body proper. According to this doctrine – which finds its topical place in the polemic of Husserl and Edith Stein against Lipps's theory of empathy – the experience of the body would be, together with the I, what is most proper and originary" (AGAMBEN, *The Use of Bodies*, 82).

[41] Ibid.

as regards the perception of the body of the other, since this latter "is not actually perceived as an inert body (*Körper*) but as a living body (*Leib*), endowed like mine with sensibility and perception."[42] The most important aspect to be noticed with respect to the *Leib/Körper* distinction is that these two terms do not designate two different entities; rather, they refer to two different modes of appearance, and, consequently, of givenness. The unsurmountable ambiguity, to which the description of the lived-living body (which is supposed to be one's own body) undergoes, stems precisely from the difficulty to discern and scientifically describe such a distinction, even in proprioception phenomena.

Michel Henry drew on the *Leib/Körper* distinction in order to formulate his phenomenology of life, based on the notion of flesh, which pushes the aforementioned ambiguity to the extreme point of a radical separation between *life* and *world*. Indeed, as Henry's phenomenological philosophy pinpoints, there are two fundamental modes of appearing, namely, two different and decisive modes through which phenomenality expresses itself in a phenomenon: the appearing of the world and the appearing of life.[43] In the former mode, every and each thing, including our body, is given from outside of us, it appears in all its properties, etymologically speaking, as *ob-jectum*, something present to us, or cast before us.[44]

This is a crucial point made by Henry, since, starting with Husserl and his research on the notions of the 'natural world' and 'life-world' (*Lebenswelt*), and particularly with his pupil Heidegger's early phenomenology, the theme of 'world' had significantly undergone a critical reappropriation by phenomenology. Indeed, Heidegger's phenomenological beginnings, as demonstrated in his first lecture courses held in Freiburg, deal with two fundamental phenomenological concepts, notably "life-world" and "event," both 'world' and 'event' being key notions observable throughout his *Denkweg*.[45] Instead of under-

---

[42] Agamben also reports that "in the notes and fragmentary drafts that make up volumes XIII and XIV of the *Husserliana* (E. HUSSERL, *Husserliana: Gesammelte Werke*, vol. 13, *Zur Phänomenologie der Intersubjektivität: Texte aus dem Nachlass. Erster Teil, 1905–1920*, ed. I. Kern [The Hague: Martinus Nijhoff,1973] and *Husserliana: Gesammelte Werke*, vol. 14, *Zur Phänomenologie der Intersubjektivität: Texte aus dem Nachlass. Zweiter Teil, 1921–1928*, ed. I. Kern [The Hague: Martinus Nijhoff, 1973]), pages and pages are dedicated to the problem of the perception of the hand of the other" (AGAMBEN, *The Use of Bodies*, 82).

[43] M. HENRY, "Incarnation and The Problem of Touch," in Kearney and Treanor, *Carnal Hermeneutics*, 128.

[44] The Latin *objectus* is the past participle of *obicere*: 'to throw before or against,' 'to cast,' 'to offer,' which is formed by the prefix *ob-* (towards, against) and the verb *jacere* (to throw, to cast).

[45] M. HEIDEGGER, *Towards the Definition of Philosophy: 1. The Idea of Philosophy and the Problem of Worldview; 2. Phenomenology and Transcendental Philosophy of Value; with a transcript of the lecture course "On the Nature of the University and Academic Study (Freiburg Lecture-courses 1919)"*, trans. T. Sadler (New Brunswick, NJ: Bloomsbury [Athlone], 2000); G. CARBONE, *La questione del mondo nei primi corsi friburghesi di Martin Heidegger* (Milan/Udine: Mimesis edizioni, 2017). In reality, the concept of 'world' takes on a fundamental position for most

standing it as a sum of beings or a collection of bodies, the phenomenological account of the world describes it, in the wake of both Husserl and Heidegger's research, as the already illuminated horizon of appearing as such, not only as the context in which every experience unfolds (which is the common feature of transcendental approaches after Kant), but as the very intertwining of world and life that hosts human subjectification.[46]

Henry's interpretation of the living body takes up such a phenomenological account of embodiment, but with the addition of a radical and critical twist. In fact, he argues that the two modes of appearing, of world and life, respectively, are not on the same plane. On the contrary, Henry emphasizes the typical phenomenological topos of the interplay between the transcendence and immanence of appearing as such, claiming that world and life are separated by the most radical difference, insofar as life, understood as "pure phenomenality" and as "the most originary mode in which phenomenality is phenomenalized," makes every other form of phenomenality possible.[47] In order to differentiate it from the phenomenality of the world, Henry calls the mode of appearing of life "revelation," arguing that, in the experience of life, the difference between appearing and what it allows to appear (between the phenomenon and the pure phenomenality) simply vanishes.[48]

---

of the phenomenological philosophies after Husserl and Heidegger, notably in those of Fink, Levinas, Merleau-Ponty, Patočka, Henry. Moreover, the phenomenological effort towards an autonomous, purely philosophical notion of 'world' becomes all the more significant the more one positions it within the context of the quintessential phenomenological task, that is, the reappropriation of the Western metaphysical tradition (L. ALWEISS, "Leaving Metaphysics to Itself," *International Journal of Philosophical Studies* 15, no. 3 (2007): 349–65, (https://doi.org/10.1080/09672550701445225) (4/22/2022), in which the concept of 'world' has always been subordinated to the two other pillars of that tradition, namely, God and Human (K. LÖWITH, *Gott, Mensch und Welt in der Metaphysik von Descartes bis zu Nietzsche* (Göttingen: Vandenhoeck & Ruprecht, 1967).

[46] According to both Husserl and Heidegger, the horizon is defined "regionally" as a topography of proximity and distance, presence and absence (S. CROWELL, "The Challenge of Heidegger's Approach to Technology: A Phenomenological Reading," in *Heidegger on Technology*, ed. A. J. Wendland, C. Merwin, and C. Hadjioannou, [London/New York: Routledge, 2018], 88). As Steven Crowell recalls, "[d]rawing out the implications of Husserl's phenomenological notion of horizon – which breaks with the 'representational' thinking of both 'empiricism' and 'intellectualism' – is a major goal of Merleau-Ponty's *Phenomenology of Perception* [M. MERLEAU-PONTY, *Phenomenology of perception*, trans. D. A. Landes (Abingdon/New York: Routledge, 2012)]" (ibid., 93).

[47] M. HENRY, "Incarnation and The Problem of Touch," in Kearney and Treanor, *Carnal Hermeneutics*, 129.

[48] Henry further argues that: "*Life reveals itself.* Life is an autorevelation. On the one hand, it is life that carries out the work of revelation; it is anything but a blind entity. On the other hand, what it reveals is itself. This is why the revelation of life and what it reveals are one and the same" (italics author's own). For this reason, life is "absolutely originary immanence" (HENRY, "Incarnation and The Problem of Touch," 129–30). On this topic, see also HENRY, *Incarnation*, in which he continues his confrontation with Christianity and the Christian notion of flesh.

From a phenomenological point of view, then, the flesh, as "auto-impression in the process of the autorevelation of life"[49] is the most essential form of phenomenality, insofar as it provides access to the phenomenality of the world, including our body. Accordingly, body and flesh are thus distinguished "through the radicality of an originary phenomenological dualism."[50] Such a phenomenological account of the flesh takes its cue from one essential fact, as Henry argues that all bodies that fall under perception, being seen, smelled, touched, or moved, presuppose another body that sees it, smells it, touches it, or moves it. The operations of this second body constitute the former and make them possible. Thus, perception, addressed as the affectivity in which life is experienced and enjoyed, traces back to what phenomenology calls "a transcendental and constituting body, a subject-body," without which the body-object would not exist. In turn, the transcendental body cannot be reduced to an object of perception, since it is instead what produces it; and this possibility relies on the "impressional self-givenness" of life in the flesh.[51]

The insurmountable contradistinction between *flesh* and *body*, which mirrors the difference between *life* and *world*, implies that the original reality of our body is not our mundane body, which is situated in the world and opens onto it; rather, such originality is given by our flesh "in the auto-impressionality through which all powers are placed in themselves and thereby able to be exercised." However, our flesh can only provide access to our body, and, through this body, to the world, *"because it first provides us with access to itself – because it is impressionally given to oneself where all self-givenness occurs, namely, in and through life."*[52]

Returning to our discussion, contrary to naturalist approaches to the mind-body problem,[53] to stress such a self-givenness of the flesh as a peculiar, unparalleled paradigm of givenness turns out to be of some use in order to philosophically understand "the flattening of the transcendent," and the fact that "objects fall into the field of total immanence," namely, the two key features

---

[49] HENRY, "Incarnation and The Problem of Touch," 130.

[50] Henry goes on to explain: "[t]he body lacks the power to make manifest; it has to seek its manifestation in the world outside-of-oneself and is thus constituted as a mundane body. The forms of the intuition of space and time along with the categories of representation under which it is subsumed are the modes of the process of externalization through which it becomes a phenomenon" (ibid., 130).

[51] Ibid., 131–32. For a critical discussion of Henry's take on the transcendental subject, see ALWEISS, "Leaving Metaphysics to Itself." As is well known, Maurice Merleau-Ponty developed an original and insightful phenomenological philosophy of flesh, which is rather different from Henry's one. See MERLEAU-PONTY, *The Visible and the Invisible*; L. VANZAGO, "The Flesh Between. Some Remarks on André Green's Remarks on Merleau-Ponty's Ontology and its Relationship to Psychoanalysis," *Chiasmi International* 18 (2016): 49–61 and R. BARBARAS, *Introduction à une phénoménologie de la vie* (Paris: J. Vrin, 2008).

[52] HENRY, "Incarnation and The Problem of Touch," 133, italics author's own.

[53] A. RONCHI, *Il canone minore: verso una filosofia della natura* (Milan: Feltrinelli, 2017), 58–63.

that we are witnessing "in what is called the technological form of life."[54] The phenomenological account of the absolute immanence of life in the flesh may serve, then, as a suitable hermeneutical tool to further investigate our symbiotic embodied interaction with digital technologies.

5. The Danger of Technicization

The present paper stems from an ongoing independent research project that is concerned with the question of what it means to be human in the digital era as we build an increasingly automated world. From a general perspective, this research aims to demonstrate how digital technology can be both sustainable and advanced at the same time: on the one hand, it can substitute, or integrate, as well as improve, older technologies, and, on the other hand, it constitutes our interface with them, opening up unpredictable, promising horizons of human-machine interaction.

How do we make use of digital technologies? How do we experience the devices that we use in our daily life, and what is the context of such experience? What does it mean to start from our embodied experience in order to organize the interaction with current and future technologies? These are some of the key questions considered by the research, which draws on the twofold meaning of 'digital,' understood both as a feature directly related to the reality of our body and to the functioning of advanced devices at one and the same time.

As argued in the previous sections, the aim of this paper has been to present phenomenology as a suitable method to philosophically approach digital technologies. This was done by stressing two basic points: first, not only does the use of technology confront us with specific kinds of objects, but, in the first place, with a mode of appearing, that is, of presence. To interpret the digital world by avoiding any naturalization of data represents the preliminary task for a phenomenological account of our symbiosis and synergy with it.

Second, interaction with technology relies on the very constitution of our own body, namely, the flesh, which shows a peculiar mode of presence, due to its fundamental self-givenness, which can be considered as a fruitful starting point for a comparison with the functioning of automata in particular. The following provisional conclusive remarks, while sketching out the historical contextualization of the research, also provide an additional point from the phenomenological perspective, which concerns the overall interpretation of the techno-ecosystem in which our life continuously evolves.

To begin with, it is worth mentioning that the question related to the entanglement between our living body and digital technology concerns the

---

[54] HUI, "What is a Digital Object?," 394.

present life-world organized into something that is increasingly computable and accessible via an attitude that in the phenomenological field has been called "calculative thinking," as opposed to "meditative thinking,"[55] or, more generally, computational rationality.[56] Furthermore, it was phenomenology itself that conceived the question concerning technology as a historical issue. In brief, as Patočka noted, while for Husserl the question concerning technology was seen within the crisis of European sciences,[57] in Heidegger's case, it was related to the notion of danger.[58] The Czech philosopher pinpoints that Husserl's phenomenological account of technology depends on his take on the crisis of modern science. Modern science, animated by a desire for universal rationality, becomes a *techne*, namely, "the art of a precise calculation of nature." Not only does the calculative attitude have an instrumental meaning, but it also flags a historical shift, in which the "subjective and unprecise" primordially given world is cloaked in "an ideational garb which transposes it into a precise universe of truths for all and so makes it calculable."[59] Thus, humanity runs the risk of losing the meaning of science understood as "the endless task of reason's immanent teleology."[60] In order to seek the root of the spiritual crisis of European culture, Patočka, in the wake of Husserl, invites us to see in the technicization of science a "radicalization of rationality."[61]

Heidegger radicalized Husserl's position, since his basic claim was that the essence of technology traces back to the history of Being, which pushes man to make use of all beings as a "standing-reserve."[62] In the technological age, 'to be' means to be used within an unceasing availability, to be caught in a

---

[55] HEIDEGGER, *Discourse on Thinking*.

[56] B. BACHIMONT, *Le sens de la technique: le numérique et le calcul* (Paris: Les Belles Lettres, 2010); S.J. GERSHMAN, E.J. HORVITZ, and J.B. TENENBAUM "Computational Rationality: A Converging Paradigm for Intelligence in Brains, Minds, and Machines," *Science* 349, no. 6245 (2015): 273–278, (https://doi.org/10.1126/science.aac6076) (4/22/2022).

[57] E. HUSSERL, *The Crisis of European Sciences and Transcendental Phenomenology. An Introduction to Phenomenological Philosophy*, trans. with an introduction by D. Carr (Evanston, IL: Northwestern University Press, 1970).

[58] Patočka expands upon this topic in his insightful conference held in 1973 in Varna (Bulgaria), devoted to the dangers of technicization in science, according to Husserl, and the essence of technology as danger, according to Heidegger (J. PATOČKA, "The Dangers of Technicization in Science according to E. Husserl and the Essence of Technology as Danger according to M. Heidegger," in *Jan Patočka, Philosophy and Selected Writings*, ed. E. Kohák (Chicago/London: The University of Chicago Press, 1989), 327–339.

[59] Ibid., 329.

[60] M. S. C. SCHUBACK, "Sacrifice and Salvation: Jan Patočka's Reading of Heidegger on the Question of Technology," in *Jan Patočka and the Heritage of Phenomenology: Centenary Papers*, ed. E. Abrams and I. Chvatík (Dordrecht: Springer Verlag, 2011), 24; R. DE MONTICELLI, *Il dono dei vincoli. Per leggere Husserl* (Milan: Garzanti, 2018), 35–37.

[61] PATOČKA, "The Dangers of Technicization," 329.

[62] M. HEIDEGGER, *The Question Concerning Technology and Other Essays*, trans. and with an introduction by W. Lovitt (New York; London: Garland Publishing, 1977), 27.

particular kind of use of beings that relies on a complex order in which both the subject and the object are involved as functions of the same "Enframing."[63] In addition, more than the use of specific things, Enframing refers to a general mode of revealing, or in other words, of coming to presence, which is why it also assumes a historical significance. The intricate system of techniques and apparatus that we call modern technology calls forth a total mobilization of beings, in which everything, including human beings, is understood as "what can be positioned anywhere and at any time, to whatever use and function, independently of all spatial and temporal determinations."[64]

In the demand for constant availability, one can easily recognize the mode of presence of digital contents in our daily and ordinary usage of digital devices. In this sense, digital technologies represent a coherent prosecution of the specific performance of modern techno-scientific development, that is, to assure the presence of all beings for unlimited usage. Accordingly, from a phenomenological perspective, digital technologies concur to the enhancement of Enframing, rather than being 'new' devices. Conversely, what is 'new' in digital technologies is the scope of the technological power expressed by the devices themselves.

Indeed, digital technologies tend to produce the organization of a new, specific "economy of presence,"[65] in terms of the demand for the ease of accessibility of things and resources, to which all beings are ideally called upon to be present under the pressure caused by calculative thinking; the latter, in turn, being a constant task elaborated by philosophy, a task that one can trace back to no less than Plato's doctrine of ideas.[66]

So, what does danger mean in this context? It is worth emphasizing, as Crowell does, that the phenomenological account of technicization as crisis and danger (particularly in Husserl, Heidegger, and Patočka) is not based on the risks related to a certain (potential or actual) misguided usage of technology, and does not focus on calamities, such as the escalation of the nuclear threat, the environmental devastation on a planetary scale, or the unregulated

---

[63] On the usage of 'Enframing' for the German *Gestell*, see the remarks by the translator of Heidegger's essay on technology: Enframing is fundamentally a "calling-forth," a "challenging claim" that gathers beings so as to reveal. This claim "enframes in that it assembles and orders. It puts into a framework or configuration everything that it summons forth, through an ordering for use that it is forever restructuring anew" (Ibid., xxix–xxxvii and 19). French translations of *Gestell* include *arraisonnement* or *dis-positif*, while in Italian it has been rendered as *impianto* or *dispositivo*.

[64] SCHUBACK, "Sacrifice and Salvation," 25. Schuback also provides a comprehensive discussion of Patočka's Varna Conference and the respective positions of Husserl and Heidegger on technology.

[65] R. SCHÜRMANN, *Heidegger On Being and Acting: From Principles to Anarchy*, trans. C.-M. Gros in collaboration with the author (Bloomington, IN: Indiana University Press, 1987).

[66] HEIDEGGER, *The Question Concerning Technology*, xxviii and 20.

technicization of labor.[67] Danger is much more radical than any risk we run in developing ever-more powerful and intelligent machines. In the phenomenological account, danger is essentially related to the prevalence of a specific mode of thinking, i. e. calculative thinking, in Enframing, according to which, as already mentioned, all beings tend to be considered as a 'standing-reserve' at our disposal. Basically, such a danger reveals itself to us in two ways. On the one hand, the calculative attitude of thinking tends to conceal the essence of thinking as meditation in a particularly persistent way,[68] with evident repercussions on research and education, for instance. On the other hand, Enframing, understood as the essence of technology, fosters the deceptive illusion of man in the position of the "lord of the earth," whereas it is precisely man's function as sovereign subject that is wiped out in the calling forth of Enframing that provokes the unlimited presence of all things for availability, in the first instance as an attitude of thinking, so that Heidegger calls this historical situation the "supreme danger."[69]

From this standpoint, when interpreted phenomenologically, digital technology brings about an expansion of the reach of technicization, by improving the mathematization of reality, which relies on the very immaterial components of the digital world. In our present time, we are witnessing an increasing demand for constant and reliable presence, not only of goods or commodities, but also of human beings, whose 'presence' is understood in terms of ease of access and availability. In this sense, digital technology contributes to the danger of technicization, insofar as it contributes to enhancing a world that is characterized by, and organized via a particular, radical rationality that goes back to calculative thinking, which is to be further investigated.

---

[67] According to Crowell, the danger concerning technology refers to a "danger of responsibility," that is, "a commitment that cannot be rationally grounded since it grounds rationality" (S. G. CROWELL, "The Challenge of Heidegger's Approach to Technology: A Phenomenological Reading," in *Heidegger on Technology*, ed. A. J. Wendland, C. Merwin, and C. Hadjioannou, 81–83). See also CROWELL, *Normativity and Phenomenology* for a wider discussion of this topic. As Patočka stressed, the danger of technicization should not be seen in "technology enslaving man." Rather, the danger is related to human beings losing the possibility (which is also a power) of establishing a relationship with the "historical character of original truth:" "And therein precisely lies the danger. The uncovering that prevails at the essential core of technology necessarily loses sight of uncovering itself, concealing the essential core of truth in an unfamiliar way and so closing man's access to what he himself is – a being capable of standing in an original relation to the truth" (PATOČKA, "The Dangers of Technicization," 330–31). In brief, in the experience of radical sacrifice, as opposed to and incompatible with both calculative thinking and the technicization of science, he sees the opportunity for the "overcoming of the technical understanding of being" (ibid., 338–39).

[68] CROWELL, "The Challenge of Heidegger's Approach," 83–84.

[69] HEIDEGGER, *The Question Concerning Technology*, 26–27.

V. Ethics

Humanity as the Development of Intersubjective Giving and Receiving

Emily Hodges

1. Introduction

This paper will argue that the idea of "humanity" can be understood as a three-part normative project of moral development. I depart from a Kantian account of morality, though I heavily reconstruct and move beyond Kant in significant ways. Section one explains humanity as a project of individual moral development, specifically the development of one's understanding of unconditional value, the construction of self-concept, and the development of virtue. Section two then discusses humanity as a project of community development that supports individual moral development. I follow Kant in calling this community "ethical community," while drawing also on the concept of Buddhist sangha. I will show that by understanding ethical community clearly, we see that we need not worry about conflicting ideas of how the project should unfold; diversity is retained, and conflict acknowledged, while a single idea of how the normative project unfolds is denied. In the third section, the concepts of giving and receptivity will show themselves to constitute the fundamental orientation within which humanity develops. I draw on Dilthey's idea of what I call the poetic attitude, Jessica Benjamin's intersubjectivity psychoanalysis, and the indigenous conceptual system of giving as described by Kimmerer. I will suggest that the normative project can only be understood when its source, the seed of humanity that brings dignity to the individual, is treated as a divine gift itself meant to be the source of giving and receiving. As such, I reinterpret the meaning of "divine grace" as explored by Kant to manifest through individual acts within ethical community.[1]

---

[1] I would like to thank Jesús Enrique Moreno for his love, support, and thoughtful discussions; Sarah Davidson for pointing me to the concept of sangha; and my mother Cathy Dugan and the participants of the 2019 Claremont Philosophy of Religion Conference for their wonderful conversations and helpful feedback.

2. Humanity as a Normative Project of Individual Moral Development

In this section I suggest that humanity ought to be understood as an *individual* project of normative moral development, wherein humanity is both an internal seed and that which is developed out of this seed. I hold that the seed is that most fundamental source of agency, morality, and creativity, and has intrinsic unconditional value – what Kant calls dignity.[2] Moral action is acting from this dignity, and the moral value of actions has its source in this dignity. In order to understand humanity, then, we must discuss value. We can have varieties of value frameworks and can value all sorts of different things, yet all valuing is sourced in the conception of unconditional intrinsic value. I will argue that the dignity framework for value must be our fundamental framework. To understand this, let us discuss value frameworks.

3. Value Frameworks

To act immorally, for Kant, is to treat oneself as having unconditional value while treating all others as means to one's own interests.[3] I suggest that this is to misunderstand one's internal seed of humanity, of which we always have a dim awareness, by interpreting it within a value framework of "price." Here, one interprets one's internal value as the only source of unconditional value, interpreting the value of others as derived from oneself.[4] Kant calls such derivative value "price." I suggest that price involves a comparative hierarchy, where all things have more or less value in light of their position in the hierarchy. Every position other than the supreme position has only conditional value and can be sold and used as a means towards obtaining other items deemed more valuable by the supreme position. The supreme position is given unconditional

---

[2] See especially 4:434–437 in I. KANT, *Groundwork of the Metaphysics of Morals*, in *Practical Philosophy, the Cambridge Edition of the Works of Immanuel Kant*, ed. and trans. M.J. Gregor (Cambridge: Cambridge University Press, 1996). See also I. KANT, *The Critique of Practical Reason*, in *Practical Philosophy, the Cambridge Edition of the Works of Immanuel Kant*, ed. and trans. M.J. Gregor (Cambridge: Cambridge University Press, 1996). The former will be abbreviated as *the Groundwork*, the later as *CrPr*. Following common practice in Kant scholarship, citations to Kant's works refer to the volume and page numbers of the Akademie edition.

[3] See *the Groundwork*, *CrPr*, and *Religion within the Bounds of Mere Reason*. The latter will be abbreviated as "*Religion*." I utilize the translation available in I. KANT, *Religion and Rational Theology, The Cambridge Edition of the Works of Immanuel Kant*, ed. A. W. Wood and translated by G. di Giovanni (Cambridge: Cambridge University Press, 1996).

[4] Wood forwards a similar interpretation in A. W. WOOD, *Kant's Ethical Thought* (Cambridge: Cambridge University Press, 1999). Here he holds that immoral action is rooted in taking oneself to have "greater self worth" than others, such that one wants "always" to be "on top" (290). He here quotes Kant at *Religion*, 6:435. I also hold that this standpoint involves seeing oneself as the creator of all value, thus denying others as sources of value-creation.

value as that which will never be traded for something else and is seen both as independent of all other positions and as the source all other values.

While immoral action involves acting from within this value framework and viewing oneself in the supreme position, the framework can also be applied to social structures. When applied in this way, I suggest that value becomes conceived as synonymous with domination – for value is accorded to the individual who is able to retain superiority, keeping others in positions of inferiority.[5] If two individuals working within the price framework interact, each will seek to dominate the other. The individual who feels dominated by the other will feel their sense of value shattered as they re-interpret themselves within the price framework as something with only conditional value. Yet this reinterpretation will conflict with their internal sense of unconditional worth, which they now see as having no avenue for being interpreted and exercised in the world. Furthermore, within complex social arrangements, an individual will find himself in positions of both inferiority and superiority. Yet the price framework only grants the supreme position unconditional value, so successful acts of domination within mid-rank positions will always be tempered by subordination to superiors, and thus cannot fully express or make sense of the internal awareness of one's own unconditional value.

We might now ask: why grant value to acts of domination? I suggest that this framework is fueled in two ways. First the need to control others is centrally rooted in fear of being dominated.[6] Such fear is based on the framework itself, where interactions are understood as competition for worth. Thus, one must fear that one's value is always threatened. But I suggest that this fear belies a deeper problem, for this framework itself relies on a concept of unconditional value while relegating it to only one position. The second source that fuels this framework, then, is misinterpretation of one's internal value. I suggested above that an individual will feel an internal conflict between his awareness of his intrinsic value and his position of inferiority. Within this framework, one can only attempt to resolve the conflict by striving to attain and then maintain the supreme position.

---

[5] The most basic form of such human interaction is that of direct domination-submission as seen in Kant's raw state of nature, the hypothetical position before social structures. Here, Kant holds that because individuals have no sense of external security, mere social proximity, that is, the possibility of interaction, involves the threat of violence and domination. See *Religion*, 6:93–4. See also I. KANT, "Toward Perpetual Peace," in *Practical Philosophy, the Cambridge Edition of the Works of Immanuel Kant*, ed. and trans. M.J. Gregor, (Cambridge: Cambridge University Press, 1996), 311–352. The footnote at 8:349 of this work is especially relevant. I suggest that such individuals must already be bringing the price framework to such interactions for the situation to lack such external security. We need not address the feeling of lack of external security, but the value framework itself, that is, the way that individuals are approaching each other.

[6] In *Kant's Ethical Thought*, Wood also mentions fear as the basis at page 290 but does not elaborate.

Nonetheless, even an individual holding the supreme position cannot fully resolve this internal conflict. He cannot feel his sense of value fully secured and expressed – for a person's value is here *externally* granted based on successful and continual exercise of domination which maintains the social position. So even the supreme dominator is not free from internal conflict; he is always at risk of losing his value if unable to retain his position. Thus, the price framework cannot make sense of *unconditional* value after all – for we see that all value is conditional upon some position; nor can it explain why we would want to take up the price framework as the guiding interpretation of value in the first place – it can only explain how, through fear and internal conflict, it can be self-maintaining.

Let us next consider what I call the moral merit framework of value. It is tempting within a certain Kantian picture to grant individuals value based on the moral actions they carry out, that is, to see the value of the individual as conditional on successful moral action. In such cases, immoral action either detracts or at the least does not add value, making individuals who have carried out more immoral actions inferior in value to "morally better" individuals. On such an account no individual has unconditional value, but only gains value by "meriting" it. The problem here is that value is again made conditional and extrinsic, something that can be achieved or lost. Furthermore, unconditional value is not something one can have more or less of; one simply has it. And if everyone, has it, one person cannot have more of it than another. So, this framework cannot help us understand unconditional value.

In contrast to accounts that grant extrinsic value based on some accomplishment, the dignity framework accounts for unconditional value as *intrinsic*.[7] Here, individuals already always are unconditionally valuable. This is called dignity, and one's dignity is the source from which all value flows.[8] One does not treat oneself as the source of the value of others but sees each individual as

---

[7] Kant famously claims right at the start of *the Groundwork* (4:393) that the "good will" is the only thing with unconditional value. He goes on to discuss the good will as a will that acts purely from respect for the moral law. At this point we might wonder: How can the self have unconditional value if it seems only to have value when it has a good will, that is, acts purely from the moral law? Kant goes on to insist that the good will is good even if not successful (4:394). He also explains that the good will is the will that is determined by pure practical reason (4:412–413). I interpret pure practical reason to be reasoning from the moral law. The moral law is what I consider the fundamental principle of action. It is what makes action possible; it is that principle from which we act. It is from this fundamental principle that we have an awareness of our own dignity. Yet we may attempt to corrupt and misuse this principle and this awareness, attempting to bury and contort them. Thus, I claim that we always already do have a good will, but it is not what Kant calls a "perfectly good will" because we can layer corruption, vice, and immoral action on top of it, losing sight of it. I am developing this interpretation in more detail in a separate paper.

[8] The source of this internal seed of dignity will be explored in the last section of the paper.

their own source of value. Here actions have moral worth in so far as they are carried out from this source of dignity, and one has dignity because the purpose of one's being is to act from dignity. As I will show throughout the rest of the paper, dignity thus has its own principle of action, which is to respect the dignity of all individuals. As such, I suggest that the purpose of action is not to attain a value we do not yet have through competition, domination and accomplishment. It is rather to express, manifest, strengthen, enrich, and deepen understanding of the internal unconditional value that we all already have.

4. Cultivating One's Inner Seed

This is the framework within which the developmental project of humanity must be guided. Kant claims that "humanity" is the source of our dignity.[9] I suggest that we understand "humanity" here as the ability to create our empirical self through our actions in a way that honors the dignity of all. In terms of value, the individual project of humanity involves developing one's understanding of the dignity framework and *acting from* a fundamental understanding of value as dignity. While Kant may have held that we all see ourselves as starting our development from the price framework, I suggest that it is irrelevant which framework an individual starts within.[10] What matters is that in any case, one always has a dim awareness and feeling of one's own unconditional value. Dignity always *already* exists in the empirical world, in so far as each of us exists. I suggest that part of our work is to develop this seed of awareness to understand the dignity framework and make it the fundamental framework within which we carry out our actions, understand ourselves, and relate to others.

Now, this seed does not automatically cause our actions or construct our sense of self in the empirical world. It is not a mechanism that controls the way we act or present ourselves in the world. Our individual project is to develop this seed into an empirical character[11], to create what I call a morally healthy self. Individual moral development, unlike a mechanical process, is thoroughly normative: we *ought* to construct ourselves from this seed, and it is our *own*

---

[9] What exactly Kant means by "humanity" is a topic of much debate in the literature. I do not have the space to engage with this debate but will merely suggest my own reconstruction.

[10] In discussing "radical evil" and original sin in "Religion," Kant sometimes seems committed to this starting place. However, I argue that this is not required for his account. Presumably, we could start within any sort of value framework.

[11] I interpret empirical character, in Kant, as developed out of the three predispositions to the good. It ought to be centered in the predisposition of personality. See *Religion*, 6:27–6:28, 6:29 fn, 6:35, 6:46–49.

work to do so. To take on the project involves claiming one's "higher vocation"[12] to develop oneself from this internal source. This does not involve following preset rules or going through the motions of what one is told to do. It involves *taking responsibility* for one's development and actions.[13] This is not the responsibility of blame, but of taking on and accepting a certain way of being that one must construct oneself. As that which has been developed, humanity is moral character, made up of ever-developing abilities and ways of being that flow from dignity.

Development of one's humanity centrally involves the cultivation of virtue and respect. Virtue involves strengthening the focus on the internal seed and remaining resolved to act from it.[14] Kant explains that the strength of virtue must be "acquired".[15] Similarly, I argue that respect is always present but must be strengthened. Respect is the feeling of awareness of the most fundamental principle of action, which is the same as the awareness of ourselves as having dignity and is itself strengthened through contemplation on this principle. Virtue, in turn, is strengthened as respect is strengthened, which in turn further strengthens respect.[16] Thus our most central work in developing our seed of humanity is contemplation: contemplation on our internal dignified humanity strengthens our feeling and understanding of that seed as it unfolds in our self-understanding, understanding of others, and our actions – thus supporting us in construction of the dignity framework, the empirical moral self, and our actions.

---

[12] Kant utilizes this terminology, especially in CrPr to discuss the moral self that has committed to self-legislating and acting from the moral law. See especially CrPr 5:87 and 5:108. Consider also 8:142 in I. KANT, "What does it mean to orient oneself in thinking (1786)," in *Religion and Rational Theology, The Cambridge Edition of the Works of Immanuel Kant*, ed. A. W. Wood and trans. G. di Giovanni (Cambridge: Cambridge University Press, 1996), 1–18. This work will be abbreviated as "Orient."

[13] This idea of "taking responsibility" is my own, though I draw inspiration from Kant's characterization of personality. See *Religion*, 6:26–28 and 6:48–49, as well as the general idea of responsibility as a virtue.

[14] In this way, it is a strength in resisting the pull of what Kant calls the inclinations. See 6:380 in *The Metaphysics of Morals*. I refer to the translation printed in I. KANT, *Practical Philosophy, the Cambridge Edition of the Works of Immanuel Kant*, ed. and trans. M. J. Gregor (Cambridge: Cambridge University Press, 1996). From now on this will be abbreviated as *MM*. Within my account, this is an indirect strength in resisting frameworks of extrinsic value.

[15] See *MM* 6:397

[16] Kant discusses this especially at *MM* 6:397–400.

5. Humanity as a Normative Project of Community

The second way of thinking about humanity is as the development of a certain kind of community. Though tempting, we should resist thinking of this community as a *collection* of autonomous individuals. It is, rather, a system constituted by intersubjective activities. I hold it is a dynamic and supportive intersubjective framework that itself can be developed and expanded through continual work, but that relies most centrally on a commitment to individual moral development.

I get inspiration for this idea from Kant's discussion of "ethical community," and will follow him in using this term. For Kant, community occurs when individuals join together under a certain principle of unity. Ethical communities are formed when individuals freely join together under the principle of supporting virtue cultivation.[17] Virtue cultivation is individual but takes place within a framework of mutual support. It is important to note that this community does not have the goal of perfect moral action.[18] Nor does ethical community *cause* moral action or make it impossible for individuals to act immorally. The role of an individual in relation to others' development is not to make others moral, "fix" others, or tell them what to do. Entering into ethical community is not a program that promises a goal. Rather, I interpret the unity of ethical community as supporting personal growth, with all of the mistakes and difficulties it will involve. The supportive roles of individuals involve providing trust, compassion, perspective, and comfort as individuals face their own challenges.

This concept can be enriched by considering the Buddhist idea of sangha. Thich Nhat Hanh describes sangha as a "refuge" we return to, within which we can find inner stability.[19] This is a voluntary spiritual community that provides an "energy" that is created by the continual work of each individual: we "contribute to that energy" through attentiveness and activity, so that "we build sangha by coming back to ourselves through mindful breathing."[20] We find centered presentness within ourselves and with those around us, bringing

---

[17] Virtue is, for Kant, "a disposition conformed with law *from respect* for law, and thus consciousness of a continuing propensity to transgression or at least impurity, that is, an admixture of many spurious (not moral) motives to observe the law, hence a self-esteem combined with humility [...]" (*CrPr* 5:128). On my account, virtue is the strength to remain focused on awareness of the fundamental principle of one's actions, the awareness of one's dignity and the dignity of all, that is, one's internal seed of humanity. This awareness involves "self-esteem" involved in having committed, and the "humility" of knowing that the work is continual.

[18] For Kant on ethical community see especially *Religion*, 6:93–96, 6:99–100, 6:101–106.

[19] T. N. HANH, *Joyfully Together: The Art of Building Harmonious Community* (Berkeley, CA: Parallax Press, 2005), 8. See also T. N. HANH, *Going Home: Jesus and Buddha as Brothers* (New York: Riverhead Books, 1999), especially 47 and 120–122.

[20] HANH, *Joyfully*, 8–9

mindful presence to the moment's activity, so that sangha is a way of living and practicing together.[21] The center of sangha is the "home" within each individual. Mindfulness is continually coming back to one's own inner center, and it is within this center that we find a sense of belonging with our surroundings. In this sense, we can be "at home" at any moment, in any place.[22] The sangha supports us in finding that inner center, such that we can "take refuge" in the sangha[23]; indeed, the central purpose of the sangha is the work of returning to this place. Sangha is thus the communal activity of continual daily practice of inner cultivation of centeredness.[24] We can see that individuals within a sangha can have conflicts and imperfections; our work in sangha is not to prove ours is the right answer or avoid conflict. Instead, the purpose of sangha is to be a supportive compassionate community for personal work.

Applying these insights to the concept of ethical community, we see that involvement in ethical community is not about acting perfectly morally but is an approach of mindful activity that involves supporting and being supported by others who are also engaged in their own process of moral development. The central principle of unity is virtue development, that is, development of committed mindful focus on developing the seed of humanity.

6. How Should the Project Proceed?

Humanity as a single universal community can be understood as the ideal system that unifies all particular ethical communities, and thus as the single community of all individuals developing the seed of their humanity and supporting each other in this development. It may seem that in moving towards unifying particular communities, conflict will be inevitable as communities argue about the "best" or "right" way of reaching this ideal universal unity. I propose that such a problem actually dissolves when we understand what ethical community truly means.

Let us start by distinguishing between ethical community and project-focused community. Project-focused community seeks to manifest certain approaches to the good life. Its members are united around a certain project, such as a hobby, interest, or product; the focus is the success or survival of the project itself. Such projects are meaningful parts of life, but they are only conditional. We can promote them, but we should not connect them to our most fundamental sense of self and value. If such projects are taken as fundamental, we treat "our" idea

---

[21] Consider HANH, *Joyfully*, 11; HANH, *Going*, 49.
[22] HANH, *Going*, 40–43.
[23] Ibid., 47.
[24] Ibid., 93.

of the good life as fundamentally superior to "theirs," which can lead to dehumanization and domination. Furthermore, when such projects fail, our sense of value is threatened if we have identified our value with the success of the project. In other words, if the central focus of humanity is taken to be a particular idea of the good life, acting from dignity has been traded for the goal of manifesting a certain kind good life, which can only work within a framework of extrinsic value that utilizes everyone towards the success of the project.

In contrast, humanity as ethical community does not seek to promote a single idea of the good life. It is focused on developing the unconditional value of the seed of humanity within each individual. Recall that this seed is the *source* of value, and it already exists within each of us. Our project is not to bring it into existence through one particular idea of the good life, but to allow it to develop within each individual, which may manifest in multitudes of different ideas of the good. This is to say that development doesn't have a goal to be reached. It is better conceptualized as an activity that continues to strengthen and unfold in a multitude of ways. Indeed, its development is not as an idea of the good, but as creative abilities to act from dignity in the variety of situations one finds in one's world. Thus, while the seed is that source of creativity, responsibility, and activity which makes it possible to pursue particular ideas of the good life, it is not defined by any particular good life.

While ethical community must be distinguished from project-focused communities, humanity does not exist removed from the embodied world. In order to develop, one must commit to certain projects, goals, and manifestations of the good. Yet because there is no single highest idea of the good life, but many different ways of manifesting the good life, an attitude of commitment but nonattachment arises: we live, work, and play in the embodied world with an understanding that the projects we have chosen are not the single correct way.

We can explore this further by considering the right. Humanity is the source of right action, and its development is the development of the ability to act from dignity in varieties of ways. This may, at times, take place within a shared project of manifesting ideas of the good. However, one must also be able to retain respect even when understanding and shared creation are not currently possible. Even within conflict between different ideas of the good, right action is possible. That is, right action – or acting from dignity – does not require shared understanding or common ideas of the good. The fundamental commitment to the idea of ethical community can hold. Each individual still has the capacity to respect the humanity in the other.

But how can one respect the humanity in the other when understanding and sharing have broken down? Respect may involve a respectful distance, an understanding that the creation of a shared project is not currently possible. Difference between projects is accepted as one continues to manifest one's own project while also respecting another's commitment to their project. I do not mean to oversimplify or idealize here, for such breakdown might devolve into fears and ideas that the other is bad, wrong, evil, or disrespectful. Furthermore, such breakdown might easily devolve into accusations that one or both sides are not committed to ethical community and are acting immorality. Finally, nonattachment means that one must sometimes realize that one must let go of or radically transform one's projects when they become outdated or inappropriate. Maneuvering this territory is tricky and part of the challenge of developing virtue in a living world. By remaining focused on acting from one's own center, one can see that the other is not in their core alien or evil, but an individual attempting to manifest humanity in the world, and as such still to be treated with respect. Such pluralism is not relativism, but an understanding of the limitations of being a human that has chosen particular forms of the good to manifest, which may lead to misunderstanding and alienation within encounters with others. We must remember that our work is *our work* – to take responsibility for our own, not others', development. The fundamental principle of interaction is not the harmony of a single shared good life, but the ability to respect and support development of humanity within every interaction.

7. Humanity as Intersubjective Orientation of Giving and Receiving: Intersubjective Orientation

This brings us to the third aspect of humanity: the first two aspects are mutually interactive, creative, and co-constructive, and this intertwining takes place through humanity as an *intersubjective orientation*. I suggest that the seed of humanity can be understood as an internal compass that orients the individual in a moral world, a world that works within the dignity framework. This orientation centers the individual in a world seen as ethical community, wherein actions are fundamentally two-directional interactions rather than one-way acts, as well as creative manifestations of dignity rather than goal-directed means towards obtaining some object of value.

We can gain some headway on understanding this orientation by drawing on Dilthey's idea of what I call the poetic attitude. For Dilthey, humans have a capacity for approaching the world poetically.[25] A developed poetic attitude involves an openness and curiosity in the present moment, but one that continually and organically draws value connections within the various aspects of one's psyche.[26] Dilthey contrasts this approach with that of pragmatic and

---

[25] See especially W. DILTHEY, *Selected Works*, Vol 5: *Poetry and Experience*, ed. R. Makkreel and F. Rodi (Princeton, NJ: Princeton University Press, 1985), 129, 243, 291.
[26] We start with a poetic predisposition which can be developed into a poetic attitude. See DILTHEY, *Poetry*, 89, 104, 241, 252.

theoretical activity, each of which approach action as goal-oriented and which thus artificially regulate activity and experience.[27] The activities that flow from the poetic attitude allow a rich experience to present itself, making connections and playing with the rich possibilities present in a given moment. I suggest the intersubjective orientation must involve such a poetic openness and curiosity that engages with the world as a rich community offering its own values and creations. I go beyond Dilthey in suggesting that we approach this richness not just as a creative kaleidoscope of imaginative processes, but as our own interpretations of the creative expressions of a world of subjects. To recognize the dignity of another is to recognize a creative being offering their own value-laden creative interpretations of life, that is, their own ideas of the good, and as a being who is capable of doing so from dignity. This is to see the world as having not a single source, but as having its source in the humanity of each individual. By cultivating our intersubjective orientation, we can creatively construct a life that can find dynamic harmony with other individuals, even when difference, distance, and diversity abound. This is not just an open mind nor empathy, but a sort of creative nonattachment that can play with and appreciate the way that others approach life and construct values of their own.

This brings me to a key point about activity within the intersubjective orientation: rather than conceiving of action as a subject acting upon an object, action is here conceived as a two-way relation of subjects. I draw inspiration from the work of intersubjectivity psychoanalyst Jessica Benjamin. Benjamin considers the starting position of interaction as recognizing another as a subject, as a "separate center of feeling and perception" and "with whom we are acting reciprocally."[28] From here, we "build relational systems" together, within interactions, as a "principle" or way of relating (not as a product).[29] This involves not "submission" but "surrender" – the ability to be with the other as a subject, allowing the other to have a perspective and role in co-constructing the relational system.[30] Breakdowns devolve into individuals feeling as if they are being treated as objects that are "done to" rather than subjects that one "co-creates" with.[31] The dynamic is like an ever-evolving dance.[32] It can accommodate things that are "bad" for an individual without equating badness to "destruction."[33]

---

[27] This is addressed particularly at DILTHEY, *Poetry*, 239–41.
[28] J. BENJAMIN, "Beyond Doer and Done: An Intersubjective View of Thirdness," *Psychoanalytic Quarterly* 73 (2004): 5–6.
[29] Ibid., 6.
[30] Ibid., 7–8.
[31] Ibid., 9.
[32] Ibid., 17–18.
[33] Ibid., 27. This is related to the idea that a subject is also always more than a single object, a single concept, a single, creative project, a single way of approaching life. Part of recognizing another as a subject is recognizing this overflow. This idea is present throughout Benjamin's work as well as Hanh's *Going Home*.

The other does not need to share the same ideas of the good, I suggest, but simply "the capacity for recognition,"[34] – on my account, the capacity to see the other as a subject that offers and receives, who allows dignity to be the source of their actions, and allows their actions to be interactions that create new aspects of relationship together.

Now, I suggest that in orienting oneself within a world of subjects with dignity, one does not orient one's actions as doing or being done to.[35] Rather, action is approached as a *simultaneous* dynamic of giving and receiving. Here one *offers* one's words, skills, creative ideas, and perspective to the interaction as co-construction, and the offering is *received* in some way. An offering can be rejected, but to reject an offering is to receive it in a certain way. To receive with dignity, it to receive its thoughtful intent, and thus to receive it as a gift in spirit, to give thanks and show gratitude for the gift, while yet acknowledging one's own needs and boundaries. Actions are not here concerned with causing the other to do something, but offering something for the other to work with, such that every response, every receiving, is also a gift.

This orientation is the fundamental way of approaching action within the dignity framework. Here acting from dignity is itself a gift; an action sourced in dignity is not domination, control, nor a means to a goal, but an offering of value and an expression of recognition of value, a gift from one subject to another. In terms of development, the orientation is woven within and between individual and community development. One approaches one's own capacities as gifts to be developed for oneself and one's community, gifts of creative shared construction and support. Ethical community itself is approached and received as a gift of support, with the gifts of others received applicably.

Botanist and writer Robin Wall Kimmerer draws a sharp distinction between a gift and a commodity, defining a gift as part of a system of relationships rather than a system of transactions. Gifts cannot be treated as property to be bought and sold; they cannot be *owned*. To utilize an item within a transaction is to make it into a commodity, to give it a price. A gift is treated always as something given with no expectation of payment; it is appreciated and honored.[36] Yet it is not simply *there*; it is given to you, for you. She says: "A gift comes to you through no action of your own, free, having moved toward you without your beckoning [...] Your only role is to be open-eyed and present."[37]

---

[34] See "Recognition and Destruction," in J. BENJAMIN, *Like Subjects, Love Objects* (New Haven, CT: Yale University Press, 1995), 31–33. Here Benjamin includes a useful discussion of the capacity for mutual recognition and its development.

[35] This framework of action involves such dualities as acting and being acted upon, activity and passivity, subject and object.

[36] See especially 26–27 of R. W. KIMMERER, *Braiding Sweetgrass: Indigenous Wisdom, Scientific Knowledge, and the Teachings of Plants*, (Minnesota, MN: Milkweed Editions, 2013).

[37] Ibid., 23–24.

But being "open-eyed and present" within a system of relationships is to be attentive in some important ways. As we will see, accepting a gift involves taking a wide and systematically sensitive perspective, allowing one to be present to the relationships strengthened by the gift and open to the joys and responsibilities involved in caring for and cultivating the gift.

Kimmerer describes the "gift economy" as a viewpoint wherein the entire world is approached as a "gift in motion."[38] Such a worldview is foundational to many indigenous cultures, including her own Potawatomi culture. On her interpretation of this viewpoint we are all recipients of the world's gifts, and as receivers we have responsibilities to do the work that enables the gifts to be received, as well as to receive with gratitude and respect.[39] Yet we are not just receivers; as participants we are tasked with cultivating and sharing the gifts we have received.[40] Indeed, gifts are meant to be kept "in motion"[41] – they are meant to be shared, for they are an abundance that belongs to the entire community. Fundamentally, the gift is not the object itself, but the activity of giving; it is the giving and receiving that is meant to be kept in motion.[42] But there is an appropriateness to the motion. The gift is for the whole community, though at any given moment it is bestowed upon a certain individual who then takes responsibility for caring for it, allowing it to support her in her work.

---

[38] Ibid., 31.

[39] Gratitude is discussed especially at ibid., 69. Showing respect for the gift and the giver by taking responsibility for caring for the gift is discussed at ibid., 166, 189. In this way, the gift involves a duty, ibid., 310.

[40] See especially ibid., 18, 30, 115, 134, and 361. See also the chapter "Skywoman Falling," where Kimmerer tells the indigenous creation story of Skywoman. This story tells of the creation of "Turtle Island" – now also known as North America. She discusses this story as providing a fundamental identity and orientation for human action and belonging in the world. Here we see that gratitude is a way of receiving, while expressing and celebrating gratitude is a way of offering a new gift, and of carrying the giving forward. This is an especially interesting story, for its content presents this framework of giving, while the storytelling itself is both a gift and an act of appreciation.

[41] See especially ibid., 165; she also uses the terminology of "circulation" at ibid., 28.

[42] Another perspective of the world as gift is articulated by philosopher Kyle Whyte in: K. P. Whyte, "Food Sovereignty, Justice and Indigenous Peoples: An Essay on Settler Colonialism and Collective Continuance," in *Oxford Handbook on Food Ethics*, eds. A. Barnhill, T. Doggett, and A. Egan (Oxford: Oxford University Press, 2018.) Retrieved from: Oxford Handbooks Online eBook. Here Whyte explains one indigenous viewpoint that views such food sources as salmon and rice as key participants in the vitality, adaptability, and resilience of an ecological system. Whyte explains that ecological systems are seen as having what he calls "collective capacities" for adaptation that are facilitated by human stewardship. As such, individuals are meant to respect and honor not a given commodity, nor just a given ecosystem, but a vital system of dynamic and interwoven processes that includes continual exercise of capacities of human stewardship and human cultural vitality. Such a system is not made up of commodities or units, but of participants, each with its own gifts to give (See especially 352–357). Thus, the salmon, the rice, and the human, for example, are each key participants with their own gifts to offer to secure the vitality of the whole system.

8. Humanity as a Divine Gift

I have presented an account of humanity as a way of orienting towards the self and others as beings with the seed of humanity, who have the responsibility to develop the gifts sourced in this seed in order to create themselves and their communities as living dynamic manifestations of dignity. But now we are ready to ask: where does the seed come from? I suggest that it can only be understood as a divine gift that has been given freely to each individual. It cannot be understood as a reward to be earned, an accomplishment to be achieved, a commodity to be purchased, nor even as a brute fact that just is. It is the source of action as giving and receiving, and itself must be received openly as a gift, indeed, as the most sacred divine gift.

In Kantian terminology this is a "predisposition" that we must claim as our "highest vocation,"[43] understanding it as having "divine origin."[44] Indeed, Kant claims we must necessarily presuppose that we are acting within a moral world wherein the internal moral principle, universal ethical community,[45] and the divine *actually* exist.[46] I interpret this as follows: 1) we take the seed of humanity as actual, including taking it as the source of value, moral development, and the fundamental principle of action 2) we take ourselves to live within an actual universal intersubjective community of individuals who can support our work, who we in turn can support, and who can orient within the world utilizing the dignity framework, and 3) we take the divine as present and actively supportive within this intersubjective framework.

It is tempting to say that we cannot take this presupposition as actual because we see too much wrongdoing in the world, but that we might instead take it as an ideal standard to strive towards.[47] This temptation should be rejected. For Kant, the presupposition is not empirically descriptive, but morally normative. That is, it is not something proven within theoretical reasoning, but something unconditional and necessary for practical reason: we must take it as fundamentally actual in order to act at all,[48] and in order to commit to our moral

---

[43] Kant calls it the predisposition to personality and defines it as the incorruptible predisposition to act from the moral principle. Consider *Religion*, 6:26–28, and 7:45–47. I suggest that this predisposition is the seed of humanity which, when taken up, is cultivated into a moral disposition and sense of self.

[44] *Religion*, 6:50.

[45] What Kant calls the highest good I interpret as the ideal universal ethical community made manifest.

[46] See "What does it mean to orient oneself in thinking," especially 8:139. This essay will be abbreviated as "Orient."

[47] It may seem that Kant holds this view in his discussion of the evil of human nature. See, for instance, *Religion*, 6:32–3.

[48] I interpret action here as including thinking, so that practical reason is more fundamental than theoretical reason. Kant seems to take this view in "Orient." See especially 8:138–143.

development.⁴⁹ It is a practical faith, a way of approaching life with the understanding that to act at all is to act within a divine moral framework; action is always morally-valued action, the self is essentially a being acting within this framework (not an empirical framework), and this framework is divine. I suggest that though at a given moment we may see ourselves as empirical beings faltering and imperfect, the most fundamental being of each of us and the most fundamental relations between us are sourced in and expressions of dignity, and this dignity is divine.⁵⁰

Now, I go beyond Kant in suggesting that we view our internal seed as a divine gift that is divinely bestowed upon us. It is meant to be received gratefully and thoughtfully, to be responsibly taken care of and cultivated. It is the gift that brings us into the world of dignity. It opens up the possibility of understanding and experiencing intrinsic value within ourselves and emanating from others, and of constructing ourselves and communities as manifestations of dignity. Like our internal seed, the moral world is a gift already actual; we do not have to earn it, win it, or accomplish it. Yet it is made apparent in embodied actions which in turn construct our empirical characters, contingent communities, practices, and ideas of the good. The moral world is thus made present or accessible to us when we are able to receive the divine seed as a gift, and from that acceptance carry forth that gift within our own activities. The ideal ethical community is not a collection of individuals who never act immorally, but the fundamental way of acting together that we strive to remain centered within. Faith is thus also the practical understanding that no matter how bad things seem to get, the world is still fundamentally, at its core, given to us already as a moral world whose source is dignity.

Our work is to help ourselves understand how to participate within such a world from our internal source, to accept the fundamental self and others as the divine expressions that they are. When interactions break down into immoral actions, the world does not cease to have its source in dignity; the source remains, ready to be taken up again. Similarly, when we falter and get lost, our dignity is not taken from us as punishment, cost, or effect, but remains the source of our actions and capacities, waiting to be properly received and taken up. Part of our work is allowing ourselves to feel worthy of accepting the gift, without thinking we must *do* something to merit it. Another part of our work is, in receiving our gift, to utilize it responsibly in order to develop ourselves and offer support to others.

At "Orient," 8:319 Kant notes that the presupposition of a divine creator applies to theoretical reasoning as well but is here only conditional: we must make the presupposition "if we want to judge" about certain things, namely first causes.

⁴⁹ "Orient," 8:142.
⁵⁰ Kant holds that the divine must be actual; it cannot be taken as a mere ideal ("Orient," 8:138–139, 8:142–143).

Though we do not have to do anything to deserve the divine gifts, I suggest that this intersubjective account helps us understand what we are meant to do in order to be able to receive divine giving – or divine grace. Kant held that we cannot achieve success in our moral work by ourselves; we require the additional "supplement" of divine grace.[51] Yet he held that we cannot wait for divine support to arrive before beginning the work. We must *prepare* ourselves to be able to receive divine grace.[52] I suggest that though divine grace is not something earned or merited, we can fail to be ready for grace by failing to be open to it and thus being unable to receive it; as such, it will not "arrive" until we are ready.[53] Within my account, divine grace flows through individual actions sourced in dignity – all acts treated as offerings of support. In order to receive such support, part of our cultivation of virtue involves cultivating openness to receptivity and finding centeredness in the dignity framework so that we can understand how to receive grace as the divine gift offered from another within intersubjective interactions as we develop ethical community together.

---

[51] While I do not have the space here to explore Kant's account of grace and my divergences from it, I retain his understanding of grace as that external supplement to our internal work of virtue. For my purposes here, we need focus on no more.

[52] See *Religion*, 6:44.

[53] Kant sometimes states that this is how we become worthy of grace. I believe that this is a mistake. I would enjoy developing my critique of this in further detail elsewhere. For now, I take seriously Kant's discussions of readiness and built upon them, while re-interpreting his discussions of becoming worthy of divine grace (such as *Religion*, 6:44 and 6:52). I also consider Kant's discussion at *Religion*, 6:174 of how we must have faith that we are supported by divine grace.

The Transformation of Human Ethics in the Age of Technological Challenges

Adriano Fabris

1. Introduction

The aim of my paper is to discuss the transformation of the concept of "ethics" in the technological environment in which we live. This transformation implies that ethics, today, *cannot* be considered connected only to human beings, or a reflection that has to do only with relations among humans, as it did in the past. According to the traditional approach, ethics is the discipline that studies the criteria and principles of action, which help distinguish between good and bad principles, providing guidance about the choices one may have to make, driving one to make a god choice instead of an assumedly bad one.

In short, the traditional task of ethics is to help human beings find their bearings when they act. It is to help us make a choice that can be defined as a "good" one. Therefore, in the past ethics concerned only human actions. Or better: human interactions. The interactions among humans are actually the space in which ethical questions arose.

This is not the case, now. This is no longer true. There are many artificial agents nowadays that can act with different levels of autonomy. Today, we – as human beings – interact on a daily basis with devices that are sometimes beyond our control. Our space of interaction has now grown bigger, it is made up not only of interactions among humans, but also, and above all, of relationships between human beings and machines.

This happens because the age in which we live is a *technological* age. Not only a technical one. We need therefore to explain, first and foremost, the difference between "technique" and "technology". We need above all to clarify the meaning and extent of the way technological devices can autonomously act and interact with human agents as well. And finally we need to point out the differences between what technological devices and humans do. This will be addressed in the first part of my paper.

In the second part, however, I will describe a specific technological environment which we find ourselves living in, nowadays. It is created by Information and Communications Technologies (ICTs). Or, better, ICTs gives us access to such environment. The possibility we have of living both in the offline and online worlds actually means that our environment is made up of a plurality of parallel and overlapping environments. We can live in them in a good way only if we properly relate them with each other.

We cannot however understand this situation unless we discuss a very important notion that does express and explain it. Here, I will mention the notion of "virtual reality". It must be discussed from a philosophical viewpoint. We need to analyse the term "virtuality" by connecting it to its etymology: its reference to the term "virtue". The relationship between virtue and virtuality, and the ethical problems that arise in a virtual dimension, will be further investigated at the end of the second part.

The complex scenario that I have described actually has important ethical consequences. In the third part of my paper and in the Conclusion, I will try to discuss some of them. Above all, I will outline the main transformations that have occurred in ethics in the age of technological challenges in which we live. We need to shift from a human-centred ethics -an ethics of interactions among humans – to a new paradigm of ethics in which interactions involve both human beings and artificial agents. This is the transformation of ethics we need today. I will discuss and develop this idea by introducing a further perspective in ethics: the ethics of relationships[1].

2. Technique and Technology

Most importantly, what is the difference between technique and technology? Let's say something about technique. *Technique* is what expands the possibilities of what human beings can do. In other words, a technical tool enhances human capabilities and allows humans to achieve results that would otherwise be unattainable. More generally, as Aristotle said, the concept of "technique" stands for a form of practical knowledge that, by using naturally available or specially-built tools, allows human beings to extend the scope of their actions[2].

What does technique stem from? Firstly, it stems from the awareness of our own limitations. Then, the prerequisite for the development of a technique is the adaptability of the human being and the ability to change our behaviour to fill that gap. Humans are structurally adaptable. Whereas a giraffe has a long neck to pick leaves and fruit that are high up on trees, a polar bear has the strength to break the bones of its preys, humans can extend the reach of their arms and break the bones of an opponent just by using a stick.

---

[1] Some of the topics herein are more thoroughly investigated in A. FABRIS, *Ethics of Information and Communication Technologies* (Berlin/New York: Springer, 2018), above all, chapters 1 and 3.

[2] ARISTOTLE, *Metaphysics* (Oxford: Oxford University Press, 1924), A, 1, 981 a, 6–8; 981 a, 25–30.

All of this is not enough to make technique come to life. We must take an imaginative approach to the world. We need to look at things and see through them. The human ability to imagine potential uses for things, the settings in which they may be possibly used, turns a mere thing into a tool. What is more, this tool fits into a context of broader relations, within which the device serves a purpose that is designed to achieve a goal[3].

Technology, on its part, is most importantly a technical *system*. This means that in technology many techniques are coordinated with one another to achieve the same goal. In the history of mankind, many examples of these instruments have been combined into increasingly complex devices, which have interacted with the human environment by transforming it. Examples include the mechanical clock (made of levers, gears, wheels, springs, all connected with each other), the factory according to Taylor's organization (based on the principle of the assembly line in which different machines are coordinated with one another) and, today, the Google Car (a driverless car that can follow a route to a given destination).

These examples, however, reveal a fundamental aspect of technology that not only makes it more distinguishable from technique, but also shows the historical progression from technique to technology. A stick needs a human hand to hold and use it. To work, a mechanical clock needs to be charged by someone, but then it works automatically. A factory consists of machines that not only work automatically and are linked with each other, but can often replace human intervention, i. e. the workers' labour-power. Last but not least, a Google Car can interact with the environment to reach its destination by avoiding obstacles, adhering to traffic rules, and using the quickest or the most convenient route.

Here we notice how a technological device gradually emancipates from the need of constant, continuous human input. The device becomes more and more capable of self-sustainment and of autonomous interaction with other parties. This sets it apart from the technical tool. The latter, actually, depends on the initiative taken by the human being and is subjected to our control. Conversely, neither the clock – when charged – or the factory system or the Google Car, each one in its own way, depend on us to work and achieve their goals.

Technological devices, then, are able to develop acts that can be largely independent from human actions and that human actions must in turn interact with. Technological equipment – especially today's most sophisticated one, like robots – is able to interact with the environment it works in and, in some

---

[3] M. HEIDEGGER develops this topic, which he takes from Aristotle, by discussing the concept of "*Zuhandenheit*" in Division One of *Being and Time*, trans. J. Stambaugh (Albany, NY: SUNY Press, 2010).

cases, even "learn" from its interactions with it. Above all, it is able to take the initiative, to achieve the goals it has been programmed for. It is with such equipment that human beings interact today.

Of course: machines are not able to act in the same way we humans do. In their activity there is no intentionality, no free will, no motivation to achieve a goal. Machines cannot choose, actually. They cannot choose because they don't have the capacity of self-reflection. Machines cannot refer to the criteria and principles that guide their activity. They are not able to criticise them and change them. At this moment, it is impossible.

This impossibility, however, doesn't mean either that only human beings can be moral subjects or that there is no machine ethics at all. In their book, for example, Wallach and Allen speak of "moral machines" and "artificial moral agents."[4] What do they mean by that? According to them, machines are not simple tools: they are precisely technological devices. That is, they have relative, increasing autonomy. Therefore, they can be considered to be "moral agents," although in a specific sense.

The expression "relative autonomy" wants to stress the fact that technological machines are programmed for interacting with humans and are able to do that. From this point of view, the term "relative" refers to a "relation." I will develop this topic further at the end of this text. However, in this day and age, machines are often partners, companions of our activity. They are programmed to act and to interact with us, although not in the same way we humans do in our mutual relationships.

Actually, if we understand the word "action" as a strictly intentional, self-reflected and motivated activity, only human beings can really act. We humans, however, very often act automatically, or – more precisely – according to the habits we adopted. From this point of view, we can say that we are "programmed:" programmed by our education, culture, and so on. We could even go as far as to say that we are "self-programmed" by the former decisions we made. Sometimes, we act automatically, like a machine, we give rise to consequences, like a machine, and we are responsible for what we do. The main difference between the automatic actions we humans can perform and the actions a machine is able to accomplish is that we can change our programme, by reflecting on it, by criticising it and by transforming it. The machine is not able to do that.

To sum up, machines act, though differently from the way we humans do (because we are able to modify the criteria of our programmed actions). If machines act, we have to interact with them and with their activity. In their activity, today, machines do have a relative autonomy, because they are tech-

---

[4] W. WALLACH, C. ALLEN, *Moral Machines. Teaching Robots Right from Wrong* (Oxford/New York: Oxford University Press, 2008).

nological devices and not merely technical instruments. Technical instruments always need human inputs.

We could say, therefore, that what happened in the history of mankind between technical tools and technological devices was not a straightforward development, but a real paradigm shift. Technique and technology are not the same thing. That is even better explained by the new horizons opened up by ICTs, especially virtual reality. I will now discuss that.

3. The Virtual Space of Communication

Within the context of ICTs, communication itself is radically transformed. For us, today, communication is not just something we do, it is a deeply-rooted way of living. Actually, instead of being just an ordinary action, communication is an activity that contributes to build the world in which we move, live, and interact. This dynamic is new. Therefore, now the concept of "communication" means something more than in the past: communication is no longer a mere transmission of information, because it has now become an environment.

As a matter of fact, the typical pattern of data transmission between sender and receiver[5] falls short of seizing contemporary communication. Data-transmission devices, such as computers, smartphones, etc. contribute to creating specific worlds and adding new environments to those we commonly live in. Structurally, the environments I am talking about consist of a global web of communication, capable of indefinite growth.

Here, communication is not just about the infrastructure that makes transmission faster and broader, day after day. What I mean is that communication – its structure definable in terms of sender, receiver, code, channel, etc. – carries along implications that go beyond its structure. It brings about something additional, something different.

What the transmission of a message involves is first and foremost the opening, maintenance and the development of a relational space. Here, the word "space" is used in a metaphorical sense, just like other notions I used or will use, such as "field," "environment," "sphere." "Space" suggests something that happens through communication and that communication gives access to. What is opened here is a network of relations, a context that regardless of its size we share, we live in, and we interact with.

In some ways, this phenomenon is not new in the history of mankind. Human beings have always interacted with the natural environment. They have transformed it to such an extent that they have often overlooked the

---

[5] See C. SHANNON and W. WEAVER, *A Mathematical Theory of Communication* (Urbana, IL: Illinois University Press, 1949).

consequences of their actions, as proven by the environmental emergencies we face today. In other words, the human species has always worked to make its world artificial by designing, creating, and using technical and technological devices. Culture itself is the result of such process. The weakening of the balance between the biosphere and the cultural sphere is what is causing today's irreversible consequences on our planet.

In the field of communication, however, the creation of specific tools has enabled us to live in the world we are already familiar with, to navigate it more conveniently, and to tell a different story about it – a story which is nothing but another tool for transforming the world. Namely, some devices have allowed us to create different worlds from the one in which we usually operate. These worlds are able to bring together specific categories and groups of human beings. Think of the novelist's ability to create exciting fiction. Or think of the screenwriter or director of a successful movie. Or, again, of a game designer and programmer.

As I mentioned, this is because of that "added bonus" that is embodied in communicative action, which has to do with different aspects of semantics, pragmatics, rhetoric, and their effects on interpersonal relationships. But nowadays that "added bonus" is going in a completely new direction. We not only see communicative actions being transformed, the communicative environment is changing too. Communication within a context of relations does not simply create and feed such context, it can also broaden and expand it. Actually, nowadays, artificial worlds are multiplied by the increasingly wide, independent, systematic spreading of the transmission of data and information[6]. It involves not only human subjects who are virtually connected from different places, but also non-human communicative agents.

The notion that best expresses the specific transformation of communication into an environment is "infosphere." Infosphere is the group of informational entities we are surrounded by. First launched in the early 1970s in connection with offline media, the notion has recently been used by Luciano Floridi to mean the environment constituted by data and information, both offline and online, that is typical of our developed societies. Clearly, this notion has been developed because of its analogy to biosphere, the field where living beings operate[7].

We should stress that this communicative space is not simply made up of data and information, their connections, and their growing ability to provide more information, faster. Such space is rather the result, as I said, of that "added

---

[6] G. WALSHAM, *Making a World of Difference: IT in a Global Context* (Chichester: Wiley, 2017).

[7] L. FLORIDI, *The Fourth Revolution. How the Infosphere is Reshaping Human Reality* (Oxford/New York: Oxford University Press, 2014).

bonus" that is embodied in communicative action, the "added bonus" that can create an artificial dimension and give it meaning. This is the dimension that we live in and that all the parties involved in communicative action, either natural or artificial, humans or machines, contribute to developing. Infosphere is made up of significant structures capable of involving our being, and in this sense they are more than data-transmission procedures. It is because of this that a specific communicative space can attract us. Only because of this can we move from one informational context to another, for example by "surfing" the web.

So far I have talked about "communicative space" and "infosphere." These notions, used in the singular, might suggest that the environment in which we live is only one. However, this is not true. Actually, another aspect of our present time is that we live in a plurality of communicative environments. The offline and online contexts produced by ICTs generate an array of further spaces that various media contribute to developing, manipulating and transforming for many different purposes.

The growing plurality of these spaces is another unprecedented feature. Today, we can live in a multiplicity of overlapping, parallel, or sequential dimensions. This means that nowadays such different spaces need to be navigated consciously and knowledgeably. This was not perceived as a problem in the past, at least not with the urgency we experience today. Most of the fantasy worlds conceived by a novel, for instance, were still tied up with the book; they were accessible only to those who could read; they were limited by the time it took to read the book, and in any case they were separated from everyday life.

It is not so easy to distinguish between offline and online situations, today. We cannot easily unplug from those devices that give us access to new worlds. Their attractiveness is due to the fact that they are in great quantity and constantly drawn to our attention. Additionally, because of the growing performance and pervasiveness of ICTs, we have become used to perceiving reality through such devices.

"Augmented" and "virtual reality" have become household names. Actually, ICTs integrates natural and cultural environments in which we have always lived. Let's take a closer look at the situation.

What does the term *virtual* mean? The adjective "virtual" comes from the Latin "*virtualis*", from "*virtus*", a noun. "*Virtus*" literally means "virtue". But this is where the first ambiguity comes into play. "*Virtus*" is not just a moral concept, it does not just mean virtue, something that helps make a human being a good being: although there is a more precise connection between virtuality and ethics. It also means a distinctive feature, an ability that something has and that has to do with its essence: as when one is told that a particular plant has beneficial virtues.

"Virtual", however, is a complex notion that only a complex definition can grasp. The meaning of "virtual" ranges from the purely possible, i.e., what differs from our everyday reality, to the potential, i.e. what has not been actualised yet. A philosophical reflection on the notions of "possibility," "reality," "potentiality," and "actuality", from Aristotle to Leibniz, can be helpful here[8]. However, the categories of "possibility" and "potentiality" are not sufficient to encompass the full meaning of virtual. Nor are they sufficient to compare the idea of the virtual to the concepts of real and actual (as Pierre Lévy does, in the footsteps of Bergson and Deleuze[9]). Actually, the virtual also implies a positive attitude: it expresses an active power that actualises things through their own resources. In other words, a virtual entity not only has a specific strength or *virtus*, it also has the power to realise it. Namely, the virtual entity is already realizing its potential, even though in a different sphere from that of everyday reality. It does not need anything else to realise it, because it fulfils itself. Then, now it's clear why "virtual" stands for a boundless ability for self-realization and a great power of involvement. It's clear why such concept fully expresses the dynamic character of artificial worlds.

"Virtual" almost acts as a synthetic agent for the notions of "possible," "potential," and "power," as defined by all Western philosophy. And "virtual" plays a similar role for those notions that are usually thought to be opposites, such as "possibility" and "reality," "potentiality" and "actuality." These oppositions do not make much sense today insofar as in a virtual environment what is possible has already been realized and what seems merely potential to me carries within itself the power to become real. This is why the expression "virtual reality," which sounds like an oxymoron in everyday language, is actually very stringent and appropriate from a philosophical standpoint.

In the concept of "virtual," however, from this perspective the reference to "virtue," in the sense of "moral virtue," implied by the Latin *"virtualis,"* is plain to see. Virtual reality actually seems to be intrinsically and instantly good, and this is precisely why it is virtuous to make the most of what it offers. It is regarded as good because it has an infinite capacity for expansion, it can encompass any other imaginable reality, and it can respond to all sorts of problems with the many solutions is carries within it. That is why virtual reality seems to be able to offer human beings that consolation and salvation from the evils of the world that used to be provided by religious beliefs.

Due to its self-affirming and self-articulating nature, virtual means therefore dissemination and multiplicity. This is why we speak of virtual mostly in the plural, of "virtual worlds." Such plurality does not depend only on the characteristics I have just described. It also depends on the fact that today a variety of technological devices provide access to the virtual spheres. In our everyday life, we can move with ease from a space to another. Given the great familiarity we have

---

[8] See M. VITALI ROSATI, *S'orienter dans le virtuel* (Paris: Hermann, 2012).

[9] P. LÉVY, *Qu'est-ce que le virtuel?* (Paris: La Découverte, 1995).

with them, we are even led to confuse them and to merge them into reality. The risk is that online and offline dimensions may become the same thing. Indifference – i.e. the loss of difference between the two dimensions – is growing.

Therefore, we are faced with a number of problems. They all hinge upon the question of what is the correct relationship among the different communicative environments in which we live. In short, these problems concern our need to coordinate our actions across the different dimensions opened up by ICTs. However, first we have to bring back the difference between online and offline environments. How to take responsibility for all the consequences of this scenario is a pressing issue, which can no longer be postponed.

4. The Transformations of Ethics

Nowadays, ethics has to tackle these problems. One of the issues we just encountered now, for example, is how to distinguish the spaces we live in, how to relate them to each other, how to move between them consciously and knowledgeably, and how to live a good life in them. Namely, the problem concerns, on the one hand, how to deal with such spaces and, on the other, how to move within them.

This twofold attitude applies to all the different ways in which we can experience an environment, a space, be it natural or cultural, merely human or technological. Generally, we can speak of the ethics *of* this space, i.e. concerning it, and of ethics *in* the environment in which we can move. The former studies the criteria and principles that are embedded in a certain structure or organization, which, once again, can be either natural or cultural, or that guide the actions that make these structures or organizations possible. The latter offers indications concerning how we should behave when we live within a specific context, whether to accept or question the rules that belong to it.

In the present situation, so deeply defined by the presence of the virtual spaces opened up by ICTs, the distinction between ethics "*of*" and ethics "*in*" these spaces becomes ever more specific. Actually, on one hand, ethics aims at studying the criteria and principles of the communicative worlds, paying special attention to the ethical and juridical problems that might arise, which may fall within the remit of professional ethics. On the other hand, ethics also has to establish how to best interact with the activities created by technological devices and how to live in the worlds which they give access to.

Shared principles and criteria for guiding human beings in their judgment and activity, when dealing with technological environments and within such spaces, need therefore be identified. How can they be defined? Three main theories were developed in the past. The traditional perspectives of philosophical ethics include above all a reference to the nature of the human being (or to the nature of the good that the human action can pursue), to the consequences of human action (consequentialism), and to the intention of the action and the duty that follows (deontological ethics)[10].

Such three scenarios, however, can only apply to human activity. Actually, nowadays ethics has a different mission. It needs to be broadened and pushed into different directions.

Firstly, the ethical challenge today is not just about assessing the different environments, both natural and artificial, one by one, it is also about learning to navigate the complexity of a simultaneous multiplicity of environments. In other words, we now need to learn how to hierarchize the spaces in which we live, how to choose, in each case, which one needs to be prioritized. Ethics, in this age of increasingly pervasive artificial and natural spaces, should teach the human being how to choose and organize them.

Secondly, today the principles and criteria that guide the activity of the technological devices should be discussed from an ethical point of view. I mean not only the principles and criteria according to which such activity is programmed, but also the principles and criteria that are part of the structure of a machine and control its actions. Actually, a technological machine can act, interact with its environment, and – as we have seen – has relative autonomy.

Finally, the scope of ethics must be broadened to include the transformations of human activity in the technological age. Actually, now human beings can not only act in their cultural and social worlds, and interact with the natural and cultural environments. Today, we also need to interact with the activity of artificial agents. This is something new, in the contemporary scenario.

Unfortunately, the traditional ethical models fall short of dealing with such issues. They might be helpful as general guidance about the option to hierarchize the online and offline worlds we inhabit. In fact, such hierarchy is still based on a human choice, even if such choice concerns both natural environments and artificial products.

The three ethical theories I mentioned, however, cannot help us develop either a machine ethics or an ethics in human-machine interaction. The Aristotelian idea of human nature and the related virtue ethics are actually unsuitable, because in this case we have to do with artificial agents. In this sense, speaking of "nature" is no longer adequate.

Consequentialism has its fatal flaws. The consequences of an action performed by a human or by an artificial agent cannot be predicted, given the numerous side effects that can happen in a complex relational context. Moreover, it is no longer clear whether the criterion of utility typical of consequentialism should be measured with respect to the human agent or the

---

[10] See, for example, P. SINGER (ed.), *A Companion to Ethics* (Malden, MA: Wiley-Blackwell, 2006).

machine. Most importantly, consequentialism does not properly apply to artificial agents, specifically with respect to their capacity to anticipate the consequences of their actions. Actually, such anticipation, even if successful, would always require an a priori decision of what cases and alternatives should be expected to happen. And such decision would be based upon additional principles, second-level principles, which the machine cannot establish by itself (even though those principles can be implemented by the programmer in the machine). In other words, the machine cannot decide autonomously by taking into account its own utility.

Lastly, neither is a deontological approach to machine ethics, and consequently to human-machine interactions, appropriate. In this case, the problem is that the agents undertake an obligation either instantly and unconditionally or for fear of punishment if they transgress. In the former case, only human beings can commit themselves to such obligation, since machines, as we have seen, have not yet developed the reflexivity required to commit themselves thus. In the latter case, the artificial agent would have to know what the punishment consists of.

In short, applying traditional ethical models to artificial agents and to human-machine interactions can be seriously difficult. The naturalistic, the consequentialist, and the deontological approaches are models built upon a scenario where the only agent is the human being. The only way to apply them to the action of an artificial agent would be by making such action conditional on a prior human action (of the designer, the programmer, the builder, the tester, the user of the machine). But this is precisely the problem that ethics is called upon to address today: the fact that the action of the machine has a certain level of autonomy, a growing autonomy, and therefore needs specific governing criteria.

5. Conclusion

In conclusion, one has to ask oneself: What is then the adequate ethical model for this situation? If it can't be the ethics of nature, or utility, or duty – still too tied up to a world in which the human agent takes centre stage – then maybe an ethics of structure is what is needed: ethics based on the structure of the action itself, whether it is performed by a human or an artificial agent. This action, on closer inspection, is always *relational*. As a matter of fact, relational is the structure of every action, both those performed by human beings and by artificial agents. The ethics that can take into account today's different environments, by navigating and choosing among them, is therefore an *ethics of relationships*.[11]

---

[11] About this, see A. FABRIS, *RelAzione. Una filosofia performativa* (Brescia: Morcelliana, 2016).

The ethics of relationships is an ethics that can regulate relationships among human beings as well as relationships between human and artificial agents. It regards action as a relationships-building event. It understands such relationships as a network in the making that can be created in many different ways, at a global level, and in multiple forms.

There are two ways in which this form of ethics can be accomplished. Again: the ethics *of* relationships and the ethics *in* relationships. The ethics *of* relationships studies the forms, environments and dimensions of acting and the way relational activity materialises in them. The ethics *in* relationships is concerned instead with the problem of how to move through these spaces in a good, reasonable way. Its responsibility is also to provide guidance on how to organize and choose within and between such different spaces. It can do that, because the dynamic, relational, and active structure of interconnected environments is always the same, whether is it organized around human or artificial agents, or both.

Additionally, the ethics of relationships lays down a normative principle for navigating the multiplicity of our complex world. Such normative principle might be worded like this: *act in such a way as to always support new relationships, to broaden and expand relationships, instead of blocking them*. Such principle is rooted in the very structure of relationships, namely, the fact that a good relationship is one that affirms itself by building new relationships. This needs to be put into practice. Hence the need to express its normative dimension.[12]

That this principle should guide our decisions, not only within each space, but more precisely across different spaces, is now clear (I hope). It emerges from the structure of every agent, which is also the structure that connects human beings and artificial agents into complex networks. This idea of ethics is rooted in the principle of relationships: the inspiring principle of our human actions (and of those of the artificial agents), which should also become the normative compass of our behaviour across the online and offline worlds.

---

[12] These last statements seem to transgress the well-known "Hume's law": that is the prohibition to mistake a description for a prescription. I confess: this is precisely my intention in this case. It is not only an idea of mine, however. I am following here, for example, what HANS JONAS says in his *The Imperative of Responsibility* (Chicago: University of Chicago Press, 1985) and what many other scholars argue against Hume's law. Actually, I think it is time to break the wall between descriptions and prescriptions, between facts and values. Formally, of course, it is a mistake to derive moral conclusions from non-moral premises. Concretely, however, values are very often embodied in facts, in our perception of them, embedded in them and in their structure (about values embodied in technological devices, see M. FLANAGAN, D. C. HOWE, H. NISSENBAUM, "Embodying Values in Technology: Theory and Practice," in *Information Technology and Moral Philosophy* ed. J. van der Hoven, J. Weckert [Cambridge: Cambridge University Press, 2008], 322–353). The awareness of that, the description of that, can – I repeat: *can* – help us make the best choice in these situations.

Inter-Being: Humanity in an Ecological Age

Joseph Prabhu

> What a piece of work is a man! how noble in reason!
> how infinite in faculty! in form and moving how
> express and admirable! in action how like an angel!
> in apprehension how like a god! the beauty of the
> world! the paragon of animals! And yet, to me,
> what is this quintessence of dust?[1]

Thus, Shakespeare in *Hamlet*, as the latter explains some of the sources of his melancholy to his friends Rosenkranz and Guildenstern. But as we know, our lives and circumstances have changed dramatically since the year 1600 CE, the time around which Shakespeare is reputed to have written these lines. The "nobility of reason" and "infinity in faculty" have taken rather more disturbing directions and the challenge today is what correctives need to be provided.

The theme of this conference is "Humanity: An Endangered Idea?" In answer to the question posed by the title, I have a complex response: On the one hand, it is true that humanity is endangered via the four-fold challenges outlined in the topic description of the conference; but, on the other hand, these challenges acquire a different focus when seen through the lens of the notion of the "anthropocene" made familiar in ecological literature – the idea that much of the danger to both natural and social ecologies comes from human activity and decisions, which in turn are driven by human hubris. This hubris makes humans more endangering than endangered, at least in any straightforward sense of endangerment. We are living with a modern Prometheanism, where the role of Zeus is in part being played by the environment. Global warming and climate change are indicating the dangers of human overreach, even as we humans have thus far remained rather oblivious of the eagles plucking at our livers. Seen through the lens of the anthropocene, it is the endangering aspect of humanity that appears to me at least as important as the "endangered" one. And through both aspects there runs a common thread – the twin syndromes of anthropocentrism and human overreach.

To counter that I propose an attitude and an ethic of Reverence for Life. The notion of reverence carries with it feelings of profound awe and respect,

---

[1] *Hamlet*, Act 2, Scene 2.

and such feelings stand at the opposite end of transactional attitudes and utilitarian modes of life, where we know the price of everything but not the value of things. Anthropocentrism is not, of course, logically or inevitably tied to an utilitarian ethic, and what Max Weber called instrumental rationality, but the transactional modes of life of modernity are nonetheless closely associated with them. By sharp contrast, we have Kant telling us in *The Critique of Practical Reason*: "Two things fill the mind with ever new and increasing admiration and awe, the oftener and the most steadily we reflect on them, the starry heavens above and the moral law within."[2] And it is no accident that Kant is a philosopher of finitude and of limits.

I want to argue in this paper that we need to recover an ethic of Reverence for Life, an ethic that has largely been lost at a time when the cult of technique is provided its logical extension in such characteristic works as that of Ray Kurzweil, *The Singularity is Near: When Humans Transcend Biology* (2005). There are other works that have succeeded Kurzweil's, such as Nick Bostrom, *Superintelligence: Paths, Dangers, Strategies* (2014) and Max Tegmark, *Life 3.0: Being Human in the Age of Artificial Intelligence* (2017), among a vast number of such books in what is now a huge industry. It is not my purpose to comment on any length on such works beyond a brief remark or two that sketches their general line of argument. The main idea in this context is indicated in the very titles of such books. Artificial intelligence and computational prowess will allow us to transcend the limits of human biology as we know them. Not only will we be able to overcome some of the barriers posed by illness and old age, but artificial intelligence will even allow us to transcend death as we have come to know it. Kurzweil posits that the exponential growth of artificial intelligence will grant us immortality of a sort. Those of us who carelessly might have missed, or might still miss, the Rapture brought to us by apocalyptic eschatologists might still be able to enjoy a secular version of it thanks to the Singulitarians. If Ingolf Dalferth had only spent more time at MIT with Ray Kurzweil, we might not be here at all discussing endangerment, but might instead have been taken up into the Rapture.

But as we are here, let me take this occasion not only for refusing the Singulitarian invitation, but also for issuing a spirited repudiation of the gestalt underlying such thinking. Such repudiation usually takes a moral-phenomenological form: we are living increasingly in an age of machines and machine-intelligence, an age when the human world, as we have hitherto known it, is seriously disrupted. Of course, the human world is also an historical world. The world of horse-drawn carriages and letters written by hand and sent through the postal service is obviously far removed from the world of the internet and

---

[2] I. KANT, *The Critique of Practical Reason*, trans. P. Guyer and W. Wood (Cambridge: Cambridge University Press, 1998), *AA* 5:161.

email. So, some technological changes significantly shift our sense of what we normatively consider to be "human." The so-called "friends" we make on Facebook differ in depth and meaning from classical definitions of friendship, which point to a concern for the good or the well-being of the other. Likewise, there are significant social changes that shift standards of normativity. We must not forget that the framers of the U.S. Declaration of Independence, who spoke of all men being equal and of possessing certain unalienable rights, were themselves for the most part slave holders. To this one must also add the vast differences across cultures regarding what counts as "human." For example, certain caste-practices that are sanctioned by a time-honored caste system in India like the treatment of widows might well be judged to be inhuman in other cultural contexts.

So, if one grants these considerable historical and cultural normative changes in what it means to be human, the question becomes whether the recent changes wrought by artificial intelligence (hereafter AI) and robotics represent a change in degree or a change in kind. Another of Ray Kurzweil's books is called *The Age of Spiritual Machines: When Computers Exceed Human Intelligence* (2000). A "spiritual" machine is not only one that has greater memory capacity and computational ability than humans, but is also said to have a "personality," such that one can have relationships with it. Not only that: these machines are also, a la Kurzweil, able to be our teachers, friends, and lovers. So, all lonely hearts can now have new hope. Have we with these "spiritual machines" moved into a wholly new phase of human existence where machines have now become are new gods?

My short and direct answer to that question is "yes:" I do believe that this age of AI will transform our lives and indeed it has already done so to a great extent. At many dinner tables these days, people are too busy looking at their smart phones to bother to have a real (in contrast to virtual) conversation, and indeed those whose express their disapproval of such a state of affairs are looked at by the phone addicts with equal measures of incomprehension and disgust. At one elite university here in Southern California – the University of Southern California – students are being taught the art of conversation, a privilege for which parents pay handsomely.

In one of the last articles that the late well-known neurologist Oliver Sacks wrote before he died in 2015, in a poignant complaint about the dehumanizing world of cell phones and virtual reality, he laments the loss of a social world of interpersonal contact and "the complete disappearance of the old civilities." Here is an extract:

Much of this, remarkably, was envisaged by E. M. Forster in his 1909 story "The Machine Stops," in which he imagined a future where people live underground in isolated cells, never seeing one another and communicating only by audio and visual devices. In this world, original thought and direct observation are discouraged – "Beware of first-hand ideas!" people are told. Humanity has been overtaken by "the Machine," which provides all comfort and meets all needs – except the need for human contact. One young man, Kuno, pleads with his mother via a Skype-like technology, "I want to see you not through the Machine [...] I want to speak to you not through the wearisome Machine."

He says to his mother, who is absorbed in her hectic, meaningless life, "we have lost the sense of space [...] We have lost a part of ourselves [...] Cannot you see [...] that it is we that are dying, and that down here the only thing that really lives is the Machine?"[3]

As philosophers and students of religion it is not enough, however, merely to describe some of the deleterious effects of the age of AI and to register our regret. Accordingly, I shall respond in a two-fold manner: (1) By providing a sketchy diagnosis of what philosophically is a very complex problem; and (2) by proferring what I hope is a constructive proposal.

1. A Critical Diagnosis

What Heidegger called "the question concerning technology" is philosophically a complex matter. Like Heidegger I could go back to Plato and talk about *Seinsvergessenheit*, the forgetfulness of Being. But I have only 40 minutes. I think a more promising prospect in this context is to invoke Max Weber and his distinction between *Zweckrationalitaet* (purposive rationality) and *Wertrationalitaet* (ethical, value-laden rationality). Weber's actual classification of the different types of rationality is more variegated, but this contrast is the relevant one for my purposes. Instrumental rationality (or purposive rationality in Weber's terminology) is means-ends rationality, concerned with the most efficient means for achieving a given end without the end itself being evaluated in terms of some non-instrumental criterion, like the good or the right. Ethical, value-laden rationality, by contrast, is concerned precisely with the good, the right, or the useful, and it is significant that Weber, unlike emotivists or other ethical subjectivists, believed that moral questions could be rationally debated. In some ways, Weber's distinction is analogous but not identical to the fact/value distinction.

Weber's notion of instrumental rationality is reworked in a different form by Max Horkheimer and Theodor Adorno in their famous text, *The Dialectic of Enlightenment*. Once again, as in the case of my mention of Weber, I am drawing very selectively on a complex text. Adorno and Horkheimer argue that under the influence of market capitalism and the commodification of culture, robust notions of reason structured toward autonomy and freedom, have become reified and made into an instrument of technocracy. The power of critical reason oriented toward freedom from authority and freedom for autonomy has become subverted into a new form of instrumental reason geared

---

[3] O. SACKS, "The Machine Stops," *The New Yorker*, February 11, 2019, 29.

toward serving market forces. Horkheimer and Adorno were concerned in that text, and in much of the work of the early Frankfurt School, in explaining the rise both of fascism in Europe and of state socialism in the Soviet Union, analyses which are beyond the scope of this paper.

I draw selectively on Weber and then on Horkheimer and Adorno merely to situate my argument. There are three essential points I wish to make: (1) The sociological current of instrumental rationality feeds a contemporary positivism where facts are separated from values; (2) This positivism is particularly noticeable in modern culture and in the social sciences which both reflect and are reflected by it; and (3) This positivism and the value-free stance it embodies encourages a "can implies ought" mentality, the reverse of the Kantian dictum that "ought implies can." Let me make brief comments about each of the three points.

No more dramatic an illustration of the spread of instrumental rationality is provided in contemporary life than the dominance of economic thinking and calculation over increasing areas of social life – from politics to education to health. The recent strike waged by the teachers of the Los Angeles public school system was for higher wages to keep up with the cost of living, for smaller classes, and for more supported services. It is a sad state of affairs when schools are drastically short of nurses and basic medical care, and their teachers have to provide classroom supplies from paper to pencils from their own pockets, and where parents have to pay for janitorial services. The main reason for the lack of funds to finance the second-largest public school system in the country serving some 700,000 students is the passing of Proposition 13, which drastically cut the property taxes that provides the revenue base for public schools, and no alternative source of funding has been democratically arrived at. The consequences of that short-sighted proposition could have been foreseen and alternatives could have been provided – if the matter of public schooling had been given due importance. But this is a reflection of the social preferences and political priorities of a democratic polity.

One knows as well about the dire state of medical care and health insurance in the USA that has been only partly mitigated by the recent passage of the Affordable Care Act, which itself took years of public advocacy to bring to fruition, and which is now again under attack. The greed of insurance and pharmaceutical companies and other vested interests has been allowed to jeopardize the health and well-being of millions of people.

The true measure of this prioritization of market forces, and economic calculation more broadly, has been well described by the economist and philosopher E. F. Schumacher:

In the marketplace, for practical reasons, innumerable qualitative distinctions which are of vital importance to man and society are suppressed Thus the reign of quantity celebrates its greatest triumphs in 'The Market.' Everything is equated with everything else.

To equate things means to give them a price and thus to make them exchangeable. To the extent that economic thinking is based on the market, it takes the sacredness out of life, because there can be nothing sacred in something that has a price. Not surprisingly, therefore, if economic thinking pervades the whole of society, even simple non-economic values like beauty, health or cleanliness can survive only if they prove to be 'economic' [...] What is worse, and destructive, of civilization, is the pretense that everything had a price or, in other words, that money is the highest of all values.[4]

No academic science is more illustrative of this turn to instrumental rationality, combined with the valorization of money, as the science of economics. Karl Polanyi has convincingly shown how exceptional the modern industrial world is in human history with regard to the separation of the economic from other aspects of life, and its emphasis on the unique predominance of the market and its ethos, from the late eighteenth century to the present. The history of economics reveals that until then, even when the scope of economic concerns was limited to material well-being, the latter was itself seen as part of a wider context of happiness or human flourishing.[5] In its self-understanding, economics, together with politics and ethics, was until the early part of the twentieth century considered one of the *moral* sciences, not just in the sense of having moral dimensions or implications, but more importantly as issuing from moral premises and being assessed in terms of moral criteria like value or utility.

Indeed, the very word "economics" comes from two Greek words, *oikos* (household) and *nomos* (law or rule). Aristotle relates the law and running of the household to a hierarchy of goods, those sought for their own sake, and those sought as means to other goods. The "master science" for Aristotle is politics, "for it is the one which uses the other sciences concerned with action and moreover legislates what must be done and what avoided." It follows for Aristotle that the good which politics seeks is the highest social good, "for while it is satisfactory to acquire and preserve the good, even for an individual, it is finer and more divine to acquire and preserve it for a people and for cities." The science of economics having the production and distribution of wealth as its immediate end is linked up with other sciences involving more basic goods. "The money-maker's life is in a way forced on him [not chosen for itself]: and clearly wealth is not the good we are seeking, since it is [merely] useful for some other end."[6] Economics for Aristotle relates closely to the study of ethics and politics, and is concerned with the good which is both instrumental and, axiologically, at the lower end of the hierarchy of goods culminating in what he considers the highest good.

---

[4] E. F. SCHUMACHER, *Small is Beautiful: Economics as if People Mattered* (San Francisco, CA: Harper & Row, 1973), 43–44.

[5] K. POLANYI, *The Great Transformation*, 2nd ed. (Boston, MA: Beacon Press, 2001).

[6] ARISTOTLE, *Nichomachean Ethics*, trans. T. Irwin (Indianapolis, IN: Hackett Publishing Company, 1985), Sections 1.2–1.43.

To the extent to which economics in recent times has wished to shore up its scientific status, it has done so by attempting to disavow its moral and political elements and by modeling itself on the natural sciences with an increased emphasis on mathematical and quantitative methods. At the same time, the scope of economics is reduced to those aspects of behavior that are quantifiable. Confining myself for the moment to Western societies, it is easy to see how the stress on quantification has gone along with the acceptance of the marketplace.

These illustrations from the spread of economic values in recent social life and the transformation of economics as a science are meant to point to the main normative thesis I wish to make in this section: We have abandoned the eternal verities of the true, the good, and the beautiful for the profitable, the convenient, and the (falsely) powerful. And we do this because of what I am calling "positivism," the tendency to go along with what our science and technology make possible, without the constraints and orientation provided by genuine moral values. Compare these two definitions of economics, and economic life, one by the famous twentieth century economist, Lionel Robbins, and the other by the late nineteenth century art historian and political economist John Ruskin, and one can see the prevalence and spread of positivism. Lionel Robbins: "Economics is the science which studies human behavior as a relationship between ends and scarce means, which have alternative uses." John Ruskin: "There is no wealth but Life. Life including all its powers of love, of joy, and of admiration. That country is richest which nourishes the greatest number of noble and happy human beings; that man is richest who, having perfected the functions of his life to the utmost, has also the widest helpful influence both personal, and by means of his possessions, over the lives of others." Contrast the utilitarian and instrumental-rational nature of Robbins's definition with the moral- aesthetic one provided by Ruskin.

This positivist context is the one where AI and the world of "spiritual machines" operate. It encourages an inversion of the Kantian deontological dictum that "ought implies can" to "can implies ought." Of course, this latter "ought" is not a moral but a pragmatic "ought" and the implication is not a strict implication. Nonetheless, "can implies ought" with these qualifications expresses the ethos of the world within which AI operates and thrives. We can clone; therefore, we should clone. We can "transcend death" a la Ray Kurzweil; therefore, we should do so. It is obvious, however, that this is a false implication and faulty logic.

This completes the diagnostic part of my argument, and I want to shift now to my constructive proposal. But before I come to the actual proposal, let me summarize the main direction of my argument thus far so as to contextualize the remaining portion of the paper. I have been making three main claims: (1) That the world of AI is indicative and a symptom of a modern Prometheanism, a hubris that has had deleterious effects, especially on the environment.

The term "anthropocene" is a code-word for this syndrome; (2) One significant form in which this hubris has expressed itself is in instrumental rationality that sees life in terms of its use rather than its value. This accounts for the preponderance of economic and transactional thinking in our time; and (3) Instrumental rationality in turn promotes a "can implies" ought," where the particular "ought" in question is a pragmatic or Promethean "ought" rather than a moral one. In this climate commercial, technological, and military considerations run far ahead of and outweigh moral deliberation and judgment.

Mention of military considerations brings up a parallel to the computer and AI, as far as technological achievements are concerned. The parallel is the case provided by the development of atomic and hydrogen bombs starting with the Manhattan Project located at Los Alamos, New Mexico in the early 1940's. Robert Oppenheimer, the brilliant physicist who led a team of outstanding scientists (including Einstein) in this project, was successful in accomplishing this particular task. But as someone who also had occasional ethical scruples, he knew he was morally responsible for leading a research program that ended not only with the dropping of atomic bombs on Hiroshima and Nagasaki in August 1945 but, as serious, with helping to set off a nuclear-arms race whose dire consequences are still with us some 70 years later. In a talk to an university audience in 1946, Oppenheimer told his listeners that when the Manhattan Project team looked back on what it had done, "we thought of the legend of Prometheus, of the deep sense of guilt in man's new powers that reflects his recognition of evil and his long knowledge of it."[7]

2. A Constructive Proposal

My constructive proposal comes out of work I have been doing for some time now at the Institute for Ecological Civilization based here in Claremont, and charged with developing and promoting a long-term research program concerned with how social, political, economic, and scientific-technological life should be reorganized so as to achieve the goal of a sustainable ecological society. It had its origins in a highly successful conference held here in Claremont in June 2015, organized by the theologian John Cobb and a large international team of co-organizers focused on the theme: "Seizing an Alternative: Toward an Ecological Civilization." It drew some 2000 people from around the world, including 5 or 6 from the Politburo of the Chinese Communist party and other high-level government functionaries. It is obviously beyond the scope of this presentation to go into any detailed description of the project

---

[7] C. THORPE, *Oppenheimer: The Tragic Intellect* (Chicago, IL: University of Chicago Press, 2006).

beyond pointing out that in talking of an entire civilization, it is aiming at a radically new organization of society grounded in a new way of viewing life and its organizing principles. It is in that sense, for example, that we talk of an industrial civilization. Some idea of the scope of the project may be provided by indicating that it is very much in accord with the thinking and the vision set out in Pope Francis's June 2015 encyclical *Laudato Si': On Care For Our Common Home*, which has a similar ambition for a sustainable ecological society.

Seen from the perspective of such a research program, I approach the topic of this conference with a single leading question: What vision of humanity and of human beings is most conducive to, and supportive of, an ecological civilization?

To get from the diagnostic or critical part of my paper to this constructive section, I am simply assuming what has been quite convincingly demonstrated in the scientific literature: namely, that it is human activity and policies which have been largely responsible for the mass extinction of many plant and animal species, the pollution of the air and oceans, and climate change more generally – among other lasting impacts. This represents yet another area of human overreach with a similar hubris underlying it as in the case of the development of AI, but now with great harm done both to the environment and to many human communities, especially from the global South.

In an influential article in 1967 entitled "The Historical Roots of Our Ecologic Crisis," the historian Lynn White Jr. laid the blame for our environmental crisis largely on Christianity with its account of creation and anthropocentric world-view both of which legitimize human insensitivity and indifference to the natural world and our consequent exploitation of nature. But precisely because the roots of the crisis are religious in nature, the solution must also be "essentially religious, whether we call it that or not." He concludes his essay thus: "We must rethink and re-feel our nature and destiny. The profoundly religious, but heretical, sense of the primitive Franciscans for the spiritual autonomy of all parts of nature may point a direction. I propose (St.) Francis as a patron saint for ecologists.

Some 50 years later, Pope Francis has heeded Lynn White's call for an "alternative Christian view" along Franciscan lines that might ground and empower a healthy natural and social ecology. He writes, "We urgently need a humanism capable of bringing together the different fields of knowledge, including economics, in the service of a more integral and integrating vision. Today, the analysis of environmental problems cannot be separated from the analysis of human, family, work related and urban contexts, nor from how individuals relate to themselves, which leads in turn to how they relate to others and to the environment."[8]

---

[8] POPE FRANCIS, *Laudato Si': On Care for Our Common Home* (London: Catholic Truth Society, 2015), §141.

There is a tendency at times to see the environmental crisis as a largely scientific-technological one having to do with reliance on different forms of energy, and questions of poverty and inequalities of power and wealth, by contrast, as a largely socio-political crisis. The Pope shows clearly the error of this way of thinking and demonstrates how both the social and environmental crises are inextricably linked and are part of one complex problem. This perception is clearer to a person from the Southern hemisphere, because much of the extraction of oil, gas and coal, and much of the deforestation required to feed modern industries have come. either from the South or from areas previously under colonial control. In particular, it is important to see how a rapacious capitalist economic system, which relies on the accentuation of desire and on consumerist lifestyles for its profits, drives the relentless extraction of resources and the exploitation of the earth, which most severely affect the poor.

If then one accepts that human activity and policies in this ecological area also have been misguided, I want, in line with the civilizational motif alluded to earlier, to address a single thematic question: What revisions in our idea of humanity do we need to support and promote a sustainable ecological society? And it is to that question I now turn in the concluding portion of my paper and introduce the idea of "Inter-being" that features in the title of this paper.

The notion of "inter-being" comes from the Vietnamese Buddhist monk Thich Nhat Hanh, the founder of the Plum Village Monastery and the Order of Interbeing in the Dordogne area of southwest France. The term is an elaboration of two key ideas taken from the Madhyamika Buddhist tradition – the related notions of *emptiness (sunyata)*, and *dependent co-origination (pratityasamutpada)*. Madhyamika philosophy, especially by propounded by Nagarjuna, its most prominent thinker, posits the primacy of relations over entities. Entities come into being because of relationships, which are themselves always in flux. The entity called Joseph Prabhu, who is standing before you, is an ensemble of relations – biological, social, and environmental – that takes a particular spatio-temporal form and is given a socially recognized name. He does not, however, exist as a permanent, independent, substantial self. Nor is he, on the other hand, non-existent. In spite of my earlier invocation of *Hamlet*, what you are seeing in front of you as the main speaker of this particular session is real, not a ghost. But he does not possess permanent, independent, substantial selfhood. Western philosophers might be acquainted with this notion of the non-self through David Hume, although Hume does not give the same ontological prominence to relations and relationality as Nagarjuna does. The doctrine of dependent co-origination spells out the chain of multi-directional relationality. Ontologically speaking, this is a significant set of ideas because it shifts out focus from entities to the relations that bring them into being and constitute them.

Inter-being thus refers to the fact that we are, precisely because of these relationships and interdependencies. We thus inter-are. More generally, inter-being refers to the interconnected nature of all reality.

The Indo-Spanish thinker Raimon Panikkar has taken this formal structure and given it specific content in terms of the metaphysical notion of "cosmotheandrism." For Panikkar the Cosmic, the Divine, and the Human are three interconnected dimensions of reality: the Cosmic points to the objectifiable, material dimension; the Human, the objectifying dimension; and the Divine, the infinite, the "always more" dimension that provides both depth and dynamism to the whole unified structure. These three dimensions do not stand on their own as independent entities but exist only in co-constitutive relationality. As Panikkar puts it

"There is no matter without spirit and no spirit without matter, no World without Man, no God without the universe, etc. God, Man, and World are three artificially substantivized forms of the three primordial adjectives that describe Reality."[9]

Panikkar has expounded and elaborated on this metaphysical picture at some length in his Gifford Lectures published as *The Rhythm of Being: The Unbroken Trinity* (2010), but in this context two features are particularly noteworthy.

First, when one considers human beings not as abstract independent entities, but as processes within and in relation to the Cosmic and the Divine and other humans, the focus shifts from independent existence to existence-in-relation-to. As I composed this essay, I do so not as an isolated individual but as the locus of a vast number of relations and forces that are concretized in me – from my parents, teachers, friends, and occasional detractors (yes, they too!), to the air I breathe, the computer that converts my thoughts into printed text, to my body, and the medical personnel who have looked after me. And from a more cosmic perspective, one may look at reality as a vast net, composed of individual knots, each vital to what the Indian tradition calls *lokasamagraha*, the maintenance of the world. Consciousness of this ontological interconnection, on the one hand, reinforces one's sense of responsibility for world-maintenance, and, on the other, evokes a deep sense of gratitude for all the forces human, divine, and cosmic that keep me and all living beings in existence. And moving beyond the personal level to the political, one can immediately see the falsity of "American First" and other chauvinistic nationalisms that strive to isolate human communities from one another. Rather, as Martin Luther King, Jr. eloquently expressed it: "We are tied together in a single garment of destiny, caught in an inescapable network of mutuality. Whatever affects one directly, affects all indirectly [...] I can never be what I ought to be until you are what you ought to be."

---

[9] R. PANIKKAR, "Philosophy as Life Style," in *Philosophers in their Own Words* (Bern: Peter Lang, 1978), 206.

Second, existing-in-relation-to carries the implication of an active, participative attitude. World-maintenance is not a spectator sport. Nor is "maintenance" to be understood in a static sense, but rather in a dynamic one of new being and new creation. Panikkar has an original, "grammatical" way of expressing this interaction:

> The Divine Mystery is the ultimate *am* of everything. Yet we also experience the *art* and the *is*. This is the cosmotheandric experience: the undivided experience of the pronouns simultaneously. Without the Divine, we cannot say *I*; without Consciousness we cannot say *Thou*; and without the World, we cannot say *it*. The "three" pronouns, however, are not three; they belong together. They are pro-nouns, or rather pro-noun; they stand for the same (unnameable) noun. The noun "is" only in the pronouns.[10]

How does this cosmotheandric picture measure up against the thematic question I posed at the beginning of this section? And how does it provide a corrective to the anthropocentrism, and associated Prometheanism, which I critiqued in the first section?

To start with, it should be obvious that this cosmotheandric account strongly refutes anthropocentrism. Humanity and human beings do not have their center in themselves, but only in relation to the Divine and the Cosmic. This is a very serious revision. Centuries of philosophical and theological tradition in the West have been built around a false and profoundly misleading idea of humanity as encapsulated both in the quote from *Hamlet* with which I began this essay, and also in this famous passage from Psalm 8 of the Bible:

> What is man, that thou are mindful of him? And the son of man, that thou visitest him? For thou hast made him a little lower than the angels and crowned him with glory and honor. Thou hast made him to have dominion over the works of thy hands; thou hast put all things under his feet. [King James Version]

For all the poetry of the psalm, I would argue, together with many others, that the consequences of taking it to be true and normative in our own day and time are disastrous. One may, of course, make a historical case for the psalmic account – as necessary, perhaps, to give humans a sense of their God-given dignity and power. Whatever its historical justification, however, given that we are talking about the present and the future, this is, I repeat, a damaging self-image of humanity at this moment of history. What I am trying to do in this paper is to point us in a different direction and in doing so, I am joining the chorus of many who are alive to our urgent ecological responsibilities.

Nor is this new "interconnected" picture that I have drawn in any way deflationary. Our dignity as a human species is not tied up with being "unique" understood as standing apart and above from the rest of the created world. I have tried to spell out some of the deleterious consequences of what the

---

[10] R. PANIKKAR, *The Rhythm of Being: The Unbroken Trinity* (Maryknoll, NY: Orbis Books, 2010), 191.

notion of "having dominion" has brought with it. The new self-image I am proposing is much more egalitarian rather than hierarchical, as in the old picture with God on top, humans below, and the non-human world still further down the chain of being. We are partners with the earth and other living beings in world-maintenance. Of course, we humans possess the gifts of reason, conscience, moral choice, and intentional action, but these gifts are shared to different degrees with other animals, and it is high time for us to discover and honor these shared gifts in other creative beings.

What this means concretely is learning the "language" of the natural world in non- anthropomorphic terms. Bird song, animal communication, the alphabet of trees – all operate at a different level and in a different register from human languages. And it is important for us humans to listen to them and heed them. All true listening requires an inner silence, a self- emptying of human concerns and preoccupations in order truly to listen and to learn. It is an interesting coincidence that the words "listen" and "silent" are anagrams of each other.

The same goes to listening to and talking about the divine. Much theology is disguised anthropology, as Ludwig Feuerbach appointed out long ago – a projection of human concerns, fears, anxieties, and desires onto God. If that premise is accepted, then Feuerbach's – and Marxes – challenge to theology still stands. Take back the projections, clear away the mystifications, and operate with a robust humanism. But Feuerbach's premise does not have to be accepted, and much recent French phenomenology of religion from Marion to Nancy to Falque is centered around notions of "grace" and "gift," and inverts the Feuerbachian challenge. It is not so much a question of our regarding God or the Divine, but the reverse: of our being regarded and viewed by God, the irregardable.

All told, my hope is that the radical shift in human self-image from dominators and controllers of the non-human world to a partnership with it, points to a new ethic of Reverence for Life. Reverence for Life is the attitude proposed more than seventy years ago by Albert Schweitzer, today a much-forgotten figure, and when remembered at all, reviled as being a racist and colonialist. There is, however, much wisdom in Schweitzer's ethic and it is well conveyed by his close friend, the Dutch doctor and artist Frederick Franck:

"Reverence for life implies the insight, the empathy, and compassion mark the maturation of the human inner process, and that implies overcoming the spilt between thinking and feeling that is the bane of our scientism and the idolization of technology that distances – estranges – us form all emotional and ethical constraints. This same distancing, the objectification of the unobjectifiable is characteristic of all Realpolitik, racism, ethnic cleansing, cruelty, and exploitation of the other by political, racial egos [...] including that free-market mentality for which all that is, is looked upon as mere material-for-profit even if it ruins our species and our earth for generations to come."[11]

---

[11] F. FRANK (ed.), *What Does it Mean to Be Human?* (New York: St. Martin's Press, 2000), 5.

What I have tried to do in the second section of this paper is to provide the lineaments of a Reverence for Life founded on a cosmotheandric basis, where the Divine, the Human, and the Cosmic join together in reverence of and care for our planet, our common home.

Who Still Deserves to Arise?

Josiah Solis

In the *Geist* of Joseph Prabhu's insightful paper[1], I find it appropriate to open my response with rather Hegelian question: if in the wake of the Anthropocene humanity is both endangered and endangering, and if what is required to counter that is what Prabhu calls the recovery of an "ethic of Reverence for Life," then *how shall humanity secure a new beginning* without falling right back into the very *gestalt* that has led to our current moment? More specifically, do we have the philosophical resources to rethink humanity for an ecological age, or are we simply doomed to repeat the same instrumental rationality that far too many Western intellectuals have built our capitalist world upon? Max Horkheimer and Theodor Adorno, who Prabhu draws on for this paper, famously open their *Dialectic of Enlightenment* with an acknowledgment that instead of enlightenment liberating human beings from fear, the "wholly enlightened earth is radiant with triumphant calamity."[2] With climate disasters already at hand, the wholly enlightened earth remains radiant with calamity, and therefore the underlying structures of the world still require critique before any constructive proposal can be offered – though time is running out. Prabhu's paper provides both this critique and a proposal and, while I cannot comment on all of issues raised in his paper, in what follows I will raise a few questions regarding both.

In the critical part of the essay, Prabhu's thesis regards what he labels as "positivism," which is the tendency to go along with what science and technology has made possible without any sort of moral values to constrain us. As he says well, "we have abandoned the eternal verities of the true, the good, and the beautiful for the profitable, the convenient, and the (falsely) powerful" (Prabhu, 9). I am in full agreement with this assessment, for it is quite clear by just taking a cursory glance at how individuals live within our current political economy that the drive for profit and convenience has dominated every aspect of our life. Put simply – I will be more specific than Prabhu is in this paper – the problem is capitalism.

---

[1] J. Prahbu, "Inter-Being: Humanity in an Ecological Age," in this volume, 363–376.
[2] M. Horkheimer and T. W. Adorno, *Dialectic of Enlightenment: Philosophical Fragments* (Stanford, CA: Stanford University Press, 2002), 1.

What I want point to out, however, is that this critique of positivism is not particularly new. It is here that I want to draw attention to Max Horkheimer's forceful account of *Traditional vs. Critical Theory*. Horkheimer argues that the traditional idea of theory is based on scientific activity carried on within the division of labor. The traditional theorist is seemingly self-sufficient, independently constructing thought and accomplishing tasks in her own sphere. Horkheimer categorically rejects this, seeing the split in traditional theory as preciously the false consciousness of the bourgeois liberal savant. Intellectual processes cannot be detached from their total societal matrix. Horkheimer is highly suspicious of categories such as "better" or "useful" and, in fact, rejects them out right. The traditional theorist may think they are simply creating new advanced forms of more useful mechanical engineering, but instead they just created the sub-atomic bomb. For our context, in our efforts to extract cheap fossil fuel as quickly as possible, we ended up destroying the ozone layer. Therefore Horkheimer, and I think it is fair to say Prabhu as well, does not only call for a radical reconsideration of the scientist or economist alone, but of the knowing individual as such.[3] The basic form of the historically given commodity economy that has defined modernity has driven humanity to barbarism and our ability to think outside of that world is incredibly difficult.

Now, while this critical attitude is challenging to argue with, we are many decades removed from its original formulation and we still lack any sort of fulfilled humanity. In a great irony of the epoch of critical theory, Bruno Latour, a critical theorist *par excellence*, has become worried that "it [critique] might not be aiming at the right target."[4] Therefore, Latour has proposed the following: that the critical mind should be found in the cultivation of a stubbornly realist attitude that deals with *matters of concern*, not *matters of fact*.[5] This is what Prabhu has done in his paper, urging us to aim at moral values that can sustain humanity for an ecological age as opposed to simply the instrumental rationality that is currently dominating humanity. But because Prabhu's diagnosis of our current moment rings so similarly to the original formulation put forth by the Frankfurt school – further back to Weber and Marx – my first question is this: what is lacking, if anything, in the early critiques of instrumental rationality that he thinks is necessary to draw out now? Following that, what continued role does he see critique playing in his call for an ecological civilization?

In the second half of the paper, Prabhu moves into his constructive proposal, which is no doubt ambitious: a radically new organization of society

---

[3] M. HORKHEIMER, *Critical Theory: Selected Essays* (New York: The Continuum Publishing Company, 2002), 199.

[4] B. LATOUR, "Why Has Critique Run out of Steam? From Matters of Fact to Matters of Concern," *Critical Inquiry* 30 (2004): 225 (http://www.bruno-latour.fr/sites/default/files/89-CRITICAL-INQUIRY-GB.pdf) (4/22/2022).

[5] Ibid.

that is grounded in a different way of viewing life and its organizing principles. The leading question underlying his proposal is this: what vision of humanity and of human beings is most conductive to, and supportive of, an ecological civilization? Here the paper's title, "Inter-Being," comes into focus. Utilizing the framework of Tich Nhat Hanh and Raimon Panikkar, Prabhu takes seriously the primacy of relations over entities and sees the Cosmic, Divine, and Human as three interconnected dimensions of all reality. Through co-constitutive relationality, the notion of inter-being posits an egalitarian counter to the hierarchical structure of the Anthropocene where life can be seen as a dynamic existing-in-relation-to. This shift in human self-image, for Prabhu, is what is needed to point to a new ethic of reverence for life.

The idea of inter-being is powerful, and I do affirm that it may have potential to lead to the reverence for life that is being called for in this paper. Still, it is important to note that statements such as "everything is connected" can also invoke feelings of absolute horror. Yes, all of life is ultimately interconnected and free from isolation, and that interconnectedness is part of why we face so many immense challenges today. For example, two researches at University College London have recently described the colonizing of the Americas and other lands as "a planet-wide human-driven evolutionary experiment" which began in the 16th century and "will continue to play out indefinitely."[6] While many philosophers have considered the origins of the Anthropocene to be relatively recent, these new studies have shown that the Anthropocene began as early as 1610, and within decades this process fundamentally altered the eco balance of the entire planet, which we can now detect in the rocks and even the air. Through human domination and colonization – *white* human domination – the global climate was changed so immensely that the entire planet continues to feel the effects today. Inter-being, indeed.

Therefore, the notion of inter-being does make great sense of the world. What Prabhu seems to be calling for is not a new conception of inter-being, but of a greater awareness of this "cosmotheandric account" that strongly refutes anthropocentrism.[7] With this cosmotheandric basis where the Divine, Human, and Cosmic join, a new reverence for life can provide grounding for an ecological civilization. This is a noble call, but my concern and question regarding this concept is simple: by emphasizing the interconnectedness of life in all its forms, how do we avoid falling into a false universalism that ends up erasing difference all together? Or is universalism exactly what Prabhu is calling for? The most prominent cases of this universalism I worry about are coming today from thinkers like Slavoj Žižek and Alain Badiou who end up invoking religious par-

---

[6] https://www.theguardian.com/science/2018/jun/10/colonialism-changed-earth-geology-claim-scientists. (4/22/2022).
[7] Prabhu, "Inter-Being," in this volume, 363–376.

adigms in their politics to set up a (Christian) universalism, whereby particular figures – Jews – end up as victims of supersessionism once again. While Prabhu rightfully warns against Christian domination in his paper, I do wonder what he might think of the universal temptation that seems to plague contemporary Continental philosophers calling for a revitalized humanity today.

The final point I want to raise regarding the "reverence for life" that is rightfully being called for is to ask specifically *whose* life is to be revered. All of humanity will face the consequences of climate change, but it is also clear that not all of humanity is blamable for climate change. Only around 100 companies are responsible for nearly 70% of all global emissions, while the 26 richest people today own as much wealth as the poorest 50%.[8] We know who is responsible for the barbarism we face, and we can call them out by name. Therefore, my fear of most calls for revering all of life is that we end up forgiving the perpetrators too quickly, while those who have suffered the most in our world are never allowed to rise to the place that they deserve. And unfortunately, all too often philosophers in particular end up returning to the scene of the crime to reassure ourselves that this moment too can be analyzed philosophically, issuing a second blow to the victims of history who we all owe our debts. What we need in this new ecological age is not simply a reverence for life, but a more rigorous and scientific discipline that, as François Laruelle calls for, establishes victims to the rightful place that they demand.[9]

So now that we are at what appears to be the end of an age, we can return to the Hegelian question I opened with: *how shall humanity secure a new beginning*? To consider new beginnings when we are at the end is always already to consider resurrection. But we must be cautious of simply resurrecting a broad and universal human, for that always leads to the temptation to solely resurrect the Christian. So, for my final question I once again call on Laruelle:

> All hope for "resurrection" is not lost. Now that the old divine plan for salvation is no more than a memory of which only a trace remains, now that the victims of history into which it was transformed bear witness in some sense to a traceability, and now that this is the sole, final message to us, a question remains to be asked: *Who still deserves to arise?*[10]

For Laruelle it is only the victim who deserves to arise. To use the language of Prabhu, it is the victim, the endangered one, who deserves to be revered. And for a notion of inter-being to bring about a true reverence for life, the victims of our age, those who have truly been endangered, must be restored to their rightful place for an ecological civilization to emerge.

---

[8] https://www.theguardian.com/business/2019/jan/21/world-26-richest-people-own-as-much-as-poorest-50-per-cent-oxfam-report (4/22/2022).

[9] F. LARUELLE, *General Theory of Victims* (Malden, MA: Polity Press, 2015), 9.

[10] Ibid, 10–11.

List of Contributors

JON BIALECKI is an honorary fellow at the School of Social and Political Science at the University of Edinburgh.

GUELFO CARBONE is a postdoctoral researcher in moral philosophy at the Department of Philosophy, Communication and Performing Arts at the University of Roma Tre.

DANIEL CHERNILO is Professor of Social and Political Thought at the Department of Social Sciences at Loughborough University, UK.

RONALD COLE-TURNER is H. Parker Sharp Professor of Theology and Ethics at Pittsburgh Theological Seminary.

DIRK EVERS is Professor of Systematic Theology at the Theologische Fakultät of the Martin-Luther-University Halle-Wittenberg.

ADRIANO FABRIS is Professor of Moral Philosophy at Pisa University.

THOMAS JARED FARMER is a lecturer in philosophy at California State University Fullerton.

PETR GALLUS is Assistant Professor of Systematic Theology at Charles University, Prague.

HASSE HÄMÄLÄINEN is a post-doctoral researcher in philosophy at the Jagellonian University, Kraków, Poland.

EMILY HODGES is a post-graduate student in philosophy at Brown University.

VELI-MATTI KÄRKKÄINEN is Professor of Systematic Theology at Fuller Theological Seminary in Pasadena, CA.

RAYMOND E. PERRIER graduated with a PhD in Philosophy of Religion and Theology from Claremont Graduate University, CA in 2018.

RICHARD LIVINGSTON is an adjunct instructor in Philosophy and Religious Studies at Chaffey College and Fullerton College.

ANSELM K. MIN (†) was Professor of Religion at Claremont Graduate University, CA.

DANIEL NELSON teaches philosophy at Reedley Community College.

JOSEPH PRABHU (†) was Professor Emeritus of Philosophy at California State University LA.

NATHAN SCHRADLE is a doctoral candidate of the Department of Religious Studies at the University of North Carolina.

WALTER SCHWEIDLER is Chair for Philosophy at the Catholic University of Eichstätt-Ingolstadt.

JOSIAH SOLIS is a doctoral student in Religion with an emphasis in philosophy of religion & theology at Claremont Graduate University.

HAVA TIROSH-SAMUELSON is Director of Jewish Studies and Irving and Miriam Lowe Professor of Modern Judaism and Professor of History at Arizona State University in Tempe, AZ.

LUCAS WRIGHT is a Ph.D. student in the Department of European Languages and Studies, University of California, Irvine.

LIU YUE is a lecturer in philosophy at the University of Macau.

Index of Names

Aach, J. 143*fn*
Adam 137*fn*, 148, 150–152, 210, 211, 236
Adorno, Th. 55–81, 209, 215, 311, 366
Anscombe, G.E.M. 163*fn*, 183*fn*
Arendt, H. 27, 37, 40, 40*fn*, 43–44, 94*fn*
Aristotle 20, 58, 174–179, 183*fn*, 286*fn*, 317–320, 352, 368
Augustine 85–99, 101, 104, 106–108, 152, 177–179
Ayer, A.J. 25*fn*

Barth, K. 147–148
Baumgarten, D.B. 175*fn*
Benjamin, W. 27
Bialecki, J. 219–234, 235–241
Böhme, J. 62*fn*
Brueggemann, W. 210*fn*
Buber, M. 204

Carbone, G. 315–334
Cassirer, E. 31*fn*, 179*fn*, 248
Cesare, D. di 33
Chernilo, D. 23–63
Cicero 3, 21, 177, 179
Claussen, G. 205
Clayton, P.C. 113*fn*, 118*fn*, 119*fn*, 120*fn*, 121*fn*, 123*fn*
Cole-Turner, R. 133–158

Dalferth, I.U. 1–10
Davis, E.F. 210–211
Derrida, J. 185, 319
Descartes, R. 261, 275–278, 286*fn*, 326*fn*
Duns Scotus 22, 22*fn*
Durkheim, E. 55, 75–76

Eckhart 60–62, 74
Edelman, G.M. 120

Fabris, A. 351–363
Fichte, J.G. 127
Fodor, J. 118*fn*, 120, 280*fn*

Follett, K. 236–237
Foucault, M. 26, 185, 311*fn*

Gagarin 32*fn*
Gallus, P. 101–108, 107*fn*
Gould, S.J. 26*fn*
Gregory of Nyssa 145, 151, 154, 163, 166
Grün, R. 134*fn*, 136*fn*
Gulick, R.V. 123*fn*

Habermas, J. 39*fn*
Harari, Y.N. 197*fn*, 198, 255, 259, 261–263, 279, 301–303
Haraway, D. 27*fn*, 143, 187
Hartshorne, C. 123*fn*
Hawking, S. 198, 245
Hegel, G.F.W. 28, 58, 70, 127
Heidegger, M. 31–37, 55–80, 318–331, 353, 366
Hobbes 254*fn*, 48–49
Hodges, E. 335–350
Horkheimer, M. 55–80, 209*fn*, 215, 311, 366–367, 377–378
Hume, D. 181, 276–277, 372
Husserl, E. 18*fn*, 22*fn*, 23*fn*, 73*fn*, 119*fn*, 276–277, 317*fn*, 324–330
Hutcheson, Th. 181
Huxley, J. 140*fn*, 140–141, 187–188

Jaspers, K. 27
Jesus (Christ) 89, 101, 106–108, 147–149, 153, 161*fn*, 161–168, 211–212, 226–241
Jüngel, E. 159*fn*, 161, 162*fn*

Kärkkäinen, V.-M. 109–132
Kant, I. 6, 12–13, 26, 37*fn*, 40, 50, 83, 126, 183*fn*, 214–215, 275–278, 283, 296, 317, 326, 335–350, 364
Keller, C. 211
Kierkegaard, S. 147, 219
Kim, J. 117*fn*, 118–119, 125*fn*

Index of Names

Kline, M. 187
Kurzweil, R. 156–157, 190, 195, 266, 302, 313, 364–365, 369

Lactantius 179
Lévi-Strauss, C. 11, 12*fn*, 20, 23, 26
Levinas, E. 13–14, 32, 55, 70–71, 205, 326
Lewis, C.S. 154, 218
Livingston, R. 235–244
Luther, M. 105*fn*, 161, 164, 373
Lyotard, J.-F. 185

Maimonides 203
Marcus Aurelius 177
Marx, K. 247*fn*, 378
Min, A.K. 81–100, 101–108
Moltmann, J. 110*fn*, 116*fn*, 123*fn*, 125*fn*, 212*fn*
Moses 163, 316*fn*, 317*fn*

Nagel, Th. 15, 120
Nicolas of Cusa 22*fn*
Niebuhr, R. 123*fn*
Nielsen, K. 231
Nielsen, R. 137
Nietzsche, F. 209*fn*
Noë, A. 214*fn*
Nussbaum, M.C. 176

O'Connell, M. 4
O'Donnell, N. 23
Oktaviana, A.A. 139

Pagden, A. 181
Pannenberg, W. 110–111, 123, 129–130
Parens, E. 193–194
Pascal, B. 5, 58
Patterson, N. 134, 137
Paul 114*fn*, 122, 125, 147, 161, 167, 212*fn*
Pearce, D. 190*fn*, 191, 193, 302
Perrier, R. 45–54
Pico della Mirandola 180
Pinker, S. 183, 280*fn*
Plato 21, 178, 256, 320, 366
Polkinghorne, J. 122*fn*, 124–131
Popper, K. 117*fn*
Prabhu, J. 363–376
Putnam, H. 118*fn*, 213*fn*, 280*fn*

Rahner, K. 97, 145, 146*fn*, 148–157, 163, 167, 212*fn*
Ricoeur, P. 12*fn*
Rosenzweig, F. 55–76

Salutati, C. 179
Sartre, J.-P. 35–44, 277–278
Schradle, N. 301–314
Schelling, F.W.J. 60–65, 74*fn*, 127
Schweidler, W. 11–24
Seneca 177
Skinner, Q. 25*fn*
Sloterdijk, P. 29–32
Smith, A. 38, 48–49, 181
Smith, J. 227, 235*fn*, 236–239
Solis, J. 377–380
Spinoza, B. 219
Stump, E. 93*fn*

Taylor, C. 28–32, 257–258, 286*fn*
Ten Elshof, G.A. 109
Thomas Aquinas 122*fn*, 296
Thomas a Kempis 99
Tillich, P. 106, 125*fn*
Tirosh-Samuelson, H. 171–208

Valla 179
Vogel, S. 172*fn*
Voltaire 26*fn*

Weber, M. 41, 55, 75–76, 136, 310, 364–367, 378
Welker, M. 110*fn*, 125, 130*fn*
Whitehead, A.N. 123*fn*, 307–308
Wittgenstein, L. 163, 216, 223
Wolfe, C. 186*fn*, 319*fn*
Wright, L.S. 55–80
Wright, N.T. 122, 212*fn*

Yang, M.A. 137*fn*
Yeshivah, M. 205
Young, S. 189*fn*, 192
Yudokowsky, E. 195
Yue, L. 271–284

Zalta, E.N. 116*fn*
Žižek, S. 96, 104*fn*, 313, 379
Zizioulas, J. 130*fn*
Zoloth, L. 199*fn*
Zuboff, S. 256*fn*

Index of Terms

absolute 4, 13, 15, 39, 45, 51, 56, 62, 167, 328
afterlife 114, 129, 132, 178, 217, 228, 232
agency 41, 112, 113, 124, 175, 209*fn*, 248, 267, 279, 289, 306
algorithm 253, 301–312
ancient 11, 25, 128, 144, 173–178, 205–211, 316–320
Anthropocene 209–218
Anthropological 5, 17, 20, 23, 28, 34, 49, 55–70, 83, 122
Anthropomorphism 55–81
Apocalyptic 198, 270, 364
Augustinian 7, 81–100, 107, 162
authenticity 34, 193, 257–264

biblical 85, 110, 113–114, 119, 132, 180, 210–212, 317
biological 4–5, 14–17, 20, 23, 38, 118, 133, 150, 196–203, 304–310
bodily 28, 86, 94, 106, 110, 113–115, 123, 178, 209, 290, 316

capitalism 49, 82–84, 96–98, 101–104, 172, 202
Cartesian 124, 127, 129, 275–280, 286, 324*fn*
causation 115–124
Christianity 70, 74, 84, 97*fn*, 144, 147–154, 215, 240, 326, 371
Christology 106–108, 153*fn*, 154*fn*, 163*fn*
climate 137, 172, 202, 216–217, 370–371, 377–380
cognitive 39, 63, 112*fn*, 141, 187, 189, 275
coherence 66*fn*, 188, 215, 224, 261
computational 196–197, 204–207, 213, 247, 251, 266–267
cosmology 38, 110*fn*, 156, 195*fn*, 211*fn*, 230, 269

cosmos 128, 131–132, 153, 155–156, 160, 167, 177
cybernetics 183–191, 303–304, 309
cyborg 143, 187, 190*fn*

dasein 57, 58, 59*fn*, 60, 62, 64–70
dataism 245–270
dehumanizing 46–48, 313, 365
deity 62, 77, 118*fn*, 239, 256
democratic 104, 190, 223, 263, 267
destiny 96, 99, 131, 157, 192, 371
dialectic 50, 60, 66*fn*, 77, 81
dialektik 68*fn*, 75, 76*fn*, 209*fn*
dignity 13–14, 45–47, 81, 122
divine 3, 56, 58, 72, 74, 120
divinity 107, 129, 154, 220
dualism 107, 110–116, 122

earth 93, 112, 131, 137, 153
ecological 363–376
economic 47–49, 81, 103, 158
egalitarian 25, 28, 33–44, 46–51
emergence 50, 112, 117–120
emotional 39, 83, 112–115
empathy 42, 47, 51–55
empirical 42, 49–50, 97, 146, 160
environmental 27, 138, 158, 172, 204
equality 26, 28, 44, 182, 199, 253, 258, 263
eschatological 88, 93, 96, 105, 267, 269
essentialism 35–40, 51, 82
eternal 5, 69, 72*fn*, 86–90, 95, 216
ethics 45–53
eudaimonia 174–177
evil 43, 83, 90, 103, 297
evolution 166–167, 173, 180*fn*
existential 50, 56, 92, 95–96
existentialism 28, 32, 35, 39
existenz 56, 61, 65*fn*, 66, 69
exploitation 172, 211, 217, 313, 371–372, 375
extropy 190, 192

faith 84*fn*, 85–89, 97, 124*fn*, 126, 161*fn*, 199, 240, 270
fear 40, 68–69, 76, 94, 334, 337–338
female 149, 161*fn*, 177, 183, 210
feminist 45–46, 186–188, 205*fn*, 228
finitude 17, 55–56, 68–69, 75, 202
flourish 175–176, 182, 182*fn*
freedom 5–6, 19, 36, 41–44, 98, 104, 180–181, 194

gender 39, 149, 187, 194, 203, 212*fn*, 253
genetic 98, 133–150, 159, 181, 191, 210, 302
givenness 320–327
godlikeness 146–147, 159, 164–167

heaven 93, 149, 191, 196*fn*
Hebrew 114, 175*fn*, 199*fn*, 211
Hellenistic 114, 176
Hermeneutics 315, 317*fn*
holy 147, 202
humanist 26–27, 32–33, 37, 45–52, 84, 170, 179*fn*

identity 36, 40–41, 62–65, 115–118, 129–130
identität 56–62
ideological 26–27, 38, 82, 220–223
imagination 50, 87, 112, 121, 143, 220–222, 240, 304
immanence 33, 74, 219, 326–328
immediacy 69, 82–83, 91, 102–104
immortality 6, 86, 106, 114, 129–131, 179–180, 194*fn*
imperative 84, 190, 195, 199*fn*, 256, 263
indeterminacy 45–54
infinite 5, 69, 104–106, 147
intersubjective 335–350
intuitive 52–54
irreducible 118, 218, 275–277, 280–282

Jewish 7, 40–42, 56–57, 71, 174, 179, 186, 199*fn*
Judaic 199–207
juridical 13*fn*, 13–18, 252–253, 359
justice 21, 27–28, 44, 47, 51, 84*fn*, 88, 98, 158, 162, 181, 202

legal 14, 23, 29, 39, 42, 172, 179
liberal 35, 44, 227, 263–264, 378
logic 45–54, 309, 311–313

machine 2–3, 82, 127–128, 143, 174
magic 23, 141, 215, 303*fn*
market 48–49, 262, 301, 311, 366
materialism 31, 117, 119, 124, 127
mathematics 52, 265, 284
mediated 95, 105, 248, 264, 324
metaphysical 20, 26, 30, 55, 117, 185, 280
monism 109–132
Mormonism 226–240

nanotechnology 4, 141, 187–189, 195, 221
neuroscience 109*fn*, 187, 193*fn*, 278, 306*fn*
non-human 3, 22, 68, 184–186, 231, 356, 375

ontological 12*fn*, 21, 35, 59, 62*fn*, 63–70
ontology 65, 120–132, 315, 318, 320, 327*fn*
orthodox 89, 155*fn*, 156*fn*, 201, 229–232

paleogenomics 134–137, 150
paradox 11–24, 155, 171, 173, 197, 252, 273*fn*
personhood 113, 124, 232, 287
phenomenological 13, 55–80, 276–277, 316, 320–331, 364
physics 61, 110*fn*, 121, 122*fn*, 177, 195*fn*, 215, 283–284
pluralistic 109*fn*, 117*fn*, 122, 128, 174, 204, 207
politics 83, 96–99, 176–179, 182, 187, 198
posthumanism 183, 186–188, 210–214, 302, 315, 319
posthumanity 146, 187–190, 196, 224

quantum 110*fn*, 118*fn*, 120, 124, 127, 232, 268

rationality 4, 31–34, 41, 48–49, 86, 113, 205–206, 306

Index of Terms

reductionism 29, 14, 117, 125, 323*fn*
relationality 67, 72–74, 85, 167, 203, 218, 323, 372–373, 379
renaissance 25, 173–186, 199
resurrection 106–108, 123*fn*, 129–131, 162, 195*fn*, 212*fn*, 232, 240–241, 380
revelation 164, 168, 205*fn*, 326
revolution 47, 49, 102, 189, 195, 203*fn*, 245–249, 254, 269–270, 302
rights 26, 38–32, 47, 81, 174, 184, 187, 285*fn*, 365
robotics 187, 191*fn*, 221, 252, 265, 289*fn*, 302*fn*, 365

salvation 99, 106–108, 152, 162–165, 228, 302, 358, 380
science 1, 3, 30, 34, 37*fn*, 42, 46, 83, 109*fn*, 121, 150, 181–191
scripture 86, 93, 132, 149, 153, 210*fn*, 240
secular 25–26, 99, 171, 174, 179, 205, 228, 263, 303, 364
self
– self-emptying 148–149, 165, 365
– self-knowledge 192, 245, 256–261
– self-reflection 245–270
– self-transcendence 19, 149, 153,190, 222
sexual 86, 91, 96, 194
singularity 67, 71, 156, 196, 198, 222, 264–302, 364
slave 47, 148–149, 161*fn*, 365
sociocultural 35–44
space 62*fn*, 66, 76, 99, 184–187, 216, 229, 231, 355

spirit 51, 70, 89, 129, 153, 161–162, 167, 240, 255
– Holy Spirit 88, 93–94, 95, 116
spiritual 85–87, 90–91, 95–98, 102, 104, 121–122, 205, 257–258
subjectivity 32–36, 66, 83–84, 97, 105–106, 232

technicization 328–331
technoscience 183, 185, 199–201
temporal 12, 16, 19–20, 39, 59, 68, 86–87, 95, 124, 216, 236, 330, 372
theological 81–100, 109–132
theosis 89, 90*fn*, 148, 162, 165, 167, 226–228, 231–232
transcend 12, 17, 34, 38, 83, 97, 105, 140, 160, 166–167
transcendence 38, 57–61, 74, 83–85, 97, 101, 105, 146, 155, 166–168, 219–222
transhumanism 171–208, 209–218, 219–235
trinity 85–88, 167, 373

universalism 45–54
universality 11, 13, 18, 39–40, 50–52, 70, 186, 309–310
utilitarian 37, 48–49, 182, 364, 369

virtue 48, 64*fn*, 74, 174–208, 352–360

well-being 174, 176, 182, 198, 203–204, 365–368
wisdom 43, 88, 92, 151, 154, 179, 182*fn*, 197, 206, 346*fn*, 375
worldliness 101–108

Religion in Philosophy and Theology

Edited by
Helen De Cruz (St. Louis, MO), Asle Eikrem (Oslo),
Hartmut von Sass (Berlin), Heiko Schulz (Frankfurt a.M.),
and Judith Wolfe (St. Andrews)

Religions are core phenomena of human life. In order to understand, evaluate and adjudicate between them, it is not sufficient to be aware of 'the facts'; it is necessary to place these facts within the context of what seems possible and plausible, to shed a critical light on the self-conception of religious realities and to explore their relationships to other forms of (dealing with) reality. This is done in a wide array of disciplines whose thematic perspectives, methods and overall objectives vary. Among these, philosophy of religion and theology are underrepresented but vital voices within international research. The main purpose of the series *Religion in Philosophy and Theology (RPT)* is to provide a forum for testing different approaches within these two disciplines, and to explore both their individual and combined theoretical potential, without giving preference to specific theological or philosophical approaches or advocating certain religious or anti-religious viewpoints. In doing so, it provides the opportunity to discuss and assess the pros and cons of widely differing religious, philosophical and theological perspectives, situated within multiple religious traditions within a globalized world. Among the essential requirements for publication in the series are clarity of presentation, rigor of argument, and the willingness to subject one's own ideas and concepts to the criticism of others. *RPT* publishes relevant specialized monographs, outstanding habilitations and dissertations as well as collected volumes.

ISSN: 1616-346x
Suggested citation: RPT

All available volumes can be found at *www.mohrsiebeck.com/rpt*

Mohr Siebeck
www.mohrsiebeck.com